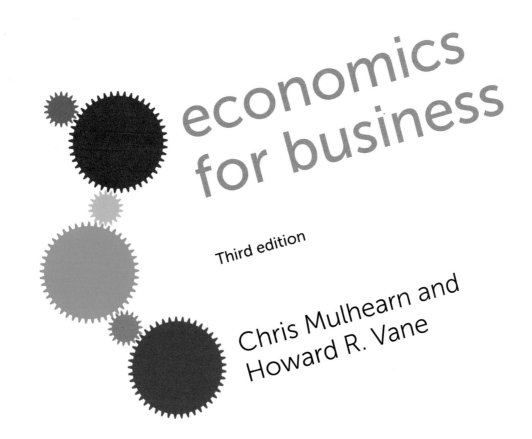

economics for business

Third edition

Chris Mulhearn and
Howard R. Vane

macmillan education   palgrave

First edition 2001
Second edition 2012
Published 2016 by
PALGRAVE

Palgrave in the UK is an imprint of Macmillan Publishers Limited, registered in England, company number 785998, of 4 Crinan Street, London, N1 9XW.

Palgrave Macmillan in the US is a division of St Martin's Press LLC, 175 Fifth Avenue, New York, NY 10010.

Palgrave is a global imprint of the above companies and is represented throughout the world.

Palgrave® and Macmillan® are registered trademarks in the United States, the United Kingdom, Europe and other countries.

ISBN 978–1–137–42922–3

This book is printed on paper suitable for recycling and made from fully managed and sustained forest sources. Logging, pulping and manufacturing processes are expected to conform to the environmental regulations of the country of origin.

A catalogue record for this book is available from the British Library.

Library of Congress Cataloging-in-Publication Data
Names: Mulhearn, Chris. | Vane, Howard R.
Title: Economics for business / Chris Mulhearn, Howard Vane.
Description: Third edition. | New York : Palgrave Macmillan, 2015. | Includes index.
Identifiers: LCCN 2015039871 | ISBN 9781137429223 (paperback)
Subjects: LCSH: Economics. | Business. | Commerce. | Managerial economics. | BISAC: BUSINESS & ECONOMICS / Economics / General.
Classification: LCC HB171.5 .M928 2015 | DDC 338.5—dc23
LC record available at http://lccn.loc.gov/2015039871

 **Chris Mulhearn** is Reader in Economics in the Liverpool Business School at Liverpool John Moores University, UK. His work has been published in a number of journals including: *Local Economy*; *Industrial Relations Journal*; *Journal of Economic Perspectives*; *World Economics*; and *World Economy*. His most recent books include: (with Howard Vane) *The Nobel Memorial Laureates in Economics: An Introduction to Their Careers and Main Published Works* (Edward Elgar, 2005); *The Euro: Its Origins, Development and Prospects* (Edward Elgar, 2008); and *The Pioneering Papers of the Nobel Memorial Laureates in Economics*, Volumes 1–5 (Edward Elgar, 2009), Volumes 6–10 (Edward Elgar, 2010), Volumes 11–14 (Edward Elgar, 2011).

 **Howard R. Vane** is Emeritus Professor of Economics in the Liverpool Business School at Liverpool John Moores University, UK. His main research interests lie in the area of macroeconomics and his work in this field has been translated and published in Bulgarian, Chinese, French, Hungarian, Italian, Japanese, Korean, Mongolian, Polish and Turkish. He has co-authored/edited 30 books and has had articles published in a wide range of journals including: *American Economist*; *Journal of Economic Methodology*; *Journal of Economic Perspectives*; *Journal of Economic Studies*; *Journal of Macroeconomics*; *World Economics*; and *World Economy*. His most recent books include: (with Brian Snowdon) *Modern Macroeconomics: Its Origins, Development and Current State* (Edward Elgar, 2005); and (with Chris Mulhearn) *The Nobel Memorial Laureates in Economics: An Introduction to Their Careers and Main Published Works* (Edward Elgar, 2005); *The Euro: Its Origins, Development and Prospects* (Edward Elgar, 2008); and *The Pioneering Papers of the Nobel Memorial Laureates in Economics*, Volumes 1–5 (Edward Elgar, 2009), Volumes 6–10 (Edward Elgar, 2010), Volumes 11–14 (Edward Elgar, 2011).

brief contents

List of figures and tables **xiv**

Preface **xix**

Tour of the book **xxii**

Online resources **xxiv**

Publisher's acknowledgements **xxvi**

1 Economics and business **1**

2 The market **35**

3 The firm **87**

4 Firms' costs and revenues **123**

5 Market concentration and market power **145**

6 Business and government **187**

7 Factor markets **219**

8 The macroeconomy, macroeconomic policy and business **253**

9 Unemployment: causes and cures **287**

10 Inflation: causes and cures **315**

11 Economic growth and business cycles **341**

12 Stabilizing the economy **373**

13 International trade **393**

14 The balance of payments and exchange rates **427**

15 Globalization **477**

Glossary **501**

Index **509**

contents

List of figures and tables   **xiv**

Preface   **xix**

Tour of the book   **xxii**

Online resources   **xxiv**

Publisher's acknowledgements   **xxvi**

1 Economics and business   1

1.1 Introduction: what is economics?   **2**

1.2 Why economics matters to business, indeed to *everyone*   **6**

1.3 Understanding the roles of firms, consumers and government in markets   **10**

1.4 Scarcity, choice and opportunity cost   **21**

1.5 Opportunity cost and incentives   **24**

1.6 Microeconomics, macroeconomics and business   **27**

1.7 Positive and normative economics   **32**

Everyday Economics 1.1 Answers   **34**
One thing you should read   **34**

2 The market   35

2.1 Introduction: the market, an old and useful institution   **36**

2.2 Consumers and demand in the market   **40**

2.3 Firms and supply in the market   **45**

2.4 The market: bringing demand and supply together   **48**

2.5 Applying market analysis 1: the example of economic integration in the European Union   **54**

2.6 Elasticity in the market   **61**

2.7 Price elasticity of demand   **62**

2.8 Determinants of price elasticity of demand   **66**

2.9 Why firms need to know about price elasticity of demand   **68**

2.10 Applying market analysis 2: OPEC and the market for oil   **69**

2.11 Other forms of elasticity   **72**

2.12 Markets and asymmetric information   **77**

2.13 Markets and the rational consumer   **81**

2.14 Markets: concluding remarks   **83**

Everyday Economics 2.1 Answers   **85**
One thing you should read   **85**

3 The firm   87

3.1 Introduction   **88**

3.2 What do firms do?   **88**

3.3 Why is the firm a necessary institution?   **90**

3.4 Different kinds of firm   **93**

3.5 Reflections on the strategies of firms: profit maximization,
economics and business strategy, organic growth,
and growth by merger and acquisition   **100**

3.6 Firms' strategies for survival: resolving the principal–agent
problem, coping with asymmetric information problems   **108**

3.7 The death of a firm   **114**

3.8 Firms and entrepreneurship: an Austrian view   **117**

Everyday Economics 3.1 Answers   **121**
One thing you should read   **121**

4 Firms' costs and revenues   123

4.1 Introduction   **124**

4.2 The short run and the long run   **125**

4.3 The short-run production function and the
law of diminishing marginal returns   **125**

4.4 Short-run costs   **128**

4.5 Production in the long run   **132**

4.6 Long-run costs   **133**

4.7 Firms' revenues   **136**

4.8 Profit maximization   **140**

Everyday Economics 4.1 Answers   **144**
One thing you should read   **144**

5 Market concentration and market power   145

5.1 Introduction   **146**

5.2 Market power   **146**

5.3 Market structures, market power, price
competition and non-price competition   **149**

5.4 Perfect competition **152**

5.5 Monopoly **158**

5.6 Imperfect competition (also known as monopolistic competition) **172**

5.7 Oligopoly **173**

5.8 Oligopoly and game theory **177**

5.9 Market structures: an institutionalist view **181**

Everyday Economics 5.1 Answers **186**

One thing you should read **186**

6 Business and government **187**

6.1 Introduction **188**

6.2 Market failure **189**

6.3 Public goods **190**

6.4 Externalities **194**

6.5 Public goods, externalities and business **204**

6.6 The liberal view: market failure and state failure **206**

6.7 Privatization **210**

6.8 Competition policy **214**

6.9 Industrial policy **215**

Everyday Economics 6.1 Answers **217**

One thing you should read **218**

7 Factor markets **219**

7.1 Introduction **220**

7.2 The labour market **220**

7.3 The demand for labour **226**

7.4 The supply of labour **230**

7.5 Issues in the labour market: bringing demand and supply together **235**

7.6 Factor incomes and economic rent **248**

Everyday Economics 7.1 Answers **252**

One thing you should read **252**

8 The macroeconomy, macroeconomic policy and business **253**

8.1 Introduction: the macroeconomic context of business **254**

8.2 Economic growth **255**

8.3 Unemployment **267**

8.4 Inflation **270**

8.5 The balance of payments **276**

8.6 A brief overview of macroeconomic policy since 1945 **282**

Everyday Economics 8.1 Answers **286**

One thing you should read **286**

9 Unemployment: causes and cures   287

9.1 Introduction: the debate over the causes and cures for unemployment   **288**

9.2 The classical approach   **289**

9.3 The orthodox Keynesian approach   **290**

9.4 The monetarist approach   **300**

9.5 The new classical approach   **302**

9.6 The new Keynesian approach   **303**

9.7 A case study: unemployment in Europe   **308**

Everyday Economics 9.1 Answers   **313**
One thing you should read   **313**

10 Inflation: causes and cures   315

10.1 Introduction: the inflation debate   **316**

10.2 The monetarist view   **317**

10.3 The non-monetarist view   **330**

10.4 A case study: maintaining price stability in the euro area   **333**

10.5 Concluding remarks   **335**

One thing you should read   **337**

Appendix   338

Keynesians, monetarists and new classicists and the expectations-augmented Phillips curve   **338**

11 Economic growth and business cycles   341

11.1 Introduction   **342**

11.2 Economic growth: an overview   **342**

11.3 The Solow growth model   **346**

11.4 The new endogenous growth models   **348**

11.5 Wider influences on economic growth   **349**

11.6 Main features of business cycles   **351**

11.7 The debate over the cause and control of business cycles   **352**

11.8 Concluding remarks   **363**

One thing you should read   **365**

Appendix   366

The Solow growth model   **366**

12 Stabilizing the economy   373

12.1 Introduction   **374**

12.2 Discretionary policy and policy rules   **374**

12.3 The rules versus discretion debate: problems of stabilization policy   **375**

12.4 Changing views on stabilizing the economy   **386**

12.5 Concluding remarks   **389**

One thing you should read   **391**

13 International trade   393

13.1 Introduction   **394**

13.2 The theory of comparative advantage   **396**

13.3 Reflecting on comparative advantage: further developments in trade theory   **401**

13.4 Patterns of trade since 1945   **408**

13.5 International trade policy   **413**

Everyday Economics 13.1 Answers   **424**

One thing you should read   **425**

14 The balance of payments and exchange rates   427

14.1 Introduction   **428**

14.2 The balance of payments accounts   **428**

14.3 The balance of payments and business   **440**

14.4 Exchange rates and exchange rate determination   **442**

14.5 Exchange rate systems   **449**

14.6 Exchange rate systems in practice   **457**

14.7 The euro   **465**

14.8 The balance of payments, exchange rates and business   **472**

Everyday Economics 14.1 Answers   **476**

One thing you should read   **476**

15 Globalization   477

15.1 Introduction   **478**

15.2 What is globalization?   **478**

15.3 How far has globalization progressed?   **481**

15.4 What are the attractions of globalization?   **490**

15.5 What threats might globalization pose?   **492**

15.6 On reflection, how new is globalization anyway?   **498**

One thing you should read   **499**

Glossary   **501**

Index   **509**

list of figures and tables

Figures

1.1 The dynamic pie: share in world exports for selected economies by development status 1980–2011 **8**

1.2 Foreign direct investment (FDI) inflows by economy type, $bn, 1995–2012 **9**

1.3 The free market and state intervention in markets **17**

2.1 The effect of a change in price on the quantity demanded of a particular good or service **42**

2.2 The effect of a change in income on the demand for a normal good or service **43**

2.3 Factors which influence the demand for a particular good: a summary **45**

2.4 The effect of a change in price on the quantity supplied of a particular good or service **46**

2.5 The effect of a change in production costs on the supply of a particular good or service **47**

2.6 Factors which influence the supply of a particular good: a summary **48**

2.7 The interaction of demand and supply in the market for a particular good **49**

2.8 A stylized representation of the market for T-shirts **52**

2.9 A stylized representation of recent developments in the UK market for canned tuna fish **52**

2.10 Gold price 1971–2014 (January) **54**

2.11 Member countries of the European Union **55**

2.12 Market intervention: the case of the Common Agricultural Policy **59**

2.13 Price elasticity of demand in the market for new cars **63**

2.14 Variation in elasticity along a demand curve **64**

2.15 Unit elasticity, perfectly inelastic demand, perfectly elastic demand **65**

2.16 Crude oil price 1970–2012 **70**

2.17 World oil production and consumption 1970–2012 **70**

2.18 US, China and Japan oil consumption 1970–2012 **71**

2.19 Price elasticity of supply **75**

2.20 Unit elasticity, perfectly inelastic supply, perfectly elastic supply **76**

3.1   Legal status of UK businesses, 2013   **95**

3.2   Value (deflated by the GDP deflator) and number of M&A deals involving UK companies, 1987 to Q1 2014   **107**

3.3   Consumers' surplus and the pricing decisions of firms   **113**

4.1   (a) The total product of labour (b) The average and marginal product of labour in the short run   **127**

4.2   A firm's short-run total cost curves   **130**

4.3   A firm's short-run average and marginal cost curves   **132**

4.4   The long-run average cost curve   **134**

4.5   The relationship between the short-run and long-run average cost curves   **135**

4.6   (a) The market price in perfect competition (b) The average and marginal revenue curves of a price-taking firm   **137**

4.7   The total revenue curve for a price taker   **138**

4.8   The average and marginal revenue curves for a price maker   **139**

4.9   The total revenue curve for a price maker   **140**

4.10   The profit-maximizing output for a price taker   **141**

4.11   The profit-maximizing output for a price maker   **142**

5.1   The revenue curves for a firm in a perfectly competitive market   **153**

5.2   Cost curves for the firm in a perfectly competitive market   **154**

5.3   The profit-maximizing output decision   **154**

5.4   The short-run position of a firm in perfect competition   **155**

5.5   The short and the long run in the perfectly competitive market and the price-taking firm   **156**

5.6   The long-run position of a firm in perfect competition   **157**

5.7   The perfectly competitive firm and allocative efficiency   **158**

5.8   Revenue curves for the monopolist   **163**

5.9   The long-run position of the monopolist   **164**

5.10   The monopolist as a misallocator of resources   **165**

5.11   From perfect competition to natural monopoly: lower prices and greater output but a misallocation of resources   **166**

5.12   Consumer surplus and price discrimination; producer surplus and *your* room to negotiate   **168**

5.13   The long-run position of the imperfectly competitive firm   **173**

5.14   Price stability under oligopoly   **176**

6.1   Traffic entering the central London charging zone during charging hours 2002–7   **193**

6.2   Private decision-making in a polluting industry   **197**

6.3   Internalizing the externalities of a polluting industry   **198**

6.4   The cap and trade approach to the reduction of CO_2 emissions   **200**

7.1   The interaction of demand and supply in the labour market   **222**

7.2   Trade union density in the G5 1960–2013   **225**

7.3   The individual firm's demand for labour   **228**

7.4   The effect of a change in the price of a firm's output upon its demand for labour   **228**

7.5   UK productivity and earnings 1975–2013   **230**

7.6   The individual's supply of labour   **233**

7.7   The supply of skilled and unskilled labour   **235**

7.8   The demand for skilled and unskilled workers   **236**

7.9   The markets for skilled and unskilled labour   **237**

7.10   Stylized labour market conditions reflecting the UK's distribution of earnings, 2013   **239**

7.11   Mean gross weekly earnings by place of work, Great Britain, scaled by number of jobs   **240**

7.12   UK workforce jobs by selected industry 1978–2014 ('000s)   **241**

7.13   Indivisibilities in the demand for labour and the impact of a minimum wage   **245**

7.14   Women and men earning less than the UK minimum wage   **246**

7.15   Economic rent in the markets for unskilled labour, capital and land   **249**

8.1   The circular flow of income   **258**

8.2   British government expenditure and income 2014–2015   **260**

8.3   UK real GDP 1948–2013, £bn, 2011 prices   **262**

8.4   Real GDP growth, G5, 1990–2014   **265**

8.5   Real GDP growth, G5, Russia and China 1990–2014   **265**

8.6   The unemployment pool: inflows and outflows   **268**

8.7   G5 unemployment rates 1990–2014   **268**

8.8   The CPI basket 2014 (%)   **271**

8.9   G5 inflation, 1990–2014   **276**

9.1   The classical approach   **289**

9.2   The consumption function   **293**

9.3   Investment and government expenditure   **295**

9.4   Import and export expenditure   **296**

9.5   The Keynesian model   **297**

9.6   The Keynesian approach   **299**

9.7   The monetarist and new classical approaches   **301**

9.8   The new Keynesian approach   **304**

9.9   Unemployment rates in the euro area and the United States 1999–2015   **308**

9.10   Minimum monthly wage 2013 for selected European countries and the US in €   **309**

10.1   The Phillips curve   **321**

10.2 The relationship between excess demand
for labour and unemployment **322**

10.3 The expectations-augmented Phillips curve **324**

10.4 The unemployment costs of reducing inflation **328**

10.5 Inflation in the euro area **334**

11.1 The short-run aggregate production function **343**

11.2 The production possibility frontier **343**

11.3 A stylized business cycle **351**

11.4 An aggregate production function relating output
per worker to capital input per worker **367**

11.5 Steady state in the Solow growth model **368**

11.6 The effects of an increase in the saving rate on capital
input per worker and output per worker **370**

11.7 The effects of an increase in the rate of growth of the labour
force on capital input per worker and output per worker **370**

11.8 The effects of an improvement in technology on
capital input per worker and output per worker **371**

12.1 Stabilization policy in the orthodox Keynesian model **376**

12.2 Time lags and stabilization policy **380**

12.3 The problem of time inconsistency **384**

13.1 Production possibility frontiers **398**

13.2 UK trade in cars, 2003–13 **407**

13.3 Selected intra and inter-regional merchandise trade flows, 2012 **412**

13.4 The World Trade Organization's agreements **420**

14.1 The effects of a fall in the exchange rate **434**

14.2 Why you can't run a personal persistent balance-of-payments deficit **437**

14.3 Current account balances 1990–2014 **439**

14.4 Current account as percentage of GDP 1990–2014 **439**

14.5 Chinese yuan per US dollar, 2005–2014 **441**

14.6 Demand and supply in the foreign exchange market **443**

14.7 Equilibrium in the foreign exchange market **444**

14.8 Long-term change in the foreign exchange market **446**

14.9 Sterling exchange rates **447**

14.10 UK, US and euro area inflation, 2007–14 **448**

14.11 A target zone in the foreign exchange market **452**

14.12 Inflation for the G7 1970–90 **461**

14.13 The widening of the ERM band in 1993 **464**

14.14 Euro area members' share of trade with EU 28, 2013 (%) **469**

15.1 Estimated size of the daily turnover of the global foreign
exchange market, weekly turnover of global share
market vs GDP of selected economies, 2013, $tn **480**

15.2   Regional shares in world merchandise exports 1983 and 2013 (%)   **482**

15.3   FDI inflows by region 1990–2013, US$bn   **483**

15.4   FDI inflows by selected countries 1990–2013, $m   **484**

15.5   Shares in world GDP: G5 and BRIC economies   **485**

15.6   Gross national income per capita 2013 (PPP 2011 US$)   **486**

15.7   Estimated international migrants at mid-year by destination   **489**

15.8   Copper price US$ per metric tonne 2000–14, monthly   **491**

15.9   Global current account imbalances   **494**

15.10   Global net foreign asset imbalances   **494**

15.11   Coffee price (arabica) US cents per pound 2000–14, monthly and illustrated Fairtrade price   **497**

Tables

1.1   Produced in the society in which you live?   **2**

2.1   Shares of regional trade flow in world merchandise exports, 2012 (%)   **58**

4.1   The total, average and marginal product of labour in the short run   **126**

4.2   The relationship between the total, average and marginal product of labour and a firm's costs in the short run   **130**

4.3   The average, total and marginal revenue for a price maker   **138**

5.1   The prisoners' dilemma   **178**

5.2   A payoff matrix for oligopolists   **179**

7.1   Economic activity in the UK, all aged 16–64; seasonally adjusted; in '000s and %   **232**

7.2   UK highest and lowest paid occupations 2013   **238**

7.3   UK Distribution of gross hourly earnings, April 2013   **239**

8.1   Economic growth rates for the G5   **264**

8.2   Openness for the G5 in current prices (total trade as % of GDP)   **277**

13.1   Hypothetical production possibilities   **397**

13.2   Germany and Ukraine in autarky   **399**

13.3   Specialization and trade   **400**

13.4   World merchandise exports by region and selected economy, 1948–2013 (%)   **409**

13.5   Leading exporters in world trade in commercial services 2013 ($billion and %)   **411**

14.1   Structure of the UK balance of payments   **429**

14.2   How the balance of payments works   **431**

14.3   UK balance of payments 2012 (£m)   **432**

15.1   United Nations Human Development Index 2013, top 10 and selected economies   **487**

15.2   United Nations Human Development Index 2013, selected economies with medium and low human development   **488**

15.3   International migrants as a percentage of the population   **489**

preface

Our approach

Today introductory courses in economics for business are taught on a range of undergraduate degree programmes, most notably business studies and management studies. While students on such programmes can turn to a number of well-established books covering the core material, they are often intimidated by the sheer length and density of these texts. For this reason our main aim in writing *Economic for Business* has been to meet the needs of students, both at undergraduate and HND or MBA level, by providing a *rigorous* yet relatively *concise* coverage of all the relevant topics. We believe that our book achieves this while using an engaging writing style to make the central concepts in economics interesting and accessible for those with no previous knowledge of the subject.

Economics for Business emphasizes the relevance of economics to business and everyday life and offers a steady stream of examples and case studies to keep students interested. For example, in Chapter 1 there is the first in a series of 'Reflecting on Economics' features that explains how, in their own words, Nobel Prize winners became interested in economics in the first place. The answers, it turns out, mostly have to do with the kind of issues most people feel strongly about: poverty, unemployment, racism and famine. We think that these stories will help to convince students of the concrete realities behind the economic theory covered in the book. Other 'Reflecting on Economics' features consider the success of central bank independence in inflation control, Edward Denison's identification of the relative strengths of the contributing factors to long-term economic growth, and the evolution of the Phillips curve, all of which encourage the student to think critically about key topics in particular chapters.

With the world of business firmly in mind, we have included two features to make sure that students grasp the connections between – on the one hand – markets, firms, consumers, workers and government, and – on the other – what may sometimes seem to be remote economic theories. Our 'Business Case Study' feature examines a variety of different business situations in which economics plays a vital role. For example:

- The imaginative use of price elasticity of demand in the pricing of admission to football matches;

- Why retailers are able to charge what appear to be exorbitant sums for optional insurance on electrical goods;
- How the 'evil' of monopoly power actually helps technological progress in the pharmaceutical industry.

We also have a series of 'Applying Economics to Business' features that explore the economic underpinnings of a number of current business issues. For example:

- The business opportunities presented by free trade areas;
- Why some currencies in the world – the Chinese renminbi in particular – are gaining in importance;
- Why asymmetric information in the labour market matters and how signalling can help to overcome it.

Each chapter begins with a set of questions to highlight the main topics to be addressed. As they are introduced, key terms and economic concepts are emboldened in the text and defined in the margins. Frequent cross-references are made to material covered in other chapters so that the student can see important links between the different topics in economics. Each chapter ends with a summary of the main issues discussed, a list of key terms, questions for discussion and *one* thing to read.

Rather than the usual list of suggestions for further reading that most students rarely undertake, we've taken the innovative step of highlighting a single item which illuminates a key aspect of the chapter. We have used some academic sources for this feature (such as a chapter from Milton Friedman's *Capitalism and Freedom*), but also extracts from novels, interviews with economists and video. Much of this material is accessible online. For example, Chapter 3 invites the student to read a section of Roddy Doyle's *The Van* in which the central characters quarrel over the running of a burger van: it's a classic principal-agent problem which students are asked to unravel. Chapter 4 asks students to watch a short video on easyJet's website to help them understand the company's business model and the crucial bearing of cost.

Content and structure

We have divided *Economics for Business* conventionally between the two interrelated areas of microeconomics and macroeconomics. In Chapters 1–7, attention is focused on microeconomic issues: the activities of business firms, operating in different market structures, satisfying consumer wants and providing employment. This part of the book also looks explicitly at the relationship between business and government. Macroeconomic issues are interpreted in Chapters 8–15 as a series of problems that require elaboration as to their nature, their (competing) underlying explanations and the range of policy options available for their resolution. Given the importance of the macroeconomic environment to business, it is crucial that students understand what causes change in the economy and what influence government policy has on the macroeconomic environment. The microeconomic and macroeconomic material is explicitly linked by the recurrent theme of the influence of government policy on business performance. In taking this approach we hope to demystify economics for students of business and management, aid their understanding of how economic analysis can be applied to 'real world' issues, and demonstrate the relevance of economics for business. A final feature used throughout the book is a series of references to Nobel Prize–winning economics that show how cutting-edge work has informed developments in economic theory and policy in *business-relevant* contexts. A comprehensive glossary can be found at the end of the book.

The third edition has been thoroughly updated with, for example, extensive discussions of the recent financial crisis and new material on PEST, Porter's five forces, behavioural economics and game theory. We've also added a new Everyday Economics feature that challenges students to identify economic themes and concepts depicted in a series of photo montages. Finally, the book is supported by a companion website which includes a number of features for lecturers and students.

In summary

Our intention is that the book should be:

- comprehensive yet concise
- academically rigorous
- business relevant
- replete with examples
- written in an engaging style

Acknowledgements

In preparing the manuscript for this book we have benefited from a number of extremely helpful comments made by a number of anonymous reviewers.

We would also like to thank Amy Grant at Palgrave. As ever, she has been a constant source of support and encouragement.

Chris Mulhearn and Howard R. Vane

tour of the book

Key issues

A set of questions that students will be able to answer by the end of each chapter, signalling the most important topics from the outset.

What are the basic economic questions every society must face?

Why must business concern itself with economics?

What does economics have ~~say about the respecti~~

Concept boxes

Core economic concepts are emboldened in the text and discussed and summarized in the margin.

■ Concept: **Resource scarcity** implies that *all* resources are scarce in relation to the limitless wants present in every society.

less ar~
ics to eng~
still present ~
economics wo~

In everyday ~
diamonds migh~
for example, is ~
might the next ~
different empl~
demands up~
currently ~
that t~

~~than th~~
that a society's ~
because of the vast ~

Because, in an eco~
with a potentially huge ~
of production and consum~
forgone. In economics the ~
of **opportunity cost**. The op~
is the value of the best altern~
opportunity cost is more tha~
rything; it allows us to und~

Consider, for example, ~
industrial countries of W~
ronmental protection w~

Opportunity cost: the cost of an action measured in terms of the best alternative action that must be given up.

Business case studies

These examine a variety of different business situations in which economics plays a vital role.

BUSINESS CASE STUDY

Pay what you like to watch I~ Town

Every football fan knows what it's li~
tration of defeat. Sometimes it's d~
you think of how much you've p~
that's left you flat and demor~
~~ht~~ even think, 'that's it~
~~ing too much~

Key terms

Highlighted in the text and defined in the margin, and listed at the end of each chapter for revision purposes.

Everyday economics

These challenge students to identify economic themes and concepts depicted in photos of everyday objects and activities.

EVERYDAY ECONOMICS 2.1

What counteracting institutions m

These are images of everyday goods and s may be asymmetric information. To overc counteracting institutions. Can you think

Answers are at the end of the chapter.

ECONOMICS AT WORK

Nileeka Gunawardene, The Bolly

Nileeka is the founder and creative direc dance company based at Pineapple Dan choreographers run weekly dance classe events, provide corporate entertainment

Visit www.palgrave.com/mu resource allocation, the impa entrepreneurs respond to

APPLYING ECONOMICS TO BUSINESS

Imagine a situation where you and a friend wer seriously considering starting up a bar business together selling a selection of beers, wines and cocktails. You have already identified premises which you both consider are ideally located to attract customers. Before going ahead you would nee to carefully consider the various cost and reven streams in order to establish whether such a b ness would be viable.

Applying economics to business

Features that discuss how economic strategies can be implemented to produce certain outcomes for the business as a whole.

Economics at work

Links to five video interviews on the companion website at **www.palgrave.com/ mulhearn3** which feature business managers from organizations such as The Bollywood Co. and The Meyer Group discussing how economics comes into play in the world of work.

ONE THING YOU SHOULD READ

At the end of every chapter we'll introduce one key on some of the key concepts we've just discussed. may not be something you've been asked to do be setting and will help you better understand the sub

John Steinbeck's *The Grapes of Wrath*, Chapte

The Grapes of Wrath was published in 1939 an ory of the Joads, a tenant farming family, of thousands of others, to leave the l' of Oklahoma to travel to different

One thing you should read

Pointers to just *one* interesting and entertaining piece of further reading per chapter, ranging from academic pieces to extracts from novels and interviews with economists to video clips to watch.

SUMMARY

- Economics is concerned with three basic *what* goods and services a society produc these are produced and *for whom* they are
- Economics matters in a business context be it explains the roles of firms, consumers and government in the market.
- All resources are scarce in the context of th demands that can be placed upon them. S therefore faced with myriad choices conc the resources it has should be used. The opportunity cost allows us to begin to choices particular societies make at
- Microeconomics deals with the individual; macroeconomics ole. Both are

Summary

Each chapter ends with a summary of the main points to consolidate learning and provide a bridge to the next chapter.

Questions for discussion

A series of questions at the end of each chapter encourages reflection and critical thinking around the chapter's main topics.

QUESTIONS FOR DISCUSSION

1. What is economics?
2. Microeconomics suggests that successful businesse need to be dynamic. Can you explain the need for such dynamism?
3. Explain how consumer sovereignty places consume at the heart of economic decision-making in capital economies.
4. How can the notion of opportunity cost help us to understand the production choices a society mak
5. Why is some knowledge of macroeconomics important for business?

Visit **www.palgrave.com/mulhearn3** to find an array of comprehensive and innovative resources for both students and instructors.

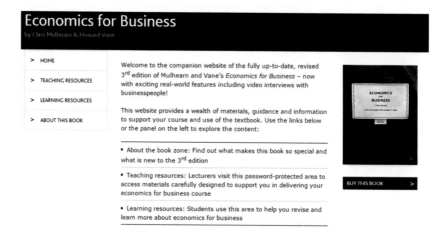

Resources for students:

- Economics at work video interviews featuring businesspeople explaining how economics has been useful in their careers
- Interactive true/false questions to test understanding of the main points in each chapter
- Bonus case studies from around the world that show how economic principles have affected real businesses
- Suggested answers to the 'one thing you should read' questions
- Animated graphs and figures to illustrate key economic concepts
- Flashcards to test your knowledge of the key terms in each chapter
- Video interviews with economic Nobel Laureates, alongside commentary relating the interviews to the themes of the textbook

Resources for instructors:

- Teaching slides for each chapter, including relevant diagrams and figures
- A comprehensive testbank of multiple choice and essay questions, with guideline answers
- Bonus tutorial materials, including handouts and teaching slides on discrete topics

The publisher and the authors would like to thank the organizations and people listed below for permission to reproduce material from their publications:

Alan Heston and Bettina Aten, for permission to reproduce data in Table 8.2 'Openness for the G5 in current prices (total trade as % of GDP).' From Alan Heston, Robert Summers and Bettina Aten, Penn World Table Versions 6.3 and 7.1, Center for International Comparisons of Production, Income and Prices at the University of Pennsylvania, August 2009 & Nov 2012. Copyright © Alan Heston, Robert Summers and Bettina Aten.

Bank of England, for permission to reproduce:
Figure 14.9 'Sterling exchange rates.' From Inflation Report, November 2014.
Figure 14.13 'The widening of the ERM band in 1993.' Adapted from Bank of England *Quarterly Bulletin*, November 1993.
Both copyright © Bank of England.

BP plc, for permission to reproduce:
Figure 2.16 'Crude oil price 1970–2012,'
Figure 2.17 'World oil production and consumption 1970–2012,'
Figure 2.18 'US, China and Japan oil consumption 1970–2012.'
All from BP Statistical Review of World Energy 2013, www.bp.com/statisticalreview Copyright © BP plc.

Controller Office of Public Sector Information (OPSI), for permission to reproduce:
Figure 6.4 'The cap and trade approach to the reduction of $CO2$ emissions.' Adapted from Lazarowicz, M. (2009), Global Carbon Trading: A framework for reducing emissions. © Crown Copyright 2009.
Figure 8.2 'British government expenditure and income 2014–2015.' From Office for Budget Responsibility, 2014-15 estimates, published in HM Treasury Budget 2014 (HC 1104) www.hm-treasury.gov.uk. © Crown Copyright 2014
Crown copyright material is reproduced with the permission of the Controller Office of Public Sector Information (OPSI).

Edward Elgar Publishing and Brian Snowdon, for permission to reproduce and adapt Figure 7.13 'Indivisibilities in the demand for labour and the impact of a minimum wage.' From Shaw, G. K. (1997) 'How Relevant is Keynesian Economics Today?', in Snowdon, B. and H. R. Vane (eds.), *Reflections on the Development of Modern Macroeconomics*, Cheltenham, UK and Northampton, MA: Edward Elgar Publishing. Copyright © 1997 Edward Elgar Publishing, Brian Snowdon and Howard R. Vane.

European Central Bank, for permission to reproduce Figure 10.5 'Inflation in the euro area.' Copyright © European Central Bank, Frankfurt am Main, Germany. Data is available free of charge via the ECB's home page.

European Union, for permission to reproduce Figure 2.11 'Member countries of the European Union.' From EUROPA website, http://europa.eu/about-eu/countries/index_en.htm Copyright © European Union, 1995-2015.

Eurostat, for permission to reproduce data in Figure 9.10 'Minimum monthly wage 2013 for selected European countries and the US in €.' From http://ec.europa.eu/eurostat Copyright © European Union, 1995–2015.

Human Development Report Office, United Nations Development Programme, for permission to reproduce:

Data in Figure 15.6 'Gross national income per capita 2013 (PPP 2011 US$)'. From UN Human Development Report 2013, www. hdr.undp.org

Table 15.1 'United Nations Human Development Index 2013, top 10 and selected economies.' From UN Human Development Report 2014, www. hdr.undp.org

Table 15.2 'United Nations Human Development Index 2013, selected economies with medium and low human development.' From UN Human Development Report 2014, www. hdr.undp.org

All copyright © Human Development Report Office, United Nations Development Programme, reprinted under the Creative Commons 3.0 IGO licence http://creativecommons.org/licenses/by/3.0/igo/legalcode The entire series of Human Development Index (HDI) values and rankings are recalculated using the most recent (revised) data and functional forms. The latest HDI rankings and values cannot therefore be compared directly to indices published in previous Reports. Please see hdr.undp.org for more information.

International Monetary Fund, for permission to reproduce:

Data in Table 8.1 'Economic growth rates for the G5.' From IMF's World Economic Outlook Database.

Data in Figure 8.4 'Real GDP growth, G5, 1990–2014.' From IMF's World Economic Outlook Database.

Data in Figure 8.5 'Real GDP growth, G5, Russia and China 1990–2014.' From IMF's World Economic Outlook Database.

Data in Figure 8.7 'G5 unemployment rates 1990–2014.' From IMF's World Economic Outlook Database.

Data in Figure 8.9 'G5 inflation, 1990–2014.' From IMF's World Economic Outlook Database.

Data in Figure 9.9 'Unemployment rates in the euro area and the United States 1999–2015.' From IMF's World Economic Outlook Database.

Data in Figure 14.3 'Current account balances 1990–2014.' From IMF's World Economic Outlook Database.

Data in Figure 14.4 'Current account as percentage of GDP 1990–2014.' From IMF's World Economic Outlook Database.

Data in 14.10 'UK, US and euro area inflation, 2007–14.' From IMF's World Economic Outlook Database.

Data in Figure 14.12 'Inflation for the G7 1970–90.' From IMF's World Economic Outlook Database.

Data in Figure 15.5 'Shares in world GDP: G5 and BRIC economies.' From IMF's World Economic Outlook Database.

Figure 15.8 'Copper price US$ per metric tonne 2000–14, monthly.' From IMF's World Economic Outlook Database.

Figure 15.9 'Global current account imbalances.' From IMF October 2014 World Economic Outlook, Legacies, Clouds, Uncertainties, Chapter 4: Are Global Imbalances at a Turning Point?

Figure 15.10 'Global net foreign asset imbalances.' From IMF October 2014 World Economic Outlook, Legacies, Clouds, Uncertainties, Chapter 4: Are Global Imbalances at a Turning Point?

Data in Figure 15.11 'Coffee price (arabica) US cents per pound 2000–14, monthly and illustrated Fairtrade price.' From IMF's World Economic Outlook Database.

All Copyright © International Monetary Fund

Office for National Statistics (ONS), for permission to reproduce:

Figure 3.1 'Legal status of UK businesses, 2013.' From Watkins, K. (2013), UK Business: Activity, Size and Location – 2013.

Figure 3.2 'Value (deflated by the GDP deflator) and number of M&A deals involving UK companies, 1987 to Q1 2014.' From Statistical Bulletin: Mergers and Acquisitions Involving UK Companies, Q1 2014 Release.

Figure 7.5 'UK productivity and earnings 1975–2013.' From Annual Survey of Hours and Earnings (ASHE), published in UK Wages over the Past Four Decades, 2014 Release.

Table 7.1 'Economic activity in the UK, all aged 16–64; seasonally adjusted; in '000s and %.' From ONS Labour Force Survey, part of Labour Market Statistics September 2014 release.

Table 7.2 'UK highest and lowest paid occupations 2013.' From ONS Annual Survey of Hours and Earnings, 2013.

Table 7.3 'UK Distribution of gross hourly earnings, April 2013.' From ONS Annual Survey of Hours and Earnings, 2013.

Figure 7.11 'Mean gross weekly earnings by place of work, Great Britain, scaled by number of jobs.' From ONS Annual Survey of Hours and Earnings, 2013.

Data in Figure 7.12 'UK workforce jobs by selected industry 1978–2014 ('000s).' From ONS data tables.

Data in Figure 7.14 'Women and men earning less than the UK minimum wage.' From Low Pay, April 2014 Release.

Figure 8.3 'UK real GDP 1948–2013, £bn, 2011 prices.' From ONS, *The Blue Book*, 2014 Edition Release.

Data in Figure 8.8 'The CPI basket 2014 (%).' From Gooding, P. (2014), Consumer Price Inflation: The 2014 Basket of Goods and Services.

Data in Figure 13.2 'UK trade in cars, 2003–13.' From ONS, *The Pink Book*, 2014 Edition Release.

Table 14.3 'UK balance of payments 2012 (£m)1.' From ONS, *The Pink Book*, 2013 Edition Release.

The figures and data above contain public sector information licensed under the Open Government Licence v3.0.https://www.nationalarchives.gov.uk/doc/open-government-licence/version/3/

Transport for London, for permission to reproduce Figure 6.1 'Traffic entering the central London charging zone during charging hours 2002–7.' From Transport for London's Sixth Annual Congestion Charging Monitoring Report (2008). Copyright © Transport for London.

The Brookings Institution, for permission to reproduce the table 'Sources of US economic growth 1929–82 (per cent).' From Denison, E. F. (1985) *Trends in American Economic Growth*, Washington, DC: The Brookings Institution. Copyright © 1985 The Brookings Institution.

The Organization for Economic Cooperation and Development (OECD), for permission to reproduce data in Figure 7.2 'Trade union density in the G5 1960–2013.' From OECD, Trade Union Density, https://stats.oecd.org/Index.aspx?DataSetCode=UN_DEN in OECD.Stat https://stats.oecd.org/ (2014) Copyright © OECD.

United Nations, for permission to reproduce:

Figure 1.2 'Foreign direct investment (FDI) inflows by economy type, $bn, 1995–2012.' From World Investment Report 2013, Global Value Chains: Investment and Trade for Development, by UNCTAD. Copyright © 2013 United Nations.

Data in Figure 15.3 'FDI inflows by region 1990–2013, US$bn.' From web table 2, UNCTAD website, http://unctad.org Copyright © United Nations.

Data in Figure 15.4 'FDI inflows by selected countries 1990–2013, $m.' From web table 2, UNCTAD website, http://unctad.org Copyright © United Nations.

Data in Figure 15.7 'Estimated international migrants at mid-year by destination.' From United Nations, Department of Economic and Social Affairs (2013). Trends in International Migrant Stock: The 2013 revision (United Nations database, POP/DB/MIG/Stock/Rev.2013). Copyright © 2013 United Nations.

Table 15.3 'International migrants as a percentage of the population.' From United Nations, Department of Economic and Social Affairs (2013). Trends in International Migrant Stock: The 2013 revision (United Nations database, POP/DB/MIG/Stock/Rev.2013). Copyright © 2013 United Nations.

All reprinted with the permission of the United Nations.

World Gold Council, for permission to reproduce the data in Figure 2.10 'Gold price 1971–2014 (January).' From ICE Benchmark Administration, World Gold Council (updated 28.4.2014). Copyright © World Gold Council.

World Trade Organization (WTO), for permission to reproduce:

Figure 1.1 'The dynamic pie: share in world exports for selected economies by development status 1980–2011.' From World Trade Report 2013: Factors shaping the future of world trade. Copyright © World Trade Organization (WTO) 2013.

Data in Table 2.1 'Shares of regional trade flow in world merchandise exports, 2012 (%).' From International Trade Statistics 2013. Copyright © World Trade Organization (WTO) 2013.

Data in Table 13.4 'World merchandise exports by region and selected economy, 1948–2013 (%).' Adapted from WTO World Trade Report 2007 and WTO World Trade Report 2014, Trade and development: recent trends and the role of the WTO. Copyright © 2007 and 2014 World Trade Organization (WTO).

Data in Table 13.5 'Leading exporters in world trade in commercial services 2013 ($billion and %).' Adapted from WTO World Trade Report. 2014. Trade and development: recent trends and the role of the WTO. Copyright © World Trade Organization (WTO) 2014.

Data in Figure 13.3 'Selected intra and inter-regional merchandise trade flows, 2012.' From International Trade Statistics, 2012. Copyright © 2012 World Trade Organization (WTO).

Data in Figure 14.14 'Euro area members' share of trade with EU 28, 2013 (%).' From www.wto.org. Copyright © World Trade Organization (WTO).

Data in Figure 15.2 'Regional shares in world merchandise exports 1983 and 2013 (%).' From the WTO website www.wto.org. Copyright © World Trade Organization (WTO).

XE Currency Services, for permission to reproduce Figure 14.5 'Chinese yuan per US dollar, 2005–2014.' From XE.com. Copyright © XE.

The publisher and the authors would also like to thank everyone who has supplied images for the book. Please refer to individual credit lines for details.

1

economics and business

KEY ISSUES

What are the basic economic questions every society must face?

Why must business concern itself with economics?

What does economics have to say about the respective roles of firms, consumers and government in the allocation of resources?

What is resource scarcity and what are its implications?

What are microeconomics and macroeconomics and why are they important for business?

CONTENTS

1.1 Introduction: what is economics?   **2**

1.2 Why economics matters to business, indeed to *everyone*   **6**

1.3 Understanding the roles of firms, consumers and government in markets   **10**

1.4 Scarcity, choice and opportunity cost   **21**

1.5 Opportunity cost and incentives   **24**

1.6 Microeconomics, macroeconomics and business   **27**

1.7 Positive and normative economics   **32**

1.1   Introduction: what is economics?

Most people can probably say what economics is about. It deals with issues such as inflation, unemployment, the profitability of firms, exchange rates, international trade and so on. But lists of this kind do not really tell us what the essence of the subject is. Economics is concerned with how societies organize the production and consumption of **goods** (physical commodities such as cars, books, food and housing) and **services** (such as those provided by banks, barbers, teachers and mobile phone companies). More precisely it tries to explain and understand:

Goods: tangible products.

Services: intangible products.

> *what* goods and services societies produce, *how* they produce them and *for whom* they are produced

Consider the society or economy in which you live. What are its production and consumption priorities? Table 1.1 lists a small range of familiar goods and services. Are they all *produced* in your economy? If so, *how* are they produced – in a business setting by firms, or does the government assist or even take primary responsibility for the production of some of them? All of these goods and services are clearly available in the developed Western economies but *to whom* are they available – everyone, or just those who are able to pay for them?

Table 1.1 Produced in the society in which you live?

Produced in some Western economies	Produced in most Western economies but in uneven quantities	Produced in Western economies in declining quantities	Produced in all Western economies in large quantities
• cars • computers • mobile phones	• tourist services • books, magazines • feature films	• footwear and clothing • sports goods • toys	• education services • healthcare • mobile phone services • digital media

Table 1.1 categorizes our selected goods and services in terms of whether and in what relative quantities **resources** in the major Western economies are **allocated** to their production. The following '*what, how* and *for whom*' patterns can be discerned:

■ **Concept:**
Resource allocation
is the commitment of a society's productive endowments, such as labour and machinery, to particular uses or patterns of use. For a society to produce a particular good or service it must allocate resources to the appropriate industry.

What is produced?

- Certain goods and services are produced in only some Western economies: cars, for example. Cars are manufactured in countries such as the United States, Japan, Germany and the UK but not in Ireland or Switzerland. Similarly, in Finland and the UK there is heavy investment in mobile phone production but, for the moment, relatively little in Denmark.
- For a second category of goods and services the production question is a matter of degree. Over the past 20 or 30 years, as international travel has become

easier and cheaper, many industrial countries have become tourist destinations and now produce the kinds of services foreign tourists want. However, for some countries, the commitment to tourism is particularly evident: France and Spain are obvious examples. Similarly, though many major film productions are American in origin, other countries have their own but mostly more modest film industries.

- Clothing and footwear provide an instance of *reduced* production by most if not all Western economies. If you check your wardrobe you will find that the labels on your clothes and shoes mostly indicate origins in the Far East and Eastern Europe. Thirty or 40 years ago, Western economies produced much more of their own clothing and footwear.
- Finally, there is a fourth category of good or service which virtually all Western economies produce in very large quantities: for example, education, health, mobile phone services and digital media.

We will have more to say in this and other chapters (see Chapter 13, especially) about *why* patterns of country specialization in production arise, but for the moment let us proceed to the noted questions of *how* and *for whom* production takes place.

How is production organized?

The form taken by production – the *how* question – can actually be discussed at two levels.

- First, we might be interested in the particular *technicalities* of production. The last 15 years have witnessed amazing changes in the actual form of some goods and services and the ways in which they are consumed. For example, prior to the early 2000s buying music meant having to buy a physical commodity: a vinyl record or CD. Internet-based music was not available. Since then physical music has had to compete with downloading and more recently with streaming services. However, the Internet has been commercially damaging to the music industry. Since 2000 the global market in recorded music has contracted sharply – by some 45 per cent – in overall revenue terms. This mostly reflects the fact that music on the Internet can be obtained without paying for it.

Communication and news services have also been technologically transformed. Texting, email, Google, Facebook and Twitter are ubiquitous; the personal letter an endangered species. The print sales of the newspaper industry are also in decline. Print journalism's lifeline may be a migration across to digital media, but can web-based news services that consumers formerly paid for in the shape of copies of the *Daily Mail* or the *Guardian* be provided profitably – *monetized* is the popular term – when so much Internet news is free? *The Times*

Digital media: a
seismic shift in the
organization of
production

and *Sunday Times* were the first of the non-specialist national newspapers in Britain to put their online versions behind a pay wall; some other papers have since followed suit while the rest are watching nervously. The technicalities of the 'how is production organized' question are clearly changing fast. Wherever there are digital applications, the threats to traditional ways of doing business appear profound and the opportunities for entrepreneurial innovation immense.

- Second, as noted, we might ask to what extent *governments* involve themselves in production decisions. Over the past 30 years, in countries such as the UK, concerted attempts have been made to reduce the influence of government over economic activity, for example through the privatization of state-owned firms and the introduction of market principles into local and central government service provision. Elsewhere, experience has been divided: in the US, to take the most obvious case, the economic impact of government has always been comparatively limited and there is consequently a greater role for the private sector in the allocation of resources. By contrast, in the Scandinavian countries the role of the state in the economy is traditionally more pervasive. As we will see, the balance between what the business sector does in an economy and what the state does is one of the key issues in economics.

One example concerns efforts in the US to reform the provision of healthcare, which is organized in the main by the private sector. Generally, Americans who can afford to do so take out insurance that will pay their medical bills should they fall ill, or insurance is provided by employers. The problem is that millions of Americans have no health insurance. The US devotes much more of its resources to healthcare compared to other advanced economies but the end result is that while most Americans have access to state-of-the-art medicine, millions of their fellow citizens are denied care because they are poor or unemployed. Some

Reproduced by kind permission of PRIVATE EYE magazine/Will Dawburn (Wilbur)

THE TIMES THEY ARE A-CHARGIN'

years ago President Clinton failed in an attempt to use government money to underwrite a universal insurance scheme. In 2010 President Obama's Affordable Care Act – nicknamed 'Obamacare' – made better progress. As of 2014 more than 7 million Americans had signed up to Obamacare. This example suggests that the boundaries between the state and the market in economies are not set in stone and that the debate over what each can competently do is a continuing and spirited one.

For whom is production organized?

The *for whom* question is often closely linked to the latter form of the *how* question. In reforming the provision of American healthcare, President Obama wanted to get the government more involved (the *how* question) in order to make healthcare more accessible (the *for whom* question). If you've watched the American TV series *Breaking Bad* you'll understand the issue in terms of Walter White's decision to finance his cancer treatment by cooking crystal meth. Walter couldn't pay his medical bills on a high school chemistry teacher's salary and his medical insurance wouldn't cover the costs (the *initial* bill was $90,000) so he became a very highly paid drug manufacturer – and serial killer – to get the money to save his life. Had Obamacare been around when Walter got sick there would have been a different answer to the question '*for whom* is US healthcare produced?' and Walter might have chosen a different career path.

This example shows that the answer to the *for whom* question is quite straightforward. When resource allocation happens through the use of the private market the only criterion determining access is ability to pay. If you want something and you can pay for it you get it. But where governments involve themselves in production decisions, they may choose to provide quantities of goods and services that otherwise might not have been available to some citizens and, moreover, provide them without charge or at a subsidized rate. In the Netherlands the government sponsors a major 'social housing' programme. This means that a large proportion (75 per cent) of the rentable housing stock in the Netherlands is publicly subsidized; many houses are built at the behest of the government according to perceived needs and rents are relatively low. As a result, Dutch citizens are less likely to be unable to find somewhere to live or find rents unaffordable. Here then, *for whom* means for people who need housing but can't afford to buy or rent privately. In the UK, to take a contrasting case, although there is some investment in public housing, much more of the housing stock tends to be privately produced and owned. Firms build houses in the expectation that they will be able to sell them at a profit. Private landlords build up property portfolios for rent. This means that the ability of an individual to become a consumer of housing – the *for whom* question – turns less on need and more on the ability to pay.

ECONOMICS AT WORK

Nileeka Gunawardene, The Bollywood Co., www.thebollywoodco.com

Nileeka is the founder and creative director of The Bollywood Co., a Bollywood dance company based at Pineapple Dance Studios in London, whose instructors and choreographers run weekly dance classes and can also be hired to perform at special events, provide corporate entertainment and appear in film/TV and product launches.

Visit **www.palgrave.com/mulhearn3** to watch Nileeka talking about resource allocation, the impact of the recession, and how successful entrepreneurs respond to market needs.

1.2   Why economics matters to business, indeed to *everyone*

In a general sense the obvious answer to the question of why economics matters to business is *context*: everything happens against an economic backdrop. BMW, Sony, a corner shop, rail and ferry firms, a small accountancy practice: all are affected as economic circumstances change. We will discuss the potential for turbulence in the general economic environment, and whether it can be moderated or tamed, later on in this chapter.

At a lower, more granular level, businesses need to think about their decisions in the light of the basic economic questions we have introduced: what should they produce, how, and for whom? Further on in this chapter we will demonstrate the intrinsic relationship between economics and business decision-making by reflecting on the case of Tesco and how its seemingly unstoppable march on the UK and, indeed, international high street was suddenly checked. Tesco got its economics stunningly right at first but then badly wrong.

Just as important, economics offers insight across a vast range of options, problems and puzzles for individuals, businesses and governments.

- Why do some people choose to buy exorbitant insurance policies on electrical goods, or go to university or to, apparently, over-consume dental treatment?
- Why do some firms, such as Apple, fiercely protect their patented innovations while others – such as the electric car maker Tesla – give away their inventions for free? Why do some firms organize production on a basis that minimizes their wage costs while others treat their workers with notable generosity and

trust, offering them higher wages than they need to, company shares and a high degree of autonomy in their work? Why is violence the trademark of the Mafia?

• Why have governments around the world clearly not succeeded in quashing the markets in illegal drugs despite the vast sums spent on enforcement and the harsh penalties faced by offenders? Might a better form of regulation involve decriminalizing drug markets?

This book reflects on all of these and many other questions using some basic economic concepts. Quite simply we will try to show that economics suffuses the business environment and indeed life in general.

One of the remarkable features of the three basic questions in economics – what to produce, how and for whom – is that the answers to them are always changing; they are in a constant state of flux. This has long been observed by economists. Capitalism was memorably characterized by Karl Marx (1818–83) as a process in which 'all that is solid melts into air', meaning that the process is never still or static but constantly evolving with a dynamism that Marx found wondrous. Though he is known as a critic of capitalism, Marx also admired its sheer capacity to produce, to do what it's supposed to do: consistently allocate and reallocate resources in new and imaginative ways. Later, the Austrian economist, Joseph Schumpeter (1883–1950), captured the fervour for renewal and growth inherent in capitalism in the paradoxical notion of 'creative destruction'. Do you think your job is safe, your business, the markets your economy relies on, your bank, your currency, in fact anything economic? Schumpeter's message is 'watch out!' These things are all potentially vulnerable to the impulse in capitalism to do things differently and better; to destroy in order to create.

But is capitalism just a wild ride? Are businesses and individuals simply at the mercy of an economic process inevitably more powerful than they are? Can capitalism be tempered or conditioned? The most influential economist of his age – John Maynard Keynes (1883–1946) – argued that it could. His view was that the destructive extremes of capitalism might be softened by government policies orchestrated at the level of whole economies. This would make for a better state of affairs where businesses and individuals would be spared the ordeals of economic crash and recession. For Keynes the task was 'to indicate the nature of the environment which the free play of economic forces requires if it is to realise the full potentialities of production'; in other words to make capitalism safe for the world.

Marx, Schumpeter and Keynes may offer ringing phrases, but do such historical figures tell us anything about today's economies? Yes they do. Table 1.1 describes something of the pattern of resource reallocation that has been happening in recent years in Western economies, but these developments have been mirrored by changes elsewhere. Figure 1.1 provides an illustration. As we will

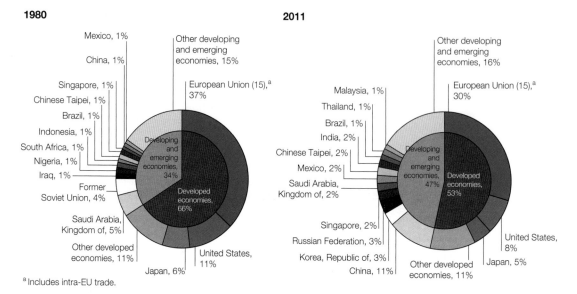

Figure 1.1 The dynamic pie: share in world exports for selected economies by development status 1980–2011

Source: WTO World Trade Report 2013

see in more detail later in this book, the ability of a country to export goods and services to the rest of the world is important. Exports promote jobs at home and earn foreign currencies needed to pay for imports. Figure 1.1 shows changes in the share of world exports for particular economies and also summarizes the share of exports between the rich developed economies and the rest. Two things stand out. First, there are individual winners and losers. In 1980 China had 1 per cent of the world export pie; by 2011 it had 11 per cent. This is a change unparalleled in modern economic history. But others gained too. For example, both Mexico and Singapore doubled their shares. On the other hand, the share of the European Union (EU) fell by 7 per cent, the US share fell by 3 per cent and the Japanese share fell by 1 per cent. The second feature of Figure 1.1 is the collective loss in export share of the developed economies (down from 66 to 53 per cent), and the collective gain of the developing and emerging economies (up from 34 to 47 per cent).

The increasing export capabilities of the developing world can be partly explained by investment: better machinery, equipment and technology and the know-how that comes with these things have all helped. Until very recently most international investment of this sort was directed towards the rich countries but Figure 1.2 shows how things have again changed. It depicts world **foreign direct investment (FDI)** flows between 1995 and 2012. FDI involves cross-border physical investment in productive capacity. When a firm opens a factory, an office, a pipeline or an educational offshoot in another country it is engaging in FDI. As recently as 2007 a clear balance of FDI favoured the developed economies but, as Figure 1.2 reveals, in

Foreign direct investment (FDI): cross-border physical investment in productive capacity.

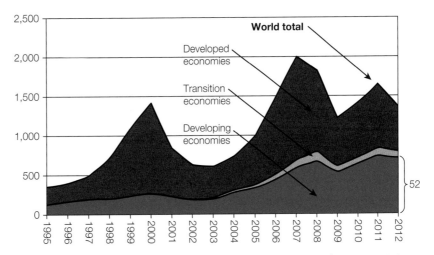

Figure 1.2 Foreign direct investment (FDI) inflows by economy type, $bn, 1995–2012

Source: UNCTAD World Investment Report 2013

2012 – and for the first time ever – the developing economies had a global edge with 52 per cent of FDI flows.

Figures 1.1 and 1.2 depict a world that is becoming increasingly globalized. Resource allocation involves global shifts in production, investment and trade that affect individual women and men, firms, economies and groups of economies. And these sometimes astonishing developments have been overlaid with others. The collapse of the Iron Curtain that until 1989 cut Europe politically and economically in half has almost doubled the membership of the European Union, and the majority of EU countries have since taken the huge step of voluntarily surrendering their own currencies for a newly created one: the euro. Other formerly communist, and in many ways remote, economies such as the Russian Federation, Vietnam and of course China are heavily integrated with parts of the world from which they were mutually isolated. The pace of technological change has accelerated: we live in a world that has in many fundamental respects been digitized. And then in 2008–9 the world economy suffered the most profound and unexpected economic shock and subsequent collapse since the onset of the Great Depression in 1929. For Marx and Schumpeter this last event may have been inevitable, but not for Keynes. His ideas had given policymakers the tools to confront this crisis and to begin to ameliorate its worst effects. We will see later that the Keynesian-inspired response to the crisis was itself controversial, but there is little doubt that in the eye of the storm many governments and policymakers around the world dusted off what had become dated and discarded economic ideas and deployed them with at least some measure of success.

The experience of the last 30 or so years might be accurately described as a 'hurricane' of creative destruction, or the modern equivalent of what Marshall

Berman called Marx's 'melting vision'. Sometimes the hurricane is tempered by governments, sometimes not. And it is through this that you (and we) must plot our course, as must everyone in any kind of business. *That's* why economics matters to business. That's why it matters to everyone.

1.3   Understanding the roles of firms, consumers and government in markets

In Section 1.1 we learned that economics is concerned with understanding how a society allocates resources – what it chooses to produce, how it produces and for whom it produces. But how are these determinations made? Which individuals or agencies, exactly, decide *what*, *how* and *for whom*? We can identify three influences on resource allocation in most economies. These are:

- firms
- consumers
- government

Market: is simply a framework that brings buyers and sellers together.

Firms, consumers and government interact through **markets**. A market is simply a nexus, a means of connection, for these different groups. It can of course, in the familiar sense, be a localized physical entity where buyers and sellers literally meet together – Billingsgate fish market in London, for example. More usually when economists speak about markets they are referring to the *process* of interaction between producers, consumers and, as we will see, government – as in the European car market, the global market in foreign currencies and so on. Let us consider the role of each of the three key agents in the market, beginning with firms.

What is the role of firms in markets?

We examine the role of firms in markets and the wider modern economy in much more detail in Chapter 3; here, a brief introduction will suffice. Firms may have a number of objectives but their central purpose is generally recognized as the organization of production for profit. In a sense, with profit as its goal, the firm must ask *itself* the three basic economic questions: what should it produce, how should production be organized, and at which customers should the goods and services it produces be aimed?

As an example, consider the declared business strategy of Tesco, Britain's largest supermarket group. Tesco is a grocer that, until about 20 years ago, traditionally concentrated on the domestic market. Its answers to the what, how and for whom questions were simple: *what* – it sold food; *how* – in supermarkets; *to whom* – British consumers. In 1997, Tesco announced much more ambitious plans. Its intention was to sell more non-food items such as clothing, computers and electrical goods. Tesco also planned to review both the form and locational focus of its UK operations, and to become much more internationally orientated:

in 1997 it had only two stores overseas. The company also intended to move further into the then new and rapidly expanding market for online shopping. Tesco's answers to the basic economic questions were thus beginning to look radically different: *what* – it would sell food and a growing range of non-food items; *how* – in different kinds of stores and different kinds of location in Britain, and it would expand into foreign markets and over the Internet; *to whom* – a wider and more differentiated British market and an increasingly global customer base.

Why did Tesco adopt this strategy? Firms cannot afford to be complacent: Tesco did not get to be Britain's premier food retailer by resting on its laurels; it was simply responding to what was happening in the marketplace. Food retailing in Britain had been transformed over the last two or three decades of the twentieth century, becoming progressively dominated by the large, often 'out-of-town' stores of a small number of companies: Tesco, Sainsbury's, Asda and so on. As these firms opened more and more stores, the level of competition between them became increasingly intense and, crucially, the possibility of further expansion was limited, ultimately by the size of the British market for superstore-based shopping. For Tesco (and the rest) then, two problems were apparent: rival firms threatening to poach its customers and something of a ceiling on the overall retail food superstore market. Tesco's new strategy would allow it to make progress on both these fronts – it would become a more attractive retailer than its competitors (or at least it would not lose ground in the face of similar moves by the other supermarket chains), selling a wider range of goods in new ways and in new places in the UK, *and* it would simultaneously gain access to a new global market with immense growth potential.

So how did Tesco's plan work out? Well, there's good news and bad. First the good. In Britain Tesco now has several distinct store formats. Its 450 'traditional' superstores are cleverly complemented by two smaller kinds of local outlet. Tesco Metro is a food retailing operation in 170 city centre stores, while around 1,000 Tesco Express stores offer convenience-store-style food shopping in a variety of residential and business locations. Note that the Metro and Express stores have taken Tesco into the heart of cities and towns, places that were not heavily served by the big supermarkets: by in a sense 'going local', Tesco has effectively begun to compete in a wholly new market and is no longer as dependent on its out-of-town traditional superstore business model.

Tesco in China

© Tesco

Tesco's UK online operation has developed to the point where it serves more than 1 million active customers and it has also ventured into the provision of financial services, insurance and a mobile phone network. Overseas, Tesco's two stores expanded to a remarkable complement of around 2200 in 12 countries in Europe, North America and the Far East. Here again, then, Tesco managed to extend its footprint – into online shopping at home and into the retail markets of other, often developing, economies such as Poland and China, where the potential for further growth is greater than in mature economies like the UK.

If that's the good news for Tesco, what's the bad? Well for a start not all of its overseas expansions have gone to plan. It sold its American Fresh & Easy food store chain in 2013 after the venture proved unprofitable. But perhaps more worryingly, Tesco has had problems in its key home market. Although it is still the market leader, Tesco's share of the market fell from a high of almost 32 per cent in 2007 to less than 29 per cent in early 2014. And it is not alone in finding trading conditions tough. Other big supermarket chains such as Asda and Morrisons have lost market share too. Why has this happened? At least part of the problem has been the effect of the recession on consumer behaviour. As the economy shrank in the wake of the 2008–9 financial crisis large numbers of people turned to the cheap discount chains such as Aldi and Lidl as they tried to stretch household budgets. In the meantime at the top end of the market Waitrose, catering for more affluent shoppers, seemed relatively immune to this trend. According to the consumer knowledge firm, Kantar Worldpanel (Kantarworldpanel.com), Aldi, Lidl and Waitrose increased their collective share of the UK grocery market by 3.5 per cent in 3 years. This might not sound a big number but Kantar Worldpanel reports that it amounts to £4.4 bn a year.

So what are the lessons from Tesco's good news/bad news story? This example demonstrates the importance of economics in a business setting in two ways. First, it allows us, from the outside as it were, to make sense of the business strategy Tesco implemented and got right before the recession hit: we can understand its business decision to try to escape the limitations of traditional British grocery retailing. But we can also explain why some of the big grocers were subsequently caught out by the recession. Second, economic principles clearly informed Tesco's own strategy, making them an

"I CAN REMEMBER WHEN AS FAR AS THE EYE COULD SEE WAS ALL TESCO SUPERMARKETS."

integral part of business decision-making. Tesco's initial success was simply down to nicely thought through economics. The later difficulties it shared with Asda and Morrisons were down to a failure to appreciate that the economic context had changed and exposed new vulnerabilities. It is worth noting too how Tesco reacted to this setback: by implementing a £200 million price-cutting initiative that directly confronted the perceived 'shopping-on-a-budget' edge opened up by Aldi and Lidl.

The Tesco case also shows that, in the pursuit of the objective of production for profit, firms are subject to two initial market-based constraints: competition from rival firms and the potentially elusive demands of consumers. We will consider what economists have to say about the role of consumers below, but let us first briefly summarize and highlight the importance of competition between firms.

For each firm, rivals are always significant because they represent an immediate threat to its continued presence in the market. A rival may improve a good or service, lower its price, practise more effective marketing, or even introduce an entirely new product that makes established ones obsolete. The point about all these eventualities is that they are best understood in the context of *resource allocation in a competitive market environment*. Every firm must ask itself what it should produce, how and for whom – in the knowledge that other firms are out there asking themselves exactly the same questions. This makes economics central to an understanding of the unfolding competitive process between firms.

A commonly used reformulation of the what, how and for whom questions – the PEST framework – is summarized in the below box.

APPLYING ECONOMICS TO BUSINESS

The PEST framework

PEST is an acronym that can be used to reflect on the environment in which the firm must compete:

- P – the *political* factors that might have a bearing on its choices and decisions
- E – the *economic* context in which it operates
- S – the *social* issues that may influence it
- T – the *technological* opportunities and threats that affect how it does business

We can use this framework to think again about the progress and problems of the large supermarkets.

One *political* problem supermarkets face is the suggestion that their size allows them too much power in markets – power over consumers who may not have a lot of choice about shopping elsewhere, and power over their suppliers who may be anxious not to antagonize such huge clients. An example of how political pressure can play out comes in the shape of the Groceries Code Adjudicator, created in 2013 by the UK government 'to oversee the relationship between supermarkets and their suppliers. It ensures that large supermarkets treat their direct suppliers lawfully and fairly, investigates complaints and arbitrates in disputes.' The Adjudicator's purpose is to limit the power of supermarkets over their suppliers.

We have already considered the most important *economic* context affecting supermarkets: the recession and extended period of slow economic growth that followed the financial crisis of 2008–9. As noted, this badly hit some of the large traditional supermarket chains such as Tesco and Morrisons.

Many businesses factor in *social* considerations when making decisions, and the supermarkets are no exception. A good current example is their treatment of the issue of foodbanks. Because they

(continued)

offer food for free they might be something super-markets frown upon or ignore. But, to demonstrate their social responsibility – an important factor in building and maintaining a good reputation – some supermarkets – such as Sainsbury's and Tesco – have offered their stores as collection points for foodbanks and encouraged their customers to donate.

One *technological* consideration for the super-markets is the development of online grocery shop-ping. This may have been a particular problem for Morrisons – which did not launch its online service until 2014, some time after its principal competitors. Morrisons acknowledges that this is one of the factors contributing to its recent relatively poor performance.

Peter Macdiarmid/Getty Images

Woolworths closes on the high street after nearly 100 years

The role of consumers in markets

Consumers are a major constraint on firms. In fact, it is ultimately con-sumers who effectively determine the way markets behave – whether they grow or decline and how fast they change. Consumers will even condition how quickly products are developed and improved in markets. How do they do this? Later today, if you pay to download a song from iTunes you are entering a market as a consumer but you would hardly perceive yourself as a major player in the music business. And this is true: on its own, your inter-est in rap, hip hop or the late John Lennon doesn't count for much. However, expressed *collectively*, purchasing power is the most powerful force at work in any market. If people decide that a particular band has had its day then the firms that produce and sell music will focus their efforts upon other more popular or potentially more popular artists.

BUSINESS CASE STUDY

The end of Woolworths on the high street

What went wrong at Woolies? More than 800 stores and almost 100 years on the British high street, but that all ended when the chain closed in 2008–9.

Can you remember what Woolies actually sold? Sweets – the famous pick 'n' mix – clothing, cheap electricals, CDs, DVDs, computer gaming, toys,

household goods, a few other things. But what would you go there *specifically* to buy? Probably nothing. That was the problem – a lack of focus to make people walk through the door in the first place.

And just as important, most of the things Woolies sold were also increasingly available elsewhere and online.

Most of the big supermarkets paralleled the majority of Woolworths' stock. This meant that the likes of Sainsbury's were able to expose customers to their non-food goods as they did their food shopping. Woolworths had little answer to this and their stores took on an increasingly tired-looking appearance.

At the same time the development of Internet-based retailing made competition in entertainment-related goods – where Woolworths had specialized – much more intensive. So Woolworths found itself caught in a kind of market-based pincer movement – between rivals in the neighbourhood and new competitors in cyberspace.

But the closure of its shops did not spell the end of the Woolworths business. The Woolworths name was bought out of administration by another company – Shop Direct – and now trades online.

■ **Concept:**
Consumer sovereignty implies that the consumption choices of individuals in competitive markets condition production patterns. Producers *must* follow the lead given by the purchasing decisions of consumers. If they produce goods and services that consumers do not want they will bankrupt themselves. Hence consumers exercise sovereignty over producers. The production of 'environmentally friendly' goods and services is an example of this kind of consumer power. The tuna fish producer who admitted to canning the odd dolphin would not remain in business very long.

■ **Concept:**
a **free market** is one in which there is no government interference or intervention.

Economists have a name for this notion of consumer power: **consumer sovereignty**. Consumer sovereignty suggests that individual consumers have ultimate control over what markets produce. As each individual chooses to buy a good or service, he or she is affirming the existence and provision of that good or service. On the other hand, if consumers generally choose not to buy something that was formerly in demand then producers will begin to withdraw it from the market. There is no point in trying to sell goods or services that people no longer want. The case study above illustrates the point: the end of almost a century of the Woolworths chain in the UK and the closure of more than 800 high street shops. All that history and tradition now counts for little – consumer preferences have changed, the market has evolved, and Woolworths' business model simply could not draw in the customers needed to help Woolies stay afloat. The same principle applies in reverse if consumers become avid purchasers of a good or service: producers then have a reason to increase the amount they produce. Witness the explosion of coffee shops over the past 15 years as evidence. The simple presence of consumers or potential consumers also gives firms an incentive to continually refine and improve the quality of their products. A firm which innovates – produces something better or cheaper – will be rewarded with more custom and thus with more profit. It *pays* firms to do as much as they can to please those who might buy their goods and services. Thus economics also matters in a business context because it is able to identify and understand the nature of the consumer-led *governance of markets*.

The role of government in markets

One way in which economists characterize markets is by the level of influence government has over them. A **free market** is one in which government has little or no influence. In a free market the key economic questions of what to produce, how and for whom will be decided mainly by interaction between individual consumers and firms. Firms will respond to the demands or anticipated demands of consumers. However, where markets are not free, resource allocation usually becomes subject to some combination of influence by consumers, firms *and* government. State intervention in markets can take two broad forms:

- The state may elect to directly produce some goods and services itself in tandem with or instead of production by private firms. Our earlier case of social housing provision in the Netherlands would be one example of mixed public and private provision: the Dutch government *and* private firms organize house building in the Netherlands. An instance of wholly public provision arose in Britain after the Second World War, when coal and steel production was taken from the private sector and run exclusively for many years by state-owned firms.

- The state may choose not to directly produce goods and services in markets but to *regulate* markets in some way. There can be a wide variety of practice here. In the European Union, agricultural production is heavily conditioned by financial subsidies paid by European governments to farmers. In fact, governments can and do choose to subsidize production by private producers in many markets. Conversely, instead of encouraging more production, government either may try to limit what it considers to be harmful or undesirable forms of output or it may seek to influence the quality of what is produced. For example, many of the world's governments are concerned about environmental pollution and have tried to regulate industry so that it pollutes less. There are more mundane but still important illustrations of the same kind of activity: for instance the empowerment by local government of health inspectors as a means to ensure that pubs and restaurants meet certain hygiene and food preparation standards.

Figure 1.3 broadly summarizes these categories of free markets and markets subject to forms of state intervention. In Panel A the market is composed only of business firms and private consumers – it is a free market. In Panel B, the *production side* of the market is composed of both firms and government. Here, then, the state has involved itself in the production of goods and services either alongside or, in some instances, perhaps instead of private firms. In Panel C, there is a layer of state regulation of the market as a whole.

Using the illustrative categories in Figure 1.3, can we say what a 'real' economy looks like – what is its typical form? In fact, **mixed economies** will be typified by the presence of markets represented by all three of the Panels A–C in Figure 1.3. Mixed economies are defined by the existence in them of some combination of public and private resource allocation: both private firms and government are involved in determining what society produces, how and for whom. Today, most of the world's countries are like this but prior to the late 1980s, economies in Eastern Europe and some in Africa and the Far East were **centrally planned** rather than mixed. This meant that there was relatively little room for private firms and resource allocation was primarily determined by the state. Bureaucrats rather than consumers and business people decided what kinds of goods and services should be produced. They also decided how production would be organized and controlled the ways in which goods and services were distributed. Most of the old centrally planned economies have now completed a process of **transition** to mixed status. This means that the

■ **Concept:** a **mixed economy** is one in which there is some role for government in resource allocation.

■ **Concept:** a **centrally planned economy** is one in which resource allocation is almost wholly determined by government.

■ **Concept:** an economy in **transition** is one in which resource allocation by the state is being eroded in favour of allocation determined by private firms and consumers.

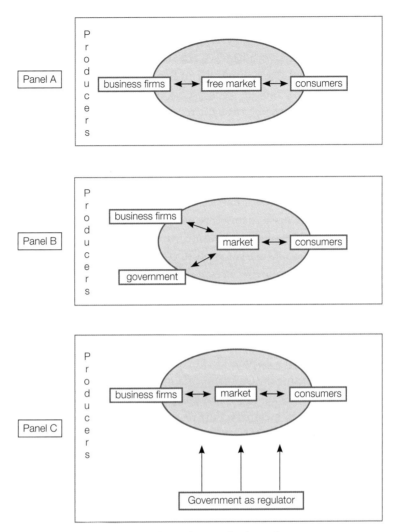

Figure 1.3 The free market and state intervention in markets

influence of the state over resource allocation has to varying extents been eroded in these economies and there are increasing opportunities for consumers and private firms to actively participate in economic decision-making. For example, in Cuba, state-run barber shops used to cut a lot of hair but now the market in haircuts has been liberalized. So Cubans have more choice in what Martin Amis calls a 'rug-rethink'. But others have not been so lucky. Reportedly, in North Korea, male university students are required to have their hair cut in the same style as the country's dictator, Kim Jong-un. *You can have any hairstyle you like as long as it's mine!*

The mixed economy can thus be defined as an arena in which key economic decisions are taken by business firms, consumers and government. In fact, under the general imperatives of consumer sovereignty, firms, consumers and government continually interact with one another across most markets in the mixed economy. In terms of Figure 1.3, this means that Panels B and C are most prevalent, with Panel A, the free market, in reality quite rare.

Consider, as examples of Panels B and C, the markets for commercial airliners, cars, mobile phone services, and top football matches. On the face of it, these might be thought to approximate reasonably 'free' markets in the sense that there appears to be relatively little government interference or intervention in them. The UK government does not, for example, try to provide airliners or flights for its citizens in the same way that it provides healthcare services. To understand the aircraft manufacturing business we might suppose that most attention would have to be paid to plane makers and their customers. Similarly, for the firms themselves, we might expect that *their* only concern would be the demands of their customers and the business strategies of their rivals. In fact, the aircraft market is more complicated than this, as are the markets for cars, mobile phone services and football matches. We will examine each in turn.

Aircraft

The market for aircraft is not a free market; it is *protected* from certain kinds of foreign competition. We explain the economics of protectionism in more detail in Chapter 13. For present purposes a simple overview will do. Rules governing the exporting and importing of goods and services in many European countries are organized collectively through the European Union on behalf of all its 28 members. One reason for doing this is that some European industries are organized on a pan-European basis. For example, the major European plane maker – Airbus – has production sites in the UK, France, Germany and Spain.

Airbus's major rival is the US firm Boeing, which complained that it has been adversely affected by a stream of subsidies Airbus received over a very long period from European governments. Putting it simply, the American accusation is that European large commercial aircraft sales have been helped by cheap or free taxpayers' money. This meant fewer sales for Boeing worldwide than would have been the case had the market not been unsettled by such subsidies. On the other hand, Airbus too claimed that Boeing receives subsidies from the US government. Both complaints were broadly upheld by the body that adjudicates such matters – the World Trade Organization – though the bigger subsidies seem to have been paid by the Europeans. In terms of Figure 1.3, the large commercial aircraft market would thus approximate Panel C – the market is conditioned (or, putting it less charitably, distorted) by the state.

Cars

Although the UK government does not itself produce cars, in the past it has done so after buying up ailing firms such as Rover. However, the UK car market remains one which is conditioned by state intervention. This usually takes two broad forms. First, in a similar way to the market in aircraft, the UK car market has been periodically protected, in this case against cars imported from Japan (protection is again administered at the level of the EU). Second, the UK government has consistently elected to subsidize investments made by big car manufacturers. Millions of pounds raised in taxes have been paid by the government to the likes of Ford and Nissan as a means to obtain or retain their production interests in Britain. The government's chief concern is the creation and retention of jobs. More recently, in an attempt to alleviate the effects of the 2008–9 recession on the car industry, the British government spent £400 million on a scheme to encourage owners of old cars to trade them in for new models with the promise of a £2000 price reduction per car. So the car market too is state regulated. Historically, it has moved from an approximation of Panel B (where government itself produces) to Panel C (with an emphasis on government regulation).

Mobile phone services

In 2013 Britain had more mobile phones than people, with some 82.7 million prepay and contract mobile subscriptions. Ofcom (the telecommunications industry regulator) reports that about half of these were third generation (3G) or fourth generation (4G) capable handsets that allow high-speed access to the Internet. The licences to operate 3G technology in Britain were auctioned by the government in 2000 to five mobile phone companies for a combined sum of £22.5 billion which, as the economists who advised on the design of the sale remarked, is a lot of money for simply 'selling air'. The 4G spectrum was auctioned in 2013 and realized a further £2.3 billion.

Regulating an industry by auctioning the right to participate in it is an interesting concept: what, besides raising a mountain of cash, were the government's objectives? Its main aim was actually to allocate resources efficiently: to try to put the mobile market in the hands of firms that would use it best. But how might best use be gauged? Informed by a context of consumer sovereignty, the principle is that those firms that can most profitably use the market by inventing, improving and selling the products will be prepared to pay most for the privilege of market entry. Of course, none of this was guaranteed in advance but, considering that in 2012 alone the retail revenues of telecom providers totalled almost £40 billion, it appears that the auction outcomes were generally very positive: the government raised an unparalleled sum of money for its own purposes and allocated licences to firms that have – if the acid test is generating and innovatively serving a market – used them well.

In terms of Figure 1.3, the mobile phone industry fits Panel C, with the government as market regulator.

Professional football

The Premier League might at first seem far removed from state concerns but there have been notable instances of intervention here too, which have had important impacts on the market. As a result of the Hillsborough Disaster in 1989, in which 96 Liverpool supporters lost their lives, the government decreed that all Premier League grounds should provide only seated accommodation.

The Bosman ruling: a magnificent result for professional footballers

DIGITAL VISION

This safety measure has had the effect of reducing the capacity of many grounds and prompted the building of a number of new stadia.

The EU has also imposed a significant, indeed infamous, change in the labour market for professional footballers. The so-called Bosman ruling prevents football clubs in the EU from 'selling' the registrations of footballers once their contracts have expired, bringing professional football in line with all other kinds of jobs. If you agree to work for a firm for 3 years you would not expect your next employer to have to pay a transfer fee to secure your services at the end of the 3-year contract. But this is exactly what happened in football before the Bosman ruling. The change vastly increased the negotiating and earning power of the best players – they are now free to choose who to work for at the end of their contracts, and their previous employers have no say or financial interest in the matter.

Taken together, there is little doubt that these two instances of state intervention in the football market have had a notable impact upon it. In terms of Figure 1.3, Panel C would be representative of this market.

These examples suggest that state intervention in markets in the mixed economy is more prevalent than might at first appear. However, it is possible to go even further. The preceding discussion considered *discrete* forms of intervention in particular markets. Most governments in the advanced economies maintain, in addition, a regulatory brief in respect of markets *generally*. There are several reasons for this; here it will suffice to highlight one. For reasons that we elaborate fully in Chapter 5, it is a commonplace among economists that monopoly – defined for now as the presence of only one firm in an industry or market – is undesirable, not least because it restricts consumer choice and impedes consumer sovereignty. Accordingly, to a greater or lesser degree, governments are concerned to prevent the achievement of monopoly status by any firm in most (not all, as we shall see) industries or markets. In a sense, then, the state regulation of markets can be said to almost always have particular and general forms. Particular in terms of, say, discrete intervention to regulate international trade in a good, or set standards for the way consumers in an industry are treated; and general as (and, to reiterate, this is but one example) in the watching brief to prevent the formation of monopolies.

On the basis of the discussion so far, we would argue that business operates in consumer-led market environments that are pervasively and sometimes subtly conditioned by government. Again, then, economics counts for business

because it helps explain this operating context. If you wish to understand business, or you are actually in business, you need some awareness of economics.

1.4   Scarcity, choice and opportunity cost

We have learned that economics concerns itself with the production choices a society has to make: *what goods and services ... produced how ... for whom*? But we also need to know why these choices are so pressing. It is painfully obvious that many societies continue to struggle with the large-scale human tragedies of poverty, malnutrition and treatable disease. The starkness of choice here needs little emphasis: people have basic needs for food, warmth and shelter and will allocate what resources they have into producing these things first. But in affluent parts of the world the general levels of production and consumption are higher now than they have ever been. Food, warmth and shelter are largely taken for granted, as indeed is the availability of an at times seemingly boundless array of other goods and services. Is there really a problem here for economics to engage with? We might of course point out that poverty and want are still present in many sections of the advanced societies, but even if they weren't, economics would still be given purpose by the notion of **resource scarcity**.

■ **Concept: Resource scarcity** implies that *all* resources are scarce in relation to the limitless wants present in every society.

In everyday usage, scarcity is interpreted simply as a lack of ready availability: diamonds might be considered scarce and therefore highly prized but alcohol, for example, is not: you can get it relatively cheaply in quantities which you might the next morning live to regret. For economists, however, scarcity has a different emphasis: it is always placed in the context of the potentially *infinite* demands upon a society's scarce resources. It is true that the advanced societies currently enjoy previously undreamt of living standards but that does not mean that there are no unmet needs or wants in these societies. In a country as rich as the US we have seen that many people still lack access to medical care, not everyone who wants one has a car, and many people would like to live in houses better than those they currently occupy. These are more than glib points: they suggest that a society's wants are in fact *limitless*. All resources must be considered scarce because of the vast range of competing uses to which they could be put.

Because, in an economic sense, resources are scarce, every society is faced with a potentially huge spectrum of choice. Committing resources to one set of production and consumption patterns necessarily means that others must be forgone. In economics the essence of resource choice is captured in the notion of **opportunity cost**. The opportunity cost of a particular resource commitment is the value of the best alternative use which must consequently be given up. But opportunity cost is more than a fancy way of saying societies can't do or have everything; it allows us to understand why *particular* production choices are made.

Opportunity cost: the cost of an action measured in terms of the best alternative action that must be given up.

Consider, for example, the issue of environmental pollution. In the advanced industrial countries of Western Europe there is a relatively high standard of environmental protection which is administered both by individual nation states and

© istockphoto/joyt

The Danube at Regensburg in Germany: don't pollute it; the opportunity cost is too high

the EU. In contrast, protection standards in parts of Africa and South America are undoubtedly lower. Why? Is it simply a question of varying degrees of interest in and commitment to the environment, or are there other forces at work here? An economic analysis would suggest the latter. A society's view of the balance between the imperative of industrial production and what is tolerable in terms of consequent damage to the environment must be set against the level of economic development of the society in question. In, say, the relatively affluent German economy it might be possible to raise industrial output by relaxing the controls over the ways in which firms dispose of liquid waste. Instead of investing in expensive equipment that treated such material, it could be pumped – cheaply – straight into rivers like the Rhine and the Danube. Here the balance between what would be gained and lost by such action becomes critical. How highly are clean rivers valued as against a *bit* more output in an already wealthy society? The likely answer is that the opportunity cost of the increase in output is too great – clean rivers are more highly valued, therefore there is an economic rationale for pollution control and a particular production choice can be understood. In much poorer countries, the value attached to extra industrial output will undoubtedly be higher and therefore the cost of some forms of environmental protection may be considered prohibitive in terms of the value of the output that must be sacrificed. If the extra output pays for necessary food, shelter or medicines, the priority it will be accorded is apparent. Here, then, the opportunity cost of environmental protection may be prohibitive and the decision to pollute becomes an economically defensible one.

Although this example contrasts rich and poor countries in the twenty-first century, exactly the same analysis could be used to compare the production priorities set by contemporary rich countries and those same countries in the nineteenth century. *Then*, industrial interests triumphed over the environment in the West too. This was because at the time the opportunity cost of lost output was higher than the value society put on the environment. Finally, note also that, in those modern economies where the opportunity cost of pollution is deemed to be too high, it is the state that intervenes in markets – usually by imposing fines on polluting firms – to try to ensure more satisfactory outcomes.

The concept of opportunity cost also allows us to understand why countries specialize in the production of particular goods and services. Switzerland, for example, has a reputation for high-quality watch-making. In fact Switzerland is the world's leading exporter of watches in value terms, presently generating more than twice the revenue of its nearest rival, Hong Kong. Why watches? There are no climatic or natural resource attributes that make Switzerland an obvious place in which to manufacture watches. However, having – over time – developed skills in their production, it is evidently an efficient use of resources to fully exploit such skills. This is because, in economic terms, the opportunity cost associated with reallocating some resources away from the production of watches into, say, the manufacture of cars – where the Swiss have no particular pedigree – would be too great. Certainly, the Swiss could make cars – they could even grow oranges if they were prepared to spend enough on the necessary kit – but they would have to switch a disproportionate volume of resources away from something they are much better at in order to do so, thus sacrificing the output of many (too many: this is the critically high opportunity cost) watches. The case is made compelling by the possibility of international trade. The Swiss specialize in the production of watches, and other things such as chemicals, machinery and financial services, and sell these on international markets in order to obtain the foreign currencies needed to buy cars, oranges and other goods and services produced more efficiently by other nations.

● **Think Point**

We mentioned above that the clothes and shoes we buy are mostly now made in the Far East and Eastern Europe rather than in Western economies as they used to be. Can you explain this change in terms of opportunity cost?

The main driver of change in these industries is the labour-intensive nature of the production process: it's not easily mechanized and so requires a significant labour input As labour costs are relatively low in the Far East and Eastern Europe (and these places are now much more integrated with the West) the opportunity cost of continuing to produce in the West is too high.

So economics is about understanding production choices in the context of resource scarcity and with an awareness of opportunity cost – societies have limitless wants: which are to be satisfied and which neglected? Economics offers a range of arguments about these possible choices which reflect the implications of doing this or that, in this or that way. Now, if we return to our earlier examples of the markets for aircraft, cars, mobile phone services and Premiership football and, indeed, some of the others we used, it is apparent that one previously mentioned issue comes consistently to the fore: *the extent to which the state should be involved in resolving the key economic questions a society faces – what, how, for whom?* Indeed, it might be argued that this is *the* issue for economics. All societies aspire to be good producers: to have modern industries, comprehensive healthcare programmes, flourishing systems of education, good housing, efficient means of communication and transport and so on. It then becomes a question of the *balance* between state and private market actors (firms and consumers) in organizing the provision of these things.

Putting it another way, we can refer to the *freedoms* the state allows private market actors in resource allocation. In some markets in the UK, such as mobile

phone services, the state normally allows much more private decision-making by firms and consumers than it does in, for example, the provision of healthcare. In the market for healthcare, the state, in conjunction with the medical profession, has a major say in the kinds of health services that are produced, how they are produced and for whom they are produced. The National Health Service is largely funded using money from taxation. The government chooses how many health professionals to train and employ, how many hospitals to build, how long waiting lists for treatment can tolerably be and so on. It also provides healthcare to patients or consumers on the basis of clinical need. People do not directly pay for the treatment they receive. On the other hand, the government does not prohibit private healthcare: in the UK there is genuinely dual provision by the public and private sectors. This means that the private sector is free to take up any opportunities it sees in the market for healthcare services. If private agents can identify any unmet healthcare needs on the part of private consumers, they have an incentive – in the form of profit – to try to meet those needs. In 2013, for example, there were more than 50,000 cosmetic surgery procedures performed privately in the UK, with breast augmentation the most popular among women, and rhinoplasty (nose jobs) the most popular among men.

From a business perspective this example suggests that an understanding of the role of the state in markets and the freedoms and opportunities it allows private actors is crucially important. The modern mixed economy is a dynamic entity. The forms of control exercised by the state over markets will evolve and change over time, not least because the control of the state itself is subject to democratic check and political influence. For business firms, then, the freedom to act in markets will be subject to review and periodic modification; this means that new business opportunities will continue to present themselves. But market dynamism has another important source we have already identified: consumers. Consumer demands are also subject to change, sometimes decisively so. Our Woolworths case provides an instance of a firm failing to take action to cope with movements in what had been a long-established market while the online relaunch of the Woolworths brand by another company offers a positive example of what can be done to stay in business. Thus, although business opportunities might be tempered by the interventionist and regulatory inclinations of the state, they are simultaneously conditioned by the imperatives derived from the sovereignty of consumers. Finally, of course, the shifting actions – real or anticipated – of rival firms are an additional consideration in business decision-making.

1.5 Opportunity cost and incentives

Opportunity cost helps us to understand the economic choices that societies and individuals make. It contrasts the benefits and costs that arise in any particular case against those from any alternative commitment. In other words, opportunity cost contrasts the choices that we have and says something about the incentives that inform these choices. For example, a person choosing to study at university is making their decision on an opportunity cost basis. The benefits of a university education include the experience itself and the career advantages it bestows over one's working life. The costs include the loss of potential earnings while studying, as well as the payment of tuition fees. A university education is something that many people in most countries aspire to because the lifetime benefits are usually thought to exceed the short-term costs: there is a strong incentive to commit to our own education. Incentives matter.

But, thinking back to our earlier discussion of the dynamism inherent in capitalism that people like Marx and Schumpeter so admired, we need to again emphasize that opportunity cost considerations are not static – they can change rapidly and sometimes profoundly. This means that incentives too can change, as in turn can economic behaviour. Returning to our higher education example, what was the effect of a trebling of annual English university tuition fees in 2012 from £3000 to £9000? The outcome was an immediate fall of 5.5 per cent in accepted university applications. Interestingly, however, this collapse was more than reversed in 2013, when a new record for accepted applications was set. How might we explain such movements? One answer could be that the eye-catching headline jump in fees altered behaviour in the short term but, in the end, despite the increased costs of higher education, many people still seem to think that the benefits it offers are greater.

Firms are acutely aware of the business possibilities that incentives provide. Think back to our earlier example of competition between supermarkets. The big chains routinely offer loyalty cards with discounts on their own or other goods, money-off petrol coupons and multiple-buy discounts. All of these things give consumers modest incentives to keep coming back. But again opportunity cost calculations can shift. Why did Tesco and others lose market share during the recession? Because, despite all the loyalty cards and petrol coupons, some consumers thought in a period when household budgets were tight that the costs of *not* moving their shopping to Aldi and Lidl were too high.

Sometimes firms can get their incentive structures spectacularly wrong. In 1992, Hoover, the vacuum cleaner and washing machine maker, introduced a promotion for its appliances offering *two* free European or even transatlantic flights with each purchase of £100. Think about opportunity cost and incentives in this case. To pay £100 for a vacuum cleaner, spend the money elsewhere, or save it. The price of the cleaner was actually a lot less than the price of the flights to the ordinary consumer. But bulk buying allowed Hoover to secure an initial allocation of flights very cheaply. What it failed to appreciate was the kind of incentive it was setting up in using these flights as a lever to persuade people to buy its cleaners. For many, the cleaners had become an utter irrelevance. People were buying them simply to get the free flights. In effect the perception was that the flights, not the cleaner, could be bought at a stunningly cheap price. The opportunity cost of not buying them was too high. But this meant a huge and

unanticipated demand for both cleaners and flights – neither of which could be easily met. Hoover resorted to 24/7 working to try to keep up but with a reported 500 jumbo jets needed to carry a stampede of customers the whole project unravelled, at a heavy cost to Hoover in terms of both money and reputation. The lesson here? Always think through incentives from the angle of the incentivized. Hoover was thinking more about the demand for its cleaners and less about the flights. Its customers were thinking the other way around.

To help you think more about the way incentives may affect behaviour, take a few minutes to reflect on the 'Everyday Economics' box below.

EVERYDAY ECONOMICS 1.1

What incentives are at work here?

These are images that illustrate incentives. What kind of behaviours are these incentives attempting to encourage? Can you think which one might not work as well as anticipated and why?

Answers are at the end of the chapter.

1.6 Microeconomics, macroeconomics and business

As we explain in more detail in the 'Reflecting on Economics' box below, modern economics is conventionally divided into two complementary parts: **microeconomics** and **macroeconomics** (or micro and macro for short).

Microeconomics: the study of the behaviour of individual households and firms, and the determination of the relative prices of particular goods and services.

Macroeconomics: the study of the economy as a whole.

- Microeconomics deals with issues at the level of the *individual* – the individual consumer, producer, market or industry, worker and so on.
- Macroeconomics, on the other hand, considers the workings of the economy *as a whole* – inflation, the overall levels of employment and unemployment, the rate at which the economy grows and how it fits into the international economic environment are all macro concerns.

REFLECTING ON ECONOMICS

Microeconomics and macroeconomics

Microeconomics focuses upon *disaggregate* and *individualistic* economic issues. In contrast, macroeconomics looks at the behaviour of the economy *as a whole*.

The concerns of microeconomics include individual consumer and producer behaviour. It looks, for example, at factors which influence people's purchasing (demand) decisions, and firms' production (supply) decisions. Microeconomics also considers the behaviour of economic agents in particular markets, such as the labour market. Wage determination is therefore an example of a micro issue. Which factors influence the level of a worker's wage? Why do wages between different occupations vary? Does a government-set minimum wage affect the numbers of people employed in particular industries? These are all questions that microanalyses are able to address.

Macroeconomics studies the behaviour and performance of the economy as a whole. It is chiefly concerned with the four major aggregates of: economic growth, unemployment, inflation and the balance of payments. Macroeconomics seeks to both understand the factors that determine these aggregates and to inform the government policies that are used to try to influence them.

In terms of our discussion so far, an emphasis on *micro* issues has been evident. We have considered the interaction of firms, consumers and government in *markets*. Markets are arenas where particular resource allocation decisions are determined. For example, the controversy that flared up in 2014 over the popular ride app Uber brought together Uber itself, its drivers and customers but pitted them against the interests of traditional taxi operators in cities around the world who see their livelihoods and the value of their taxi assets threatened. Governments have an interest here too, as taxi operators tried to claim that Uber may be offering an illegal service in an industry in which pay-by-meter systems are written into the frameworks of law governing the industry. However, because what happens in the market for personal transport is not an issue for the economy as a whole or business in general, this, along with developments in most other such markets, remains a focus of microeconomics.

From Chapter 8 onwards, we will turn our attention to macroeconomics. Our interest will still be in the three familiar sets of actors – firms, consumers and government – but it will be situated at the more general level of the whole economy instead of in this or that particular market. Although it would be premature to enter into too detailed an explanation of the significance of macroeconomics at this stage in the book, for illustrative purposes it is worth reflecting on two macro concerns that impact heavily on business – *interest rates* and *exchange rates*. We couch our discussion in the context of the 2008–9 **recession** and conclude it with some thoughts on the important links between microeconomics, macroeconomics and government policy that the recession has brought into sharp focus. You may be unsurprised to learn that the common denominator here is the banking sector.

Recession: a decline in real GDP that lasts for at least two consecutive quarters of a year.

Interest rates

Generalizing for a moment, we can say that interest rates are set by governments or their agents for some specific macroeconomic purpose. If, for example, a government wished to stimulate economic activity it might lower interest rates. This would make borrowing for firms and consumers in the economy less expensive and encourage them to invest and consume more. Interest rates are therefore a key tool of macroeconomic policy. In March 2009 British interest rates were set at 0.5 per cent, the lowest they had ever been since the institution that sets them, the Bank of England, was established in 1694. Roughly speaking, rates were slashed and then kept at an historic low for more than 5 years because the UK experienced its worst recession since the Great Depression of the 1930s.

But there may be a cost in using 'cheap money' to try to stimulate the economy. Lower interest rates, coupled with other measures designed to encourage more activity, may push up inflation in the future. This is a worry to both policymakers and businesses. We explain why it is important to keep inflation low and stable in later chapters but we can give a hint here. As we discuss in Chapter 2, markets are coordinated by *price signals*. Prices inform firms and consumers about conditions in markets. When prices are rising in a particular market this may signal to firms that the market is buoyant and encourage them to produce more goods to sell in it. However, when significant inflationary pressures are also present in the economy as a whole, the price signals from all markets become less reliable as guides to conditions in those markets. Do rising prices in markets provide grounds for optimism about the prospects for particular goods, or are they just part of the general increase in prices across the economy as a whole? Where should firms direct their investment? The difficulty is that when inflation is high and rising, changes in the *relative* prices of goods are harder to discern. A relative price change is simply the extent to which one good changes in price in relation to another good. In these circumstances it becomes easier for firms to make mistakes that may turn out to be costly: they might produce too much of something and be left with unsold stocks, or they might produce too little and miss an opportunity to make profits. One problem associated with inflation is therefore the degree of uncertainty it introduces into economic decision-making. Firms prefer a low and stable rate of inflation because it minimizes such uncertainty.

So, despite the immediate attraction of lower interest rates in the face of a protracted and deep recession, there is a recognition that inflationary dangers may be lurking just around the corner. This means that the decision about when and how far to raise interest rates to suppress any nascent inflationary pressures must be carefully judged. Matters become even more complicated when the link between interest rates and the exchange rate is taken into account. The exchange rate too is important from a business perspective.

Exchange rates

We deal extensively with exchange rate issues in Chapter 14. For present purposes we will only highlight the significance of the exchange rate for firms selling goods or services in foreign markets. Taking Sweden as an example, if the value of the krona depreciates (falls in value against other currencies) it becomes easier for Swedish firms to sell abroad. Why? Simply, foreign residents have to spend less of their own currencies to obtain a given amount of krona as the krona exchange rate falls. For example, if the krona and the euro exchanged at 1SEK: €0.20, a Swedish car costing 200,000SEK would retail in the Netherlands or Belgium for €40,000. However, if the krona weakened against the euro to the point where 1SEK is worth €0.15, it should be clear that the same car will now retail at €30,000 in the euro area. In other words, a fall in the exchange rate of a currency drives down the (foreign currency) prices of the issuing country's exports. One implication for business is immediately apparent: a depreciating currency makes exporting potentially easier.

There is also a connection between interest rates and the exchange rate: they tend to move together. In other words, a fall in Swedish interest rates may promote at least a short-term depreciation of the krona. This is because lower interest rates discourage international investors from buying Swedish financial instruments as they now carry a lower yield in comparison to those in countries with unchanged interest rates. As investment of this sort in Sweden decreases so too does the demand for krona, thus driving down its value or rate of exchange.

We've seen this kind of thing happen in Britain. Given the two consecutive years of recession in 2008 and 2009, in which the British economy contracted by −0.1 and −4.9 per cent respectively, the interest rate cuts implemented by the Bank of England were broadly welcomed by UK businesses. In the early summer of 2008 the pound was trading against the US dollar at around $2 and against the euro at around €1.25. The rate cuts prompted the pound to depreciate fairly sharply against both currencies. By February 2009, £1 was worth a little over $1.40 and about €1.10. When the Bank of England once again begins to raise interest rates it is possible that the fall in the pound's value will be sharply reversed, making exports more expensive and imports cheaper, consequently producing a more testing environment for British businesses.

Confronting the 2008–9 recession

Deep cuts in interest rates and a depreciating pound were just two of the measures that the British government used to try to arrest the sharp deterioration in the performance of the economy. It also implemented a year-long cut in the rate of value added tax (VAT) from 17.5 to 15 per cent, and even more controversially

Apparently its good for growth.

it electronically printed money: some £375 billion in a process it called quantitative easing, which was used to improve the balance sheets of UK firms in the anticipation that cash injections would raise their levels of activity. Other policies included the noted support for the car industry, and the infamous interventions and outright rescues in the banking sector. It is worth reflecting a little more deeply on the last of these.

By the autumn of 2008 the world's financial markets effectively stopped working. In normal times banks and other financial institutions lend heavily to one another as well as to firms and consumers. As a result of problems that began with large-scale mortgage failures in the American housing market, many of the world's major financial institutions began to realize that both they and their competitors had accumulated significant amounts of bad debt. Exactly how much was uncertain. In an increasingly febrile climate the mutual trust necessary to keep the banks lending among themselves and to others simply evaporated. The outcome was aptly named the *credit crunch*: bank lending, the flow of credit, had ceased.

The British government's reaction to the financial crisis was profound. It provided cash and guarantees, some of it in secret and worth potentially around a *third* of the country's national income, to the UK banking sector. It also took into public ownership – or part ownership – such household names as Northern Rock, Lloyds and the Royal Bank of Scotland. Finally, it even guaranteed the deposits of UK residents in several doomed Icelandic banks. The government was not alone in this kind of activity. Banking systems around the world have been underwritten and supported in various ways by public authorities.

The need for governments to ride to the rescue of the banks reflects the centrality of the financial system to modern capitalist economies. On the face of it, what happens in the banking system is a microeconomic concern – the focus is on a particular industry. But there is an obvious difference between a crisis in, for example, quarrying in an economy and one in banking. A catastrophic failure in quarrying would badly affect in the main only those engaged in the industry, or who live in localities where quarrying is a major employer. A banking crisis, on the other hand, poses a *systemic* risk to the economy as a whole because most other forms of economic activity directly depend on it. This was why problems in the world's financial markets quickly spilled over into huge implosions in whole economies. As credit flows dried up businesses and consumers lost confidence; the former cut production and jobs, and the latter bought fewer goods and services: recession was the inevitable result.

To return to an earlier theme, given what happened in 2008 and 2009, how are we to characterize the balance between firms and government in UK banking? One possibility would be to think of the government as a kind of banks' guardian angel – there just in case things go very wrong. In periods of crisis there is no doubt that this is a legitimate function for government. To do nothing might lead to the unthinkable. But it's also important to illustrate an interesting tension between the microeconomic concept of **moral hazard** and the urgency with which the banks may in the future need to be saved. Moral hazard refers to dangerous or even reckless behaviour by a person or firm in an economic context where the consequences of that behaviour are indemnified or insured by others. One lesson of the financial crisis is that banks can and do behave recklessly: many clearly took on stupid risks and were caught out. But in business the usual penalty for failure is the death of the firm. This happened recently on the high street for Woolworths but not for Northern Rock, which couldn't be allowed to fail because of the potential impact on the UK financial system and the wider British economy. So Northern Rock, the Royal Bank of Scotland and, indeed, the whole UK banking sector are protected from the consequences of their own actions. The question then becomes: what's to stop the banks behaving recklessly again in the future when their executives know that the personal rewards of success are so huge and that, in any case, the government and the taxpayer are there to bail them out should they get into trouble? If the answer is 'nothing', then the problem of moral hazard in banking may well be repeated. Perhaps the acid test of any banking reform process that evolves over the next few years is whether or not it provides for – or even demands – the demise of badly behaved banks, and whether risky behaviour by bank executives is made to carry some personal risk to salaries and bonuses.

For business then, interest, exchange rates, and the possibility of recession are clearly crucial issues. Our discussion in this section suggests that business needs to retain a focus on both microeconomic and macroeconomic issues. At the micro level, the short- and long-term conditions of the market in which the firm operates are its immediate concern but no less significant will be factors operating at the macro level such as interest and exchange rates. To refine an earlier conclusion: if you are studying business or in business, you need to know about micro *and* macroeconomics.

■ Concept:
Moral hazard refers to undesirable or reckless behaviour in an economic context where there are no incentives to avoid such behaviour. An example would be if you take out insurance and then act carelessly with your belongings because, should you lose them, you're insured.

Heather, ring my therapist, I just felt a twinge of guilt

Reproduced by kind permission of PRIVATE EYE magazine/Tony Husband

1.7 Positive and normative economics

To complete our introduction we need to mention one final issue. Economics seeks to be a **positive** discipline: that is, one concerned with matters of *fact*, not opinion. That Britain's retail opening hours have become much more liberal over the past 20 years is a positive observation. Some shops now trade 24 hours a day, every day. Thirty years ago, very few shops opened on Sundays and many closed on Wednesday afternoons. Whether or not more liberal retail opening is a good or bad thing is a **normative** question. The Archbishop of Canterbury probably has a view about Sunday opening, possibly not shared by shareholders in Sainsbury's. Economists do not claim to be able to answer such normative questions. What they *can* say is something about the impacts of this change: on the structure of the retail market for example, on the profitability of retail businesses, on the changing form of retailing – the development of Internet shopping – and so on. These are all positive issues.

Coming up with positive answers to normative concerns is an area where economics can make an enormously important contribution. If you think that unemployment in your economy is too high, or that incomes in poor countries are

Positive issues: those that are factually based.

Normative issues: those that are a matter of opinion.

REFLECTING ON ECONOMICS
Why I became an economist

The five people mentioned in this box have all won the Nobel Prize in Economics.

Amartya Sen was born in India. As a child he witnessed the harrowing Bengal famine in which 3 million people died. This shocking number was estimated later in his professional life by Sen himself. He has also written about seeing a Muslim man murdered because he was looking for work in the 'wrong' neighbourhood. This made Sen think about extreme poverty and the risks it forced people to take. When asked years later why he chose to study economics Sen replied, 'For someone from India, it is not a difficult question to answer. The economic problems engulf us.'

Milton Friedman, the world's most famous monetarist economist, was born in 1912 in New York. He graduated from college in 1932 at the height of the Great Depression and had a choice between graduate

study in economics or mathematics. Why did he choose economics? 'Now put yourself in 1932 with a quarter of the population unemployed. What was the urgent problem? It was obviously economics so there was never any hesitation on my part to study economics.'

James Mirrlees also trained in mathematics as an undergraduate before switching to economics 'because I kept discussing it with economist friends, and they didn't make sense to me; and because poverty in what were then called the underdeveloped countries seemed to me what really mattered in the world and that meant economics'. Mirrlees was advised to read Keynes's *General Theory* (one of the most famous books in economics but not an easy read) and later wrote, 'That may not have been the best advice, but it did me no great harm and one day I hope to finish it'.

(continued)

Robert Merton, a financial economist, remembers that: 'As early as 8 or 9 years of age, I developed an interest in money and finance. I created fictitious banks ... At 10 or 11 I drew up an "A" list of stocks, and bought my first one.' At college he studied engineering and mathematics but dropped out of a Ph.D. programme to take up economics because he thought it a force for social progress and even more because he felt an intuitive connection with the subject. Right through college he continued to play the stock market, rising early to put in a couple of hours before attending classes.

The microeconomist **James Heckman** was drawn to the discipline after witnessing the institutionalized racism still practised in the American South in the 1950s and 1960s. 'The separate water fountains, park benches, bathrooms and restaurants of the Jim Crow South startled me [Jim Crow is the term used to describe the laws of institutionalized racism then prevailing in Southern states]. These experiences motivated my lifelong study of the status of African Americans, and the sources of improvement in that status.'

too low, economics can offer both explanations of such problems as well as their potential solutions. Worrying about important concerns like these was the reason why many eminent economists chose to study the discipline in the first place. The box, 'Reflecting on Economics', explains why some of the most influential members of the profession became economists.

SUMMARY

- Economics is concerned with three basic questions: *what* goods and services a society produces, *how* these are produced and *for whom* they are produced.
- Economics matters in a business context because it explains the roles of firms, consumers and government in the market.
- All resources are scarce in the context of the infinite demands that can be placed upon them. Society is therefore faced with myriad choices concerning how the resources it has should be used. The concept of opportunity cost allows us to begin to understand the choices particular societies make at given times.
- Microeconomics deals with the economics of the individual; macroeconomics deals with the economy as a whole. Both are important from a business perspective.

KEY TERMS

- Market
- Resource allocation
- Positive issues
- Normative issues
- Free market
- Mixed economy
- Scarcity and choice
- Opportunity cost
- Microeconomics
- Macroeconomics
- Moral hazard

QUESTIONS FOR DISCUSSION

1. What is economics?
2. Microeconomics suggests that successful businesses need to be dynamic. Can you explain the need for such dynamism?
3. Explain how consumer sovereignty places consumers at the heart of economic decision-making in capitalist economies.
4. How can the notion of opportunity cost help us to understand the production choices a society makes?
5. Why is some knowledge of macroeconomics important for business?

EVERYDAY ECONOMICS 1.1 ANSWERS

1. **A small charge to use a public toilet**. Why charge? A charge does three things.
- It generates revenue to pay a toilet attendant to keep the toilets clean.
- Existing cleanliness and the presence of an attendant encourages users to keep the facilities clean.
- A charge deters some users who may be anti-social abusers of such facilities.

2. **A 5p charge for every plastic shopping bag used in Northern Ireland**. Shopping bags have traditionally been free in the UK.
- If something is free people generally consume a lot of it as there is no incentive not to do so.
- But plastic bags are an environmental problem.
- Where a small price per bag has been imposed – so far in Northern Ireland, Wales and Scotland – the demand for bags has fallen by as much as 75 per cent.

3. **Parking restrictions outside schools**. Such measures are intended to safeguard schoolchildren by prohibiting cars from parking near school entrances.
- The problem here is that such restrictions alter the behaviour only of responsible drivers.
- Irresponsible drivers are aware that there is always likely to be a space to park illegally right outside a school where it will be convenient to drop off their own children.
- So such restrictions might not work very well as they incentivize irresponsible drivers to park dangerously in a space the parking restriction has kept free for them!

ONE THING YOU SHOULD READ

At the end of every chapter we'll introduce one key – and short – reading or other reference that will help you to reflect on some of the key concepts we've just discussed. Some of these readings, like the one below, are works of fiction. This may not be something you've been asked to do before, but we think this approach brings economics alive in a business setting and will help you better understand the subject.

John Steinbeck's *The Grapes of Wrath*, Chapter 5

The Grapes of Wrath was published in 1939 and tells the story of the Joads, a tenant farming family, forced, like tens of thousands of others, to leave the uneconomic 'dustbowl' of Oklahoma to travel to California in search of a new life and a different future. It's set against the backdrop of the Great Depression in the 1930s when a quarter of all Americans were without jobs. The book is a great read, winning Steinbeck a Pulitzer Prize and helping him to win the Nobel Prize for Literature.

Chapter 5 is an intercalary chapter, the function of which is to provide the reader with a general context for the central story. Steinbeck alternates chapters on the Joads' experiences with intercalary chapters throughout the book. In this case we learn about the meagreness of the dust-dry states like Oklahoma in the 1930s and the bleakness of the lives of those trying to farm in such places. But what's worse is their looming expulsion from the land. Small farms don't appear to make sense any more but big mechanized ones might, so the owners of the land or their agents come to tell the poor tenants and their families that they have to leave. But when they ask where they should go, the answer is vague – 'out west' to California, where it's always warm and there is good land that needs plenty of people to work it. But the tenant farmers are angry and confused;

why should they go, who's going to make them, what's going to happen to 'their' land, the place where they were born and where their parents and grandparents are buried?

Read the chapter (only 10 pages double spaced) and then reflect on the questions below. All questions are based on economic concepts we've learned about in this introductory part of the book.

1. What resources are at issue in this chapter (land is one but not the only one) and how are their allocation decisions made?
2. What kind of market is depicted here: free, mixed or planned?
3. Can you explain landowners' decisions to evict the tenant farmers in terms of opportunity cost? Pay particular attention to *changes* in opportunity cost over time. These are the key drivers of the processes described in the reading.
4. Labour is being evicted from the land and there are few alternative employment opportunities for the displaced farmers (unemployment is at 25 per cent in the US at the height of the Great Depression). Can labour still be considered a scarce resource during something like the Great Depression?

2

the market

KEY ISSUES

What is a market and what is its purpose?

What factors determine the demand for a good or service?

What factors determine the supply of a good or service?

How do demand and supply interact?

How can market theory be applied to the real world?

What factors determine how consumers and business firms respond to price changes?

CONTENTS

2.1	Introduction: the market, an old and useful institution	**36**
2.2	Consumers and demand in the market	**40**
2.3	Firms and supply in the market	**45**
2.4	The market: bringing demand and supply together	**48**
2.5	Applying market analysis 1: the example of economic integration in the European Union	**54**
2.6	Elasticity in the market	**61**
2.7	Price elasticity of demand	**62**
2.8	Determinants of price elasticity of demand	**66**
2.9	Why firms need to know about price elasticity of demand	**68**
2.10	Applying market analysis 2: OPEC and the market for oil	**69**
2.11	Other forms of elasticity	**72**
2.12	Markets and asymmetric information	**77**
2.13	Markets and the rational consumer	**81**
2.14	Markets: concluding remarks	**83**

2.1   Introduction: the market, an old and useful institution

Wander around any town or city in any country in the world and sooner or later you'll see a market. Someone who lived 1000 years ago would know what a market looks like. Someone who lived 2500 years ago would recognize a market. Markets are *old* institutions and we've been using them for thousands of years because, generally, they work. And they work in all kinds of situations. People use them to buy and sell books, fish, education, foreign currencies, clothing, drugs, chocolate, land, blood, water, sex, medicine, weapons, in fact anything. Markets are everywhere. Some are global and many are international or national; others exist in cities, towns, villages, prisons, schools and armies in wartime; there were markets even in the terror and horror of Auschwitz.[1]

© Chris Mulhearn

The market: an instantly recognizable institution

Markets allow buyers and sellers to exchange goods and services, usually for money but sometimes for other goods that become forms of money. In prisons, for example, where cash does not circulate, people use cigarettes; in schools kids have variously used marbles, pogs and football picture cards; in wartime armies it's often alcohol. But markets are more than places of exchange – they have some other important attributes. Because they are everywhere and provide potentially anything they facilitate and encourage specialization and the development of an extended division of labour. They also help us to manage risk.

Specialization: a focus on one form of activity by an economic agent.

Division of labour: the separation of economic activity into different but complementary tasks.

Specialization means concentrating on the production of something. Your teachers, for example, concentrate on the production of an education service. Because that's all they do and because they've been well trained we expect they'll produce a good service. What teachers generally don't do is grow their own food, make their own clothes or generate their own electricity. They use markets to obtain these things – and everything else they need – from others who specialize in their production and who are therefore probably good at it in the same way that most teachers are good at teaching. The more of this kind of thing that goes on the greater the potential for us all to be good at what we do; in other words, our economies become more productive through what is a greatly extended division of labour.

1 Primo Levi's book *If This Is A Man* describes his experiences as a prisoner in Auschwitz. Markets were forbidden by the SS but, despite the risks, they still emerged inside the camp and between the camp and the outside world. *If This Is A Man* is the best book on the Holocaust we know. Sometime in your life you should read it.

Think about your day so far. You were awoken by an alarm on a device made in China; you dressed in clothes made in Eastern Europe or the Far East. A barista at Starbucks made you a coffee that might have been grown by farmers in Vietnam, Brazil or Africa. Someone drove the bus on which you travelled. Someone at Subway made your favourite sandwich. Later you'll watch videos from Europe or the US on YouTube and tonight you'll sleep in a bed sold by the Swedish firm IKEA but fabricated in Poland. This means that lots of people, many of whom you'll never meet, have been specializing on your behalf. Why are they doing this and how are they able to do it? Because they make a living by specializing, and because others reciprocate by doing the same. Most of this fantastically complicated web of interaction takes place in markets. If markets didn't exist your day would be very different: you'd oversleep, there would be none of the cheap clothing you like, no coffee, no bus ride, no sandwich, no YouTube entertainment and no comfy bed. Unless you managed to sort out all these things for yourself, which would be near impossible. Or the government did it, which is improbable.

How does all this activity for mutual benefit actually come about? Who's in charge? Actually, no one is. It all happens spontaneously. To understand how remarkable this is, imagine that you were given the job of organizing tomorrow's food production – all of it – for a city like Paris. Could you do this? No, not even with a few hundred people or even 1000 to assist you. The task is simply too big, too daunting. Yet tomorrow it will be accomplished. Every single person who visits Paris or lives there will benefit from some food shopping or go to a restaurant and get the things they want to eat. And the same will happen the day after, and the day after that. And it won't just happen for food but for myriad other things too. All this gets done through what the founder of modern economics, Adam Smith (1723–90), called the *invisible hand* of the market. It is as if some unseen force hovers over the economy orchestrating the allocation of scarce resources to deliver to everyone the kaleidoscope of goods and services they want to buy.

Markets are also able to process information that helps buyers and sellers to make informed economic choices. This happens through the setting of prices. As we'll see, prices act as signals to consumers and producers to behave in particular ways. The crucial thing here is that what might be complex changes in matters of resource scarcity are distilled into simple but very useful signals. Later in this chapter we look in some detail at the oil market. Let's briefly pre-figure that discussion now. The world's oil supply is finite. Sooner or later there will be no more oil. How will this information be reflected in the oil price? As oil supplies dwindle the price is likely to rise. A rising oil price is likely to alter behaviour in the market as it affects the incentives faced by oil consumers, oil producers and others in the wider market for energy. We highlighted the importance of incentives in economic life in Chapter 1. What are the incentives that begin to emerge more strongly in the oil market as oil prices increase?

Consumers will be incentivized to buy less oil but they will also have an incentive to look very favourably on anything that helps them use oil more economically, such as cars with hybrid – petrol and electric – engines, or better insulated homes. Oil producers will have an incentive to explore oil fields that might have been previously too difficult and expensive to exploit. The higher oil price removes this obstacle. Others in the energy market have a stronger incentive to develop sources of non-oil energy, such as gas, solar or wind power and to innovate in these areas as much as they can. Where have fracking and solar panels on roofs come from? Partly from oil price pressures. Note too that non-energy markets are affected. Innovation in the car industry and the way we build our homes are both driven by the prospect of a world with very expensive oil, or none. Changes in the oil price have therefore set in train a complex set of responses in markets that result in the reallocation of scarce resources. By using price signals, markets cope when circumstances in the economic environment change.

Another way to look at this is to think about markets as mechanisms for managing and reducing *risk*. Some markets are specifically designed to do this. Insurance markets, for example, allow us to pool risk: many people pay a relatively small premium against the risk that they may be burgled, which allows the few who actually are to be compensated. Investment markets help us to hold income that we earn in diversified and therefore risk-reducing forms such as stocks, bonds and property. Pension investments allow us to securely defer income until retirement so that the risk of penury can be avoided when we can no longer work. We can also bring income forward into the present by borrowing to buy somewhere to live (also an asset that may appreciate in value), or to invest in our own education to avoid the risk of exclusion from some labour markets. The oil example above is a study in the market management of risk in energy.

So markets are old institutions that seem to do a good job in bringing buyers and sellers together, extending the productivity-raising division of labour, managing risk, and helping economies allocate and reallocate their scarce resources. But markets are not without their problems. In this and later chapters we'll discuss some of these. For now here are some possibilities.

In Chapter 1 we introduced the idea of consumer sovereignty which suggests that markets are ultimately driven by consumers. Firms need to produce things that people want to buy; those that don't fail. But consumer sovereignty depends on the existence of *competitive* markets where there are numbers of firms chasing customers. We also assume that markets are populated with consumers who are independent and competently aware when they act. Finally, we trust that the incentives established in markets are not warped so as to risk a fevered breakdown of the allocation process. Should these conditions not be fulfilled markets may function less well and allocate resources poorly. Consider the following examples.

- What happens in a market where there are many buyers but only one seller – a monopoly? In this case the principle of consumer sovereignty will be infringed. A monopolist may not need to respond to consumer demands because consumers have no alternative sources of supply. A competitive firm that treats its customers poorly will fail and the resources the firm used real-located. A monopolist may not fail in the same circumstances which means that monopoly may result in a questionable use of resources.

- The consumption of certain goods can affect other non-consumers of such goods in a detrimental manner – others are in effect *forced* to consume. Non-smokers may smoke passively against their will. Here there is too much consumption of tobacco but, as we will see in more detail in Chapter 6, the market has no means of recognizing that it is allocating, from society's perspective, too many resources to this activity.

This driver's passengers are forced to consume the harmful chemicals in cigarette smoke

- In many markets consumers are competent and aware in exercising choice. But in some markets they are less well informed. When you buy shoes you can make an informed choice. When you visit the dentist you cannot. We accept the dentist's word that we need the treatment they recommend. But if the dentist's income reflects the amount of work they do might not unscrupulous dentists do unnecessary work? In these circumstances resource allocation in the shoe market might be about right but too many resources might be used in dentistry.

- The financial crisis of 2008–9 was the outcome of markets gripped by what the then US Federal Reserve chairman, Alan Greenspan, memorably called *irrational exuberance*. This was a belief that, amongst other things, property values would continue to rise unchecked, and that economic agents would miss out were they not to borrow heavily to get in on the deal. But property did not keep rising in value – property markets collapsed as did the financial markets that were tied to them, and the world economy teetered for a time on the edge of meltdown.

Each of these bullet points represents a case where markets *fail*. We will reflect further on such possibilities later in this chapter and in Chapters 5 and 6.

For the remainder of this chapter we offer a more detailed analysis of how the market is supposed to work in theory, and we see how real markets actually work in practice. We concentrate here on markets for goods and services: so-called goods markets. These are composed of two sets of economic agents: consumers

Goods markets: markets in which goods and services can be bought and sold.

who demand goods and services; and producers, or firms, who supply them. In order to understand how goods markets work, we need to begin by thinking about the respective aspirations and motivations of firms and consumers in the market process.

2.2   Consumers and demand in the market

Quantity demanded: the amount of a good or service that consumers wish to purchase at a particular price (*ceteris paribus*).

For a particular good or service, which factors influence the precise quantity demanded by consumers over a given time period? One obvious factor is *price*. If we assume that all other influences upon demand remain unchanged (the so-called ***ceteris paribus*** assumption), then higher prices will usually be associated with a lower quantity demanded. Similarly, lower prices will usually be associated with a greater quantity demanded. The box 'Applying Economics to Business' below explains the basis of this claim in terms of the behaviour of the individual consumer.

APPLYING ECONOMICS TO BUSINESS

Individual consumer behaviour, marginal utility and market demand

Think about your demand for chocolate. Like most people you're probably fond of the odd Freddo or Aero. So consuming a Freddo gives us satisfaction. What about having a second Freddo? They're not very big so that would be good too. How about a third, fourth or a fifth? Our guess is that the extra satisfaction people derived from eating a fifth Freddo would be less than the satisfaction they got from the first. Generally, satisfaction from consumption of goods declines as we consume successively more of them. Occasionally we've all thought, *'I wish I hadn't eaten those last few chips, had that extra helping or drank that last beer'*, at which point the extra satisfaction is zero or even negative.

Economists call the satisfaction we get from consumption utility and the extra satisfaction we get from consuming extra units the marginal utility of each unit. The marginal utility of a good declines as we consume more of it.

So how many Freddos would you like today? Freddos cost 25p. If you buy one you think the satisfaction you get from it is at least 25p. It can't be less or you'd spend your 25p on something else that you thought was worth this amount. So you

buy a Freddo. Would you like a second one? The extra satisfaction or marginal utility you get from it is likely to be less than you got from the first but if it's greater than 25p a second Freddo is worth buying. A third might also be worth buying. But what about a fourth? By now you've had your daily chocolate fix and you think a fourth would bring less than 25p's utility so you stop at three. In effect you're buying Freddos up to the point at which the marginal utility of the last unit is equal to its price.

Now, what happens tomorrow if the price of Freddo Frogs changes? We know something about your declining marginal utility: it caused you to stop buying at three when the price was 25p.

- If the price increases to 40p will you buy more or fewer? Clearly you'll buy fewer as the third Freddo brought you only around 25p's worth of satisfaction and that unit now costs 40p.
- On the other hand if the price falls to 10p you'll be likely to buy more than three Freddos as a fourth will have a lower marginal utility than the third but as long as this is not less than 10p the fourth is worth buying.

This reasoning enables us to make the claim that an individual's demand for a good will vary inversely with its price as will the market demand for a good which is simply the demand expressed by all individuals in the market together.

Reproduced by kind permission of PRIVATE EYE magazine/Paul Shadbolt

Declining marginal utility?

Utility: the satisfaction an individual derives from the consumption of a good.

Marginal utility: the extra satisfaction an individual derives from an additional unit of a good.

■ Concept:
Ceteris paribus:
a commonly used assumption in economics. It means 'other things remaining the same'. Its purpose is to allow us to examine the influence of one factor at a time on something – in this case, price on quantity demanded – we are trying to explain or understand.

Contractions or extensions in the quantity demanded: movements along a demand curve that result from a change in the price of the good.

Demand: the quantity of a good or service consumers wish to purchase at each conceivable price (*ceteris paribus*).

We can illustrate the *inverse* nature of the relationship between price and quantity demanded graphically.

In Figure 2.1, the price of a good is depicted on the vertical axis, while the quantity demanded is depicted on the horizontal axis. At price P_2, the quantity Q_2 is demanded. However, if the price increases to P_3, the quantity demanded falls, or contracts, to Q_1. Conversely, if there is a reduction in price from P_2 to P_1, the quantity demanded rises, or extends, to Q_3. If several such links between price and quantity demanded are established, it becomes possible to discern a *demand curve* (D_1), which shows, *ceteris paribus*, the *entire* relationship between price and quantity demanded for the particular good in question. It should be clear that the relationship is indeed an inverse one. In other words, higher prices are associated with contractions in the quantity demanded and lower prices prompt extensions in the quantity demanded. The convention in economics is to refer to *movements* along a single demand curve as either contractions (where the quantity demanded is falling) or extensions (where it is rising).

So, the particular price of a good determines, over a given time period, the precise quantity demanded: 50 aircraft, 2 million cars, 20 million mobile phone contracts and so on. But, beyond price, there are other factors that have some bearing upon the demand for a good, again over a given time period. Here demand refers not to a particular quantity and a particular price but to *all* possible prices and quantities demanded. Consider, for example, the influence of a change in the *incomes of consumers* on demand.

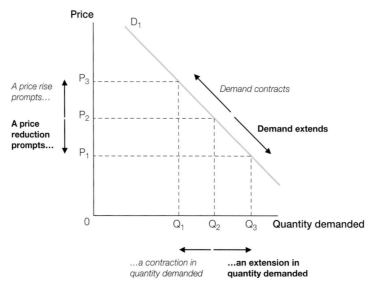

Figure 2.1 The effect of a change in price on the quantity demanded of a particular good or service

Normal good: one for which demand increases when income increases.

If incomes rise, *ceteris paribus*, we would anticipate that the demand for a **normal good** would increase whatever its particular price. Conversely, a fall in consumer incomes would prompt a decrease in the demand for a normal good.

It is possible to illustrate the effects of a change in income on demand graphically. In Figure 2.2, the demand curve D_2 represents the range of possible relationships between the price of a normal good and the quantity demanded at an initial level of consumers' incomes. For example, at price P_1, the quantity demanded is Q_2. Now, what happens if the incomes of consumers rise? The higher levels of income prompt consumers to increase their demand for the good. Note that this is the case *regardless of the level of the assumed price*: if it was higher or lower than our arbitrary selection, P_1, the outcome would be the same. The increase in demand that results from the higher level of consumers' incomes is captured graphically by a *rightward shift* of the demand curve from D_2 to D_3. At each and every possible price demand will increase. For example, at a price P_1, quantity demanded increases to Q_3. Conversely, because it prompts a decrease in demand, a fall in consumers' incomes is associated with a leftward shift of the demand curve. In the diagram this is captured in the shift of the curve from D_2 to D_1. At price P_1 the quantity demanded is Q_1. To distinguish them from the extensions and contractions in the quantity demanded caused by a change in the price of a particular good, changes in demand, which are associated with *shifts* in the demand curve, are conventionally referred to as **increases or decreases in demand**.

Increases or decreases in demand: shifts of the demand curve.

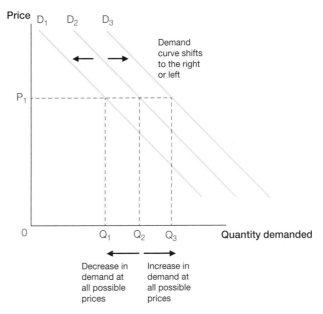

Figure 2.2 The effect of a change in income on the demand for a normal good or service

Substitute: a good that can replace another good.

In addition to changes in consumers' incomes, there are a number of other factors that also prompt shifts in the demand curve for a particular good or service and consequent increases or decreases in demand. Among the most important of these are:

Watch a movie at the cinema or download it at home? A choice between substitutes

• *Prices of other goods and services:* Goods and services generally have substitutes. For example, viewing a downloaded film at home might be thought of as substitute for a visit to the cinema to see the same film. Downloaded films might

not be *perfect* substitutes for the cinema – many people prefer the cinema experience and new releases tend to be shown in cinemas first – but they are certainly *close* substitutes. So, considering the demand for cinema seats, what would we expect to happen if the download charges for films increase? The answer is that, *ceteris paribus*, the demand for cinema seats should increase. In other words, following the logic of Figure 2.2, the demand curve for cinema seats would shift to the right as demand by consumers increases. Similarly, if download charges fall, we would expect to see the demand for cinema seats decrease and the demand curve for them shift to the left.

- On the other hand, some other goods and services are said to be complementary, in the sense that they are consumed jointly. For example, apps for an iPhone are useless without an iPhone to activate them. So, considering the demand for paid-for apps, what would be the outcome of a fall in the price of iPhones? The expectation is that, *ceteris paribus*, the demand for apps would increase as more people demand iPhones and the apps that enhance them. In terms of Figure 2.2, this would be reflected in a rightward shift of the demand curve (for apps). Alternatively, a rise in the price of iPhones would, *ceteris paribus*, lead to a fall in the demand for them and an associated decrease in the demand for apps. In Figure 2.2 this would be depicted by a leftward shift in the demand curve.

- *Preferences or tastes of consumers:* At different times, consumers take different views as to the attractiveness of particular goods and services. In virtually every city in Britain over the past decade or so there has been an explosion in the number of internationally branded coffee shops: Starbucks, Costa Coffee, Caffè Nero. People clearly like drinking coffee in places like these, so more and more of them have opened. There may come a time when the coffee shop wanes in popularity. If and when this happens the resources presently given over to it will be reallocated to different uses.

This is one example of the possible effects on demand (and resource allocation) of changes in consumer preferences but other interesting cases are not hard to find. For instance, over the past decade or so, consumers have become much more aware of the ethical implications of some of their consumption decisions. This has led to increases in the demand for goods and services that complement consumers' perceptions of appropriate corporate behaviour (demand curve shifts to the right). On the other hand, questionable social or environmental activities by firms or even countries may negatively influence demand. During the years of apartheid in South Africa an effective consumer boycott of South African goods allowed people to signal their opposition to a particularly odious regime (the demand curve for South African goods shifts to the left). Ethical Consumer is a UK-based organization that researches corporate behaviour and uses the information it obtains to draw up free ethical shopping guides and rankings for a wide range of products and services (ethicalconsumer.org). It also encourages boycotts of firms that fail to adhere to certain standards. At the time of writing it has Amazon and Starbucks in its sights for 'outrageous tax avoidance'. To the extent that Ethical Consumer informs market behaviour, the demand curves for Amazon and Starbucks products shift to the left.

A summary of the main factors influencing demand is given in Figure 2.3.

Complement: a good that is used with another good.

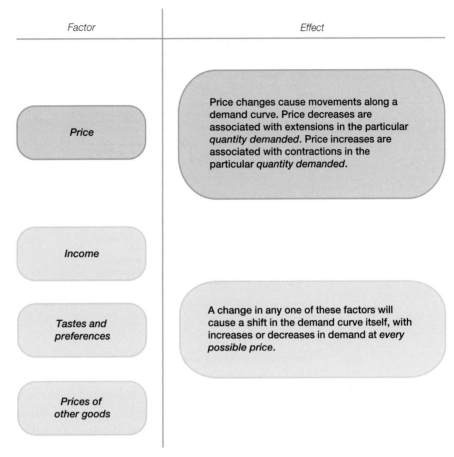

Figure 2.3 Factors which influence the demand for a particular good: a summary

2.3   Firms and supply in the market

Quantity supplied: the amount that firms wish to sell at a particular price (*ceteris paribus*).

The second economic actor or agent in the market is the producer or firm. The role of the firm is to supply goods and services to the marketplace. So what influences firms' decisions regarding the quantity supplied of a particular good or service? The issue of price is again relevant. The proposition is that the higher the price of a particular good, the greater the incentive for firms to supply it. What is the reasoning behind this statement? We know from Chapter 1 that the motive force of capitalism is self-interest. For firms this translates as profit. We will see in later discussion that the standard assumption made is that firms seek to maximize the profits they earn and they do this by producing as many profitable commodities as they can. The profit on an individual good is simply the price it fetches less the cost of its production. Now, it follows that when the price of a good increases then, *ceteris paribus*, it will generate more profit. Thus, a higher price for a particular good will prompt firms to raise the quantity supplied in the pursuit of greater profit.

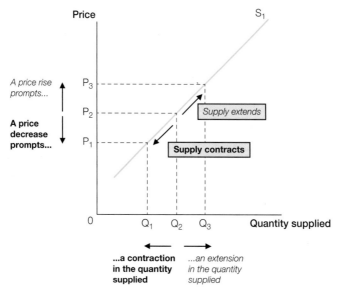

Figure 2.4 The effect of a change in price on the quantity supplied of a particular good or service

The relationship between the price of a good in a market and the quantity supplied over a given time period can be illustrated graphically. In Figure 2.4, as for our discussion of demand, price is depicted on the vertical axis. The horizontal axis depicts the quantity supplied. At price P_2, firms are motivated to supply Q_2 of the good or service in question. If price increases to P_3, then the quantity supplied extends to Q_3. On the other hand, if price falls from P_2 to P_1, then the quantity supplied contracts from Q_2 to Q_1. If we examine a range of such links between price and quantity supplied, it becomes possible to distinguish a *supply curve* (S_1), which shows the *entire* relationship between price and the quantity supplied. It can be seen that the relationship is *positive* in nature: that is, price and quantity supplied move in the same direction. Increases in price prompt extensions in the quantity supplied; decreases in price prompt contractions in the quantity supplied (as for demand, the convention is that *movements* along a given supply curve are referred to as extensions or contractions).

So, the particular price of a good determines, over a given time period, the precise quantity supplied: 5 ships, 2 million cinema tickets, 5 million canned drinks and so on. But, as for demand, there are other factors beyond price that have some bearing upon the supply of a good, again over a given time period. Here, supply refers not to a particular quantity and a particular price but to *all* possible prices and quantities supplied. We have already noted that firms are interested in the profit yielded by their output and that this is a function of both price and the cost of production. It follows that lower production costs will prompt increases in supply. If, for example, firms producing baked beans find that the costs of factor inputs such as tin, beans, sugar or tomatoes fall,

Contractions or extensions in the quantity supplied: movements along a supply curve that result from a change in the price of a good.

Supply: the quantity of a good or service that producers wish to sell at each conceivable price (*ceteris paribus*).

Factor inputs: any goods and services used in the process of production.

then, *ceteris paribus*, they will be motivated to supply more tins of baked beans at each and every possible price. This is simply because the profitability of baked beans has increased. The nature of the link between the cost of production and supply can be illustrated graphically.

In Figure 2.5, the supply curve S_2 represents a set of possible relationships between price and quantity supplied with a given set of production costs. Operating with this supply curve, it can be seen that at, say, price P_1, firms are motivated to supply Q_2. The effect of a fall in production costs is to shift the supply curve to the right from S_2 to S_3. Operating with the new supply curve, S_3, and the given price P_1, it can be seen that firms wish to supply an increased output Q_3 to the market. Note that this is the case regardless of the price of the good. In other words, at each and every possible price, supply increases. Conversely, an increase in production costs reduces the profitability of beans at any given price; so, if costs rise, firms will be motivated to decrease supply. In Figure 2.5, higher production costs have the effect of shifting the supply curve to the left (from S_2 to S_1). With S_1 operating, at a price P_1, firms are motivated to supply Q_1 to the market. Note that the terms increase and decrease in supply refer to changes arising from *shifts* of supply curves, as opposed to extensions and contractions in the quantity supplied which arise, as noted, from price-related movements along given supply curves.

Changes in production costs that shift the supply curve for a good or service can also result from a change in technology. In terms of Figure 2.5, an improvement in technology that reduces production costs shifts the supply curve to the

Increases or decreases in supply: shifts of the supply curve.

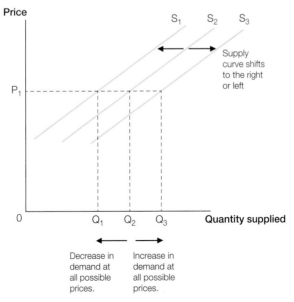

Figure 2.5 The effect of a change in production costs on the supply of a particular good or service

Factor	Effect

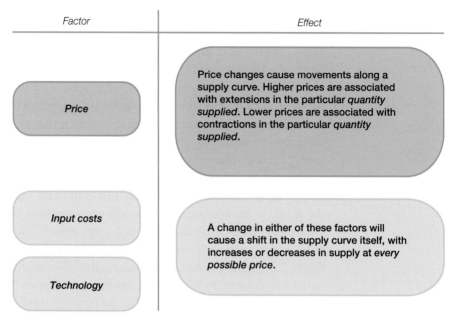

Price

Price changes cause movements along a supply curve. Higher prices are associated with extensions in the particular *quantity supplied*. Lower prices are associated with contractions in the particular *quantity supplied*.

Input costs

A change in either of these factors will cause a shift in the supply curve itself, with increases or decreases in supply at *every possible price*.

Technology

Figure 2.6 Factors which influence the supply of a particular good: a summary

right. This is because, at each possible price, profitability has increased, prompting increases in supply. For example, the production and consumption of books may be revolutionized by the development of devices such as the iPad. Should Apple negotiate with publishers the rights to download books *very* cheaply relative to their price in physical form, one might imagine an explosion in digital supply (the supply curve shifts decisively to the right). A summary of the main factors influencing supply is given in Figure 2.6.

2.4   The market: bringing demand and supply together

The equilibrium price and market equilibrium

■ **Concept:**
A **market** is said to **clear** when the quantity demanded equals the quantity supplied.

Having reviewed the two sides of the market in isolation we are now in a position to see how they interact: it is this *interplay* between consumers and firms – or demand and supply – that produces market conditions satisfactory to both. The analysis is easiest to conduct graphically. Figure 2.7 represents the market for a particular good or service. Price is again depicted on the vertical axis, while the quantities demanded and supplied are depicted on the horizontal axis. At price P_2 notice that the quantity demanded (Q_2), as given by the demand curve D_1, *exactly matches* the quantity supplied (also Q_2), as given by the supply curve S_1. Thus, at price P_2 the **market** is said to **clear** in the sense that, in any given time period, demand equals supply. This situation appears to have some intrinsic merit as there are no gluts or shortages in the market: no consumers are left with demand unsatisfied and no firms are left with stocks they cannot sell.

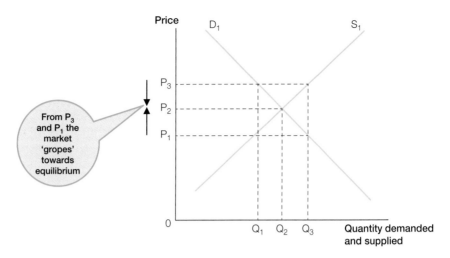

Figure 2.7 The interaction of demand and supply in the market for a particular good

The price P_2 can also be shown to be an equilibrium price. In economics, the term equilibrium is used to describe a state of balance from which there is *no tendency to change*. How does P_2 prompt equilibrium? Consider the prices P_1 and P_3 also shown in Figure 2.7. At P_3, the quantity supplied (Q_3) exceeds the quantity demanded (Q_1) and there is said to be excess supply in the market. Now, because they are saddled with unsold stocks, this situation leaves some firms dissatisfied (those consumers in the market at price P_3 are able to buy all they desire, so we judge them content). In order to change things, the most obvious option open to firms is to reduce the price they charge. As this happens and price starts to fall below P_3, the quantity demanded begins to extend and the quantity supplied contracts. Eventually, as price falls to P_2, quantity demanded will have extended and quantity supplied contracted sufficiently to entirely eliminate excess supply, leaving demand and supply perfectly matched. The market has groped to equilibrium. We can draw an important general implication from this analysis:

At any price above P_2 there is a tendency for price to decrease. Excess supply will encourage firms to initiate price reductions until demand and supply are harmonized.

When this happens, the market is said to be in equilibrium.

So much for prices above P_2, but what of those below it? Consider a price below P_2: P_1, for example. At price P_1 there is excess demand over the supply firms choose to make available. Now, while firms are content with this situation (as they sell all they wish to offer to the market), the same cannot be said of consumers. At P_1, consumers wish to buy Q_3 of the good or service in question but only Q_1 is available: the demand of some consumers is left unsatisfied. Now, as their output is rapidly and avidly swallowed up by consumers, firms will be aware that there is excess demand in the market. This results in the price being 'bid up'. Notice that, as price rises above P_1, the quantity demanded begins to contract and the quantity supplied extends. The market is once more groping towards equilibrium. However, it is only when price reaches P_2 that the excess demand in the market is entirely eliminated. Again, we can draw an important general implication from this analysis:

> At any price below P_2 there is a tendency for price to increase. Excess demand will encourage firms to initiate price increases until demand and supply are harmonized.

Moreover, it is now evident that P_2 is in fact a *unique* equilibrium price in the market depicted in Figure 2.7. All other possible prices are associated with either excess supply or excess demand conditions, which result in spontaneous movements back towards the market-clearing equilibrium price.

Reflections on equilibrium price and market equilibria

We now want to extend our analysis of how the actions of consumers and firms are harmonized by market processes. We will do this using case studies of the interplay between demand and supply in three 'real world' markets: those for T-shirts, canned tuna fish, and gold. Although the outcomes in each case are different, these illustrations demonstrate that markets do have the ability to produce equilibrium positions across a range of varying economic circumstances.

T-shirts

Let's begin with an experiment. We have an idea what the outcome will be but we're not absolutely sure, so bear with us. The paragraph you're reading is being written at a desk in Liverpool John Moores University. In a moment we're going to stop writing and take a 5 minute walk into the centre of Liverpool to buy a men's T-shirt. How much might we expect to pay? While you pause to think about this we'll go shopping.

Right, we're back. We bought a T-shirt from the popular retailer Primark, for £2. That's *cheap*. Of course, we might have paid more elsewhere. If you look at the website of the renowned British fashion designer Paul Smith you'll see T-shirts that start at £35 but can cost around £100 or more: www.paulsmith.co.uk. So, one £100 T-shirt from Paul Smith or 50 from Primark; that seems to be a choice the market is offering. How can the market analysis we've introduced make sense of T-shirt prices that vary so widely; they're just T-shirts, aren't they? It's actually not quite that simple. We actually have two *separate* markets here, with different products on offer and different conditions prevailing in each. If this were not the case people would be unwilling to pay 50 times as much as they needed to for a T-shirt and Paul Smith would not be the fashion icon he undoubtedly is.

Primark claims that its clothing and accessories are the cheapest on the high street and that its low prices arise from bulk purchasing and costless word-of-mouth advertising. Primark's prices are also low because it sources its products globally and this allows it to take advantage of low labour cost locations; not untypical in the clothing industry which tends to use labour-intensive manufacturing methods. Because labour is the largest cost input, much of the world's clothing production now takes place in countries where wages are low. It appears that Primark has a cost-driven business model: it identifies the fashions that it thinks will sell and then gets them into its shops in significant quantities as quickly and as cheaply as possible.

Paul Smith's business model is different. His products are organized in a number of distinct collections with design based in Nottingham and London, and materials sourcing and production mostly in Britain, Italy and France. Here then there is less emphasis on cost control and more on bespoke design, material and product quality and the personal imprimatur that Paul Smith himself places on a relatively limited range of goods.

By now you may be able to see where we're going with this. On the one hand, we have a bulk producer that sources globally and aspires to get price-competitive fashion into (and out of) its shops as quickly as possible. The result is crystallized in the £2 T-shirt, the £10 dress and so on: high-turnover fashion for the majority. On the other hand, there is the design-intensive Western European producer of a limited range of clothing and related products in relatively constrained quantities. The result is the £100 T-shirt, the £300 shoes, and the £650 dress: fashion for the discerning and affluent. In the market in which Primark competes, demand is relatively high, reflecting both very low prices and Primark's ability to anticipate and match its customers' tastes. In the market in which Paul Smith competes, higher prices reflect the supply considerations of higher costs of design, materials and manufacture. These factors also serve to limit supply. Clearly, high prices will also constrain demand in the design-intensive market but the important point is that it won't even come close to eliminating it: the rich and fashion-aware ensure that the market will certainly bear the £100 Paul Smith T-shirt. The two markets are depicted in Panels A and B of Figure 2.8. In Panel A, relatively high demand and supply conditions combine to produce a relatively low price P_1, as compared to the more constrained demand and supply conditions in Panel B which together result in a relatively high price P_2.

Tuna fish

The UK market for canned tuna fish enjoyed a long period of demand-led growth in the 1980s and 1990s. Research by the industry suggests that consumers see tuna as a low-cost, high-protein food and an attractive alternative to meat. Diagrammatically, the increase in demand can be represented by a rightward shift of the demand curve in Figure 2.9, from D_1 to D_2 across the supply curve S_1. The outcome in the market, *ceteris paribus*, was an increase in the equilibrium price from P_1 to P_3 and a higher equilibrium quantity Q_2 bought and sold. However,

PANEL A

PANEL B

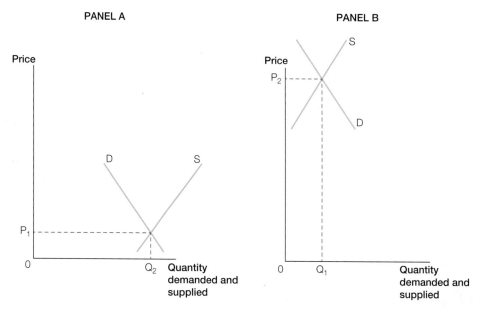

Figure 2.8 A stylized representation of the market for T-shirts

demand changes were not the end of the matter. To meet rising demand most major tuna producers invested heavily in new modernized plant and equipment. Recall that technological improvements in a market have the effect of shifting the supply curve to the right (from S_1 to S_2). When we incorporate this feature into Figure 2.9, the result is given by the intersection of D_2 and S_2: an equilibrium price of P_2 and an equilibrium quantity of Q_3. This is broadly consistent with what happened in the tuna market: a marked increase in the equilibrium quantity demanded and supplied with a moderate increase in price.

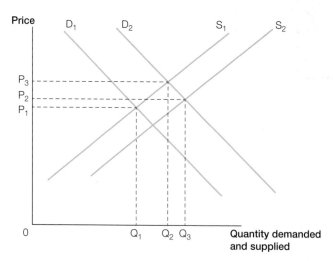

Figure 2.9 A stylized representation of recent developments in the UK market for canned tuna fish

More recently, demand and supply conditions have been rather static but there are concerns in the industry that new supply constraints may begin to drive up tuna prices. The main problem here is that, since the mid-2000s, catches of higher-quality yellowfin tuna have fallen sharply. Supplies in cold storage have compensated for some of the shortfall but as these near exhaustion there will be renewed pressures on price. Moreover, more environmentally friendly and sustainable fishing methods such as pole and line may cause prices to increase as they are less efficient than net fishing. In Figure 2.9 this possibility is captured in the leftward shift of the supply curve *back* to S_1 and an increase in the equilibrium price to P_3, with an equilibrium quantity demanded and supplied of Q_2.

Gold

Four ounces of gold? That'll be about $5,000 please

©iStockphoto.com/Donall O Cleirigh

Recent developments in the world gold market have been heavily conditioned by the severe fright given to investors by the 2008–9 world recession. Gold is a robust and highly prized metal. It is held in three principal forms. About half is used as jewellery; a further 10 per cent is used in dentistry and industry – especially electronics; and the rest is devoted to investment by the private sector, or held by the world's central banks and other official institutions.

Figure 2.10 depicts monthly movements in the world gold price, expressed in US dollars, since 1971. One notable feature is that in 2009 the price of an ounce of gold moved beyond the $1,000 mark for the first time ever. This was certainly due to a surge in demand from investors concerned to diversify away from riskier assets such as shares and property that were falling sharply in value as a result of the world recession. As rising demand came up against a relatively stable short-term supply, prices were forced up.

Will gold prices remain above $1,000? One argument suggests that they might. The crucial issue is the nature and pace of the world economy's recovery from recession. Should this remain uncertain and weak, investors' demand for gold is likely to remain strong because of the continuing risks attached to rival assets. On the other hand, a sharp upturn in the world's economic prospects may spark fears about the macroeconomic phenomenon of inflation, which erodes the purchasing power of money. Again, in these circumstances, gold's status as a haven asset makes it attractive to investors. Moreover, renewed economic growth would also underpin the jewellery-based demand for gold. The recent softening of gold prices probably reflects a market view that, in the near future, neither a return to recession nor a surge in inflation is likely.

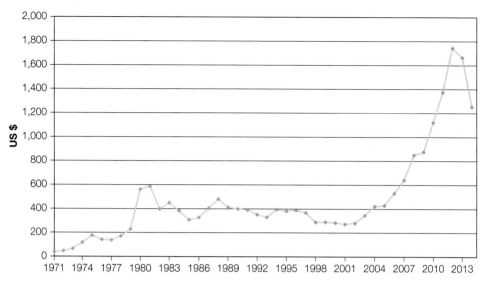

Figure 2.10 Gold price 1971–2014 (January)

Source: Data from ICE Benchmark Administration, World Gold Council

A closer examination of Figure 2.10 suggests that gold has also been an asset of choice in other turbulent periods. For example, the sevenfold increase in its price during the 1970s probably reflected both the protracted slowdown in the world economy during that period, as well as the appearance of the (then) new and apparently intractable problem of worldwide inflation. In contrast, the slackening of the gold price to under $300 per ounce in 2001 may be explained by the achievement of relatively stable world economic growth without any attendant inflationary pressures – simply, investors were in much less need of a safe-haven asset.

2.5   Applying market analysis 1: the example of economic integration in the European Union

■ Concept: The single market programme is an attempt to create, across the EU, a unified market in goods, services, capital and labour. In an economic sense, national boundaries inside the EU were abolished at the end of 1992.

If markets can work as our theoretical arguments have so far suggested – prompting equilibria in the face of various forms of change and disruption – we might expect to see them promoted and supported in many 'real world' situations. Using policies adopted by the European Union (EU) towards the organization of markets as an example, let us now see if this is the case. In fact our findings will demonstrate that the EU appears to be somewhat *ambiguous* in its attitudes towards the free market. On the one hand, it has introduced the so-called single market programme and an entirely new currency – the euro – which together are intended to harness the market mechanism in a positive way, using it to coordinate the production and consumption of many goods and services across Europe, and to make European labour and investment markets work more effectively. On the other hand, however, in the market

Laissez-faire: a situation in which there is little or no state interference in the market economy. Here all decisions are taken by individual firms and consumers.

for some foods, the EU prefers intervention to laissez-faire or free enterprise. In what follows, we use the principles of demand and supply to explain such ambiguity.

The EU is currently composed of 28 member states. Of these 15 are longer-standing members from Western Europe. In the mid-2000s ten formerly communist countries from Eastern Europe joined, together with two Mediterranean island states: Malta and Cyprus. Croatia joined in 2013. And the EU is still expanding. Macedonia, Montenegro, Serbia and Turkey are official candidate countries for membership. Figure 2.11 depicts EU members and candidates.

A central aim of the EU is to enhance the economic prospects of its members. This is being achieved by binding their separate national territories together to form a *single market* in Europe. The result will be the creation of a unified

*member countries in dark green, EU candidate countries in grey

Figure 2.11 Member countries of the European Union

Source: EU

economic space, which, it is anticipated, should enjoy the kind of cohesiveness presently evident inside the separate national economies. Consumption and production decisions, decisions about where to live and work, decisions about where to invest – *all* are now being taken more and more across the whole EU map in Figure 2.11. Technically, the single market has been in existence since the end of 1992. However, it is one thing to create the framework for a market: the extent to which the single market actually flourishes will depend on the actions of European firms, consumers and state agencies. As part of the process, 19 EU member states so far have also elected to join the euro area and share the same currency. In 2015 Lithuania became the latest country to adopt the euro. Can you think why the euro should greatly enhance market processes across the many economies that use it? Here's one answer.

■ **Concept: Price transparency** refers here to how easily consumers in one country can understand prices in another country.

A major argument for the euro is the price transparency it generates across different countries. Think about the last time you used a price comparison website. You were able to make a very informed choice about a product or service because you were presented with a list of alternative prices for the item you wanted. If you're a UK resident you saw these prices in pounds; in Russia you'd see them in roubles; in China the currency is yuan, and so on. In each case the market is a *national* one. Quotations in other currencies would not make much sense because they're not easily understood.

We can easily demonstrate this. Here's an offer: want a new laptop? We can offer you one for 7,500 Hungarian forints. Deal? We know you're hesitating – *er, what's that in pounds?* Too late, we withdraw the offer. You missed a real bargain – a laptop for about £20.

Now, for consumers in the euro area things are very different – prices across 19 countries are instantly understood and it's increasingly likely that their price comparison websites – which are really just a representation of their markets – will be articulated at the widest level, meaning more choice for consumers and more opportunities for firms.

The drive to create a single market in Europe was born out of a concern that, over the 1970s and early 1980s, the existing form of the so-called 'Common Market' was unable to sufficiently help its members to match the economic performances and potential of other advanced nations: the United States and Japan in particular. The source of the problem was thought to be the increasingly fragmented nature of the European economy. The Common Market was an economic space that provided for the free movement of goods and services between member nations. Since its creation in 1957 as part of the Treaty of Rome, citizens in member states all over Europe could buy and sell freely to one another, without the hindrance of any barriers to trade such as tariffs, which are taxes on traded goods. Commercial freedom of this sort should in theory have brought substantial benefits. German citizens would no longer tend to buy goods and services from mostly German firms; they could buy just as easily from French firms if these offered better or cheaper products. Similarly, (say) Italian and Dutch firms would be encouraged to sell wherever in Europe their products merited a demand. In this way, a more open European market would allow European consumers to buy from firms that offered them the best value. Moreover, because the best firms would tend to be rewarded with more custom, they would thrive at the expense of their inferior rivals, reaping the benefits of economies of scale as they grew larger. The long-term effect of the Common Market would therefore be the encouragement and promotion of the best producers: Europe would become a more productive and competitive place.

How did the concern over the fragmentation of the European economy arise? The problem was that, in some important respects, Europe appeared by the late 1970s and early 1980s to be *retreating back* into its national economic components. For example, it was felt that the free movement of goods and services was increasingly hampered by various kinds of what we might term 'administrative' trade barriers, such as those concerned with national standards for certain classes of good. For example, both the Danish and German governments have, at times in the past, sought to prevent their citizens from importing foreign beers that did not match established domestic production standards. In addition, it was evident that despite their apparent commitment to European integration, national governments themselves tended to purchase along very nationalistic lines. Thus, the British government usually bought from British firms, the French government from French firms and so on. In this context, the single market, introduced in 1992, was an attempt to *refresh the integration project*. Its intention was to sweep away all forms of trade barrier in the markets for goods and services and, in addition, to allow the free movement of labour and capital in Europe too. By opening up economic opportunity in this way, it is hoped that the single market will re-establish the EU's competitive edge in the world economy.

The single market has now been developing for nearly 25 years and the euro has been in existence for 15 years, so how have things progressed – is there a truly single European market? It is certainly possible to argue that Europe looks more like a single market than any other group of countries anywhere else in the world. Table 2.1 summarizes the extent of trade within and between the world's principal regions and shows that 66.8 per cent of European countries' exports are to other European countries. In contrast intra-North American exports represent only 37.9 per cent of total exports by Canada, the US and Mexico.

Just as telling perhaps are the views of businesses that operate in the single market. A widely reported view comes from the airline easyJet. EasyJet acknowledges that its origins lie in the creation of an open European market: 'easyJet is a product of the EU's deregulation of Europe's aviation market. Without deregulation we would not exist'.

While the EU seeks to reap the benefits of laissez-faire from its single market project, in other areas *intervention* in markets is the preferred option. As noted, heavily state-managed food production in Europe is the most obvious

■ Concept: Economies of scale arise when a larger output is produced without a proportionately equal increase in the costs of production. In the single market, as the more successful firms grow in size they are able to produce more efficiently by, for example, purchasing inputs in bulk quantities, or sharing business services such as marketing across European countries.

Table 2.1 Shares of regional trade flow in world merchandise exports, 2012 (%)

Destination origin	World	North America	South and Central America	Europe	CIS	Africa	Middle East	Asia
World	100	100	100	100	100	100	100	100
North America	13.2	37.9	27.6	5.8	3.3	6.5	10.5	9.2
South and Central America	4.2	6.2	25.6	1.9	1.5	3.6	2.4	3.2
Europe	35.6	16.2	15.7	66.8	44.6	36.3	29.2	12.0
CIS	4.5	1.2	0.9	6.6	27.0	2.4	3.0	2.4
Africa	3.5	2.4	3.9	3.7	0.3	13.9	2.4	3.0
Middle East	7.5	3.9	1.4	2.3	1.3	6.8	16.2	13.7
Asia	31.5	32.1	24.9	13.0	21.9	30.4	36.5	56.5

Source: Data from International Trade Statistics 2013, courtesy of WTO

and – with associated claims of 'butter and beef mountains' – notorious case. We can again use supply and demand here to follow what is going on.

Agriculture in the EU is regulated by the Common Agricultural Policy (CAP). The CAP is actually a determined attempt to *prevent* the operation of market forces in European agriculture. This, of course, must mean that a free market in agriculture would produce outcomes that the EU does not want. In effect, the CAP works to preserve the kind of localized production that, for the most part, the EU would like to sweep away in its single market programme. If the CAP were abolished, a free market in European agriculture would tend to drive less efficient farmers out of business and, in the search for economies of scale, encourage the creation of much larger farms. These would be necessary to compete with low-cost food producers outside Europe who, given free market conditions, would be able to export greater volumes of output to meet European demand. So why does the EU wish to preserve relatively small-scale, fragmented and less efficient localized production? Historically, part of the answer concerned the need to guarantee food supplies in Europe after the Second World War but now the simple reason is that the EU wants to protect the jobs and incomes of its farmers. Let us see how this is achieved.

Figure 2.12 depicts the EU market for a particular agricultural commodity such as sugar. The supply and demand curves therefore represent the dispositions of *EU* producers and consumers respectively. Assuming there is no possibility of trade between the EU and the rest of the world, the equilibrium in this market is given by price P_e and quantity Q_e. Now, let us also assume that sugar can be produced more cheaply in the rest of the world (which, as it happens *is* actually the case). This means that the prevailing world price for sugar is lower than P_e. But if free trade between the EU and the rest of the world were possible, European consumers could buy sugar at the lower world price. In this case, the quantity demanded would be Q_4 but European producers would offer only

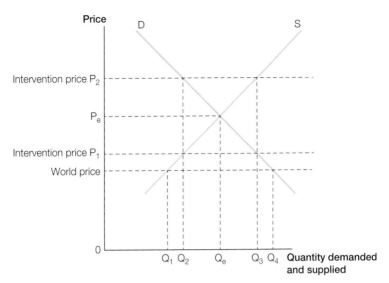

Figure 2.12 Market intervention: the case of the Common Agricultural Policy

Q_1. At the world price, therefore, sugar imports into the EU would amount to $Q_4–Q_1$. In a completely free market for sugar the relatively low world price would benefit European consumers, who would pay less and consume more. On the other hand, the EU's output of sugar would fall and so would the number of EU farmers in the now 'world articulated' sugar market.

This means that for the CAP to fulfil its noted objective – the retention of the jobs and incomes of EU farmers – it must insulate or protect EU agricultural markets from those of the rest of the world. This is done by setting an intervention price for the agricultural commodities it wishes to protect. Clearly, in Figure 2.12, there is a big difference between the world price for sugar and the EU's intervention price P_2, which means that EU consumers must be prevented from obtaining sugar at the lower world price (because they would not then buy EU sugar). This is done by the imposition of a tariff on sugar imports into the EU. A tariff is a tax on traded goods and, in this case, it has the effect of raising the price of the EU's imported sugar close to the level of the intervention price (if importers have to pay a tax on sugar they ship to the EU, the assumption is that they will pass the costs of the tax on to EU consumers in the form of higher prices).

In Figure 2.12 note that at intervention price P_2 there is excess supply in the EU sugar market. As we have seen, disequilibrium prices of this sort are unstable. The accumulating unsold stocks they are left with should prompt farmers to sell at lower prices until the equilibrium price P_e is attained. To prevent this happening – and EU farmers leaving the market – *the EU itself arranges the purchase whatever excess supply arises at the intervention price*. In Figure 2.12, this amounts to $Q_3–Q_2$. Purchases of this kind are the source of the infamous food 'mountains', for which the EU has been criticized. Because there is no demand for these agricultural surpluses, they are simply stored indefinitely at the EU's expense.

In summary, the effect of the CAP is to raise the prices of agricultural commodities in the EU. This encourages more farmers to remain in business than would be the case in a free market, fully integrated with the rest of the world. The positive outcome of the policy is, therefore, a higher number of farmers supported by subsidized incomes. The less attractive implications of the policy include the higher prices EU consumers have to pay for agricultural produce, the sheer cost of the policy (alone it consumes roughly 40 per cent of the EU's total budget) and its distortion of world trade (as, for example, the rest of the world has its capacity to export to the EU restricted).

Criticisms of the economics of the CAP, together with its rising costs as the EU added 10 Eastern European countries with significant agricultural sectors to its membership in the mid-2000s, have prompted some reforms. For certain commodities – such as beef, arable crops and olives – payments to farmers have been 'decoupled' from an obligation to produce unwanted food so that intervention stocks are not the problem they once were. In the sugar sector the intervention price has been lowered by more than a third and the EU sugar market made freely open to the exports of least-developed country sugar producers, which means that the gap between the intervention price and the world market price represented in Figure 2.12 has narrowed. For example, at intervention price P_1, the EU produces less sugar at Q_2 and imports $Q_3 - Q_2$.

On the basis of the cases reviewed in this section, the EU appears to have a rather inconsistent view on the usefulness of the market mechanism. For industry in general, it anticipates that the articulation of market processes at the widest level will serve to enhance Europe's competitiveness in the world economy. However, for agriculture, the same market processes are to some extent judged to be harmful. Why the difference? The answer lies in the conditions of industry and agriculture in the EU *relative* to their conditions in the rest of the world. European industry *already* enjoys a level of overall competitiveness which is equivalent or very close to the world's best and it is *currently* integrated into international markets in the same general way that, for example, American and Japanese industries are. Further progress for European industry might well be predicated on the market-based improvement of an existing highly creditable performance.

However, when compared to the rest of the world, the relative performance of the agricultural sector in the EU is generally inferior. The integration of European agriculture into the world market is therefore difficult for the EU to accept because it would expose the meagre competitiveness of European farmers and many of them would be driven out of business. The reason why this has not been allowed to happen has much to do with the political and lobbying strength of agricultural interests in the EU: witness, for example, the familiar spectacle of European capital cities clogged by the tractors or sheep of demonstrating farmers. The agricultural community is an able defender of the CAP, while those who have most to gain from its removal – EU consumers who would benefit from lower food prices – are largely without a collective voice.

2.6   Elasticity in the market

The concept of elasticity is a further element to be introduced to our analysis of the operation of markets. What is elasticity? In Sections 2.2 and 2.3, we reviewed the respective sets of factors that determine the demand for and supply of a particular good or service. For example, following the usual *ceteris paribus* assumption, higher prices reduce the quantity demanded and lower prices push it up (the analytical terms we used were contractions and extensions of the quantity demanded), but what about the *strength* of response? When, for example, the price of a good increases by, say, 5 per cent, by how much does the quantity demanded contract – about the same, more, much more, or less? This is clearly a significant question, both for economists who want to understand how markets work, and particularly for firms who are active participants in them. If a firm is considering a price change for a product it makes, it will want to know the likely effect of the change. Will a price reduction allow it to sell a lot more units of output or only a few more, and what will be the effect upon the overall level of revenue? The concept of elasticity provides answers to such questions.

We conceptualize the response of supply and demand to other economic changes as the *elasticity* of supply or demand. When the quantity supplied or demanded is relatively unresponsive to a particular stimulus – such as a price change – it is said to be *inelastic*. On the other hand, when it is more responsive and changes substantially it is said to be *elastic*. We define and extend these categories more carefully below.

2.7   Price elasticity of demand

Price elasticity of demand: the proportionate (or percentage) change in the quantity demanded of a good divided by the proportionate (or percentage) change in its price that brought it about.

The most commonly used form of elasticity is price elasticity of demand. This measures the responsiveness of the quantity demanded of a particular good or service to changes in its price. More formally, the price elasticity of demand of a good or service (P_{ed}) is measured by the proportionate change in its quantity demanded divided by the proportionate change in price which brings this about:

$$P_{ed} = \frac{\text{Proportionate change in quantity demanded}}{\text{proportionate change in price}} \tag{2.1}$$

Price elasticity of demand can be illustrated diagrammatically. In Figure 2.13 we show a hypothetical market for new cars. Two among many possible prices are considered, together with the respective quantities demanded at each price. Now, we wish to use the concept of elasticity in this market, which means, following the equation above, that we have to find proportionate changes in quantity demanded and price. But there is a snag here. The proportionate change in price will depend upon whether we are considering a price *increase* (from £12,000 to £15,000 per car) or a *decrease* (from £15,000 to £12,000). When price increases, the proportionate change is one quarter or 25 per cent (an increase of £3,000 over the original price of £12,000). But if price falls from £15,000 to £12,000, then the proportionate change is one fifth or 20 per cent (a decrease of £3,000 on the original price of £15,000). In order to overcome this problem and arrive at the same number for a proportionate price change in either direction, we express the change in price as a proportion or percentage of the *average* price over the range in which we are interested. In this case, the average price is £13,500 ((£12,000 + £15,000)/2). We follow the same procedure when calculating proportionate changes in quantity demanded.

We now have a slightly more sophisticated means of calculating price elasticity of demand. In Figure 2.13, following equation (2.1), we arrive at a value for price elasticity of demand in our example of −4.77 (correct to two decimal places). But what does this number tell us? In fact, it indicates that, for the range in question, demand is price elastic; in other words, the price change (in either direction) will produce a *more than proportionate response* in the quantity demanded. Notice also that, as price is cut, there is an increase in the net revenue earned on the sale of cars. This increase is derived from the combination of the area of revenue loss (£3,000 × 10,000 cars = £30m per month) and the area of revenue gain (£12,000 × 22,000 cars = £264m per month) and amounts to £234m per month. For a price increase from £12,000 to £15,000, there would be a net revenue loss of £234m per month.

Price elastic: where the proportionate change in quantity demanded is greater than the proportionate change in price; elasticity is greater than 1.

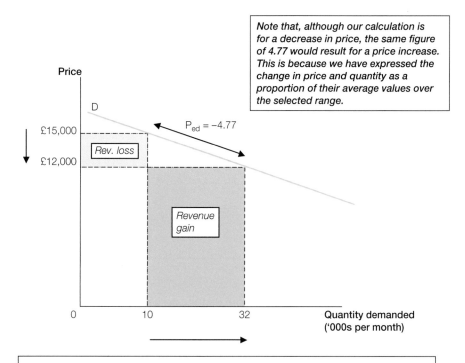

Note that, although our calculation is for a decrease in price, the same figure of 4.77 would result for a price increase. This is because we have expressed the change in price and quantity as a proportion of their average values over the selected range.

Price elasticity of demand (P_{ed}) is calculated across a selected range of the demand curve.

P_{ed} = proportionate change in quantity demanded ÷ proportionate change in price

For a fall in price from £15,000 to £12,000 ...

$$P_{ed} = \frac{\text{(change in quantity} \div \text{average quantity over selected range)}}{\text{(change in price} \div \text{average price over selected range)}} \quad (2.1)$$

$$P_{ed} = \frac{22 \div ((10 + 32) / 2)}{-3 \div ((15 + 12) / 2)}$$

$$P_{ed} = \frac{(22 \div 21)}{(-3 \div 13.5)}$$

$$P_{ed} = \frac{1.05}{-0.22}$$

$$P_{ed} = \mathbf{-4.77}$$

Figure 2.13 Price elasticity of demand in the market for new cars

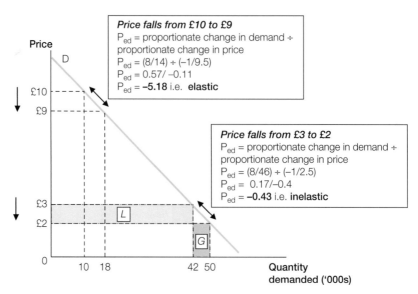

Figure 2.14 Variation in elasticity along a demand curve

Figure 2.14 presents two further worked examples of price elasticity of demand. In the first case, as price falls from £10 to £9, demand can again be seen to be price elastic. The gain in net revenue associated with the price reduction is also clearly evident in this case. However, when price falls from £3 to £2, price elasticity of demand is calculated at −0.43. This is a case of price inelastic demand, in that the price change induces a *less than proportionate response in the quantity demanded*. Notice here that the price reduction is clearly associated with a net loss in revenue (the areas of revenue loss and gain for this price reduction are marked *L* and *G* respectively). We have now uncovered the two *main* classes of elasticity. When the quantity demanded responds more than proportionately to a price change it is said to be *elastic* and will carry a value *greater than 1*. On the other hand, when the quantity demanded responds less than proportionately to a price change it is said to be *inelastic* and will carry a value *less than 1*. Although, given the inverse relationship between price and quantity demanded, the values of price elasticity of demand are negative, the convention is to omit the minus sign to avoid any possible confusion. We will follow this custom from now on.

Beyond the two main cases of price elastic and inelastic demand, the prescient reader may have anticipated other possibilities. The quantity demanded may respond *proportionately* to a change in price. Here $P_{ed} = 1$. This is known as unit elasticity. An example of unit elasticity is presented in Figure 2.15, panel (a). Notice, incidentally, that here the loss and gain in revenue resulting from changes in the price and quantity demanded are identical. Of course, it may be that quantity demanded is completely *unresponsive* to changes in price. In such cases demand is said to be perfectly inelastic. On the other hand there may be

Price inelastic: where the proportionate change in quantity demanded is less than the proportionate change in price; elasticity is less than −1.

Unit elasticity: where the proportionate change in quantity demanded is equal to the proportionate change in price; elasticity is 1.

Perfect inelasticity: where the quantity demanded does *not* respond to a change in price; elasticity is 0.

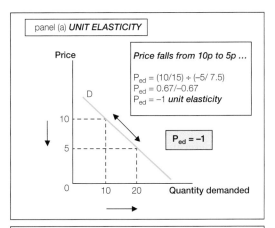

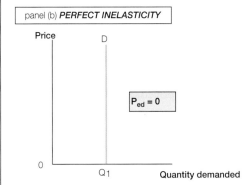

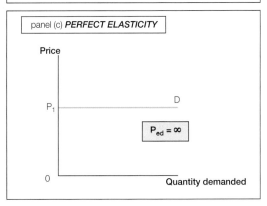

Figure 2.15 Unit elasticity, perfectly inelastic demand, perfectly elastic demand

a *perfect response*, inasmuch as the quantity demanded is infinitely large at one unique price and zero at all other possible prices. Here demand is said to be perfectly elastic. Figure 2.15, panels (b) and (c), also depicts examples of these two cases. Notice that, for the vertical perfectly inelastic demand curve, regardless of whatever price is set over the range of the curve, the quantity demanded remains static at Q_1. Here P_{ed} = zero, consistent with the complete unresponsiveness of quantity demanded to a change in price. In the case of the perfectly elastic curve, at price P_1 there is an infinitely elastic demand for the good or service but at all other prices quantity demanded evaporates completely. Here $P_{ed} = \infty$ (that is, infinity), consistent with an infinitely large response of quantity demanded to the change in price.

In summary then, price elasticity of demand can range in value from zero (perfectly unresponsive) to infinity (perfectly responsive) as follows:

perfectly inelastic demand – quantity demanded fails to respond to price changes $(P_{ed} = 0)$
inelastic demand – the response of quantity demanded is proportionately smaller than the price change $(P_{ed} < 1)$
unit elastic demand – the response of quantity demanded is proportionately equal to the price change $(P_{ed} = 1)$

Perfect elasticity: where the response of quantity demanded to a price change is infinitely large; elasticity is ∞ (infinity).

The sign < indicates 'less than'.

The sign > indicates
'greater than'.

elastic demand – the response of quantity demanded is proportionately
greater than the price change ($P_{ed} > 1$)
perfectly elastic demand – the response of quantity demanded to the price
change is infinitely large ($P_{ed} = \infty$)

2.8   Determinants of price elasticity of demand

The most important determinants of price elasticity of demand are:

The availability of substitutes
The proportion of income spent on a good or service
Time

The availability of substitutes

Goods and services that have *close substitutes* tend to have relatively price-*elastic*
demand structures; those with only distant substitutes tend to be more price
inelastic. There are, for example, many brands of soft drink sold in Europe and
most tend to be similarly priced. Manufacturers are generally unwilling to raise
their prices for fear that custom will leak to their competitors' products. This
is an implicit acknowledgment that the demand for any particular soft drink is
price elastic, and is so precisely because consumers enjoy a wide range of choice.
Incidentally, where a market is characterized by a high degree of choice-driven
price elasticity, producers have a great incentive to develop *brand loyalties*.
Brand loyalty establishes the superiority of a particular good or service over its
rival products in the mind of the consumer and serves to reduce its price elasticity: people may be willing to pay a little more for it because of its perceived
qualities. We return to this issue when we discuss asymmetric information
problems later in this chapter.

Oil is an often quoted example of a good with *few close substitutes* (at least
in the short run) and, as a consequence, a relatively *inelastic* demand structure.
In 1973–4 and 1979, a group of the world's leading oil producers – the OPEC
nations, in what became known as 'oil shocks' – effectively quadrupled and then
doubled the world price of oil. The industrialized non-oil producing nations
had little immediate choice except to meet the inflated oil prices as their economies were highly oil-dependent. This, of course, led to significantly increased
flows of revenue from oil-importing countries to the oil producers. We will have
more to say about the market for oil in Section 2.10 below.

The price-inelastic demand qualities of tobacco and alcohol are equally well
known, not least by those governments that choose to tax these commodities
in order to raise revenue. Such taxes are passed on by producers to their customers in the form of higher prices. The working assumption here, of course, is
that the higher prices, because they brush up against inelastic demand, do not
significantly reduce consumption. Again, inelastic demand arises in these cases

because, for smokers and drinkers, there are few, if any, close substitutes for tobacco and alcohol. Governments could not tax, say, crisps or peanuts with the same degree of impunity: people would snack instead on the dozens of alternative savouries available in the shops.

● **Think Point**

Which other goods and services might governments feel able to tax because the demand for them is perceived to be price inelastic?

In addition to tobacco and alcohol the British government levies particular taxes on fuels, gambling, insurance policies and air travel. History throws up some weird-sounding examples of tax decisions by authorities. Taxed in the past: beards in Russia (actually as a deterrent; Peter the Great didn't like beards); windows in England (simply to raise revenue) and urine (used for industrial cleaning purposes) in ancient Rome: taxing the p*ss!

"He's convinced they'll bring back window tax!"

Reproduced by kind permission of PRIVATE EYE magazine/Roger Latham

© iStockphoto/borer

Please don't tax my beard!

The proportion of income spent on a good or service, or *why have Freddos more than doubled in price?*

When only a small portion of income is spent on a good, purchasers are thought to be relatively indifferent to price changes in terms of their demand for it: demand in such cases will be more inelastic. Here's a popular example: Cadbury's Freddo. Our students tell us they're avid consumers but with one moan thrown in which usually runs along the lines of: '*they used to be 10p each but now they're 25p; what's going on?*'

Well, what's going on is that the people at Cadbury's know a little about the determinants of price elasticity of demand. Freddos are now indeed 25p – a 150 per cent price increase on the original – but do you still buy them? Most people will probably say yes because 25p isn't a great deal in the wider scheme of things so demand here is almost certainly price inelastic.

However, what might be the demand reaction to a significant rise in the price of, say, a washing machine or a smart TV? Because goods like these cost at least hundreds of pounds even a modest percentage increase in price could involve spending an extra £100 or so. This would be likely to more significantly affect the quantity demanded: the response in other words would be more *elastic* in nature because the purchase takes up a much greater proportion of income.

One last thing that may make you feel better. Although Freddos more than doubled in price they got bigger too, so the actual price increase in terms of chocolate consumed was a lot less than 150 per cent!

Time

Demand patterns often do not respond instantaneously to price changes. Take, for example, the demand for national newspapers. Newspapers have substitutes readily available in the form of rival titles and rival news media such as radio, television and the Internet. This suggests that the demand for particular newspaper titles should be price elastic and this, indeed, is the case. However, demand is not *instantaneously* elastic. If the price of one title rises, those who customarily buy it may not at first notice because they have the paper delivered and pay for it weekly or because they're not particularly alert in the shop first thing in the morning. They continue to buy it for these reasons and also perhaps because it reflects their views, they like a particular commentator whose byline it carries and so on. However, some readers will notice the price rise – certainly after a day or two, or when they next pay their paper bill – and they may then begin to sample rival titles, or even decide not to regularly buy a newspaper at all. This *gradual* change means that price elasticity of demand is likely to be more inelastic immediately after a price rise than later on. Once consumers have had time to register the price change in their minds they *then* begin to seek out close substitutes for the good or service in question.

2.9 Why firms need to know about price elasticity of demand

An awareness of price elasticity of demand is clearly essential for firms if they are to understand consumer responses to the pricing structures they set in particular markets. We are already aware that firms cannot afford to misread market conditions. If, for example, price is set above its equilibrium level, the market will fail to clear: there will be excess supply and firms will be left with unsold stocks. However, the extent of excess supply will increase as price elasticity of demand increases. This means that if firms fail to appreciate the nature of elasticity in the market they can make poor commercial decisions even in apparently very favourable market conditions. On the other hand, reading elasticity correctly can pay off handsomely.

As an illustration of this possibility, the case study below reviews the very imaginative pricing structure set by Mansfield Town for a match in the Blue

Square Premier League. The club allowed fans to pay whatever price they liked at the turnstile. Had people paid less than normal and the match attendance figure not changed much (because it was price inelastic), Mansfield might have had the makings of a mini financial disaster on their hands. But as the example shows, things turned out rather well. The club made a shrewd judgement that for this game demand was likely to be price elastic.

BUSINESS CASE STUDY

Pay what you like to watch Mansfield Town

Every football fan knows what it's like to feel the frustration of defeat. Sometimes it's doubly galling when you think of how much you've paid to watch a match that's left you flat and demoralized. Sometimes you might even think, 'that's it, I'm not going again – it's just costing too much'.

Football clubs are not insensitive to the prices they charge fans to watch games. Some Premier League clubs raise prices to reflect the importance of particular fixtures, knowing, for example, that when Manchester United visit they can charge more without much risk that the attendance will fall. The demand for tickets for games against Manchester United is considered somewhat price inelastic.

On the other hand, for a Premier League club, an early round and possibly highlights-televised Carling Cup home fixture against a team from the bottom of league two on a wet Wednesday night is a tricky proposition. Here a Premier League-style ticket price may cause a collapse in demand. Clubs are aware of this and usually offer cheap tickets to try to prevent attendances from falling too much. Here demand is price elastic.

So football clubs know a little about price elasticity of demand and try to set prices to make this knowledge work in their favour. But one club – Mansfield Town of the Blue Square Premier League – has gone a lot further than the rest. It's left pricing decisions to the fans themselves.

For a match against promotion rivals, Gateshead F.C., Mansfield allowed fans to pay *any* amount they wanted to gain admittance. A risky strategy? Possibly. The club presented the offer as a thank-you to the fans for their support and as an attempt to get more people along to cheer on the team in an important game.

Mansfield's previous home match had seen 3368 people come to watch, and the season's average was 3159. But for the Gateshead fixture 7261 fans squeezed into the Field Mill ground. And crucially for the club the gate receipts went up so that more income was generated than on a normal match day, even though most people were probably choosing to pay less than the normal ticket price. Demand for this game was clearly price elastic.

Unfortunately, as for the game itself, Mansfield lost.

2.10 Applying market analysis 2: OPEC and the market for oil

In Section 2.8 we mentioned that, because it has few close substitutes, oil may be classed as a good with low price elasticity of demand. In the 1970s it became commonplace that the possession of substantial oil reserves was a very welcome economic advantage for a country. As noted, in 1973–4 and 1979 OPEC, the group of major oil exporting nations, orchestrated dramatic increases in the price of oil. These first two 'oil shocks', as they became known, are highlighted

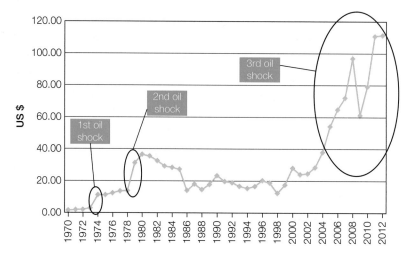

Figure 2.16 Crude oil price 1970–2012
Source: BP Statistical Review of World Energy 2013

in Figure 2.16. We can see in Figure 2.17 how these higher prices were achieved. By cutting its own output OPEC reduced the world's supply of oil and the market price consequently increased on both occasions. Figure 2.17 also shows that the shocks caused oil demand (consumption) to slacken as prices increased but not by much in proportionate terms. For example, during the second oil shock, demand fell from 64 million barrels a day in 1979 to 60 million barrels in 1981 against a relatively larger price increase from $32 to $37 a barrel. Price elasticity of demand in this case comes out at −0.4. OPEC clearly took advantage of oil's price-inelastic demand.

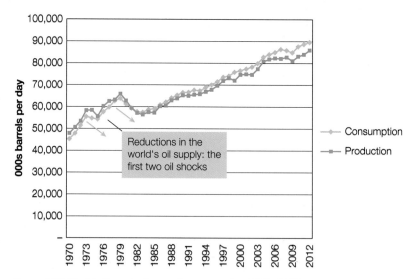

Figure 2.17 World oil production and consumption 1970–2012
Source: BP Statistical Review of World Energy 2013

Higher oil prices greatly enriched OPEC members and caused major problems for economies that were highly dependent on imported oil. At first at least, oil importers simply had to pay more for this important commodity. But this is not the end of the story. Subsequent developments in the market for oil provide a good illustration of how market processes come to constrain even the most powerful producers. The possession of something as vital as oil to modern industrial economies is certainly desirable but it does not allow producers to evade the ultimate sanction of the laws of supply and demand.

Figures 2.16, 2.17 and 2.18 capture the essence of this problem for the OPEC nations. In response to the first two oil shocks (see Figure 2.16) some significant shifts occurred in oil consumption. Oil-importing nations had a growing incentive to economize on the use of oil, to exploit their own oil deposits more intensively (in many instances, the previously low OPEC price had meant this was not worthwhile), and to further develop alternative energy sources. Over time then, the relatively price-inelastic demand structure of OPEC's oil began to melt away as demand for oil slackened and new non-oil energy supplies became more economic. In effect OPEC, in 1973–4 and 1979, had attempted to impose its will on the long-run development of the market. It wanted permanently higher prices for its oil. Unfortunately for OPEC, markets are not amenable to this kind of manipulation much beyond the short term. All OPEC succeeded in doing was to incentivize the development of new oil and non-oil energy supplies outside its jurisdiction. As is evident from Figure 2.17, oil demand did not pass its 1979 peak for almost a decade, while Figure 2.18 shows that demand in the US – the world's largest economy and principal consumer of oil – did not regain its 1978 peak for nearly *twenty* years. The resultant depression in the oil price from the early 1980s is depicted in Figure 2.16. After peaking in 1980 at $36 a barrel, the oil price did not rise above this level again until 2004. Over time the laws of supply and demand simply reasserted themselves.

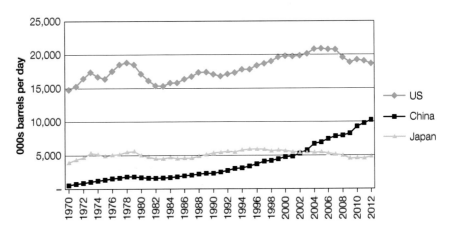

Figure 2.18 US, China and Japan oil consumption 1970–2012

Source: BP Statistical Review of World Energy 2013

Before we leave this example, it is worth saying a few words about the more recent developments in the oil market. Figure 2.16 shows that from a low of $13 in 1998, the price of a barrel of crude oil surged to almost $100 by July 2008. The recession of 2008–9 caused the price to then slacken as the demand for oil waned in the worst-hit countries, but the $100 barrel mark was breached in 2011. In effect the world has experienced a third oil shock which, again, has been conditioned by the interplay between supply and demand. Since the end of the recession the gap between world oil production and demand has widened. In 2010 and 2011 oil consumption outstripped world oil production by its widest-ever modern margin. A principal source of the rising demand for oil is shown in Figure 2.18. Together, the US, China and Japan account for around 37 per cent of the world's total demand for oil. Although demand from the US was weakened by the start of recession and demand from Japan has been broadly flat since the 1970s, oil consumption in China accelerated from the early 1990s. This, together with rising demand in other large economies, such as Brazil, Russia and India, has underpinned the demand for oil in the world economy as a whole and again confirmed its price-inelastic characteristics. The fact that the so-called BRIC countries (Brazil, Russia, India and China) are rapidly industrializing means that their energy demands are for the moment heavily invested in oil and alternative sources are not yet well developed – note from Figure 2.16 that the relatively low oil price until the mid-2000s provided little incentive to develop non-oil energy.

What will happen to the oil price in the future? If previous experience is a reasonable guide, a likely scenario would see the BRIC economies reduce their oil dependencies, incentivized to do so by soaring oil prices, much as the Western economies reduced their demand for oil in the 1980s and 1990s. The oil price would then fall over the medium term as, for example, the development of alternative sources of energy made demand less inelastic. But this possibility must be set against the life cycle of the world's oil supply. A recent estimate suggests that the world's oil reserves-to-production window is less than 40 years. That is, if oil use continues at its present rate, current reserves will be exhausted around 2055. Looming oil shortages could more than offset the effect of reduced demand so that, unless viable alternatives to oil-based energy are quickly developed and widely applied all around the world, the demand for oil may remain price inelastic in the longer term. Meaning that in the long term oil prices will be pushed higher.

2.11   Other forms of elasticity

Income elasticity of demand

In Section 2.2, we considered a range of factors other than price that influenced the demand for a good or service. These factors too can be placed in an elasticity framework. We suggested, for example, that demand can vary positively with consumers' income: higher incomes, *ceteris paribus*, prompted the demand curve for a normal good to shift to the right, while lower incomes caused it to shift to the left (see Figure 2.2). The question now arises – how *responsive* is the quantity demanded of a good to a change in income? We can resolve this issue using the concept of income elasticity of demand.

Income elasticity of demand: the proportionate change in the quantity of a good demanded, divided by the proportionate change in consumers' incomes.

Income elasticity of demand (Y_{ed}) measures the responsiveness of the quantity of a good demanded to changes in income. It is calculated using an approach similar to that which allowed us to calculate price elasticity of demand. The equation for income elasticity of demand is:

$$Y_{ed} = \frac{\text{Proportionate change in quantity demanded}}{\text{proportionate change in income}} \qquad (2.2)$$

Inferior good: one for which demand decreases when income increases.

Generally, we would expect Y_{ed} to be *positive*. In other words, higher incomes would be associated with an increase in demand (and vice versa). However, this is not always the case; in some circumstances, higher incomes can prompt a decrease in the demand for particular goods and services. In such cases Y_{ed} will be *negative*. For example, rising incomes in Britain over the past 50 years have substantially altered the way people spend their holiday time. As many more people can afford to travel abroad for longer periods, the demand for holidays in traditional seaside towns – such as Blackpool – has declined. Where Y_{ed} is negative, the relevant goods and services are said to be inferior. In contrast, as noted in Section 2.2, *normal* goods are those for which demand increases as income increases. We can identify two sets of normal good:

You're more likely to holiday here when your income rises; the demand for foreign holidays is income elastic

First, that for which Y_{ed} is *inelastic* (<1). An obvious example here is the demand for basic foods. In Europe, where incomes are already relatively high, the demand for basic foods is unlikely to increase much even when incomes rise still further. Consumers are more likely to spend their extra incomes on high-end goods such as cars and foreign holidays. Of course, there may be changes in the *way* people consume food as incomes rise – they will be more likely to eat out, for example – but the actual level of basic food consumption will increase relatively slowly.

MEDIO IMAGES

The second kind of normal good possesses an *elastic* Y_{ed} (>1). Here, when incomes rise, there is a proportionately greater increase in demand. Examples of income-elastic goods would typically include the kinds of high-end items mentioned above. In the richer societies, most basic needs – such as those for food and housing – are already amply met and so further increases in income tend to be directed towards cars, foreign holidays and so on.

Applying income elasticity of demand

The concept of income elasticity of demand can usefully contribute to, among other things, an understanding of the patterns of specialization and development that have emerged in the international economy over the past 50 years. Before this period there was a clear and long-established international division of labour within which, broadly speaking, the industrial countries produced manufactured goods while most other developing countries specialized in the production of agricultural output and raw materials. However, during the 1960s and 1970s, a number of (then) *newly industrializing countries* successfully reallocated productive resources away from old dependencies on agriculture and raw materials and switched them instead into manufacturing. Foremost among this group were South Korea, Hong Kong, Singapore and Taiwan. All these countries have now assumed fully developed status. Other economies have since followed in their wake, most notably China. The point here is that the economic success of all these countries is to some extent underpinned by their awareness of the pattern of *world* income elasticity of demand. Despite regrettably wide differences in economic growth between its different regions, the world itself is, as a whole, a richer place than it has ever been hitherto. This implies that, especially in its most advanced European, North American and Far Eastern economies, most basic needs are met. Any growth in incomes in these places is then inevitably translated into higher demand for income-elastic goods, many of which are manufactured: cars, laptops, mobile phones, fridge freezers, sports equipment, clothes, children's toys and so on. This of course means that the decision to switch resources into the production of such goods was extremely wise: the demand for them will continue to increase at a faster rate than the growth in world income. Meanwhile, those countries that continue to rely on exports of agricultural goods and raw materials will usually find the more sedate (*income inelastic*) demand for them constraining wider national prospects for faster economic growth and development.

Price elasticity of supply

Price elasticity of supply: the proportionate change in quantity supplied of a good divided by the proportionate change in price that brought it about.

As the reader will expect from our discussion in this section so far, price elasticity of supply (P_{es}) measures the responsiveness of quantity supplied to changes in price. It is given by the following equation:

$$P_{ed} = \frac{\text{Proportionate change in quantity supplied}}{\text{proportionate change in price}} \qquad (2.3)$$

Figure 2.19 provides two worked examples of price elasticity of supply. These follow precisely the same general principles as those introduced in Figure 2.13 for the calculation of price elasticity of demand. It can be seen from Figure 2.19 that price elasticity of supply can vary along a single supply curve. In this case, we observe both an instance of price-inelastic supply, where the proportionate

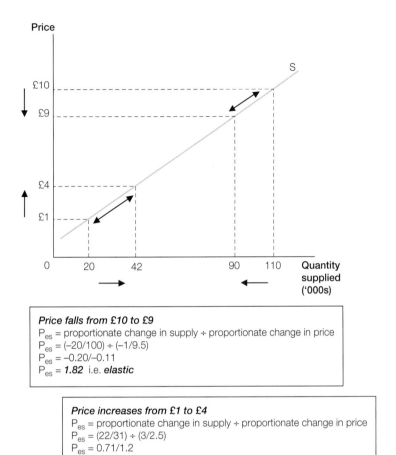

Price falls from £10 to £9
P_{es} = proportionate change in supply ÷ proportionate change in price
P_{es} = (−20/100) ÷ (−1/9.5)
P_{es} = −0.20/−0.11
P_{es} = **1.82** i.e. **elastic**

Price increases from £1 to £4
P_{es} = proportionate change in supply ÷ proportionate change in price
P_{es} = (22/31) ÷ (3/2.5)
P_{es} = 0.71/1.2
P_{es} = **0.59** i.e. **inelastic**

Figure 2.19 Price elasticity of supply

response of quantity supplied is less than the proportionate change in price that brings it about; and an elastic response, where the proportionate change in quantity supplied is greater than the proportionate change in price. Instances of unit elastic, perfectly inelastic and perfectly elastic supply are also possible. These are depicted in Figure 2.20. Notice that, as in panel (a) of this figure, any supply curve that passes through the origin will have unit-elastic supply characteristics. In panel (b), a situation of perfectly inelastic supply indicates that the quantity supplied will not respond regardless of the scale or direction of any price change. Finally, in panel (c), where supply is perfectly elastic, all prices other than P_1 induce an infinitely large fall in the quantity supplied:

Determinants of price elasticity of supply

There are two principal determinants of elasticity of supply:

Time
Elasticity of supply of factor inputs

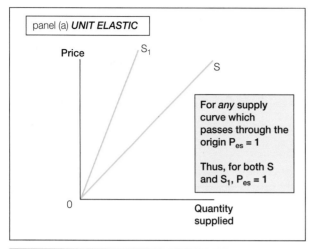

panel (a) **UNIT ELASTIC**

Price

For *any* supply curve which passes through the origin $P_{es} = 1$

Thus, for both S and S_1, $P_{es} = 1$

Quantity supplied

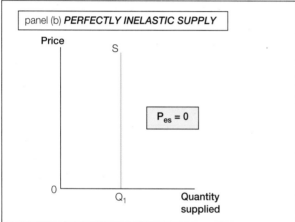

panel (b) **PERFECTLY INELASTIC SUPPLY**

Price

$P_{es} = 0$

Quantity supplied

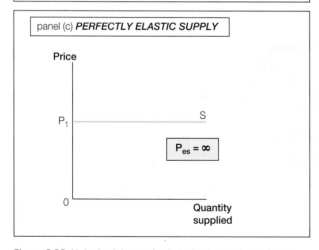

panel (c) **PERFECTLY ELASTIC SUPPLY**

Price

$P_{es} = \infty$

Quantity supplied

Figure 2.20 Unit elasticity, perfectly inelastic supply, perfectly elastic supply

Time

We noted earlier that the demand for many goods and services does not respond instantaneously to changes in price; a similar constraint operates on supply. In some markets, such as that for newspapers, output may be increased (or decreased) relatively quickly in response to a new market price – it is simply a matter of extending the print run; all the requisite machinery and raw materials will already be in place. In other markets, however, the task is more difficult. A given season's total supply of seats at football matches is highly inelastic. The only way to increase the quantity of seats supplied is to extend football grounds or build new ones: a process that can take several years. Incidentally, this makes apparent the economic basis of ticket touting at big games: a strong demand meets an inelastic supply.

The elasticity of supply of factor inputs

The responsiveness of the supply of a particular good or service to changes in price will also depend on the degree to which additional factor inputs are readily available. To take an extreme example, the prime factor input to paintings by Van Gogh is the labour of the artist himself. No more work by Van Gogh will ever be produced and, therefore, its supply is perfectly inelastic (again this, coupled with strong demand, accounts for the high prices his art commands). On the other hand, the supply of Internet content is much more elastic because the principal inputs – motivated suppliers and their access to the Internet – are not constrained to anything like the same extent.

2.12 Markets and asymmetric information

■ Concept:
Economists generally recognize four factor inputs – or factors of production – some or all of which are required in order to supply a good or service. These are: land, labour, capital and entrepreneurial – or business – skill.

So far in our discussion we have made the implicit assumption that producers and consumers have all the knowledge they need to properly discern their own best interests when they enter a market. For example, when you last bought a mobile phone you were probably aware of the range of models available, the tariffs set by different network providers and so on. Information about mobiles comes from a variety of reliable sources: your own experience of using one, the experiences that your friends share with you, advertising and visits to shops to see what's on offer. The market might be fast-changing and a little complex but it's not too difficult to make a reasonably informed choice. But not all markets are like this. Some things are easier for one side of the market to see and a little hazy or even opaque for those on the other side.

■ Concept:
Asymmetric information alludes to a situation in which one party to a transaction has more information about a product than his or her counterpart.

Take, for example, medical services. A visit to the dentist for a check-up sometimes results in a filled tooth. But the service you pay for at the dentist is not like buying a mobile phone – the consumer's awareness of why they are engaging in the transaction is very shallow. Information is unevenly distributed or asymmetric: the dentist has plenty; the worried patient – mouth open in the chair – has virtually none. But we take dentists at their word and accept that they have our best interests at heart, don't we? They're professional people, properly qualified and regulated.

As it happens, since 2006, dentists working in the UK National Health Service have had to meet agreed targets for their work, which are measured in 'units of dental activity' (UDAs). A check-up is one UDA, filling a tooth is three. Dental practices are paid according to their annually contracted allocation of UDAs. Should a practice undershoot its target for the year, it must pay back money received for work that it has not done. Work above contract is done for free.

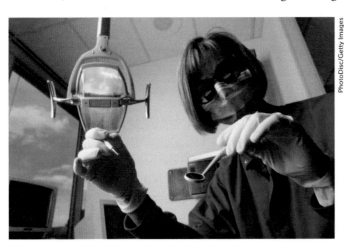

Dentists have lots of information about your dental health, you have less; information is asymmetrically distributed

Think about the incentives this arrangement offers to dentists. Practices that make a mistake in over-estimating their UDAs for the year won't have provided enough treatments – to fulfil their contracts, balance their books and justify their incomes they have to provide more treatments. But are any of these extra treatments necessary? A 2009 NHS review into dental services in England argued: 'The incentives for dentists are not as precisely aligned as they could be to a goal of oral health and consequently there are inefficiencies within NHS dentistry'.[2]

2 NHS Dental Services in England, An independent review led by Professor Jimmy Steele, 2009.

In the same review a practising dentist summarized matters a little more starkly: 'There are two things you think: how can I do the best for the patient and how can I maximize the UDAs?' So unnecessary dental treatment *is* probably provided under the UDA arrangements and because information in dental surgeries is asymmetric patients are in no position to question what goes on.

The importance of asymmetric information in markets was first highlighted in a famous paper by George Akerlof that he titled 'The Market for "Lemons".[3] Akerlof won a Nobel Prize for this work. Lemons, in American slang, are poor-quality second-hand cars. Akerlof's initial interest was in the link between sales of new cars and the performance of the whole economy. Variations in new car sales seemed to have influence on the business cycle: better sales helped the economy to grow, weaker sales threatened that growth. This got Akerlof interested the determinants of the demand for new cars and why people might prefer to buy a new car rather than a cheaper second-hand one.

Asymmetric information seemed to play a key role here. In the used-car market sellers hold all the aces: they know about the quality and reliability of the vehicles they are offering; car buyers generally know very little. Worried about buying a lemon, potential buyers desert the market (preferring the security of a new car), leaving it flat and depressed. This in turn has the effect of deterring sellers of good-quality used cars who will not obtain the relatively higher prices they think their cars merit. As they too leave, the used-car market becomes dominated by an **adverse selection** of lemons.

■ **Concept:** An **adverse selection** arises in a market when asymmetric information problems drive out higher-quality goods or services.

Akerlof's paper highlighted asymmetric information problems in other market contexts such as credit finance in less developed economies. Here Akerlof noted the extortionate rates of interest charged by moneylenders to local people who would otherwise not be able to get credit from conventional financial institutions. Banks would be reluctant to lend small amounts in poor communities about which they knew little. Here asymmetry works against the banks that fear they would not be repaid.

APR: annual percentage rate of interest. The APR allows easy comparison of different interest rates and must be quoted by finance providers in the UK.

Interestingly, we can adapt this example to understand some widely different rates of interest charged for credit in the UK today. Does an interest rate of 5853% **APR** sound attractive, or even feasible? At the time of writing, it's the typical rate advertised by wonga.com. In contrast, the Nationwide building society presently offers an interest rate of 5.9% APR. How can Wonga possibly compete with what looks like an ultra-high price on its lending? Wonga offers small (up to £400) short-term loans meant to help 'if you're short of cash due to an unexpected bill, emergency or opportunity you can't miss'. Wonga also advises that its loans are only for occasional use and must be repaid within weeks. Nationwide's loans are bigger (£7500–£14,999) and offered for longer periods (up to 5 years).

The immense gap between these two lenders might suggest that there is room in the credit market for firms to do something in between, to offer relatively

---

3 Akerlof, G.A. (1970) 'The Market for "Lemons": Quality Uncertainty and the Market Mechanism', *Quarterly Journal of Economics*, 84: 488–500.

LOOK CHARLIE, IT'S AN EVERLASTING DEBT!

WILLY WONGA

small sums repayable, say, in 6 months but at a much more competitive APR than Wonga offers. The concepts of asymmetric information and adverse selection help us to understand why this is unlikely to happen. Were firms to offer a Wonga-style service at a much lower typical APR they would likely attract a large adverse selection of customers with poor prospects of timely repayment; 'lemons', to put it crudely. Here the asymmetry problem would again run against the credit provider who would be unable to discern the good borrowers from the bad. Developing a larger and much riskier loan book in this way does not look like good business.

In 'The Market for "Lemons"', Akerlof also reflected on the kind of *counteracting institutions* that have arisen in markets to offset the problems of asymmetric information. Examples include product guarantees, the cultivation of reputation by brand loyalty, and the establishment of professional bodies. He also included educational qualifications in this list and, presciently, given the accolade his paper would eventually win him more than 30 years later, even the Nobel Prize. All these institutional forms serve to reassure or indemnify market participants that their less-than-full knowledge about a seller, buyer or product will not work to their disadvantage. The below box provides an example of an unusual counteracting institution used by the Mafia: violence.

Counteracting institutions in *The Sopranos*

How do Tony Soprano and friends in the Mafia overcome concerns that customers for their loansharking business might not pay back – with interest – the money that they owe? How does the Mafia avoid attracting an adverse selection of lemons? By severely hurting or even murdering anyone who fails to pay up!

This means that *everyone* who does business with the mob knows exactly what the stakes are and won't renege on debt. So for Tony Soprano violence, actual or threatened, is a counteracting institution that eliminates any uncertainties about the likely behaviour of his customers. He knows he'll get paid; there's very little chance of information asymmetries working against him.

Everyday Economics 2.1 below depicts a range of goods and services. Can you think of the counteracting institutions that might reassure participants that asymmetric information will not work to their disadvantage?

EVERYDAY ECONOMICS 2.1

What counteracting institutions might be at work here?

These are images of everyday goods and services but they're sold in markets where there may be asymmetric information. To overcome this problem these markets have developed counteracting institutions. Can you think of examples in each case?

Answers are at the end of the chapter.

1

2

3

Finally, think for a moment about the effect that asymmetric information has on the market. In the introduction to this chapter we talked about markets as institutions that broadly do a good job in allocating scarce resources. We rely on them because they seem to be able to organize the right amount of stuff that we want to buy and that firms want to produce. And when circumstances change they seem to be able to cope by altering price signals and the incentives that these transmit. What happens when oil begins to run out? What happens if there's a very poor coffee harvest? What happens when people buy many more digitized books instead of paper ones? The market seems to be able to answer lots of questions like these. But if there is asymmetric information in a market things go less smoothly. Our dentistry example suggests that too many treatments may be performed because consumers are poorly informed. On the other hand, before the rise of firms like Wonga how was the demand for small short-term loans catered for? And we think there may be unsatisfied demand for loans pitched somewhere between the offers made by Wonga and the likes of Nationwide. Our conclusion then is that asymmetric information undermines the capacity of markets to allocate resources efficiently. In dentistry the market provides too many; in personal lending it may allocate too few.

2.13   Markets and the rational consumer

Asymmetric information problems may mean that markets do not allocate resources as well as they might. In the used-car market asymmetric information causes fewer transactions than would occur were knowledge to be evenly distributed; in dentistry it may mean extra unnecessary treatments. But in the absence of asymmetric information can we simply assume that markets will always function well? This is what we implied earlier in the chapter: for example, in relation to the behaviour of consumers when we suggested that the demand for a good is based on a menu of price, the prices of other goods, tastes and incomes (see Figure 2.3). Where consumers have a decent knowledge of each of these factors we presume that they act sensibly and in their own best interests. Their behaviour in other words is rational.

■ Concept: Rational behaviour implies that economic agents act in their own best interests.

That economic agents – consumers, firms, workers and so on – behave rationally is one of the cornerstones of economics. Were economists to admit to irrational behaviour the discipline would potentially be in a lot of trouble and certainly it would become much more complex and messy, with agents acting in ways that defied conventional self-interest. How in such circumstances could behaviour be analysed, still less predicted? But in recent years economists and psychologists have begun to research and document economic agents' sub-rational behaviour.

Here's an example that originated in the work of the psychologists Daniel Kahneman and Amos Tversky. At the start of the previous section we made the slightly flattering assumption that when you last bought a mobile phone you made a reasonably well-informed choice. We would hope the same of ourselves: no one likes to be thought of as foolish or gullible. Now, think for a moment about the price you paid. You may not remember it exactly but we think you'll have a rough idea. Drawing on Kahneman and Tversky's work, behavioural economists would call this price your *anchor* for future decision-making in the mobile phone market. In other words, the price you paid last time will have a bearing on the choices you make when next shopping for a phone. And, indeed, for your phone purchases for some time into the future.

If you reflect on a range of things that you buy you may begin to discern other pricing anchors. Do you regularly take a taxi for certain journeys rather than a cheaper bus? Does £40 for a bottle of perfume or cologne sound about right? How about £7 for a cocktail, or £3.20 for a glossy magazine? A yes to one or more reveals some of your anchors. If you gave a decisive 'no' then you will have different anchors, which may be higher or lower. For example, to us a £7 cocktail appears, well, ridiculous; what's wrong with £2.50 for a pint of beer in your local? You see, we're anchored like everyone else. One last experiment. Tell your oldest relative the price you last paid for a haircut and watch them wince – different anchors again.

But what's to say that this kind of decision-making is not just something that economics has known about for a long time – taste? You might just have a taste for expensive clothes or shoes; there's nothing necessarily sub-rational about it. There might be a case here but experiments have shown that the anchors that condition our choices may be entirely arbitrary. Should you enjoy a small lottery win of say £50 would it change your life? Of course not, but it may well alter your behaviour if you spend the £50 on a very nice scarf and this turns into an anchor for decisions about subsequent accessory purchases. In fact experimentation suggests, bizarrely, that simply having a number in one's head – not a price, just a random number – can affect the economic choices we make.

What are we to make of behaviour that's skewed by anchoring? It's not rational: consumers apparently don't function in a cold and calculating way when they make decisions; to some extent we let our personal economic history decide. You may have slightly shocked yourself when you first paid £150 for a phone or £9 for a couple of drinks and modest cakes in Starbucks or Costa Coffee but, hey, the next time it seemed more like the thing to do. But if it's not rational, is anchoring irrational? Well it's not that either, in the sense that consumer behaviour becomes hopelessly chaotic, anarchic and unpredictable. Instead, what we're left with is something in between: *bounded* rationality, where consumer decision-making is affected by particular traits or biases – such as anchoring – that operate in fairly consistent ways. That they're consistent means that they're predictable and open to analysis; just as importantly it suggests that we can become more self-aware and condition our anchors if we're dissatisfied with their influence. Think a little about your own anchors. Are there any that, on reflection, you'd like to shake free of?

Before we conclude this chapter there's one last angle on human behaviour that we'd like to introduce. The work of Thomas Schelling – a Nobel Prize winner in 2005 – explores the fascinating issues of self-command (the capacity to control one's own actions) and the consistency of our decisions. We know that, contrary to the economist's notion of the rational consumer, we sometimes make ourselves better off by *denying* ourselves consumption opportunities. Usually we think we're better off with more goods and services but consider some persuasive and thought-provoking examples of denial offered by Schelling:[4]

> *Do not give me a cigarette when I ask for it, or dessert, or a second drink. Do not give me my car keys. Do not lend me money. Do not lend me a gun.*

But are we always so steadfast in these choices? One of Schelling's themes here is that people have *alternating* preferences that affect their decision-making over time. A shopping binge might be highly pleasurable, but cutting up the credit cards later on might be a resolutely affirming way of tackling the incurred debt. Schelling's question is the *true* identity of the individual – is it the binger or the chastened debtor? As he puts it:

> *We can say that it looks as if different selves took turns, each self wanting its own values to govern what the other self or selves will do by way of eating, drinking, getting tattooed, speaking its mind, or committing suicide.*

But, Schelling asks, if turns were taken what happened to the individual's well-being; was it maximized? Did they end up better off? 'Or can we only argue that one of the selves enhanced its utility at the expense of the other?' Schelling confesses that, for him, this is an open question.

2.14 Markets: concluding remarks

From a business perspective markets are both interesting and useful. They are the vital frameworks through which firms can reach their customers but they are also the means by which consumers assert their authority over firms. It is impossible for any single firm, or indeed firms in general, to evade the basic laws of supply and demand in markets. The basic lesson for business seems to be that prosperity may follow where market priorities are respected; where they are not, there is missed opportunity.

Many markets may be distorted or conditioned by the presence of asymmetric information but where this happens counteracting institutions can serve to alleviate concerns on both sides of the market. Even where there are no information problems consumers may still behave with degrees of bounded rationality.

We will see later that there are some economic questions to which markets cannot provide answers. In such instances we noted that it is often the case that the state intervenes to restrict the commercial freedoms of firms or to otherwise moderate their behaviour, even to the extent that the state may act as a producer itself. However, before we move on to explore these possibilities we must first begin to examine the firm itself in much more detail.

---

4 Schelling, T.C. (1984) 'Self-Command in Practice, in Policy, and in a Theory of Rational Choice', *American Economic Review*, 74(2): 1–11.

SUMMARY

- Markets are old institutions that bring buyers and sellers together, extend the productivity-raising division of labour, manage risk, and help economies allocate and reallocate their scarce resources.
- The point at which price, the quantity demanded and the quantity supplied are in balance is said to be the point of equilibrium. All other prices indicate positions of disequilibrium in the market where firms and consumers are motivated to change their behaviour.
- The articulation of markets at wider levels raises the possibility of greater choice in production and consumption decisions.
- The EU's single market programme is an example of the wide-ranging application of market analysis to the real economic problem of slower growth in Europe.
- Nonetheless, where it feels it is justified and in response to strong producer lobbies, the EU continues to intervene heavily in certain agricultural markets.
- The concept of price elasticity of demand allows us to analyse the strength of the relationship between changes in price and corresponding changes in the quantity demanded. Similarly, price elasticity of supply allows us to analyse the strength of the relationship between price and quantity supplied.
- Income elasticity of demand measures the responsiveness of quantity demanded to changes in incomes. It may be used to understand the basis of contemporary shifts in the international division of labour.
- Asymmetric information may distort markets and undermine participants' confidence in them.
- Counteracting institutions reduce the problems associated with asymmetric information.
- Consumer behaviour in markets may exhibit the characteristics of bounded rationality.

KEY TERMS

- Market
- Demand
- Supply
- Equilibrium
- Excess supply
- Excess demand
- Disequilibrium
- The single market programme

- Market intervention
- Price elasticity of demand
- Income elasticity of demand
- Price elasticity of supply
- Asymmetric information
- Adverse selection
- Bounded rationality

QUESTIONS FOR DISCUSSION

1. What are the principal determinants of the demand for a particular commodity?
2. What are the principal determinants of the supply of a particular commodity?
3. Explain the process by which disequilibrium prices in a market give way to one unique equilibrium price.
4. For a particular good, what will happen to the equilibrium price and quantity bought and sold following:
   i.   an improvement in technology
   ii. a change in tastes away from the good
   iii. an increase in the cost of producing it
   iv. an increase in consumers' incomes?
5. Explain the basis of the single market programme in Europe.
6. How can governments offset movements toward equilibrium in markets?
7. Use the concept of price elasticity of demand to explain why governments are able to continually raise the tax they levy on tobacco. Why might it not be sensible to levy a tax on boxes of matches or cigarette lighters?

EVERYDAY ECONOMICS 2.1 ANSWERS

1. **The Mercedes logo.** Mercedes is one of the world's most familiar brands and a brand is a counteracting institution.
- It reassures customers about the quality of the product they're buying.
- In Mercedes's case the brand does more: it suggests a certain cache and whiff of exclusivity that people value

2. **Licensed taxis.** Think how asymmetric information may lead to too big an allocation of resources in this case.
- If you're in a cab in an unfamiliar city and the journey goes on for a bit do you get a bit suspicious? *Where are we going? Is this the long way? Am I being ripped off?*

- Well, you might be (the longer journey is the market producing too much) but, if you're in a licensed taxi, you have some grounds for reassurance.
- Fares are usually regulated and published inside the cab; the driver's details will be on display and the cab will have a number in case there's a dispute that you want to resolve with the help of the licensing authority.
- All of these are counteracting institutions that help to give you confidence in the service you're buying.

3. **Selling insurance (not buying it).** This is a trickier case. Here the asymmetric information problem affects the insurance firm. Think about travel insurance.
- When you buy a travel insurance policy the firm has a problem. It doesn't know if you're careful with your belongings when you go on holiday or whether you're careless because, after all, you're insured! (This is also an example of moral hazard.)
- To reduce their exposure to reckless travellers insurance firms usually impose modest excesses (say £50) against claims as a counteracting institution.
- This incentivizes policy holders to behave more responsibly because in the event of a claim they have some financial loss to bear.

ONE THING YOU SHOULD READ

John Steinbeck's *The Grapes of Wrath*, **Chapter 7**

We introduced *The Grapes of Wrath* and the Joad family at the end of our first chapter. The extract we would like you to read now is another short scene-setting piece. The Joads have decided that they must migrate to the promised land of California. They need to buy a car to carry them on this long and difficult journey. They need something they can rely on but have little money to spare. Steinbeck fictionalizes the kind of market they and others like them had to enter. It's one bedevilled by asymmetric information. At one point a salesman says, 'Listen, Jim, I heard that Chevvy's rear end. Sounds like bustin' bottles. Squirt in a couple quarts of sawdust. Put some in the gears too. We got to move that lemon for thirty-five dollars.' The market for lemons indeed.

When you've read the chapter answer the following questions.

1. The writing style conveys the impression of a frenetic selling environment: why is this? What is Steinbeck trying to convey about the nature of this market? To whose advantage does the atmosphere of the market work?
2. What references are there to counteracting institutions? Are these institutions effective in this market?
3. What examples are there of salesmen themselves succumbing to the perils of asymmetric information? How do they resolve this problem?

Getty Images/iStockphoto
Thinkstock Images/Robert Churchill

3

the firm

KEY ISSUES

What is the role of the firm in
the modern economy?

Why do *firms* necessarily have
to fulfil this role?

What different kinds of firm exist
in the modern economy?

What strategies exist for the
growth, survival (and even
death) of firms?

What is the significance of
entrepreneurship?

CONTENTS

3.1	Introduction	**88**
3.2	What do firms do?	**88**
3.3	Why is the firm a necessary institution?	**90**
3.4	Different kinds of firm	**93**
3.5	Reflections on the strategies of firms: profit maximization, economics and business strategy, organic growth and growth by merger and acquisition	**100**
3.6	Firms' strategies for survival: resolving the principal–agent problem, coping with asymmetric information problems	**108**
3.7	The death of a firm	**114**
3.8	Firms and entrepreneurship: an Austrian view	**117**

3.1   Introduction

Market structure: characterizes a market according to the degree of competition in it. Monopoly is an example of a market structure where there is an absence of competition.

Monopoly: exists where a firm has the ability to exclude competing firms from the market. Competition is the process that empowers consumers: each firm in a competitive market seeks to offer a better deal to consumers than its rivals. Monopoly removes this incentive and may leave the firm less responsive to consumer interests.

The first two chapters of this book were primarily concerned with the operation of markets. Markets allow producers to pursue their own economic ends by serving the consumption needs of others. Up to this point, however, we have not considered in any detail how market processes actually influence producers or, indeed, reflected upon the institution of the *firm*, the most common organizational form which capitalist production assumes. In this chapter and Chapters 4 and 5 we fill in these gaps. Here we provide an overview of the contribution firms make in answering the basic economic questions of what to produce, how and for whom.

In Chapter 4 we introduce the parameters economists use to interpret and measure the performance of firms: cost, revenue and profit. Chapter 5 offers a framework for analysing the different kinds of **market structure** in which firms are located. It also considers the extent to which firms actually match up to the ideals conventional economics supposes that they follow. There are, for example, serious doubts about whether consumer sovereignty can prevail in the presence of firms that are monopolies. **Monopoly**, the argument runs, permits the firm – rather than consumers – to direct the general course of production.

3.2   What do firms do?

Firms are organizations that buy or hire *factors of production* in markets in order to produce goods or services which can be sold for profit in markets. As noted in Chapter 2, economic theory recognizes four factors of production. These are:

- land
- labour
- capital
- entrepreneurship

We assume that a firm will require some combination of all four factors in order to produce goods or services. Let us reflect briefly on the nature of each.

- *Land* embodies all natural resources. It includes the physical space in which production occurs and all the unprocessed materials present in the environment. For economists, houses and factories are built on land; animals, minerals and vegetables can be reared, extracted and grown on it; even fish swim in it.
- *Labour* is the time and effort of people hired by firms to perform specialist production tasks and to increase the scale of production of the individual firm.
- *Capital* consists of all those goods that are used to produce other goods and services. Thus laptops, the paper cups in Starbucks, taxi cabs, tools, cinema theatres, machines and factories may all be forms of capital: their value lies not in immediate consumption but in what can be produced for the market using them.

- Finally, *entrepreneurship* – the ability to read the market, anticipate the demands of consumers and manage land, labour and capital to meet these demands – is *the* pivotal factor of capitalist production. If a firm is lacking in entrepreneurship, it risks destruction simply because it will fail to correctly judge economic conditions in the market. Most obviously, it may produce goods and services for which there proves to be little or no demand. On the other hand, the entrepreneurial firm must, by definition, be profitable: it effectively produces things consumers want. Entrepreneurial skill enables firms, in their thousands, to dovetail production to complex patterns of demand; it also encourages them to continually refine what they produce and how they produce it so that they can better meet demand in the future. Because of its centrality to the market process, we elaborate upon the role of the entrepreneur within the firm in a later section.

Factor intensity: refers to the emphasis in production towards the use of one particular factor of production above others.

The particular *factor mix* – how much land, labour and capital – used by a firm will, of course, reflect the nature of the production process the firm is engaged in. Economists recognize that certain forms of production favour particular **factor intensities**. For example, the manufacture of chemicals is a *capital-intensive* process in that the typical firm employs relatively more capital than labour or land. On the other hand, the manufacture of footwear and clothing is a *labour-intensive* activity. What about agriculture? On the face of it, agriculture appears *land intensive*. And for the most part it probably is. But think back to the 'One Thing You Should Read' exercise at the end of Chapter 1. This described a great shift in American agriculture around the Great Depression. The labour-intensive and small-scale tenant-farming system gave way to much larger farming operations serviced by *capital-intensive* tractor technology. This happened because opportunity cost considerations had changed. The owners of the land were under pressure because of the Depression. Improvements in technology allowed the land to be worked in new ways. This meant that, despite the human cost in displacing tenant-farming families, resources were reallocated in a particular direction. Our point here is to reinforce an understanding of the *dynamic* nature of capitalism. The ways in which societies produce things are often subject to change, sometimes quickly and dramatically. Contemporary examples? Think GM crops, renewable energy, smart watches, virtual media, online shopping, call centres half way around the world, 3D printers. *All that is solid melts into air.*

Finally in this section, we should note the payments that firms make for the factors of production they employ. The returns paid to each factor are as follows:

- land earns *rent*
- labour is paid a *wage*
- capital earns *interest*
- entrepreneurship is rewarded with *profit*

We elaborate upon the earnings of land, labour and capital in Chapter 7; for the moment we concentrate here upon profit.

As noted, a firm's entrepreneurial ability is rewarded in the form of profit. If, by organizing land, labour and capital, the firm produces goods that consumers are willing and able to buy at a price that exceeds the cost of production, then the difference between price and cost is retained by the firm as profit. The conventional assumption is that firms attempt to *maximize profits*. Now, this might appear to place the firm and the consumer slightly at odds, given that higher profits could simply result from firms increasing the prices they charge. However, such a view neglects the significance of the *competitive environment* in which firms, in theory at least, operate. Because firms must compete with one another for customers, no single firm can risk speculative price increases for fear that its rivals will not follow suit and will maroon it in an uncompetitive position. At the same time, the competitive environment places a *cost control* imperative on firms. No firm can absolve itself of the need to produce as efficiently as possible for fear of the competitive disadvantage it would incur in the presence of more cost-conscious rivals. The competitive environment makes profit maximization advantageous both for the firm *and* the consumer. Recall also our discussion of the constraining influence of markets upon producers. In Chapter 2, using the example of oil we saw that even a body as powerful as OPEC was unable to defy the laws of supply and demand in the long run.

3.3 Why is the firm a necessary institution?

We begin here with an obvious question: what is the *purpose* of firms – why do markets not simply consist of large collections of individual (sole) producers and consumers? By way of an answer, consider the following example. If a person wishes to obtain a new house, one option open to them is to personally organize the details of its construction. Land would need to be purchased and an architect commissioned to design the house. The requisite materials and tools would also have to be obtained and a bricklayer, joiner, plumber, roofer and so on hired. Overall, the project might take a year to complete and it would probably require a good deal of management attention from our potential house owner.

This kind of approach involves building the house directly through the *use of the market:* the consumer hires the skills and experience of capable people and puts them to work on designated tasks. Now, in the UK, some houses might be built

Can you make sense of this? Probably not; that's why we have firms

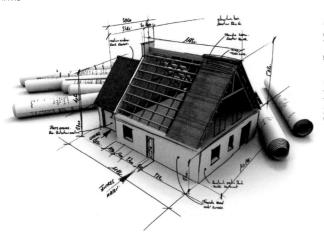

© istockphoto.com/Franck Boston

in this way but most are not. This is because most buyers of new houses find it more convenient and cheaper to rely on building firms instead. In our example, the individual must devote months of their time to construction management. The opportunity cost of this work would include the loss of income from employment which must be given up while building is going on. Moreover, the individual would have to have confidence in their ability to effectively manage and coordinate the project. Because few people find it possible to easily open up long windows in their working lives and because few are likely to have building-management skills, the favoured option for many is to buy from an established house-building firm. All of which means that firms are a good way of answering the *how* question in resource allocation.

But opportunity cost and the questionable managerial abilities of consumers are not the only factors that militate against market-coordinated production and therefore give rise to the existence of firms. Firms also offer a range of additional advantages as organizers of production. The most important of these are:

Transaction costs: costs associated with undertaking business activities or other forms of economic exchange.

- Savings on **transaction costs**
- The capacity of firms to extend the division of labour
- The potential of firms to innovate

Savings on transaction costs

A building firm that constructs thousands of houses a year will contract for consistently large volumes of building materials; it will not order individual loads of sand, cement, bricks and timber for each house. To repeat small orders would clearly be less efficient: it would cost more in time and in paperwork. Similarly, the workers the firm employs will not be issued new contracts as they move from house to house and the tools and equipment they use will not be rehired each time a house is finished: *one* set of contracts or transactions would cover a year's work or more for the firm. If houses were built one at a time by their eventual owners through the market the number of transactions taking place could be multiplied several thousand-fold. Therefore, in terms of transaction costs, firms appear to offer a much more efficient means of organizing production when compared to a market without firms. The transaction cost rationale for the existence of firms was first highlighted by Ronald Coase (1910–2013) in work for which he was awarded a Nobel Prize. Coase characterized firms as 'little planned societies'. Put in these terms it's easy to see why they're so useful. You might build a house, make some furniture or grow some food but if there are thousands of little planned societies around to do these and lots of other things for you isn't it easier to let them get on with it?

● **Think Point**

The ability of firms to reduce transaction costs is a compelling reason for their existence. However, given that some transaction costs have to do with information and communication requirements, is the Internet beginning to challenge the role of firms in some industries? Can you think of any examples?

Here are two.

Travel agents may find some of their activities threatened by Internet-enabled independent travel. It's now very easy for people to book a flight, a hotel or hire a car online. On the other hand the travel business has itself migrated online, meaning that it can still bulk-buy flights and hotel rooms and offer the resultant savings to its customers. Think Expedia, lastminute. com, Travel Republic and so on.

In Chapter 1 we noted the damage done to the music industry by music piracy and the growing convention that things on the Internet are 'free'. The creation and distribution of recorded music and video has in many ways been democratized by the Internet: anyone can record a song with highly sophisticated but very cheap software and then put it on YouTube or iTunes. The role played by record companies in the time of vinyl and CDs – signing and promoting bands – appears rather dated.

The capacity of firms to extend the division of labour

If production was predominantly organized by individuals through the market process then some or all of the signal leaps in productivity that have occurred over the last 250 years might never have been realized. One of the most famous of these was the utilization, by Henry Ford in the early 1900s, of 'flow-line' car assembly. This process involved the fragmentation of car making into very simple tasks that could be repeated easily and quickly. The flow-line enabled the cars themselves to move at a given pace while the stationary workers repeated their allotted tasks on each unit. Ford demonstrated that cars could be made in their millions in this way at a *much lower cost per car than had ever been achieved before*. Subsequently, this method of production – sometimes known, after its originator, as Fordism – spread beyond car making into many other branches of industry and provided the basis for a general and marked improvement in productivity in the advanced economies. The point here is that the flow-line principle, resting on an extended division of labour, could not have been put into practice outside the firm. To produce efficiently, Ford's output needed to be at least in *the hundreds of thousands* per annum. Car production (and, by implication, most forms of industrial production) on any meaningful scale is most efficiently done by firms.

The motor industry also provides an example of the way in which firms can extend the *external* as well as their internal division of labour. Although most of the world's cars are now produced by a fairly limited number of large **multinationals**, these firms usually rely on supplies of auto parts from other specialist producers. Car radios, tyres, windscreen wipers, upholstery and electrical components as well as other items are bought in by carmakers. This arrangement allows the car firms to concentrate on the central tasks of design and body, engine and transmission production, as well as final assembly, while the specialist suppliers refine their own particular product contributions. Again, such a complex and highly integrated production system would be unlikely to emerge in the absence of the institution of the firm.

Multinational: a firm that owns and controls assets (usually production facilities) in more than one country.

The potential of firms to innovate

Where do new products come from? How can we account for the vast array of goods and services modern societies make available? Part of the answer is *invention*. Invention can, of course, be driven by solitary genius. For example, the vulcanizing process that makes rubber malleable and therefore usable in so many ways in heat or cold was discovered after a long and lonely struggle by one individual: Charles Goodyear. Tellingly, though, Goodyear died in poverty. It took the firm that bears his name (and its competitors) to actually develop and market rubber tyres, making them the ubiquitous product they are today. Invention may also result from military imperatives. It is well known that the design and manufacture of aircraft was revolutionized as a result of pressures that emerged during the First and Second World Wars. But research and development into new products and processes is most often sponsored by firms: Microsoft, Apple, Ford, McDonald's, Walt Disney, Google, BP, Coca-Cola, Amazon, Pfizer and so on became the success stories that they are by coming up with things the rest of us want to buy.

While invention has a variety of sources it is usually firms that *apply* advances in technology to the marketplace, regardless of how these arise in the first place. Indeed, for many branches of production, it is difficult now to imagine how it could be otherwise. While an individual consumer might be capable of hiring the factors of production they need to build a house or repair a car, following the same process to obtain the equivalent of an iPad would be impossible. Indeed, it would be impossible for a complex society to successfully organize production as a whole in this way.

Although our reference here is to *private-sector* firms, there are areas in capitalist economies where *public-sector* institutions such as nationalized industries, hospitals and universities bear some burden of both product development and production. However, it still appears reasonable to conclude that the firm is the uniquely important source of *marketable* innovation – the introduction of new goods and services to markets where individuals pay directly for what they consume. Note also that this still leaves the firm subservient to the market and therefore preserves the central principle of consumer sovereignty. A new product that fails to bring forth sufficient demand is itself destined for oblivion, regardless of any other considerations.

3.4 Different kinds of firm

In this section we describe the main kinds of firm that exist in the modern economy. Although the examples and data we use are primarily UK-specific, the general patterns they reveal are applicable to other advanced capitalist economies, such as those in other parts of Western Europe and in North America.

Firms are legally distinguished by their forms of *ownership*. There are three main categories of private ownership:

- Sole proprietorship
- Partnership
- Companies

Sole proprietorship

A firm owned by one individual is a sole proprietorship. The firm's owner receives all the profits it makes but these are taxed as income, in the same way as wages and salaries. The owner is also responsible for any debts or losses which the firm may incur; in fact, they have **unlimited liability** for such losses. This means that the entire personal wealth – savings, a house, a car or any other asset – of the owner is at risk if losses are sufficiently large. Sole proprietorships are typically small and are most common in the *service sector*, in areas of work such as retailing, property and business services (especially plumbing, electrical work and so on).

Unlimited liability: places the entire personal wealth of the owner of a firm at risk in respect of losses the firm may incur.

Partnership

A partnership divides ownership of the firm between two or more individuals. This is a more complicated arrangement than that which obtains for the sole proprietorship, as the management of the firm and the distribution of its profits must be the subject of agreement between the partners. However, partnerships also allow more individuals to participate in the firm, perhaps bringing in more money and a wider range of business expertise. As for the sole proprietorship, the profits of a partnership are taxed as the income of its owners. Partners are also subject to *joint* unlimited liability. This means that the personal wealth of all partners is at risk if the firm runs into financial difficulty. In the UK, partnerships predominate in retailing, agriculture and property and business services (typically in firms of accountants and solicitors).

Companies

Companies are owned by their shareholders. The more shares that are held the greater the proportion of ownership that the holder enjoys. Shares in *private* limited companies can only be bought and sold when there is mutual agreement to do so among existing shareholders. On the other hand, shares in *public* limited companies (PLCs) may be bought and sold openly by anyone on the stock exchange.

Shareholders also enjoy the important advantage of **limited liability**. This means that, unlike sole proprietors and partners, their financial exposure is limited to the value of the company itself. In the event of poor trading and a decision to wind up the company, any debts that cannot be covered by selling stocks of goods, plant and machinery and so on will remain unmet. Creditors of the company are not entitled to any claim on the personal wealth of shareholders. In the UK, the government levies corporation tax (currently at 20 or 21 per cent)

Limited liability: in the event of losses incurred by a firm, the personal wealth of its owners is not at risk. Liability is limited to the value of the firm.

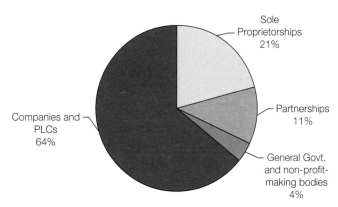

Figure 3.1 Legal status of UK businesses, 2013
Source: ONS, UK Business: Activity, Size and Location – 2013

on the profits earned by companies. After the payment of corporation tax, profits are disbursed among shareholders as dividends on each share held. For shareholders, these dividends are then subject to income tax. One evident disadvantage of shareholding is therefore that profits may be subject to *two* taxes compared to the single tax on income from profits that sole proprietors and partners pay.

Figure 3.1 summarizes the distribution of the three main types of private firm for 2013, together with government-sponsored businesses and non-profit-making bodies. Although the majority of UK firms are either limited companies or PLCs, all three types of private firm have some representation. Roughly one third is made up of sole proprietorships or partnerships without limited liability status. This suggests that no one type of firm has an overwhelming advantage over the others.

ECONOMICS AT WORK

Geoff Gorst, The Meyer Group Ltd, www.meyeruk.com

Geoff is the Business Development Director for Meyer Group Ltd, a company which designs, manufactures and markets cookware on a global scale. Meyer Group Ltd supplies all the major department stores, such as Debenhams, John Lewis and House of Fraser, supermarkets such as Tesco, as well as mass merchants like Argos. Geoff is responsible for all business throughout Continental and Central Eastern Europe, the Middle East and Africa.

Visit **www.palgrave.com/companion/mulhearn3** to watch Geoff talking about his firm's strategies for growth.

The relative advantages and disadvantages of different forms of ownership

In sifting through the three main forms a private firm might assume, the decisive factors of choice are:

- the taxation of the firm's profits
- the extent of liability of the firm's owners for any losses that might arise
- how easily capital can be raised
- the way the firm is to be managed

Let us reflect on each of these factors in turn.

The taxation of the firm's profits

As noted, the profits of sole proprietorships and partnerships are taxed – once only – as the personal income of the firm's owners. Company profits, on the other hand, are subject to tax twice: corporation tax is levied initially and, subsequently, any dividends paid to shareholders are liable to income tax.

Liability

Although tax arrangements might appear to favour sole proprietorships and partnerships over companies, the issue of liability works in the opposite direction. While shareholders risk nothing more than the stake that they own in a company, sole proprietors and partners lay open their entire personal wealth should their firms collapse. While this might appear a major burden under which to conduct business, it must also be remembered that most sole proprietorships and partnerships are relatively small and their financial exposure is therefore limited. Moreover, as these firms are usually under the immediate supervision and control of their owners, any risk-taking will presumably not be done in a cavalier manner.

Raising capital

New and existing businesses need money for investment to help them grow. For sole proprietorships and partnerships additional capital may come from the owners themselves, their families and friends or the banks. Generally, however, *large* injections of capital will not be available from these sources. This helps to explain why sole proprietorships and partnerships tend to be small. Companies, on the other hand, find it easier to secure substantial amounts of new money. One way that they can do this is by selling shares on the open market – the stock market. Shares are attractive to individuals and investment institutions because, if the company performs well, they will yield a stream of dividends. Moreover, because the value of the shares may rise as demand for them increases they can often be sold at a profit. Note that limited liability underpins the attractiveness of shareholding as the purchaser shoulders a risk equivalent only to their investment. Indeed, this explains the origin of the principle of limited liability: it was devised as a means to help firms secure larger amounts of capital at minimal risk to investors.

The management of the firm

For sole proprietorships and partnerships, management and ownership of the firm are usually fused into one. In tandem with their generally smaller scale of operations, this makes for relatively simple management and decision-making. However, in the case of companies, both the typically larger scale of the firm and its diversified form of ownership may make for more complex and unwieldy management structures that may have some worrying effects on performance. We will begin to review this problem shortly.

First, however, we further illustrate issues around firm ownership by reflecting upon the legal status of three well-known firms:

- the John Lewis Partnership
- Facebook
- Sunderland Football Club

Our intention here is to reflect upon the reasons behind particular choices of status and to understand pressures which might favour a change in a firm's status. We begin with the John Lewis Partnership.

The John Lewis Partnership

The John Lewis Partnership is a department store group owned by its 91,000 staff (the group includes Waitrose and Greenbee). Periodically, it is in the news because of rumours that the firm could be floated on the stock exchange. A stock market listing could bring substantial windfalls to John Lewis staff, possibly up to £100,000 each. Not surprisingly some staff favour a sell-off. This example makes clear one of the possible advantages of a public listing: it releases capital that the owners of a business have tied up in it. However, a sell-off has been consistently resisted by John Lewis management which takes the view that it may be counter-productive in a business sense to sell the company. Management also points out that the partnership arose in the first place because of an act of generosity by the previous owner, Spedan Lewis. It would be legally difficult and morally questionable to break up the partnership he founded.

The business argument is easy to understand. The John Lewis shops have strong traditions and are patronized by many customers because of a jealously guarded reputation for quality and value. A change of ownership might well undermine all this. There is also the issue of what the John Lewis partners (that is, the staff) risk *losing* in a change of ownership. They enjoy a range of benefits that is very unusual in retailing. After 5 years' service, partners are guaranteed a job for life; after 25 years, there is 6 months' paid leave. All partners receive an annual salary bonus based on profits. In 2014, this was set at 15 per cent – about eight weeks pay. There is more, but the reader will get the general idea. It might be expected that new owners might quickly push working practices and staff benefits towards (that is, *down* to) the more familiar level for retail employees. So, while floatation might bring obvious immediate cash rewards for John Lewis partners, it might also put at risk at least some of their jobs and possibly the whole basis of the business itself. The question of which legal status to adopt is clearly a more difficult one than it might at first appear.

Facebook

If you've seen the very watchable film *The Social Network*, you'll know something about Facebook's origins in 2004 at Harvard University. Facebook was created by Mark Zuckerberg and some fellow students. Zuckerberg's share in Facebook is now estimated to be worth around $20bn. That's about the same as the annual national income of countries such as Bolivia and Paraguay, and considerably more than the incomes of, for example, Zambia, Nepal and Cambodia. How did Zuckerberg get to be so rich?

Bloomberg/Getty Images

The development of the Internet changed the economics of many markets but perhaps most profoundly altered the market in communication. The genius of Facebook was to bottle digital communication into a form that gained almost instant and pretty much global popularity. But

Facebook has made Mark Zuckerberg very wealthy but he's given away $1billion

the surprising thing was that, at first, it didn't make money. To an extent this was a matter of choice. Facebook's priority was to grow and enhance the kinds of service it offered. That meant reinvesting what it earned and supplementing this revenue with investments from other firms. For example, in 2007 Microsoft bought a 1.6 per cent stake for $240m. This gave Facebook a market capitalization (the collective worth of its shares) of about $15bn. The attraction of Facebook to outside investors was obvious. It was on course to reach one *billion* active users: the biggest digital market on the planet and it was only three years old. Who wouldn't want to be part of that?

Now put yourself in Mark Zuckerberg's shoes. Everyone seems to want a piece of the company you and a few others *privately* own. Were you to offer shares in Facebook on the open market – turning it into a PLC – the demand would be tremendous and the value of your holdings would rocket. At the same time the generation of a lot of extra capital would allow Facebook to further consolidate its position at the top of the social networking food chain. Facebook's shares were offered to the public in 2012 with its market capitalization at the time of the sale working out at $104bn. Although this did indeed make Facebook's owners even richer, Zuckerberg's argument is that the primary reason for the initial public offering (IPO) was to grow the business: to attract talented people and reward them with salaries and shares that will increase in value alongside the company's growth. Facebook's strategy since the IPO seems to prove his point. In 2014 Facebook paid $19bn for the messaging service, WhatsApp. WhatsApp allows users free text messaging, an attractive alternative to paying for SMS messaging. Zuckerberg admits that $19bn seems to be a high price for a firm with a revenue stream that is far below this figure. So why pay so much? Because, Zuckerberg says,

> There are very few services in the world that reach a billion people; they're all incredibly valuable, much more valuable than that [$19bn].

So his eyes are on the commercial potential of this newly acquired service, but notice too that had Facebook not become a PLC the possibility of it coming up with $19bn for WhatsApp would have been much more remote. All of which means that Facebook's decision to relinquish private status and opt for an IPO made sense for both Facebook's owners and the long-term future of the business.

Finally, does Mark Zuckerberg really need all that money? In 2013 he gave about 5 per cent of his net worth to charity. That's a cool $1bn.

Sunderland football club

For Sunderland Football Club, competitive pressures have brought a changing set of answers to the question of whether or not to alter the basis of ownership of a business. Sunderland was floated on the stock market at the end of 1996. This move was intended to help the club compete in the Premier League alongside the traditionally bigger clubs, some of which had already opted for public company status. The capital raised by the sale was intended to help Sunderland strengthen its team *and* underpin investment in the wider business. The two went hand in hand. If Sunderland performed well in footballing terms, then match attendances would increase, their games would be televised more (earning substantial fees) and they would sell more replica kits and other club merchandise. In this case then, the existing owners of a business were happy to sell some of their shareholdings on the open market in order to generate new monies for investment.

Unfortunately, things did not work out quite as well as the club hoped. Although the floatation generated enough capital to help Sunderland finance a new stadium, the performance of the team was poor. An ignominious record-low-points relegation from the Premier League in 2003 meant revenue streams from television and match attendances dwindled and the status of the club as an investment prospect became highly questionable. After initially listing at 585p, shares in Sunderland plc slumped to 60p just prior to the decision to leave the stock exchange: simply, there was little investor interest in the club. This meant that the major reason for the stock market listing – to attract new investment – was no longer valid; hence the decision to withdraw from the market. Although

Sunderland remained a public limited company, there was no active trade in its shares. In 2008, substantial new investment was provided by Ellis Short, an American businessman, who now effectively owns Sunderland.

Note that, in each of our examples, there is no right or wrong solution. Decisions concerning the legal status of a firm will be taken by the owners of the firm in their perceptions of their own and the firm's best interests. In the John Lewis case the owning partners clearly see a degree of uniformity between their personal interests and the long-term vitality of the business and the outcome for the moment is the preservation of the partnership. For Mark Zuckerberg the decision to take Facebook to an IPO was informed by precisely the same reasoning but with a different outcome: he thought it better for the owners and the business to go public. Similarly, for the owners of Sunderland, the ambition was to see shares in the club actively traded on the stock market, allowing them to attract new investment that could be spent on improving the team and the club's infrastructure. Although a stock market listing met with some initial success, the anticipated investment stream ultimately failed to materialize. So, unfortunately for Sunderland, a nice try but no cigar.

One final point. Emerging evidence suggests that combining different forms of ownership can make commercial sense. For example, consider the growth in *franchising* in Western economies in recent years. Franchising involves a firm selling or leasing the right to produce or sell its brand of goods to a third party. In the UK, it has been estimated that 10 per cent of retailing is franchise based. Perhaps the world's most famous franchising operation is McDonald's: the majority of McDonald's restaurants are actually run by franchisees. *You* could buy a McDonald's franchise. Want to know more, what it's likely to cost, what the returns might be, what time commitments are necessary? Check out the possibilities at www.mcdonalds.co.uk.

The attraction of franchising is that it can combine the resources, experience and expertise of a large company with the energy and investment of the franchisee. The franchisee can take the same kind of risks as, say, a sole proprietor but does so in the knowledge that he or she is treading on *proven* ground. It must be hard to mess up a McDonalds. At the same time, the franchiser is assured that each individual franchisee has a direct personal stake in the development of the business and is therefore highly committed to it.

3.5   Reflections on the strategies of firms: profit maximization, economics and business strategy, organic growth and growth by merger and acquisition

Are firms profit maximizers?

The conventional assumption underlying orthodox microeconomic theory of the firm is that firms seek to maximize the profit they earn. Firms compete with one another for the patronage of the consumer, profit being the indicator of success. Those firms that neglect the profit motive risk bankruptcy at the hands of rivals that respect it. The greater the degree of competition, the higher the likelihood that non-profit-maximizing firms will fail to survive. Pursuing the objective of profit maximization is seen as the best guarantee that the firm will continue in business.

Profit is determined by the difference between the total revenue and the total costs of the firm over a given period of time. In Chapter 4 we examine firms' costs and revenues, and specifically in Section 4.8 discuss the level of output at which profit maximization is achieved. But before we do this it is worth briefly considering a number of *alternative* views on the objectives of firms that have appeared in the literature. We begin our discussion with an overview of the behavioural approach in which firms do not aim to maximize a single goal (namely profit), but instead seek to achieve *satisfactory* performance over a range of objectives.

According to Richard Cyert and James March the firm acts as a *coalition* between different groups: managers, workers, shareholders, creditors and customers. These groups make competing demands on the firm. For example, workers may want high wages, whereas shareholders may want high dividends. Goals are set and are modified over time through a complex process of bargaining as the firm's managers try to contain and resolve the conflicting demands of different groups or stakeholders. In contrast to the conventional theory firms are seen as *satisficers* with multiple goals, rather than maximizers pursuing the single goal of profit. Cyert and March's work is in the tradition pioneered by Nobel Prize–winning economist Herbert Simon. The box below, 'Applying Economics to Business', briefly summarizes Simon's work.

We now turn to managerial theories that retain maximization as an objective, but downplay the profit motive. In what follows we outline three such theories

APPLYING ECONOMICS TO BUSINESS

Herbert Simon's pioneering insights into firms' decision-making

Herbert Simon (1916–2001) was awarded the 1978 Nobel Prize in Economics for 'his pioneering research into the decision-making process within economic organisations'.

In work first published in the 1940s, Simon criticized the traditional theory of the firm, which, as we have seen, is based on the assumption of a rational, profit-maximizing entrepreneur. In his alternative approach, the single entrepreneur is replaced by a constellation of decision-makers whose rationality is limited and who cooperate to find mutually satisfactory solutions to the problems they face.

Simon argued that, in reality, people in large organizations cannot obtain or process all the information needed to make fully rational decisions. In consequence, firms are unable to maximize profits. Instead, people 'satisfice' by making decisions that result in acceptable outcomes.

Simon's view of human decision-making, based on limited rationality, or what he subsequently called 'bounded' rationality, results in satisficing, not optimizing, behaviour.

associated with the work of, respectively, William Baumol, Oliver Williamson and Robin Marris. These theories are based on the separation of ownership (by shareholders) from control (by managers) of the firm, and an understanding that the objective that is maximized depends on the motives of the top managers. The commonly highlighted factors that motivate managers are their desires for status, power, income and security.

William Baumol developed a theory of the firm in which some managers seek to maximize sales revenue, subject to a minimum level of profit being earned. Baumol based his theory on his experiences as a consultant for a number of large firms where he observed that some managers were more interested in expanding turnover rather than profits. The reason for this is that the status, power and income of top managers are often more closely related to sales revenue than they are to profit. It is, however, important to note that the objective of sales revenue maximization is subject to a minimum profit constraint that allows shareholders' dividends to be high enough to keep them content.

A complementary approach advanced by Oliver Williamson (a Nobel Prize winner in 2009) involves 'managerial discretion' in which managers aim to maximize their own *satisfaction* or utility, subject to a minimum level of profit being earned that will keep shareholders content. Williamson argued that executives derive satisfaction, or utility, from certain kinds of expenditure on, for example, emoluments (such as generous expense accounts and luxurious company cars), discretionary investment and staff. Such perks and discretionary investment are more likely to enhance image than be justified on the grounds of profit maximization. Increased expenditure on staff may also enhance the status, influence and standing of those at the top. One recent example of this kind of empire building came to light after the collapse of the Royal Bank of Scotland (RBS) during the 2008–9 financial crisis. The former boss of RBS, Fred Goodwin, was reported to have insisted that the colour of a fleet of executive cars had to match the corporate blue of the bank and the cars' interiors had to be in beige to match the bank's carpets!

The final managerial theory we will briefly outline is that put forward by Robin Marris. According to this theory, managers seek to maximize the *growth rate* of the firms they control in order to increase their own status, power and income. As managers also desire job security they have an interest in minimizing the risk of mergers and takeovers that might threaten their security. The danger of a firm being taken over will increase the lower is the market value of the shares of the firm compared to the capital or book value of the assets of the firm (for example buildings, capital equipment, land and so on). Given that the risk that the firm will be taken over is greater the lower the **valuation ratio**, managers will need to pay shareholders adequate dividends to maintain the market value of the firm's shares at a relatively high level.

Valuation ratio: the market valuation of the firm, expressed by the price of its shares, divided by the book value of assets.

Economics and business strategy: the case of Google

Presently, in terms of market value (number of shares times price), Google is the third largest firm in the world behind Apple and Exxon Mobil. Google has around 50,000 employees and it operates in more than 50 countries. But the most stunning statistic is that the basic service it provides – organizing information and making it easily accessible – is used around the world more than 100 billion times a *month*. Google's size, its saturation in our societies and the billions of dollars in profit it earns present this firm with choice opportunities. But Google also faces threats. In Chapter 1 we reflected on the competitive environments firms find themselves in using two complementary approaches:

- We suggested that firms had to continually think through the economics of their business, attending to what they produce, how and for whom.
- We also used the PEST framework to explore the **P**olitical, **E**conomic, **S**ocial and **T**echnological contexts in which firms operate.

Here we offer a third way to understand the competitive environment of the firm: Michael Porter's famous five forces model. We use Porter's work to briefly explore Google's business strategy.

Porter's interpretation of the firm's environment centres on the industry at issue with the incumbent firms in direct competition with each other. This is the first force that governs competition in the industry. Key considerations here include the number of rival firms, their relative sizes, the rate of growth of the industry and the presence of brand loyalties. Ranged around the industry are four additional forces:

- the threat of new entrants into the industry
- the bargaining power of customers
- the threat of substitute products or services
- the bargaining power of suppliers

How might this model help us to understand the business choices facing Google?

Let's start with competition in the industry. Who are Google's competitors? Google offers a huge range of information-based products but it also makes things on its own or with partners: smart watches, smart glasses, driverless cars, even Star Trek-like tricorders are all here or in development. Google's rivals are other firms doing similar things: Apple, Microsoft, Facebook and Amazon. The key factor affecting competition between these firms from Porter's model is probably the sheer dynamism of the industry. It's growing and innovating at a breathtaking speed. This suggests Google's chief concern is what it can do differently or better in the future and much less that Microsoft will displace its search engine or some other product. Strategically then the competitive forces between firms in the industry tend to drive them forward as innovators. For Google this imperative is partly realized through acquisition: buying up other

■ Concept: Economies of scale: arise when a larger output is produced without a proportionally equal increase in the costs of production. In the single market, as the more successful firms grow in size they are able to produce more efficiently by, for example, purchasing inputs in bulk quantities, or sharing business services such as marketing across European countries.

Economies of scope: arise when firms are able to provide goods and services *collectively* at a lower cost than would be possible were they to provide them discretely.

smaller innovating firms that can help push back particular information or product frontiers. It has a $30bn reserve set aside for purchases of this sort outside the US.

Turning to the threat posed by new entrants to the industry Porter highlights two factors that are of particular relevance in the Google case. First, where incumbent firms have developed strong brands it is very difficult for new entrants to encroach upon the market. The brands in this industry are deeply embedded. Think of how we unconsciously use the word 'google'. Certainly it's a firm and a brand but it's also a verb in commonplace usage in multiple languages. This makes it a very tough nut to crack. The same would apply to the other big brands in the industry. So accessing this industry as an entrant is difficult.

Second, very large firms like Google also benefit from **economies of scale** and economies of scope. An example of a scale economy for Google is its cloud infrastructure. Google's products require a lot of computing power. This comes from very large data centres and the computers that equip them. Google designs and builds both from the ground up. This gives it great cost advantages. It buys chips and other components in bulk – and therefore very cheaply – to make machines and everything else specific to its needs. The alternative of buying finished hardware from others would be more expensive and the hardware itself would not be bespoke. Google is then able to offer cloud services to customers at a fraction of the costs they would incur were they to choose to establish their own infrastructures.

Economies of scope emerge when firms use their existing infrastructures to lever themselves into new markets. Large firms can do this extremely effectively. Think about Google as a provider of advertising and other web-based content. It anticipates that it will be able to serve this material in a few years on refrigerators, car dashboards, thermostats, glasses, and watches, meaning that Google has a new means of commercial access to these formerly quite separate markets.

All these factors – immensely powerful brands and economies of scale and scope – make the task of entry into the industry on a scale that would challenge any of the incumbents very daunting.

Next in Porter's list is the bargaining power of customers. Here Google, along with other firms in the industry, presently has an issue. A few years ago most people were accessing Google's services via desktop PCs but now things have changed as mobile technologies have suffused the market. One of the industry's principal revenue streams is generated by paid clicks. When you click on an advert the content provider earns some money. The problem is that advertisers are unwilling to pay as much for adverts on mobile devices as they pay on PCs, hence the potential threat to revenue. The industry's difficulties are compounded by uncertainty over the very nature of what is mobile. To combat this problem Google's business strategy is to make its services 'device agnostic'. It won't matter if your content is coming from your phone, your glasses or your fridge. Adaptions like this will make the industry less vulnerable to the shifts in device habits that are bound to come along in the near future.

Does this industry need to worry about substitute products, the fourth of Porter's forces? Complacent firms fail – Woolworths, banks too lazy to think beyond a frenzy of property-based speculation, Comet, Blockbuster – so, yes, substitute products are a concern. But the difference in the history of Google and its competitors is that they appear to be defined by innovation. They themselves are a primary source of substitute products. This is possibly the key element in their competitive strategies.

Finally we come to the bargaining power of suppliers. In the case of Google two points are worth making. First, as noted, Google designs and builds its own infrastructure so for the key element of its business concerns about suppliers may be vanishingly small. Second, the key input for the industry – the Internet – is owned and supplied by no one. But there are supply limits here in the sense that not everyone can access the Internet. Roughly 2 billion people can but another 4–5 billion can't. This is both a problem in human terms and a strategic business question: can these people be reached? Google's answer is to try to increase the supply of the Internet to unserved regions using a network of balloons at the edge of space in what it calls Project Loon.

By now you should be able to see the usefulness of Porter's model. It's an easy way to review the constellation of business strategy considerations facing an industry. Looking at Google through the prism of this model we find several platforms of secure-looking development and few weaknesses. Given the growth of this firm and others in the industry this is about what we'd expect. If you'd like to test your understanding a little further think back to our Woolworths case study in Chapter 1 and run Porter's model across the strategic imperatives facing this firm just before it crashed.

So we know something of why firms try to grow – because of the considerable material advantages growth brings, but *how* do they grow?

Horizontal, vertical and diversified growth

Horizontal growth occurs when a firm expands by doing more of the same kind of activity. For example, the travel company Trailfinders began as a small overland tours operation in 1970. It had a staff of just four and did not record its first profit until 1977. Today it has 30 travel centres in the UK and Ireland and has served more than 12 million customers. It's got bigger by working very successfully in a market it clearly knows well.

Trailfinders has also grown **organically**, in other words its expansion has been generated from its own resources. Another way that firms can engineer growth is by **merging** with other firms or **acquiring** them in a takeover. In 2010, the UK airline BA agreed to

---

Sidebar definitions:

Horizontal growth: occurs when a firm expands its existing form of activity.

Organic growth: the growth of a firm from its own resources.

Merger and acquisition: the process in which one firm combines with or takes over another.

Trailfinders: growing horizontally and organically

a merger with the Spanish carrier Iberia. This too is horizontal growth, as the new larger company will continue to compete in the same market as its parents.

One motive for the merger is to cut costs in a very competitive industry. Hit by the aggressiveness of budget airlines such as easyJet and Ryanair, and the threats to European short-haul flights from high-speed rail travel, the large national airlines have responded by moving towards a global business model. This has allowed them to regionalize their operations in new ways. The BA–Iberia merger will mean that Latin America can be serviced by the Iberia arm of the new company, leaving BA to concentrate on its more traditional long-haul destinations. As BA no longer has to devote resources to cover a few Latin American hub destinations there is a cost saving to the merged operation. Such synergies are shortly expected to generate savings of up to £350m a year.

Firms can also grow by entering markets upstream or downstream from their principal form of activity. This is known as **vertical growth**. A simple example is the farmers' market. This allows farmers, who might never usually see the people who eat the food they grow, to move down the production chain and act as very simple retailers. Appropriately, this kind of firm growth is also organic – farmers don't have to merge or buy up other firms, they just need a van and a bit of basic equipment.

Vertical growth: occurs when a firm engages in activity in another part of the production process or market in which it has an interest.

On the other hand, when Rupert Murdoch's News Corporation wanted to gain a platform in digital media to complement its print and television operations it paid $580m in a takeover of the social networking site Myspace. One reported attraction of this kind of vertical integration is that sites like Myspace can be used to generate marketing synergies by, for example, pushing users towards a firm's more traditional media: Fox television in the case of News Corporation. But this was an acquisition that didn't work out. Facebook's domination of social media rather left Myspace behind and News Corporation sold the firm in 2013 for only $35m.

Diversified or conglomerate growth: occurs when a firm engages in activity in another market or industry in which it has no prior interest.

A final source of growth for firms comes from **diversification** or **conglomeration**, where firms move into entirely new markets or industries – most often through a process of merger and acquisition. A simple example of diversified organic growth comes again from farming. Taking advantage of the natural attributes of their land, farmers sometimes lease ponds or stretches of river to angling clubs, or diversify into other forms of recreation such as riding, shooting, or even golf.

In contrast, the Virgin group is a global conglomerate. A conglomerate is a collection of firms under one owner, and in Virgin's case, one brand. Founded as a mail-order record retailer in 1970 by Sir Richard Branson, the group now has more than 50,000 employees in 50 countries, with brand revenues in 2012 of £15bn. And many of its companies do *very* different things. There is still a Virgin music business but there are also – among a long list – airline and train companies, and financial and media services. Exceptional conglomerate and risk-diversifying growth of this kind is heavily fuelled by merger and acquisition.

Growth by merger and acquisition

Figure 3.2 summarizes merger and acquisition (M&A) activity involving UK companies between 1987 and 2014. The red line – measured on the right vertical axis – indicates the number of deals. The blue line – measured on the left vertical axis – indicates the real-terms value of these deals. Three features of Figure 3.2 are worth noting. First, there is the pronounced surge in the *value* of deals in 1999–2000. Because corporate acquisitions can be hugely expensive there is always the possibility that events in a single industry or sector can dominate the whole picture. This is largely what happened in 1999–2000, reflecting consolidation in the global mobile phone market. In 1999 Vodafone, a UK company, merged with the American firm Airtouch in a deal worth £40bn that created the world's largest mobile phone provider. A year later, Vodafone paid £112bn to complete a takeover of the German communications company Mannesmann; at the time this was the biggest acquisition in corporate history. There was a further upturn in UK-related cross-border corporate acquisitions in the period 2005–7, conditioned by improved performances just prior to the crash in European economies, such as Germany and France, and the United States, as well as by sustained economic growth in the UK (acquisitions in the UK from abroad come overwhelmingly from EU and US firms). Increased merger and acquisition activity is often fuelled by strong general national and corporate economic performance.

A second feature of Figure 3.2 is the long-term downward trend in the number of deals compared to their relatively steady value. The Office for National

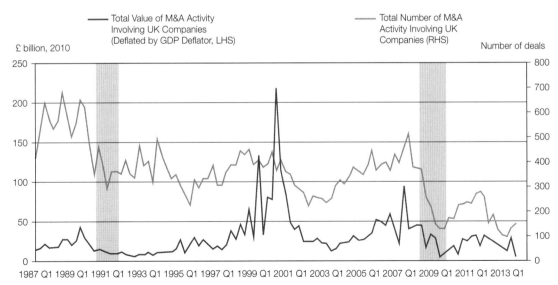

Figure 3.2 Value (deflated by the GDP deflator) and number of M&A deals involving UK companies, 1987 to Q1 2014
Source: ONS: Statistical Bulletin, 2014

Statistics points out that this means the average value of each deal has risen over time. Finally, notice that the sharpest fall in deal numbers coincided with the 2008–9 recession. An unfavourable economic climate may prompt the takeover of acutely distressed firms by their more resilient competitors but, broadly speaking, a collapse in world economic activity such as occurred in 2008–9 would be expected to dampen corporate appetites for acquisition.

3.6 Firms' strategies for survival: resolving the principal–agent problem, coping with asymmetric information problems

The principal–agent problem

The basic premise of the principal–agent problem is that firms may not always behave in the profit-maximizing way anticipated by economic theory. This is because firms are often not simple organizations: their structures are riven by relationships between diverse economic groups that can pull the individual firm in different directions. We have noted, for example, the possible tensions between a firm's managers and its shareholder owners, but probably the most quoted instance of the principal–agent problem concerns the relationship between the managers of a firm and its workers. Here, the managers assume the guise of principals and are responsible for setting the agenda for the firm while the workers as their agents carry out major parts of that agenda. If the objective of the firm is indeed profit maximization, what happens when worker-agents choose not to perform their allotted tasks as well as they might? Workers may not be as zealous about production or quality targets because it is managers who are directly responsible for these, not the workers. Here, the firm's effectiveness and therefore its profits will be compromised by the establishment of two disparate agendas: the managers' (principals') and the workers' (agents').

The solution to the principal–agent problem in this case involves binding the objectives of the agents to those of the principals. This can be done in a variety of ways. For example, the distribution of shares to workers – giving them a direct stake in the firm – may serve to focus their attention on business performance. This means that the objectives of workers and managers run in parallel and a degree of unanimity about the need for profitability can be achieved. The case study on Promethean World offers an example of this kind of approach.

Another common strategy to overcome the principal–agent problem in respect of workers as agents has involved the reorganization of work itself. In the manufacturing industry especially, managers have tried to define more autonomous and challenging roles for production workers. The objective here is to push more responsibility for the organization of work and for the quality and quantity of what is produced onto the worker-agents; in other words, to make

BUSINESS CASE STUDY

Promethean World: bonuses, shares and the principal–agent problem

In 2010, Promethean World – a supplier of educational technologies such as interactive whiteboards – listed on the stock market for the first time. As part of the process the company decided to reward its staff with £3 million in bonus payments, distributed according to length of service.

Employees with six months in post received £750 but anyone in post for more than a year got £1000 for each year's service. This meant that some workers benefited to the tune of £30,000.

Not unnaturally, press reports of Promethean World's generosity highlighted these cash handouts but they were actually not the major part of the story.

Promethean World also introduced an employee share scheme as part of its strategy, which is potentially worth around £7 million to the company's employees, about half of whom were awarded share options.

No doubt Promethean World's workers welcomed the firm's decision to reward them. Think how you would feel in a similar position – gratified, certainly; but *valued* too. The company made it plain that its stock market listing – a mark of successful expansion – reflected its employees' efforts.

The cash rewards were one way to acknowledge this but the additional and more substantial share options also turned a lot of the company's workers into its *owners*. This gave them a more direct personal stake in the future of Promethean World, potentially making them think and behave like principals as much as agents.

---

them behave more like (self) managers or principals. Once again, the solution to the principal–agent problem is an attempt to fuse the agent to the principal.

A good example of this kind of strategy is provided by the car industry and, in particular, innovative working practices among Japanese car manufacturers such as Nissan. Nissan's first British car plant was located in Washington in the north-east of England – a place with no history of carmaking. This was no accident. Nissan wanted to make cars in ways not previously seen in Britain. It supposed that this would be best done in a place where traditional methods of manufacturing would not have to be challenged or 'unlearned'. Nissan television advertisements at the time boasted of car factories 'where no one goes on strike, and where no one is made redundant either', and that 'work wasn't just about getting a better pay packet, but about working together to make something you could be proud of'. Nissan wanted management and workers to meet daily to discuss possible improvements in car production. It saw work as achieving something, fostering a pride in the product. The firm had still further ambitions. It saw all its employees – management and workers alike – as part of the same team. Everyone at Nissan would wear the same uniform and eat in the same canteen. There would be no clocking in, no 'us and them'; and a consequent blurring of the principal–agent distinction.

All this was a long way from traditional working arrangements and industrial relations in British car plants where large numbers of workers were engaged in boring, arduous and repetitive tasks on an assembly line under the direct supervision and control of chargehands, foremen and managers. It was the job of these authority figures – principals – to *extract* work from agents on the line.

The result was a continuing antagonism between management and labour that translated into poor industrial relations and problems for car firms in their attempts to organize profitable production.

Now, whether or not the attempts by Nissan and, following its lead, many other car producers, has *fundamentally* changed the organization of work is an open question and not one we have the opportunity to explore further in a book of this kind. However, what we can say is that the Nissan case provides a useful illustration of how firms may attempt to confront the principal–agent problem in a notoriously difficult setting.

Everyday Economics 3.1 considers some other possible solutions to the principal–agent problem.

EVERYDAY ECONOMICS 3.1

Solutions to the principal–agent problem

These images depict different ways in which firms try to overcome the principal–agent problem. Can you explain how each works?

Answers are at the end of the chapter.

1

Clocking in at work.

2

A duvet day.

3

A production line.

Firms and asymmetric information

In Chapter 2, we introduced the concept of asymmetric information – the notion that knowledge in markets is not always evenly distributed and that sometimes this can significantly disadvantage consumers or producers. In George Akerlof's Nobel Prize-winning analysis, asymmetric information problems work against the buyers (and some sellers) of second-hand cars. Unsure of the quality of what they might be buying and worried about getting stuck with a lemon (a poor-quality car), people desert the market and buy new cars instead. At the same time, suspicious purchasers mean that sellers of good used cars can't realize the prices their vehicles are worth, so they too withdraw from the market, leaving it dominated by lemons. Asymmetric information warps resource allocation in the second-hand car market.

In work that also helped to win him a Nobel Prize, Joseph Stiglitz extended Akerlof's approach to consider the management of risk by insurance firms. Stiglitz explored the information asymmetries in insurance markets where, typically, insurance providers have less information about the risks faced by their customers than do customers themselves. You know if you're a fast driver, a traveller who is routinely careless with your belongings, or if you sometimes forget to set your burglar alarm at night – but your insurer doesn't. To combat this kind of problem Stiglitz showed that insurance firms try to shape the choices faced by their customers so that they purchase policies in accordance with firms' preferences.

In the presence of perfect – and therefore symmetric – information, insurance companies would offer individual customers policies specifically tailored to the level of known risk they carry. Careless travellers would pay more to insure against the loss of their belongings, lower-risk careful travellers would pay less. But because information is asymmetric and the careful and the careless are hard to tell apart, insurance providers offer policy permutations that 'screen' the market such that different risk groups *reveal themselves* and gravitate towards the right kind of policy.

You're not uninsurable if you're a careless driver but you will pay more for insurance

Stiglitz shows that high-risk individuals are willing to pay a higher premium on the understanding that they will receive full compensation in the event of a loss that *they* know to be more likely ('I'm happy to pay £100 for travel insurance that will completely cover my losses because I know I might very well need it'). On the other hand, low-risk individuals choose a lower-cost policy but one that carries an excess or deductible which, because they know *they* are low risk, these people are willing to accept given the attraction of a lower premium ('I'll accept an excess of £150 and pay only £30 for travel insurance I probably won't need').

Stiglitz calls the outcome that arises from this self-selection process a 'separating equilibrium' – that is, one that generates different kinds of policy for different groups of high- and low-risk consumers. He also shows that there is no 'pooling equilibrium' – that is, where all individuals opt for the same policy. There is an analogy here with Akerlof's 'lemons' analysis. Were they to offer a single policy to the market, insurance firms would set a premium too high for low-risk individuals (who would leave the market) and thus attract only an adverse selection of high-risk customers. Again, asymmetric information would distort resource allocation in the market.

Insurance pricing has other interesting quirks. The chapter's final case study takes a brief look at the optional, and sometimes very expensive, extended insurance cover offered by many electrical goods retailers.

BUSINESS CASE STUDY

Behavioural economics and optional insurance

In the run up to Christmas a few years ago, the department store John Lewis offered free 2-year guarantees on the computers it sold. One such computer was a Dell Mini 10 netbook, priced at £299.95. John Lewis has a reputation for good-quality merchandise and relatively generous guarantees. Dell's computers also enjoy a reputation for performance and reliability.

Most people buying electrical goods nowadays will be familiar with the option to buy additional periods of insurance against defective performance. John Lewis offered such an option with their Dell Mini 10 netbooks. An extra year's guarantee could be purchased for what looks to be the astonishing sum of £145 – about half the original purchase price. Presumably some people bought this insurance – John Lewis is a retailer that knows its market – but how can the relatively high price be justified or explained? One clue comes from behavioural economics.

Much standard economic theory is premised on the view that consumers and firms behave in a *rational* manner according to their own interests. In the case of firms, rationality translates into the pursuit of profit. But we have already come across approaches that suggest that firms may not always be profit maximizers. They may at times prioritize other objectives such as size or market share.

In the case of consumers, the standard assumption is that some measure of satisfaction or utility is maximized and that this is commensurate with the consumption of goods and services in the light of available income.

Behavioural economics takes issue with this rather robotic maximizing approach. It suggests, for example, that consumers make judgements in markets not with any great precision but mostly with rough and ready, *simplified* processes. Gut instincts if you like. The advantage for analyses of consumer behaviour – and the firms that might want to make commercial use of it – is that many of these gut instincts appear systematic and therefore predictable.

A relevant example is the concept of *loss aversion*, one form of which simply suggests that people become more attached to an item or asset once they own it and value it more highly as a consequence.

Think again about John Lewis's offer of an extra year's insurance but this time picture yourself in the shop. You've just got your shiny new red netbook in your hands and you're comfortable with the price you're paying and the free guarantee, but now you're being offered something more. This bit of state-of-the-art kit you now *own* can be instantly given more life as a pristine working tool. It's yours; you don't want to think about the possibility of it breaking down or the cost of replacing it should it break down. Suddenly, you're *loss averse*, and the additional insurance perhaps no longer seems quite as expensive as it did before you owned your netbook.

Firms try to overcome asymmetric information problems by encouraging customers to reveal themselves in other markets too. One basic question for firms is the price they can charge for a good or service given their lack of knowledge of the prices customers would be prepared to pay. Differentiation in prices and products can sometimes be used to induce customers to disclose their preferences and produce commercially advantageous separating equilibria. For example, a business-class flight to Australia from the UK is priced at around £3800; flying in economy costs about £1800. The more expensive ticket sometimes gets you chauffeured to and from the airport, it buys you a seat that folds down flat so you can sleep comfortably, and the food and drink you are served is of a higher quality. The point here is to get travellers who are prepared to indulge themselves with a more refined service to do so (and pay more for the privilege), while simultaneously presenting more frugal passengers with the opportunity to fly at a lower price. An airline that offered only business-class seats would struggle to fill its planes (with an adverse selection of only wealthy customers), whereas one that offered an economy-only long-haul service might generate strong demand (with an adverse selection of the cost-conscious) but its ticket revenue would be relatively low.

Other examples of product and price differentiation-induced separating equilibria include cinemas that offer premier and standard seating in their theatres, executive and standard rooms in hotels, first and standard class rail travel and even different levels of service at the carwash.

The demand-curve analysis we introduced in Chapter 2 allows us to demonstrate the advantages to the firm of separating equilibria. In Figure 3.3 the demand curve indicates that at price P_1 quantity demanded is Q_2. But imagine that the market is composed of 100 different consumers each buying one good. In these circumstances it is only the 100th consumer buying the last good who is willing to pay the price P_1 and no more. Given the demand curve, *all* other consumers would be willing to pay more for the good. For example, the consumer buying the Q_1th good would be willing to pay price P_2. Because all but the last consumer appear to be getting a price lower than they would be willing to pay, we consider that the market is generating an amount of **consumer surplus** given by the triangle ACP_1.

Consumer surplus: the amount consumers would be willing to pay for a good or service above the price that they actually pay.

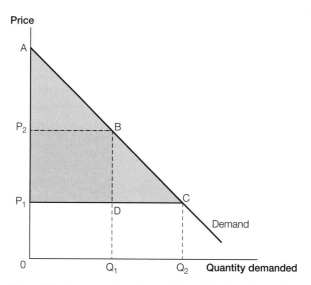

Figure 3.3 Consumers' surplus and the pricing decisions of firms

Were firms able to arrange individual prices with each consumer in this market they might be able to charge so as to claim all consumer surplus for themselves but this is usually not possible. One alternative is to charge different prices and allow customers to choose which they would prefer to pay. To return to our flights-to-Australia example, P_2 might represent a business-class fare and P_1 economy class. Under this arrangement a portion of consumers' surplus given by the rectangle P_2BDP_1 is gained by firms as they generate separating equilibria in the market.

In this section we have reflected on the ways in which firms may try to cope with the principal–agent problem and asymmetric information issues. The underlying assumption has been that firms may be threatened by such difficulties. What we have yet to do is consider the consequences of a strategic failure to address the common corporate imperatives. Such consequences may include the death of the firm.

In the next section we discuss the death of one notable firm: Lehman Brothers, the fourth-largest investment bank in the US. The bankruptcy of Lehman can be best understood in the context of an event – the US sub-prime mortgage crisis which triggered the 2008–9 world recession, and by using the concept of asymmetric information.

3.7   The death of a firm

Type the name Lehman Brothers into a search engine. The Lehman.com web address takes you to a single page that announces the bankruptcy in the US of Lehman Brothers Holding Inc. Lehman was one of the most high-profile casualties of the credit crunch. In January 2008 it was worth more than \$30bn; by September of the same year it was effectively dead. How did this happen? The answer mostly lies in Lehman's very poor business decision-making but there is an asymmetric information context to the story too.

In Chapter 1, we discussed the implications of the UK government's nationalization of a number of banks during the financial crisis. Concerns that the failure of one or more banks might have posed a systemic risk to the integrity of Britain's entire financial system led the government to embark on a

*Not **THE** Lehman Brothers ?*

HUNTer

Reproduced by kind permission of PRIVATE EYE magazine/James Hunter

series of bank rescues. In the US matters unfolded a little differently. While the US government moved to save some institutions, such as the giant insurance firm AIG with a bailout costing $182bn, it let Lehman fail. As we suggested in Chapter 1, there are actually sound reasons for accepting corporate failure. Many banks were badly exposed during the credit crunch because they had taken excessive risks. If governments were known to be ready to bail out any and every bank that indulged in hazardous behaviour, the incentive *not* to indulge in such behaviour would be greatly reduced. So the death of Lehman might be construed as morally instructive for the rest of Wall Street.

Lehman sowed the seeds of its eventual destruction with a 2006 decision to intensify a strategy that characterized it as a 'growth firm in a growth industry'. It was Lehman's upbeat reaction to the realization that the US sub-prime mortgage crisis was causing growth in the financial services industry to falter that sealed its fate. It didn't worry that prospects in property and in finance were looking a little bleak – Lehman's ambitions were bigger than ever.

But before we look at what Lehman did as the sub-prime crisis unfolded, let's pause for a moment to think about an aspect of the crisis itself. One important feature at the heart of the sub-prime mortgage market was asymmetric information. In an environment of low interest rates, and where the government had actively encouraged the extension of home ownership, millions of Americans entered the property market for the first time. In 2006 about half of US mortgage originations, worth about $1.5 *trillion*, were classified as sub-prime. Many

*"Also from the New World, Your Majesty,
a portfolio of sub-prime mortgages"*

of these mortgages were what might be termed 'liar' loans, or less impolitely, ninja loans (where ninja stands for no income, no job or assets). Quite simply, people exaggerated their capacity to meet the costs of the mortgages they were taking out. Now, the sellers – or brokers – of the mortgages were on straight commission for each mortgage they arranged, so they were paid regardless of what happened once the deal had been done (which, incidentally, is a principal–agent problem). Indeed, in the event that the borrower became concerned that they might not be able to meet their mortgage payments, brokers were happy – for another fee – to remortgage the property in question, *on the assumption that its price was still rising in value*. As house prices were rising fast there was no apparent problem.

Here's where the asymmetric information problem comes in. Briefly, all of these sub-prime loans were then bundled together with others and sold to the big investment banks – like Lehman – who unpacked and repacked them again with other assets and sold them on to investors. But notice there is *no* connection at all between those taking out sub-prime loans and the institutions on Wall Street parcelling them up and selling them on. The investment banks had historic data on rates of mortgage default and the security of rising house prices that suggested the whole process was rock solid, but once defaults began to cascade and house prices plummeted it quickly became apparent that the whole edifice was built on quicksand. And at the heart of the crisis was a lack of information on Wall Street about the real status of millions of liar and ninja loans: in other words, asymmetric information.

© istockphoto.com/narvikk

Mayhem on Wall Street: not wholly a bad thing?

Now back to Lehman Brothers. Lehman supposed that the sub-prime crisis presented it with a business opportunity to cheaply acquire property-based and other assets on its own account, and, before the true extent of the crisis became apparent, it borrowed massively and over the *short term* to fund these purchases. According to its bankruptcy examiner, Lehman accumulated $700bn in assets in this way, with equivalent short-term borrowing liabilities. The problem was that the assets it had bought were *long term*. They were mostly illiquid – they could not be sold quickly or easily and, as the financial crisis unfolded, they were also falling in value. But Lehman's new and enormous liabilities – the sums it had borrowed – left it needing to refinance billions of dollars on a *daily* basis just to stay afloat. In 2006 this looked 'doable'; in 2007 it became difficult; during the 2008 credit crunch it became impossible: Lehman ran out of money, out of institutions willing to do business with it and out of business.

What lessons might be drawn from the death of a firm like Lehman Brothers? There's an asymmetric information context certainly, but this applies to the whole financial services industry both in the US and around the world. The real message is very simple: Lehman's downfall lay in its excessive appetite for risk. It saw an opportunity in a newly distressed property market and was too slow to understand that the sub-prime crisis would eventually jam up the credit markets upon which it had suddenly made itself wholly dependent. As its property-based asset portfolio began to lose value Lehman took on the aspect of a bad credit risk. But this time there was no asymmetric information: Lehman knew it was in trouble and so did everybody else. As an administrator of the firm in London memorably said, 'What it underlines to me is the importance of market confidence. If no one wants to do business with you ... there's no way back'.

We have discussed a range of motives for the growth of firms – diversification, the realization of economies of scale and of scope, the desire to access new markets and, perhaps above all, the management of risk. It was the last of these that Lehman got horribly wrong. Lehman's administrator was right, there was no way back, and by the rules of capitalism nor should there have been. This is a view that Austrian economists would certainly endorse; we explore some Austrian perspectives on entrepreneurship in the next section.

3.8   Firms and entrepreneurship: an Austrian view

Earlier in this chapter we defined entrepreneurship as the capacity to organize the remaining factors of production: land, labour and capital. We also argued that it is the pivotal factor in capitalist production in so much as it is uniquely able to discern the demands of consumers. This latter claim is derived from the Austrian School of economic thought and merits further elaboration here. Austrian economics emerged in Vienna in the 1870s in the works of Carl Menger (1840–1921), Ludwig von Mises (1881–1973) and Friedrich Hayek (1899–1992). As a result of Nazism, the school's leading proponents moved abroad, especially to the US. The major contemporary figure in Austrian economics is Israel Kirzner (b. 1930) who has written extensively on entrepreneurship.

For pre-Austrian economists, the *organizational role* of the entrepreneur was of primary interest: he or she assembled the necessary factors of production in the appropriate form and received the appropriate reward – profit – for so doing. With its emphasis on the attainment of market equilibrium (as detailed in Chapters 1 and 2), mainstream economic thought has tended to reinforce this view that the entrepreneurial task is not possessed of any particular dynamism. The market process balances supply and demand – all entrepreneurs have to do is produce the appropriate quantities of goods and services at the appropriate price while controlling their costs. Rather like an engine that has been set running, each firm can simply 'tick over' with the entrepreneur supplying the fuel and the occasional tune-up as required.

In the Austrian view, this kind of conceptualization of entrepreneurship is far too *passive*. For Austrians, entrepreneurs – whether individual producers or firms – anticipate and help to shape the market, they do not meekly follow it. To illustrate, think about the two different car markets in the former East and West German economies. In East Germany, the car industry and car market were both state-run. Demand for the single model produced – the Trabant – generally tended to run ahead of supply. East German carmakers were not dissatisfied with this arrangement – whatever output they produced was sold. Most importantly there was no competition from the west: western models could not be imported, not that many people in East Germany could have afforded them anyway. The result of this state of affairs was a notable degree of industrial complacency and lethargy: the Trabant, made partly from cardboard, changed hardly at all over 30 years. In the West German car market, however, things proceeded on an altogether different basis. West German carmakers were (indeed, still are) private-sector firms operating in a highly open and competitive environment. They must compete both with each other and with overseas firms for the domestic and foreign markets. This means that they cannot simply parcel up factors of production and churn out a given model range indefinitely: they must continually strive to outperform their rivals, both on price and in terms of the quality of product. In a word, these firms must be *entrepreneurial*. The outcome is that names like Mercedes and BMW have become bywords for quality and excellence, while Trabants, shorn of state protection following German reunification, are no longer made.

While this example gives us a flavour of what Austrians mean by entrepreneurship, it doesn't quite capture their interpretation completely. Entrepreneurial firms must certainly observe the imperatives of consumer sovereignty and follow the patterns of demand that consumers lay down. But, crucially from the Austrian perspective, they also help to *anticipate* demand. The key here is the ability of the entrepreneurial firm to *innovate*. For example, the impressive range of mobile communication devices that continue to emerge are all available because of the entrepreneurial skill of firms. Note again that this does not mean that all or even many firms have to invent new goods; their contribution is to find

The Trabant - Is that the best they could do? Er, in the absence of competition, yes

© istockphoto.com/Wouter van Caspel

market applications for technologies as they appear. Thus, Google didn't invent the Internet; it developed a way of effectively searching it. Indeed, innovation does not necessarily have to embody sophisticated new technologies at all. In the UK for at least a decade there has been a phenomenal interest in cooking. All the major TV channels showcase celebrity chefs and screen cooking shows and there are numerous promotional spin-offs in 'book of the series' publications, magazines and even cooking holidays. The entrepreneurial skill here was to *anticipate* the level of popular demand for this kind of activity and to *persuade* and even *educate* people that cooking is something most of us can enjoy doing. But again, regardless of the strength of persuasion, the consumer remains the final arbiter. If demand is not forthcoming, the product or products will inevitably fail.

Now, the Austrian version of entrepreneurship has some interesting implications for the notion of market equilibrium. Recall the definition of equilibrium we offered in Chapter 2: a position from which there is no tendency to change. At a market-clearing equilibrium price, the quantities of a good demanded and supplied are perfectly matched. Accordingly, because both consumers and producers are satisfied with existing conditions, there is no pressure from either group that might result in changes in the quantities demanded or supplied. Yet entrepreneurs, in the Austrian view, are clearly *never* satisfied with the existing state of affairs in a given market. Prompted by the pressure of a competitive environment and the prospect of profit, they are continually seeking to engineer changes in the market, to introduce modified or wholly new goods and services to make consumers aware of wants and needs they did not know they had. In this sense, equilibrium is always just out of reach, and inevitably so. A market in equilibrium would be one in which entrepreneurship was dead: an impossibility under capitalism but a state of affairs Austrians would recognize in, say, the former East German car industry. In the Austrian view then, markets are dynamic and uncertain arenas in which entrepreneurs innovate and compete under the ultimate sanction of the consumer; entrepreneurship is in effect the motive force of capitalism.

SUMMARY

- Firms are a key institution in capitalism. They use factors of production to produce goods and services that can be sold for profit. Economic theory assumes that firms attempt to maximize profits.
- Profit maximization, while self-evidently beneficial for the firm, is also held to serve the interests of consumers. Firms operate in a competitive environment and must produce goods and services that consumers demand at an appropriate price. Thus the most successful and most profitable firms are those best able to satisfy the consumer.
- Firms exist because they offer a number of advantages as organizers of production that individuals operating through the market cannot attain. Thus, firms provide savings on transaction costs; they facilitate the extension of the division of labour; and they are accomplished innovators.
- There are three main categories of firm, as defined by ownership: sole proprietorships, partnerships and limited companies. Sole proprietorships and partnerships are generally smaller, simpler to manage and taxed less than limited companies but they find it harder to raise capital and their owners have unlimited liability for losses. Companies tend to be larger, more difficult to manage and are subject to heavier taxes. On the other hand, they can raise capital more easily as their shareholders' risk is limited to the size of their immediate investment. All three categories are well represented in most advanced capitalist economies, suggesting a fairly even balance of advantage and disadvantage between them.
- A number of alternative views on the objectives of firms have appeared in the literature. Aside from profit maximization these include achieving satisfactory performance over a range of multiple objectives, maximizing sales revenue, maximizing managerial satisfaction and maximizing the growth rate of firms.
- The growth of firms may be organic or occur as a result of merger and acquisition. Firms seek to grow because of a number of risk-reducing and other advantages growth brings.
- The principal–agent problem is an acknowledgement that, in the real world, firms may not always approximate the seamless profit-maximizing entities of economic theory. Managing the principal–agent problem is an issue for many firms.
- Asymmetric information is an additional difficulty that many firms must address; they may do this by inducing consumers to generate separating equilibria in markets.
- Firms die when they get business decisions seriously wrong. In that it reduces moral hazard, bankruptcy is a necessary and positive feature of capitalism.
- In the view of Austrian economists, the central attribute of the firm is its entrepreneurial skill. Motivated by profit, entrepreneurial firms, operating in a competitive environment, are at the dynamic and innovative heart of capitalism. This conceptualization of the firm leaves the consumer as the ultimate arbiter of the course of capitalist production but it sits rather uneasily with the notion of equilibrium as defined by mainstream economic theory. For Austrians, equilibrium is always just out of reach as entrepreneurs consistently reshape what they produce and how they produce it in the search for more profit.

KEY TERMS

- Firms
- Entrepreneurship
- Factors of production
- Profit maximization
- Limited and unlimited liability
- Objectives of firms
- Organic growth
- Growth by merger and acquisition
- Principal–agent problem
- Asymmetric information
- Austrian approach to entrepreneurship

QUESTIONS FOR DISCUSSION

1. What is the prime function of the firm and how is it motivated?
2. What advantages do firms, as opposed to individuals, offer as organizers of production?
3. What are the relative merits of the three main types of firm?
4. What is the principal–agent problem and what implications does it have for the firm?
5. How do firms cope with problems of asymmetric information?
6. Should we regret the bankruptcy of firms like Woolworths or Lehman Brothers?
7. What perspective do Austrian economists have on entrepreneurship?

EVERYDAY ECONOMICS 3.1 ANSWERS

1. **Time-keeping**. Clocking in and out of work is a common practice. Its purpose is to strictly regulate the length of the working day and monitor the number of hours worked by employees. It also indicates lateness. Firms use time-keeping to save on supervision costs (workers register their own hours) and to devolve the responsibility for time-keeping onto workers themselves. Workers know that if they're late or they leave early it will be noted so they have an incentive as agents to accept whatever timeframes are set by the principals.

2. **Duvet days**. These are days employees can take off with an employer's blessing at short notice. Late night? Hangover? Take a duvet day. At first sight they look like an indulgence. Employers might offer them to appear sympathetic so they get a better-disposed agent when they do turn up for work. But there is also evidence that duvet days actually reduce the propensity of workers to take sick days. Instead of telling a white lie about having a cold they just opt for a duvet day which is then taken from their annual leave. This means that principals see the number of days lost to agents' sickness fall.

3. **The production line**. Principals would like agents to work solidly and consistently. In many work settings this is hard to achieve. Think about your experience in a class or lecture. Does the person teaching the class always begin on the hour and finish precisely 50 minutes later? No. Our own classes are often marked by a short delay while we shuffle papers, check something on the computer or, frankly, just look out of the window. The production line limits this kind of porosity in work time. Agents are in given positions and the work moves at a pace set to allow them just enough time to do the job required: there is little possibility that time will be wasted. So agents work with the level of intensity desired by principals.

ONE THING YOU SHOULD READ

Roddy Doyle's *The Van*, pp. 216–31

This is a funny book, as in laugh-out-loud funny. Its central character is Jimmy Sr. and the story is of his loose partnership in a burger van with his friend Bimbo. Their business is launched in working-class Dublin against the backdrop of the 1990 World Cup, when Ireland reached the quarter finals.

One business problem for Jimmy Sr. is that, although he and Bimbo are informal partners in the van, it was Bimbo who actually bought it, filthy and engine-less, with some of the redundancy money he'd been paid when he lost his job. Jimmy Sr. and Bimbo make a success of things for a while – selling burgers and chips outside their local pub, the Hikers – but Jimmy Sr. becomes worried about the enterprising ideas to generate more business that Bimbo's wife, Maggie, keeps dropping on them. Some of these he and Bimbo resist; others they go along with. But a principal–agent issue quickly begins to emerge, with Bimbo and Maggie on one side and Jimmy Sr. on the other.

Finally, a warning – if you're offended by swearing, you might want to skip this one.

The extract begins 'Maggie had a great head for ideas' and has a flyer for 'Bimbo's Burgers'. After reading it think about the following questions.

1. How well does Herbert Simon's view of the decision-making process in firms capture the essence of the relationships between Bimbo, Jimmy Sr. and Maggie in their management of the burger van?
2. Jimmy Sr. conspires with Bimbo to puncture Maggie's plan for them to offer early-morning breakfasts to commuters. How might Maggie as principal have tried to ensure that her strategy was properly carried out?
3. Can you find some examples that show Jimmy Sr.'s awareness that he's becoming an agent?
4. Jimmy Sr. tries and fails to resolve his emerging status as an agent; how does he do this and why, in the end, do you think he fails?

© iStockphoto/maxsattana

4

firms' costs and revenues

KEY ISSUES

What determines a firm's short-run costs of production?

How are a firm's long-run costs affected by the scale of production?

What factors determine a firm's revenues?

At what level of output will a firm maximize its profit?

CONTENTS

4.1	Introduction	**124**
4.2	The short run and the long run	**125**
4.3	The short-run production function and the law of diminishing marginal returns	**125**
4.4	Short-run costs	**128**
4.5	Production in the long run	**132**
4.6	Long-run costs	**133**
4.7	Firms' revenues	**136**
4.8	Profit maximization	**140**

4.1   Introduction

In the previous chapter we considered the role of the firm in a modern advanced economy and explained that firms exist because they offer a number of advantages as organizers of production that individuals operating through the market cannot realize. We also discussed how firms – a key institution in capitalism – buy or hire factors of production in order to produce goods or services that can be sold for profit. As profit is determined by the difference between total revenue and total cost, in this chapter we examine firms' costs and revenues. This will allow us to consider the level of output at which profit maximization is achieved.

Before considering firms' costs and revenues in subsequent sections of this chapter you should first read the box below, 'Applying Economics to Business', and think about what costs you would face if you decided to set up a bar after you graduate.

APPLYING ECONOMICS TO BUSINESS

Imagine a situation where you and a friend were seriously considering starting up a bar business together selling a selection of beers, wines and cocktails. You have already identified premises which you both consider are ideally located to attract customers. Before going ahead you would need to carefully consider the various cost and revenue streams in order to establish whether such a business would be viable.

The costs involved in your business would include rent and rates on the premises; lighting, heating, Internet and phone costs; equipment (beer pumps,

glasses, chiller cabinets, tables and chairs etc.); the drinks and drink ingredients you are going to sell; the cost of any bar staff you employ etc. Now this list isn't exhaustive but it will prompt you to think about all the various costs involved in running your business. Once you have produced what you consider to be a full list of *all* your costs you next need to think about a number of questions. For example:

- Which of these costs are fixed costs?
- Which costs will vary over time?
- How will the costs you have identified vary depending on the number of customers you attract?
- What ways are open to you to reduce the costs of running the business?

Having thought about the costs of running the bar you next need to reflect upon your main source of revenue: drinks sales.

- How much would you have to sell each week to cover your costs?
- How could you attract more customers to come to the bar in order to generate more revenue?
- At what point would you maximize your profit?

We will now consider the costs involved for a firm that has already been set up to manufacture beds. In examining the nature of firms' costs we begin by distinguishing between two main time periods facing a firm: the short run and the long run.

4.2   The short run and the long run

To illustrate the distinction between the short run and the long run, imagine a firm that has been set up to manufacture beds. It has factory space and the appropriate machinery in place, and employs a given number of workers. For ease of exposition we assume that the firm uses only two factors of production: labour and capital. Suppose the firm decides that it wants to increase its current level of production in a situation where all machinery is in use and its given labour force is employed working a full or normal working week. In the short run the firm can take on more labour – either by hiring additional workers or by paying overtime to its existing workforce – in order to produce more beds. What it can't do in the short run is buy and install more machinery or build and equip a new factory. Such actions take time to implement. The **short run** is a period of time in which some factors of production – such as capital and land – are fixed, while others – such as labour – can be varied.

In contrast the **long run** is a period of time in which all factors of production can be varied. If our bed manufacturer wants to increase production, it could both expand and equip its existing factory space and hire more workers. It could also, if it chose to do so, build and equip a new factory at a different location. In making this distinction between the short run and the long run it is important to note that the length of each time period will vary from one firm to another, depending on the nature of the production process involved.

In the next two sections we consider production and costs in the short run before turning to discuss long-run production and costs in Sections 4.5–4.6.

Short run: a period of time in which some factors of production such as capital and land are fixed, while others such as labour can be varied.

Long run: a period of time in which all factors of production can be varied.

4.3   The short-run production function and the law of diminishing marginal returns

In the short run a firm's production is subject to the law of diminishing marginal returns. In order to understand this law, consider the relationship between a firm's output and the inputs it uses in the production process. This relationship is known as the **production function**.

Returning to our example, in the short run the bed-making firm's capital stock – in the form of its factory space and all machinery within it – is fixed and the only variable factor of production is labour. The relationship between the number of workers (L) the firm employs and the total output of beds produced (TPL) over a given period of time is illustrated by the hypothetical data presented in Table 4.1.

What happens to bed production as the firm employs more and more workers is shown in the first two columns of Table 4.1. When the firm employs no workers whatsoever the factory, and all equipment within it, will lie idle

Production function: a functional relationship between the output of goods or services produced and the inputs used in the production process.

Total product of labour: the total output produced by a given number of workers.

and total output will be zero. As the first worker is taken on, total output – or the **total product of labour** – rises from zero to 30 beds. When a second worker is employed output increases from 30 to 70 beds and so on. What the data illustrates is that, initially, as additional workers are taken on, the production process becomes more efficient as each worker specializes in performing specific tasks in the production process. However, although total output increases as more and more workers are employed, beyond a certain point (the employment of the fifth worker) output increases less and less rapidly as **diminishing marginal returns** set in. This is because – with a given factory space and a fixed amount of capital equipment – the production process will eventually become less efficient and the productivity of workers will begin to fall. In other words, as the opportunities for task specialization are exhausted additional workers who are taken on start to duplicate tasks and get in each other's way, resulting in diminishing marginal returns.

Diminishing marginal returns: occur when the extra output produced from employing additional units of a variable factor alongside the fixed factors of production diminishes.

Using this data we can draw a graph of the total output produced against the number of workers employed. This relationship is also known as the short-run production function and is depicted in panel (a) of Figure 4.1. Let us consider two other important terms associated with the short-run production function: the average product of labour and the marginal product of labour. These terms are illustrated in columns three and four of Table 4.1 and presented as graphs in panel (b) of Figure 4.1.

Table 4.1 The total, average and marginal product of labour in the short run

L	TPL	APL	MPL
0	0		
			30
1	30	30	
			40
2	70	35	
			50
3	120	40	
			60
4	180	45	
			70
5	250	50	
			50
6	300	50	
			36
7	336	48	
			32
8	368	46	
			19
9	387	43	
			13
10	400	40	

Average product of labour: the average quantity of output produced by each worker employed.

The **average product of labour** (APL) can be found by dividing the total output produced (TPL) by the number of workers employed (L):

$$APL = TPL/L \tag{4.1}$$

For example, when four workers are employed, 180 beds are produced. The average output of each of the four workers is therefore 45 beds; that is, 180/4. As can be seen from Table 4.1 and panel (b) of Figure 4.1, the average product of labour initially rises before beginning to fall as employment is increased from 6 to 7 workers and beyond.

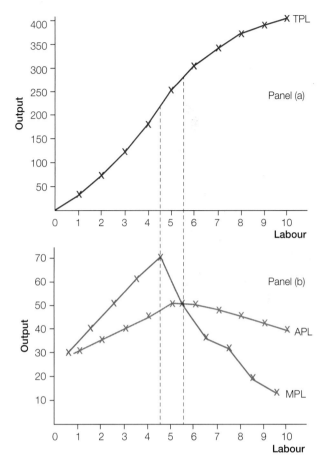

Figure 4.1 (a) The total product of labour
(b) The average and marginal product of labour in the short run

Marginal product of labour: the change in total output produced as a result of employing one more worker.

The **marginal product of labour** (MPL) is the change in total output produced (ΔTPL) as a result of employing one more worker (ΔL):

$$MPL = \Delta TPL/\Delta L \qquad (4.2)$$

where the Greek letter delta (Δ) is used to denote 'the change in' a variable.

For example, when employment is increased from zero to one worker, total output increases from zero to 30 beds, giving an MPL of 30 for the first worker. If a second worker is employed, output increases from 30 to 70 beds. In other words, the MPL of the second worker is 40. Initially, as more and more workers are employed the MPL rises, reaching a maximum of 70 when employment is increased from four to five workers. Thereafter the employment of additional workers results in diminishing marginal returns. It is important to note that both in the fourth column of Table 4.1 and in panel (b) of Figure 4.1 the

PHOTODISC

When the marginal age of a student joining a tutorial changes so does the average age

data for MPL is presented and drawn *between* the reference points of all other data in the table and graph. The reason for this is because the MPL is the change in output that results from employing one more worker. For example, the change in output *between* employing eight and nine workers is 19; that is, 387 − 368.

Before we turn to examine the costs a firm faces in the short run there are two connections between the data graphed in panels (a) and (b) of Figure 4.1 worth highlighting:

- The slope of the short-run production function measures the MPL. Where the MPL is at its maximum, the slope of the short-run production function (TPL) is at its steepest. Beyond that point MPL falls as diminishing marginal returns set in and the slope of the short-run production function becomes less and less steep and becomes progressively flatter.
- When MPL is above APL, APL rises. Conversely, when MPL is below APL, APL falls. Only when MPL is equal to APL will there be no change in APL, which is at its maximum point.

● **Think Point**

A simple example may help to conceptualize the relationship between marginal and average values. Suppose you are in a tutorial class where the average age is 20 years.

- What happens to the average age of the class when someone who is 25 arrives late?
- Alternatively, what happens if the latecomer is 18?

In the first case the average of the class age will rise because the marginal age (25) is higher than the average.

In the second case the average age will fall because the marginal age (18) is less than the average. Only where the additional (marginal) person has exactly the same age as the average will the average age of the class remain unchanged.

Having considered production in the short run and the law of diminishing marginal returns, we are now in a position to examine a firm's short-run costs.

4.4   Short-run costs

Variable costs: costs that vary with the quantity of output produced; also sometimes referred to as direct costs or avoidable costs.

In the short run a firm's costs of production will be determined by the cost of the factors of production it uses and the productivity of labour. In our example we have assumed that the bed-manufacturing firm uses two factors of production: labour, the only factor input that can be varied in the short run; and capital, which is fixed in the short run. This allows us to make a distinction between variable and fixed costs. **Variable costs** (in our example the cost of labour) vary

Fixed costs: costs that do not vary with the quantity of output produced; also sometimes referred to as overhead costs or unavoidable costs.

Total cost: the sum of the costs of all inputs used in producing a firm's output; total cost can be divided into total fixed costs and total variable costs.

with the quantity of output produced. In contrast, **fixed costs** (in our example any costs associated with renting or leasing the factory buildings and the cost of machinery) do not vary with the quantity of output produced.

A firm's **total cost** (TC) of production is the sum of its total fixed costs (TFC) and its total variable costs (TVC):

$$TC = TFC + TVC \qquad\qquad (4.3)$$

These terms are illustrated numerically in Table 4.2, the first four columns of which are reproduced from Table 4.1. The reader may have noticed that the second column of Table 4.2, which shows the total output produced, is now headed Q (for quantity of beds produced) rather than TPL as it was in Table 4.1. For simplicity we assume that:

- total fixed costs (column 5 of Table 4.2) are £500, regardless of the level of output produced
- each worker that the firm employs is paid £100 per period of time. For example, in producing 250 beds (Q) the firm incurs total variable costs of £500, as five people are employed (L).

The TC (column 7) of producing 250 beds is therefore £1000, the sum of TFC of £500 (column 5) and TVC of £500 (column 6).

It is also possible to illustrate these terms graphically. However, rather than meticulously plotting the data presented in columns 5–7 of Table 4.2 onto a scaled graph, in Figure 4.2 we trace the shape that the three short-run total cost curves would take. What is important is that you understand why a firm's total cost curves in the short run are depicted this way.

The total fixed cost (TFC) curve will be a horizontal straight line as these costs are fixed regardless of the level of output produced. The total variable cost (TVC) curve will start from the origin (with zero output produced variable costs are also zero) and rise as the number of units of output produced increases. The shape of the TVC curve is determined by the law of diminishing marginal returns. Initially as additional workers are employed, output increases more and more rapidly. As a result, before diminishing marginal returns set in, the TVC curve rises less and less rapidly as the extra output produced will be costing less and less in terms of the firm's wage costs. Once diminishing marginal returns set in, the TVC curve will start to rise more rapidly; that is, it gets steeper. The total cost (TC) curve is exactly the same shape as the TVC curve as it involves shifting the TVC curve vertically upwards by the addition of TFC; that is, it is in line with equation (4.3) TC = TVC + TFC.

We next consider a firm's short-run average and marginal costs. These costs involve average cost, average fixed cost, average variable cost and marginal cost. Numerical examples of these costs are presented in columns 8–11 of Table 4.2. Let's start with average cost (AC), which is shown in the tenth column.

Table 4.2 The relationship between the total, average and marginal product of labour and a firm's costs in the short run

L	Q	APL	MPL	TFC	TVC	TC	AFC	AVC	AC	MC
0	0			500	0	500				
			30							3.3
1	30	30		500	100	600	16.7	3.3	20	
			40							2.5
2	70	35		500	200	700	7.1	2.9	10	
			50							2.0
3	120	40		500	300	800	4.2	2.5	6.7	
			60							1.7
4	180	45		500	400	900	2.8	2.2	5.0	
			70							1.4
5	250	50		500	500	1000	2.0	2.0	4.0	
			50							2.0
6	300	50		500	600	1100	1.7	2.0	3.7	
			36							2.8
7	336	48		500	700	1200	1.5	2.1	3.6	
			32							3.1
8	368	46		500	800	1300	1.4	2.2	3.6	
			19							5.3
9	387	43		500	900	1400	1.3	2.3	3.6	
			13							7.7
10	400	40		500	1000	1500	1.3	2.5	3.8	

Note: Columns 5–11 are denominated in £, with columns 8–11 correct to one decimal place.

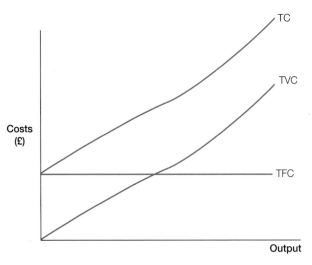

Figure 4.2 A firm's short-run total cost curves

Average cost:
the total cost of producing any given output divided by the number of units produced; average cost can be divided into average fixed costs and average variable costs.

The **average cost** (AC) per unit of output can be found by dividing the total cost of producing any given quantity of output by the number of units produced:

$$AC = TC/Q \tag{4.4}$$

For example, as the total cost of producing 250 beds is £1,000, the average cost of producing each bed is £4. In the same way that total cost can be divided into total fixed costs and total variable costs, average cost can be split into average fixed costs (AFC) and average variable costs (AVC). The average fixed cost per unit of output is found by dividing the total fixed cost by the number of units produced:

$$AFC = TFC/Q \tag{4.5}$$

For example, when the firm produces 250 beds it incurs a total fixed cost of £500. In consequence, the average fixed cost of producing each bed is £2. Average variable cost per unit of output is found by dividing total variable cost by the number of units produced:

$$AVC = TVC/Q \tag{4.6}$$

For example, when the firm produces 250 beds it incurs a total variable cost of £500; that is, the wage bill of employing five workers. In consequence, the average variable cost of producing each bed is £2. The astute reader will have already spotted that

$$AC = AFC + AVC \tag{4.7}$$

Marginal cost: the change in total cost resulting from increasing production by one unit.

The final term we need to consider is marginal cost. The **marginal cost** (MC) is the change in total cost resulting from increasing production by one unit. In other words, the cost of producing one more unit of output is

$$MC = \Delta TC/\Delta Q \tag{4.8}$$

For example, suppose our bed manufacturer, currently producing 250 beds per time period, decides to increase production to 300 beds. In line with equation (4.8) the marginal cost is also £2; that is, £100/50.

Although it has been helpful to illustrate these terms numerically using the hypothetical data presented in Table 4.2, as with the total cost curves what is far more important is that you understand the shape that the average and marginal cost curves will take in the short run. The shape of each of these curves is depicted in Figure 4.3.

The average fixed cost (AFC) curve falls continuously because as output increases total fixed costs are spread over an increasingly greater quantity of output produced. The shape of the average variable cost (AVC) curve is determined by the marginal product of labour (MPL). AVC initially falls as output increases due to increasing MPL, but will eventually increase because of diminishing MPL. This

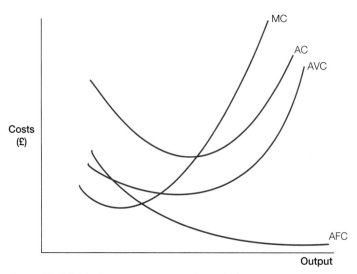

Figure 4.3 A firm's short-run average and marginal cost curves

gives rise to a U-shaped AVC curve. As labour is the only variable factor of production in the short run, there is a relationship between the APL curve depicted in panel (b) of Figure 4.1 and the AVC curve. When APL rises, AVC (the average variable, or average labour cost, per unit of output) falls, and vice versa.

The average cost (AC) curve also has a U shape since it is the vertical sum of the AFC and AVC curves (see Equation 4.7). However, given that the AFC curve continuously falls as output increases, the gap between the AC and AVC curves narrows as the quantity of output increases.

The J shape of the marginal cost (MC) curve is determined by the law of diminishing marginal returns. Initially as more and more workers are employed, marginal cost falls. However, once diminishing returns set in, marginal cost starts to rise as each additional unit of output costs more and more to produce; that is, the MC curve will start to rise sharply once diminishing marginal returns set in.

Finally, in discussing short-run costs it is important to recall the relationship between average and marginal values we illustrated earlier in Section 4.1 with our example of the average age of a group of students in a tutorial class. Reference to Figure 4.3 reveals that when MC is below AC, AC falls, but when MC is above AC, AC rises. As depicted, the MC curve crosses the AC curve at its minimum point. At this point MC is equal to AC, and AC is unchanged. The same relationship exists between the MC and the AVC curves.

In the next two sections we discuss how production and costs will be affected when all factors of production can be varied.

4.5   Production in the long run

Unlike the short run, in the long run both labour and capital are variable. In the long run the relationship between a firm's output and its inputs is determined by the scale of production. Suppose, for example, that our bed manufacturer

Increasing returns to scale: occur where a given percentage increase in all factor inputs results in a larger percentage increase in output.

Constant returns to scale: occur where a given percentage increase in all factor inputs results in the same percentage increase in output.

Decreasing returns to scale: occur where a given percentage increase in all factor inputs results in a smaller percentage increase in output.

Economies of scale: occur where the average cost per unit of output falls as the scale of production increases.

decides to increase the scale of its operations by doubling both its capital stock (its factory space and all machinery within it) and labour force. In this situation output would clearly increase, but the amount of the increase is determined by the returns to scale. Three possibilities arise:

- **Increasing returns to scale** occur where a given percentage increase in all factor inputs results in a larger percentage increase in output. In our example of a bed manufacturer, output of beds would more than double (that is, increase by more than 100 per cent) when capital and labour are doubled.
- **Constant returns to scale** occur where a given percentage increase in all factor inputs results in the same percentage increase in output. In our example, output of beds would double following a doubling of capital and labour.
- **Decreasing returns to scale** occur where a given percentage increase in all factor inputs results in a smaller percentage increase in output. In our example, output of beds would increase by less than 100 per cent following a doubling of capital and labour.

Whether a firm experiences increasing, constant or decreasing returns to scale has a crucial bearing on the firm's long-run costs. In what follows we focus our discussion on the shape of the long-run average cost (LRAC) curve.

4.6 Long-run costs

Capital is variable only in the long run

The assumption most commonly made is that as a firm expands it will initially experience increasing, then constant and finally decreasing returns to scale. For

a firm that initially experiences increasing returns to scale, its output increases at a faster rate than its inputs. This means that as the firm expands its production, it will be using fewer units of factor input per unit of output. In consequence, *ceteris paribus*, its average cost per unit of output will fall. In this situation a firm is said to be experiencing **economies of scale**. Economies of scale can arise for a number of reasons. For example, as the scale of production increases, economies can often be made because specialization allows workers to become more efficient in performing their assigned jobs and less time is lost with workers switching between tasks (remember our example from Chapter 3 of Henry Ford's use of flow-line assembly and an extended division of labour as a means to raise productivity). Another potential source of economies of scale concerns the more effective use of an indivisible factor input. In agriculture this might involve, for example, the more intensive use of existing machinery – such as a combine harvester – as a farm extends its cultivated acreage. As a result, the average cost per unit of output falls as

the scale of production increases. For further examples of potential economies of scale associated with the single market programme see Chapter 2, Section 2.5.

As the firm continues to expand it is likely to reach a certain level of output where these economies are exhausted. At this point the firm experiences constant returns to scale and its average cost per unit of output produced will also be constant. If the firm continues to grow it may experience decreasing returns to scale, in which case its long-run average cost per unit will begin to rise due to **diseconomies of scale**. Such diseconomies may arise because as a firm increases in size, beyond a certain point it becomes more and more difficult to manage and coordinate.

The shape of the long-run average cost curve is illustrated in Figure 4.4. Like the short-run average cost curve the long-run curve is also U-shaped, but much flatter than in the short run. The reason it takes this shape is not, however, due to the law of diminishing returns; instead it is due to a firm experiencing economies of scale up to output Q_0, constant costs between Q_0 and Q_1, and diseconomies of scale beyond output Q_1.

Diseconomies of scale: occur where the average cost per unit of output increases as the scale of production increases.

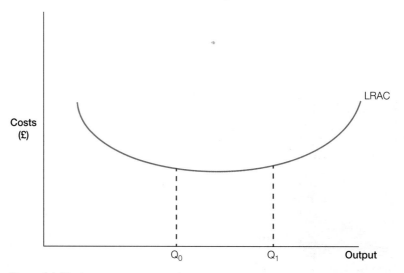

Figure 4.4 The long-run average cost curve

Figure 4.5 depicts the relationship between the short-run and the long-run average cost curves. $SRAC_1$ represents the average cost curve over a range of output facing a firm in the short run. You will recall that in the short run, average cost will eventually start to rise because of diminishing marginal product of labour. In the long run a firm can change the scale of its production by increasing both its factory space and machinery, and its workforce. Having expanded the scale of its production the firm would now be operating on a new SRAC curve such as $SRAC_2$. Following a further increase in the scale of production the firm would move to a new SRAC curve such as $SRAC_3$. As can be seen from Figure 4.5 the much shallower LRAC curve will form an envelope around a series of possible SRAC curves; that is, the LRAC curve lies at a tangent to the SRAC curves.

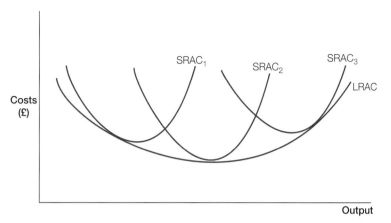

Figure 4.5 The relationship between the short-run and long-run average cost curves

EVERYDAY ECONOMICS 4.1

Short and long-run costs

These images depict different kinds of costs that firms incur in the production process. Which are short-run costs and which are long-run?

Answers are at the end of the chapter.

Having completed our discussion of firms' costs in both the short and the long run, we now turn to examine firms' revenues.

4.7   Firms' revenues

In discussing revenues we can make a distinction between a firm's total revenue, average revenue and marginal revenue.

Total revenue: the amount of money that a firm receives from the sale of its output; it equals the price of output multiplied by the number of units sold.

- **Total revenue** (TR) is the amount of money that a firm receives from the sale of its output over a given period of time. For example, if a firm sells 100 units (Q) of a good at a price (P) of £10 per unit, it will receive total revenue of £1000.

$$TR = P \times Q \tag{4.9}$$

Average revenue: the total revenue divided by the number of units sold; it also equals price.

- **Average revenue** (AR) is the amount of money that a firm receives per unit of output sold. For example, if a firm receives £1000 (TR) from the sale of 100 units (Q), it receives £10 per unit. In other words, average revenue equals price.

$$AR = TR/Q = P \tag{4.10}$$

Marginal revenue: the amount of money that a firm receives from the sale of one more unit of its output.

- **Marginal revenue** (MR) is the amount of money that a firm receives from the sale of one more unit of its output over a time period. For example, if a firm's total revenue increases from £1000 to £1100 (ΔTR = £100) as a result of an increase in sales from 100 to 110 units (ΔQ = 10), it will receive an additional £10 (MR) for each extra unit sold.

$$MR = \Delta TR/\Delta Q \tag{4.11}$$

Although this distinction between total, average and marginal revenue can be applied to all firms, an individual firm's revenue will vary depending upon the degree of market power the firm has. To highlight why this is the case we will consider the revenue curves of two kinds of firms: those that are unable to influence the market price of their goods – so-called **price takers**; and those that can determine the price they charge for their goods – so-called **price makers**.

Price taker: a firm that has to take the market price of its product as given.

Price maker: a firm that can determine the price it charges for its goods.

Revenues and price takers

A price-taking firm is one that has to take the market price of its product as given. The reason for this is that each firm produces a homogeneous good and is *very* small relative to the total market and cannot therefore influence the market price of the goods it is producing. As we will discuss more fully in Chapter 5, these are *two* of the key assumptions underlying a market structure referred to as perfect competition.

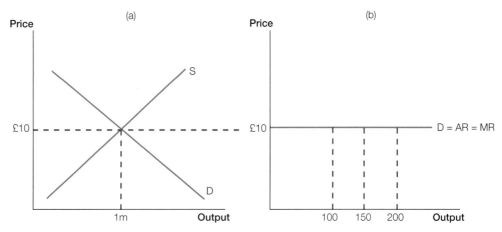

Figure 4.6 (a) The market price in perfect competition
(b) The average and marginal revenue curves of a price-taking firm

The situation facing a price-taking firm is illustrated in Figure 4.6. In panel (a) the market-clearing price (£10) is established at the intersection of the market demand and supply curves. A price-taking firm must observe the price set by the market. If it were to raise its price above £10 it would lose all demand, as customers would buy from other firms that charge the (lower) ruling market price. Furthermore, it would not be in the interest of any firm to lower its price below £10 as each firm can sell as much as it can produce at the prevailing market price. Being so small any change in an individual firm's output will not have any impact on the market price. In these circumstances the demand curve (D) for an individual firm will be a horizontal line (perfectly elastic) at a price of £10. This is illustrated in panel (b) of Figure 4.6. A firm can produce and sell 100 units, 150 units, 200 units of output and so on at the prevailing market price of £10 per unit. Each additional unit of output produced would be sold at a given price of £10 per unit. In other words, for a price-taking firm operating within a perfect competition:

$$D = P = AR = MR \qquad\qquad (4.12)$$

What about the total revenue received by a price-taking firm? As each unit of output is sold for £10 – recall that price is set by market conditions – total revenue will increase at a constant rate as more of the good is sold. As illustrated in Figure 4.7 the total revenue curve will be a straight line through the origin. When there are zero sales of output total revenue is zero; when 100 units are sold total revenue is £1,000; when 150 units are sold total revenue rises to £1,500; and when 200 units are sold total revenue is £2,000.

Revenues and price makers

The shapes of the three revenue curves we have been discussing take on a different form for a price-making firm. When a firm has a significant share of the total

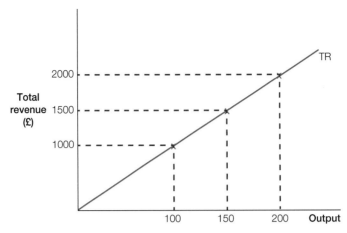

Figure 4.7 The total revenue curve for a price taker

market for a good, it has a degree of market power and will face a downward-sloping demand curve. In what follows we review the revenue curves facing a firm that is the *only* firm in the market, and that therefore has a monopoly in producing a particular good. For a monopolist, there is no distinction between the market and the firm's demand curve. The firm is the market. In Chapter 5 we discuss the assumptions underlying this particular market structure more fully. As you will come to appreciate, the market structures of perfect competition and monopoly are at two ends of a spectrum concerning firms' market power.

Because a price-making firm – in our example a monopolist – faces a downward-sloping demand curve, it will have to lower the price of its output in order to sell more. The hypothetical data presented in the first two columns of Table 4.3 shows that if the firm wishes to sell 100 units of output it must charge a price of £10 per unit (recall from our earlier discussion that P = AR). If, however, the firm wishes to sell 150 units, it must lower the price to £9 and so on. In Figure 4.8 we plot this data to derive a downward-sloping demand curve (D = AR).

Next we consider the firm's marginal revenue curve. Earlier we defined marginal revenue (MR) as the amount of money a firm receives from the sale of one more unit of its output. You should recall from equation (4.11) that MR is found by dividing the change in total revenue (ΔTR) by the change in output (ΔQ). When the firm sells 100 units at £10 per unit, it receives total revenue of £1000 (see column 3 of Table 4.3). In order to sell 150 units it must lower the price to £9 per unit, generating total revenue of £1350. As marginal revenue is calculated as ΔTR (£1350 – £1000 = £350) divided by ΔQ (150 – 100 = 50), MR is therefore £7 (£350/50). It is important to note that because the

Table 4.3 The average, total and marginal revenue for a price maker

Q (units)	P = AR (£)	TR (£)	MR (£)
100	10	1000	
			7
150	9	1350	
			5
200	8	1600	
			3
250	7	1750	
			1
300	6	1800	
			–1
350	5	1750	
			–3
400	4	1600	

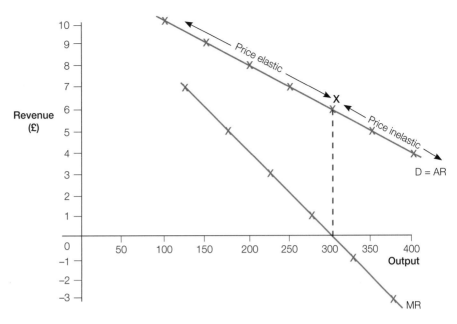

Figure 4.8 The average and marginal revenue curves for a price maker

demand (AR) curve that the monopolist faces is downward sloping, in order to sell an extra (marginal) unit the price on *all* units must fall. In consequence the MR curve has a much steeper slope than the AR curve (see Figure 4.8). In order to test your understanding of this analysis you should check the accuracy of the data for MR presented in column 4 of Table 4.3.

Finally, Figure 4.9 depicts the total revenue curve facing a price-making firm, which – unlike that of a price-taking firm where the TR curve is a straight line – initially rises and then falls. Reference to Figures 4.8 and 4.9 reveals that, where TR is at its peak at an output of 300 units (see Figure 4.9), MR equals zero (see Figure 4.8). The astute reader will have spotted that a relationship exists between marginal revenue, total revenue and price elasticity of demand. You will recall from Chapter 2, Section 2.7 that where demand is price elastic, a decrease in price will bring about a more than proportionate increase in the quantity demanded and an increase in total revenue. Conversely, where demand is price inelastic, a decrease in price will result in a less than proportionate increase in the quantity demanded and a decrease in total revenue. In other words, where demand is price elastic (that is, to the left of point X along the demand curve shown in Figure 4.8), marginal revenue will be positive and, as shown in Figure 4.9, total revenue will increase as output increases. On the other hand, where demand is price inelastic (that is, to the right of point X on the demand curve shown in Figure 4.8), marginal revenue will be negative and, as shown in Figure 4.9, total revenue will fall as output increases. Total revenue will be at its peak (that is, at an output of 300 units in Figure 4.9) where marginal revenue equals zero (that is, at an output of 300 units in Figure 4.8).

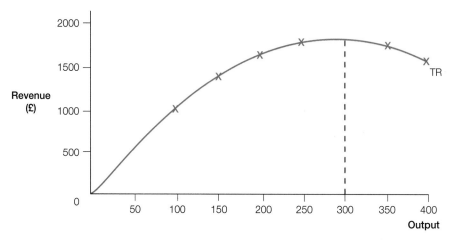

Figure 4.9 The total revenue curve for a price maker

Having completed our discussion of firms' costs and revenues we are now in a position to determine the level of output at which a firm will maximize its profit.

ECONOMICS AT WORK

Ben MacKinnon, e5 Bakehouse, http://e5bakehouse.com

Ben is the founder of e5 Bakehouse, an independent bakery in London. The bakery uses artisan methods, local, organic products and energy from renewable sources in the creation of its fresh bread and cakes. The bakery also encompasses a café and a space for evening cookery classes.

Visit www.palgrave.com/companion/mulhearn3 to watch Ben talking about how he kick-started the business, the market for his products, the relevance of price elasticity, and how the bakery manages supply and demand.

4.8   Profit maximization

Any firm – regardless of whether it is a price taker or a price maker – will maximize its profit by producing at that level of output where marginal revenue and marginal cost are equal to one another. In what follows we explain this rule and illustrate the profit-maximizing output for both a perfectly competitive

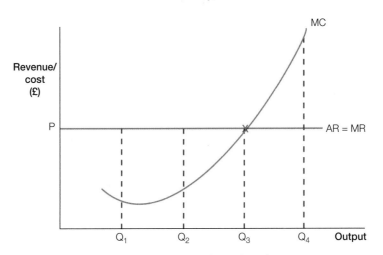

Figure 4.10 The profit-maximizing output for a price taker

firm (our price taker) and a monopolist (our price maker). To maximize profit, produce where marginal cost equals marginal revenue.

In Figure 4.10 we show the profit-maximizing output for a price-taking firm. For the reasons discussed earlier in this chapter, a price-taking firm faces a horizontal demand curve, where $P = AR = MR$. The J-shaped MC curve is also shown on the diagram. Profits will be maximized at an output level of Q_3 where the MC and MR curves intersect. To see why this is the case, consider the circumstances underlying the other marked output positions. At all output levels between Q_1 and Q_3, marginal revenue (MR) is greater than marginal cost (MC). In these circumstances the firm should continue to expand production up to Q_3, as each additional unit of output produced would add more to the firm's revenue than it would to the firm's costs and would, in consequence, add to the firm's profit. In contrast, at all levels of output above Q_3, MC exceeds MR and each additional unit of output produced beyond Q_3 would add more to the firm's cost than to its revenue, reducing the firm's profit. For example, at Q_4 MC is greater than MR and by reducing its output to Q_3 the firm can increase its profit. Where the MC and MR curves intersect marks a boundary between units of output that add to or reduce a firm's profit. In other words, where the two curves intersect establishes the level of output at which profit is maximized.

Before we consider the profit-maximizing output for a price-making firm, two points are worth highlighting, namely:

- For the price-taking firm, at the level of output at which profits are maximized $P = MC$ (we will examine the significance of this in the next chapter).
- The profit-maximizing rule (that $MC = MR$) applies only when the MC curve is rising; that is, where the MC curve cuts the MR curve from below. Although we have not shown the MC curve in its entirety, it will actually cut the MR curve twice – the first time at a level of output when it is falling.

How is the profit-maximizing output established for a price maker? For exactly the same reasons, for a price maker profit is maximized according to the rule that MC = MR. The profit-maximizing rule holds true for any firm operating in any form of market structure. What is different between price takers and price makers is the shape of their AR and MR curves. In Figure 4.11 we show the AR, MR and MC curves facing a monopolist. The profit-maximizing output (Q_M) occurs where the MC and MR curves intersect. As can be seen from the diagram the monopolist's profit-maximizing price (P_M) is greater than its MC. This contrasts with the situation facing a price taker where P = MC. We will explore the significance of this in the next chapter where we will also discuss *how much* profit a firm – whether it be a price taker or a price maker – will actually make (both in the short run and the long run) at the level of output at which profit is maximized.

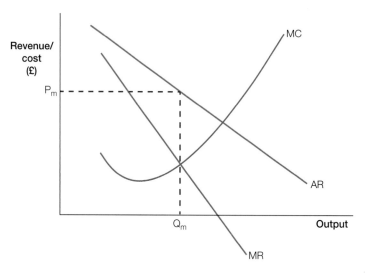

Figure 4.11 The profit-maximizing output for a price maker

We turn in the next chapter to considering the behaviour of firms operating in different market structures, and in doing so we focus our discussion on the issue of market concentration and power.

SUMMARY

- Firms buy or hire factors of production in order to produce goods and services. In the short run, a firm is only able to expand production by employing more labour; its other factors of production – capital and land – are fixed. Eventually, as more and more workers are employed diminishing marginal returns set in. When this happens each additional worker employed adds progressively less to total output than the previous worker.
- In the short run, a firm's costs of production will be determined by the cost of the factors of production it uses and the productivity of labour. A distinction can be made between a firm's variable costs and its fixed costs. In the short run, a firm faces a U-shaped average cost curve and a J-shaped marginal cost curve.
- In the long run, all factor inputs are variable and the relationship between a firm's output and its inputs is determined by the scale of production. Whether a firm experiences increasing, constant or decreasing returns to scale has a crucial bearing on the firm's long-run costs. In the long run, a firm faces a U-shaped average cost curve but one that is much flatter than in the short run.
- The revenue a firm receives depends on whether it is a price taker or a price maker. A price-taking firm has to take the market price of its output as given. It can produce and sell as much as it likes at the prevailing market price. Price-taking firms face a horizontal, perfectly elastic demand curve. A price-making firm can determine the price it charges for its goods. It faces a downward-sloping demand curve as it has to lower the price of its output in order to sell more.
- Any firm – regardless of whether it is a price taker or a price maker – will maximize its profit by producing at that level of output at which the cost of the last unit of

output produced is equal to the revenue gained from the sale of the last unit of output produced.

KEY TERMS

- Short run
- Long run
- Production function
- Total product of labour
- Diminishing marginal returns
- Marginal product of labour
- Average product of labour
- Variable costs
- Fixed costs
- Total cost
- Average cost

- Marginal cost
- Increasing returns to scale
- Constant returns to scale
- Decreasing returns to scale
- Economies of scale
- Diseconomies of scale
- Total revenue
- Average revenue
- Marginal revenue
- Price taker
- Price maker
- Profit maximization

QUESTIONS FOR DISCUSSION

1. In the short run, why will the marginal cost and average cost curves of a typical firm be J-shaped and U-shaped respectively?
2. What underlies the distinction between a price taker and a price maker?
3. Why will any firm maximize its profit by producing at that level of output where marginal cost and marginal revenue are equal?

EVERYDAY ECONOMICS 4.1 ANSWERS

1. **An office setting**. There are actually three sets of cost in this image. The worker on the phone represents a variable cost that can be changed in the short run. On the other hand the equipment in view – the computing hardware and the phone – are long-run costs.

2. **A screwdriver**. Equipment is usually taken to be capital so, strictly speaking, we suppose this is a long-run cost but in practical terms it's probably not. It's easy enough to purchase a screwdriver so our interpretation is that this particular item is a variable cost.

3. **A worker with his van at a petrol station**. The van is capital so is a long-run cost but the worker and the fuel he's putting in the van are short-run costs. Again though, the real world may be a bit more complicated than our theoretical model of costs. Many firms lease rather than buy their vehicles which means they're probably a variable cost in the short run.

4. **A shop renovation**. This is a long-run cost. Physically expanding its commercial footprint takes a firm some time.

ONE THING YOU SHOULD READ

Founded in 1995, easyJet is the UK's largest airline. EasyJet is a low-cost airline which aims to provide a friendly, efficient service at an affordable price for its customers. In June 2013 it announced plans to upgrade and replace its existing fleet by purchasing new generation aircraft from Airbus to run from 2017 to 2022. To understand the strategy behind easyJet's plan you should watch a short (10 minute) video that can be found on its website at: http://corporate.easyjet.com/investors/video/easyJet-plc-fleet-plans.aspx?sc_lang=en

Having watched the video, answer the following questions.

1. What are the main cost savings easyJet will derive from investing in the larger Airbus A320 planes?
2. What is the projected cost advantage per seat to easyJet of investing in the new generation aircraft compared to its existing fleet of Airbus A319 planes?
3. How does EasyJet plan to pay for the new aircraft?
4. How has EasyJet been able to build in a degree of flexibility into its plans to accommodate for potential changing market conditions?

5

market concentration and market power

KEY ISSUES

What are the main sources of market power?

What are the major market structures in the modern economy?

What implications do different market structures have for competition?

How does game theory help us to analyse firms' strategic behaviour?

Do competitive or uncompetitive market structures dominate in the real world?

CONTENTS

5.1	Introduction	**146**
5.2	Market power	**146**
5.3	Market structures, market power, price competition and non-price competition	**149**
5.4	Perfect competition	**152**
5.5	Monopoly	**158**
5.6	Imperfect competition (also known as monopolistic competition)	**172**
5.7	Oligopoly	**173**
5.8	Oligopoly and game theory	**177**
5.9	Market structures: an institutionalist view	**181**

5.1   Introduction

This chapter introduces the different market types or structures in which firms operate and reflects on the implications of each of these structures for the firm, the consumer and wider society. There are four such market structures:

- perfect competition
- imperfect or monopolistic competition
- oligopoly
- monopoly

As we will see, despite the outlined claims of mainstream economic theory in favour of firms as effective organizers of production, certain real-world market structures place clear limits on their ability to efficiently allocate scarce resources. Firms, it appears, may not always 'get it right' as far as the consumer and wider society is concerned. Moreover, because firms in some market structures can misallocate resources by producing too much or too little, governments may choose to regulate their activities in various ways.

5.2   Market power

Market power: the capacity of a firm to influence the market price of a good or service.

Market power refers to the capacity of a firm to influence the market price of a good or service. We know from Chapter 4 that there are firms that are price takers and other firms that are price makers. Price takers must accept the ruling market price because they are very small in relation to the market and because they produce a homogeneous product – milk, butter, paint, water – indistinguishable from other goods in the market. A small milk supplier has to accept the ruling market price. If they charge a higher than market price demand simply melts away as consumers buy milk elsewhere. The milk supplier has no incentive to charge less as they can sell the small quantity they produce at the market price. All of which means that price takers have no market power: they cannot in any way influence the market price.

On the other hand price makers have the capacity to choose the prices they set. If they charge less they'll sell more. If they charge more they'll still sell something. This means they have at least some market power. It may be vanishingly small but what these firms do in setting independent prices impacts upon the market in a way not achievable for price takers.

Market power in the real world

Market power has two general forms. It comes from various forms of monopoly or from consumer preferences, branding and reputation.

Monopoly and market power

The term monopoly conjures up images of well-resourced firms dominating markets but not all monopoly is underpinned by large scale. Where might

You'd expect to pay a little more for the convenience of shopping here

you buy some essentials late at night? Possibly a small local shop or petrol station. Outlets like these are great when you've run out of milk or need some bread. The prices they charge may not be as low as in the big supermarkets but customers are prepared to pay a bit more to get what they need locally at 11 pm on a wet Wednesday. So a monopoly on convenience gives corner shops a little market power and prices in the market are different as a result.

To take another example, imagine sitting at home, bored, when the thought occurs that you'd like to buy a book a friend's recommended to you. Let's experiment here. Say the book is *The Van* by Roddy Doyle, which we used as one thing you should read at the end of Chapter 3; it's laugh-out-loud stuff. Anyway, you want this book, where might you buy it? We've just checked and it's available online from Amazon at £5.51 with the possibility of free delivery though it will take at least a few days to arrive. But let's say you want the book today. We're now going to leave our desk in Liverpool John Moores University to trot down to Waterstones to find out the price of an immediate purchase.

Right, we're back and *The Van* was £6.39. So pay £6.39 now or £5.51 later? The monopoly on off-the-shelf availability that Waterstones has would cost you an extra 88p – this premium is a reflection of the market power Waterstones enjoys as a result of its near-monopoly presence on the high street.

On the other hand, the changing technology of book production and consumption allows our example to be read a little differently. Downloading means that immediate access to books is no longer a high street monopoly and we know that e-book downloads are outselling hardbacks. Trends like these will reduce the market power of traditional booksellers.

One final example. There were dramatic media reports a few years ago that an unknown trading group had bought and taken physical delivery of Europe's *entire* supply of cocoa beans – the basic ingredient in chocolate. Why attempt to corner the market in cocoa beans? To gain *immense* market power. And what subsequently happened to the world market price of cocoa? It went up. If a firm controls a substantial proportion of the world's supply of a commodity it will, as a monopolist, enjoy a degree of market power that arises because of the absence of competitors. The firm can set cocoa prices right across the market according to its own preferences secure in the knowledge that buyers have limited alternative sources of supply. Of course, this does not mean that *any* price can be set. All price-making firms still face downward sloping demand or average revenue curves (refer back to Figure 4.8 for a reminder). This means that if a price above the range of the demand curve is set, demand will shrivel away. Who would buy chocolate at £40 or £50 a bar? As we emphasized in Chapter 2 when discussing OPEC oil price increases, even the most powerful producers are ultimately constrained by the market context in which they operate.

Market power in the context of branding, reputation and consumer preferences

Brands and the reputation they confer in the eyes of consumers matter. Here's an example. *Which?*, the consumer interests campaigning organization, gave a recent best airline award to Air New Zealand, noting that 98 per cent of its passengers had indicated that they would recommend the company to a friend. On the other hand, *Choice* – an Australian equivalent of *Which?* – in a satisfaction survey of 9,000 people, rated British Airways worst in an 11-strong field of carriers from Australia to the UK. Respondents were reported to be particularly critical of BA's in-flight service. What do these results imply for market power? It *may* be that if its reputation as a quality airline is sustained Air New Zealand could edge up its UK route ticket prices without seeing a significant fall in demand, suggesting possibly considerable influence on the market price. For BA in Australia, the same opportunity may not presently be available if BA really is for the moment held in relatively low regard by its customers. Its market power is constrained by a poor reputation.

Generally, firms that are able to positively differentiate their goods or services from those supplied by their competitors may be able to set higher or much higher prices because consumers are willing to pay more where they perceive higher quality, better durability, superior design, more attentive customer service, or some other attribute. Think about your own tastes and preferences. Do you tend to gravitate to Costa Coffee or Starbucks? Is it Google, Yahoo or Bing? Primark or Topshop? Apple or android? What about the rest of your family; any notable leanings there? In business, reputation and brands matter. They're like mini-monopolies. They convey market power.

5.3 Market structures, market power, price competition and non-price competition

A market structure is a means of characterizing a market by reference to the *level and intensity of competition* that prevails between firms in it. Think about the kinds of competition that exist between firms in the markets for the following goods and services:

- haircuts
- pubs, bars and restaurants
- new cars
- train travel

Competition actually varies quite considerably in form and intensity across these markets. Let us briefly consider each in turn.

Haircuts

Barber shops and hairdressing salons are numerous and they offer a fairly uniform service. True, customers may elect to patronize one establishment regularly (reputation and brand again) but if it closes, there are many others to choose from. Because they are plentiful and generally small barber shops are in fairly intense competition. This may manifest itself in several ways – for example in the form of investment in furniture and fittings to improve the appearance of the shop. Most obviously, however, barber shops have to be competitive in terms of the price they charge. In any given city or district, there will be a 'going rate' for a haircut which few barbers will exceed by more than a modest amount. To do so would entail the risk of losing customers to rivals. Note that the main connection we have established here is between, on the one hand, the large number of small firms competing in the market and, on the other, the wide range of consumer choice and consequent need for firms to remain price competitive. This, of course, is another way of saying that barbers have relatively little market power.

Pubs, bars and restaurants

Pubs, bars and local restaurants appear similar. In cities there are plenty of them and consequently there is lots of consumer choice. On the other hand there may be more opportunities for the cultivation of reputation and brand. Sites such as TripAdvisor help with this, as do other forms of endorsement. Pubs are recommended by the Campaign for Real Ale; restaurants have their hygiene standards independently assessed and publicly displayed. So there are probably more opportunities for product differentiation in the retail food and drink industry which means that there is more market power present than there is amongst barbers. But because the firms here are usually still relatively small in relation to the market there will still be fairly intensive price competition between them.

New cars

Market concentration: the extent to which a market is dominated by a small number of firms.

Cars are produced on a *world* scale by a small number of very large firms: Ford, BMW, Toyota, Renault and so on. Clearly, these firms are in competition with one another, but because there are probably less than 20 of them in total the market is highly concentrated. This means that the ways in which they compete may be different and less intense than if there were hundreds or thousands of carmakers. So how does competition between carmakers manifest itself? Unlike haircuts, or to a lesser extent beer, or a meal in an Italian restaurant, cars are highly differentiated products with a host of particular design features. Most models come in several versions and with a range of optional extras. Typically, because they are few in number and because they make highly branded products, carmakers tend to compete *less* on price and much more on the intrinsic merits of the product. BMW does not suggest that its cars are cheaper than Toyota's or Renault's. Its advertising asserts that BMWs are *better* cars. Here then there is less price competition but more persuasion of consumers through the medium of advertising. In other words *non-price* competition is prevalent and appears to be based in part on the restricted number of firms in the industry.

It is important to stress here that we are *not* arguing that carmakers think that competitive pricing is unimportant. Indeed, in certain segments of the car market – those of the family saloon or the economy hatchback for instance – manufacturers do sometimes compare their models favourably in price terms with those of their rivals. What we would stress however is that even here there are more pronounced emphases on reliability, versatility, exhilaration, gender, sexual assertiveness, environmental protection, safety and so on. You can probably even 'pin the car' on such a list. This general approach tends to give carmakers greater freedom to set prices independently and leaves non-price competition as the primary lever of customer interest.

Train travel

Usually, suppliers of train travel have no immediate competitors in the shape of rival train firms. Of course, train firms *are* in competition in the wider travel market – alternative forms of transport are offered by coach firms, airlines and private motoring. However, it is the absence of *immediate* rivals that gives train operators more market power and relative freedom from the imperatives of price competition. Train operators tend to advertise speed, standards of service and comfort rather than direct fare or cost comparisons with other forms of transport. Thus, in a market where there are very few firms (here arguably only one train operator per route – concentration could not be higher), price competition is at its lowest relative intensity – train firms have a lot of market power – and non-price competition appears to dominate.

© Chris Mulhearn

A train leaves Berlin's Hauptbanhof: trains are quick, convenient and comfortable but less intensive competition may mean higher prices

To what use can we put this discussion of different market types? Economic theory *also* recognizes four major market structures. These are differentiated by the intensity of price and non-price competition. Now, as we will see, although the examples we have just given are *not* literal illustrations of each theoretical market structure, there are some good parallels between them. The four major market structures identified by theory are:

- *Perfect competition:* This is a benchmark or ideal type with which other market structures may be compared. It is characterized by an infinitely intense level of price competition – to the extent that all firms in the market are forced to charge the *same* price. The number of firms in a perfectly competitive market is large and, as suggested by our examples, this has an important bearing on the form and intensity of competition that prevails. Firms in perfect competition have no market power.
- *Imperfect competition:* Here, although the number of firms is still high, the relative intensity of price competition is somewhat moderated by the presence of slightly differentiated products. As noted, differentiated products enable firms to charge different prices to those of their competitors. Firms that elect to charge higher prices may do so in the knowledge that consumer preferences for their particular product will, to some extent, safeguard the level of demand. Imperfectly competitive firms have some limited market power.
- *Oligopoly:* An oligopolistic market is dominated by a small number of firms, each large in relation to the market it serves. Because they have market power

oligopolistic firms tend not to engage in intensive price competition, focusing instead on non-price competition.

- *Monopoly:* A pure monopoly exists where there is one firm in a market selling a good or service for which there are no close substitutes. Here, as might be anticipated, price competition is extremely weak and non-price competition for brand and reputation management purposes will dominate.

For ease of analysis, we confine *detailed* discussion of market structures in this chapter to a contrast between perfect competition and monopoly. Although we also consider imperfect competition and reflect at greater length on oligopoly, the essential understanding of firms that we wish to elaborate here can be made by reference simply to the most and least competitive market structures.

5.4   Perfect competition

Perfect competition: a market structure most notably characterized by a situation in which all firms in the industry are price takers and there is freedom to enter and leave the industry.

A perfectly competitive market is characterised by the following assumptions:

- The market is composed of a large number of independent profit-maximizing firms, each of which is small in relation to the market. As such, none is in a position to influence market conditions. There are also many consumers, each small in relation to the market.
- Any firm may leave the market if it chooses to do so and other firms are free to enter it.
- Factors of production enjoy perfect mobility. This means that land, labour, capital and enterprise can move with ease between uses.
- There is perfect knowledge in the market. All firms and consumers are constantly aware of all prevailing economic conditions.
- Firms in the perfectly competitive market produce a homogeneous product; that is, one with no identifiable brand. This assumption means that loyalties to particular firms cannot be developed.

These assumptions are not reproduced in their entirety in any typical market. While the first two might be observable in the real world, the possibility of the simultaneous existence of perfect mobility and perfect knowledge is clearly remote. The final assumption is, moreover, probably the antithesis of concrete business practice. Virtually every firm tries to persuade the consumer that its product or service is in some way superior to that of its competitors. Facebook is a notable success in brand assertion with more than 24 million active users in the UK; that's more than half of the country's adult population.

The perfectly competitive firm as a price taker

While perfect competition might be a little hard to reach it is still useful as a means to assess the performance of actual market structures. What then are the implications of the restrictive assumptions we have just outlined? The most important of these is that firms in a perfectly competitive market are *price takers*.

All perfectly competitive firms must observe the single equilibrium price set by the market. Any firm that imposed a higher price for its output would quickly cease to trade because it would immediately lose all demand. This is because consumers in the market would instantly be aware (given the assumption of perfect knowledge) that they could buy exactly the same product elsewhere at a lower price. Nor would it be in the interest of any individual firm to try to raise demand for its output by charging a price below the ruling market price, given that it can sell all it wants at the ruling market price.

The revenue and cost curves of the perfectly competitive firm

You will recall from our discussion in Chapter 4 that, as a price taker, the perfectly competitive firm faces a perfectly elastic demand curve. This is because, by assumption, every firm must respect the prevailing equilibrium market price, meaning that demand for the firm is perfectly responsive to a change in price. The firm's demand curve is the equivalent of its average revenue curve. Average revenue simply indicates the amount a firm receives per unit of output sold. The average revenue curve for a firm in perfect competition is also its marginal revenue curve. The marginal revenue curve indicates the extra revenue associated with each additional unit of output produced. Figure 5.1 reproduces the revenue curves for a perfectly competitive firm. You should check back to Chapter 4, Section 4.7, to confirm why the average revenue curve and the marginal revenue curve are also the demand curve for the firm.

If we assume that the firm's objective is to maximize profits, it will produce up to the point where marginal revenue and marginal cost are equal. Figure 5.2 depicts the average cost curve and marginal cost curve faced by a representative firm in a perfectly competitive market. Once again you should check back to Chapter 4, Sections 4.3–4.4, in order to make sure you understand how

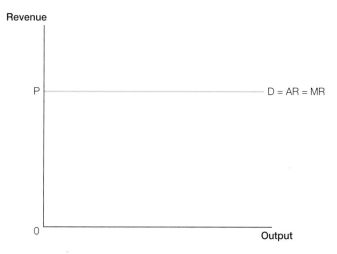

Figure 5.1 The revenue curves for a firm in a perfectly competitive market

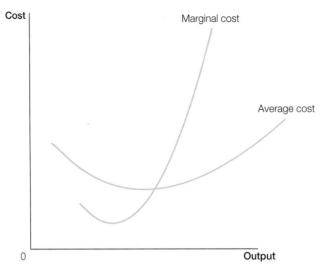

Figure 5.2 Cost curves for the firm in a perfectly competitive market

these curves are derived. Average cost falls at first because, as the firm begins to produce, although total costs will rise, fixed costs are shared over (that is, divided by) an increasingly large output. Eventually, despite further increases in the output total, average costs begin to rise because of the law of diminishing returns. Diminishing returns imply that, after a certain point as more variable factors are added to a given set of fixed factors, the marginal and average costs of production begin to increase.

Figure 5.3 reproduces Figure 4.10 in order to show exactly where the firm will maximize profit. Figure 5.3 illustrates the firm's marginal revenue and

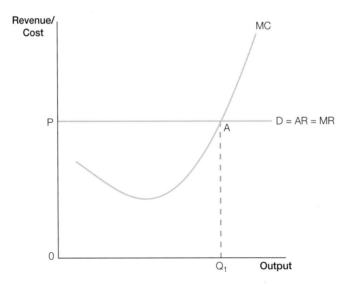

Figure 5.3 The profit-maximizing output decision

marginal cost curves. Profit is maximized at the output level Q_1, (point A) where marginal cost (MC) and marginal revenue (MR) intersect and where the MC curve cuts the MR curve from below.

The short-run position of the perfectly competitive firm

In Figure 5.4 we consider the short-run position of the perfectly competitive firm. The firm's output decision reflects its assumed desire to maximize profits and, accordingly, it produces at Q_1 where MC = MR. From the vertical axis it is evident that the average cost of this level of output is at point A, while the average revenue associated with it is at P_1. Total cost is indicated by the rectangle $0ABQ_1$ (average cost multiplied by the number of units produced), while the rectangle $0P_1CQ_1$ indicates total revenue (average revenue times the number of units produced). Thus the shaded area AP_1CB – total revenue minus total cost – represents the (maximum) profit earned at Q_1. For reasons that we will explain shortly, this level of profit is also known as supernormal profit.

Supernormal profit: profit that exceeds the minimum amount a firm must earn to induce it to remain in the industry.

As noted, this is a short-run position for the firm. Remember that the short run is that period in which only variable factors of production, such as labour, can be altered. In the long run all factors are variable which also means that, should they wish to, firms can enter (or leave) the market. The question is: why would they choose to enter? The answer, of course, is the existence of super-normal profit. Given our assumption of perfect knowledge, other firms will be aware of the level of profit in the market; they can enter it by securing the requisite factors of production. As new entrants come into the market, conditions change and the short run gives way to the long run.

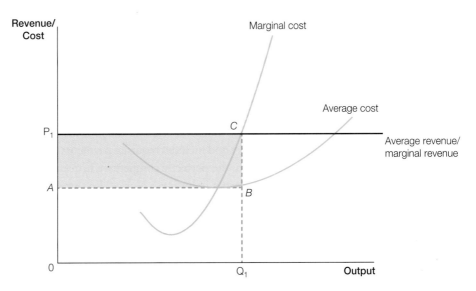

Figure 5.4 The short-run position of a firm in perfect competition

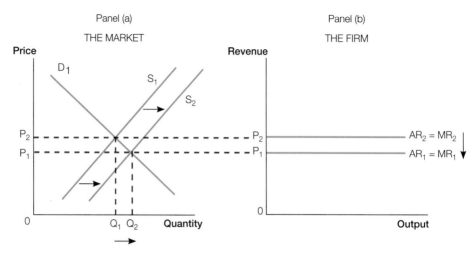

Figure 5.5 The short and the long run in the perfectly competitive market and the price-taking firm

The long-run position of the perfectly competitive firm

Some of the details of the movement from the short to the long run are sketched out in Figure 5.5. In panel (a) of the figure we see the effect of the new entrants on the market. The supply curve shifts to the right from S_1 to S_2. This results in a fall in the market-clearing equilibrium price from P_2 to P_1 and an increase in the equilibrium quantity demanded and supplied from Q_1 to Q_2. For the representative firm, the implications of this change in market conditions are clear. As a *price taker* the firm must observe the new equilibrium market price. Accordingly, in panel (b), its demand curve (which, remember, is also its average revenue and marginal revenue curve) shifts downward from AR_2, MR_2 to AR_1, MR_1.

The remaining question is what effect this has on the supernormal profit that the firm was earning in the short run. In Figure 5.6 the representative firm's AR/MR schedule has fallen in line with panel (b) of Figure 5.5. The firm still seeks maximum profit and, therefore, output is fixed at Q_{PC}, where MC = MR. Here, however, we can see that the rectangles of total revenue and total cost are one and the same: $0P_1AQ_{PC}$. This means that the firm is now *covering its costs* but is no longer earning supernormal profit. In fact, economists refer to this as a position where normal profit is being earned. Normal profit is the return required to keep the firm in the market and includes requisite payments to all factors of production. In the long run then, the perfectly competitive firm earns only normal profit but this *is* sufficient to keep it in business. Notice also that should *too many* firms enter the market, to the extent that each firm's AR/MR schedule falls below the average cost curve, all firms will incur losses. This will provide an incentive for firms to leave the market until normal profit positions are achieved for those that remain.

Normal profit: the minimum amount of profit a firm must earn to induce it to remain in the industry.

The perfectly competitive firm and allocative efficiency

Finally, it is important to emphasize that, in both the short run and the long run, the representative firm is producing at a point at which price equals marginal cost. This

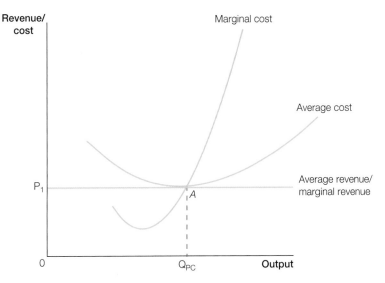

Figure 5.6 The long-run position of a firm in perfect competition

means that the firm is efficiently allocating resources as far as *wider society* is concerned. In other words, the firm is producing exactly the amount of output that society as a whole would like it to. This is a big claim which we need to explain and justify.

In Figure 5.7 we present the marginal revenue and marginal cost curves of a perfectly competitive firm. The firm produces at Q_2, the output that equates MC and MR and at which price (P_2) equals marginal cost (P_2). Notice that at output Q_1, price (P_2) is greater than marginal cost (P_1). Our contention is that, socially, Q_1 would be an undesirable output; it would be preferable if the firm produced at Q_2 (which it will anyway in order to maximize profits). Consider the *single unit* of output at Q_1. How does society value this unit? If we assume that the firm's MC curve is a good representation of society's view of the marginal costs of production,[1] we can say that society's estimate of the cost of the unit at Q_1 is P_1. What of the value society places on the unit at Q_1? Given that the MR/demand curve of the firm indicates the price consumers are willing to pay for this unit (P_2), we can say that P_2 is a good approximation of society's valuation of it. We now know society's estimate of the cost of the unit (P_1) and its valuation of it (P_2). Since the value placed on the unit is greater than its cost, the unit is deemed to be socially desirable. Notice that other units beyond Q_1, such as Q_Y, are similarly desirable (value P_2, cost P_L). In fact, above Q_1 all units are socially desirable up to and including Q_2. However, units beyond Q_2, such as Q_N, are socially undesirable because, socially, their costs of production exceed the valuation placed on them (Q_N costs P_H but is only valued at P_2). The general conclusion is the anticipated one: the socially desirable output for the firm is at that output where price equals marginal cost. As we will see, this rule applies to *all* firms in *all* forms of market structure.

1 This is on the assumption that there are no externalities associated with the firm's activities. Briefly, externalities are costs or benefits that a firm generates which affect third parties who are not directly engaged in transactions with the firm (see Chapter 6 for more on externalities).

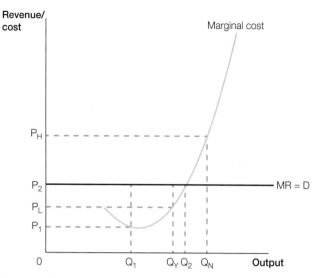

Figure 5.7 The perfectly competitive firm and allocative efficiency

Perfect competition: a summary

The perfectly competitive market produces some highly desirable outcomes. In the long run, it provides sufficient incentive in the form of normal profit to retain firms in the market. At the same time, the output firms produce can be seen to be set at a socially desirable level. We assume that the perfectly competitive firm in the free market is an effective means of allocating scarce resources. Yet perfect competition is only a *model*; its assumptions are not validated, in their entirety, in any real markets. Its usefulness, therefore, lies in the establishment of standards against which to judge market reality. Let us now compare perfect competition with the *least* competitive market structure: monopoly.

5.5 Monopoly

The word monopoly conjures up images of gigantic firms that dominate markets and consumers. For economists, this is not an appropriate way to conceptualize monopoly. Monopoly is defined by *market exclusion*. Whenever a firm can take advantage of barriers that prevent others from entering the market, it is in a position to exploit market power and influence prices. This means that the size of the firm has no necessary bearing on whether or not it is a monopoly – big or small, what counts is its ability to keep potential rivals out.

Exclusion can happen in a variety of ways. Buffet cars on trains possess market power because, for the duration of a journey, passengers have no other place to go for refreshment. Motorway service stations have market power because they are the most readily available source of fuel for those driving long distances. In cases such as these, market power arises because of a lack of close substitutes. The train passenger could make some sandwiches and a flask of coffee before leaving for the station;

Do you leave the motorway in search of cheap fuel or pay more at the services?

and the driver could leave the motorway to search for cheaper petrol. But these options involve delays, or work the consumer would rather not do – thus he or she patronizes the supplier with market power. Because market power involves some lessening of the intensity of competition, the monopolist is able to charge higher prices than would otherwise be the case. Hence, one would normally expect to pay more for food and drink on trains and fuel at a motorway service station.

To test your understanding of possible sources of monopoly power have a look at Everyday Economics 5.1. Can you identify the barriers to entry illustrated in these photos?

EVERYDAY ECONOMICS 5.1

What kinds of barrier to market entry are illustrated here?

Monopoly is created by barriers to entry. See if you can identity each of the barriers illustrated in the images below.

Answers are at the end of the chapter.

1

2

3

4

Before examining the economic implications of monopoly in detail, let us complete our review of the forms it can take.

Pure monopoly: a market structure in which there is a sole supplier of a good or service that has no close substitutes and for which there are barriers to entry into the industry.

- **Pure monopoly**: A pure monopoly exists where there is a sole supplier of a good or service in a market for which there are no close substitutes. The qualification concerning substitutes is an important one. There is, for example, only one tunnel under the English Channel. However, Eurotunnel, its operator, does not have a pure monopoly on cross-channel travel because of the presence of a number of rival ferry operators. In the UK, until recently, Royal Mail enjoyed the status of a pure monopoly as the government forbade any other operator to carry post for less than £1 per item. This privilege had endured for 350 years. However, the market has now been liberalized and Royal Mail presently has scores of licensed postal operators to compete with.

Legal monopoly: arises in the UK when a firm enjoys a market share of 25 per cent or more.

- **Legal monopoly**: In the UK, a monopoly is effectively defined in law as a market share of 25 per cent or more. When a merger of firms or an acquisition of one firm by another threatens to breach the 25 per cent threshold, the process is liable to investigation by a government body, the Competition Commission. The Competition Commission has the power to prevent mergers, require that large firms sell off parts of their business, or behave in other ways that sustain competition in the industry.

Natural monopoly: arises when a single firm is the most efficient structure for the production of a particular good or service.

- **Natural monopoly**: Some industries, because of their technical characteristics, tend to be most efficiently organized under the mandate of a single firm. The most common examples of natural monopoly are the electricity, water and gas industries. It would be wasteful if an economy had several rival firms in, say, the supply of gas. Each firm would have its own separate supply network, running pipelines to the homes of customers or potential customers – a pointless duplication when one network would suffice. In the UK, until the 1980s, in order to protect consumers, these industries were publicly owned. Now they are all in private ownership but subject to forms of public regulation and accountability. We examine the issues surrounding privatization in Chapter 6.

Sources of monopoly

We have seen that the existence of monopoly requires exclusivity in a market for goods or services with no close substitutes. As was the case for Royal Mail, such exclusivity can be granted by the government. There are a number of other instances of government-sanctioned monopoly. For example, monopolies may be created where this encourages artistic or technological innovation. Thus musicians and authors are granted copyrights on their work and new inventions are similarly protected by patents. Without the right to exclusively exploit their creativity for a period, innovators would not have an incentive to commit scarce resources to the processes of research and development. This implies that, though monopoly might be associated with certain problems, it is acceptable for (say) the duration of a patent because of the wider long-term benefits it brings. The case study below considers why patent protection is necessary in the pharmaceutical industry.

BUSINESS CASE STUDY

Monopoly power and advances in medicine

The leading pharmaceutical company Pfizer considers patent protection essential to the way it does business.

Without patents this firm would not have the incentive to invest huge sums in research and development – Pfizer estimates that each new medicine it brings to the market costs, on average, £400m to develop, money that has to be spent *before* any profit can be realized. That's a big speculative outlay.

Patents in medicine are granted for 20 years, but this usually occurs early in the development stage, without any guarantee that the patented item will become clinically proven and make it onto the market.

On average, by the time a medicine is fully licensed, Pfizer reports that its patents only have around eight years left to run. This is the period that makes investment in research and development worthwhile because production rights are exclusive to Pfizer.

After a patent expires other firms are able to produce generic versions of a medicine, based on Pfizer's research – which it is obliged to make available for public health reasons. A generic medicine is one that does the same job as the original but carries a different name.

Pfizer's most famous medicine? Probably Viagra. Patents on Viagra that Pfizer holds around the world are close to ending. When this happens other companies will be free to manufacture and sell generic versions of the drug.

Is this fair? Well, yes. Pfizer has been rewarded with temporary monopoly power for coming up with a new and important medical treatment. But were the monopoly to be permanent consumers may suffer because competition would be stifled.

In the end a temporary monopoly underpinned by the conferment of a patent provides the best of both worlds. Pfizer has sufficient incentive to invest very large sums of money in medical research, a lot of which will not pay off. Consumers' interests are also protected because competition eventually brings down the price of the generic medicine.

In the UK a government body, the Intellectual Property Office, offers safeguards to innovation and creativity under four headings. These are:

- Patents: As noted in our Pfizer example, patents granting exclusive rights in production, sales, use and even importing can last for up to 20 years.
- Trademarks: A trademark is something that distinguishes a company or product from its competitors. Look at the logo of most big corporations and you'll see one of the following symbols near the lower right hand corner: ® or ™. This means the symbol has been registered as a trademark and can't be copied by rivals. Trademarks are important because they establish and reflect the brand image of a firm and the goods and services it produces. What's the world's most recognized symbol? It's generally thought to be the trademark

of Coca-Cola. Interestingly, can you name a trademark that actually has no written name? How about the Nike 'swoosh'?

- Copyrights: A copyright prevents someone reproducing music, lyrics, plays, books, photographs and other similar works that have been created by others. J.K. Rowling took years to write the first Harry Potter book which, when published, became an almost overnight sensation. Since then there have of course been more Harry Potter books, films, games and toys. But once Rowling had opened up a whole new and massively popular wizards and sorcery genre, plenty of other wizardy-style books and paraphernalia began to appear. This shows that there is no copyright in an idea. But J.K. Rowling's versions of wizardry – her books and characters – are copyrighted. This protection lasts for the author's life plus 70 years, protecting both J.K. Rowling and the inheritors of her estate. The copyright symbol is ©.

- Designs: A design right prevents the copying of a three-dimensional product's visual appearance including, shape, contours and textures. The range of products covered by design rights is vast and includes things like the shape and texture of biscuits, the outline form of a car, a torch, or a child's toy. Design rights can last up to 15 years.

The economic implications of monopoly

On the familiar assumption of profit maximization, we begin here by reviewing the cost and revenue curves of the monopolist in order that the profit-maximizing output might be determined. Note that, as for perfect competition

It's like an illness with you, isn't it?

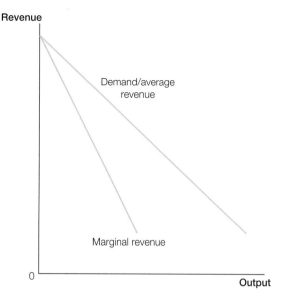

Figure 5.8 Revenue curves for the monopolist

and all other market structures, the profit-maximizing output for monopoly is where the marginal cost and marginal revenue curves intersect.

We have seen that, in perfect competition, the firm is a *price taker*: It must take the ruling market price as given. For the monopolist, no such restriction applies. In the case of pure monopoly, the firm is the industry. The monopoly firm can determine its own price. In Chapter 4 we discussed why such a firm is known as a price maker. The monopolist faces a demand curve that slopes downwards from left to right, as in Figure 5.8. The demand curve is also the monopolist's average revenue curve, as it indicates the revenue received per unit of output (and this must be the selling price).

Figure 5.8 also depicts the MR curve for the monopolist. As the demand (average revenue) curve that the monopolist faces is downward sloping, in order to sell an extra (marginal) unit the price on *all* units must fall. Hence, the marginal revenue curve has a much steeper slope than the average revenue curve. Check back to Chapter 4, Section 4.7, if you are unsure why this is the case.

The monopolist's output decision

In order to maximize profits, the monopolist will produce at an output that equates MC and MR. Figure 5.9 illustrates the monopolist's output decision. Figure 5.9 is remarkably similar to Figure 4.11. The profit-maximizing output is at Q_M. At Q_M the monopolist will set price at P_1, which will also be the average revenue associated with this output. The average cost is at point *A*. We are now in a position to determine the level of *supernormal* profit earned by the monopolist. The total revenue associated with Q_M is the price of this

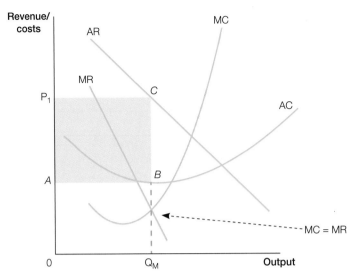

Figure 5.9 The long-run position of the monopolist

output times the output itself. Thus, total revenue is represented by the rectangle $0Q_MCP_1$. Total cost on the other hand is given by the rectangle $0Q_MBA$. Taking total cost from total revenue leaves the shaded area $ABCP_1$, which represents profit. Significantly, because monopoly is defined by barriers to entry, this position (and the supernormal profits that go with it) is a *permanent* one. Unlike the case of the perfectly competitive market, here there will be no new entrants and therefore supernormal profits will not be competed away by other firms.

Monopoly and allocative efficiency

In perfect competition we saw that the output generated by each firm maximized profits at a point where price equals marginal cost. You will recall that the price of a good can be taken to represent society's marginal valuation of it, while its marginal cost approximates society's view of the costs of its production. Thus, where price is above marginal cost, the output concerned is deemed to be socially desirable, but when marginal cost exceeds price, that unit of output should not be produced. It follows that the output at which price and marginal cost are equal is the socially efficient one as it marks the boundary between socially desirable and socially undesirable output.

In Figure 5.10 we can see that the output for profit maximization, which the monopolist will select, is Q_M (where MC = MR, and price is P_2). However, a socially efficient allocation of resources demands that output be set at a higher level: Q_2 (where price = MC). This means that the economic implication of monopoly is that it *misallocates* resources: the social preference would be for more resources to be committed to the industry and a greater output produced (Q_2) at a lower price (P_1).

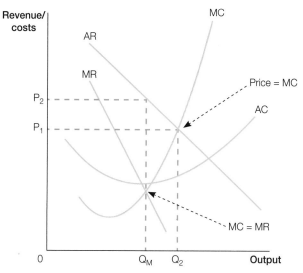

Figure 5.10 The monopolist as a misallocator of resources

We must stress here that the problem with monopoly is that, compared to the perfectly competitive market structure, it misallocates resources. If a monopolist took over a perfectly competitive industry, it might be expected to restrict output and raise prices but this is not necessarily so. Take, for example, the case of an industry which is a natural monopoly but which is organized along perfectly competitive lines. Recall that the single supplier is the most effective form of organization for a natural monopoly. In perfect competition, with output divided between a large number of small firms, costs are unnecessarily high as each firm maintains its own (say) infrastructure of gas pipelines. With the emergence of the monopolist only one set of pipelines is retained and the cost basis of the industry falls sharply.

This possibility is illustrated in Figure 5.11. In a perfectly competitive industry, equilibrium occurs where supply (the summation of individual firm's marginal cost curves, MC_1) equals demand (AR). A perfectly competitive output Q and price P are established where $P = MC_1$. If the industry is monopolized, with the monopolist facing the *same* cost and demand conditions as previously prevailed when the industry was perfectly competitive, output would fall to Q_1 and price would increase to P_3 (as the monopolist employed the MC = MR rule). If, however, costs were reduced following monopolization, say from MC_1 to MC_2, it is possible for the price to fall below, and output increase above, that which would prevail under a perfectly competitive industry; that is, P_2 compared to P and Q_2 compared to Q. This, of course, means that the economic effect of monopoly is *not*, as is sometimes claimed, always to lower output and increase price. Monopoly does, however, *consistently* misallocate resources. Notice in Figure 5.11 that a socially efficient allocation of resources for the monopolized industry would require an output of Q_3 (where price $= MC_2$) and price set at P_1.

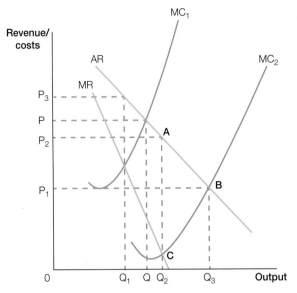

Figure 5.11 From perfect competition to natural monopoly: lower prices and greater output but a misallocation of resources

Deadweight loss: arises in the case of monopoly when society is denied output it would prefer to see produced and consumed.

The triangle ABC indicates the deadweight loss associated with a monopoly operating under MC_2. The deadweight loss in this case is a cost imposed by the monopolist on the society as a whole in the sense that the output between Q_2 and Q_3 is denied to consumers who value it more highly than the output costs to produce. However, they can't buy it because the monopolist has set a prohibitive price of P_2 for the good in question.

Monopoly and price discrimination

We know that monopoly is defined by market exclusion – monopolies have the capacity to keep potential rivals out. So far we've seen that this allows monopolies a degree of market power in that, unlike perfectly competitive firms, they can choose what prices to set. They are price makers. But there's a further possibility here. Monopolies may be able to charge *different* prices to different sets of customers for the *same* product. The attraction is obvious: charge high prices to customers willing to pay more and lower prices to others. Overall the monopolist's revenue stream will be enhanced by such price discrimination.

Price discrimination: charging customers different prices for the same product.

The key to successful price discrimination is market segmentation. There must be some means of keeping customers apart otherwise when faced with a choice they would pay the lower rather than the higher price. So how is this done? Here are some examples.

- Discounts by age group

    Care for a new Apple Mac or iPad? If you're student anywhere around the world you can get both of these products at a discount. Apple has a dedicated

Store for Education that presently offers savings of up to £175 on a new Mac, and up to £32 on a new iPad. According to Apple,

> Education pricing is available to university students, students accepted into university, parents buying for university students, teachers and staff at all levels.

Pensioners are another age group favoured by heavy discounting. Bus and train firms, barbers and hairdressers, lots of shops and so on all offer lower prices to senior citizens. Notice that such discounts are, not surprisingly, dressed up in positive language: *look what we can do for you now you're retired*. But what's not said is that everyone else is charged a higher price.

Think about the economics behind the example of Apple. Our guess is that Apple thinks that many students would like to buy a Mac or iPad but find them too expensive. A lower price for just this group, though, may have a big effect on demand. In other words for *this* group demand may be price elastic. On the other hand, for everyone else, demand may be less price elastic so cutting prices for everyone would leave Apple worse off.

- Peak and off-peak travel: trains, taxis

Train travel in the morning and early evening usually carries a price premium; travel during the middle of the day or very early or very late is cheapest. Taxi fares are higher late at night. The ride-hire app Uber offers fares that vary according to the level of market activity in a particular city at a particular time.

The economics of price discrimination here have a slightly different emphasis. The travel demands of commuters who need to get to and from work are probably more price inelastic so providers can charge more. Late at night when public transport is infrequent the demand for transport becomes more price inelastic so private-hire fares rise.

- Hotel bookings with different cancellation possibilities

Want a cheaper hotel room? Many hotels offer discounts to customers willing to pay some weeks in advance for a room booking that cannot be cancelled later. If you want to pay at the time of your stay with the right to cancel in the meantime the room will cost more.

- Happy hours in pubs and bars

This is another example of market segmentation by time. In the traditionally quiet period between 5 pm and 7 pm bar owners often seek to attract more customers by heavily discounting drinks.

We can use the concept of consumer surplus from Chapter 3 to better understand the attraction of price discrimination to the monopolist. Figure 5.12 shows demand and supply schedules for a good in a market. The equilibrium price is $20 and the quantity demanded and supplied at this price is 14,000 units. Let's just remind ourselves of the way consumer surplus is interpreted.

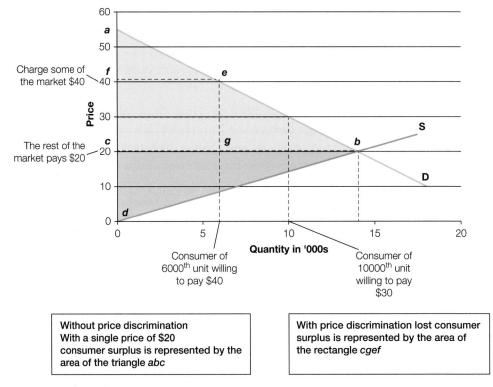

Figure 5.12 Consumer surplus and price discrimination; producer surplus and *your* room to negotiate

Notice that a consumer in the market who buys the 6000th unit pays the market price of $20 but, from their vertical intersection with the demand curve, is willing to pay up to $40. Similarly, the buyer of the 10,000th unit pays $20 but is willing to pay up to $30. In fact it is only the final 14,000th customer who is willing to pay no more than the market price of $20. Adding up all the prices that consumers are willing to pay but don't actually pay gives us total consumer surplus in this market (the triangle *abc*).

If this market is supplied by a monopolist the possibility of price discrimination arises. If the monopolist charges only the market price, consumer surplus in the market amounts to the area of triangle *abc*. Without price discrimination the monopolist would sell 14,000 units at a price of $20 per unit generating $280,000 in revenue. But if the first 6000 customers can be placed in a unique market segment and charged $40 a unit this will generate $240,000 in revenue, while the remaining 8000 customers face a lower price of $20 a unit generating $160,000 in revenue. As a result, the monopolist gains an extra $120,000 in revenue from consumers in the form of appropriated consumer surplus (the rectangle *cgef* in Figure 5.12). Price discrimination pays.

Figure 5.12 also depicts **producer surplus**. This is the total amount suppliers in a market receive above that necessary to induce them to supply the goods in the first place. Take the 6000th unit. The supplier of this unit gets $20 for it

Producer surplus: the total amount suppliers in a market receive above that necessary to induce them to supply the goods in question.

but only needs $8. The supplier of the 10,000th unit also gets $20 but would supply it for $14. The total volume of producer surplus in the market is given by the triangle *dcb*.

● **Think Point**

Is producer surplus a concept worth knowing about? Can you imagine how you might put it to some personal use?

Look again at the 10,000 unit. The minimum amount a supplier wants to supply this unit is $14. The maximum the consumer of this unit would pay is $30. So the transaction potentially happens at a price *anywhere* between $14 and $30. Next time you make a purchase, especially of a big ticket item, think about this. The advertised price may be £250, $750 or €900 but that needn't be the price *you* pay. Unless they're on the extreme right of the likes of Figure 5.12 your supplier will potentially accept a below-market price, just as you may potentially pay an above-market price. So don't just accept the price you're quoted: there's a sound economic basis behind the process of haggling.

Reflections on monopoly

Although allocative inefficiency is a major problem of monopoly, it is not the only one. By definition, monopoly involves some restriction of competition. This has wider significance because competition is the ultimate guarantor of consumer sovereignty. In a competitive market, no single producer is able to set excessively high prices or offer substandard goods or services because others will always be prepared to better meet the perceived demands of consumers. Now, as the whole canon of conventional economic theory rests on the certainty that free markets are indeed created and conditioned by the demands of consumers, the impairment of consumer sovereignty raises some serious questions concerning the validity of economic theory itself. So, just how serious are these questions?

For many economists, there is actually little cause for alarm here. Even where there is an absence of competition and monopoly exists, wider interests usually, at some level, prevail. Consider the following two examples.

Cartel: a group of firms or producers that agree to act as if they were a single firm or producer, for example with regard to pricing and output decisions.

● First, the outcome of the pricing policies of the oil cartel, the Organization of Petroleum Exporting Countries (OPEC) in 1973–4 and 1979. OPEC, which controls a large proportion of the oil consumed by the advanced Western economies, is without doubt a very strong monopoly. For industrialized societies, oil is an important fuel with no readily available substitute. Knowledge of this fact permitted OPEC to reap the rewards of a *fourfold* increase in the price of oil in 1973–4, followed by a further *twofold* increase in 1979. The *initial* response in the oil-importing nations was stoicism: oil was vital and nothing could replace it, so the higher prices simply had to be met. OPEC's monopoly seemed then to have placed it in an extremely powerful position and further price increases might have been expected. However, although OPEC was not threatened by any serious competition, its ability to control events in the market was sharply curtailed in the first half of the 1980s and the price of oil actually *fell* over this period. Why? The answer lies in the response of the oil-importing nations to the price rises: they scaled back their demand for oil as, for instance, people began to run cars with smaller engines.

This example reveals the limits to monopoly. Even where something close to a pure monopoly exists, the monopolist is not free to set *any* price he or she likes without suffering the consequences. The basic law of demand – that at higher prices less will be demanded (and *vice versa*) – will assert itself through the actions of consumers. Yet even if consumers are the ultimate source of authority in the face of monopoly, this does *not* mean that monopoly can simply be ignored as an economic issue. In the OPEC case, the oil price increases caused major problems of adjustment for the oil-importing nations. Countries all over the world experienced difficulties in adapting to the changed relative price of oil. Monopolies may cause significant *disruption* to markets for a time, which would be less likely to occur in more competitive environments.

- Second, what of the noted encouragement of monopolies by governments? How does this policy – implemented through the granting of patents, trademarks, copyrights and design rights – square with the notion that monopolists dominate markets and act contrary to social preferences over resource allocation? It is not that governments favour the creation of monopolies per se, rather that they recognize monopoly as an important potential source of *innovation* in the economy.

Innovation is a challenging process. As we saw in the Pfizer case study, it may require years of effort and heavy investment to develop a new marketable product or piece of technology. There would be little point in a firm spending decades and large sums of money in, say, coming up with a cure for the common cold if, as soon as it was put on the market, rival manufacturers simply made a generic copy to sell. However, an incentive to undertake the necessary research and development is created when firms are granted patents on their inventions for a period of time. This argument was first advanced by Joseph Schumpeter. Schumpeter also suggested that the greater size of the typical monopolist would enable it to finance research and development on a scale beyond the capabilities of smaller firms. In this view then, while monopoly might indeed restrict output, raise price and misallocate resources, these are not the only criteria by which it should be judged. Monopoly may also an important source of innovation in the modern economy.

Government control of monopoly

Market failure: arises where the market either fails to provide certain goods, or fails to provide them at their optimal or most desirable level.

We now turn to the question of the extent to which monopoly should be controlled or regulated by the state. If monopolies can disrupt markets, if they can set high prices because competitors are absent or, indeed, if they are able to offer poorer quality goods or services because the consumer has little other choice available, should the state – recognizing a case of market failure – step in and do something to rectify matters? In practice, most governments in Western economies do, though as we shall see in Chapter 6, some economists of the *liberal school* think that state intervention to control monopoly may actually create bigger problems than monopoly itself.

As noted, in the UK, issues of monopoly are investigated by the Competition Commission. This agency decides whether or not a monopoly – or potential monopoly in the case of a proposed merger between firms – is likely to be against the public interest. A second government agency, the Office of Fair Trading, has the job of initially recommending that particular monopolies or mergers should be investigated. This rather convoluted process is designed to prevent the Competition Commission becoming 'judge and jury' in a case. The chapter's final case study summarizes a recent interesting instance of local monopoly regulation involving Tesco, the UK's largest supermarket chain.

BUSINESS CASE STUDY

Competition Commission forces Tesco sell-off

Tesco's slogan 'every little helps' has been given an unusual twist in Slough, Berkshire, where the Competition Commission has prompted Tesco to give a little help to its competitors by requiring it to sell off a prime retail site to one of its closest rivals.

Tesco bought the site from the Co-op and used it as a temporary home while its major Slough superstore underwent a refit.

After the refit Tesco indicated to the Office of Fair Trading that it was actively seeking to sell the Co-op site to another supermarket chain, allowing competition and choice for Slough consumers to be restored to their former levels.

However, Tesco missed an Office of Fair Trading (OFT) deadline to complete the sale and, concerned about the effect of the loss of the Co-op store on competition in grocery retailing in Slough, the OFT referred the case to the Competition Commission for investigation.

The Competition Commission reviewed a number of issues including:

- whether the absence of a retailer on the Co-op site made it possible for Tesco to 'unilaterally increase prices or otherwise worsen its retail offer to consumers'
- whether the closure of the Co-op 'may have reduced the competitive pressures faced by all the stores in the relevant market'.

Ultimately the Commission concluded that Tesco's purchase of the Co-op site did threaten a 'substantial lessening of competition' in the Slough grocery market in particular because a competitive constraint on the existing Tesco superstore had been removed by the closure of the neighbouring Co-op.

The Competition Commission's remedy was to require Tesco to sell the site so that a competitor might make use of it, with the proviso that Tesco would not be expected to accept too low a price for an asset which had cost it time and money.

Subsequently, the site was sold to Sainsbury's for redevelopment to host a new superstore – a direct rival to the neighbouring Tesco superstore and a general stimulus to competition in the Slough grocery market.

Monopsony: arises where there is a dominant buyer in a market.

Before leaving the topic of monopoly it is worth noting that market power arising from the exclusivity that a firm possesses in a market as a seller can also result when the firm is an exclusive or dominant *buyer*. Such a firm is known as a **monopsony**. For example, Amazon distributes very large numbers of goods through the post, making it a major purchaser of postal services all over the world. This means that suppliers of postal services to Amazon, while they're fortunate to be dealing with a rock-solid multinational company, may at the same time have to accept any hard bargains that Amazon may occasionally drive.

5.6 Imperfect competition (also known as monopolistic competition)

Imperfect competition[2] and oligopoly (see Section 5.7 below) are the two intermediate market structures that lie between the *extremes* of perfect competition and monopoly. Both exhibit a greater degree of competition than monopoly. Like monopolies, imperfectly competitive firms and oligopolies are *price makers*. They are, in other words, able to set prices independently of their competitors. Recall that *price-taking* firms in perfect competition must all take the market price as given.

Imperfectly competitive firms are price makers because they sell *differentiated* products. Differentiated products are similar to each other but they do possess some distinguishing features. As noted, city-centre pubs and bars, for example, might be thought to be in imperfect competition. There are plenty of them and they mostly sell the same beers, wines and spirits. The market is also relatively easy to enter and leave. The distinguishing features here might be the ambience of any particular establishment, its opening hours, particular clientele, or the price and quality of its cocktails or beer.

As price makers, imperfectly competitive firms face a normal downward sloping demand/average revenue curve, such as that depicted in Figure 5.8. They also have a marginal revenue curve of the same general form as the MR curve in the figure. Moreover, we know that the average and marginal cost curves of all firms are similar to those in Figure 5.2. Putting all this information together, and assuming profit maximization, we arrive at a supernormal profit position for the imperfectly competitive firm that is identical to that of the long-run position of the monopolist (as depicted in Figure 5.9). However, for the imperfectly competitive firm, this is a *short-run* position only. An imperfectly competitive market allows firms freedom of entry and exit (without freedom of entry monopoly is created). Thus, because supernormal profits attract new entrants, the demand/AR curves of all firms in the market shift to the left as the level of demand is 'shared out' between more firms. This means that imperfectly competitive firms will, in the long run, earn only *normal profits*. New firms continue to enter the market until all supernormal profit is eroded. The long-run position of the representative imperfectly competitive firm is depicted in Figure 5.13. As always, the profit-maximizing output, at Q_1, is determined by the MC = MR rule. That only normal profits are earned here is evident because total revenue and total cost are equal (both are represented by the rectangle

---

2 Imperfect competition is also sometimes referred to as monopolistic competition as it blends elements of monopoly with competition.

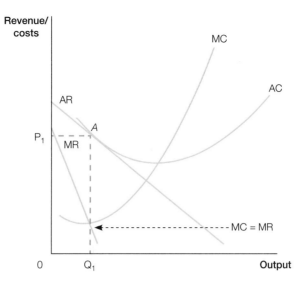

Figure 5.13 The long-run position of the imperfectly competitive firm

$0P_1AQ_1$). Notice also that, unlike the firm in a perfectly competitive industry, the firm is not producing at the lowest point of its average cost curve.

5.7   Oligopoly

Oligopoly: a market structure in which a small number of firms compete with each other.

Oligopoly arises where there are a small number of firms in an industry, each large in relation to the overall size of the market that the firms serve. Oligopoly is also typified by barriers to entry that make access to the market difficult for new firms. This means that profits earned by oligopolists are not easily eroded, as is the case in imperfect competition. On the other hand, oligopolistic markets are not impossible to enter. We can identify several ways in which oligopolists protect their markets.

- Some oligopolistic markets may be difficult to enter because of the size of the incumbent firms. For example, the *global* manufacturing of mobile phones was for a long time dominated by just three firms: Samsung, Apple and Nokia, which together accounted for about 50 per cent of the market. To have competed effectively with these firms even in the medium term would have been extremely difficult and very risky. Any new firms would have to produce (and sell) in enormous volumes relatively quickly and at immense cost, with the chance that their business strategies might fail. Note however that entry is far from impossible. Firms with a winning product – such as Apple's iPhone – can certainly enter the market and grow organically. Alternatively, it's also possible, as Microsoft has recently done with its enormous $4.6bn purchase of Nokia, to buy a handset manufacturer and lever yourself into the market at an incumbent's expense.

Organic growth: the growth of a firm from its own resources.

- Oligopolistic markets may also be difficult to enter because of the production and sales strategies of incumbent firms. A famous example here is the UK soap powder industry which has just two main players: Unilever and Procter &

Gamble. Unilever brands include Persil, Surf and OMO, while Procter & Gamble produces Ariel, Bold, Daz and Fairy. These products are also usually available in a variety of forms – biological, non-bio, liquid and tablet. All this means that a new entrant to the market with an ambition to compete on an equal footing with Unilever and Procter & Gamble would probably need, from the outset, to produce and market at least three distinct laundry products, each in a variety of bio, non-bio and other forms – in total that's a *dozen* or so products for just a third of the market. Again, not impossible but the cost and associated risk is much higher than if the incumbent firms did not follow a sophisticated strategy of product diversification.

- Another barrier to entry arises from the weight and authority that oligopolists lend to their products through the creation of brands. Because they are usually well resourced and dominant in the market, incumbent firms are able to establish levels of brand recognition that new entrants would find difficult to effectively challenge or dislodge. Sometimes branding can be so successful that the brand becomes the product. For example, a common or even preferred name for a vacuum cleaner? A hoover. But this is actually a firm with a brand and registered trademark that's passed into language, as in: 'Seven-year-old Layla was so hungry she simply hoovered up her Spaghetti'.

Brand dominance can be challenged – the success of the Dyson range is testament to that, with Dyson vacuum cleaners remarkably gaining UK market dominance less than two years after their launch. But it must be galling for James Dyson to hear his revolutionary product casually referred to as a hoover. Still, language develops at a slower pace than technology so perhaps one day Layla's grandchildren will be dysoning up their spaghetti.

Is this a hoover? No, it's a Dyson

Courtesy of Dyson

Oligopoly and price stability

An unusual characteristic of the oligopolistic market is the degree of *price stability* it is sometimes thought to exhibit. An example? Think about cinema ticket prices. Is there much price competition between different cinemas in your experience? We suggest not. Prices may vary according to the time of day, or whether you choose a particular seat or a 3D film but, generally, there doesn't seem much point in going to a particular cinema because it's cheaper. They all charge more or less the same. So there appears to be an absence of price competition between cinema operators.

What about forms of *non-price* competition between oligopolists? It's hard to discern many in

Image Source/Image Source/Jasper White CM

How does Vodafone compete? By advertising VIP access to events rather than by simply offering cheaper airtime

cinemas; the service tends to be pretty standard and, anyway, once you're there in the dark with your popcorn it's the quality of the film that counts. But this isn't the case in some other oligopolistic markets. Mobile phone service providers are an example. These companies are selling something that is homogeneous: airtime. What's the difference between EE's airtime and Vodafone's? Customers may not discern any, so service providers compete by heavily advertising the extras they offer with their networks.

Remember Orange Wednesdays and two-for-one cinema tickets? O_2? Top-up surprises and priority concert tickets, as that bloke from the first season of *Game of Thrones* keeps reminding us. Vodafone? The chance to get VIP access to 'some of Britain's best events'. So fairly elaborate, intensive and, not least in terms of advertising, costly competition of a non-price form.

Why is there a tendency towards price stability in oligopoly?

The examples we've looked at so far tend to suggest that oligopolistic firms have a unique business problem – they must continually think about and react to the actions and even anticipated actions of their rivals in a way that firms in other market structures don't have to. For example, the pure monopolist is insulated from such worries because, in this case, the firm and the industry are one and the same thing and competitor firms do not exist. Similarly, we know that imperfectly competitive firms are price makers so they have the capacity to make independent pricing and output decisions that may impact upon their competitors but, because each is relatively small in relation to the market, it is unlikely that such decisions could affect the plans of large numbers of rival firms. One tanning salon out of 100 in a large city that doubled its prices would go out of business pretty quickly. If it halved its prices it would be swamped with tan-seekers and couldn't cope in the short run (where capital inputs are fixed). Either way, the other 99 tanning salons would in all likelihood continue serenely on. What other firms do doesn't matter much in this market structure. Finally, in perfect competition because firms are price takers, they simply accept the ruling market price and cannot make independent pricing decisions. Here, rival firms don't matter because they *can't* do anything differently.

But the defining characteristic of oligopoly – a small number of firms that are large in relation to the market – means that the pricing strategies of each firm are of *vital* concern to its competitors. If Orange suspects that O_2 is about to cut its tariffs should it do the same? Were Orange not to follow O_2's lead it would

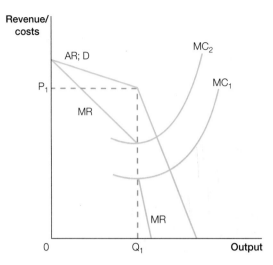

Figure 5.14 Price stability under oligopoly

probably lose business. On the other hand, is it wise for O_2 to cut tariffs if it anticipates that Orange and other network providers will simply do the same? Here prices fall across the market but relative market shares are unchanged so all firms are probably worse off. You see the problem? Doing *nothing* in price competitive terms begins to look the safest business strategy and again we come back to the price stability of the oligopolistic marketplace.

Figure 5.14 offers a slightly more formal interpretation of the tendency for price stability to emerge among oligopolistic firms. The key feature here is the *kinked* AR or demand curve which is steeper below price P_1 and flatter above it. Why is the curve kinked? The answer has to do with the kind of strategic uncertainties we referred to in our Orange/O_2 example above.

- Any oligopolist contemplating a price cut below P_1 may worry that, should some or all of its rivals follow suit, the demand curve it faces below P_1 may be relatively price inelastic. This means that price cuts will produce a less-than-proportionate extension in quantity demanded and leave the firm worse off. So price reductions don't look good.
- On the other hand, the firm may also worry that if it increases price, few or none of its rivals will follow its lead, meaning that above P_1 demand is relatively price elastic. In other words price increases will prompt a more-than-proportionate contraction in demand, again leaving the firm worse off. So price increases don't look good either. The oligopolistic firm's preferred strategy may therefore be price stability.

Nash equilibrium: a situation where economic agents optimize their actions, given the choices made by other parties.

If price stability does emerge this is an example of a Nash equilibrium, named after the Nobel Prize winner (for work done at age 21) John Nash. Nash equilibrium occurs when economic agents choose a preferred course of action given the choices made by others. Remember that equilibrium means no tendency to change. In the case of oligopoly this translates as price stability given the trepidation of each firm about the responses of its rivals to any price change it might make.

There is one further twist in Figure 5.14. Notice that the kinked demand curve produces a gap or discontinuity in the marginal revenue curve at the profit-maximizing output level Q_1, where MC = MR. This gap makes it possible for the firm to absorb modest increases in cost (in the range MC_1 to MC_2) without these prompting changes in price or output.

5.8   Oligopoly and game theory

Oligopolies are *interdependent* – what other firms in this market structure do matters in ways that do not arise in perfect competition, imperfect competition or monopoly. So far, we have suggested that this interdependence produces a degree of price stability that is particular to oligopoly. In this section we introduce an approach – game theory – that allows us to analyse the relationships between oligopolists in a rather different and interesting way.

Game theory is a powerful tool that can be used to explore a wide variety of economic and non-economic relationships. Chess and poker are examples of games of strategy. How do you win? By anticipating the possible reactions of opponents to your moves and by revealing as little about your intentions as you are able. Lots of things in life are done in a similar way. Here are some examples.

- Have you renewed your car insurance lately? The renewal process usually goes something like this. Your insurance company sends you a letter inviting you to renew at a price that's possibly a bit higher than last year. 'What?' you think, 'I haven't made a claim, why should I pay more? They're having a laugh.' Hugely irritated, you find a cheaper quote on a comparison website and phone your existing provider to decline their rather insulting offer. Instantly, they're placatory. 'We don't want to lose your business, Madam, please bear with me while I see if I can get you a better rate.' And, amazingly, they can! They also cheekily ask about the best offer you've had from the comparison site. What's happening here? Well, you're actually in a *game* with your insurer. The game might have ended with your simply accepting the original quote, or it might go through several stages with new and better offers from several insurers during which they try to get you to reveal game-pertinent information about yourself and each other.

- Two drivers are approaching each other down a narrow street that's partially blocked by a parked car. The driver that should give way accelerates aggressively to try to squeeze by. Does the other driver

Would you give way to this nutcase or take him on?

© iStockphoto.com/Kirk Johnson

slow down, or assert their right and accelerate too? This is another game. Does the game change if the aggressive driver has a shaven head and is in a 4 × 4? What might happen if the second car is old with lots of dents and scrapes and the 4 × 4 is pristine? (This example comes from Thomas Schelling, a Nobel Prize–winning game theorist.)

- The British government continues to wrestle with the problem of whether to replace its very costly submarine-based nuclear deterrent. Might a reduced nuclear capability make UK citizens more or less safe from nuclear attack? Possessing these weapons would make an attack on the UK by a belligerent very risky. But, on the other hand, a non-nuclear-capable UK might not be a target should a nuclear exchange occur. The defence choices of countries can also be analysed using game theory.

The most famous illustration of game theory is known as the *prisoners' dilemma*. In this scenario two people have been detained for alleged crimes they committed together. Their interrogators make it clear to each separately held prisoner that they have enough evidence to secure a guilty verdict on one crime that carries a light sentence. But the prisoners are each given a choice. If they confess and implicate their partner in other crimes they will go free while the partner gets life imprisonment. But if both confess to other crimes then both will receive medium-term sentences. It's a tricky choice which turns on trust in your partner. Table 5.1 shows the outcomes for each prisoner in a payoff matrix.

Kate knows that denying the crime carries both the promise of a light sentence and a risk of life. If she trusts Libby she'll deny the crime and if she's right to do so they both get a light sentence as in the top-left quadrant. But if she's wrong and Libby confesses, then in the top-right-hand quadrant the result is life for Kate and freedom for Libby because Libby's done the dirty and implicated her partner. Were Kate to confess, on the other hand, she would be exposed at worst to a medium sentence and at best she'd go free depending on Libby's choice (the bottom right and left quadrants respectively).

So what should Kate do? If she thinks Libby will deny the crimes she should confess and go free. But if she thinks Libby will admit them and implicate her, Kate's best option is *still* to confess so she gets a medium sentence rather than life. Kate has a **dominant strategy** to confess whatever Libby does. A dominant strategy in a game is one that is best regardless of the choices of another player.

Dominant strategy: a course of action that a player in a game follows regardless of the decisions of other players.

Table 5.1 The prisoners' dilemma

		Libby	
		Deny	**Confess**
Kate	**Deny**	light sentence, light sentence	life, freedom
	Confess	freedom, life	medium sentence, medium sentence

Following the same line of reasoning Libby too has a dominant strategy to confess in order to avoid the risk of a life sentence. Confessing may bring freedom but at worst it carries a medium sentence. So both confess. But note that had they trusted each other and denied the other crimes both Kate and Libby would have been better off, each receiving a light sentence instead of a medium one.

How does game theory help us to understand the interactions between oligopolistic firms? It seems that the quandaries of the prisoners' dilemma are echoed in the strategic business questions that confront oligopolies. Table 5.2 sketches out some alternative scenarios for two fictional firms in an oligopolistic market: Red Bus Ltd and Blue Bus Ltd. The choice these firms face is whether to raise fares. Let's think about each in turn.

- **Red Bus** decides to increase its fares; it will gain £4m should Blue Bus do the same. But if Blue Bus keeps its fares unchanged, Red Bus will suffer a fall in revenue of £2m.
- What if **Red Bus** decides to keep its fares unchanged? It gains £3m if Blue Bus puts its fares up. If Blue Bus also keeps its fares unchanged, Red Bus experiences no change in revenue.
- *Conclusion?* **Red Bus** has a dominant strategy (that is, one that disregards the Blue Bus decision) to keep its fares unchanged to avoid the risk of a major collapse in revenue.
- For **Blue Bus** the same argument holds. If it increases its fares, it will gain £6m if Red Bus follows its lead. But if Red Bus doesn't follow suit and keeps its fares at their current level, Blue Bus will lose £4m.
- If **Blue Bus** keeps its fares unchanged it will gain £5m should Red Bus raise fares, but will experience no change in revenue if Red Bus also keeps its fares steady.
- *Conclusion?* **Blue Bus** too has a dominant strategy to keep fares at their current level to avoid the risk of a substantial revenue loss.

But, as per the prisoners' dilemma, there is an apparently better option for both firms were they to trust each other. If both raised their fares, each would make a substantial gain in revenue. Trust implies some kind of collusive agreement or cartel. In certain circumstances this might be possible. As we have seen, OPEC is a cartel of oil-producing countries. In Chapter 2 we discussed OPEC's manipulation of international oil production and through this the world oil price.

Table 5.2 A payoff matrix for oligopolists

		Blue Bus Ltd	
		Raise fare	No change
Red Bus Ltd	Raise fare	+**£4m**, +£6m	−**£2m**, +£5m
	No change	+**£3m**, −£4m	**same revenue**, same revenue

However, for our two bus firms matters are likely to be more difficult. First, because they seriously inhibit competition and work against the interests of consumers, cartels are illegal in many countries. In the UK a firm that is found to be a member of a cartel can be fined up to 10 per cent of its worldwide turnover and its executives convicted of a *criminal* offence that carries a sentence of up to 5 years' imprisonment. Second, there is every chance that cartel members will renounce one another. Indeed, in the UK, the authorities actively encourage cartel members to voluntarily admit what they have been doing with the promise of complete immunity from prosecution so that the remaining firms in the cartel and their executives bear the full brunt of the law – a kind of confessors' charter. So maintaining a cartel is a very risky business. It may make you better off but for how long can you trust your partners?

The answer is about a year if a case in the airline industry is anything to go by. In 2007 British Airways was fined £121.5m by the authorities after it admitted to collusion with Virgin Atlantic over the level of fuel surcharges it required passengers to pay. The fine was the heaviest on record for anti-competitive behaviour in the UK. Virgin Atlantic avoided any penalty because although it was the other partner in the illegal cartel it had informed the authorities about the price-fixing arrangement the two companies had entered into. Price fixing had pushed up fuel surcharges from £5 to £60 between 2004 and 2006. Following this civil case criminal proceedings were launched against four BA executives but their trial collapsed.

Real-world dominant strategies in oligopoly

Though the rigging of markets in cartel-type operations is anti-competitive and illegal there are lots of other ways in which oligopolistic firms may choose to strategically cooperate rather than aggressively compete. A little earlier in this chapter we noted the economic rationale behind patents. Patents are a source of monopoly power but they are also the principal way in which firms are incentivized to innovate. Usually, then, we would expect firms to jealously guard patents they own. A famous recent case involves the claim and counter-claim between Apple and Samsung over the ownership of aspects of smartphone and tablet technology. In 2012 Apple sued Samsung for patent infringements and won $1bn; in 2014 it sued again, this time for $2bn. Samsung countered that *its* patents have been infringed by Apple. Given the scale and dynamism of the smartphone and tablet markets the stakes here are enormous; our guess is that the lawyers will be busy for some time yet.

Apple's dominant strategy is clear: *sue the pants off anyone that we think rips off our technology.* Apple's boss, the late Steve Jobs, once promised a 'thermonuclear war' to this end. In game-theoretic terms the approach has much to recommend it. Thomas Schelling argues that any bargaining position may be strengthened by permanently surrendering freedom of choice *and being seen to have done so.* If the rest of the industry took Jobs at his word – and Apple's willingness to litigate is proof of its seriousness – then the wider industry's strategic considerations in dealing with Apple might soften. Schelling offers a memorable example to illustrate his point:

> If a man knocks at the door and says that he will stab himself on the porch unless given $10, he is more likely to get the $10 if his eyes are bloodshot.

In other words you believe the door-stepper not just because he sounds crazy but because he *looks* crazy. Metaphorically, Steve Job's nuclear war threat was the 'sound crazy' element but Apple's readiness to sue is the equivalent of corporate bloodshot eyes. You *know* what's going to happen should you infringe Apple's patents.

But, thinking strategically in an oligopolistic setting, is such a decisively aggressive approach the only way? Actually, no. In the car industry the move from petrol and diesel engines to those powered by electricity is a key technological issue. It might be expected that innovating firms would be fiercely protective of new engine designs. But this hasn't been the case for Tesla, an American electric car maker. In an imaginative leap, Tesla has effectively decided to rip up the patents it holds and share its technology on an open-source basis. Such a move might at first glance seem odd: why render valuable assets in intellectual property worthless? Tesla's concern is the vested interests of the traditional big car firms in preserving fossil-fuel power. The company claims that the big car firms' output of non-hydrocarbon vehicles is less than 1 per cent of their total production. Tesla on its own can do nothing about the industry's hydrocarbon bias but if it shares its research and motivates other firms to also engage in electric vehicle research there is a much better chance that this alternative technology platform will develop to the point where it challenges the status quo and the global economy gets a new and viable electric car market. So Tesla's dominant strategy is to cooperate with its rivals rather than compete in the traditional patent-safeguarding manner.

5.9   Market structures: an institutionalist view

Having reviewed the four major market structures identified by economic theory – perfect competition, imperfect competition, oligopoly and monopoly – an obvious question now arises as to the relative importance of each in the real economy. Although perfect competition has been presented as an ideal, its near neighbour – imperfect competition – appears to possess some important attributes that might be thought to recommend it over both oligopoly and monopoly. In particular, the imperfectly competitive market retains a high degree of openness and intensity of competition and firms operating within such a market structure have few powers of market exclusion. The key to their survival must, therefore, be their ability to remain competitive, one against the other, in the way that they satisfy consumer demands. It follows that, if an economy is characterized by the presence of many imperfect markets, the pre-eminence of consumer sovereignty is still firmly established. Such an economy will be close to, if not quite at, Adam Smith's ideal. So what do modern advanced economies actually look like? Do they approximate imperfect competition or do they tend to be dominated by oligopoly and monopoly?

Of the various schools of economic analysis, *institutionalism* has the most decisive perspective on such questions, particularly in the writings of J.K. Galbraith (1908–2006). Galbraith's work concentrated on the American economy but its generalities are applicable to the other advanced capitalist nations in Europe and the Far East. Galbraith's primary claim is that, in many respects, these economies are *increasingly* dominated by relatively small numbers of extremely large and therefore *powerful* firms. Power here means the ability to manipulate and control one's own environment. Thus, Galbraith argued, the largest firms are able to organize the markets in which they are situated to the exclusion of other interests, such as those of smaller firms and – especially – the consumer.

This situation is a relatively new one. The capitalism of the eighteenth and nineteenth centuries was not of this form – it was typified by the kind of imperfectly competitive markets characterized above. *Then*, the tenet of consumer sovereignty generally applied. But in the interim, and especially since 1945, the key *institutions* of capitalism – including the firm – have undergone profound change. This postwar period has witnessed not only the emergence of giant firms but also the development of 'big' government and large trade unions. Galbraith argued that the reshaping of these key institutions of capitalism has important implications for the way the system actually works and, moreover, in *whose interests* it works. Here we concentrate on his analysis of firms.

The emergence of significant numbers of large firms across a variety of industries in the advanced capitalist economies since 1945 is, in the institutionalist view, the result of rapid *technological development* over this period. We noted in Chapter 3 that Henry Ford's adoption of the flow-line method of car assembly, while making cars cheaper and easier to produce, required the overall scale of production to be much bigger than it had ever been before. As elements of 'Fordism' were taken up by other industries, they too increased their scales of production. In industries unsuited to the flow-line, other forms of technological change with associated high investment costs also tended to make the efficient scale of production higher such that, again, the size of firms tended to increase.

So how far has this process gone? In Galbraith's view, about *half* of private-sector production in the United States rests in the hands of large firms that are either monopolies or oligopolies. The other half can be attributed to firms that broadly conform to the rules of imperfect competition. In this latter segment then, the principle of consumer sovereignty still applies: in attempting to maximize profits, firms must prioritize the interests of consumers and the course of production is strongly conditioned by consumer demand. Galbraith called the uncompetitive part of the economy the *planning system* and the competitive part the *market system*. The term 'planning' is appropriate because firms in this sector are able to plan and direct the development of their own markets. This is clearly a very strong assertion and, moreover, one that flies in the face of the orthodoxy of consumer sovereignty; how is it justified?

As noted, the institutionalist approach suggests a link between the *size* and *power* of a firm. Now, there can be no doubt that the leading firms in the advanced economies are indeed extremely large. For example, the total annual sales of the US oil giant ExxonMobil have in recent years been greater than the national incomes of countries such as Norway, Denmark and New Zealand. But how *precisely* does scale translate into power? Galbraith's claim is that the largest firms enjoy a measure of influence over consumers, costs and prices that escapes smaller firms. Let us think about each of these spheres of influence in a little more detail.

Consumers

To take the first case, consumers are clearly receptive to advertising, or firms – large and small – would not bother to do it. The largest and best-resourced firms will be able to afford the heaviest advertising – this is also clear. But what does advertising do? In the conventional view, it allows the individual firm to provide information about its product in the hope of persuading people of its particular merit. Ford promotes the Focus in the hope that car buyers will prefer it to a Toyota or a Renault. For Galbraith, however, the picture is complicated when one considers the combined and cumulative effect of advertising by the car industry as a whole. This amounts to continuous persuasion not that this car or that car is better but that *private motoring* is desirable in itself. While this might indeed be the case, private motoring is only one way of getting from place to place. An obvious alternative would be to take an environmentally friendly bus. But are bus services promoted as extravagantly as new cars? The answer is no, because bus firms are generally smaller and not so well off as carmakers. The effect of plentiful car advertising is then to affirm a psychological desire for private motoring above other forms of transport when, in fact, the material *need* is only for mobility. Now, although virtually all firms can and do advertise, the superior resources of the planning sector mean that only its members are likely to be able to generate persuasion on a scale sufficient for general product affirmation, such as that achieved by the giant car firms. None of this means that consumers become mere dupes of the planning system but it does suggest that firms in the planning system can fix the interests and generate the allegiance of consumers in ways denied to the smaller firms in the market system.

Costs and prices

Their scale also permits firms in the planning system to exert unusually strong influence over costs and prices. A good example of cost control is the power that the major UK supermarkets have over the producers of food and other goods that they sell. Because the largest supermarkets now account for the vast proportion of retail sales their suppliers are forced into a subordinate business relationship for want of many alternative outlets for the goods they produce.

Turning now to prices, we have already characterized imperfectly competitive firms, oligopolies and monopolies as price makers but there is an important difference between the first of these and the other two in the extent to which the prices they set have significance in the wider market. The ability of the imperfectly competitive firm to establish a unique price is conditioned by the degree of product differentiation it can achieve in a crowded and fairly competitive market. Even when substantial product differentiation permits relatively high prices to be set compared to the market norm, these have no general market relevance: consumers can elect to buy the product in question or choose a readily available and cheaper alternative. In markets dominated by oligopoly and monopoly the situation is rather different. Here, because most production is (at best) shared among a small number of large firms, whatever prices are set tend to be significant for the market as a whole because consumer choice is relatively limited. This is most apparent in the case of pure monopoly but it is also a familiar trait in oligopoly where there tends to be a degree of price stability among firms, with competition, such as it is, tending to assume non-price forms. Once again then, firms in the planning system enjoy a measure of market control far beyond that available to their counterparts in the market system.

The implications of this analysis are profound. Galbraith referred to the notion of consumer sovereignty as the 'accepted sequence', meaning that the chain of command in a market economy flows from the consumer to the producer. As we have seen, Galbraith's work contends that, in the market system at least, the accepted sequence works largely as anticipated and the firm is subordinate to the consumer. However, given the conditions outlined above, in the planning system there is a dramatic reversal of influence. Here, the firm has the *power* to shape and control the market and to impose its priorities and preferences on the consumer; in Galbraith's phrase there is then a 'revised sequence' as consumer sovereignty is replaced by *producer* sovereignty. While conventional economics does not wholly ignore the concept of power – independent price making and market exclusion are clearly forms of power – in the institutionalist view it fails to recognize the extent of the power of the planning sector and its negative implications for the trumpeted ideals of competitive capitalism.

SUMMARY

- Firms that are able to set their price independently are said to possess a degree of market power.
- Economic theory recognizes four market structures: perfect competition, imperfect competition, oligopoly and monopoly. Perfect competition provides an idealized view of how markets would work given the highest possible level of competition between their constituent firms. Its principal attributes are absolute consumer sovereignty and the socially efficient allocation of resources. Although the assumptions of perfect competition are not all met in the real economy, it provides a useful benchmark against which the relative merits of actual market structures may be assessed.
- In contrast to perfect competition, pure monopoly is characterized by an absence of competition. This inevitably entails a misallocation of resources. However, it is not the case that monopolies always restrict output and raise prices to the detriment of the consumer. In the case of natural monopoly, a single supplier may raise output and lower prices to levels that could not be achieved in a competitive environment. Nor need monopolies be especially large. Monopoly is defined by barriers to entry, not size. Finally, monopolies necessarily impinge upon the sovereignty of the consumer.
- Firms in the two remaining market structures are, like monopoly, price makers. Arguably, oligopoly is characterized by lower levels of competition and weak consumer sovereignty, while imperfect competition, because it retains competitiveness, necessarily prioritizes consumer interests.
- Finally, the work of J.K. Galbraith contends that large parts of modern capitalist economies tend towards oligopolistic and monopoly organization. This poses serious questions as to the ultimate *raison d'etre* of the contemporary capitalist system: whose interests does it primarily serve – those of the consumer or the producer?

KEY TERMS

- Market power
- Market structure
- Perfect competition
- Monopoly
- Resource misallocation
- Deadweight loss
- Monopsony
- Imperfect competition
- Oligopoly
- Price taker
- Price maker
- Normal and supernormal profit
- Game theory
- Nash equilibrium
- Institutionalism
- Planning system
- Market system
- Accepted sequence
- Revised sequence

QUESTIONS FOR DISCUSSION

1. Why should the profit-maximizing firm always produce at that output which equates marginal cost with marginal revenue?
2. To what extent might the following exert monopoly power – a late-night corner shop; a 'local' pub; the *Financial Times* newspaper; British Gas; the Channel Tunnel?
3. Do monopolies tend always to raise price and lower output?
4. What is the significance of Galbraith's notion of the 'revised sequence'?

EVERYDAY ECONOMICS 5.1 ANSWERS

1. **The Great Wall of China** The Great Wall is a UNESCO World Heritage Site and one of the most visited tourist attractions in China. Of itself the Great Wall is a barrier to market entry because it's unique. This gives economic activity connected to Great Wall tourism a degree of market power: prices can be set somewhat higher because of an absence of close competition.

2. **Luis Suarez** Luis bites people so that's not good. But he seems to be able to play football very well. Possibly better than anyone else in the world according to some people. Luis's skill is a barrier to entry to the elite levels of professional football faced by the less-skilled. This means he's able to charge very high prices

for his services: to football clubs choosing to employ him and to firms that want him to endorse their products. There may be fewer of the latter in future. Following Luis's chomp on an Italian opponent at the World Cup in Brazil, 888poker promptly ended his sponsorship deal. Good!

3. **The Sydney Harbour Bridge** Like the Great Wall of China, the Sydney Harbour Bridge is a spectacular sight but the economic issue here is more its function than its appearance. The bridge crosses the Parramatta River and links Sydney to North Sydney and beyond. To drive between these two places there's no other choice than to use the bridge or its sister tunnel, both operated by the New

South Wales state government. This is a considerable barrier to entry that allows the bridge and tunnel operator to levy tolls on its customers.

4. **Noma Restaurant, Copenhagen** Copenhagen, the capital of Denmark, is stuffed with restaurants of all kinds so why should we pick out this one? In 2014 Noma regained the title of the world's best restaurant. There can only be one of these at a time, so, while it lasts, it's an impermeable barrier to entry. Copenhagen's a pricey city and Noma is, given its market power, a very pricey restaurant. Private dining there comes in at a minimum spend of 25,000 krona (about £2700 or €3400), though this is for up to 18 people.

ONE THING YOU SHOULD READ

J.K. Galbraith's *Economics and the Public Purpose*, Chapter 9 'The Nature of Collective Intelligence'

This book is the third in a trilogy in which Galbraith's critique of large and powerful corporations is developed. In Chapter 9 Galbraith offers a summary of the nature and importance of the *technostructure*. This is a term he uses to describe the agents who collectively control and direct the modern corporation.

   Read the chapter and answer the following questions.

1. What kind of people make up the technostructure and how are they able to gain decisive influence over the firms in which they work?
2. What are the motivations of the technostructure and how do these affect the assumption of conventional economics that firms maximize profit?

3. What do you think of Galbraith's arguments? Their apparent implication is that the influence of business leaders of the calibre of, say, Sir Richard Branson or Rupert Murdoch on their own firms is limited. Do you agree?
4. After answering question 3, have a look at the websites of News Corp and 21st Century Fox and see how far these firms, both chaired by Rupert Murdoch, stretch across cable networking, filmed entertainment, television, satellite television, publishing and other activities. Now what do you think? (newscorp.com and 21cf.com).

6

business and government

KEY ISSUES

Do markets sometimes fail to produce desirable outcomes in coordinating the demand and supply of some goods and services?

If markets do 'fail', can the state intervene to correct the problem?

Or might the state itself similarly fail when it intervenes in markets?

What kinds of relationship between business and government are implied by market failure?

What kinds of policy might governments pursue to help business perform better?

CONTENTS

6.1	Introduction	**188**
6.2	Market failure	**189**
6.3	Public goods	**190**
6.4	Externalities	**194**
6.5	Public goods, externalities and business	**204**
6.6	The liberal view: market failure and state failure	**206**
6.7	Privatization	**210**
6.8	Competition policy	**214**
6.9	Industrial policy	**215**

6.1   Introduction

Chapters 1 and 2 of this book discussed the view that the free and competitive market system can be an effective means of resolving the basic economic questions surrounding the use and allocation of scarce resources. However, in Chapter 5 we saw that once the implicit assumption that free markets are necessarily competitive is relaxed, established certainties as to the inherent strengths of laissez-faire begin to melt away. In many *real* markets the existence of monopoly and oligopoly directly undermines consumer sovereignty and may be inimical to general consumer interests. From a business perspective such apparent shortcomings in market-based resource allocation are highly important because they provide a rationale for government intervention in markets. Business must therefore accept that it will have various forms of relationship with government.

Market failure: arises where the market either fails to provide certain goods, or fails to provide them at their optimum or most desirable level.

In this chapter we begin to examine the nature of the relationship between government and business by introducing the notion of **market failure**. Conventional economic theory recognizes three *main* forms of market failure:

- monopoly
- public goods
- externalities

We saw in Chapter 5 that the existence of monopoly, because it is perceived to distort the proper functioning of the market, may give rise to various forms of state intervention. For example, the government may take steps to limit the commercial freedom of monopolists, or it may choose to assume the ownership of a monopoly by nationalizing it. Because public goods and externalities are also forms of market failure, they provide an additional rationale for state intervention, adding new dimensions to the relationship between business and government.

Yet some *liberal* economists claim that market failure is a relatively rare occurrence and that the problems associated with its particular forms can be overstated. The liberal school also raises the issue of *state* or *government* failure. The argument here is simply that, in intervening to 'solve' a particular case of market failure, the government itself often gets things wrong and the economic problem becomes worse rather than better. This suggests that market failure should be tolerated because in many instances it is preferable to state failure. In effect liberals argue that governments intervene far too much in markets. Their preference is to let business get on with its role in resource allocation unencumbered by state interference. This chapter also considers this view.

In many economies, the belief that the market – regardless of certain shortcomings – is the *best* means by which to allocate scarce resources has informed the policy of *privatization*. Privatization involves the surrender of some aspects of state influence over economic activity and the consequent reassertion of market priorities. We use an overview of the privatization process in the UK as a means to further illustrate issues around the relationship between business and government, which is the core theme of this chapter.

Finally, we also consider attempts by government to improve business performance. This kind of state activity has two contexts. First, primarily as a safeguard for consumer interests, governments may attempt to establish rules for the preservation of competition in markets. In Chapter 5 we reviewed government policy in respect of monopoly – in most instances monopolies are perceived as economically undesirable and their formation is resisted. A more general form of such **competition policy** is practised alongside government attempts to control monopoly. Here, one emphasis is on promoting competition to ensure that consumers are treated properly and fairly. Second, as well as improving the performance of firms in a 'consumer protection' sense, governments may also be minded to address the issue of business performance in the sense of *achievement*. Thus the Danish government may have concerns about the vitality of Danish firms in comparison (say) to their rivals elsewhere in Europe, the United States or Japan. What the Danish government can do about such concerns is the preserve of its **industrial policy**.

■ Concept:
Competition policy
involves attempts by government to promote competitive practices between firms in markets.

■ Concept:
Industrial policy
involves attempts by government to enhance the performance of firms in markets.

6.2   Market failure

What does market failure mean? A successfully functioning free market is based on the tenets first identified by Adam Smith in *The Wealth of Nations* (1776). These have undergone remarkably little modification in more than 200 years. Smith supposed that free markets were composed of many independent producers and consumers. This makes markets *competitive* and *individualistic*. Producers compete against one another to try to secure the business of each individual consumer. When a transaction takes place, it assumes the form of a *discrete* contract between the producer and the consumer in which a clearly identifiable volume of goods or services changes hands. These are not trite observations, they closely define the necessary elements without which the market would not work as anticipated: it would indeed then exhibit signs of failure.

We have already seen that competition is an important source of dynamism in the market. Without competition the incentive for producers to be entrepreneurial and innovative is reduced; they can churn out the same old goods and services and earn a profit unconcerned that their lethargy will be exposed by the dynamism of rivals simply because there are no current rivals. Such stagnation certainly merits the charge of market failure. Monopoly is an obvious way in which competition can be undermined and is a prime source of market failure.

Similarly, free markets must be *individualistic* in the sense that the goods and services bought and sold pass privately from producer to consumer. It would not be possible for a market to exist in cases where the nature of particular goods and services prevents individuals from exclusively owning or consuming

Public good: one that, once produced, can be freely consumed by everyone.

them. As we will see such **public goods** do exist and the market fails because it is unable to coordinate their production and consumption.

Finally, Smith's notion of the successfully functioning market rests on its *discreteness*. When individual producers and consumers participate in market transactions, they do so willingly and voluntarily because they expect to gain from such transactions. Smith supposed that as the millions of individual economic agents present in society toiled away, undertaking more and more transactions, the overall volume of gain would increase. The general effect would therefore be a more productive and contented society. There is, however, a crucial and implicit assumption here that each and every transaction affects *only* those who directly participate in it. But what if there are, as it were, 'innocent bystanders' at the edge of a transaction who are in some way harmed or advantaged by it? When such *external effects* (**externalities** for short) arise, the free market, with its working assumption of discrete individualism, fails to recognize them.

Externalities or third-party effects: costs incurred or benefits received by other members of society not taken into account by producers and consumers.

These then are the senses in which free markets can fail: where the underlying *necessary* assumptions of competition, individualism and discreteness– which are at the heart of the Smithian framework – break down. We have already reviewed (in Chapter 5) aspects of market failure that can be attributed to monopoly. Although we return to this issue in our discussion of privatization and competition policy, for the present we concentrate on the remaining two forms of market failure: *public goods* and *externalities*.

6.3   Public goods

Many kinds of goods and services are consumed privately and exclusively. If I drink a pint of beer no one else can drink the same pint. If you visit the cinema to watch a film I cannot sit in the same seat as you at the same screening. In each case the good and service are comprehensively and exclusively 'used up'. In fact, as we will see, these **private good** characteristics are essential if the market is to be employed as the framework for their delivery.

Private good (or service): one that is wholly consumed by an individual.

However, some goods and services do not have such private attributes. Take, for example, street lighting. If I take a walk at night I consume street lighting but my consumption does not diminish the supply available to anyone else: thus, street lighting is said to be *non-rival* in consumption. At the same time, once street lighting is provided, it is difficult to imagine how individuals could be prevented from consuming it if they wished to: they would simply have to step outside on a dark evening. Street lighting is therefore also *non-excludable*. These two public good characteristics make it very difficult to see how a street lighting service could be made available via the market mechanism.

■ **Concept:**
The **free rider problem** refers to the possibility that public goods will be underprovided by the market because individuals rely on others to pay for them.

The central obstacle to private provision is what is known as the **free rider problem**. If a private firm chose to supply street lighting who would buy it? Every potential consumer would know that if just *one* person agrees to pay for the service everyone else can consume it for free: its supply will not be eroded

Street lighting in Paris:
a public good

with consumption (it is non-rival), nor can the provider or the paying consumer prevent free consumption by others (it is non-excludable). Thus, the public characteristics of the service mean that no one has an incentive to buy it – everyone is content to be a free rider. And if there is no private demand there will be no private supply. Now, because public goods are not available through the market, if they are judged to be intrinsically desirable we have an economic rationale for their provision by government. Effectively, the government *forces* society to pay collectively through taxation for something it will not or cannot buy privately. Of course, in democratic societies there is an electoral mandate for such action.

Other examples of public goods include national defence, the justice system and roads. Let us consider this list a little more closely in the context of the noted public good characteristics of non-rivalness in consumption and non-excludability. National defence, to take the first case, effectively blankets any society for which it is provided. Whether they like it or not all UK residents are *equally* safeguarded by the UK's defence system. Even those who are pacifists or members of the Campaign for Nuclear Disarmament consume the services of the armed forces and they do so just as intensively as any general or admiral. National defence is therefore a *pure* public good because it exhibits *perfect* non-rivalness and non-excludability.

oh, we don't really need it, it's one of life's little luxuries.

Similarly, the justice system is administered on behalf of all citizens equally. Every individual is protected by the police and the courts from criminal activity. However, notice here that it is possible for the private sector to become independently involved in *some* aspects of this service. Private security firms, for example, offer protection to individuals, shops and businesses in exactly the same way as, say, cleaning firms offer their services. This means that part of the security element of the justice system – effectively the criminal dissuasion work of the police – has limited non-rivalness and non-excludability. In this respect then, aspects of the policing service may be thought to lie somewhere between a pure public good and a private good. Overall, however, police responsibilities in the administration of justice and the maintenance of public order elevate the essential public good characteristics of the service.

Roads are a rather different matter. Non-rivalness applies here only up to a point. On a road where traffic is flowing freely, additional vehicles may join without undue hindrance to other road users. However, a motorway such as the M25, which orbits London, has a notorious congestion problem, which means, by definition, that consumption has become rival. As more and more vehicles join particular hotspots on the M25, traffic flow slows down, ultimately to a stop. But it is also possible to exclude traffic from roads. Some stretches of motorway in the UK and large parts of the French and Spanish motorway networks are tolled, as are American turnpikes; only those who pay get access. So non-rivalness or excludability does not apply with any degree of completeness here.

Conventionally though, roads are still generally classed as public goods despite the fact that their form is less pure than both national defence and the justice system. The main reasons for their public good status are the practical and political difficulties that would be associated with systematic exclusion and wholly private provision. Thus, while tolling systems might be appropriate for motorways, they could hardly be installed on most roads. Moreover, given the cultural significance of private motoring in Western societies – typically embodied in notions of the freedom of the open road – systematic exclusion would hardly be likely to command a popular mandate. The implication is that, for the most part, governments must indeed assume responsibility for road provision.

However, there are limited signs of change even here. There is a basic problem with public road provision: roads are *free* at the point of use for car owners. This means that there is no price constraint on consumption and motorists are incentivized to freely consume as much of the road network as they like (to instantly see why this is a potential problem think about how your consumption behaviour might alter were all apps to be suddenly free). Motorists have to pay for fuel and meet the other costs of car ownership but though these vary with mileage they are not directly related to road use in the sense that they are constant whether drivers are contributing to congestion on the school run or using a quiet road on a Sunday evening. Motorists also have to pay a road or emissions tax but this is levied on a lump-sum basis and not according to the intensity of car use. In the UK in 2014 there were 35.3 million licensed motor vehicles, 29.4 million of which are cars. When we couple the free availability of roads with high and rising levels of car ownership there can be only one outcome: a road network choked with traffic.

What can be done about traffic congestion? An obvious solution is to build more roads. In a market sense, this means increasing supply to try to meet demand. The difficulty here is that demand too may continue to rise. As the economies grow so does car ownership. Congestion cannot be tackled only in this simplistic way. An alternative is to try to regulate demand by making the market for road use behave more like a private market. This has been done in several cities around the world by forms of road pricing. Singapore, Rome, Stockholm, Gothenburg and London all charge drivers to consume their roads. Here the emphasis has switched from increasing supply to meet a rising demand to trying to limit demand.

A congestion charge in London was first introduced in 2003. Access to a defined zone in central London now costs a daily fee of around £11.50 between the hours of 07.00 and 18.00 on weekdays. The aim is to dissuade some people from driving into London and encourage them instead to use public transport, cycle or walk. The charging zone is policed by a camera network. Has the congestion charge worked? Figure 6.1 provides some evidence. Notice that in 2002 when motorists could drive into central London for free more than 180,000 chose to do so on weekdays between 07.00 and 18.00. After the introduction of the charge this figure fell to around 120,000. This means that the congestion charge dissuaded about 60,000 motorists from driving into London. What did they do instead? Figure 6.1 suggests that some of them may have used taxis, buses or pedal cycles – the frequency of access for each of which increased after the introduction of the charge. This looks like a success story but the authorities accept that, after some initial

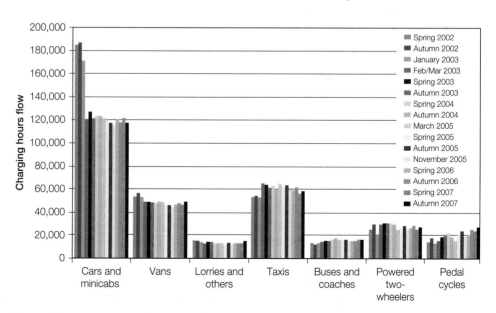

Figure 6.1 Traffic entering the central London charging zone during charging hours 2002–7

Source: Transport for London (2008), *Congestion Charging: Impacts Monitoring,* Sixth Annual Report

improvement, congestion in central London is now back up to pre-charge levels. In the absence of the charge, however, matters would undoubtedly be a lot worse.

One objection to this kind of road pricing is that it might be considered unfair. Those who can afford to pay road charges do so and benefit from easier journeys. In San Diego in California solo drivers can use faster lanes usually reserved for cars with at least one passenger (car-pooling lanes) if they pay a charge. These so-called 'Lexus lanes' must be an irritant to people who can't afford to pay stuck in traffic while they watch the wealthy zoom by. And it's not just road pricing that's open to this charge. Demand for cars in the city state of Singapore is regulated by a quota scheme that strictly limits the number of cars on what is after all just a small island. To buy a car in Singapore you must first have a Certificate of Entitlement (COE) issued by the government. These are distributed through a bidding process. Prices have recently touched nearly 80,000 Singapore dollars – that's about £38,000 or €47,000. And then you need to pay for the car! Does this policy unfairly favour the wealthy? Possibly, though an economic argument would be that the high prices of COEs accurately reflect their true value. Equity considerations like these are recognized by economists but whether or not the equity costs of a particular policy are outweighed by its other benefits is a normative judgement that is to be made through the political process.

6.4   Externalities

The third form of market failure arises because many apparently market-based, private transactions between individuals affect other third parties or innocent bystanders. The result may be welcome or unwelcome but in either case the market is unable to comprehend what is happening. Generally, the market produces too many transactions that have negative externalities and too few that have positive externalities. As in the case of public goods, the appearance of an externality provides a rationale for state intervention in the market. It is the state's purpose to reduce negative externalities and promote positive ones.

Negative externalities

Environmental pollution is a notorious form of negative externality. If a firm uses a river as a sink into which it releases waste products, the firm's activities clearly impact upon those who use and value the river. Ornithologists, anglers and those who simply like to take a riverside walk will all be adversely affected by the firm's decision to pollute. The firm's interests clearly lie in organizing production as efficiently as possible, so, from its own standpoint, polluting the river is sensible if cleaner methods of waste disposal are expensive. Similarly, for those who consume the firm's products the decision to pollute may also be preferred as they will wish to pay lower prices rather than higher ones. The key point here is that both the firm and its customers are acting rationally in the individualistic world of the market. Their focus is entirely upon the cost of the private transaction to which

River pollution: a negative externality

they are party: the interests of river users – third parties – simply do not register economically.

This is clearly a problem because a clean river *does* have value to those who use it or who might use it in the future. If the firm could be made to recognize this it would presumably take steps to dispose of its waste in an environmentally friendly but more expensive manner. This would mean that the firm appreciated both the private and wider social costs of its activities. In such circumstances, the firm's output would become more expensive – higher prices reflecting higher production costs – but only because the pollution externality had been *internalized*. So how can the firm be forced to take account of the externalities it generates? This is where the state comes in. If, for example, river pollution carried a financial penalty of sufficient weight, then all potential polluters would have an incentive to find clean methods of waste disposal even where these carry higher costs – better to meet the higher cost than the even higher fine.

BUSINESS CASE STUDY

Norwegian drivers do it better...

What are the negative externalities associated with driving?

- Congestion is one. Drivers think about the costs and benefits to themselves of driving, not whether their decision to drive affects the driving experience of other road users. Road pricing is one way that governments try to solve this problem.
- Road accidents are another. A pedestrian hit by a driver has no interest in the economic transactions that, unintentionally, led to their injury but they certainly bear costs as a result of *others* choosing to make and drive cars. Again, the state gets involved to try to reduce externalities like this with a battery of measures to prevent accidents: traffic calming, speed limits, speed and signal cameras, police patrols, tachometers, breath and drug tests, careless and dangerous driving penalties, licence points and fines, disqualification.
- Pollution is a third negative externality generated by driving. Car emissions damage the environment. In Norway the government is trying to do something about this by encouraging people to drive electric cars instead of ones that run on fossil fuels. In Norway (population 5 million) there are about 35,000 electric cars on the road; in the UK (population 60 million) there are 4000. The difference has a lot to do with policy. Here are the government-sponsored perks for Norwegians who drive electric:

- Free electricity
- No VAT
- No car tax
- Use of bus lanes
- Free parking
- Free use of toll roads
- Free ferries (all those fjords!)
- Lower insurance costs

These perks have been estimated to add up to the equivalent of £5000 or €6000 per year per car. That's a subsidy – a bribe if you like – that the Norwegian government is prepared to pay to encourage drivers to switch to cars that don't carry a set of externalities. Remember our discussion about the importance of incentives in economic life in Chapter 1. The opportunity cost of *not* switching to electric looks very high. If your government offered you the equivalent of €6000 a year to alter an aspect of your economic behaviour what would be your response?

Here are some other examples of negative externalities and government reactions to them.

- Do you smoke? Do you know people who smoke? Let's think about the economics of smoking. The market for cigarettes, like any other, is composed of consumers and producers. It reaches equilibrium and consumers pay £7 or whatever for a pack of 20 cigarettes that tobacco firms are happy to supply in the quantities required. Is that it? Far from it, because the activity in this market spills over to adversely affect many people who don't smoke and who have no interest of any kind in smoking. In other words smoking carries negative externalities. These include the dangers to the health of non-smokers caused by passive smoking, the unpleasant smell of tobacco smoke inflicted on non-smokers and the costs to society of caring for smokers who develop smoking-related diseases.

In trying to suppress the negative externalities of smoking governments around the world have implemented a selection of the following measures:

- Bans on selling cigarettes to minors
- Bans on cigarette advertising
- Bans on the open display of cigarettes in shops
- Bans on smoking in public places
- Requiring plain cigarette packaging
- Requiring health warnings and alarming pictures of smoking-related disease to be displayed on cigarette packs
- Heavily taxing cigarettes to push up their price (this has the added attraction of generating revenue for government)

- Do you chew gum? What do you do with the gum once you're finished with it? If you spit it out on the pavement you're creating a negative externality. People who don't buy gum might get your gum on their shoes or might not appreciate the chewing-gum strewn vistas now evident in most of our city centres; but not all cities are like this. If you fly into Singapore you'll see the usual customs warning signs about prohibited goods that the Singapore government won't allow you take into the country. On the list of prohibited goods, alongside drugs and guns, is chewing gum. The government's aim is simply to suppress the negative externalities associated with this good.

- Finally, what about recreational drugs? The market in these goods is often illegal and heavily policed with severe penalties for offenders. But outlawing the market doesn't eliminate it: consumers and producers are still out there. For example, cocaine is banned in the Netherlands but the EU estimates that the total annual consumption of cocaine in the Netherlands ranges between 2.08 and 3.22 metric *tons*. What are the negative externalities generated by recreational drugs? Addiction is a particularly dangerous one. As addiction is experienced by drug consumers who presumably know the risks this is not obviously a problem for a third party. But what about the families of addicts – children in particular?

Drugs are also generators of crime: users need money and may undertake criminal activity to get it; suppliers may engage in organized and violent crime.

● **Think Point**

Is criminalizing the drugs market the only or best way to suppress the negative externalities it generates? Don't just fasten on the criminal justice issues; reflect on the market and how it might be conditioned using economic reasoning. Think about prices, opportunity cost and incentives in a legalized drugs market.

We don't have all the answers here, no one does, but what would happen in a legalized drug market? Supply might increase as new providers saw an economic opportunity. This would push prices down. Not good for existing (criminal and violent) suppliers who now might leave the market as their profits collapse. But wouldn't lower prices stimulate more demand? Yes, but in a legal market governments could tax consumption and use the revenues to pay for drug education and treatment programmes. Has this kind of approach ever been tried? There have been some instances of the decriminalization of soft drugs, such as cannabis. Cannabis consumption has long been tolerated in the Netherlands and it has recently been made legal in the US states of Colorado and Washington. In Colorado it is treated in a way similar to alcohol: it's sold in licensed premises in limited quantities for private use and is taxed.

Perhaps there's an attempt here to learn from the case of Prohibition in the US in the 1920s and early 1930s. Prohibition involved criminalizing the production side of the market in alcohol. The American government was persuaded that sobriety would reduce crime and boost the economy. In fact crime went up. People didn't stop drinking and millions of thirsty customers created enormous opportunities for organized crime to flourish in supplying the alcohol they wanted to buy. The end of Prohibition removed such opportunities.

We can illustrate the economics behind externalities using supply and demand analysis. In Figure 6.2 the demand curve D and the supply curve S represent the preferences of consumers and firms in an industry that generates pollution – of air, land, water, as noise; the form isn't really important. The equilibrium output of the industry Q is satisfactory to all private participants in the

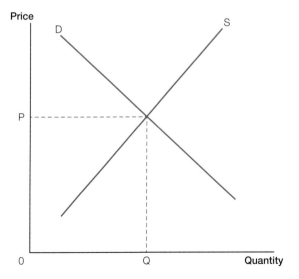

Figure 6.2 Private decision-making in a polluting industry

market. Why? Because at the equilibrium price P consumers are motivated to buy just this amount and firms to supply it. But what of the wider social costs of this industry? The market has no way of understanding that it is a polluter as it only recognizes private estimations of value and cost. In Figure 6.3 the supply curve S_1 represents both the private *and* social costs of production. The vertical distance between S and S_1 represents the cost of the pollution externality that the industry imposes on the rest of us. When both private and social costs are taken into account we can see that the equilibrium for the industry should be Q_A rather than Q. The externality costs of the industry are therefore given by the triangle *ABC*. We derive the triangle as follows. Take the unit of output at Q, just this marginal unit. Society measures its cost at P_M but the value of this unit to whoever consumes it is only P. So there's a net cost to society in producing the unit. The same applies to all adjacent units between Q and Q_A. The unit at Q_A doesn't carry any net social cost and all units below it carry a net benefit as the social and private cost curve is below the demand curve over this range. So Q_A is where we want to be. How do we get from Q to Q_A? Think about some of our examples of negative externalities. The government may fine river polluters, thus raising industrial costs (pushing up the supply curve from S to S_1 in Figure 6.3). It might, as in the case of Norway, subsidize non-externality generating substitute goods (electric cars). This would be the equivalent of a negative technology shock to traditional cars again pushing their supply curve to the left. It might tax cigarettes per pack sold or ban chewing gum.

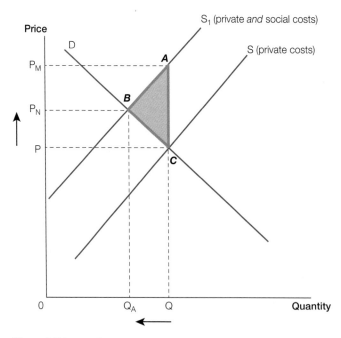

Figure 6.3 Internalizing the externalities of a polluting industry

All these measures involve the state attempting to direct the market in particular, but this is not the only way of getting externality generators to adapt their behaviour to limit the damage it does. Global warming is arguably the most serious externality problem facing humankind. How is this being tackled? One initiative is the European Union's Emissions Trading System (EU ETS). The EU ETS is an example of a *cap-and-trade* scheme, the purpose of which is to set an absolute limit on harmful emissions and then allow firms to buy and sell emissions allowances to each other. Here the state effectively creates a market in the *right* to pollute with a limit to how much pollution is acceptable overall. It then lets firms trade these pollution rights in a market anticipating that incentives not to pollute will arise. Here's how it works.

The EU ETS, part of Europe's commitment to the Kyoto Protocol for the prevention of global warming, aims to achieve a 20 per cent reduction in EU greenhouse gas emissions from their 1990 levels by 2020. Under the ETS each EU member country develops an allocation plan that distributes emissions allowances to emission-heavy industries. In the UK these are the electricity generators and energy-intensive industries such as food and drink, engineering and carmaking. At the end of each year, firms are required to submit allowances (permits in effect) to account for their emissions. In theory, firms that can reduce their emissions cheaply will do so in order to sell the allowances they no longer need to other EU firms that have exceeded their allocations. Cap-and-trade therefore incentivizes firms to reduce their emissions so that they can sell their allowances, or avoid having to buy additional ones. Whatever the outcome of the trading process, the overall cap should ensure that CO_2 emissions in the EU fall.

The process is illustrated in Figure 6.4. Firm 1's emissions are 0E. Its allowances are above this level at 0A, leaving Firm 1 with a set of surplus allowances it does not need in this time period. For Firm 2, however, matters are rather different. Its emissions at 0E* are above its allowances, which have been set at 0A*. To comply with the cap-and-trade system, Firm 2 needs to purchase additional allowances from other firms in the scheme that do not require their whole allocation, such as Firm 1. In the event that many firms exceed their allowances there will be a high demand for surplus allowances, forcing up their price and thereby raising still further the incentive for all firms to seek emission reductions.

Is the EU ETS working? It's certainly true that emissions in Europe have been falling, with an overall reduction estimated at about 10 per cent. Unfortunately, the EU acknowledges that much of the fall can be accounted for by the reduction in overall economic activity associated with a stagnant European economy. The overall message appears to be that the scheme has made a promising impact so far but there is still a long way to go.

Positive externalities

A positive externality arises when a private transaction produces *unintended* benefits for economic agents who are not party to it. Because the market does

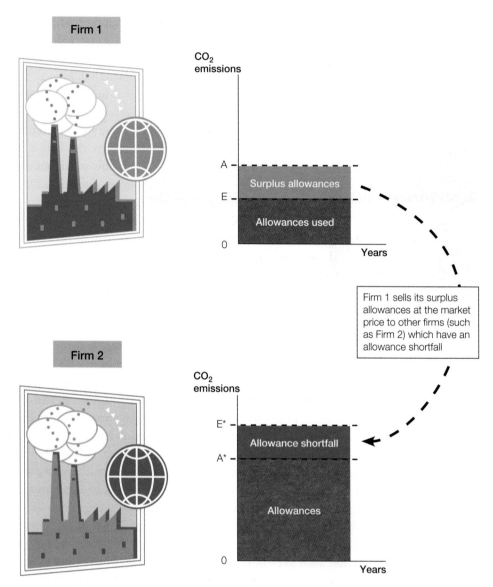

Figure 6.4 The cap and trade approach to the reduction of CO_2 emissions
Source: Adapted from Global Carbon Trading 2009, Crown Copyright

not recognize anything beyond the immediacies of the transaction itself, it is unable to appreciate its true (higher) value. For society as a whole, private transactions that generate positive externalities are clearly a good thing. However, the problem is that, because they are *private* transactions, they occur entirely at the discretion of individuals. Now, as some individuals may choose not to undertake the transactions in question, some wider social benefit will inevitably be lost – in other words, the market underprovides transactions that carry positive externalities. Again, this creates a rationale for the state to intervene in the market to ensure that the extra transactions do take place so that their associated external benefits can be realized.

A WHO poster celebrating the eradication of smallpox in Somalia – and consequently the world – in 1979

From http://www.who.int/features/2010/smallpox/posters/en/index4.html © WHO

An example is in order. Before 1958, many people in the world faced the threat of contracting smallpox: a fatal disease. In 1977 smallpox disappeared entirely: now no one will ever die of this disease again. The worldwide eradication of smallpox was achieved by a vaccination programme sponsored by the World Health Organization (WHO). This is a supranational health promotion body which is funded by most of the world's governments.

Smallpox eradication is a majestic example of the externality principle. Vaccination for smallpox, or indeed any other contractible disease, could be left to the market. Individuals would then subjectively balance the costs and benefits of vaccination. The costs would include the price, the discomfort of consumption (own up, who's scared of needles?) and, of course, the risk of catching the disease. The benefit to the individual would be *personal* immunity from infection. Given such costs, some individuals would choose not to be vaccinated, or – more to the point in less developed parts of the world especially – would not be able to afford vaccination. They would not therefore gain the benefit of personal immunity. But there is also a wider benefit here that the individual (and hence the market) fails to take into account. This is that everyone who is vaccinated achieves both a personal safeguard against disease and the status of a *non-carrier* – that is, someone from whom disease cannot be caught. The point, of course, is that non-carriers benefit everybody; they reduce the risk of disease being passed on. In this sense, the private vaccination decision has clear potential social benefits and the more people who are vaccinated the better, from *society's* point of view. Here then is the rationale for state intervention of the kind undertaken by the WHO. If the state provides free vaccination, the level of consumption may rise to the point at which the risk of contracting disease is very small or even, as in the case of smallpox, eliminated entirely.

We encountered a widely applicable business example of a positive externality in Chapter 5 – the benefits that all of us derive from creative people and organizations. Whether it is the vacuum cleaner technology invented by James Dyson, Pfizer's Viagra, the novels of J.K. Rowling or the music of John Lennon and Yoko Ono, the patents and copyrights that protect new science and art provide a great incentive for more of it to be produced. Without protection, plagiarizing free riders would quickly destroy the reward systems underpinning creativity, leaving all of us materially and spiritually poorer.

EVERYDAY ECONOMICS 6.1

What kinds of externalities are illustrated here?

The images below all depict different kinds of externalities. See if you can identify what they are.

Answers are at the end of the chapter.

1

2

3

4

Externalities and the work of Ronald Coase

We first encountered the work of Ronald Coase in Chapter 3 when we discussed the transaction costs reduction argument for the existence of firms. Coase also made a notable contribution to the analysis of externalities. So far in this chapter we have taken an approach that generally suggests market failure may be corrected by government intervention. In the case of externalities governments try to suppress negative ones and promote those that are positive. Coase suggests that there may be other ways. For example, where there are no transaction costs, it may be possible for parties to successfully negotiate mutually satisfactory outcomes that resolve externality problems without the need for governments to become involved.

Let's take the example of dog mess. We're not sure about you but we *loathe* it. It so happens that in some public parks there has developed a culture of social responsibility among dog owners – many of them now bag the mess their dogs produce. This minimization of a negative externality is a good thing for all park users. Now, to some extent this is a stretched example because there are notices in many cities that advertise fines for dog-fouling which means the state is trying to address the problem. But to our knowledge such fines are seldom applied. So why have some dog owners apparently become more aware of the wider consequences of their pets? The answer seems to be a combination of sometimes loud complaints in the direction of offenders from people with children and joggers, publicly expressed gratitude to the responsible owners and the example to their peers set by the growing band of socially aware dog walkers. All of these transactions in information are costless.

The point is that the government alone has not solved what is a ubiquitous externality problem; its reduction in some localities may be partly explained by a combination of costless tacit and explicit bargaining between victims and perpetrators. A really interesting related contribution here comes from Elinor Ostrom (1933–2012). In work that won her a Nobel Prize – so far the only one awarded in economics to a woman – Ostrom considered the problem of resources that may be held in common, such as water, fish stocks in the sea, or tracts of land on which animals graze. The big issue here is over-exploitation as private individuals motivated by their own narrow benefit deplete the resource. If everyone behaves in this way the resource may be degraded or destroyed. The biologist Garratt Hardin memorably labelled this 'the tragedy of the commons'.

Ostrom's work did two things. First, she demonstrated that the conventional ways of safeguarding common resources may not actually work. The traditional safeguards are:

• to privatize the resource so that its owners have a clear incentive to organize its consumption by themselves and others in a way that preserves its value;
• to take the resource into state ownership and charge those who consume it so that they ration their consumption; or limit consumption by quota.

In a case study – one of many – of land used for grazing in central Asia, Ostrom showed that privatization and state ownership generated rather than solved the problem of over-exploitation. Both 'safeguards' encouraged communities of land users to replace traditional nomadic ways of living with settlement in villages. Where settlement occurred land was used more intensively and degraded but where there was no government intervention patterns of nomadic life continued and the quality of the land was preserved.

Findings like this meant that Ostrom's work was also able to provide a challenge to the notion that there is, *necessarily*, a tragedy of the commons. It happens that, in many cases, users themselves develop mechanisms – sometimes as simple as communication or what Ostrom calls 'cheap talk' – that preserve resources held in common. Cheap talk may also be read as relatively low transaction costs.

Notably, Ronald Coase also recognized that issues around externalities can be complicated by both the presence of significant transaction costs and some degree of ambiguity as to which party is actually responsible for the generation of an externality in the first place. In such cases private bargaining will be inhibited because it is too costly. More importantly, the crucial question in addressing the externality then becomes the assignment of property rights. In such instances the state assumes an important role.

Following McCloskey's (1998)[1] argument we might as an example consider the case of airport expansion in South East England. Building a third runway at Heathrow is an obvious way to increase flight capacity for London. But this would mean more noise and inconvenience for tens of thousands of people living near Heathrow. McCloskey points out that the readily identifiable generator of the externality is supposedly the airport. But Heathrow has been an airport for a long time. People who choose to live near it cannot easily claim its presence took them by surprise. Paraphrasing McCloskey, their ears are as much a cause of the externality as the noise of aeroplanes. Coase's work suggests that the state's role is to decide on the rights and obligations of the deadlocked parties. Do the airport authorities have the right to develop land they own? Should their neighbours have to live with more noise and disruption? Is it imperative for London and the wider UK economy that Heathrow expands? Sorting out these questions is a complex and politically charged task.

6.5   Public goods, externalities and business

The public goods and externality principles we have outlined so far may generally imply a pronounced role for government in certain kinds of market. While, as a corollary, this might suggest restrictions on business freedom, it is important to recognize that – as Coase and Ostrom argue – there are no hard and fast rules here. In this section we examine two instances of established forms of public service delivery where the British government has elected to surrender ground to business but, in the light of changing circumstances, has done so rather hesitantly.

The two cases we have in mind are railways and air traffic control. The common thread that joins them is the issue of public safety. Both services were deemed by government to be suitable for delivery by the private sector. In the case of railways, privatization first commenced in the mid-1990s. Air traffic control was part-privatized in 2001.

1 McCloskey, D. (1998) 'The So-Called Coase Theorem', *Eastern Economic Journal*, 24(3): 367–71.

Let us begin by briefly reviewing the economic case for the delivery by the state of these services. The externality principle applies in both instances, the public goods argument in one of them. In a modern economy, both services clearly have a great deal of merit. Mobility is important – we want a reliable and safe rail system that connects our towns and cities and we also wish to fly safely. The proposition is that if we wish to *guarantee* the provision of a good and safe railway network and adequate air traffic control, these services should be organized and underwritten by the government. To rely on the market is to risk some degree of underprovision to the extent that the services become *less* safe; and if the railways and skies become more prone to accidents this clearly may have negative impacts on both their direct users and third parties.

There is also the possibility that private-sector delivery may mean that important external benefits carried by the railways in particular will be unrealized: for example the easing of road congestion and lower CO_2 emissions as more people and businesses use trains for their transport needs instead of cars, vans and lorries. Air traffic control, in contrast, has a public goods dimension associated with it. If one airline elected to finance a system of air traffic control it would instantly benefit all other users of airspace, and for that matter people on the ground: it is non-rival in consumption and in practice non-excludable – air traffic control that excluded some aircraft would be positively dangerous.

If these are valid claims and both services may be justifiably retained in the public sector because of the externality principle, why have they been privatized? In fact, the assumption is that privatization should lead to an improvement in the delivery of rail and air traffic control services *beyond* a level attainable by the public sector. In the case of railways, the government argued that public ownership had been associated with long-term underinvestment in most forms of rail infrastructure. The result was a poor service with declining passenger numbers. The government's view was that private rail operators would be in a position to revive investment in the network. They would have a strong motive (profit) to provide a standard of service that attracted people back to the railways. For air traffic control, similar arguments about more profit-motivated investment applied.

These *were* the government's plans up until the autumn of 1999; however, rail disasters at Paddington (October 1999), Hatfield (October 2000) and Potters Bar (May 2002), in which a total of 42 people were killed and many others injured, appeared to change matters somewhat. These terrible events – in which driver training and track maintenance were highlighted as causes and for which private firms were fined millions of pounds – had the effect of refocusing attention upon the issue of public safety. A consensus emerged that the public sector still had an important role to play in providing acceptable guarantees of *safe* service delivery. In effect, the externality principle (the suppression of negative externalities) – underpinning state intervention – was reasserted. Although the privatization of air traffic control still went ahead, the government's legislative programme made it clear that public safety regulation would remain in public hands and that the (public) Civil Aviation Authority would retain its responsibility for the development of airspace policy.

In the case of the railways, we had the remarkable spectacle of the government putting Railtrack – the privatized company responsible for rail infrastructure such as bridges, stations and track – into administration after it asked to be partly renationalized because it did not think it was possible to raise the amount of money needed to 'improve the safety and quality of Britain's antiquated rail network'. In 2002 Railtrack was replaced by a new body, Network Rail, which although a private company, is obliged to retain whatever profit it makes for investment purposes; it has no shareholders that expect dividends. How this arrangement fits with the idea of profit as an incentive to improve corporate performance – the underlying logic behind privatization – isn't very clear.

6.6 The liberal view: market failure and state failure

Despite the existence of an established case for forms of state intervention in the modern economy, a mixture of private and public resource allocation is not the preference of every group of economists. The *liberal school*, for example, contends that economies that adhere as closely as possible to free market principles are inherently superior to those that permit the state to substantially encroach on questions of resource allocation. This view rests on three propositions:

- That the state too 'fails'
- That state failures may be worse than those of free markets
- That the failures of the free market are, in any case, invariably overstated

Let us examine each of these propositions in turn.

State failure

The notion of state failure has one central theme: that the presence of the state in resource allocation ruptures the vital *individualist* connection between consumer and producer. Markets we know are organized on *voluntary* principles. Every consumer who enters a market does so because he or she wants to, because there is a good or service in that market for which he or she is willing to pay. Liberals argue that voluntarism is extremely important. It is in fact the *only* way we can be sure that markets are delivering goods and services that people actually want. When the state involves itself in a market – such as transport or housing – it may, for example, tax individuals in order to provide them with the transport or housing *it* thinks that they should have. In the liberal view, the individual's perceptions of his or her own needs are replaced with bureaucratic interpretations of those same needs. This, the liberals claim, is an insurmountable problem. The state seems to be asking: 'Who knows best what *you* should spend *your* money on?', and replying '*We* do'.

There are three particular aspects of state failure that flow from this analysis.

- First, it seems quite obvious that the state's interpretation of the needs of the individual can be mistaken. Indeed, how can a bureaucracy assess with any accuracy the highly nuanced desires of an entire society? The liberals argue that only the market can do this because it does actually respond to each and every individual's expressed demand. But is the corollary true: does the state actually provide things that people do *not* want? Consider the following example. In the field of housing, it is not unreasonable to point to the 1960s and 1970s government preoccupation with the construction of huge blocks of flats as a solution to a perceived housing problem. Now widely viewed as a mistake, such flats are no longer built and many have been demolished because people simply do not want to live in them; they are, literally, a monumental example of state failure.

iStockphoto.com/Jonathan Barton

A monumental example of state failure

- The second aspect of the liberal interpretation of state failure is *coercion*. The market, we know, operates on voluntary principles: economic agents engage in market transactions because they want to. For liberals, this means that markets underscore both economic and personal freedom. However, as the state involves itself in various ways in the provision of goods and services, it necessarily impinges upon the freedom of individuals to dispose of their own resources in ways that they themselves choose. Individuals find themselves taxed by the state so that it can service what the leading liberal, the late Friedrich Hayek (1899–1992), called 'abstractions' such as 'the good of the community'. Yet although taxpayers may vehemently resent what is done with *their* money (recall our earlier example of taxes levied on members of the Campaign for Nuclear Disarmament helping to finance nuclear weapons, regardless of their evident disapproval), they have no choice in the matter.

Those who evade taxation are liable to be fined or even imprisoned. In the liberal view, this is coercion pure and simple.

- The third and last aspect of state failure arises when state intervention in part of a market has the effect of subverting the efficient operation of the whole of that market. For example, local authorities in the UK have been active in the provision of public housing for more than 100 years. The liberal claim is that this has had a devastating effect upon the general functioning of the UK housing market. The problem here is one of **crowding out**. There are three generally recognized types of housing tenure: owner-occupied, privately rented and rented from the state. However, for a long time, the housing market in the UK was dominated by owner-occupation and state rented accommodation, with only a relatively small private rented sector. How did this situation come about? Partly, the answer lies in the determination of the state that there should be more collective housing provision. As more public housing was built and let at relatively low rents subsidized by the taxpayer, the effect was to reduce the level of demand for private rented accommodation; consequently less private rented accommodation was supplied. Moreover, at the same time, the state also saw fit to give tax relief to owner-occupiers on their mortgage interest payments. This had the effect of simultaneously raising the demand for owner-occupied property. The private rented sector was caught in the middle of these two broadening avenues of intervention and (hence the phrase) crowded out. This state-inspired distortion of the housing market has also had consequences for the effective functioning of other parts of the UK economy. For example, the liberals claim that unemployment could be more easily reduced if the unemployed were better able to move around in search of work. At present this is difficult because the most flexible element of the housing market – the private rented sector – may be too small.

■ **Concept:** Strictly, **crowding out** refers to the reduction in private expenditure that results following an increase in government expenditure. Here we are using the concept in a more general way to describe the relative suppression of private-sector activity by an expansion in related state sector activity.

State failure versus market failure

Liberalism accepts aspects of the conventional economic argument that markets can fail: monopoly, public goods and externalities are all valid concepts that may justify state intervention. However, we are also aware of the liberal notion of state failure. This creates an interesting dilemma: if a market is not able to function effectively, should we use this as justification for state intervention, with its attendant risk of state failure; or should we simply tolerate market failure itself? Effectively, what we have here in the liberal view is a competition between two inferior options. The preferred situation may be a properly functioning free market; thereafter it becomes a choice between state intervention and possible failure and the failing market – which is worse? The liberal position is that each case should be judged on its merits. This may be contrasted with the conventional view, which, liberals imply, seems to proceed on the intrinsic assumption that when the state intervenes to 'correct' a market failure, it is usually effective in doing so.

Reflecting on the liberal view of market failure

Liberal economists do not deny that markets can fail. They usually concede that, because of their innate indivisibility, pure public goods such as national defence and the greater part of the public road network must be provided by the state; markets that operate on an individualist basis cannot deliver goods and services that must be consumed collectively. However, beyond this, the liberal view is that market failure can be overstated. Consider, for example, the externality issue. Here the liberal school argues that, while certain externalities clearly demand government intervention, many others are merely conveniences that permit the state to involve itself in markets that would be better served by laissez-faire.

A leading liberal, the late Milton Friedman, for example, argued that while the provision of city parks is an appropriate 'externality justified' activity for government, the maintenance of national parks is not. Urban public parks are an unlikely private-sector interest. They certainly provide benefits to many city dwellers. Some will use them directly; others might simply walk past or live nearby and enjoy the view. The problem for the potential operator of the private city park is that he or she will not be paid for benefits accruing to the latter group. Even direct users may not be prepared to pay if their intention is simply to take a brief stroll past some greenery on their way to another destination. So although most citizens will gain from a city park, it is unlikely to be profitable. This, Friedman conceded, means that the state may usefully provide such amenities in order that their external benefits may be realized.

However, he thought that national parks are different. Generally, people do not walk past them or live overlooking them. Nor do they use them as pleasant short-cuts. Thus, users of national parks are usually purposeful visitors who could be charged – via an entrance fee – for the benefits they derive from such use. For Friedman, this is the decisive point. Because individuals can be made to pay for the benefits of consumption, if there is a demand for a national park the market will have an incentive to provide it and there is no need for state involvement at all. If, on the other hand, there is insufficient demand then why should the state tax individuals to provide them with something they do not wish to have? Here then, the externality justification for state intervention has been stretched too far. Friedman argued that this has happened in a range of markets to erroneously justify, inter alia, public housing, price support in agriculture (see discussion of the EU's Common Agricultural Policy in Chapter 2) and legislation imposing minimum wage levels (see Chapter 7).

Liberalism: a summary

Conventional economics supposes that the main areas of market failure readily justify state intervention. The state should control or regulate monopoly, arrange for the provision of public goods and attempt to control negative externalities while simultaneously promoting positive ones. The liberal position is that this interpretation of state competencies is too simple. Liberals dispute the presence of some externalities that are used to justify intervention in the real economy. They also harbour doubts about the ability of the state to correct actual instances of market failure. For liberals, the state too can fail and its failures may be more serious than those of the market. Ultimately then, state intervention should always be both a matter of careful judgement and, because of its potentially adverse consequences, one of last resort. In the liberal view, the restriction of state activity gives the freest reign to the superior allocative mechanism of the market.

6.7   Privatization

Privatization entails the surrender of some aspect of state influence over economic activity and the consequent reassertion of market priorities. There are many examples.

- Over the past 30 years in the UK, successive governments have adopted policies intended to return most nationalized industries to the private sector. BP, BT, Rolls-Royce, British Airways, and the water, gas and energy industries all used to be in public hands. The latest item on the UK's privatization agenda is Royal Mail, sold in 2013. Elsewhere, the process has been even more profound. In the formerly planned economies of Eastern Europe and the Far East, where economic activity was under very extensive state control until 1989, privatization programmes involving whole countries have taken place.
- Privatization can also assume more subtle forms. Rather than selling whole firms or industries, the state may allow market process to develop in areas of public provision. For example, until recently the funding for British universities was largely underwritten by government. But now students provide universities with most of their revenue in the form of tuition fees; for undergraduates, fees are capped at £9000. This is the maximum price of a year's university education. Some universities have argued that the cap should be removed entirely, allowing them to set whatever fees they like. What effect might this proposal have? One outcome could be the development of price competition in the sector. Cambridge, the world's top-ranked university, could raise its fees significantly (for example, those at Harvard University, which is second in the world rankings, are about £20,000 a year). Other universities, fearful that the demand for their courses is much more price elastic, may be hesitant to do likewise. But the bigger question is whether the university sector would gain from uncapped fees. The meaning of 'gain' takes us into normative territory but let's say that the main criterion is the overall international status of British universities, rather than some other objective such as the proportion of school leavers entering higher education.

    George Orwell once wrote that the problem with competitions is that somebody wins them. In the case of price competition between universities, the winners would include the highly prestigious institutions such as Cambridge, some colleges of the University of London, and Oxford. They could raise fees and the resulting higher income streams would allow them to further improve

Oxford University would gain from uncapped fees

facilities, attract more world-class staff and, should they choose, raise student numbers. Some of the least prestigious universities could find it very hard to survive in a more competitive climate where income is increasingly derived from students, but their ability to raise fees without driving away applicants is very limited. Indeed, Vince Cable, a prominent if at times conflicted member of the 2010–15 coalition government, argued that it would be no bad thing were some universities to go out of business in the way that firms do [except, Vince, the banks!]. The end result might be a smaller university sector, educating fewer students but one that is better resourced because it is able to tap into a substantial stream of fee-based income.

- Since the 1990s, *local* government in Britain has also been subject to forms of privatization. For example, compulsory competitive tendering (CCT) required local authorities to allow bids from private firms for work that was formerly done by the authorities themselves. If a private firm could do the job cheaper than the local authority then it obtained the contract for a given period. As a result of CCT, services such as refuse collection, street cleaning and the provision of school meals in many towns and cities were undertaken by private firms. As the state still financed and retained ultimate responsibility for such services, this fell short of local 'denationalization' but it did admit private-sector influences into what had been a wholly public domain.

More recently local services have come to be provided by public–private partnerships between local authorities and firms. One of the largest of these was Liverpool Direct, a private company jointly owned by Liverpool City Council and BT for 15 years. The ethos of the public–private partnership model is that local government service provision can be better organized with some measure of private-sector input. This is because placing service provision relationships on a commercial basis may provide the necessary incentives – and resources – to ensure their efficient delivery. The corollary is that the absence of market force pressures in 'old style' local government accounted for its reputation as a failing local service provider.

The rationale for privatization

Why privatize? The answer to this question, captured in the examples we have just considered, lies in the purported advantages of the free market as sketched out in Chapters 1–3 of this book. The market empowers the consumer, it promotes the division of labour and it sparks the entrepreneurial zeal of the profit-motivated producer. The case for privatization is that it extends these features into new areas of economic activity and, at the same time, it necessarily compresses the boundaries of less efficient state-determined resource allocation.

But on what *necessary* basis are forms of state-determined resource allocation rejected? The proponents of privatization argue that, historically, when the state assumes responsibility in particular for *whole industries*, chronic poor performance and decay are the inevitable result. Nationalized industries, it is argued, tend to suffer from the general deficiencies that arise as a result of the insulation of the (state) producer from the 'realities' of the market. Private firms, on the other hand, *must* respond to consumer demands; they *must* introduce new technologies and new working practices in order to remain competitive; they *cannot* pay workers more than their competitive position allows; they *cannot* tolerate indolent or incompetent management. The suggestion is that these and other strictures do not apply with anything like the same force in industries that are nationalized. In the public sector, the state is always able to excuse poor performance because the ultimate market sanction of bankruptcy is removed.

While state ownership might protect industry at one level, it can also dangerously frustrate its development at another. Nationalized industries like the former British Telecom (now BT), privatized in 1984, had their ability to raise investment capital strictly controlled. This is because governments usually wish to constrain the rate of growth of public expenditure. At the same time, the capacity of nationalized industries to enter foreign markets is limited – in the BT case it was clearly not politically acceptable for the British government (in its BT guise) to start to compete with, say, Deutsche Telekom in the German domestic market. Now, in an extremely dynamic internationalizing industry such as telecommunications, the ability to innovate and achieve economies of scale is crucially important. Therefore it was argued that, if it was to become a leading-edge telecommunications provider, BT had to be freed from the constraints imposed by nationalization: it needed to raise adequate amounts of investment capital and gain access to bigger markets. Privatization enabled both of these imperatives to be realized.

So far we have concentrated on the *microeconomic* benefits of privatization: the stimulus it gives to firms as they are forced to compete in the market and the opportunities for better resourced growth it also provides for them. However, privatization has also been defended on macroeconomic grounds. Since 1979, the privatization programme in the UK has yielded over £60bn. As this sum is regarded as negative government spending, its effect has been to substantially reduce government borrowing – sometimes thought to be a desirable outcome for macroeconomic management reasons.

The case against privatization

The central weakness of the privatization view is that a change of ownership in itself confers no obvious benefits. Where the privatized firm is a monopoly, the normal rules of competitive practice remain suspended. Because it lacks competitors, a private monopoly is just as insulated from the realities of the market as the nationalized industry; indeed, given the freedom to more assiduously exploit its exclusive position, a private monopoly might be considered to pose more problems than a public one. This means that the acid test for the success of privatization must be the extent to which it promotes competition.

In the UK, the privatization process has been attended by the creation of a number of regulatory watchdog organizations, such as the Office of Communications (Ofcom) for the telecommunications, broadcasting and postal sectors and the Office of Gas and Electricity Markets (Ofgem) for the gas and electricity industries. The purpose of these and other similar bodies has been to prevent the privatized monopolies from exploiting their dominant positions and to underpin competitive environments in each industry. Yet, as the following case study suggests, progress on the latter front has been uneven as, for example, the domestic gas market in the UK has lurched between competitive behaviour and the kind of price stability that might be expected of an oligopolistic market structure. Again, this suggests that privatization is desirable only to the extent that it enhances competition. Adam Smith would surely have agreed.

BUSINESS CASE STUDY

The UK's domestic gas market – how price competitive is it?

It may be difficult to imagine now when we're continually bombarded with advertising that suggests we can save by switching gas supplier, but before 1999 consumers in the UK had *no* choice at all – the government-owned British Gas was the sole supplier.

Now things are very different. There are six major UK gas suppliers – British Gas, Scottish Power, Npower, EDF Energy, e.on, and Scottish and Southern Energy.

In theory this should be very good for customers: a monopoly has been replaced by a more competitive supply arrangement. But has the presence of six firms rather than one really increased competition and lowered gas prices?

The answer, at least for a time, seemed to be yes. A 2007 commentary on the development of the privatized UK energy market by Ofgem – the industry regulator – reported that:

A record number of customers are switching suppliers – this is driving energy suppliers to offer more competitive prices, improve customer service and innovate by offering new products both to retain existing customers and win new customers. Our analysis reveals a dynamic market where a supplier's competitive position can change *quickly and where the best suppliers are seeing significant increases in their market share by delivering superior service at competitive prices.*

But more recently matters have become less clear-cut. In 2009 there was a stunning *two-thirds* fall in wholesale gas prices – that is, the prices paid by suppliers for their gas. This should have been good news for consumers. In a competitive market, falling wholesale prices might be expected to stimulate competition among the big six gas suppliers.

So what happened to domestic gas prices? They fell, but only by about 7 per cent compared to the 66 per cent fall in wholesale prices. And the price cuts announced by the big six were all closely grouped around this average. In 2015 the same thing happened again. A 30 per cent fall in wholesale gas prices resulted in – at best – 5 per cent reductions in the prices charged to households.

Any thoughts as to what's going on here? If you reflect back on the discussion of oligopoly in Chapter 5, you might be inclined towards the view that the domestic gas industry has begun to exhibit a degree of price stability.

Recall that oligopolists may tend to keep prices stable as they try to second-guess the reactions of their competitors to any price changes they might make.

In conclusion then, privatization may stimulate competition but it may also create the conditions for less competitive forms of behaviour by oligopolistic firms.

6.8   Competition policy

Competition in markets is important. It underwrites the sovereignty of consumers and it is the process through which 'good' firms (in the sense that they are good at serving the interests of consumers) drive out bad ones. We saw in Chapter 5 how governments may seek to control monopolies because of the threat these firms pose to the competitive process. Many governments actually go much further than this – they try to ensure that there are satisfactory levels of competition in *all* markets, not just those where there may be problems posed by monopoly.

The Competition and Markets Authority is one of the main government bodies charged with safeguarding competition in the UK. It was launched in 2014 and replaced the Competition Commission and the Office of Fair Trading.

The Competition and Markets Authority

The Competition and Markets Authority's job is to make sure that markets work in a free, open and competitive manner. To this end it can investigate mergers between firms that may lessen competition, review the broad operation of markets, bring criminal proceedings against cartels, and work with industry regulators such as Ofgem.

As the Competition and Markets Authority is a very new institution it has, as yet, little in the way of a track record of achievement. As an example of the kind of work it will engage in we consider below an intervention by one of its predecessors, the Office of Fair Trading (OFT), in the financial services industry.

"Don't regulate me, you wouldn't like me when I'm regulated."

Reproduced by kind permission of PRIVATE EYE magazine/Grizelda

BUSINESS CASE STUDY

The OFT secures a better deal for savers

Many people want to save – for a deposit for a house, for retirement, for a holiday. Since 1999 they have been able to use individual savings accounts (ISAs) to keep the interest on their savings out of the hands of the Inland Revenue.

ISAs are tax-free savings accounts. Millions of people have ISAs.

In 2010 the consumer protection campaigning body Consumer Focus brought a super-complaint about the conduct of cash ISA providers – the banks, building societies and others. The complaint argued that the interest rates paid on cash ISAs had fallen to meagre levels: on average less than half a per cent. This was because:

- Providers did not make it easy for savers to transfer their ISAs from one bank or building society to another to secure a better interest rate.
- Information about interest rates on ISAs was often unclear.
- Many providers used the lure of high interest rates to attract savers only to lower them later on.

The super-complaint process is governed by law. It requires the OFT to discover whether consumers are being unfairly treated and do something about it if they are.

In this case the OFT found that parts of the super-complaint were justified and it secured agreement with the financial services industry to change its practice in two key respects.

- First, from 2012, all providers will publish interest rates on the face of cash ISA statements so that savers will be fully aware of what rate their ISA is earning.
- Second, from 2011, cash ISA transfers between providers should take a maximum of 15 working days – down from the earlier figure of 23.

The OFT found that the lure of an initially high cash ISA interest rate was not an underhand practice as savers were aware that introductory rates were likely to give way to lower rates later.

Moreover, the greater transparency over interest rates and the easier process of switching between providers means that savers will no longer be stuck with a poorly performing ISA – they can simply transfer their money to someone offering a better deal.

6.9   Industrial policy

This chapter has so far reflected upon a number of different kinds of relationship between business and government. The existence of public goods, externalities and anti-competitive practices all give rise to state action in a market context, the primary purpose of which is either to replace business or regulate it. Here, we introduce a form of state intervention that is concerned not to supplant business or moderate its behaviour but to *boost* it – to improve business performance. As we have just seen, competition policy does this to some extent but only by focusing upon the more reprehensible elements in the business world. In contrast, industrial policy involves government working *positively* with business: offering it the right kind of environment, acting as its advocate and providing it with resources.

Many kinds of government action fall under the heading of industrial policy and in a book of this sort we cannot do justice to them all. Rather than try to summarize here everything the government tries to do for business, we instead briefly reflect on the Strategy for Sustainable Growth outlined by the UK's coalition government. This has three broad planks:

- The promotion of well-functioning markets
- The fostering of investment in productive capacity
- Encouraging entrepreneurship

The promotion of well-functioning markets

The Strategy recognizes that markets are central to guiding investment and generating the growth both of firms and the economy as a whole but it also acknowledges that markets can fail in, for example, the generation of externalities and where non-competitive structures, such as monopoly, emerge. So the intention appears to be to promote competition and regulate markets as appropriate.

The fostering of investment in productive capacity

Among the issues highlighted are two of potential market failure. In the aftermath of the credit crunch, there is a concern about the capacity of the financial sector to respond adequately to the future investment needs of business. The government has indicated its intention to explore how the financial sector can become more attuned to the wider imperatives of the economy as a whole. The second issue is investment in higher education and skills. The government acknowledges that Britain remains a middle-ranking country in terms of educational attainment. As we will see in later chapters, the long-term growth of an economy is partly conditioned by its human capital – the accumulated skills and competencies of its workforce. So there is an ambition here to enhance higher education and skills in the UK.

Encouraging entrepreneurship

The government's view is that the small business sector, the health of which is conditioned by the level of entrepreneurship in society, is an important driver of growth and employment. The government suggests that its role here is to help provide local support and information networks that foster entrepreneurial activity and small business growth.

Reflecting on industrial policy

A final note of caution is appropriate before we leave the issue of industrial policy. The general strategy we have discussed was that preferred by the 2010–15 coalition government. It is important to be aware that alternative perspectives to industrial policy do exist. Indeed, this should not surprise us. For example, we have seen in the present chapter how the liberal school harbours deep suspicions about state intervention in most of its forms. In the liberal view, many of the coalition government's objectives were questionable, for example the idea that the state should try to lead or condition lending by the financial sector. If there is a market-based demand for capital that can be profitably met by financial institutions then *they* will discern it and respond appropriately. The liberal position is that it is not the state's responsibility to take the lead here. The liberals would ask: what do government ministers and career civil servants know about the *fine detail* of this or that lending arrangement or investment proposal? A less interventionist industrial policy might then emphasize the regulation of markets in order to promote competition but it would not extend to government meddling in markets. By all means restrict monopolies and prevent cartels but do not proceed to more grandiose schemes in which governments begin to direct how society allocates its scarce resources.

SUMMARY

- The existence of clear forms of market failure provides a rationale for state intervention in free markets.
- The three main forms of market failure are monopoly, public goods and externalities.
- Not all economists share this orthodox view. One branch of dissent comes from the liberal school. Liberals raise doubts about the real extent of market failure and introduce the issue of state failure. On the other hand, we saw in Chapter 5 that the institutionalist school raises a different set of questions about monopoly in particular. In the institutionalist view, orthodox approaches understate both the extent and dangers of concentrations of monopoly power in modern economies.
- Privatization appears to sympathize with a laissez-faire perspective. However, the important conclusion is that the extent of competition in a market matters more than the distribution of ownership between the public and private sectors.
- Competition policy is used by government to improve the effectiveness of markets. Its main emphasis is on the prevention of cartels and other market 'distortions' which are inimical to consumer interests.
- Industrial policy involves attempts by governments to improve the performance of the supply side of the economy. Industrial policy may encompass wide forms of intervention and spending by government. This is not welcomed by some groups of economists.

KEY TERMS

- Market failure
- Monopoly
- Public goods
- Free rider problem
- Negative externalities
- Positive externalities
- Coase theorem
- Liberal view

- State failure
- Freedom
- Crowding out
- Privatization
- Competition
- Competition policy
- Industrial policy

QUESTIONS FOR DISCUSSION

1. Explain the significance of the 'free rider' problem.
2. In most economies, taxis are licensed by the state for externality reasons. What externalities might unlicensed taxis generate?
3. What is state failure? Give some examples.
4. What are the implications of state failure for orthodox economics?
5. Why is the privatization of a nationalized industry, such as the railway network, no guarantee in itself of improved economic performance?
6. What is competition policy?
7. Why would virtually all economists agree competition policy is a good idea but disagree about the usefulness and validity of industrial policy?

EVERYDAY ECONOMICS 6.1 ANSWERS

1. **Litter.** An obvious negative externality. People buy something, rip off the packaging and simply throw it away. The cost to them of the item they've bought is recognized by the market as the equilibrium price. But the cost to the rest of us who think litter unsightly is ignored.

2. **Street theatre – some dude apparently levitating.** Many people might suppose this a positive externality. You walk past, see him, and are briefly entertained. It doesn't cost you anything to look. As long as a few people give some money he'll carry on levitating and the rest of us get free enjoyment.

3. **Christmas lights.** Lots of houses are decorated at Christmas or other festivals. Some of them ostentatiously. When others enjoy private decorations there is a public benefit so this might be thought of as an example of a positive externality. But there's another way to read both this and the street theatre example. There are some curmudgeons out there who don't like the inconvenience of street theatre when crowds gather or who don't like being surprised by people pretending to be statues. They might not like the 'look at me' element of house decoration either. Here, private acts generate negative externalities. So examples 1 and 3 are possibly ambiguous.

4. **University education.** Why do people go to university? To better themselves in career and personal development terms. But the consumers of higher education help everyone else too. They become more productive, making their societies more prosperous as well as themselves. So university education generates positive externalities.

ONE THING YOU SHOULD READ

Milton Friedman's *Capitalism and Freedom*, Chapter 6 'The Role of Government in Education'

This book was first published in 1962 and is based on lectures Friedman gave in the 1950s. So it's old, but the ideas it contains have a continuing relevance. Friedman was an economic liberal, someone who believes in the ability of the market to efficiently allocate scarce resources and who thinks the state or government generally makes things worse when it interferes in economic life.

The recommended chapter is about education and whether this is best provided by the market or the government. Friedman considers education to generate positive externalities or what he calls 'neighbourhood effects'. However, these do not lead him to suppose that the collective provision of education is desirable.

Read the chapter and answer the following questions.

1. What are the externalities or neighbourhood effects that Friedman associates with education?

2. Why do only certain forms of education generate positive externalities in Friedman's view?

3. Even where he accepts that the state should fund education, Friedman argues that it should be provided by a competitive market process. How would this work? Can you see any problems with this approach?

4. What parallels can you detect between Friedman's recommendations about increasing the amount of what he calls professional and vocational schooling and the decision of the British government that from 2012 students should largely fund the costs of university education using a government-backed loan scheme?

© iStockphoto/DNY59

7

factor markets

KEY ISSUES

Do factor markets work in the same way as markets for goods and services?

Which factors in the labour market determine demand and supply?

How is skill in the labour market rewarded?

Do minimum wages destroy jobs?

CONTENTS

7.1	Introduction	**220**
7.2	The labour market	**220**
7.3	The demand for labour	**226**
7.4	The supply of labour	**230**
7.5	Issues in the labour market: bringing demand and supply together	**235**
7.6	Factor incomes and economic rent	**248**

7.1   Introduction

In previous chapters much of our discussion tended to concentrate on markets in goods and services. In this chapter, we extend some of the concepts we have already introduced to the analysis of **factor markets**. Recall that there are four factors of production, the services of which are combined by firms in order to produce an output. These factors of production are:

Factor market: a market for a factor of production.

- labour
- capital (factories, machines and so on)
- land (all natural resources used in production)
- entrepreneurial skill

Factor markets are clearly of interest in themselves. It is important, for example, to understand the operation of the labour market. If the labour market fails to clear, unemployment may result. In such circumstances we need to consider what if anything can be done (see Chapter 9). An analysis of factor markets also allows us to understand how the income a society generates is distributed among the groups that comprise it. In other words, such analysis will tell us why particular social groups – workers, entrepreneurs, the owners of capital and land – earn what they do. However, as we considered entrepreneurship in conjunction with the theory of the firm in Chapter 3, we will concentrate here on the markets for capital, land and, especially, labour. We begin with an analysis of the labour market.

7.2   The labour market

Before we consider how the labour market works it's important to briefly think about why labour matters so much in a business context. We do this in the box 'Applying Economics to Business', below.

Essentially, factor markets and goods markets work in the same general way. The principles underlying the interaction of demand and supply are as applicable to labour markets as they are to the markets for furniture, cinema tickets or any other good or service. A useful way to start looking at the labour market would therefore be to examine it as a perfectly functioning *abstraction*. We began our analysis of market structures and firms in precisely the same way with a model of perfect competition. The purpose behind this kind of approach is to allow us to see how a market might work under 'ideal' conditions and to contrast this with the much greater – and more problematic – complexity of the real world.

One of the by now familiar tenets of conventional economics is that free markets clear. In other words, markets are possessed of forces that push them towards situations in which the quantities demanded and supplied are perfectly matched. At such points in every market, because there is no tendency for further change to take place, each prevailing price is by definition an equilibrium

APPLYING ECONOMICS TO BUSINESS

Why the labour market matters to business

Labour is a crucial business resource. Just how crucial can be easily seen by reflecting on the proportion of business costs accounted for by labour.

Approximate percentage of revenue (or costs) paid in wages

70.0	
60.0	
50.0	
40.0	
30.0	
20.0	
10.0	
0.0	Chelsea Manchester Liverpool Tesco Vodafone Barclays NHS AstraZeneca
	Utd John
	Moores
	University

The wages paid in the top ranks of professional football are often thought remarkable. And they are in the sense that individual footballers may earn £100,000 a week or even more. But, as the chart shows, the proportion of the revenues of Chelsea and Manchester United taken up by wages is not hugely out of line with what goes on in other industries.

Private firms, universities and the NHS all face significant wage burdens. For example, Liverpool John Moores University's (LJMU) latest accounts reveal that its wage bill swallows up almost 59 per cent of its revenue. For Barclays Bank and the NHS the equivalent figures are around 43 and 45 per cent.

The shares of wages paid by AstraZeneca, Tesco and Vodafone are smaller but they are not insignificant.

● **Think Point**

Why does LJMU pay its workers a much bigger slice of its income than Tesco pays to its employees? LJMU's main business is degree-level teaching. It needs a lot of highly qualified people to do this work. Highly qualified people are in relatively short supply so they tend to be relatively well paid. This is *one* reason for LJMU's proportionately high wage bill. Tesco's main business is selling groceries. Many of its employees are less qualified and not in relatively short supply so Tesco's wage bill is proportionately smaller.

price. Given certain assumptions, we can reproduce exactly the same kind of analysis in the context of the labour market. Thus, if we assume:

- that work is not qualitatively different between occupations
- that labour is (like a good in perfect competition) homogeneous
- that there exist perfect mobility and perfect knowledge in the labour market
- and, finally, that there exist large numbers of independent buyers (firms) and sellers (individual men and women)

it follows that *the* labour market in an economy – our assumptions mean that there would be only one – can be represented as in Figure 7.1.

In Figure 7.1, the wage rate – the *factor price* firms must pay to hire the services of labour – is depicted on the vertical axis, while the quantity of labour demanded and supplied is depicted on the horizontal axis. The market is in equilibrium at wage rate W_e, with the quantity demanded and supplied at Q_e. From our discussion in Chapter 2, the reader should be able to verify that at

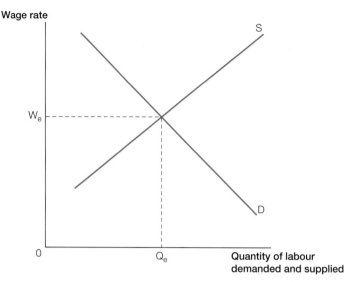

Figure 7.1 The interaction of demand and supply in the labour market

all possible wage rates below W_e, there will exist an excess demand for labour. This will be eroded as firms begin to offer higher wage rates in an attempt to overcome labour shortages. Higher wages encourage more workers to enter the market, and supply extends. However, at the same time, higher wages also cause the demand for labour to contract. Eventually, a point will be reached where the quantities demanded and supplied are equal: this will be at wage rate W_e. Conversely, at all possible wage rates above W_e, there will be an excess supply of labour. In other words, some workers who are willing to work at the prevailing wage rate will not be able to do so because the requisite demand is not there. Recognizing such conditions, firms will begin to offer lower wages knowing that they will still be able to recruit all the labour they need. Wages will continue to fall until W_e is again reached and the quantities demanded and supplied are equal. We consider the influences on the *positions* of the demand and supply curves for labour in later sections.

For the moment, consider the familiar implicit message that this analysis delivers. The suggestion is that if markets are left alone and are competitive then they will tend to clear. In the case of the labour market, this means that labour is in neither excess demand nor excess supply. Competitiveness in the labour market entails both the capacity for individual workers to freely enter and leave the market and flexibility in wage rates. As we will see in Chapter 9, some economists claim that many problems in labour markets can be overcome if they are characterized by openness and if wages are sufficiently flexible.

Let us now examine the effects of relaxing some of our highly restrictive assumptions. To begin with the first assumption, there are plainly significant differences in the *quality* of work between occupations. For example, miners and people who work on oil rigs are exposed to more physically arduous and dangerous working environments than teachers, librarians and others in what we might term the indoor professions. This means that, if all jobs were rewarded with the same generally determined equilibrium wage, many miners, oil rig workers and others would choose to take up less arduous and less hazardous jobs instead. So, because occupations vary greatly in quality, wage rates must differ to compensate those who undertake the less pleasant tasks. The level of compensation is conditioned by something called the *principle of net advantages* or the *principle of compensating wage differentials*. This requires that the pecuniary (monetary) and non-pecuniary advantages of different jobs should, when taken together, tend to be equal. When the principle of net advantages applies, workers will not be collectively repelled from the least attractive jobs. The implication of this first concession to the real world is that we have not one uniform labour market but a *series* of labour markets in which different wage rates are paid, reflecting differences in job quality.

iStockphoto.com/teekid

Living and working here has to be relatively well rewarded

Yet some very pleasant jobs are extremely well paid. This suggests that differences in the quality of work should not be our only concession to reality. In professional football, for example, the most successful players are amply rewarded for doing what many people would joyfully do for nothing. Unfortunately, however, Everton or Liverpool are not going to sign you (probably) or us (definitely) for the simple reason that, in the real world, our second assumption does not apply. Labour is *not* homogeneous. To be a professional footballer requires a natural talent that most people do not possess. This means that the supply of top-class footballers is extremely limited and, as we know, when restrictions on supply are coupled with strong demand, higher market prices result.

For the purposes of comparison, let us also consider the ability requirements of another occupation: a bus driver. Here the natural talent element of the job is relatively modest: many if not most people of working age could be quickly trained to drive a bus. Even if labour is not homogeneous it would seem that the potential supply of drivers is very large. Now, when plentiful supply is coupled with relatively weak demand, lower market prices result. However, there is an additional issue here. Most bus operators tend to recruit trainee drivers not from the general labour force but from only the male half of it. Why? Although women are clearly capable of this kind of work, it appears that reciprocally confirming social and institutional barriers prevent them from participating in it to any significant extent. Driving a bus is socially regarded as 'men's work'. Accordingly, bus operators have a tradition of recruiting and training men. There are many such examples of *gendered* work and most similarly incline against employment opportunities for women. Our point is that these further separate or segment the labour market into discrete elements. Indeed, the greater the degree of natural, social and institutional *heterogeneity* of labour, the greater the degree of **labour market segmentation**. Of course, social and institutional heterogeneity in the labour market is socially constructed and includes all forms of discrimination, whether on the basis of ethnic origin, religious belief, disability, sexual orientation or gender; it has no independent objective existence.

Labour market segmentation: arises when labour faces barriers to entry to a particular labour market.

Our third initial simplifying assumption is that there is perfect mobility of labour and perfect knowledge in the market. We have just discounted one element of the first part of this assumption: that labour is able to move freely between occupations. But, in addition to natural talent and the kinds of social and institutional barriers to work mentioned above, many jobs require specialist qualifications. For example, to obtain a licence to drive a Hackney Cab in London it is first necessary to 'do the knowledge'. This entails learning, usually over a period of years and in great detail, the layout of London's major roads and principal destinations. Similarly, people are not permitted to fly aircraft, pilot ships, or practise medicine, law or accountancy without the appropriate training.

It is also important to recognize the existence of *geographical* barriers to mobility in the labour market. An excess demand for labour and excess supply can coexist in different parts of an economy simply because unemployed workers cannot (perhaps because of a lack of affordable housing), or do not want to move to where the jobs are. The degree of labour mobility in the European single market is an interesting case in point. All citizens of the European Union (EU) are now free to live and work in any EU country, but how many actually choose to search for work abroad is a very open question (see Chapter 2 for a discussion of the single market). The implication here is that labour markets can also be geographically segmented as individuals restrict their search for work to familiar localities. Finally, the segmentation of markets may be compounded by poor information flows. Our initial simplifying assumption was perfect knowledge but workers cannot compete for jobs they do not know exist.

Collective bargaining: involves negotiations between a trade union and one or more employer over pay or workplace conditions.

The final assumption in our specification of a perfectly competitive labour market is the presence of many independent workers (the suppliers of labour) and firms (the institutions that demand it). But, in the UK for example, a little over 25 per cent of workers belong to trade unions whose aim is to provide a **collective** presence in labour markets for their members. In so far as trade unions are successful in **bargaining** higher wage rates than the market would bear in more competitive circumstances (say above W_e in Figure 7.1), the effect of their action is to reduce the numbers employed while securing more favourable returns for those who remain in work.

Interestingly, evidence from some countries suggests that the influence of trade unions on labour markets may be in long-term decline. Figure 7.2 presents data on **trade union density** for the G5 economies (France, Germany, Japan, UK and US) since 1960. Trade union density measures the percentage of employees in an economy who are trade union members. Notice that for all of the G5, union density is trending downwards.

Trade union density: the percentage of employees in an economy who are trade union members.

● **Think Point**

Can you suggest reasons why trade union density is falling in the G5?

There are likely to be several factors at work here. For example, the turning point for the UK at the start of the 1980s was probably conditioned by deindustrialization – the loss of manufacturing jobs which tended to be heavily unionized. Deindustrialization almost certainly explains much of the general pattern in Figure 7.2. Some factors, though, are likely to be country-specific. For example, governments in the UK during the 1980s developed a legislative programme designed to reduce the power and influence of trade unions – hence the marked fall in density in the UK during this period. The jump in German trade union density at the beginning of the 1990s looks a little odd but was a product of the reunification of West and East Germany. Communist East Germany's high trade union density was simply absorbed by the new Germany.

Real-world labour markets are, then, far removed from our idealized model. What we appear to have is a complex set of labour markets with a range of uneven barriers between them. The barriers include: natural talent or skill, training, qualifications, age, forms of discrimination, distance, information and trade union membership.

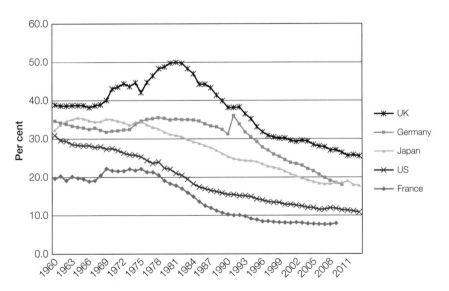

Figure 7.2 Trade union density in the G5 1960–2013

Source: Data taken from OECD, Trade Union Density https://stats.oecd.org/Index.aspx?DataSetCode=UN_DEN, in OECD.Stat https://stats.oecd.org/, (2014)

Now, recall our definition of market power from Chapter 5. Market power can arise wherever there are barriers to entry in a market. This means that, in reality, many labour markets are characterized by the presence of market power. Of course, in those cases where there are the most stringent and daunting barriers to entry, labour will enjoy the highest levels of market power and may find its rewards magnified accordingly. But what does all this mean for our opening remarks about the governance of the labour market by the familiar laws of demand and supply? Are the propositions concerning excess demand and supply, and notions of the equilibrium market-clearing wage depicted in Figure 7.1 now irrelevant? Fortunately, they are not. What we must recognize, however, is the changed context in which they operate. Within each segmented labour market, *particular* demand and supply conditions will determine the *particular* equilibrium wage rate for that market. In the next two sections of this chapter we consider the determinants of labour demand and supply in more detail. This analysis then allows us to conclude our discussion of labour as a factor of production by reviewing the operation of some real-world labour markets.

7.3   The demand for labour

Derived demand: arises for a factor of production because of the demand for the output that the factor helps to produce. The factor in itself does not generate demand.

The firm's demand for labour – and, indeed, for any factor of production – is a **derived demand**. This means that firms do not hire labour for itself but for the services it can perform in the production process. Labour is demanded because it helps to produce goods and services that can then be sold, yielding the firm revenue: the source of profit. Let us now examine how it is possible to derive the individual firm's demand curve for labour.

Recall from Chapter 4 (Section 4.8) that a firm maximizes profit by producing an output at which the marginal or extra cost (MC) associated with the last unit produced equals the marginal or extra revenue (MR) derived from the last unit sold (the MC = MR rule). We can apply this principle to the individual firm's demand for labour. We begin with an analysis of the firm's *short-run* demand for labour. In the short run, we assume that the quantities of some factors of production are fixed, while others can be varied. Thus, a firm can increase output relatively easily by hiring more labour but it takes time to buy and install new machinery. On the basis of this assumption, labour is often referred to as a *variable* factor of production in the short run, while capital is a *fixed* factor, again in the short run. In the long run all factors of production are variable.

The firm's demand for labour in the short run

In the short run, the question of how much labour the individual firm demands turns on the contribution each extra worker makes to profit. In other words, for every extra worker, the firm asks itself: is this person adding more to revenue than he or she is costing to employ? If the answer is yes, then the person is employed; if no, then he or she is not. The contribution an extra worker makes to the firm's profit depends on three things:

1. How much additional output he or she produces.
2. The price of this extra output.
3. His or her wage.

Marginal physical product: the change in a firm's total output resulting from a unit change in the variable factor.

The first of these – the additional output he or she produces – is called the **marginal physical product** (MPP). As we saw in Chapter 4, the law of diminishing returns states that, as additional units of a variable factor are used by a firm in the context of a given volume of fixed factors, the marginal product of the variable factor will eventually begin to fall. Here, the implication of the law of diminishing returns is that MPP falls as extra workers are employed. The second issue is the price at which the extra worker's additional output is sold. If we assume the firm to be perfectly competitive, this price will be given: the perfectly competitive firm can sell as much as it likes at the prevailing market price; that is, MR = P. Putting 1 and 2 above together, we can now say that the extra revenue associated with each additional worker hired by a perfectly competitive firm will be given by his or her MPP multiplied by the market price of the product in question. This extra revenue is called the **marginal revenue product** of labour (MRP).

Marginal revenue product: the change in a firm's total revenue resulting from the sale of output produced by one more unit of the variable factor.

© iStockphoto.com/gerenme

Marginal revenue product: how many extra computers does the employment of these two people generate?

Figure 7.3 depicts the individual perfectly competitive firm's marginal revenue product schedule, MRP. At a market wage W, for example, its demand for labour will be set at Q_2. At this point, the contribution made by the last worker to the firm's revenue is identical to his or her wage (W). This means that earlier workers over the range of the schedule MRP will be contributing more to revenue than cost. For example, for the worker at Q_1 the cost/wage is still the market rate W but the MRP is 0B. The 'profit' on this worker is therefore 0B–0W. On the other hand, for workers beyond the point Q_2, MRP is below the market wage rate. It is clearly not in the firm's interest to extend employment beyond Q_2 because workers in this range add more to cost than revenue. For example, at Q_3, the wage W exceeds the MRP by 0W–0A. The MRP schedule is the individual firm's demand curve for labour. A fall in the wage rate will *ceteris paribus* engineer an extension in the quantity of labour demanded, while an increase in the wage rate will be associated with a contraction in the quantity of labour demanded by the firm.

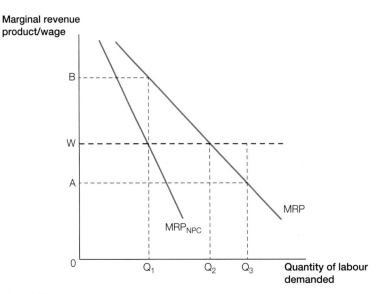

Figure 7.3 The individual firm's demand for labour

For a perfectly competitive firm, when the market price increases the marginal revenue product of labour also increases. Simply, the goods produced by each worker bring in more revenue. This causes the MRP schedule to shift to the right and leads to an increase in the firm's demand for labour. In Figure 7.4, we depict an MRP schedule shift from MRP_1 to MRP_2. At a market wage W the quantity of labour demanded increases from Q_2 to Q_3 as a consequence. Conversely, a reduction in the market price of the perfectly competitive

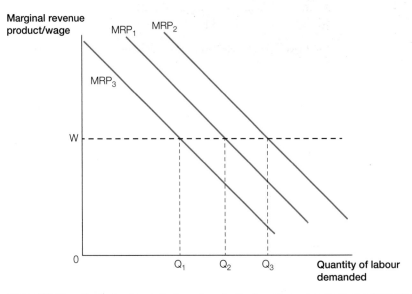

Figure 7.4 The effect of a change in the price of a firm's output upon its demand for labour

firm's output causes the MRP schedule to shift left (from MRP_1 to MRP_3 in Figure 7.4), resulting in a decrease in its demand for labour. At a market wage W, the quantity of labour demanded falls from Q_2 to Q_1.

What happens to the individual firm's demand for labour when we relax our assumption that it is perfectly competitive? The essential difference concerns point 2 above – the selling price of the firm's output. As discussed in Chapters 4 and 5, a *non*-perfectly competitive firm faces a downward sloping demand curve because it produces a non-homogeneous product. Like the perfectly competitive firm, it is small in relation to the overall market but it cannot sell as much as it wants at a given market price because it understands that consumers have to be persuaded to buy more of its particular product by the attraction of a lower price. For the non-perfectly competitive firm, extra output means a *lower* selling price. The implication here is that the extra output produced by an additional worker will reduce the price of all of the firm's output and thus steepen the slope of its MRP curve as the MRPs of all employed workers fall. In Figure 7.3, the non-perfectly competitive firm's MRP curve is labelled MRP_{NPC}. At the market wage W, the quantity of labour demanded by the non-perfectly competitive firm will be Q_1. Note that, assuming the non-perfectly competitive firm and the perfectly competitive firm have the same technology (that is, they're equally efficient), this is less than the quantity of labour demanded by the perfectly competitive firm at the same wage rate.

The firm's demand for labour in the long run

As noted, the difference between the short and the long run is that in the long run *all* factors of production become variable. This means it is possible for the firm to increase (say) the amount of capital it employs in the long run. Two kinds of effect upon labour demand can then occur.

- First, if the price of capital relative to labour changes, the firm will alter its demand for labour. If capital falls in price, relative to the price of labour, then *ceteris paribus* the firm will elect to introduce more mechanized production methods at the expense of labour (that is, there will be a decrease in the demand for labour) and vice versa.
- Second, changes in production technologies may also cause the demand for labour to change. For example, an improvement in technology that results in an increase in the marginal physical product of labour will lead to an increase in the demand for labour.

Labour productivity and wages: some evidence

One of the main conclusions arising out of the theory of labour demand is that firms will pay more when labour is more productive: when it generates more output per hour worked. The evidence for this claim is pretty conclusive. Figure 7.5 depicts productivity and earnings in the UK for the

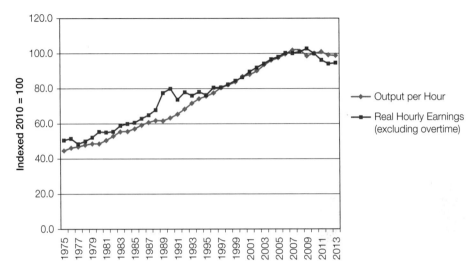

Figure 7.5 UK productivity and earnings 1975–2013

Source: ONS: Annual Survey of Hours and Earnings, 2014

four decades since 1975. Over the period as a whole, workers have produced increasingly more goods and services per hour and they've been rewarded with higher wages. Note that in the late 1980s earnings increased sharply above the rising trend in productivity. This reflected very fast growth in the wider economy and a tightening labour market that improved the bargaining position of labour.

● **Think Point**

Since 2010 earnings have been falling. This may be partly explained by falling productivity in 2012 and 2013 but what else might account for lower earnings?

7.4   The supply of labour

The supply of labour in an economy

The total supply of labour in an economy is conditioned by changes in population and international migration. For example, the population of the UK is presently increasing by about 400,000 a year, while net inward migration adds about another 200,000 annually. Inside the general constraint of population growth, institutional and social factors will also influence the supply of labour in an economy. For example, an increase in the school leaving age or a lowering of the retirement age will compress the population of working age. Similarly, longer holidays and a shorter working week will also reduce labour supply. While these factors have traditionally been decided at the national level, it is worth noting that, for EU member countries, they are now increasingly

A lower retirement age may constrain the supply of labour

Economically active individuals: those people of working age who are either in work or actively seeking it. People of working age not in employment and not seeking it are deemed to be economically inactive.

Participation rate: the proportion of economically active workers in a particular group of the population.

determined collectively through the EU itself. The length of the working week is a case in point. Under the Social Chapter of the Maastricht Treaty (1991) it was agreed that the length of the working week in most EU countries should be restricted to a maximum of 48 hours.

While what we might term the 'boundaries' of the working population are conditioned by the socially acceptable and institutionally determined ages of entry and exit, the duration of the working week and holiday entitlement, these factors do not wholly determine actual labour supply. To be of working age is one thing, to be **economically active** in the labour market is another. The economically active are those people of working age who are either in some kind of paid employment or who are actively seeking it.

Table 7.1 describes economic activity in the UK in 2012 and 2014. Notice from the table that the economic activity rate for women over this period increased from 71.5 to 72.4 per cent, whereas for men the rate fell from 83.7 to 83.5 per cent. This means that the **participation rate** for women in the labour market has increased, while that of men has decreased. More women of working age are engaging with the labour market either by working or searching for a job; but more men of working age are taking themselves out of the labour market altogether.

Table 7.1 also allows us to explore some of the gender-specific labour supply dynamics of the recovery from the 2008–9 recession. Between 2012 and 2014 the number of women of working age increased by 0.38 per cent but, possibly because of improving labour market conditions associated with the recovery, the number of economically active women increased by 1.6 per cent. The number of women in jobs increased by 3.3 per cent and female unemployment fell from 7.6 to 6.0 per cent.

The total number of men of working age also increased between 2012 and 2014 by 0.85 per cent but the male participation rate went up by only 0.59 per cent. The male unemployment rate decreased from 8.8 to 6.6 per cent. Unfortunately some of this fall may be attributable to men of working age permanently leaving the labour market. Notice that the number of economically inactive men increased by 2.18 per cent, whereas the number of economically inactive women decreased by 2.68 per cent.

To sum up, it appears that both men and women have experienced improving labour market conditions in the context of the wider economic recovery. Unemployment has fallen for both groups. However, at least part of the reduction in male unemployment is explained by men leaving the labour market. The

Table 7.1 Economic activity in the UK, all aged 16–64; seasonally adjusted; in '000s and %

		All aged 16 to 64	Total economically active	Total in employment	Un employed	Econo- mically inactive	Economic Activity rate (%)	Employment rate (%)	Unem- ployment rate (%)	Economic inactivity rate (%)
People										
	May–Jul 2012	40,187	31,174	28605	2569	9013	77.6	71.2	8.2	22.4
	May–Jul 2014	40,434	31,504	29507	1998	8930	77.9	73.0	6.3	22.1
	% change	0.62	1.06	3.15		−0.92				
Men										
	May–Jul 2012	20,018	16,749	15273	1476	3269	83.7	76.3	8.8	16.3
	May–Jul 2014	20,189	16,849	15734	1115	3340	83.5	77.9	6.6	16.5
	% change	0.85	0.59	3.02		2.18				
Women										
	May–Jul 2012	20,169	14,425	13332	1093	5744	71.5	66.1	7.6	28.5
	May–Jul 2014	20,245	14,656	13773	883	5590	72.4	68.0	6.0	27.6
	% change	0.38	1.60	3.30		−2.68				

Source: ONS: Labour Force Survey, 2014

number of women leaving the labour market has actually fallen so the reduction in female unemployment is the result of women finding jobs.

The individual's supply of labour

The general law of supply, introduced in Chapter 2, states that supply varies positively with price. At first sight, we might expect the same relationship to hold in the labour market: the greater the reward in terms of the wage rate, the more hours we would expect an individual to be willing to work. However, we must also recognize that the opportunity cost of work is the leisure time that the individual must surrender in order to work. The issue of the individual's supply of labour now becomes the more complex one of balancing the rewards gained from work against the subjective value that he or she places on the leisure which must be given up.

Consider the position of someone who is unemployed. Such a person clearly has a lot of free time but a relatively low income comprising (say) some form of welfare benefit. This means that they would be likely to value some extra income gained from work (they currently have little) more than a few hours of leisure forgone (they have leisure in abundance). Thus, if a wage rate in excess of benefit is offered, the rational decision is to begin to work. Of course, the difference between the benefit rate and the wage rate must be sufficient to convince the individual that work is worthwhile.

Figure 7.6 represents the individual's supply of labour. Notice that the supply curve here intersects with the vertical axis at £5 per hour. This is the **reservation wage**; that is, the rate required to induce this person to begin to work. A rate of £4 per hour would not be enough. It might be too close to

Reservation wage: the minimum rate required to induce an individual to accept a job.

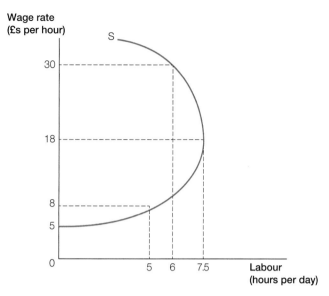

Figure 7.6 The individual's supply of labour

the benefit rate, such that the opportunity cost of work (lost leisure) is valued more highly than £4 per hour.

If the wage rate is £8 per hour, the individual wishes to work 5 hours per day. The £40 they earn (5 × £8) is of greater subjective value than the 5 hours of leisure per day forgone. So far then, the relationship between the wage rate and labour supply is of the expected positive form: the higher the wage rate, the more hours worked. However, it is important to understand that there are *two* effects taking place here.

- As the wage rate increases, there is positive incentive to work more hours as the marginal benefit of work compared to leisure increases: the so-called *substitution effect*.

Should your hourly wage rate increase, would you work more hours or fewer?

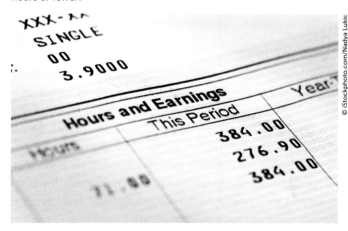

- On the other hand, an increase in the wage rate will also generate a disincentive to work more hours because a higher wage rate reduces the number of hours required to obtain a given income: the so-called *income effect*.

When the substitution effect dominates, a higher wage rate increases the number of hours the individual is willing to work. At a wage rate of £18 per hour, the 7.5 hours worked represents the maximum length of the working day desired by our subject (who earns £18 × 7.5 = £135 per day). Thereafter, despite higher wages, they wish to work *fewer* hours and the supply curve takes on a negative or backward sloping form. In this situation, the income effect dominates the substitution effect. Quite simply, the individual has reached a point where their dwindling leisure time now has a very high subjective value and further improvements in the wage rate afford the opportunity to maintain a satisfactory income while reducing the number of hours worked. Another way of putting it is to say that the relatively high income associated with the high wage rate stimulates the individual's demand for all goods and services, including leisure: effectively they now have the money to 'buy' more leisure by working less. In Figure 7.6, when the individual is paid £30 per hour, they wish to work 6 hours per day. Notice that, at this rate, the daily wage of £180 (£30 × 6) does allow our subject to take more leisure while more than preserving their income.

The supply of labour to a particular occupation

Having discussed both the supply of labour to the economy as a whole and an individual's supply of labour, we now turn to consider the supply of labour to a particular occupation. Here we need to be aware of two issues.

- First, different occupations will offer qualitatively different forms of work. As noted, work on an oil rig is likely to be more dangerous and unpleasant than a 9 to 5 desk job. Thus, in order to retain workers, occupations that offer work that is less attractive must offer higher monetary compensation. This implies some degree of segmentation between different occupations, with *ceteris paribus* higher wages being paid in the more dangerous ones. Clearly then, different occupations will have different labour supply curves. Supply conditions between occupations may also differ for other reasons. We have already seen, for example, that variations in natural talent, training and trade union membership may act as constraints on labour supply.
- Second, the supply curve for an occupation is likely to be positively sloped such as S in Figure 7.1. In order to induce an increase in the quantity of labour supplied to a particular occupation, the wage rate will need to be increased.

The elasticity of labour supply

Elasticity of labour supply: measures the responsiveness of the quantity of labour supplied to changes in the wage rate.

The **elasticity of labour supply** measures the responsiveness of the quantity of labour supplied to a change in the wage rate. The elasticity of supply in a particular occupation will vary according to the degree of skill and training involved and the time period under consideration. For certain highly skilled occupations, such as those in medical practice, it would be difficult or impossible for the quantity supplied to *immediately* extend following an increase in the wage rate. In these occupations the supply curve will be relatively inelastic. On the other hand, for relatively low skilled occupations such as shop assistants, the quantity supplied will be much more responsive to an increase in the wage rate.

7.5 Issues in the labour market: bringing demand and supply together

Skilled and unskilled labour

In Figure 7.7, the supply curve S_1 represents the supply of unskilled labour. Notice that it has a positive slope, indicating that the supply of labour is not perfectly elastic. At a wage rate W_1, the quantity of unskilled labour supplied is Q_1. A modest proportionate increase in the wage rate from W_1 to W_2 induces a relatively large proportionate increase in the quantity of labour supplied from Q_1 to Q_2. Thus, over this wage rate range, supply is elastic (recall from Chapter 2 that price elasticity of supply is given by the proportionate change in quantity supplied divided by the proportionate change in price or, in this case, wage).

Next consider the supply curve S_2. This represents the supply of skilled workers. It has a slope slightly steeper than S_1 and lies above it. Why? The *position* of S_2 reflects the higher wage rate required by skilled workers. If they were paid at the same rate as unskilled workers there would be less incentive for skill acquisition. In order to encourage workers to spend time and money obtaining a skill (which can often necessitate leaving the labour market and paid employment for a period) there have to be adequate rewards. Thus, to induce the supply of Q_1 skilled workers require a wage rate of W_3. The only slightly steeper slope of S_2 *suggests* that the elasticity of supply for skilled workers may not be much different from the elasticity of supply of unskilled workers. Note, however, that the response of labour supply to changes in wage rates cannot be simply 'read' from the slope of the supply curve. In every case it is a question of the *particular* change in the wage rate and the *particular* change in supply that follows.

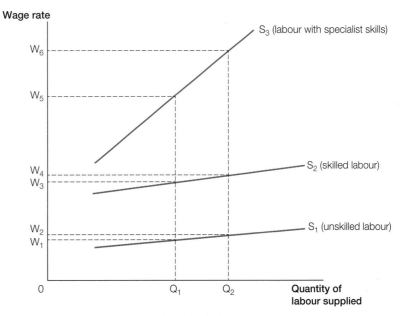

Figure 7.7 The supply of skilled and unskilled labour

Finally, the supply curve S_3 represents the supply curve for highly specialized labour. It lies above both S_1 and S_2 because specialist skills are still more difficult and costly to obtain and therefore require even higher wage rates to make skill acquisition worthwhile. In order to induce the quantity of Q_1 specialists, the wage rate W_5 must be paid. The much steeper slope of S_3 *suggests* that the elasticity of supply of specialist labour may be not be quite as responsive over the same period when compared to the other two categories, though in our diagrammatic presentation it is still elastic.

Let us now introduce demand into the analysis. In Section 7.3 we saw how the demand for labour reflects labour's marginal revenue product (MRP). The profit-maximizing firm will recruit additional workers up to the point at which the MRP equals the wage rate. The MRP curve is in effect the firm's demand curve for labour. It follows that if we sum all of the quantities of labour demanded at each wage rate by all firms active in a particular labour market, we arrive at the demand curve for that market.

We can also distinguish between the market demand for skilled and unskilled labour. Remember that the demand for labour is a derived demand. Firms value labour for its contribution to the production process. It is the case, therefore, that skilled labour will be more valued than unskilled labour because of its greater capabilities as manifested by its marginal revenue product. Accountants sell specialist services that command a high price and this justifies the relatively high wage rates they are paid. On the other hand, waiting and bar staff sell services that command a relatively low price; accordingly, because workers in this occupation are less productive, their wage rates will be lower. *Generally then, the demand curves for skilled workers will be above those of unskilled workers.*

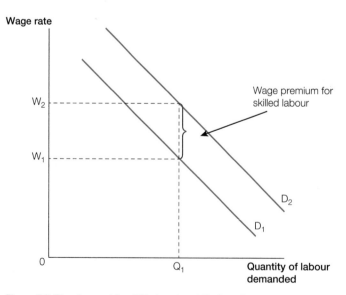

Figure 7.8 The demand for skilled and unskilled workers

Figure 7.8 illustrates the point. The curve D_1 represents the demand for unskilled labour. At a wage rate W_1, Q_1 workers are demanded. The demand for skilled labour is represented by the curve D_2. The higher marginal product of skilled labour justifies the payment of a higher wage rate W_2, at which the demand for labour is also Q_1. Thus the wage premium for skilled labour is the distance $0W_2 - 0W_1$.

Let us now combine our analyses of supply and demand. In Figure 7.9 we reproduce the supply curves from Figure 7.7 for unskilled and highly skilled labour and add two demand curves that correspond to the demand in a market for unskilled (D_U) and highly skilled labour (D_S). For unskilled labour, lower productivity and elastic supply conditions combine to produce an equilibrium wage rate W_2 and quantity Q_2. On the other hand, the higher productivity of highly skilled labour coupled with the wage premium for skill and a much less elastic supply yields a much higher equilibrium wage W_5.

Table 7.2 provides some evidence on the salaries paid in a variety of occupations which tends to support this theoretical analysis. From the table we can see that among the higher paid jobs are those in the executive, air-related, marketing, medical, legal and financial professions. The rewards here reflect *both* the high prices charged for the services of highly qualified accountants, pilots, engineers, doctors, solicitors – the high marginal revenue products of these people – *and* the fact that there are relatively few of them in the labour market (because their training is very demanding and lengthy). The poorer paid jobs – hairdressing, waiting, bar work and so on – have much less robust demand and supply conditions. Low marginal revenue products, low skills and relatively elastic supply all combine here to depress wage rates.

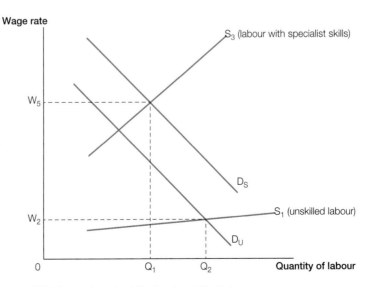

Figure 7.9 The markets for skilled and unskilled labour

Table 7.2 UK highest and lowest paid occupations 2013

Full-time employees on adult rates whose pay for the survey period was unaffected by absence; excludes occupations with small numbers of jobs	
Highest paid	**Median full-time gross weekly pay (£)**
1. Chief executives and senior officials	1594.4
2. Aircraft pilots and flight engineers	1528.1
3. Air traffic controllers	1328.2
4. Marketing and sales directors	1289.2
5. Legal professionals	1257.6
6. Advertising and public relations directors	1221.7
7. IT and telecommunications directors	1194.2
8. Medical practitioners	1159.6
9. Senior police officers	1107.1
10. Financial managers and directors	1094.2
Lowest paid	
1. Hairdressers and barbers	257.0
2. Waiters and waitresses	257.3
3. Bar staff	258.0
4. Kitchen and catering assistants	262.2
5. Retail cashiers and checkout operators	269.3
6. Launderers, dry cleaners and pressers	270.2
7. Other elementary service occupations	272.2
8 Leisure and theme park attendants	277.2
9. Cleaners and domestics	281.7
10. Nursery nurses and assistants	286.0

Source: ONS: Annual Survey of Hours and Earnings, 2013

Low marginal revenue product, low skill content, elastic supply – impersonating a chicken leaves you poorly rewarded

© iStockphoto.com/Lisa F. Young

Consider, finally, Table 7.3 and Figures 7.10 and 7.11. These bring together some evidence on the distribution of UK salaries and the theoretical precepts we have built up on the workings of labour markets. Table 7.3 summarizes a distribution of hourly earnings in the UK. It shows that 10 per cent of workers earned less than £6.56 per hour, half earned less than £11.56 per hour and 10 per cent earned more than £25.42 per hour. The table also shows that men's earnings were slightly higher for each of these categories.

Table 7.3 UK Distribution of gross hourly earnings, April 2013

		£ per hour
		All
Men	10% earned less than	6.90
	50% earned less than	12.86
	10% earned more than	28.88
Women	10% earned less than	6.40
	50% earned less than	10.33
	10% earned more than	22.13
All	**10% earned less than**	**6.56**
	50% earned less than	**11.56**
	10% earned more than	**25.42**

Source: ONS: Annual Survey of Hours and Earnings, 2013

Figure 7.10 is a representation of some *stylized forms* of UK labour market conditions. Market type 1 is intended to typify the demand and supply conditions for unskilled labour. The equilibrium wage rate we illustrate in this market is £6.56 per hour. From Table 7.3 we know that 10 per cent of workers earn less than this figure. This does not mean that our stylized labour market is a simple homogeneous group of the bottom 10 per cent of earners. These people will be spread across a *variety* of industries and regions in what are, in reality, *distinct* labour markets. These markets will, however, be of the same general form. For Market type 2, where demand and supply conditions are more robust, the equilibrium wage rate is £11.56 per hour. Table 7.3 shows that half of UK workers – roughly 15 million people – earn

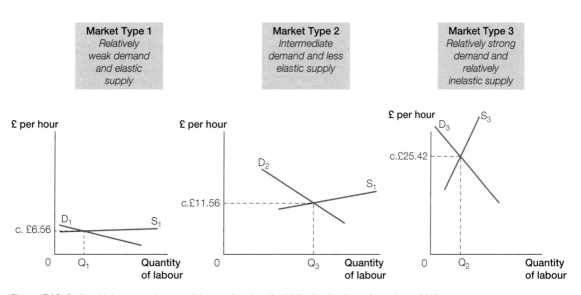

Figure 7.10 Stylized labour market conditions reflecting the UK's distribution of earnings, 2013

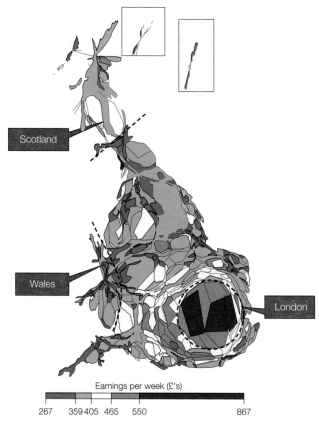

Earnings per week (£'s)

267   359 405 465   550   867

Figure 7.11 Mean gross weekly earnings by place of work, Great Britain, scaled by number of jobs

Source: ONS: Annual Survey of Hours and Earnings, 2013

up to this level. For Market type 3, where demand conditions are stronger and supply conditions less elastic, the stylized equilibrium wage rate is £25.42 per hour. Table 7.3 shows that only 10 per cent of UK workers earn at a higher rate than this.

Figure 7.11, from the Office for National Statistics, gives a fascinating glimpse of the geographical distribution of earnings and jobs in Great Britain. The distortion in the map is accounted for by the sheer economic gravity of London which pulls in people, jobs and, especially, high-earning jobs from other parts of the country and indeed the rest of the world.

Human capital

Human capital is the reserve of skill and knowledge a worker can gather. Our discussion so far suggests that it can boost the wage-earning potential of the worker from both the demand and the supply side. On the demand

Human capital: the skill and knowledge that a worker can gather. Note that some forms of human capital will be more valuable than others. The crucial factors are again demand and supply: is what you can do strongly demanded, and how many others can do the same thing?

side, it raises the worker's marginal revenue product as he or she becomes capable of more challenging tasks. On the supply side, it provides the means of entry into a select group of workers, whose relatively small numbers cannot be easily increased. For those who fail to invest in their own human capital or who have in the past invested in what has become the wrong sort of human capital, both earning and employment prospects are relatively poor.

The point is exemplified by the changing patterns of employment in the UK over the past 20 or so years, as illustrated in Figure 7.12. The most striking change in the chart is the dramatic fall in manufacturing jobs. Of the 6.5 million jobs in manufacturing in 1978 roughly 4 million had disappeared by 2014. On the other hand, employment in some industries expanded rapidly. For example, 2 million jobs have been created in human health and social work activities; a million and a half in professional, scientific and technical activities; and another million in education. The suggestion here is that labour market demand and supply conditions in the UK and many other developed countries have moved in favour of those who have invested not just in human capital but in what has turned out to be the right *sort* of human capital. The secular (a useful word meaning slow but persistent) decline in manufacturing employment may have rendered many traditional craft and low-level 'factory skills' increasingly redundant, whereas the growth of service activities in health, science and education continues to underpin a rising demand for those with what we might broadly term professional skills with a high human capital content. In terms

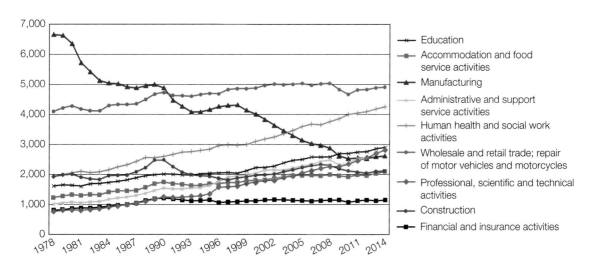

Figure 7.12 UK workforce jobs by selected industry 1978–2014 ('000s)

Source: Data from ONS tables

of Figure 7.9, labour markets in the UK and elsewhere may be dividing into those that are moving towards a situation typified by the curves D_S and S_3 (high human capital content of the right sort) and, unfortunately, those that more readily approximate D_U and S_1 (lower human capital content that may be increasingly obsolescent).

But before the educated and professional classes among us get too comfortable, we should note here an additional complication highlighted by the American economist Alan Blinder. He warns that between 30 and 40 million US jobs – out of a total of 140 million – may be vulnerable to *offshoring*, in the sense that they can be performed more cheaply by workers in many other parts of the world, with no appreciable loss of service quality, and delivered digitally to American consumers and firms. The implication of Blinder's analysis is that what counts as valuable human capital in the developed countries in particular is presently in a state of flux because of the possibilities opened up by the Internet.

Look again at Figure 7.12. The increases in service jobs depicted here are not unusual. In many European economies, Japan and the US the share of service sector jobs in total employment has been rising for decades. But many of these jobs are potentially at risk. Consider the following two examples among several that Blinder offers. On the one hand, medical professionals can feel pretty happy with their career choices. Most people would probably not be satisfied with a consultation delivered remotely, and surgical or dental treatment cannot be delivered digitally – you have to be there. But what about the work done by teachers in universities? While we might like to think our presence in the classroom is indispensable, it's not hard to see that high-quality, digitally based distance learning and teaching is both possible and increasingly attractive, especially in economies where the costs of higher education are rising sharply. These trends and possibilities suggest that people need to think through their choices in education and training very carefully to ensure that they acquire human capital that will both pay off and endure. In particular, it may be unwise to invest in skills that don't absolutely require immediate personal contact with your customers.

"We don't believe a word of this CV...and we'd like to offer you a job"

Before we leave the subject of human capital, we need to consider one last issue that goes back to the problems of imperfect market information and adverse selection we introduced in Chapter 2. We look again at information asymmetries in a specifically labour market context in the box 'Applying Economics to Business', below.

APPLYING ECONOMICS TO BUSINESS
Information signals in the labour market

In Chapter 2, we introduced George Akerlof's pioneering work on the economics of information. Akerlof's famous 'Market for "Lemons"' paper showed that where information is asymmetric, markets don't work as well as they might.

Asymmetric information simply means that some groups in a market are better informed than others.

In the labour market it is workers – the suppliers of labour – who hold many of the cards. They know what their own strengths and weaknesses are; what they are capable of and what they can't do. Employers are less well informed about workers' abilities and may find it difficult to distinguish between the productivity potential of different prospective employees.

This creates a problem. If employers fail to offer adequate rewards to high-productivity individuals because they can't easily recognize these people, the labour market will become dominated by an adverse selection of lower-productivity workers (in the same way that Akerlof's car market became dominated by an adverse selection of lemons).

Building on Akerlof's original contribution, Michael Spence showed that educational attainment could be used by workers to *signal* information about their abilities to potential employers, thus overcoming asymmetric information problems in the labour market.

He also suggested that for different groups in the labour market the costs of education are not the same. In particular, for high-productivity individuals, education costs – measured in terms of effort, time or expense – are lower than for low-productivity individuals.

This means that high-productivity workers have both cost and reward incentives to acquire an education and signal their distinctiveness to prospective employers.

Spence also argued that it is important that employers' perceptions about the relationship between educational attainment and productivity are mutually reinforcing. So long as employers' faith in the reliability of the signals they receive is maintained, they have an incentive to operate a system of differential reward – in effect *not* to underpay workers who have invested in their own education.

This means that, overall, signalling acts to preserve what Spence calls 'multiple equilibria'. In other words, the presence of reliable market signals overcomes the adverse selection problem by preventing segmented labour markets from collapsing into one another.

Spence won a Nobel Prize for his work on signalling.

Minimum wages: do they raise the wages of the low paid; do they destroy jobs?

In virtually all developed countries, governments choose to intervene in labour markets to set legally enforceable minimum wage rates. The UK's national minimum wage from October 2014 was £6.50 per hour for workers aged 21 and over, and £5.13 per hour for those aged 18–20.

Why set a minimum wage? The debate about minimum wages clearly has some *normative* aspects to it. Many people think it is unfair of employers to pay workers relatively low wages: low wage rates exploit those who do not have the skills to move up in the labour market. On the other hand, others argue that governments are wrong to interfere in employment arrangements freely entered into by workers and firms. The *positive* dimension is, however, rather different. The key questions here are:

- Does a national minimum wage rate raise the incomes of low-paid workers?
- What is the effect of a minimum wage on the level of employment; does it destroy jobs?

These questions are closely related. Let us see why by first examining the economic case against the imposition of a national minimum wage. We should begin by putting this issue into context. Remember that we are dealing not with one labour market but many, variously segmented by occupation, geography, industry, gender and so on. Recall also from Table 7.3 that the majority of Britain's full-time workers are not in markets where relatively low pay dominates. This means that, on the reasonable assumption that the minimum wage is intended to raise the pay of those at the bottom of the wage range, the minimum wage is an *irrelevance* in many labour markets.

That said, its opponents argue that where it has an impact, its effect is to raise the wages of some low-paid workers at the expense of the jobs of other low-paid workers. This conclusion derives from simple market analysis. If, in a given labour market, there is a relatively low *equilibrium* wage rate, any attempt to raise wages will cause the quantity of labour demanded to contract and the quantity supplied to extend. The inevitable cost of the improvement in the wage rate is job loss. Referring back to Figure 7.1, the reader should be able to verify that any wage rate above W_e will produce an excess supply of labour. Moreover, the higher the minimum wage is above W_e, the greater the resultant excess supply of labour. So, the central conclusions of its critics are that, in markets where it has an impact, the minimum wage destroys jobs, improves the wages of those still in work and lowers the incomes of those made unemployed.

Finally, we should note the claims of some employers that the minimum wage spills over into labour markets where it has no formal influence. We have seen how skilled workers require compensation in the form of higher wages for the costs of acquiring those skills. This creates a **pay differential** between skilled and unskilled work. Where unskilled workers have their wages boosted by a minimum wage, the differential that skilled workers enjoy will be partially eroded. In these circumstances skilled workers may press employers to restore lost differentials. To the extent that they are successful, the impact of the minimum wage may ripple through to labour markets where low pay is not an issue.

There are, however, problems with the basic argument that the main economic effect of minimum wage legislation is to destroy jobs. In the first place, it assumes that labour is paid according to the value of its marginal revenue product. This may not always be the case. In Figure 7.13, the firm's MRP curve does not slope smoothly down from left to right in the expected fashion but

Pay differentials: exist where there are wage rate premiums attached to particular kinds of work. The most common pay differentials are between skilled and unskilled work.

follows a path with abrupt changes in it. This reflects *indivisibilities* in the employment of labour. Indivisibilities arise when it is not possible to add relatively small amounts of labour to that already employed. According to Shaw (see source of Figure 7.13 for reference), this limitation may apply particularly to small firms.

Take the example of a firm that employs only two people, both of whom have many years of work experience. This sets their marginal revenue product contributions to the firm at a given level. If the firm were to recruit a third worker who is inexperienced, his or her MRP will be at a level below that of the first two and not, as we have previously assumed, merely on a downward sloping MRP curve. In terms of Figure 7.13, the MRP of the first two workers is at W_3, while that of the third is at W_1. Now, if the wage level set in the market is W_2, the firm will set demand at Q_2 and not employ the third worker because his or her MRP is below the wage: this individual's cost of employment would be above the revenue he or she brought in. Notice, however, that the MRP of the first two workers is *above* the market wage level. The point here is that a minimum wage could be set at any level above the market wage and up to W_3, *without* causing the firm to reduce its demand for labour.

So what has been the impact of the minimum wage in the UK? Our two criteria for assessing it are its effect on low pay and its potential to destroy jobs. Taking the job-destruction issue first, most studies seem to suggest that there is little evidence that it has caused any reduction in employment. Government data shows that the total number of jobs in sectors where low pay tends to dominate has increased at broadly the same rate as jobs in the economy as a

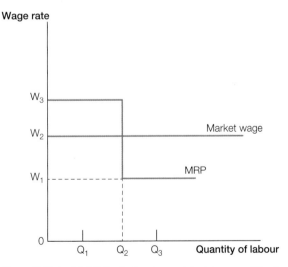

Figure 7.13 Indivisibilities in the demand for labour and the impact of a minimum wage

Source: Adapted from Shaw, G.K. (1997) 'How Relevant is Keynesian Economics Today?', in Snowdon, B. and H.R. Vane (Eds.), *Reflections on the Development of Modern Macroeconomics*, Cheltenham, UK and Northampton, MA: Edward Elgar Publishing

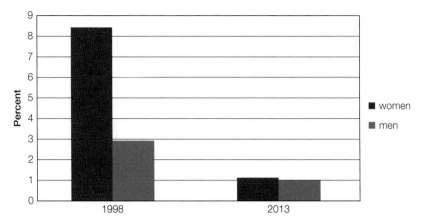

Figure 7.14 Women and men earning less than the UK minimum wage

Source: Data from ONS: Low pay, 2014

whole since 1999 when the minimum wage was introduced. On the other hand, there is *some* evidence that the minimum wage has reduced the numbers of workers – particularly women – earning very low pay. Figure 7.14 shows that the proportion of women paid less than the minimum wage fell from 8.4 per cent just prior to its introduction to 1.1 per cent by 2013. The proportion of men earning less than the minimum fell from 2.9 to 1.0 per cent over the same period.

The labour market as a shock absorber

One of the features of markets is their capacity to respond to shocks. For example, as discussed in Chapter 2, oil shocks – involving abrupt changes in either demand or supply conditions – can be coped with over time. Problems with the supply of oil push up oil prices. In turn these incentivize producers to exploit oil reserves that were hitherto neglected because oil extraction was technically challenging and costly. At the same time higher oil prices incentivize oil consumers to become more energy efficient and to invest in non-oil energy sources. Labour markets too have an ability to cope with shocks. One of the most often quoted examples is the influence of the bubonic plague on wage rates in medieval Europe. The plague killed perhaps *forty* per cent of Europe's population. So the European economy was a lot smaller and more miserable after the plague than before it but what about the position of the surviving workers – might they have been materially better off?

● **Think Point**

Can you express the outcome in a simple labour market diagram? What happens to labour supply and the real wage?

The plague caused a notable leftward shift in the labour supply curve and therefore pushed up real wages in medieval Europe – a boon for surviving workers and a huge incentive for employers to reallocate resources so as to use labour as productively as possible.

The development of the Chinese economy provides more up-to-date cases of shocks to the labour market. Before it began its transition to capitalism China's economy was largely isolated from the West. What went on in China economically did not matter much in Europe and North America. But the advent of an open, capitalist China changed things. China has a population of 1.3 billion – about twice as big as Europe and four times larger than the US. That's a huge addition to the *world's* supply of labour. Although the world's labour market is segmented by national boundaries, language, culture and all the other characteristics we discussed earlier in this chapter, hundreds of millions of new workers have still had some big impacts. Here are two.

- The world's labour supply curve has shifted to the right. More people are employed but the increase in labour supply may have suppressed real wages in the world economy. On the other hand, because wages have been constrained, many goods are now cheaper on world markets than they would otherwise have been. We can see this most directly in the prices we pay for goods from China and other lower-wage cost countries.

- As China continues to develop, the wealth it generates will vastly improve the human capital of China's workers – leading to greater international competition in more skilled labour markets, many of which may be levered open by further developments in offshoring. But as China's human capital develops so will the marginal revenue products of China's workers. Remember that a worker's MRP is conditioned by their productivity. This means that the low-cost edge of the Chinese economy will fade as its workers' rising productivity prompts rising real wages.

A notable feature of the China's labour market is the policy of the Chinese government to restrict its growth. This is one consequence of its one-child-per-family policy. There are some exceptions but since 1979 most couples living in cities have only been permitted to have one child. The policy is enforced by a system of heavy fines. But this could be about to change with a proposal that families may be allowed to have two children where one of the parents is an only child. What effect will such a policy relaxation have on the Chinese labour market? Assuming that couples choose to have more children the move would imply a rightward shift of the Chinese labour supply curve with resultant downward pressure on Chinese and – given the size of the Chinese labour market – possibly world real wages.

All these examples illustrate the capacity of labour markets to absorb major shocks. Whether labour supply increases or catastrophically decreases process are set in train that in time restore equilibrium and put a price on labour that reflects its scarcity relative to other factors of production.

7.6 Factor incomes and economic rent

Having discussed the labour market in some detail, we now finally and briefly consider the operation of capital and land markets. As noted at the beginning of this chapter, a number of key principles are common to all factor markets. Thus, the demand for capital and land is, like that for labour, a *derived demand*. This means that the notion of marginal revenue product – the change in a firm's total revenue from employing an additional unit of a factor – is again relevant when studying the individual firm's demand for capital and land. It follows that the quantity of capital or land demanded by a profit-maximizing firm will be that which equates the MRP of the relevant factor with its price (expressed as interest for capital and rent for land). If, for example, the return from the installation of one more machine by a firm exceeds the interest the firm must pay on the funds it borrows to make this investment, then the investment should proceed. In other words, the firm's MRP of capital is currently above the price of capital and the firm can, therefore, make additional profit by raising its demand for capital. On the other hand, a farmer who rents an extra field on which to grow more crops will break the rental agreement if he or she finds that the price the crop can be sold for is less than the season's rent on the field. Because the MRP of land is below its price, the demand for land will fall.

Economic rent: payment to a factor of production above that necessary to retain it in its present use.

While we used basic demand and supply analysis to analyse the labour market, all factor markets can also be studied using the concept of **economic rent**. This is not the same as rent, the reward to land. Economic rent can be earned by *any* factor of production. It is defined as payment to a factor over and above that which the factor requires to remain in its present use.

For example, although the best professional entertainers – top actors, footballers and musicians – are very well paid, do they really need all that money to keep them in the jobs they probably enjoy doing anyway? Would they work for less? How much less? If they were offered a lot less they might even wonder if they could earn more doing something else entirely. But what might they do instead of acting and so on? Let's assume that they're averagely qualified, and in an average job would therefore attract the average UK salary of around £26,000. This means that most if not all of the multimillion pound incomes earned by people like 007 actor Daniel Craig, Wayne Rooney and Cheryl Fernandez-Versini is economic rent. The non-star alternative jobs are, for them, relatively very poorly paid and in all likelihood they would still continue to act, play football and sing for an average salary if that were all that was on offer. It would still be enough to keep them doing what they do.

If rent is the income a factor of production earns that is above the level required to keep it in a given occupation, what about the *minimum* income level the factor demands to keep doing the job? Welders in the UK are paid around the UK average salary of £26,000. Remember that this will reflect on the demand side the marginal revenue product of welders, and on the supply side influences such as training content and the principle of net advantages (which here suggests that welding is not a particularly pleasant job and people need to be paid a bit more to do it). Were welders' salaries to fall below £26,000, some people in this occupation might decide that driving a bus or coach is, for them, a more attractive proposition. This means that their **transfer earnings** are probably close to £26,000, in the sense that when this threshold is breached they may switch to a different occupation. So might Cheryl Fernandez-Versini forsake recording and celebrity were her wages to fall from millions to £26,000? Might she take up welding? On the principle of net advantages, possibly not. Being on telly with Simon Cowell apparently carries its own non-pecuniary compensations.

Transfer earnings: payments to a factor of production required to retain it in its present use.

Applying the concept of economic rent to different factor markets

Figure 7.15 depicts three factor markets: for unskilled labour, finance capital and land. Consider first the market for unskilled labour. We assume here that supply is perfectly elastic because the hypothetical pool of workers is extremely large. At higher levels of supply it is conceivable that the curve will turn upwards (and then resemble the supply curve in the first panel of Figure 7.10), but for our purposes it remains flat over the relevant range. In this case, the total value of wages paid to labour (the wage rate W_1 multiplied by the number of hours worked) is represented by the rectangle $0W_1AQ_1$. The earnings of labour here are all transfer earnings: there is no element of economic rent. This is because, for Q_1 hours labour to be supplied, the volume of wages paid must be *exactly* $0W_1AQ_1$. Given that supply is perfectly elastic, if a lower wage were paid no labour would be forthcoming.

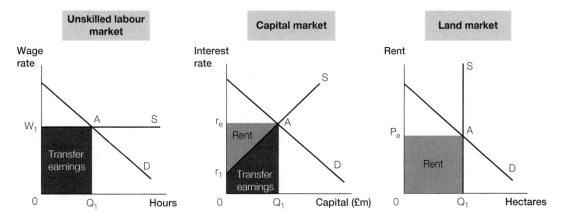

Figure 7.15 Economic rent in the markets for unskilled labour, capital and land

The market for finance capital on the other hand has normally sloped demand and supply curves: S and D respectively. At the equilibrium interest rate r_e, the demand and supply of capital is Q_1. The volume of revenue generated for the providers of this amount of capital is the return on it (at the rate r_e). However, notice that the rate r_e is necessary to induce the supply only of the *very last* unit of capital advanced. All the preceding units of capital would still be supplied at rates between r_e and r_1. This means that, except for the last unit, all capital advanced earns economic rent in the form of unnecessarily high rates of return. The transfer earnings, in this case the combination of interest rates that would be *just* sufficient to bring forth a supply of Q_1, are given by the rectangle r_1AQ_10. Economic rent on the other hand is represented by the triangle r_1Ar_e.

Finally, consider the supply of land. A given piece of land is in fixed supply, which does not vary regardless of the rent paid for it: the land is always supplied. This means the value of the land is *wholly* dependent upon demand and all of its earnings take the form of economic rent. This explains why land values are exceptionally high in central London relative to other places in the UK. In London, intensive demand is forthcoming from business, government and relatively affluent residents; elsewhere, the levels of demand from equivalent sources are much lower. In Figure 7.15, the market for a given piece of land is in equilibrium at rent P_e, with supply at Q_1. Thus the rectangle $0P_eAQ_1$ is pure economic rent. If rent was halved or even set at zero, the land would still be in supply, there are no minimum transfer earnings necessary to induce its supply.

EVERYDAY ECONOMICS 7.1

How much economic rent; what level of transfer earnings?

Here are some jobs and associated salaries. What might be the rough division of economic rent and transfer earnings in each salary?

Answers are at the end of the chapter.

1

Vicars earn about £21,000

2

Butlers can earn more than £100,000

3

Prison Officers start on £18,720

The significance of economic rent lies in its influence on the potential earnings of factors of production. Where no economic rent is earned, as in our unskilled labour market example, factor returns are effectively fixed by *supply* considerations at the level of transfer earnings. There is no scope for improvement unless supply conditions change. At the other extreme, where earnings are all economic rent, returns are wholly *demand* driven. If demand increases then so, commensurably, does economic rent. As modern Premiership footballers know, this can be hugely advantageous. Even a moderately talented Premiership footballer can now enjoy millionaire status. How is this possible when only a few years ago such rewards were unthinkable? The answer is that, as noted, footballers' wages are mostly economic rent and, therefore, demand driven. The last and most crucial piece in the jigsaw is that the demand for Premiership footballers has ballooned because of the vast sums television companies are willing to pay for the right to screen top football matches. Should companies like Sky grow lukewarm about football, the premium rewards for top players will melt away.

SUMMARY

- Factor markets, like the markets for goods and services, are governed by the laws of supply and demand. Demand in factor markets is a derived demand: it is dependent upon the demand for the output factors produce.
- The labour market is segmented because of barriers to labour mobility. Labour may be prevented from moving freely between different market segments by the presence of, inter alia, skill or training requirements, the need for natural ability, trade unions, distance, poor information and discrimination.
- In the short run, the firm's demand for labour is regulated by the level of the wage. The firm will employ labour up to the point at which the marginal revenue product (MRP) of labour and the wage are equal. In the long run, changes in the price of capital and technological advances can affect the MRP, which is also the firm's demand curve for labour.
- The supply of labour in an economy is governed overall by the rate of population growth. It is also conditioned by a range of social and institutional factors affecting participation rates. In most industrialized countries, the participation rates of women have been rising, while those of men have fallen.
- The supply of labour to a market will be positively sloped. The elasticity of labour supply is dependent upon time and the possibility of new workers acquiring the skills or aptitudes necessary to join the market.
- The highest market wage rates will be paid to workers in occupations for which there is a strong demand and relatively inelastic supply.

- Investing in the right sort of human capital gives workers the best chance of earning a relatively high wage, though it also makes sense for firms to invest in their workers.
- In industrial countries such as the UK, minimum wage legislation has no relevance in many labour markets. While, theoretically, minimum wages may help the low paid at the expense of job destruction, in practice there is little evidence that they significantly impede the functioning of market processes.
- The concept of economic rent helps us to understand why factors in inelastic supply can earn relatively high returns.

KEY TERMS

- Net advantages
- Barriers to labour mobility
- Segmented labour markets
- Bargaining power
- Derived demand
- Marginal revenue product
- Economically active
- Participation rates

- Reservation wage
- Substitution and income effects
- Elasticity of labour supply
- Human capital
- Trade union density
- Minimum wage
- Pay differentials
- Economic rent
- Transfer earnings

QUESTIONS FOR DISCUSSION

1. Why is the concept of labour market segmentation useful in explaining wage rate variation between occupations?
2. Why is the demand for labour a derived demand and how does this influence our analysis of the demand for labour by a firm?
3. Which factors govern the supply of labour in an economy?
4. Which factors govern the supply of labour to the German building industry? (Hint: labour migration may be important here.)
5. Your ability to read this book is in part a reflection of the skills of the primary school teachers who taught you reading. Why should a job as socially, culturally and economically important as teaching young children be so poorly rewarded relative to the jobs done by David and Victoria Beckham?

EVERYDAY ECONOMICS 7.1 ANSWERS

1. **The clergy.** Vicars earn an average of around £21,000 a year. Is any of this economic rent? Probably most of it. Rent is payment over and above that required to keep resources in their present use. Would vicars desert their churches if pay dropped to £15,000 or the minimum-wage level salary of £13,520? Some might but our guess is that most are vocationally driven and would not. So vicars do earn a fairly substantial portion of economic rent relative to their overall salary. What about transfer earnings – the payment necessary to keep vicars in post? Are vicars in it for the money? Almost certainly not. The religious life is not motivated by pecuniary concerns so transfer earnings are probably vanishingly low.

2. **Butlers.** You may be surprised to learn that experienced butlers can be very well paid with salaries of £100,000 or more reported for some. Again, a good proportion of this may be economic rent if butlers could still be recruited at say £50,000 – which is twice the average UK salary. What about transfer earnings? A butler's post must be a very demanding one in terms of time: on constant call, few weekends off; almost a vicarious existence. Considerations such as this might suggest that a salary close to the national average would not be enough to justify a life in service so transfer earnings may be relatively high. Overall then butlers may be paid a roughly even split between economic rent and transfer earnings.

3. **Prison officers.** If you've ever watched *Porridge* you'll remember Mr McKay. The starting salary for prison officers is £18,720. Is any of this rent? Very little of it in our view. Were this figure to be cut our guess is that many prison officers would be motivated to seek alternative occupations so most prison officers' salaries are likely to be composed largely of transfer earnings.

ONE THING YOU SHOULD READ

Robert Tressell's *The Ragged Trousered Philanthropists*, Chapter 2, 'Nimrod: a Mighty Hunter before the Lord'

This book is a fictionalized account of the lives of a small group of working-class builders in England in the early 1900s. It is funny, tragic, uplifting and provocative. Its central theme is the conflict between capitalists, who own the land, money and machinery that are necessary to produce goods and services, and workers, who own nothing but their capacity to work.

Tressell has read Marx. Chapter 21, 'The Reign of Terror. The Great Money Trick', is as good an interpretation of the basic Marxian relation between capital and labour as you will find. However, it is Chapter 2 that we're interested in here. This introduces one of the book's villains – the foreman, Hunter – and explains the source of his power as lying in part in the labour market conditions prevailing in Mugsborough, the town where the story is set.

Read the chapter and answer the following questions.

1. How do we know that there is an excess supply of labour in the market?
2. In what ways does Hunter make this work to his firm's advantage? There are least three.
3. Hunter is cast throughout the book in an unsympathetic light but how different is his situation from those he supervises? Should you read the whole book, you'll find he comes to a grizzly end.
4. This labour market existed more than 100 years ago. Are the relationships described merely historical curiosities, or do they still have some contemporary relevance?
5. This market is also one largely unconditioned by the state or trade unions. What differences do these institutions make in contemporary labour markets?
6. A final question – what is the meaning of the book's title?

8

the macroeconomy, macroeconomic policy and business

KEY ISSUES

What are the main objectives of macroeconomic policy?

How can the objectives of macroeconomic policy be measured?

What are the costs of failing to achieve each objective?

What potential conflicts exist between the main objectives of macroeconomic policy?

CONTENTS

8.1	Introduction: the macroeconomic context of business	**254**
8.2	Economic growth	**255**
8.3	Unemployment	**267**
8.4	Inflation	**270**
8.5	The balance of payments	**276**
8.6	A brief overview of macroeconomic policy since 1945	**282**

8.1   Introduction: the macroeconomic context of business

The first half of this book dealt with microeconomics. You will recall that this involves the study of the behaviour and performance of particular or individual aspects of the economy, such as the individual market, consumer, firm or worker. **Macroeconomics,** the subject matter of the second half of the book, is concerned with the study of the behaviour and performance of the economy as a whole. Thus, for example, the microeconomic focus upon the level of output produced in particular markets is generalized at the macro level into an analysis of the overall or *aggregate* level of output produced in the economy. Similarly, micro analyses of the number of people employed in particular markets are, in macro terms, transformed into concerns about the total levels of employment and unemployment in the economy.

> **Macroeconomics:** the study of the economy as a whole.

While macroeconomics takes in the complete picture of the way in which the economy works, it is important to recognize at the outset that such a broad approach is also associated with the some loss of detail. An analysis of the general trend in the level of unemployment, for example, inevitably glosses over unevenness in its distribution. Thus, in both the UK and the EU as a whole, there are long-established concerns over sharp differences in regional unemployment rates. This kind of problem is not immediately apparent from an inspection of aggregate data on unemployment. Similarly, while an increase in national output is usually to be applauded, we might also have a legitimate interest in the relative performances of different sectors in the economy: manufacturing versus financial services, for example. The macro focus tends to neglect this in its preoccupation with the output total.

The profitability of business is critically affected by the macroeconomic environment in which firms operate. By way of illustration, imagine a situation in which an economy is experiencing an upturn in the level of domestic economic activity. During an upturn, output improves and unemployment falls, and the potential for firms to raise their profits increases. However, as demand in the economy increases, upward pressure on wage costs and prices may have a damaging effect on, respectively, the costs of production and sales, and hence on business profitability. Moreover, as the price of domestic goods increases, consumers may begin to buy more imported goods. Domestic firms may also lose custom from declining export sales as their goods become less competitive abroad. Such changes in the macroeconomic environment may have further consequences. Long-term investment decisions may be adversely affected as greater uncertainty over both future revenue flows and the rate of interest (as the government reacts to higher inflation) makes firms increasingly cautious.

> **Macroeconomic policy:** policy used by governments to try to influence overall economic performance.

Given the importance of the macroeconomic environment to business it is crucial that students taking degree courses in subject areas like business studies and management understand what causes changes in the macroeconomy and what influence government policy has on the macroeconomic environment. **Macroeconomic policy** is concerned with the attempts of policymakers to influence the behaviour of macroeconomic aggregates in order to improve the overall performance of the economy. As subsequent chapters will make clear, there is much controversy surrounding the appropriate mix of policies required to improve economic performance.

The remainder of this book is organized as follows. In Chapters 9 and 10 we examine the macroeconomic problems of unemployment and inflation and, in particular, explore debates over their causes and cures. In Chapter 11 we consider the factors that determine long-run economic growth and the different theories economists have put forward to explain short-term fluctuations in aggregate economic activity. In Chapter 12 we discuss the continuing debate between economists over the issue of whether the authorities need to, can and should stabilize the macroeconomy. In the final three chapters we turn to a more detailed consideration of the international macroeconomic environment. In Chapter 13 we consider such key issues as the gains from international trade, changing patterns of trade, and how policy has been used to shape the trading environment. In Chapter 14 we reflect on the nature and significance of the balance of payments and exchange rates. Finally, in Chapter 15 we discuss issues around globalization and business.

The purpose of this chapter is to provide a context for the more detailed discussion of macroeconomics that follows in Chapters 9–15. In particular we will examine the four *main* objectives of government macroeconomic policy, which are

- a stable and satisfactory rate of economic growth;
- a high and stable level of employment;
- a low and stable rate of inflation;
- balance of payments equilibrium in the medium term.

In each case we describe the nature of the objective and explain why it is thought to be desirable. We also briefly consider the extent to which these policy goals can be achieved simultaneously. The chapter concludes with a brief historical overview of the changing policy priorities that have operated at the macro level since the end of the Second World War.

8.2   Economic growth

Economic well-being or *welfare* is a decisively materialist concept. In a micro context we have seen that the amount of goods and services an individual is able to consume is the conventional criterion of satisfaction: 'more is usually better'. At the macroeconomic level a similar logic applies: the greater the level of output produced and consumed in an economy the higher will be its living standards in relation to a given population. One way of measuring overall economic performance is to aggregate – just add up – the value of goods and services produced in a country over a given time period, usually a year. The total that results is known as the **gross domestic product** or **GDP**.

Gross domestic product: the total value of goods and services produced in a country by the factors of production located in that country.

GDP is the total value of goods and services produced in a country by the factors of production located there – regardless of who owns these factors. It can be measured in three *equivalent* ways: on the basis of output, income and expenditure.

The output method

Final output: goods and services that are sold to their ultimate users.

The *output* method of measuring GDP involves aggregating the value of final output of new goods and services (production goods such as machinery and computers, magazines, meals in restaurants, tattoos, tanning-salon sessions and so on) produced within an economy over a given time period, usually a year. We are interested in final output because of the problem of double counting. To illustrate, think about the production of a car. Its principal components include steel, plastic and glass. But if we counted the value of the steel, plastic and glass in GDP *and* also the value of the car in the showroom, we would be double counting the car's components: once on their own and once again as part of the assembled car.

With this pitfall in mind, the output method sums the *value added* in the production process by each sector of the economy. Value added is the difference between the cost of the inputs a firm buys and the value of the output it produces. So the value added by Ford is the value of its cars and trucks minus the value of the materials it uses to make them. Notice though that when Ford buys a metal press this *is* considered a final good to be included in the GDP total – it is not an intermediate component that becomes embodied in a later final good.

DIGITAL VISION

GDP is calculated by adding together the value of everything that's produced in an economy each year, including tattoos

Because they are produced using the resources of other economies, imports are excluded from GDP. On the other hand, exports are the product of domestic economic activity and therefore are counted as an element of GDP.

The output method calculates GDP at *factor cost*. This simply means that values are represented by the actual cost that is paid at each stage of the production process by producers and consumers.

The expenditure method

GDP can also be measured by adding together all *spending* on final goods and services, including spending by foreign residents on goods and services exported abroad. Expenditure on imported goods and services is excluded because imports are the result of production in other economies.

The expenditure method initially measures GDP at *market prices*; that is, the prices at which final goods and services are purchased. But many market prices are distorted by government because it levies an indirect tax such as value added tax (VAT) on most classes of goods or services. VAT typically raises the market price of goods and services by the standard rate of 20 per cent. Think why this poses a problem for the calculation of GDP. Were the government to increase the VAT rate to 22.5 per cent, market prices would typically rise by 2.5 per cent but this would not reflect an increase in the number of goods and services produced, meaning that market prices are not a good guide to production in an economy. So to calculate GDP at *factor cost* – as per the output method – it is necessary to subtract all indirect taxes. Market price distortions also arise where the government chooses to subsidize production. For example, during the 2008–9 recession the British government sought to support the car industry using a scrappage scheme that had the effect of reducing the prices paid by customers for new cars. Because subsidies typically lower market prices, they must be added to the GDP total to cancel out their influence.

The income method

The final measure of GDP involves adding together all of the *incomes* paid to the factors of production in an economy. The act of production in an economy over a year clearly generates incomes for those that undertake it. So labour is paid a wage to reflect its contribution and, similarly, capital is paid interest, land earns rent, and enterprise is rewarded with profit. These incomes are also measured at factor cost – for example, the cost of labour to a firm is simply the total it pays in wages – which makes the income method equivalent to both the output method and the expenditure method after government price distortions have been eliminated.

As noted, GDP measures the total value of goods and services produced in a country by the factors of production located in that country *regardless* of who owns them. But it may be of interest to know what is produced by the British, French or Australian economies in the sense of *national* factors of production. Gross national product (GNP) measures the value of goods and services produced by domestically owned factors of production. GNP is calculated by adding *net property income from abroad* to GDP. Net property income from abroad is income from assets and property owned and held abroad, minus equivalent payments made to overseas residents.

The relationship between the three methods of measuring GDP can be visualized using the circular flow of income presented in Figure 8.1. For ease of exposition, we assume initially that there is no government or international trade. In our highly simplified economy there are only two sectors that

Gross national product: the value of final goods and services produced by domestically owned factors of production.

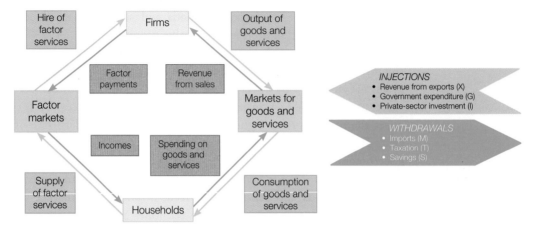

Figure 8.1 The circular flow of income

contribute to the flow of goods and services: firms and households. Households consume a range of goods and services produced by firms. In order to produce these goods and services, firms hire the services of factors of production (labour, capital and land) in factor markets from households. Payments made by firms to the factors of production (wages, profits and rent) flow as incomes to households. Households then spend their incomes on the goods and services produced by firms in goods and services markets. Household expenditure flows back to firms in the form of revenue that firms receive from the sales of final goods and services to households.

In Figure 8.1 a real – *physical* – flow of factor services, and of goods and services, repeatedly circulates around the economy in a clockwise direction between households and firms. These real flows are matched by repeated corresponding *money* flows of income and expenditure from firms to households in an anticlockwise direction. If households spend *all* their incomes on firms' final output of goods and services, and firms use *all* the revenue they received from such sales to buy factor services from households, then income continuously flows around the economy at an unchanged level.

Notice, finally, that Figure 8.1 demonstrates the equivalence of the three methods of calculating GDP. The output of goods and services is met in goods markets by a corresponding level of expenditure, which is in turn generated by a corresponding level of household income.

We will now drop our initial simplifying assumptions and consider how this circular flow of income is affected when an economy has both a government sector and engages in international trade. This more complex picture introduces a set of injections of income into the circular flow and a set of withdrawals of income from it.

Spending on goods: a component of the circular flow

Injections into the circular flow of income

There are three main injections of income into the circular flow, as depicted in Figure 8.1.

- First, firms sell some of their output abroad. The revenue from such export sales (X) enters the circular flow as an injection of income.
- Second, government expenditure (G) on goods and services is an injection of income into the circular flow. Governments undertake both *current* expenditure on, for example, the incomes paid to public-sector employees, and *capital* expenditure, for example on hospital building in the NHS. Government transfer payments – monies transferred between different sections of the community such as jobseeker's allowance – are excluded as they are not paid in return for the production of goods and services.
- Third, private-sector investment expenditure (I) enters the circular flow as an injection of income. Investment expenditure includes purchases of fixed capital such as machines and warehouses, inventory investment that occurs when firms increase their stocks of finished goods, and residential investment: the purchase of new houses.

Total injections of income into the circular flow therefore consist of exports (X), government expenditure (G) and private-sector investment expenditure (I).

Withdrawals from the circular flow of income

Figure 8.1 also illustrates the three main withdrawals from the circular flow. These are:

- First, both households and firms purchase imported goods and services (M). Such expenditure is a withdrawal from the circular flow of income.
- Second, households and firms are unable to spend all the income they receive via the circular flow since they have to pay taxes (T) to the government.
- Third, some income is taken out of the circular flow through savings (S).

Total withdrawals from the circular income flow thus consist of imports (M), taxes (T), and savings (S).

If injections are greater than withdrawals, the level of income in the economy will rise, and vice versa. Income will only circulate at an unchanged level when total injections are exactly matched by total withdrawals. The importance of this equilibrium condition will be discussed more fully in Chapter 9.

Injections and withdrawals in the circular flow – the significance of government involvement

Before we leave the circular flow it is important to note the extent of the government's contribution to it. This is large (and controversial) in many economies, including the UK. For example, in 2014–15 GDP in the UK was estimated to be £1750bn of which £732bn – about 42 per cent – was accounted for by expenditure by the British government. The major categories of spending are summarized in the top half of Figure 8.2. The bottom half of the figure summarizes the sources of government income from which this spending was financed. Notice that government receipts at £648bn meant that the government had to borrow some £84bn to cover all its spending commitments for the year.

Look again at Figure 8.1, the circular flow diagram. Although government injections and withdrawals are depicted in tabs off to the side of the circular flow, it should be clear that many aspects of what the British government

Total expenditure = £732bn

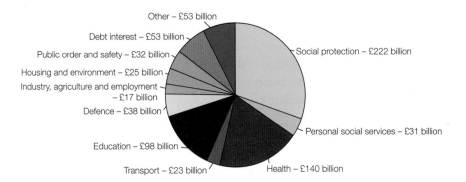

Total income = £648bn

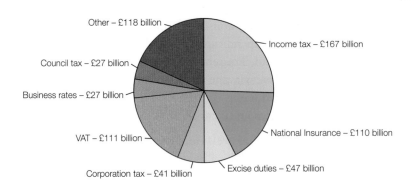

Deficit of income minus expenditure = £84bn

Figure 8.2 British government expenditure and income 2014–2015

Source: Office for Budget Responsibility, 2014–15 estimates. Crown copyright material is reproduced with the permission of the Controller Office of Public Sector Information (OPSI)

chooses to do are actually an integral part of it. For example, although we have followed convention in labelling the box that hires factors of production and produces output 'firms', it might more accurately be labelled 'firms and public-sector institutions', as hospitals, schools, universities, police forces and so on all hire labour and produce services that are components of the circular flow.

The circular flow, microeconomics and macroeconomics

The circular flow diagram also makes plain one aspect of the link between micro- and macroeconomics. The essence of the macroeconomy is captured in the diagram as a whole: in, for example, the total output of firms, or the total spending by households on goods and services. But at the same time the circular flow also illustrates the microeconomic foundations of the grand macro landscape. For example, total expenditure on goods and services is, in the end, simply the expression of the consumption preferences of tens of millions of individual households, together with the investment decisions of millions of firms, and the spending undertaken by thousands of central and local government authorities, departments and agencies. The macroeconomy is, in the end, simply the microeconomy summed.

Further reflections on GDP

Real GDP: the value of gross domestic product measured in terms of the prices that prevailed in some particular base year; also known as GDP in constant prices.

Nominal GDP: the value of gross domestic product measured in terms of the prices prevailing at the time; also known as GDP in current prices.

Economists are particularly interested in real GDP. Real GDP measures output at the prices prevailing in some particular base year – in other words at constant prices. Real GDP will only change if there has been a change in the quantity of goods and services actually produced, so increases in real GDP always indicate that *more* goods and services are being produced. On the other hand, nominal GDP measures GDP at the prices prevailing at the time – in other words at current prices. Nominal GDP may change from one year to the next because of a change in the quantity of goods and services actually being produced and/or a change in the prices of goods and services. This means that nominal GDP may rise simply because prices have risen and not because more output has been produced, hence the greater interest in real GDP which unambiguously indicates changes in output.

Figure 8.3 depicts the movement of real GDP (at constant 2011 prices) for the UK economy since 1948, showing the change in the actual *volume* of goods and services produced. We can make two observations concerning the way in which real GDP has changed over this period. Firstly, the established trajectory of real GDP is clearly upwards. This means that, over the long term, output and income in the UK have tended to increase incrementally.

Economic growth: an increase in real GDP over time.

Economic growth refers to an increase in real GDP, while the annual percentage change in real GDP is known as the *rate* of economic growth. As we will see, *long-term* economic growth can be observed in most economies and reflects changes in factors such as the form and use of technology in new capital equipment, refinements in the organization of production and increases in the supply of labour.

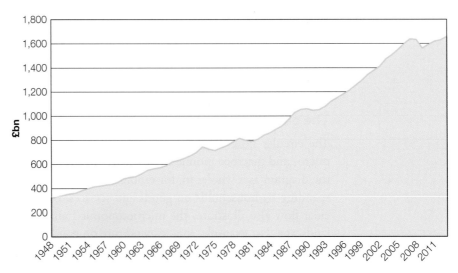

Figure 8.3 UK real GDP 1948–2013, £bn, 2011 prices

Source: ONS: The Blue Book, 2014

The second observation we can make about Figure 8.3 is that there are a number of periods when the real GDP growth path moves decisively away from its long-term trend. In some cases real GDP actually falls, indicating a reduction in the output total in comparison to earlier achievements. For the UK, periods of negative growth occurred in 1974–5 and 1980–81, following the quadrupling of oil prices by the Organization of Petroleum Exporting Countries (OPEC) in 1973–4 and the second OPEC oil price increase in 1979, together with the introduction of the Conservative government's anti-inflation strategy, at the start of the 1980s. The most recent periods of recession in the UK occurred in 1991–2 and 2008–9. Notice that GDP only again reached its 2007 peak in 2103. On the other hand, there are also several instances of relatively rapid economic growth, or boom, when real GDP moved sharply above its trend. In the period 1985–8, for example, real GDP in the UK grew at an annual average rate of 4.4 per cent.

The presence of a long-term growth trend mixed with such short-term fluctuations gives rise to the question of what is a *desirable* rate of economic growth. If rapid growth generally equates with strongly rising living standards, should government policy not have as one of its prime objectives the pursuit of as fast a rate of growth as is possible? Similarly, given that severe recessions are associated with falling output and a drop in the standard of living as fewer goods and services are produced and consumed, should governments not seek to avoid such episodes at all costs? In answering these questions, it is important to be clear about certain constraints under which government policy operates in both the long and the short term. As noted, the long-term growth path reflects, among other things, the technological and organizational sophistication of production, together with the volume of inputs – such as labour – that it is able to command. Because of their very nature, governments can influence these so-called

Recession: a decline in real GDP that lasts for at least two consecutive quarters of a year.

supply-side factors only gradually over time. This means that the established trend in economic growth can be conditioned upwards only very slowly.

On the other hand, *short-term* growth is much more open to the influence of government policy. Thus, governments may try to engineer faster growth in periods before elections in order to curry favour with voters. Why then can they not sustain the rate of expansion over a longer period? One answer is that they are *constrained by other macroeconomic policy objectives*. A high rate of growth, for example, results in higher incomes, some of the increases in which people may choose to spend on imported goods and services from abroad. If the higher import bill is not matched by increased export earnings, a balance of payments deficit problem may emerge. As we will see, balance of payments deficits must ultimately be corrected and, therefore, a more moderate rate of economic growth may have to be actively sought. Periods of rapid expansion can also be associated with higher rates of inflation and, again, policies to trim the rate of economic expansion might be necessary in order to help bring inflation down towards more tolerable levels. It is interesting to note that the historically high rates of growth experienced in the UK in the late 1980s were associated with both inflation and balance of payments problems and that these were subsequently addressed by the 1991–2 recession.

Although governments are constrained from operating the economy at short-term growth rates far above the long-run growth trend, it will be equally evident that there is no advantage in accepting meagre expansion below this trend. Slower short-term growth will entail only marginal increases in output and income for the economy as whole and – in consequence – minimal improvements in living standards. Moreover, if growth becomes slower it is likely to be associated with higher levels of unemployment as falling output prompts firms to reduce the number of people they employ.

Higher growth = higher incomes = more imports of French perfume and Belgian chocolate = potential balance of payments difficulties

Perfume: PhotoDisc/Getty Images. Chocolate: Getty Images/Thinkstock/Monkey Business Images Ltd

If there are constraints on the extent to which the rate of economic growth can be raised in the short term and it is also recognized that slow growth may have some serious disadvantages, what can be said about the objective of macro-economic policy in respect of growth? Generally it is accepted that governments should aspire to a *satisfactory* rate of economic growth. As a policy target, 'satisfactory growth' may appear a little vague or imprecise but let us briefly consider its meaning in the context of our earlier discussion. A wildly variable rate of economic expansion, oscillating between rapid growth – which has to be curtailed because of its adverse inflationary or balance of payments implications – and severe recession, which is associated with rising unemployment and falling living standards, would clearly not be desirable. This suggests that a satisfactory rate is one that is *economically sustainable in the light of the broader framework of macroeconomic objectives.*

The G5 is a group of leading economies in the world: the US, Japan, Germany, France, and the UK.

The comparative performance of similarly advanced industrial economies might also be considered to be important when attempting to assess the adequacy of a given growth rate. Table 8.1 compares real GDP growth rates since 1990 for the so-called G5 group of the world's largest industrial economies – the United States, Japan, Germany, France, and the United Kingdom. The table shows that the average rates of growth for these economies from 1990–2007 ranged between 2.5 per cent for the US to 1.1 per cent for Japan. It is probably reasonable to suggest that growth rates that average less than 2 per cent over the long term are to some extent unsatisfactory. Certainly, Japanese growth over two decades now has with the odd exceptional year been notoriously sluggish. The scale of the 2008–9 recession is also apparent from the table. The Japanese economy shrank by 1.2 per cent in 2008 and then by a further 5.2 per cent in 2009 – the worst performance among the G5. But 2009 was a catastrophic year for all these economies. The period since has produced mixed results. Recovery appears to be reasonably solid in the US and UK but much weaker in the other three economies.

Table 8.1 Economic growth rates for the G5

	1990–2007 annual average	2008	2009	2010	2011	2012	2013	2014
US	2.5	0.4	−2.4	2.5	1.6	2.3	2.2	2.2
Japan	1.1	−1.2	−5.2	4.7	−0.5	1.5	1.5	0.9
Germany	1.6	1.2	−5.0	3.9	3.4	0.9	0.5	1.4
France	1.7	0.3	−2.2	2.0	2.1	0.3	0.3	0.4
UK	2.0	0.5	−4.9	1.7	1.1	0.3	1.7	3.2

Source: Data from IMF's World Economic Outlook Database

Figure 8.4 places the economic collapse of 2009 in longer-term context. Notice that for each of the G5, 2009 sees an unparalleled contemporary fall in real GDP; in fact this is the worst collective performance by the leading economies since the Great Depression of the early 1930s.

Figure 8.5 compares the growth performances of the G5, China – now the world's second-largest economy – and Russia since 1990. The Chinese economy

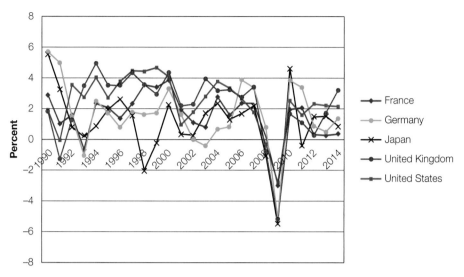

Figure 8.4 Real GDP growth, G5, 1990–2014

Source: Data from IMF's World Economic Outlook Database

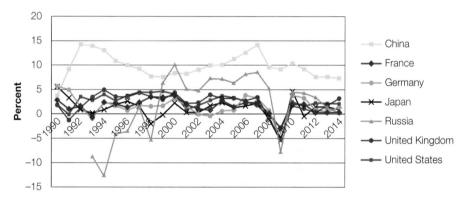

Figure 8.5 Real GDP growth, G5, Russia and China 1990–2014

Source: Data from IMF's World Economic Outlook Database

Note: Data for Russia starts in 1993

has grown on average by 10.1 per cent over the period as a whole. Russia also expanded rapidly for a time after 2000 but it also appears susceptible to deep recessions – its performance in 2009, with growth of *minus* 7.8 per cent, was worse than any of the G5. One obvious question concerns how China and to a lesser extent Russia are able to sustain such comparatively high rates of economic growth. The answer has to do with their relative underdevelopment as market-based economies. While, for example, the UK economy has been maturing since the Industrial Revolution in 1750, China and Russia are very new to the table. Consequently their resource allocation processes are still in a state of flux and undoubtedly still improving, which means that these economies have much more 'room' for growth than do the G5.

Finally in this section we note some qualifications regarding the use of real GDP as a proxy measure or indicator of living standards. As we have seen, real GDP provides a simple measure of the overall economic performance of a country in terms of its material output of goods and services. However, a more reliable indicator of average personal living standards is provided by data on real GDP *per capita*. Real GDP per capita is real GDP divided by the total population of the country. For any given level of real GDP, the smaller the population the more goods and services are available for each person in the economy. Real GDP per head will only remain constant if real GDP is growing at exactly the same rate as the population of the country. If a country's real GDP is growing at a slower rate than its population, then real GDP per head will fall, and vice versa.

Furthermore, while real GDP per capita figures provide a rough indicator of average living standards they don't tell us anything about the *distribution* of income in a country or how that distribution changes over time. This is an important consideration that needs to be borne in mind when using real GDP per capita figures as an indicator of average personal living standards. Real GDP per capita would only provide a reliable measure of what each person in the economy actually received if income was equally distributed among the total population of a country.

Aside from these qualifications it is also important to reflect briefly on whether data on real GDP, and real GDP per capita, provides a complete picture of economic welfare and quality of life in a country. Here we note two main problems. First, data on real GDP does not include non-market activities such as leisure. People's happiness depends not only on the consumption of material goods and services but also on the amount of time spent at leisure. Second, data on real GDP does not include the output of negative *externalities* such as pollution, traffic congestion and noise, all of which have an adverse effect on people's happiness and welfare. Given these two most fundamental omissions, it is important to remember that figures on real GDP provide only a *crude* measure of national economic welfare.

● **Think Point**

What makes you happy? Our focus on GDP suggests that societies are happier when they have higher real incomes. Do you personally agree that more money would make you happier?

Richard Layard, a pioneer in the economics of happiness, makes some interesting points.

- For decades, despite rapidly rising real incomes, happiness in most Western economies has either been flat or actually fallen.
- Higher real incomes may make us feel better at first but once we're habituated to having more money the positive feeling quickly fades.
- People care about *other* people's incomes, not just their own. Layard offers the telling example of East Germany where, since German reunification in 1990, incomes have rocketed but happiness has almost evaporated. Why? Because East Germans used to compare themselves to other countries behind the iron curtain but now they compare themselves to West Germany.

Layard's conclusion is that GDP is actually a *hopeless* measure of welfare.

8.3   Unemployment

Unemployed: people who are available for work and are actively seeking jobs but cannot find them.

An internationally recognized definition of unemployment considers the **unemployed** to be people of working age who are jobless but who are both available for work and actively seeking employment. Note that the definition requires *active* participation in the labour market on the part of the unemployed: the unemployed person's situation must impact upon overall market processes. An unemployed person who sits at home every day and does not look for work makes no impression on the labour market. People who regularly submit job applications and attend interviews tend to condition the operation of the market. Even if it takes time for them to find work their active participation may affect the behaviour of both employers – who are aware that there are jobseekers available for hire – and workers, who understand that there are competitors in the market for the posts that they currently hold.

Unemployment rate: the percentage of the labour force unemployed.

Out-of-worker bee

Reproduced by kind permission of PRIVATE EYE magazine/Rusell Herneman

The **unemployment rate** is the proportion of the total labour force – the total of those employed and unemployed – currently out of work. The unemployment rate is measured at a point in time. At the time of writing (autumn 2014) the unemployment rate in the UK is 6.2 per cent. But such a precise figure as this is in some ways misleading as it rather fails to capture the inherent dynamism of the labour market in a modern economy. One way to capture the fluidity of the processes behind the unemployment rate is to conceptualize, for the economy as a whole, a *pool* of unemployed labour. The pool has inflows that cause it to deepen, and outflows making it shallower. The unemployment rate rises or falls depending on the relative strengths of the pool's inflows and outflows.

The pool is illustrated in Figure 8.6. It has six main inflows. Four of these involve people previously employed who become unemployed because they are made redundant, are sacked, temporarily laid off, or voluntarily quit their existing job. Two further inflows into the pool involve new entrants, such as school leavers, and re-entrants – for example people who have raised a family and are now returning to the labour force.

There are three main outflows from the pool. Some people previously unemployed find new jobs, some who have been temporarily laid off are recalled, while others withdraw from the labour force by retiring or, perhaps disheartened at the prospect of ever finding work, they stop actively seeking employment.

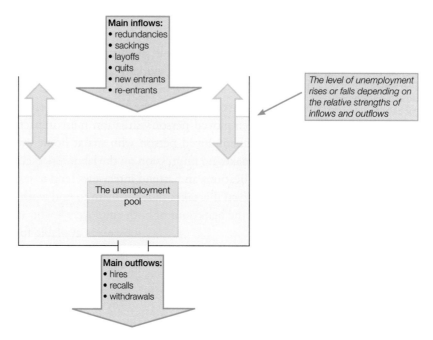

Figure 8.6 The unemployment pool: inflows and outflows

Figure 8.7 summarizes the experience of unemployment in the G5 economies since 1990. Three points emerge from the trends evident in the table. First, the best and most consistent record is that of Japan. The Japanese unemployment rate over the whole period remains below 6 per cent. This is something of a puzzle when we reflect upon Japan's relatively poor growth rate since 1990, as illustrated in Figure 8.4 and Table 8.1. Second, unemployment from the mid-1990s has been stubbornly high in France, while its neighbour Germany, after experiencing similar problems for a long time, has recently seen unemployment

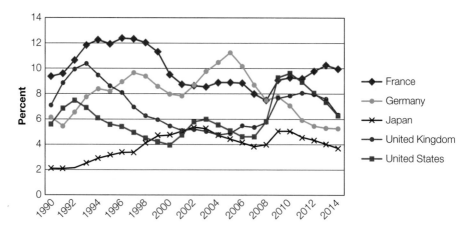

Figure 8.7 G5 unemployment rates 1990–2014

Source: Data from IMF's World Economic Outlook Database

fall below 6 per cent for the first time in 20 years. Finally, the 2008–9 recession pushed up unemployment rates in all the G5 economies but the increase was sharpest in the US. Note that the recoveries in growth in the US and UK have since fed through to improved performances in the labour markets of these countries. We should also emphasize that the data in the table conveys only the broadest picture of the course of unemployment in each country. The more detailed nuances of its distribution by age, gender, social class, and locale must be left to finer, more disaggregate analyses.

Unemployment is a serious policy problem for both economic and social reasons. Economics, as we know from Chapter 1, is concerned with resource allocation: how are the resources a society has being used; are they deployed as effectively as they might be? Unemployment means that a proportion of one particular resource, perhaps the most important one, labour, is not put to any use whatsoever. This waste is compounded by the need to devote still more resources, such as the money tied up in the benefits system, to alleviate the plight of the unemployed; and by the loss of tax revenue to the state that unemployed people would contribute if they had jobs. Far better from an economic perspective is to have a situation in which all who are willing to work have the opportunity to do so. In such circumstances, the welfare – defined by higher incomes and consumption levels – of individuals who might otherwise be unemployed is raised.

For society as a whole, greater employment means more people producing more output, thereby adding to real GDP. As is evident from Table 8.1 and Figure 8.7, the relatively healthy growth performances of the US and UK economies since 1990 and the relatively low US and UK unemployment rates are not a coincidence. On the other hand, lower employment means fewer people producing less output, thereby reducing real GDP.

The social and economic problems associated with unemployment fall into two main categories: those that impact directly upon the unemployed themselves and those that are borne by society as a whole. The first and most obvious burden of unemployment for the individual is financial hardship. Although there is relatively wide variation in the benefit levels set in, for example, the major European countries, in most cases the benefits paid to the unemployed are substantially below the average level of wages. Low incomes may be the precursor of a further set of difficulties for the unemployed and their families: poor standards of health and educational underachievement, for example. *Long-term unemployment* in particular is also recognized to have significant psychological consequences, such as increased stress and low self-esteem.

The wider social costs of unemployment arise because a proportion of the population is, or may perceive itself to be, economically and socially disenfranchised from the mainstream. If some people feel excluded from society and the kinds of material welfare it appears to offer to the majority, then a range of consequences may emerge: increases in political and ethnic tensions and rising crime have all been associated with higher levels of unemployment.

Full employment:
a situation in which all unemployment is frictional and structural, and cannot be reduced by increasing aggregate demand.

Structural unemployment: unemployment that arises from a mismatch between the skills or location of existing job vacancies and the present skills or location of the unemployed; also known as mismatch unemployment.

Frictional unemployment: unemployment that arises because it takes time for workers to search for suitable jobs; also known as search unemployment.

Unemployment is a serious macroeconomic problem and the objective of policy in this area, noted at the beginning of the chapter, is to maintain a high and stable level of employment. However, the notion of full employment does not mean that every member of the working population will always be in a job. Clearly, in a dynamic and changing economy, as new industries emerge and older ones mature, there will be a periodic refocusing of employment opportunity. This is likely to give rise to structural unemployment as some workers, newly released from declining industries, may not have the skills and aptitudes demanded by employers in industries that are growing and offering new employment opportunities. Over time, the required skills can be learned and people can then move back into work. In this sense, structural unemployment may be considered to be a consequence of changes that inevitably occur in a dynamic economy. Similarly, it might be expected that, even in the absence of any structural economic shifts, a competitive labour market will embrace a fair degree of fluidity as people move from job to job, seeking promotion, new challenges or new working environments. In the midst of the many job changes that are constantly taking place in the economy, some people will find themselves temporarily unemployed or *between* jobs for a short period: this is known as frictional unemployment.

In a competitive and ever changing economy some unemployment is inevitable; the question is, how much? In the UK, for example, full employment in the 1950s and 1960s was associated with an achieved rate of unemployment of around 2.5 to 3 per cent. However, since the mid-1970s the UK, along with many other economies, has experienced a significant rise in the level of unemployment. As is evident from Figure 8.7 this is particularly the case for Germany and France. In Chapter 9 we consider possible reasons why unemployment has risen, what level is now believed to be consistent with full employment and the range of policies open to governments to reduce unemployment.

8.4   Inflation

Inflation rate: the rate at which the general level of prices increases; expressed as a percentage on an annual basis.

Inflation is a process of continually rising prices. The inflation rate in an economy thus denotes the pace at which the price of goods and services on average has risen over a given period of time. Although negative inflation (deflation) sometimes occurs, the experience in most economies for most of the time since 1945 is that of positive inflation.

Measuring inflation

Price index: a measure of the average level of prices of a set of goods and services relative to the prices of the same goods and services in a particular base year.

Inflation is measured by reference to movements in a price index. The UK's principal measure of inflation is the Consumer Prices Index (CPI). The CPI measures inflation as the increase in the price of a basket of goods and services over a year. The usual practice is to try to define what a typical household spends its income on and weight the items in the basket according to how much is spent on each. The *broad* weighted contents of the 2014 basket are shown in Figure 8.8, but there are about 650 individual items in the basket altogether.

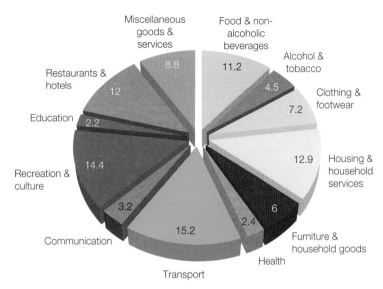

Figure 8.8 The CPI basket 2014 (%)

Source: Data from ONS: Consumer Price Inflation

At 15.2 per cent, transport is the largest single category in the basket. Transport includes car purchase, maintenance and fuel, as well as public transport by road, rail, sea and air. In contrast, health and education are among the smallest categories, each at 2.4 and 2.2 per cent respectively. Neither features significantly in the basket because most education and health services in the UK are provided collectively through the state; consumers are not directly charged for them.

Revisions to the basket are sometimes interesting as, over a longer period, they reflect a combination of changing consumer tastes and product innovation. Notable additions in 2014 reflect changes in the technology behind certain classes of good. When, for example, did you last think about buying a camera? Our guess is a long time ago. Most people have excellent cameras on their mobile phones so the demand for compact digital cameras has dwindled. But, among camera enthusiasts the popularity of cameras with interchangeable digital lenses has grown so these have been added to the CPI basket. Similarly, some DVD-based products have been replaced in the basket by the now more popular streaming-based alternatives.

DVDs: no longer in the CPI basket

Bananastock

The inflation objective

Governments tend to have as an objective a low and stable rate of inflation. Some governments also declare a precise inflation target. For the UK, this is defined as an annual CPI rate of inflation of 2 per cent. For Sweden, the target figure is also 2 per cent; in the euro area it is less-than-but-close-to 2 per cent; for Poland, the target is 2.5 per cent. Canada has a target range of 1 to 3 per cent. We could go on, but you get the picture.

Why is it important to keep inflation low and stable? We will discuss a number of specific problems associated with inflation in a moment but first we want to briefly reflect on inflation from a broad business perspective. In Chapter 2 we saw how markets are coordinated by price signals. Prices provide incentives to producers and consumers to behave in particular ways. For example, higher prices may signal the possibility of greater profit to firms and encourage them to expand output. On the other hand, some consumers may respond to higher prices by leaving a market. But what defines a good signal? One important property is stability. Think what would happen to road traffic flows if traffic lights – another form of signal – had their timings randomly set. You pull up at a red light and you're unsure if you're going to be stuck there for one minute, three minutes, or even ten. The same is true for all other drivers. Our guess is that this would soon result in chaos, with gridlock and accidents as people jumped traffic lights and made poor driving decisions. Traffic signals do a good job when they're predictable and people feel they can rely on them. In markets, price signals are also better if they're reliable and people feel they can use them to make informed choices; this happens more regularly when inflation is low and stable.

© iStockphoto.com/hero30

Traffic signals keep traffic moving; price signals keep markets moving. Both need to be stable and reliable

Perfectly anticipated inflation: arises when the actual rate of inflation is equal to the anticipated or expected rate of inflation.

Problems associated with inflation

Take first a hypothetical situation in which the agents in an economy – consumers, employers, workers, government and others – are aware of the future course of prices. In this case, the rate of inflation could be said to be *perfectly anticipated* and it would be possible to effect movements in other nominal variables such that real economic circumstances remained unchanged. Thus, if the rate of price inflation turned out to be as expected; say, 15 per cent over a future period, equivalent increases in the money value of wages, benefit levels and other incomes would leave the real purchasing power of people receiving such incomes unchanged. Inflation, even though relatively high, would not appear to have any concrete impact. In fact, economists identify two problems that can still occur even if inflation can be perfectly anticipated in this way: so-called shoe leather and menu costs.

Shoe leather costs

Shoe leather costs arise because, in the presence of inflation, cash is continually losing its real purchasing power. This provides people with an incentive to hold as little cash as possible and instead put their money into a bank or some other financial institution where it will earn interest. However, because they need cash for everyday purchases, people will be continually withdrawing small amounts from their accounts, wearing out shoe leather on each visit to the bank or ATM. Of course, 'shoe leather' is a metaphor for the general costs of inconvenience and administration associated with many cash withdrawals.

Menu costs

Menu costs reflect the time and resources used in continually repricing goods and services in shops, vending machines, parking meters and so on, in line with the prevailing inflation rate.

Given the relatively moderate inflation rates experienced in most Western industrial economies since the Second World War, there is general agreement that such shoe leather and menu costs are relatively small. However, such costs become more significant as economies begin to experience more rapid rates of inflation.

While shoe leather and menu costs would arise even in the hypothetical case of inflation being perfectly anticipated, in reality inflation is imperfectly anticipated – for example, the actual rate of inflation turns out to be higher than expected – and, as a result, an additional more important set of costs arises. These costs are the dangers of *hyperinflation*, *market distortion*, *deteriorating international competitiveness*, and problems associated with the *redistribution of income*.

Imperfectly anticipated inflation: arises when the actual rate of inflation differs from the anticipated or expected rate of inflation.

Hyperinflation

Inflationary surges, unless checked, can develop a momentum of their own and may eventually lead to extremely rapid rates known as hyperinflation. The most widely known instance of hyperinflation occurred in Weimar Germany in 1923, where prices were rising at an annual rate of 1 billion per cent. Now, given that the market is perhaps *the* central institution of competitive capitalism and that markets are coordinated by price signals, it follows that the extreme distortion of prices by cumulatively higher rates of inflation is a direct challenge to the integrity of the capitalist system itself.

To put it another way, consider a situation in which money is constantly and quickly drained of its value. As soon as income is earned the imperative will be to spend it before its purchasing power is diminished. At the same time, there will be frantic pressures on all social groups to negotiate and struggle for higher money incomes in order to try to offset imploding real incomes. The apocalyptic consequences for economy and society of the intensification of this

Hyperinflation: arises when the rate of inflation is extremely high.

Photo by Three Lions/Getty Images

Money's not a toy but it was in Germany in 1923 when hyperinflation made it worthless

Relative price: the ratio of the price of one good to the price of another good; expressed as the number of units of one good that one unit of another good will buy.

kind of process, as inflation surges ever higher, are not difficult to imagine: ultimately, the payments system would collapse, leaving exchange to be coordinated by the process of barter.

This actually happened in Weimar Germany. The photograph shows children playing with blocks, as children all over the world have always done. Except, if you look closely, you'll see that these blocks are made of German banknotes. Inflation had so eroded the real value of money people no longer used it to buy things with; it was better used as a children's toy.

Market distortion

Inflation does not need to reach 'hyper' proportions for it to be sufficient to distort and weaken the way in which markets work. The late American economist Milton Friedman argued that as the rate of inflation increases, so too does its variability. Greater variability of inflation generates more *uncertainty* as to what the actual rate will be at any given time. This makes it more difficult for economic agents to distinguish between changes in the general price level and changes in the **relative prices** of different goods and services. Accordingly, economic agents will make mistakes.

For example, imagine a situation where the price of a particular good, good X, is £30 and the price of another good, good Y, is £10. The relative price of good X to good Y is 3:1. Now if prices increase across the economy by 10 per cent, the price of good X will increase to £30.30 and that of good Y to £10.10, but relative prices will remain unchanged. However, higher prices in the market for good X might prompt firms to enter in the anticipation of higher profits. The overall level of output in the market increases accordingly but, if price rises are occurring right across the economy and there is no new or extra demand present, unsold stocks of good X will pile up.

The possibility of errors of this sort breeds distrust as to the reliability of price signals and encourages economic agents to spend time and resources unproductively trying to discern what is really going on. Ultimately then, markets become less efficient than they would otherwise be in the absence of high and rising inflation, and Friedman argued that lower output and higher unemployment is the inevitable result. Friedman also suggested that similar consequences follow when increased uncertainty induced by higher rates of inflation makes economic agents more cautious: they become more reluctant to take the consumption and investment decisions that would occur in periods of greater price stability.

Deteriorating international competitiveness

A further major problem associated with a high rate of inflation concerns the damage inflicted upon international competitiveness. An economy that experiences rapid increases in prices will find it more difficult to trade successfully in an environment where its trading partners enjoy more moderate rates of inflation. Very simply, the price of its exports will be rising faster than the price of substitutes in foreign markets; and, at home, the price of domestic goods will be rising faster than the price of imports. *Ceteris paribus*, this means that the balance of trade in goods and services for the more inflationary economy will deteriorate and, as we explain below, trade deficits, where imports surge ahead of exports, cannot be sustained much beyond the medium term. What is crucial here then is not the rate of inflation per se but the rate of inflation experienced in one country relative to that experienced elsewhere.

The redistribution of income

When inflation is imperfectly anticipated it raises another set of redistributive problems because of its differing impacts upon different groups of people in society. In financial markets, for example, inflation helps borrowers but penalizes lenders. Just as inflation drains money of its value, so it reduces the real value of debt. A sum borrowed at the beginning of a period of high inflation will, in real terms, be worth much less when the debt comes to be subsequently repaid. For those in debt this is clearly a substantial boon: they can borrow and spend now but the real value of the sum they have to repay in future will be diminished in direct proportion to the inflation rate. Similarly, the expected real value of the interest paid on a debt will be eroded when inflation turns out to be higher than anticipated. For lenders, the implications are reversed: inflation reduces the real value of their capital tied up in loans and it similarly erodes the real value of interest earnings when inflation is imperfectly anticipated. Overall then, inflation has the effect of redistributing income from lenders to borrowers.

Unanticipated inflation has similar redistributive effects among other groups in society. For example, it disadvantages those with incomes that were fixed in less inflationary times. Thus, people who are retired may have saved capital to provide for their old age. If inflation diminishes the real value of their savings, and any income stream they derive from such savings, they will be severely disadvantaged because they have no further access to other sources of income, such as wages, that may be easier to adjust for inflation. At the same time, wage earners, if they are in a strong enough bargaining position, may actually increase the real value of their incomes if they can negotiate an increase in money wages above the rate of inflation. Here, redistribution would be from the non-waged to the waged. Generally, in distributive terms, we may conclude that inflation injures those who are unable to defend or raise their real incomes and advantages those in debt or who have the capacity to revise their real income levels.

Inflation performances

Figure 8.9 describes the inflation performances of the G5 economies since 1990. From the figure, it is evident that none of the G5 has had much difficulty in controlling inflation over this period: in general it has been low and stable. Indeed, if anything, there has been a problem in Japan of *deflation*, with

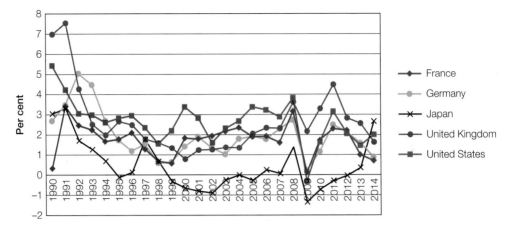

Figure 8.9 G5 inflation, 1990–2014

Source: Data from IMF's World Economic Outlook Database

periodic negative movements in overall prices. One difficulty here is that when prices are falling in an economy, consumer demand may become fragile. People prefer to put off purchases to buy cheaper at a later time. But if many consumers do this then demand overall falls and growth falters.

8.5   The balance of payments

Balance of payments: a record of the transactions that take place between the residents of one country and the rest of the world over a given time period (usually one year).

The balance of payments is a record of the transactions that take place between the residents of one country and the rest of the world over a given period, usually a year. Balance of payments transactions come in a variety of forms. The most obvious category is trade in goods and services. Imports and exports of goods are known as *visible* trade, while service transactions are called *invisible* trade. Other balance of payments transactions include foreign borrowing and lending, buying and selling financial assets such as shares abroad, and buying and selling real assets such as firms in international markets. A full discussion of the various components of the balance of payments accounts can be found in Chapter 14.

Why are balance of payments considerations an important element of macroeconomics? To help answer this question, think about the range of goods you will use or consume today. Many of the clothes you are wearing, for example, will have been manufactured abroad, probably in the Far East as well as in other parts of the EU. The television on which you watch an American-made film tonight might be Japanese and the bed you sleep in Swedish. This kind of exercise gives us some idea of how interdependent most of the world actually is. We live in an international economy that is characterized by increasing openness. This means that more and more of the output individual economies produce is being sold in other countries. For the most part, such openness, because it

Where was the bed you sleep in made?

is associated with increasing market accessibility, faster economic growth and wider consumer choice, is viewed very positively.

Table 8.2 illustrates the increasing openness of the world's major economies over the postwar period. The data expresses the combined money value of exports and imports as a percentage of *nominal GDP*; that is, GDP valued in the prices ruling in each year. Although some economies, the US and Japan for example, have a lower relative dependency on trade, all have seen a growth in openness over the period in question. For the European nations of Germany and France, the increase is particularly marked. This probably reflects their collective participation in the long process of economic integration that began in the 1950s.

We can identify two main reasons why such openness is likely to increase still further over the next decade and beyond. First, economic integration is gaining momentum. In particular parts of the world, formerly separate economies or groups of economies are coalescing to form unified or single markets and free trade areas. The single market in Europe, for example, provides for the free movement of both goods and services and factors of production among all European Union member states. Prior to the establishment of the European Economic Community (EEC) in 1957, the countries of Europe were much more fragmented with a host of restrictions on both the range and form of cross-border transactions their citizens were permitted to engage in. Now, for economic purposes at least, we are all citizens of the single market rather than our respective 28 economies. Similarly, the North American Free Trade Area (NAFTA), created in 1993, binds together the economies of the US, Canada and Mexico into a unified market, which has no internal barriers to trade, although separate markets in factors of production, such as labour, continue to exist. The box below, 'Applying Economics to Business', reflects on some of the business opportunities that trade agreements between nations may offer.

Table 8.2 Openness for the G5 in current prices (total trade as % of GDP)

	1950	1960	1970	1980	1990	2000	2010
France	28.23	27.22	31.32	44.38	43.85	56.63	53.27
Germany	19.7	29.0	33.5	44.42	49.57	66.46	88.18
Japan	17.73	20.56	20.0	27.94	19.77	20.52	29.26
United Kingdom	45	41.96	43.79	51.67	50.02	57.1	62.55
United States	8.21	9.46	11.27	20.76	20.54	25.95	29.05

Source: Alan Heston, Robert Summers and Bettina Aten, Penn World Table Versions 6.3 and 7.1, Center for International Comparisons of Production, Income and Prices at the University of Pennsylvania, August 2009 and November 2012

APPLYING ECONOMICS TO BUSINESS

Free Trade Areas and Business Opportunity

Most of the world's economies practise various forms of trade protection by, for example, using tariffs – which are taxes on traded goods – to restrict the flow of imports and preserve more of the domestic market for domestically produced goods.

But at the same time, policymakers also recognize that, because they limit competition and consumer choice, tariffs are economically harmful. This is why by 2010 there were more than 250 regional trading agreements (RTAs) in force throughout the world. These agreements create free trade between partner economies.

In reaching an RTA, signatory countries usually agree to eliminate all tariffs and other trade policy measures that may restrict mutually beneficial trade flows.

RTAs create notable opportunities for business by, in effect, increasing the size of the domestic market to encompass the economies of all partners. For example, when Bulgaria and Romania joined the European Union in 2007, they secured open access to each other's markets and those of the EU's incumbent 25-strong membership.

The Toyota Tacoma

Courtesy of Toyota

From the perspective of Bulgarian and Romanian firms, this is a positive development. They have the opportunity to sell in a very large and very affluent market, and their exposure to healthy competition should provide an incentive for them to reflect on what they do and improve how they do it.

RTAs also generate other kinds of business opportunity. For example, the Japanese car firm Toyota has a truck-making plant on the Baja peninsula in Mexico that produces approximately 50,000 Tacoma trucks annually. Toyota also has a plant in Canada making approximately 200,000 Corolla and Matrix passenger cars combined. But Toyota doesn't build these vehicles just to sell them in Mexico and Canada.

The North American Free Trade Agreement (NAFTA) allows Toyota to freely sell its Mexican and Canadian output in any of the three North American economies, which means its Mexican-built trucks can be shipped to both Canada and the world's largest national market, the US. The same opportunity applies to its Canadian-build cars. Toyota opened its Mexican and Canadian operations only after NAFTA was created.

So NAFTA has generated business opportunities for Toyota but it has also helped the Mexican and Canadian economies too. Both have attracted substantial overseas investment, partly because of their open access to the affluent American market.

The second factor promoting accelerated openness in world markets is the liberalization of many of the former centrally planned economies such as China, Vietnam and those in Eastern Europe. Markets in these economies are increasingly open to Western investment and goods and the West itself is available as a potentially lucrative market for the outputs these fast-growing economies produce. Indeed, for the more dynamic of the Eastern European states, such as Slovenia and Slovakia, there is already deep integration with the European single market and active participation in the euro area.

Because of the high and increasing degree of openness in world markets, balance of payments problems are clearly a significant macroeconomic issue. What then are the policy objectives that arise in this area? In order to simplify the discussion we will concentrate here on the balance of payments as represented

© iStockphoto.com/Nikada

Shanghai: China offers a dynamic new market for Western investment and goods

by trade in goods and services. Initially, three possibilities arise for the balance of payments position of an economy:

- *deficit,* where the total value of imports exceeds the value of exports
- *surplus*, where export revenues are greater than the total import bill
- *balance*, where the values of exports and imports are roughly equal.

In the case of a deficit, it follows that domestic residents have an appetite for imports that is not matched by their ability to sell goods and services abroad: they are, in other words, net importers. At this point, the fact that different currencies are involved in international trade becomes significant. Exports are a means of generating the reserves of foreign currency or foreign exchange necessary to pay for imports. If the residents of a country are – collectively – net importers, it follows that they have a need to acquire foreign currency to pay for imports which is not matched by the level of foreign currency earnings that their exports currently generate: they have, in other words, a foreign currency 'gap'.

This gap can be filled in two ways. Either residents can draw on currency reserves that they have accumulated in previous periods or they can borrow the foreign currency that they require. Now, while both courses of action are possible in the short term neither is sustainable indefinitely: foreign currency reserves and the goodwill of lenders are both finite. This means that balance of payments deficits cannot be sustained in the medium term because of the exhaustion of the supplies of foreign currency necessary to finance them; *a persistent balance of payments deficit is, therefore, a policy problem.*

A surplus on the balance of payments, on the other hand, has the effect of augmenting the reserves of foreign currency held in the domestic economy. Because domestic residents are net exporters, it follows that they will be more than meeting the foreign currency requirements of their current level of imports. The extra foreign currency their net exports generate, because it is not immediately needed, is simply added to any existing reserves. A balance of payments surplus might thus appear to be relatively attractive, particularly when the positive knock-on effects of strong export demand on economic growth and domestic employment levels are also taken into consideration. However, this is not the whole story. A consistent surplus – and the piling up of foreign currency reserves – also represents missed consumption opportunities. It would be possible for domestic residents to comfortably finance more imports – and thereby raise their welfare – from the revenues generated by current export performance. Alternatively, they could increase investment abroad or provide more overseas aid.

A balance of payments surplus therefore, even though it might represent export dynamism is, in itself, no real achievement. A surplus can also be a sign of considerable economic weakness. In a recessionary period when real GDP grows more slowly, the capacity to import is constrained by a slowdown in the growth of income. At the same time, assuming export markets are unaffected – their strength is in part a function of foreign incomes – the balance of payments may improve sharply – that is, move away from deficit – but, clearly, this is far from any kind of achievement. Further caveats concerning the desirability of balance of payments surplus are considered in Chapter 14.

Given that a deficit is a problem and a surplus is hardly laudable, it follows that the objective of policy in respect of the balance of payments is *balance in the medium term*. Balance equates the import-derived foreign currency demands of domestic residents with their export-derived foreign currency earnings. This means that there is no foreign currency 'gap' to close, nor any potential consumption or investment forgone. The emphasis is on balance over the medium term, rather than every year, because individual years' deficits and surpluses have the effect of cancelling each other out.

Finally in this section, we briefly consider the relationship between the balance of payments and the other objectives of macroeconomic policy. To some extent this has been anticipated by earlier discussion. We have already indicated, for example, that improvements in the balance of payments can be achieved from the implementation of domestic austerity measures: if domestic residents are made poorer by the onset of recession they cannot afford to buy as many imports as in previous periods. We also noted, in our discussion of growth, that a rapidly expanding economy with rising income levels will usually be associated with a deterioration in the balance of payments: in other words, a movement towards or into deficit. Such links between the balance of payments and other macroeconomic targets give rise to a wider definition of the notion of balance of payments balance or *equilibrium*. We may consider the balance of payments to be in a desired equilibrium over a period of years if a balance is achieved without the need for slower growth, with all its attendant disadvantages, to make this happen. In Chapter 14 we offer further revisions of this definition.

Austerity: a programme of public expenditure reduction.

1

© Chris Mulhearn

2

© iStockphoto/clu

3

© Chris Mulhearn

EVERYDAY ECONOMICS 8.1

What's the macroeconomic issue in each of these photographs?

Here are some images that represent some fundamental issues in the macroeconomy. Can you explain them?

Answers are at the end of the chapter.

Hint for photo 1: this is the Liverpool Tobacco Warehouse, the largest brick building in the world. It's on Liverpool's Dock Road once an area of thriving economic activity and high employment. The warehouse has been derelict for decades.

8.6   A brief overview of macroeconomic policy since 1945

It is a commonplace that economic ideas are *reactive* in that they change and develop to confront new or emergent economic problems. If the macroeconomic objectives we have discussed are, broadly speaking, met for many economies over a sustained period, then there will be little pressure to search for new forms of understanding and policy: economists and governments will seemingly have 'got it right'. On the other hand, when targets are missed, perhaps disastrously so, there will be an obvious need to revise the thought behind and conduct of macro policy.

The first major instance of this kind of shift in macroeconomic thinking and action occurred as a result of the Great Depression of the early 1930s. During this **depression**, output and employment in most of the world's major industrial economies fell dramatically. For example, in the US, real GDP fell by 35 per cent between 1929 and 1933, with unemployment reaching a peak of 25 per cent in 1933. Previously, although cycles of fast and slower growth had been experienced, economic progress had proceeded relatively smoothly on a generally uninterrupted upward path. This meant that the prevailing economic orthodoxy of **classical economics**, seemingly having 'got it right', was not open to serious challenge. The Great Depression offered hugely changed circumstances and the opportunity for the advancement of radically different theory and policy.

As a response to the new economic problems posed in the 1930s, the British economist John Maynard Keynes wrote *The General Theory of Employment, Interest and Money*. This book, published in 1936, contained the seeds of a revolution in macroeconomics; indeed, it is often credited as the first work to be framed in a conscious macro dimension. Keynes argued that governments, through managing the total or **aggregate demand** for the output of an economy, could vanquish depression and produce full employment (see Chapter 9 for a much more detailed explanation of this approach).

Keynes's work proved to be exceptionally influential in both academic and government circles to the extent that during the 1950s and 1960s both macroeconomic thought and policy came to reflect the broad thrust of his views. Moreover, his influence was not confined to Britain; rather it assumed the proportions of a new ruling orthodoxy in all the advanced Western economies. **Keynesian economics** or **Keynesianism** – as the new approach became known – set its sights firmly on maintaining a high and stable level of employment in order to avoid the social, economic and political costs of unemployment. Accordingly, as governments absorbed and put into practice Keynesian ideas, the major short-term policy objective of the early postwar period became full employment. Because there is a correlation between higher levels of employment and faster short-term economic growth, this too became an objective associated with Keynesianism. However, recall our earlier qualification that growth over the longer term is much less open to the influence of government policy.

What of the other macroeconomic objectives under Keynesianism? We have noted that the balance of payments can act as a constraint upon the successful

---

Depression: a very severe and prolonged recession.

Classical economics: a pre-Keynesian approach based on the assumption that wages and prices adjust to clear markets and that monetary policy does not influence real variables, such as output and employment.

Aggregate demand (AD): the total planned expenditures of all buyers of final goods and services; comprises consumer expenditure, investment expenditure, government expenditure and net exports.

Keynesian economics: an approach based on the belief that capitalist economies are inherently unstable and can come to rest at less than full employment for prolonged periods; Keynesian economists favour the use of discretionary aggregate demand policies to stabilize the economy at, or near, full employment.

attainment of both employment and growth objectives. When more people are employed and incomes are rising quickly, there will be a consequent increase in imports without any necessary compensatory movement in exports. In this situation the balance of payments will worsen. Because balance of payments deficits cannot be tolerated beyond the medium term, it may prove necessary to trim the growth rate and accept higher levels of unemployment.

The final policy objective – inflation – tended to remain comfortably low in most economies for the period of the 1950s through to the mid-to-late 1960s when Keynesianism was dominant and, therefore, following the problem–response notion introduced at the beginning of this section, the issue of inflation was not the focus of a great deal of attention. Where slightly faster inflation did provoke mild concern, it tended to be addressed as a constraint on employment and growth in a similar manner to the balance of payments.

Keynesianism was coincident with an era known as the *postwar boom*. This lasted from the end of the Second World War until about 1970. The postwar boom was characterized by the general experience in most economies of historically rapid rates of economic growth, full employment and low inflation. Whether or not Keynesianism can be credited with some or all of these achievements is, however, a matter of some dispute. The period since 1970 has been one in which economic progress has faltered somewhat. Growth rates have been lower, unemployment higher on average and, in particular, inflation has been higher and more variable. Furthermore, the inflationary surge experienced in major Western economies at the end of the 1960s and beginning of the 1970s was so radically different from the gradual rates that prevailed during the postwar boom that it served to undermine the Keynesian orthodoxy, clearing the ground for a second comprehensive revision of macro thought and policy.

The changed economic circumstances after 1970 served to expose two major weaknesses in Keynesian theory. First, in its understandable preoccupation with unemployment, Keynesianism had tended to neglect inflation both as a phenomenon, which needed explanation, and as a problem for policy. Second, in a limited theorization, Keynesianism posed inflation as an 'alternative' to unemployment; in other words, economies could suffer from high unemployment *or* high inflation but not both at the same time. The new 1970s phenomenon of stagflation thus provided a set of circumstances for which Keynesianism had no ready analysis or answers.

It should be clear that a theoretical approach that could explain the emergence of virulent inflation rates and higher unemployment would challenge Keynesianism for the economic high ground. This is what the revived doctrine of monetarism, associated with the work of Milton Friedman, actually did. As we will discuss in Chapter 10, Friedman argued that inflation is essentially determined by the rate of monetary growth relative to the rate of real output growth and he stressed the need for monetary control to combat inflation. Moreover, if inflation is kept low and stable by government policy it is suggested that markets can then be relied upon to produce favourable outcomes in

Stagflation: a situation where high unemployment and high inflation occur simultaneously; a combination of stagnation and inflation.

Monetarism: an approach based on the belief that capitalist economies are inherently stable unless disturbed by erratic monetary growth, and will return fairly rapidly to the neighbourhood of the natural level of output and employment when subjected to some disturbance.

respect of the other three macroeconomic variables introduced in this chapter. To a great extent, the view many governments have distilled from this approach over more recent years is that inflation should be accorded priority in respect of the conduct of macroeconomic policy.

In summary then, the second half of the twentieth century was successively dominated by two different macroeconomic perspectives, which gave rise to two sets of policy imperatives. During the postwar boom the work of Keynes inspired an approach that emphasized the policy problem of unemployment; while, since the 1970s, the work of Friedman has shifted the policy consensus firmly towards the control of inflation. This refocusing of policy was paralleled by a move away from the Keynesian management of aggregate demand in favour of inflation targets and the management of the supply side of the economy – areas we will explore more fully in subsequent chapters.

We conclude this chapter with a brief reflection on the impact of the 2008–9 recession on macroeconomic thought and policy. Recall our opening sentence in this section – that economic ideas are *reactive*; they change and develop in response to new macroeconomic problems. In one sense we were wrong. Macroeconomic thought and policy in the context of the 2008–9 recession were actually *recursive*, meaning that the recession prompted the recycling of some old – Keynesian – approaches to macroeconomics.

These mainly involved revisiting the idea that governments could arrest and reverse decline by stimulating the level of aggregate demand in the economy. Governments can manage demand in two principal ways: by spending more themselves even if this means incurring debt, and by encouraging individuals and firms to spend more by cutting taxes and lowering interest rates.

In response to the global downturn, governments around the world have done all of these things and more. For example, the British government either directly or through the Bank of England:

- initiated an increase in government spending in 2009–10 equivalent to almost 5 per cent of GDP
- cut the rate of VAT from 17.5 to 15 per cent for 2009
- reduced interest rates to their lowest ever level of 0.5 per cent
- printed £200bn – about 12 per cent of GDP – which was used to push liquidity into the UK's private sector, encouraging firms to spend and invest.

Did these Keynesian measures work? We think the broad answer is yes in the sense that the UK and other economies began to come slowly out of recession towards the end of 2009. There was no 1930s-style prolonged slump. Recovery though has been slow and patchy and some European economies have lapsed back into intermittent periods of negative growth.

What is also interesting is the rapid reassertion of what had up to the financial crisis been the monetarist orthodoxy in macroeconomic policy. In many economies, including the UK, this has been embodied in a fervent attachment to programmes of austerity; in short, the urgent cutting of public expenditure to reduce the deficits accumulated during the Keynesian-inspired reaction to the crisis. An extended discussion of why this happened is beyond the scope of an introductory textbook in economics for business, but some fascinating work by Henry Farrell and John Quiggin offers the following.

The re-emergence of Keynesianism was propelled by the vocal arguments of a small number of world-renowned economists, some of whom had been persuaded that the scale of the crisis demanded that the doubts they themselves harboured about deficit spending had to be set aside. This provided a veneer of unanimity that appeared to endorse Keynesian intervention. Subsequently, as the recession receded and a greater plurality of views came to be heard, the appearance of a Keynesian consensus melted away. (Search online for Henry Farrell and John Quiggin, *Consensus, dissensus and economic ideas: the rise and fall of Keynesianism during the economic crisis*, 2012.)

SUMMARY

- Macroeconomics involves the study of the economy as a whole. Macroeconomic policy is concerned with the efforts of policymakers to influence the behaviour of four key variables: the rate of economic growth, the level of unemployment, the rate of inflation and the balance of payments position. We must recognize that macroeconomic policy objectives in respect of each of these variables cannot be pursued independently. For example, efforts to raise the rate of economic growth in the short term must be tempered with an acknowledgement of its potentially negative effects upon inflation and the balance of payments.
- Failure to achieve macroeconomic objectives carries a variety of consequences. Attaining slower rates of economic growth than desirable will entail only modest increases in general living standards and may be associated with rising unemployment. In turn, unemployment carries economic and social costs. It wastes scarce human resources and it inflicts poverty and a sense of hopelessness on the unemployed.
- Inflation is economically undesirable as it can distort and undermine a central feature of capitalist resource allocation: the price mechanism. It also disadvantages those on fixed incomes and may threaten the trading position of the economy as a whole.
- Adverse balance of payments positions may necessitate actions that undermine other objectives. For example, balance of payments deficits usually require some moderation in the rate of economic growth.

- There is a strong correlation between the emergence of new macroeconomic problems and the development of macroeconomic thought and policy. Since 1945, macroeconomic policy has been dominated successively by the development and application of first Keynesianism, then monetarism, and most recently by a *brief* resurgence of Keynesianism as a response to the recessionary implications of the 2008–9 financial crisis. Keynesianism promotes the widespread involvement of the state in many aspects of the economy. Monetarism, on the other hand, demands much more circumspect forms of state intervention.

KEY TERMS

- Macroeconomics
- Macroeconomic policy
- Economic growth
- Unemployment
- Full employment
- Inflation
- Hyperinflation
- Balance of payments surplus and deficit
- Balance of payments balance
- Keynesianism
- Postwar boom
- Stagflation
- Monetarism

QUESTIONS FOR DISCUSSION

1. What are the main objectives of macroeconomic policy?
2. Why are fast rates of economic growth not necessarily desirable?
3. What are the main costs of unemployment? Are there any circumstances in which firms might benefit from a rise in the level of unemployment in the economy?
4. How important is it to control inflation?

5. In what ways will an increase in the rate of inflation adversely affect firms?
6. Why is a surplus on the balance of payments undesirable?
7. What potential conflicts exist between the main objectives of macroeconomic policy?
8. What is the link between economic performance and the development of economic thought and policy?

EVERYDAY ECONOMICS 8.1 ANSWERS

1. **The derelict warehouse represents the problem of *structural* unemployment**. Tens of thousands of dock workers were employed in Liverpool up to the 1950s. Now there are just a few hundred. The port turns around more cargo than it ever did but containerization means that dock activity is now capital- rather than labour-intensive. So Liverpool and cities like it have had to find new sources of jobs as old industries die away as major employers. One of the job-generating growth industries in Liverpool is tourism and the Tobacco Warehouse complex is now being redeveloped as a hotel, apartments, shops, restaurants and bars.

2. **A billion mark note from Germany in 1923**. Hyperinflation destroyed the German currency – the Reichsmark – but before the end came the authorities were printing money in ever higher denominations as the prices of even everyday items were counted in billions!

3. **Our friend has Bolivian bolivianos and wants to spend them in a pub in the UK.** He can't do this because the pub only accepts pounds. He can exchange his bolivianos for pounds in the foreign exchange market but what makes this exchange possible? The only reason that non-Bolivian residents (and therefore the foreign exchange market) will accept bolivianos is that Bolivia produces goods and services that the rest of the world wants to buy. If Bolivia produced nothing of interest to anyone outside Bolivia its currency would be internationally worthless. Because Bolivia does produce things the rest of us want to buy (such as natural gas and silver) there is a demand for the boliviano in the international economy and it can be exchanged for other currencies.

ONE THING YOU SHOULD READ

Paul Krugman on the Macroeconomics of a Space Alien Invasion
http://www.youtube.com/watch?v=nhMAV9VLvHA

A 90-second reflection on how the US government should have confronted the 2008–9 economic crisis. Paul Krugman offers a Keynesian-style argument that the depth of the recession in the US and the high unemployment that it has caused necessitate urgent action. Unemployment in the US hit 10 per cent at the end of 2009 – the highest for 25 years.

The video opens with an argument by Kenneth Rogoff that public spending on infrastructure is a good thing to do in a recession: classic Keynesianism. But Rogoff states that this should not be done without regard to costs – he counsels against 'Boston Big Dig prices'. This is a reference to the most expensive road engineering project in US history.

What's really interesting though is how Krugman then develops the infrastructure spending case. He talks about the 'negative social spending' of World War II but then you can see him visibly hesitate before suggesting that a 'space alien' threat might do the trick this time. Of course, he's not serious but the underlying point is.

Watch the video and then answer the following questions.

1. How does the TV anchor respond to Kenneth Rogoff's point that infrastructure spending should not be exorbitant? Do you agree?
2. What does Paul Krugman mean by 'negative social spending'?
3. What is Krugman's underlying point: what does he want the government to do and why?

Another thing you might like:

Loudon Wainwright III singing 'The Krugman Blues':
http://www.youtube.com/watch?v=hZSor-w3yJk

© iStockphoto.com/Henrik Jonsson

287

9

unemployment: causes and cures

KEY ISSUES

Are the causes and cures for unemployment to be found *inside* or *outside* the labour market?

What are the main theories that economists have put forward to explain unemployment?

How can governments reduce unemployment?

How have economists sought to explain the substantial rise in unemployment that has taken place in Europe since the 1970s?

CONTENTS

9.1 Introduction: the debate over the causes and cures for unemployment **288**

9.2 The classical approach **289**

9.3 The orthodox Keynesian approach **290**

9.4 The monetarist approach **300**

9.5 The new classical approach **302**

9.6 The new Keynesian approach **303**

9.7 A case study: unemployment in Europe **308**

9.1   Introduction: the debate over the causes and cures for unemployment

In the previous chapter we discussed the nature and measurement of unemployment, together with its economic, social and political costs. Furthermore, we highlighted that the profitability of business is critically affected by the macroeconomic environment in which firms operate. Changes in unemployment, for example, can have a substantial effect on the success of firms. During an upturn in the level of domestic economic activity unemployment falls and the potential for firms to raise their sales and profits increases. In contrast during a downturn – given that unemployment results in financial hardship for the vast majority of those concerned – rising unemployment reduces the level of overall demand within the economy, adversely affecting business profitability. In addition rising unemployment results in a loss of tax revenue to the state and increased payments of state benefits, and is associated with a range of social and political problems – in areas such as crime, health and inequality – that need to be addressed by costly social policies. The purpose of this chapter is to look at the main theories put forward by economists to explain unemployment and consider the policy implications that derive from these competing theories.

While there is a general consensus that the maintenance of a high and stable level of employment is an important objective of macroeconomic policy, there is considerable debate over why unemployment exists and what governments can do to reduce it. At the outset it is worth emphasizing that the central question underlying this continuing debate is whether the cause of unemployment is largely to be found *inside* or *outside* the labour market. We saw in Chapter 7 that the labour market in reality is not perfectly competitive. If unemployment is essentially due to imperfections inside the labour market, then government policy to reduce unemployment needs to be directed to alleviate such imperfections. If, on the other hand, the cause of unemployment is largely to be found outside the labour market – because of insufficient spending in the goods market – then government policy needs to be directed to stimulate aggregate demand in the economy.

Historically, economists have applied many adjectives to the term 'unemployment'. These include voluntary, involuntary, classical/real wage, frictional/search, structural/mismatch and demand-deficient/cyclical, to name but a few. In addition, some economists refer to a natural rate of unemployment, while others prefer to speak of a non-accelerating inflation rate of unemployment (NAIRU). It is hardly surprising that, given such a plethora of terms and concepts, students often find the issue of unemployment one that is particularly difficult to get to grips with. In attempting to shed light on the causes and cures for unemployment, we will trace how economists from the nineteenth century through to the present day have put forward new and often controversial theories to explain unemployment. In sketching out the history of unemployment theory in this way it is possible to identify the development of *five* main approaches within mainstream economics, namely the:

- classical approach
- orthodox Keynesian approach
- monetarist approach
- new classical approach
- new Keynesian approach

9.2 The classical approach

Real wage: the money wage divided (or deflated) by the price index; the amount of goods and services that a money wage can buy.

Economists who adhered to the so-called classical approach – an approach widely held by economists writing from around the middle of the eighteenth century to the mid-1930s – maintained that so long as money wages and prices were flexible, and free to adjust, the labour market would always tend to clear at full employment equilibrium. Given a perfectly competitive labour market, anyone able and willing to work could do so at the ruling market-clearing **real wage** rate.

This situation is illustrated in Figure 9.1, where the aggregate demand for labour (D_L) equals the aggregate supply of labour (S_L) at the market-clearing real wage rate $(W/P)_{mc}$ and employment (N) is at its full employment level (N_F). Now, if the real wage rate is initially set at $(W/P)_1$, above its market-clearing level, the supply of labour (N_2) exceeds the demand for labour (N_1). Competition among the excess supply of unemployed workers $(N_2 - N_1)$ to find work would then lead to a reduction in money wages and hence a reduction in the real wage rate (assuming prices remain unchanged) until such time as full employment was restored.

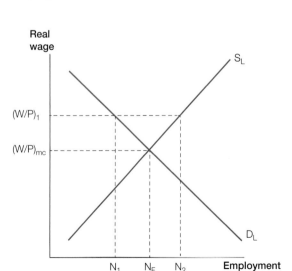

Figure 9.1 The classical approach

In classical analysis, **Say's Law** (named after the French economist Jean-Baptiste Say) guaranteed that aggregate demand would be sufficient to absorb the full employment level of output produced. According to this law 'supply creates its own demand' in that the act of production yields income that will be sufficient to purchase *whatever* level of output is produced. Given a competitive labour market, in which full employment was the normal state of affairs, Say's Law ruled out the possibility of any deficiency of aggregate demand: demand would always be sufficient to purchase the full employment level of output produced. Aside from some short-term temporary unemployment, which may occur as the real wage rate adjusts to its new market-clearing level following a change in demand or supply conditions in the labour market, the *only* source of unemployment in this classical approach is *voluntary unemployment*, which arises because there are people who, while they are capable of working, for various reasons choose not to work.

How then did classical economists explain the mass unemployment experienced in Western economies in the 1930s? Classical economists attributed the persistence of such mass unemployment to the downward inflexibility of money (and real) wages due to the actions of trade unions and argued that full employment would be restored only if money (and real) wages were cut to their market-clearing level. In Figure 9.1, *classical unemployment*, or what is sometimes referred to as *real wage unemployment*, occurs when the real wage rate is kept too high, resulting in an excess supply of labour equal to N_2-N_1 at $(W/P)_1$. In this situation unemployment exceeds the level that would prevail at the market-clearing real wage rate $(W/P)_{mc}$.

The leading British economist John Maynard Keynes (1883–1946) attacked the classical explanation of the cause of unemployment and also the solution classical economists put forward to solve the problem. In his *General Theory of Employment, Interest and Money*, published in 1936, he put forward a new, and at the time, revolutionary theory which provided a very different explanation of, and remedy for, the then-prevailing severe unemployment. In contrast to classical economists, Keynes placed the cause of the mass unemployment of the 1930s *outside* the labour market: he argued that it was, in fact, essentially rooted in a deficiency of aggregate demand in the goods market. In Keynes's view, the cure for unemployment required government intervention to increase aggregate demand in order to restore the economy to its full employment level of output. We now turn to discuss the Keynesian approach to unemployment in more detail.

9.3   The orthodox Keynesian approach

Keynesians have traditionally identified three *main* types or categories of unemployment, namely: frictional, structural and demand-deficient unemployment.

Frictional unemployment occurs because it will take time for a newly unemployed person to obtain information on job vacancies and find a new job.

Frictional unemployment: unemployment that arises because it takes time for workers to search for suitable jobs; also known as **search unemployment**.

Because frictional unemployment occurs when individuals are changing jobs and searching for new employment, it is also sometimes referred to as **search unemployment**. Even though there will be search costs involved (for example loss of earnings, expenditure on postage and phone calls and so on), such behaviour is entirely rational as newly unemployed individuals will need to spend time familiarizing themselves with both the monetary and non-monetary features of available jobs.

© iStockphoto/zakokor

Frictional unemployment happens when people are searching for new jobs

Structural unemployment: unemployment that arises from a mismatch between the skills or location of existing job vacancies and the present skills or location of the unemployed; also known as **mismatch unemployment**.

What can the government do to reduce this type of unemployment? Measures that reduce the search time moving between jobs will reduce the amount of frictional unemployment. One way to reduce search time is to improve the provision of information about employment opportunities. In the UK this is done through job centres. But it is not only the government that has a role here – there are also commercial opportunities in the creation of information networks in the labour market. For example, employment agencies such as Reed, Adecco and Randstad offer tens of thousands of jobs on behalf of employers all over the world.

Structural unemployment happens because economies are dynamic entities. The kinds of activities they support constantly change. Think about the way communication has evolved over the last couple of decades. Twenty years ago the principal means of communication included the landline, the letter and the paper memo. Now we use mobile phones, Skype, email, Facebook and a host of online ordering and billing services. The basic structures of communication have been fundamentally altered.

What has this done to the communications industries? For a start, wholly new ones have, to use Marx's memorable phrase, been conjured out of the ground, creating a torrent of new job opportunities. But, at the same time, other industries have waned – most evidently those involved in traditional postal services, putting the jobs of postal workers at risk. For example, in the UK, mail volumes have been falling annually by almost 10 per cent in recent years. Structural unemployment arises when postal workers leaving a declining industry find themselves without the skills or aptitudes to quickly pick up work in expanding sectors. A postie who's been doing delivery rounds for 30 years might not find it easy to slip into an online communications business. Retraining is probably a must, as might be a simple period of adjustment – accepting that old forms of work are disappearing and coming to terms with the shock of the new.

Note that structural unemployment can happen as *any* industry stagnates and sheds workers. In the UK it's been associated with the slow disappearance of industries such as coal mining, steel making, shipbuilding and the

'LORD BLESS YOU SIR. THE E-CIGARETTE BOOM HAS HIT OUR BUSINESS SOMETHING ROTTEN"

manufacture of textiles and clothing. One additional difficulty has been that most of these industries are regionally concentrated, so that their decline badly affects particular localities. Mining has to take place where the coal is; shipbuilding happens in towns and cities on major rivers. Interestingly, our example of the post office is one of structural unemployment that is much more diffuse: postal workers are distributed pretty evenly throughout the country.

Because structural unemployment arises from a mismatch of skills and geographical job opportunities, following underlying changes in demand and supply, it is also sometimes referred to as **mismatch unemployment**. What can the government do to reduce this type of unemployment? One way to reduce both the extent and duration of structural unemployment is to design policies aimed at improving the occupational mobility of labour (for example retraining programmes) and geographical mobility of labour (for example providing financial assistance to help cover the costs of moving from one area to another).

In addition, policy measures that encourage firms to invest in areas of high unemployment will help to reduce structural unemployment. For example, in 2010 the British government announced £360m in state aid for the carmaker Ford to support the development of low-carbon emission engines, helping to protect around 2800 jobs. The government also provided £20m to Nissan to support the development of its new electric car, the Leaf. The Nissan plant employs 4000 people in Sunderland, a place in which unemployment has been a significant problem in the past. Finally, government loan guarantees of £270m were provided to Vauxhall, securing more than 2000 jobs at its plant in Ellesmere Port near Liverpool.

These cases are particularly interesting because of the changing economics of car production. The car industry is still one typified by mass production, employing large numbers of people on production lines. But it is no longer the mass *employer* it once was. In the 1960s, the Ford factory at Halewood in Liverpool employed 16,000 people; Nissan's Sunderland plant with 4000 workers is now the UK's largest. Carmakers have been closing production facilities and shedding workers for decades. The greener cars that the government is helping Nissan and Ford to build are a way of extending the life of the car industry in the UK, so that it remains internationally competitive, producing vehicles for which there is a secure demand into the future. In this way UK carmaking may avoid the slow death of industries such as coal mining and shipbuilding and the structural unemployment their crises generated.

Demand-deficient unemployment: unemployment that arises because aggregate demand is insufficient to provide employment for everyone who wants to work at the prevailing real wage; also known as **cyclical unemployment**.

Aggregate demand: the total planned expenditures of all buyers of final goods and services.

We now turn to consider the third main type or category of unemployment, namely **demand-deficient unemployment**, or what is sometimes referred to as **cyclical unemployment**. In the Keynesian approach, the level of real national income/output and hence employment is *largely* determined by the level of aggregate expenditure or demand in the economy. As such, the economy may come to rest at less than full employment equilibrium due to a deficiency of aggregate expenditure. In contrast to the classical model, the Keynesian view is that less than full employment equilibrium is the *normal* state of affairs. Let us now examine why this is the case.

Aggregate expenditure or **aggregate demand (AD)** is the sum of the following major categories of expenditure: consumer expenditure (C), investment expenditure (I), government expenditure (G) and expenditure on net exports (X − M). More formally, we can express this in the following way:

$$AD = C + I + G + X - M \tag{9.1}$$

In order to explain why – in the simple Keynesian model – the level of real output and employment is essentially determined by aggregate demand, and why the economy may come to rest at less than full employment equilibrium, we first need to consider briefly what determines each of these components of aggregate demand.

Consumer expenditure

In the Keynesian model the main determinant of aggregate consumer expenditure is the level of national income: the higher the level of national income the higher the level of total consumer expenditure undertaken. This relationship between aggregate consumption and aggregate income, which is known technically as the consumption function, is depicted in Figure 9.2.

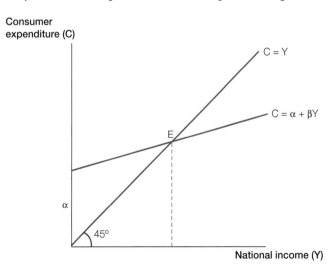

Figure 9.2 The consumption function

In Figure 9.2 consumer expenditure (C) and national income (Y) are shown on the vertical and horizontal axes respectively. The 45° line shows points of equality between the two axes. In consequence, where the consumption function crosses the 45° line at point E, consumption equals income (C = Y). You may have spotted that, in order to further simplify our discussion, we have drawn a linear consumption function. This allows us to express the relationship between aggregate consumer expenditure and national income in the form of an equation of a straight line, namely:

$$C = \alpha + \beta Y \qquad\qquad (9.2)$$

Autonomous expenditure: expenditure that does not depend on the level of national income.

Marginal propensity to consume: the change in consumption expenditure resulting from an additional unit of income.

In equation (9.2) the intercept (α) shows the level of aggregate consumer expenditure undertaken independently of the level of national income. Such expenditure is said to be *exogenous* or **autonomous** consumer **expenditure** and depends on factors such as the level of wealth. The important point to note about autonomous consumer expenditure is that it is *not* determined by the level of national income. Returning to the equation of a straight line, the slope of the consumption function (β) indicates the extent to which consumer expenditure changes when national income changes. Economists refer to this as the **marginal propensity to consume.**

Investment expenditure

What determines the level of investment expenditure undertaken in the economy? The main determinants of investment expenditure include:

- firms' past and current sales
- expectations about future sales and factor prices
- the cost of capital equipment
- the rate of interest

Ceteris paribus, investment expenditure will tend to rise following an increase in firms' current sales, an upward revision of business expectations about the future profitability of investment, a fall in the cost of capital equipment, or a fall in the cost of borrowing funds to finance such expenditure and vice versa.

In the simple Keynesian model, investment expenditure is assumed to be autonomously or exogenously determined. Because, in Figure 9.3, it is assumed to be independent of the level of national income, investment expenditure is depicted as a horizontal line.

Government expenditure

Having considered briefly the main determinants of consumer expenditure and investment expenditure, we now need to comment on government expenditure. For the purposes of constructing the Keynesian model, it is sufficient to note

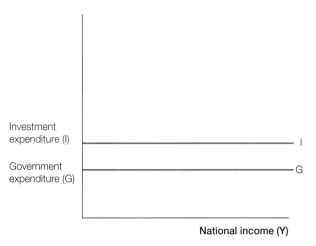

Figure 9.3 Investment and government expenditure

that government expenditure, like investment expenditure, is assumed to be independent of the level of national income. Such expenditure depends on government policy. In consequence, government expenditure is also depicted as a horizontal line in Figure 9.3.

Net export expenditure

Finally, we need to consider what determines net export expenditure. The three main determinants of the level of export and import expenditure are:

- income
- relative prices
- non-price factors such as tastes

These determinants are discussed more fully in Chapter 14. At this point in our discussion we focus on how income affects expenditure on imports and exports. The income variable relevant to imports is domestic national income. As national income rises, some part of this increase will be spent on buying more imports from abroad. This positive relationship between imports and national income is illustrated in Figure 9.4. The slope of the import function depicts the **marginal propensity to import** and indicates the extent to which import expenditure changes when national income changes. In contrast, the income variable relevant to exports is not domestic national income but rather income in the rest of the world. *Ceteris paribus*, as world income increases the demand for a country's exports will increase. Because exports are determined independently of the level of domestic national income, the export schedule in Figure 9.4 is depicted – as it is for investment and government expenditure – as a horizontal line.

Marginal propensity to import: the change in import expenditure resulting from an additional unit of income.

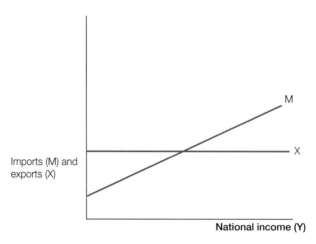

Figure 9.4 Import and export expenditure

The equilibrium level of national income in the Keynesian model

Having briefly discussed what determines each component of aggregate demand, we are now in a position to consider what determines the equilibrium level of national income in the Keynesian model and why the economy may come to rest at less than full employment equilibrium. This analysis is illustrated in Figure 9.5.

The 45° line in the top panel of Figure 9.5 shows points of equality between aggregate demand (vertical axis) and aggregate output or national income (horizontal axis). Where aggregate demand and aggregate output are equal (AD = Y), firms will be selling all the goods they produce and in such circumstances there will be no tendency for income to change. We encountered this equilibrium condition in a slightly different form in Chapter 8 where we explained how the level of income will only remain unchanged when injections (G + I + X) are matched by leakages (T + S + M). The three main injections of investment expenditure, government expenditure and gross export expenditure are assumed to be determined independently of national income, while consumer expenditure increases as national income increases. In consequence, the aggregate demand schedule (C + I + G + X − M) shown in Figure 9.5 slopes upwards to the right. The equilibrium level of national income is established where the aggregate demand schedule crosses the 45° line; that is, where aggregate demand (AD) equals aggregate supply (Y).

Let us assume that the economy is initially operating at its full employment equilibrium level of national income (Y_F) with aggregate demand equal to AD_0; that is, where AD_0 crosses the 45° line at point E_0. By referring to the bottom panel of Figure 9.5, which shows the short-run aggregate production function, we can trace the implications of the level of income (determined by aggregate demand) in terms of the level of employment – in this case full employment (N_F).

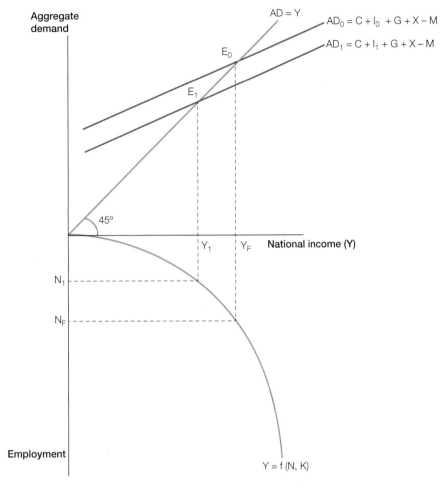

Figure 9.5 The Keynesian model

Now suppose investment expenditure decreased from I_0 to I_1 causing the aggregate demand schedule to shift downwards from AD_0 to AD_1. Investment expenditure might decrease due to a downward revision of business expectations of the future profitability of investment. In his *General Theory* (1936), Keynes suggested that investment could be influenced by tides of irrational pessimism and optimism, which he referred to as a change in investors' 'animal spirits', causing large swings in the state of business confidence. Following the fall in investment and associated fall in aggregate demand, a new equilibrium level of national income (Y_1) would be established where AD_1 crosses the 45° line at point E_1. Reference to the bottom panel of Figure 9.5 reveals that the level of employment (N_1) required to produce the new equilibrium level of national income (Y_1) is now below its full employment level. In other words, at Y_1, aggregate demand is insufficient to provide employment for everyone who wants a job resulting in so-called *involuntary unemployment*. You should note that income and employment will be affected in the same manner, *ceteris paribus*, following an autonomous decrease in consumer expenditure, government expenditure or net export expenditure.

How could the government intervene to eliminate the resultant demand-deficient unemployment and restore the economy to its full employment income level (Y_F, N_F)? The solution lies in **aggregate demand management**: the government needs to change its stance with respect to fiscal and/or monetary policy. Traditionally, orthodox Keynesians have emphasized **fiscal policy** measures involving changes in government expenditure and/or tax payments. Such changes act *directly* on the level of aggregate demand and are believed by orthodox Keynesians to be both more predictable and faster-acting on the level of economic activity than monetary policy measures. For example, increased government expenditure or reduced direct taxation (stimulating increased consumers' expenditure as households' disposable income increases) is held to have a strong and predictable effect on the level of income and employment, as the initial increase in spending leads to successive rounds of further increases in expenditure. Following such expansionary fiscal policy, income will rise by more than the initial increase in spending, to a new equilibrium level where aggregate demand and aggregate supply are again equal. This phenomenon, known as the multiplier process, is discussed more fully in Chapter 11.

In contrast, **monetary policy** changes are held to operate indirectly mainly through changes in the rate of interest, which affect aggregate demand by causing a change in investment expenditure. In a recession, when firms' expectations about profitable investment opportunities are depressed, the response of investment expenditure to a fall in the cost of borrowing funds may be small. In such circumstances, the power of monetary policy will be limited. In consequence, orthodox Keynesians express a preference for fiscal policy, rather than monetary policy measures, to restore full employment.

At this stage it would be useful to draw together our discussion of the Keynesian approach to unemployment and consider the three main types of unemployment within the context of the labour market. The demand for labour (D_L) comprises the level of employment (N) plus the level of vacancies (V), while the supply of labour (S_L) comprises the level of employment (N) plus the level of unemployment (U).

$$D_L = N + V \tag{9.3}$$

$$S_L = N + U \tag{9.4}$$

It follows that when the labour market clears and the demand for labour (D_L) equals the supply of labour (S_L), then vacancies (V) will equal unemployment (U). In this situation all unemployment will fall in the category of frictional and structural unemployment (that is, non demand-deficient unemployment) and demand-deficient unemployment will equal zero. As illustrated in Figure 9.6,

Aggregate demand management: the use of fiscal and monetary policies to influence the level of aggregate demand.

Fiscal policy: entails measures that alter the level and composition of government expenditure and taxation.

Monetary policy: entails measures that alter the money supply and/or interest rates.

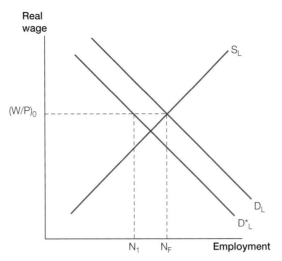

Figure 9.6 The Keynesian approach

this occurs at a real wage rate $(W/P)_0$ at the intersection of D_L and S_L; that is, where the labour market clears.

Now, suppose as before that investment expenditure decreases, causing output and employment to fall. As the aggregate demand for goods and services within the economy falls, the demand curve for labour will shift to the left from D_L to D^*_L, resulting in demand-deficient unemployment at the prevailing real wage rate $(W/P)_0$. This would be an *additional* source of unemployment on top of any existing frictional or structural unemployment. Note that in Figure 9.6 there are N_F workers willing to work at the prevailing real wage rate $(W/P)_0$ but demand from firms (which in our example have collectively cut investment) would produce a level of employment of only N_1. This demonstrates that Keynesian demand-deficient unemployment occurs when there is an excess supply of labour at the ruling wage rate; in other words, when the real wage rate is above the market-clearing wage rate. Now, the important point to make about demand-deficient unemployment is that its cause lies *outside* the labour market: people who want to work cannot find jobs not because they are in a search process (which would involve frictional unemployment), or because they need retraining to take jobs in new industries (which would involve structural unemployment) but because *there are not enough jobs to go around* – the demand is not there to sustain them. Finally, we should again emphasize that, in the Keynesian view, it is of course possible for all three types of unemployment to exist simultaneously.

The Keynesian approach to unemployment stands in bold contrast to the classical approach discussed earlier. In the classical approach full employment is determined within the labour market, with Say's Law ruling out the possibility of any deficiency of aggregate demand. Classical economists argued that as long as money wages and prices are free to adjust, the labour market would clear with any excess supply of labour being eliminated by downward pressure on the real wage rate. Why then does the labour market fail to clear in the Keynesian approach? The answer to this question lies in the assumption made by Keynes that workers would not be prepared to accept a cut in money wages when there is unemployment. The reason he advanced for this is that workers are concerned to maintain their real wage *relativities*. Workers would strongly resist a cut in money wages that only affected their section of the workforce because such a cut would adversely affect their real wage relative to other workers. Given the assumption that money (and hence real) wages tend to be sticky in a downward direction, the labour market will fail to clear. Furthermore, cutting everybody's wages would fail to restore labour market equilibrium. According to Keynes, a generalized cut in wages would merely reduce aggregate 'effective' demand in the economy and result in a further fall in output and still higher unemployment. In the orthodox Keynesian approach both the cause of, and cure for, unemployment is largely to be found outside the labour market.

Natural rate of unemployment: the rate of unemployment that exists when the labour market clears and is in equilibrium; composed of frictional and structural unemployment.

9.4 The monetarist approach

The monetarist approach to unemployment derives from the highly influential work of the late American economist Milton Friedman (1912–2006) who, in his Presidential Address to the American Economic Association in 1967, coined the term the **natural rate of unemployment**. According to Friedman, the natural rate – or what can alternatively be thought of as the long-run *equilibrium* rate of unemployment – depends on both the structure of the economy and the institutions within it. He specifically highlighted such factors as market imperfections in the labour and goods markets, the cost of gathering information on job vacancies and labour availability, and the costs of mobility as determinants of the natural rate of unemployment.

Milton Friedman

Courtesy of the University of Chicago News Office

The natural rate of unemployment is associated with equilibrium in the labour market at the market-clearing real wage rate. This situation is illustrated in Figure 9.7 where the equilibrium or natural level of employment (N_N) is established at the market-clearing real wage rate $(W/P)_{mc}$. The natural rate of unemployment corresponds to the amount of unemployment that would exist where the aggregate supply of and demand for labour are equal. Although monetarists do not approach unemployment in terms of the sum of various types or categories, it is possible to define the natural rate as a situation where

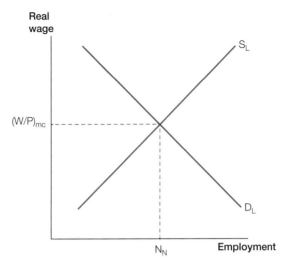

Figure 9.7 The monetarist and new classical approaches

there is no demand-deficient unemployment. As such, the natural rate can be conceptualized as embracing the two main types of non-demand-deficient unemployment, namely frictional and structural unemployment.

How can the government reduce the natural rate of unemployment in order to achieve higher output and employment levels? Rather than the macro-economic (demand-management) policies favoured by orthodox Keynesians, monetarists advocate that governments should pursue *microeconomic* (supply-management) policies designed to improve the structure and functioning of the labour market (see Chapter 7). Within the labour market any policy that leads to either an increase in the supply of labour (that is, shifting the supply curve to the right) or the demand for labour (that is, shifting the demand curve to the right) will increase the equilibrium level of employment and reduce the natural rate of unemployment. Among the wide range of policy measures that have been advocated are policies designed to increase the:

- incentive to work (for example through tax and social security reforms)
- flexibility of wages and working practices, and reduce distortions that prevent the labour market from working efficiently (for example through trade union reform)
- geographical and occupational mobility of labour
- efficiency of markets for goods and services (for example by privatization – see Chapter 6) and for capital (for example through the abolition of various controls on activity in financial markets).

Many of these proposed measures are, of course, highly controversial. For example, the reform of social security or welfare payments to unemployed people may entail cutting such benefits. The purpose here is to lessen the relative 'attractiveness'

of unemployment in comparison to low-paid work. While this measure might increase the supply of labour (shifting S_L in Figure 9.7 to the right), raise the equilibrium level of employment and thereby reduce unemployment, it would also raise equity or fairness questions about low pay and the impartiality of the state vis-à-vis the unemployed and less scrupulous employers.

In summary, given that in the monetarist view, the natural or long-run equilibrium rate of unemployment derives essentially from labour market imperfections, reducing the natural rate necessitates measures designed to increase competitiveness in the labour market.

Before turning to discuss the new classical approach to unemployment it is important to note that, while monetarists argue that the labour market will clear in the long run with a corresponding equilibrium or natural rate of unemployment, in the short run actual unemployment may be above or below the natural rate. In other words, for monetarists, the labour market may be in disequilibrium in the short run. In the next chapter, when we come to discuss the relationship between inflation and unemployment, commonly referred to as the Phillips curve, you will see how in the short run unemployment may be temporarily reduced below or raised above its natural rate following expansionary or contractionary aggregate demand policies. However, in the long run, monetarists argue that there is no trade-off between inflation and unemployment. As such the natural or equilibrium level of employment and unemployment is held to be independent of the level of aggregate demand, and is associated with a stable rate of inflation.

9.5   The new classical approach

During the 1970s, a highly controversial new classical approach to unemployment emerged. In the US, the most prominent new classical economist is Robert Lucas, Jr (University of Chicago), the 1995 Nobel Laureate in Economics; while in the UK the new classical approach is mainly associated with the work of Patrick Minford (Cardiff Business School). In contrast to both Keynesian and monetarist approaches, the assumption underlying the new classical approach to unemployment is that the labour market *continuously* clears. In other words, in line with the classical approach discussed earlier, new classical economists assume that anyone wishing to find work can do so at the market-clearing real wage rate; that is, at $(W/P)_{mc}$ in Figure 9.7.

Courtesy of the University of Chicago News Office

Robert Lucas, Jr

As we will discuss in Chapter 11, in the new classical approach fluctuations in employment are held to reflect voluntary changes in the amount that people want to work. Unemployment is treated entirely as a *voluntary* phenomenon, with those who are unemployed voluntarily choosing not to work at the current market-clearing real wage rate. Moreover, any unemployment that results from trade union bargaining and higher real wages in a particular sector is also considered to be voluntary in that workers have chosen unions to represent them. Viewed in this way, new classical economists argue that those who are unemployed could find jobs if only they were prepared to lower their sights and accept inferior or less well paid jobs.

If all unemployment is regarded as being voluntary as new classical economists argue, is there anything governments can do to reduce unemployment? In the new classical view, any policy measure that increases the *microeconomic incentive* for workers to supply more labour will reduce unemployment. For example, it is claimed that by reducing the real value of unemployment benefits unemployment will fall as: (1) unemployed workers spend less time looking for the 'right' job, and (2) certain low-paid jobs become more attractive, compared to the reduced benefits that can be obtained when out of work, ensuring that fewer job vacancies remain unfilled.

One clear objection to the new classical explanation of unemployment is the weakness of its interpretation of *mass* unemployment. During the Great Depression of the 1930s, unemployment in the US reached 25 per cent. In Spain in 2014, unemployment was also nearly 25 per cent. Can new classical economists really persuade us that a quarter of depression-era Americans *chose* not to work or that one in four Spaniards did the same in 2014? Some have suggested that, on this account, the Great Depression really ought to be renamed the Great *Vacation*.

9.6   The new Keynesian approach

During the 1980s, a new Keynesian approach to unemployment was developed to challenge the new classical view that unemployment is entirely a voluntary phenomenon. Within the extensive new Keynesian literature, a number of models have been put forward to explain why an 'equilibrium' real wage rate can emerge that is above the market-clearing real wage rate. Such models are therefore capable of generating involuntary unemployment in long-run

equilibrium. In what follows we shall outline two such new Keynesian explanations of real wage rigidity in the labour market: namely, efficiency wage and
insider–outsider theories.

Efficiency wage model

The essence of efficiency wage theories is that the productivity (effort or efficiency) of workers depends positively on the real wage rate workers are paid.
In consequence, it is both profitable and rational for firms to pay a so-called
efficiency wage that is above the market-clearing real wage rate. Efficiency wage
theories suggest that, even in the face of an excess supply of labour, it will not be
in firms' interests to lower the real wage rate as to do so would lower productivity and raise costs. Before we outline the main reasons why firms may pay an
efficiency wage above the market-clearing real wage rate, it would be useful to
consider the implications of this analysis by reference to Figure 9.8.

In Figure 9.8 full employment (N_F), where the aggregate demand for labour
(D_L) is equal to and matched by the aggregate supply of labour (S_L), would
occur at a market-clearing real wage rate $(W/P)_{mc}$. If, however, firms pay an
efficiency wage $(W/P)^*$ above this market-clearing real wage rate, there will be
an excess supply of labour (N_2–N_1) and involuntary unemployment will result.
Suppose now that a shock occurs, which shifts the aggregate demand for labour
to the left from D_L to D^*_L. In this situation, if the efficiency wage remains at
$(W/P)^*$, the excess supply of labour will increase from N_2–N_1 to N_2–N_3 and
the amount of involuntary unemployment will increase.

Let us now outline the four versions of efficiency wage theory that have been
put forward.

- The *labour turnover model* suggests that quit rates are a decreasing function
  of the real wage rate paid to workers. In consequence, firms have an incentive

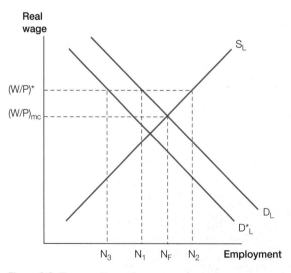

Figure 9.8 The new Keynesian approach

to pay an efficiency wage in order to deter workers from quitting and reduce costly labour turnover, for example the costs involved with hiring and training new employees. At the same time, the existence of involuntary unemployment that results from the payment of an efficiency wage above the market-clearing real wage rate also acts as a disincentive to workers to quit their job.

- The *adverse selection model* suggests that firms that offer higher wages will attract the best or most productive applicants for a job. Job applicants have more information about their ability, honesty and commitment than do employers before they are hired. Given hiring and firing costs, firms clearly prefer not to hire workers and then find they need to fire those with low productivity. If workers' abilities are closely related to their reservation or minimum wage (which would induce them to take a job), by paying an efficiency wage, firms will attract the most productive job applicants. Furthermore, paying higher wages will also deter the most productive workers from quitting. The astute reader will recognize that the labour market provides an excellent example of a market where asymmetric information predominates. For further discussion of adverse selection associated with asymmetric information see Chapter 2. For a discussion of information signalling in the labour market see the box 'Applying Economics to Business' in Chapter 7.

- The *shirking model* suggests that, in many jobs, workers can exercise considerable discretion with respect to how well they perform their job and that there is a real possibility that some workers will shirk their work effort. Such behaviour may be difficult to detect and/or costly to monitor, especially where teamwork predominates. In a fully employed economy where firms pay the market-clearing real wage rate, the threat of dismissal for workers caught shirking will fail to act as an effective deterrent since they can easily find alternative employment at the same real wage rate. If, however, firms pay an efficiency wage above the market-clearing real wage rate (as depicted in Figure 9.8) then there will be a disincentive for workers to shirk since if they are caught and are subsequently dismissed they will not readily find employment elsewhere but will join those who are already involuntarily unemployed. In other words, by paying an efficiency wage, firms discourage shirking and raise worker productivity or effort. In addition to acting as a disciplinary device, an efficiency wage also allows firms to reduce costs in monitoring workers' performance. For further discussion of the issue of moral hazard associated with asymmetric information see Chapter 1.

Hands up, who hasn't shirked when they're supposed to be hard at work?

BRAND X

- The *fairness model* suggests that workers' productivity or effort is closely connected to their morale, which is in turn linked to the notion of being treated fairly with respect to pay. By paying an efficiency wage above the market-clearing real wage rate, the morale and loyalty of workers will increase and workers will respond by working harder, increasing their productivity.

In the four versions of efficiency wage theory outlined above, it is firms who decide to pay an efficiency wage above the market-clearing real wage rate because it is both profitable and rational for them to do so. We next consider a model in which no positive effect of real wages on productivity is assumed and where the focus shifts away from firms as employers to the power of employees in partially determining wage and employment outcomes.

Insider–outsider model

Within the insider–outsider model of real wage rigidity, the so-called *insiders* are the incumbent employees and the *outsiders* are the unemployed workers. The power of insiders arises from labour turnover costs. As mentioned earlier, these costs include hiring and firing costs (such as those associated with advertising and severance pay) and also the costs of training new employees. In addition, the power of insiders is reinforced by the fact that they can refuse to cooperate with or even harass new employees. As a result, insiders can affect the productivity of new employees. In these circumstances, it is argued that insiders have sufficient bargaining power to raise real wages above the market-clearing rate without the fear of losing their jobs and being undercut by outsiders. Unemployed outsiders are unable to price themselves back into work, by offering to work for a lower real wage than incumbent employees, because of the power of insiders. In consequence, the insider–outsider model is able to explain why real wages are set which result in involuntary unemployment. One policy implication to reduce unemployment that derives from this model is to increase the market power of unemployed outsiders. For example, measures targeted at the long-term unemployed (those people who have been out of work for a year or more), such as government retraining programmes, would help to increase the power of unemployed outsiders.

Hysteresis effects and unemployment

So far in discussing the new Keynesian approach to unemployment, we have focused our attention on various theoretical models that can help account for the existence of involuntary unemployment as an *equilibrium* phenomenon. In this context equilibrium is defined as a situation where there is no incentive for economic agents to change their behaviour. In other words, as illustrated in Figure 9.8, equilibrium can occur in the labour market where there is an excess supply of labour and involuntary unemployment persists. We now turn to consider new Keynesian hysteresis theories where the resultant long-run equilibrium level of unemployment is affected by the path taken by the actual level of unemployment.

Earlier, in discussing the monetarist approach to unemployment, we introduced Friedman's concept of a natural rate of unemployment to describe the long-run equilibrium rate of unemployment. We also noted that the natural rate of unemployment is associated with a stable rate of inflation (see Chapter 10, section 10.2). While aggregate demand shocks can influence the actual rate of unemployment in the short run, in the long run the natural rate is determined by supply-side influences independently of aggregate demand. Rather than refer to the natural rate, many Keynesians prefer to speak of the **non-accelerating inflation rate of unemployment (NAIRU)** to describe the long-run equilibrium rate of unemployment that is consistent with stable inflation. However, in marked contrast to monetarists, new Keynesians argue that the natural rate (or NAIRU) *is* affected by the path taken by the actual rate of unemployment. In other words, the natural rate (or NAIRU) is affected by the level of aggregate demand.

NAIRU: the rate of unemployment at which inflation is stable.

EVERYDAY ECONOMICS 9.1

Reducing the rate of unemployment

There are differences between economists over the way in which policy can be used to reduce the rate of unemployment. Each of the images below characterizes a particular form of policy. Can you identify them?

Answers are at the end of the chapter.

1

2

3

In order to explain why this is the case, suppose the economy is initially operating at its natural rate of unemployment. If the economy experiences, for example, a contractionary aggregate demand shock, the economy may then undergo a prolonged recession. In circumstances where the actual rate of unemployment remains above the natural rate for a prolonged period the natural rate (or NAIRU) will tend to increase due to so-called **hysteresis** effects. Such effects act like a magnet pulling the natural rate in the same direction. Not only will those who are unemployed suffer a deterioration of their human capital (skills), exacerbating the problem of structural unemployment, but the number

Hysteresis: the proposition that the equilibrium value of a variable depends on the history of that variable.

of long-run unemployed, who exercise little influence on the wage bargaining process, is also likely to increase. Both forces will raise the natural rate (or NAIRU). Following our discussion based on the insider–outsider model, outsiders will be unable to price themselves back into work even in the face of high and rising unemployment. As such, hysteresis effects provide a strong case for the authorities to stimulate aggregate demand during a protracted recession.

9.7   A case study: unemployment in Europe

While estimates of the natural rate (or NAIRU) diverge and are themselves fraught with difficulties, most economists agree that the natural rate of unemployment in Europe has increased from around 3 per cent in the 1960s to over 8 per cent in the present decade. Some indication of this phenomenon is provided by Figure 9.9, which depicts the unemployment rate in the euro area and the US over the period 1999–2015. Figure 9.9 indicates that since the launch of the euro in 1999, euro area unemployment has seldom been below 8 per cent while, over the same period, unemployment in the US has seldom been above this figure.

Figure 9.9 also shows that although the gap in unemployment performance between the euro area and the US narrowed during the 2008–9 recession – the impact of which was particularly hard felt in the US – a sharply divergent pattern re-emerged once recovery commenced in the US economy. We now turn to consider how economists have sought to account for the substantial rise in unemployment that has taken place in Europe since the 1970s. Before doing so it is worth noting that there are significant differences in unemployment rates experienced in individual European countries. For example, in 2014 unemployment in Spain was almost five times that experienced in Germany.

Two main theories have been put forward to explain the rise in European unemployment. One theory explains high European unemployment in terms of labour market rigidities. Among the specific changes that it is

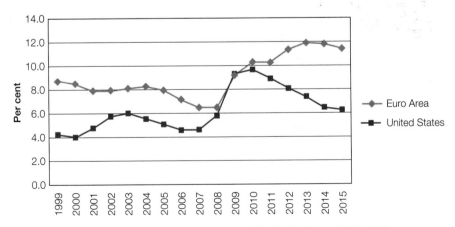

Figure 9.9 Unemployment rates in the euro area and the United States 1999–2015

Source: Data from IMF's World Economic Outlook Database

alleged have reduced the flexibility of the labour market and resulted in higher unemployment are:

- minimum wage laws, which have made it unprofitable for firms to hire unskilled workers
- more powerful trade unions, who by obtaining real wage increases above the increase in the value of output produced per worker, and by imposing restrictions on working practices limiting firms' ability to adjust to changes in economic circumstances, have raised firms' costs
- higher unemployment benefits, which have acted as a deterrent for the unemployed to find a job, especially for unemployed unskilled workers to take up low-paid jobs.

Changes in technology, it is argued, have further reduced the demand for unskilled relative to skilled workers.

For illustrative purposes let us briefly reflect on the first point in the bulleted list. Figure 9.10 depicts minimum monthly wages in a number of European economies and the US in 2013. Notice that minimum wage levels in the US are closer to those in Greece and Spain. In contrast, minimum wages in Ireland, the Netherlands, Belgium and France are roughly a third higher than the US rate. The suggestion here is that relatively low minimum wages in the US give that country a degree of labour market competitiveness that is not shared by some European economies, with the end result that unemployment in Europe has on average and for fairly substantial periods been higher than unemployment in the US.

Eurosclerosis: a term used to describe the belief that Europe suffers from excessive labour market rigidities.

The term **Eurosclerosis** has been applied to describe such developments. In other words, labour market rigidities are, it is suggested, leading to the *sclerosis* (a term applied to describe a hardening of the tissues) of the economic system in Europe, resulting in high unemployment. While some of these factors may explain part of the rise in European unemployment in the 1970s, many economists doubt that they offer a full explanation of European unemployment

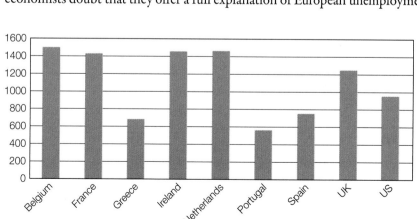

Figure 9.10 Minimum monthly wage 2013 for selected European countries and the US in €

Source: Data from Eurostat © EU

experience since the 1980s when many of these rigidities had been reduced. For example, trade union density (the percentage of the labour force that is union-ized), which can be used to proxy trade union power, has declined in most European countries since the early 1980s (see Figure 7.2).

The second main theory explains high European unemployment in terms of hysteresis effects in that following prolonged periods when actual unemploy-ment has been high the natural rate (or NAIRU) has itself increased. Two episodes are highlighted. First, in the 1970s, unemployment in most European countries rose sharply following the OPEC oil price increases that occurred in 1973–4 and 1979. Second, in the early 1980s, following the lead given by the Thatcher government in the UK, most European countries sought to reduce inflation via monetary contraction resulting in recession and rising unemploy-ment (see Chapter 10). For example, actual unemployment in the UK rose from 4.7 per cent in 1979 to 11.1 per cent in 1982. In particular, adherents of this second main theory argue that periods of prolonged recession in Europe have led to an increase in the number of long-term unemployed who have not only lost skills/work habits but who also exercise little influence on the process of wage determination (in line with the insider–outsider model). According to this theory, prolonged unemployment has led to an increase in long-term unemployment, which has in turn caused an increase in the natural rate of unemployment (or NAIRU). It remains to be seen whether the aftermath of the 2008–9 recession will cause an increase in the natural rate of unemployment. Given that unemployment remains stubbornly high in the EU as a whole this is a real possibility particularly in countries like Spain where unemployment has been much higher than the EU average.

What tentative conclusions can be drawn from our overview of unemploy-ment in Europe? Most economists tend to take an *eclectic* position between the two main views we have outlined. As such they recognize that the substantial rise in European unemployment can be attributed in part to:

- changes in the labour market on the *supply side*
- two major adverse (OPEC) supply shocks
- the pursuit of deflationary policies on the *demand side* to reduce inflation in the early 1980s.

In the latter case, the evidence suggests that there are significant output/employ-ment costs involved in reducing inflation (see Chapter 10) and that such costs can be sustained by hysteresis effects. A major problem facing policymakers in Europe is to reduce persistent unemployment. While some economists argue that this may require some reform of the unemployment benefit system with respect to the level of and duration that benefits are paid, it is especially important that *active* labour market policies are pursued which are targeted at the long-term unemployed, for example retraining programmes, the payment of recruitment subsidies to employers who take on long-term unemployed workers and so on.

Furthermore, in a prolonged recession where actual unemployment has risen significantly above the natural rate (or NAIRU), governments should seek to stimulate aggregate demand. But the main lesson to learn above all else is not to let unemployment increase in the first place. Once unemployment has been allowed to rise, as it has in the EU, it is extremely difficult to bring down again.

● **Think Point**

To conclude our discussion of unemployment, in 'Applying Economics to Business', below, we outline the main initiatives adopted by the UK government in response to the 2008–9 recession. Once you have carefully read the material you should consider the following two questions:

1. Are the measures outlined in the box aimed inside or outside the labour market?

2. Advocates of which of the main approaches to unemployment would you anticipate would support these measures?

APPLYING ECONOMICS TO BUSINESS

The UK government's response to the 2008–9 recession

In addition to the support given to the banking system following the financial crisis associated with the credit crunch in the autumn of 2008, the UK government adopted a number of policies aimed at boosting spending and protecting jobs. These initiatives included:

- a temporary reduction in the standard rate of value added tax (VAT) from 17.5 per cent to 15 per cent, from 1 December 2008 until 31 December 2009
- the introduction of a temporary car scrappage scheme from mid-May 2009 until March 2010. Under the scheme owners of cars that were at least 10 years old could get £2000 off the price of a new vehicle and their old car would be scrapped. Half of the money off the price of a new vehicle was paid by the government and half by the car manufacturer. The UK government put £400m into the scheme, thereby creating an upper limit of 400,000 vehicles that could be scrapped. Interestingly, both the US and the German governments ran similar scrappage schemes in an attempt to arrest the decline in new car sales and support the motor industry in their economies
- the introduction of a policy known as quantitative easing – announced in March 2009 – by the Bank of England's Monetary Policy Committee (MPC) designed to inject money directly into the economy in order to boost spending and

prevent inflation falling below its 2 per cent target. The 2008–9 recession witnessed a sharp fall in demand as both households and firms reduced their spending. Given that interest rates were already at historically low levels (0.5 per cent), and couldn't be reduced below zero per cent, the MPC decided that it needed to inject extra money into the economy in order to support higher consumer spending and investment, and meet its inflation target. From March 2009 to July 2012 the Bank of England injected some £375bn new money into the UK economy by buying assets – such as government and corporate bonds – from private-sector businesses, including insurance companies, pension funds, high-street banks and non-financial firms, through its quantitative easing programme. Although at the time of writing (autumn 2014) the UK economy appears to be on the road to a sustained recovery, there is no consensus view among analysts as to what part has been played by the introduction of this new policy initiative. Some critics have suggested that quantitative easing has failed to boost spending to the degree required; while others fear that the policy will lead to a future sustained increase in the rate of inflation. In truth it is impossible to establish what part quantitative easing has played in preventing the economy from experiencing a severe depression. If, however, the UK economy continues to recover from recession, and inflation remains in check over the medium-to-long term, then a consensus view is likely to emerge that the policy worked.

SUMMARY

- The central question underlying the debate over unemployment is whether the cause of, and consequently cure for, unemployment is essentially to be found inside or outside the labour market.
- Orthodox Keynesians identify three main types or categories of unemployment: frictional, structural and demand-deficient unemployment. Each type of unemployment requires a different policy solution. In the Keynesian approach, the level of employment is largely determined outside the labour market by the level of aggregate demand in the economy. Because aggregate demand may be too low to guarantee full employment, governments need to stimulate aggregate demand to maintain high and stable levels of employment.
- Monetarists refer to a natural or long-run equilibrium rate of unemployment, which is independent of the level of aggregate demand and is consistent with a stable rate of inflation. The natural rate depends on a number of factors and can be reduced by measures that improve the flexibility of the labour market.
- In the new classical approach the labour market is assumed to be cleared continuously. Unemployment is treated entirely as a voluntary phenomenon.
- New Keynesian economists have put forward efficiency wage and insider–outsider theories to explain the existence of involuntary unemployment as an equilibrium phenomenon. The long-run equilibrium rate of unemployment or NAIRU, which is consistent with stable inflation, is affected by the level of aggregate demand. Where the actual rate of unemployment remains above NAIRU for a prolonged period, NAIRU will increase due to hysteresis effects.
- Two main theories have been put forward to explain the rise in European unemployment. One view focuses on labour market rigidities that have led to an increase in the natural rate (or NAIRU), the other focuses on hysteresis effects pulling NAIRU up following periods when actual unemployment has been high. What is needed to reduce the present high level of unemployment in the EU is a set of solutions that involve both aggregate supply and aggregate demand policies.

KEY TERMS

- Classical/real wage unemployment
- Frictional/search unemployment
- Structural/mismatch unemployment
- Demand-deficient/ cyclical unemployment
- Natural rate of unemployment/NAIRU
- Efficiency wages
- Insiders versus outsiders
- Hysteresis
- Eurosclerosis

QUESTIONS FOR DISCUSSION

1. What is the difference between frictional and structural unemployment? What policies can help to reduce each type of unemployment?
2. What is demand-deficient unemployment? How can the government reduce this type of unemployment?
3. What is meant by the term the 'natural' rate of unemployment? What policies might be used to reduce the natural rate?
4. Why may firms find it profitable and rational to pay a so-called efficiency wage which is above the market-clearing real wage rate?
5. How might hysteresis effects cause a rise in the natural rate of unemployment?
6. How have economists sought to explain the rise in unemployment that has taken place in the EU since the 1970s? What can governments do to reduce unemployment?

EVERYDAY ECONOMICS 9.1 ANSWERS

1. **To be counted as unemployed you have to be actively seeking work.** In many economies there are audit procedures to ensure that people receiving unemployment-related benefits are searching for jobs. If they are not their benefits may be reduced or stopped. This increases the incentive to look for work and tends to reduce the rate of unemployment.

2. **Income tax reduces net income.** Therefore higher income tax rates may reduce the incentive to work as they close the gap between income from work and income from unemployment-related benefits. So lower income tax rates may improve the incentive to work and reduce unemployment.

3. **The photo is of a new hospital, one of two under construction in Liverpool.** Public works programmes such as these were precisely the kind of activity that Keynes recommended to tackle demand-deficient unemployment.

ONE THING YOU SHOULD READ

Go to www.nationalaffairs.com/publications/detail/crisis-economics where you will find an essay entitled 'Crisis Economics' that appeared in *National Affairs* in Summer 2010. The essay was written by Greg Mankiw, Professor of Economics at Harvard University, USA, who from 2003 to 2005 served as Chairman of the President's Council of Economic Advisers. After you have read the essay consider the following questions:

1. What approach to unemployment lay at the heart of President Obama's 2009 stimulus package to tackle the problem of unemployment in the USA?

2. Why is government spending commonly assumed to be more effective in stimulating aggregate demand than reducing taxation?

3. Aside from leaving consumers with more disposable income, in what other ways may tax cuts stimulate spending?

4. Why does Professor Mankiw suggest that macroeconomists should adopt a greater degree of humility?

10

inflation: causes and cures

KEY ISSUES

What causes inflation?

How can the authorities reduce the rate of inflation?

Is it necessary to increase unemployment in order to reduce the rate of inflation?

CONTENTS

10.1 Introduction: the inflation debate   **316**

10.2 The monetarist view   **317**

10.3 The non-monetarist view   **330**

10.4 A case study: maintaining price stability in the euro area   **333**

10.5 Concluding remarks   **335**

Appendix: Keynesians, monetarists and new classicists and the expectations-augmented Phillips curve   **338**

10.1 Introduction: the inflation debate

In Chapter 8 we defined inflation as a process of continually rising prices and outlined how it can be measured. In addition we discussed the economic, social and political costs associated with inflation. You will recall that changes in inflation can have a substantial effect on the success and profitability of firms. In Chapter 8 we discussed how higher inflation may cause higher unemployment because as the rate of inflation increases the more it varies. Greater variability of inflation results in greater uncertainty surrounding economic transactions, causing unemployment to rise. Not only will the price system become less efficient as a communication system resulting in increased unemployment but increased uncertainty may cause a fall in consumption and investment. For example, long-term investment decisions may be adversely affected as increased uncertainty – over both future income flow and the interest rate – diminishes firms' incentive to invest. In Chapter 8 we also discussed how if inflation in the home economy is greater than abroad then, *ceteris paribus*, domestic producers will experience a loss in price competitiveness in both home and foreign markets causing domestic output to fall and unemployment to increase, with adverse consequences for the profitability of business.

Given these considerations, in this chapter we turn to the debate over the causes and cures for inflation. This debate can be conveniently divided between two main explanations of inflation involving monetarist and non-monetarist views. In Section 10.2 we discuss the monetarist explanation – which embodies two of the most famous relationships that exist in macroeconomics, namely the quantity theory of money and the (expectations augmented) Phillips curve – before turning to consider the non-monetarist explanation in Section 10.3. Given the importance of money in the monetarist explanation it is first worth reflecting on what constitutes money and the functions it serves (see box 'Reflecting on Economics').

Money: anything which is generally accepted in exchange for goods and services and in the settlement of debt.

Medium of exchange: an instrument that is accepted in exchange for goods and services.

REFLECTING ON ECONOMICS

Money: what it is and what it does

Buying a good or paying a bill is done with money. You might use cash or a bank card that draws money from your account and gives it to the seller. So when we think of money we generally think of either notes and coins or the balance we have at the bank. But money can sometimes assume other forms. In Chapter 2, when we reflected on the propensity of markets to emerge in very different kinds of setting, we noted that what passed for money in these contexts could sometimes be unusual. Someone serving a jail sentence lives in a place where money does not circulate in the familiar manner. But there is still money in prison.

Here, cigarettes are commonly used to purchase other goods and services. Cigarettes are money.

We can define **money** as anything that generally allows us to buy goods and services in the society in which we live. Note that this means that cigarettes are *not* money in most places. If you tried to settle a restaurant bill in cigarettes how far would you get? If you swap a pair of shoes you own for a friend's coat the shoes aren't money either. This is a case of exchange by barter. Shoes aren't money because they're not *widely* accepted as money.

We have a definition of money but what precisely does money do? Money has three generally recognized uses. We've already described one of these: money is a **medium of exchange**. It's readily accepted in exchange for all the goods and services

(continued)

the economy produces and in the settlement of debts. Money also acts as a **store of value**. If you have £100 in your purse or £500 in the bank, you know that over the next few days or weeks you have enough to get by. Because everyone thinks like this, societies find money a very convenient way to parcel up buying power for the future. Finally, money is a **unit of account**. It allows us to measure the values of myriad different goods and services using a society-wide framework.

Let's finish by thinking about a £10 note and, in prison, 20 cigarettes. Both can be used to buy goods and services: both can be used as a store of value to be spent next week, next month or next year; and both can be used to measure the value of goods and services. A bar of chocolate might cost £2 in a shop or 10 cigarettes in a prison. This week and next week £10 will buy five bars of chocolate; 20 cigarettes will buy two. Both pounds and cigarettes are money in their respective contexts.

10.2 The monetarist view

The quantity theory of money

Store of value: an instrument which allows people to defer purchasing power to the future.

Unit of account: an instrument that allows us to measure the values of different goods and services.

The monetarist view of inflation is best summarized by Milton Friedman's pronouncement that 'inflation is always and everywhere a monetary phenomenon in the sense that it can be produced only by a more rapid increase in the quantity of money than in output'.[1] This belief is embodied in the quantity theory of money, a body of doctrine concerned with the relationship between the money supply and the general price level.

The traditional quantity theory of money

If the supply of money increases faster than output, inflation will increase

The traditional quantity theory, which has taken a variety of forms, has a long history dating back to before the seventeenth century. Rather than discuss any one particular formulation of the theory, in what follows we present a stylized version of the old (classical) quantity theory. This stylized version of the old quantity theory of money can be described by the equation:

$$MV = PY \qquad\qquad (10.1)$$

where M = the nominal money supply

V = the income velocity of circulation of money during a given time period (the average number of times money circulates throughout the economy in exchange for final output)

P = the average price of final output

Y = the real quantity of final output produced during a given time period

By definition, the nominal money supply multiplied by the average number of times it circulates in exchange for final output *must* be equal to the average price of the final output multiplied by the real quantity of final output produced during a given time period (see box 'Reflecting on Economics: the quantity theory of money' for a simple numerical example of this relationship).

---

1 Friedman, Milton (1970) *The Counter-Revolution in Monetary Theory*, IEA Occasional Paper No. 33, London: Institute of Economic Affairs.

© iStockphoto.com/Emilia Szymanek

Narrow money: notes and coins in circulation plus reserve balances held by banks at the central bank.

Broad money: notes and coins plus a range of deposits held by individuals, firms and other organizations in banks and similar financial institutions.

Reserve requirements: the minimum amount of reserves banks must hold against deposits.

Open market operations: the purchase and sale of government bonds by the central bank.

Base rate: the interest rate on loans the Bank of England makes to the banking sector.

To turn the quantity equation $MV = PY$ into a theory we must discuss what determines each of the four variables, M, V, P and Y. Classical economists argued that the authorities controlled the nominal supply of money in the economy. As such, M was determined independently of V, P and Y in the quantity theory relationship. The income velocity of money was thought to depend on institutional factors, such as the length of the payments period, and was also treated as being independent of the other variables. As institutional factors were held to change slowly over time, V was assumed, for practical purposes, to be constant. Turning to the right-hand side of the quantity theory relationship, classical economists believed that the level of real output was determined by real forces, such as the supply of factors of production. Furthermore, they believed that output would always return to full employment in the long run. In consequence, Y was assumed to be constant at the full employment level of output.

Given these assumptions, classical economists argued that in the *long run* P, the average price of final output, would be determined solely by the supply of money and that any change in the money supply would lead to a proportionate change in the general price level. For example, with V and Y assumed to be constant, a 10 per cent rise in the money supply would lead to a 10 per cent rise in the general price level (see box 'Reflecting on Economics: the quantity theory of money'). Classical economists thereby postulated a purely monetary explanation of the determination of the general price level and its rate of change: inflation. In the latter case, the old quantity theory relationship can be rewritten and expressed in terms of percentage rates of change. Maintaining the assumption that V and Y are constant, we obtain the old quantity theory prediction that, in the long run, the rate of inflation ($\dot{P}$) is determined by, and equal to, the rate of growth of the money supply ($\dot{M}$).

$$\dot{P} = \dot{M}$$

(10.2)

Before considering the modern quantity theory of money it is worth reflecting on how the money supply is regulated by the actions of both the banking sector and the economy's central bank.

REFLECTING ON ECONOMICS

Thinking about the money supply

What is the money supply? An economy's money supply is pretty much what it sounds like – how much money there is out there. But this is still a little vague. If someone asks their wealthiest friend or relative how much money they've got the reply is likely to run along the following lines: 'Right now I've got so much in cash and in my current account, but if you give me 48 hours I could get a much larger amount by drawing money from less accessible accounts.' We measure the money supply in the economy in a similar way. **Narrow money** focuses primarily on notes and coins in circulation plus reserve balances held by banks at the central bank, whereas **broad money** encompasses notes and coins plus a range of deposits held by individuals, firms and other organizations in banks and similar financial institutions.

The money supply is regulated by the actions of both the banking sector and the economy's central bank. For example, in the UK the Bank of England is the central bank; in the euro area it's the European Central Bank. Let's begin by considering how the banking sector influences the money supply.

Regulating the money supply – the role of the banks

Deposits in banks are the largest and most important element of the money supply. Few individuals or firms retain large amounts of money in cash: it's easier to lose if they do and bank deposits are also preferred because they earn interest. The fascinating thing is what banks do with all the money deposited with them. Obviously they lend money out: that's how they earn profits. But how much can be lent? This is the artful bit. They can't lend everything they take on deposit as most bank customers will need to draw money out from time to time and, in any case, banks have a reserve requirement imposed on them by the central bank (more on this below). But say banks choose to retain 10 per cent of deposits in reserve and lend out the rest. In this instance a bank with £1m in deposits will retain £100,000 and lend £900,000. What's happened to the money supply? Depositors still have £1m showing on their accounts

and the bank has enough in reserve to service their cash needs but the bank has lent £900,000 to borrowers. This means that the bank has *created money* by adding £900,000 to the money supply.

Notice that this has happened with just *one* bank. The borrowing customers of this bank may use their cash to buy goods whose sellers bank their revenues, which means that there are new deposits in the banking sector of which 10 per cent (of £900,000) will be set aside as reserves but the rest can be lent out as more newly created money. For a 10 per cent reserve ratio this continuing (but diminishing) process will eventually create a tenfold increase in the money supply so that the banking system as a whole uses the original £1m to increase the money supply by £10m.

Regulating the money supply – the role of the central bank

Should the central bank be concerned about excess money creation by the banking sector one moderating influence it can use is to alter banks' **reserve requirements**. In the aftermath of the 2008–9 financial crisis many central banks around the world agreed to raise reserve requirements to prevent banks from running out of money as many had actually done. A potential unfortunate side effect of this prudent measure is that it may restrict bank lending in many countries.

A second way the central bank may influence the money supply is through **open market operations**. Should it wish to increase the money supply the central bank will buy government bonds from the private sector (issuing interest-bearing bonds is one way for the government itself to raise money). Bond buying puts cash in the hands of the private sector, some of which will then be deposited with the banks. In turn, the banking sector creates new money via additional lending.

Finally, the central bank sets an interest rate on the loans it makes to the banking sector. In the UK this is the Bank of England's **base rate**. The base rate allows the central bank to condition the cost of borrowing. If the banks are charged more when they borrow their lending in turn becomes more expensive. *Ceteris paribus*, as interest rates rise, the demand for loans by the private sector falls thus causing a fall in the money supply.

The modern quantity theory of money

In the mid-1950s Friedman reformulated the old quantity theory of money relationship. Although his restatement of the theory was, in the first instance, a theory of the demand for money, the modern quantity theory of money provides the basis for the monetarist explanation of inflation. In contrast to the old quantity theory, in which V and Y were assumed to be approximately constant over time, in the modern quantity theory, V and Y are held to be *stable* and *predictable* in the long run. Once the assumption that Y is constant is relaxed, then, in the long run, the rate of inflation is determined by, and equal to, the rate of growth of the money supply minus the rate of growth of real output.

$$\dot{P} = \dot{M} - \dot{Y} \tag{10.3}$$

The policy proposal that follows from this modern quantity theory approach is that the authorities should seek to control the rate of growth of the money supply, in line with the underlying rate of growth of real output, in order to ensure long-term price stability.

Our discussion so far has focused on how, according to the monetarist view, the rate of monetary expansion essentially determines the rate of inflation in the *long run*. We now turn to consider how, in the *short run*, the effects of a change in the rate of monetary expansion are divided between changes in output and inflation. This involves an examination of the relationship between unemployment and inflation, commonly referred to as the **Phillips curve.**

Phillips curve: depicts the relationship between the inflation rate and the unemployment rate.

The original Phillips curve

The statistical relationship between inflation and unemployment

In 1958 the results of a *statistical* investigation undertaken by A.W. Phillips into the relationship between unemployment (U) and the rate of change of money wages ($\dot{W}$) in the United Kingdom, over the period 1861–1957, were published in *Economica*. Phillips found evidence of a *stable* relationship between these two variables that appeared to have existed for almost a century. The negative (non-linear) relationship between unemployment and wage inflation is depicted in Figure 10.1. The estimated average relationship indicated that, when the level of unemployment was approximately 5.5 per cent, the rate of change of money wages was zero. Furthermore, at an unemployment level of approximately 2.5 per cent, the rate of change of money wages was approximately 2 per cent, which was roughly equal to the then-average growth of productivity (output per worker). In consequence a 2.5 per cent level of unemployment was compatible with price stability. For this reason the Phillips curve is presented in some textbooks with price (rather than wage) inflation on the vertical axis, with the curve cutting the horizontal axis at an unemployment level of 2.5 per cent.

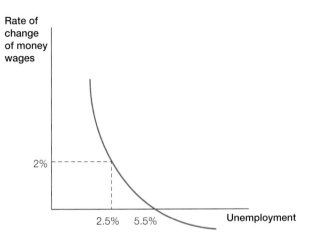

Figure 10.1 The Phillips curve

The economic rationale for the original Phillips curve

Now, as noted, Phillips's study was a statistical investigation and the economic rationale for the curve was provided by Richard Lipsey in an article subsequently published in *Economica* in 1960. Utilizing standard demand and supply analysis we first encountered in Chapter 2, Lipsey argued that money wages will rise when there is an excess demand for labour. Moreover, the greater the extent of excess demand for labour, the faster the rate or speed at which money wages will increase. While it is straightforward to illustrate a state of excess demand diagrammatically, it is more problematic to actually measure excess demand for labour. To get round the problem that excess demand for labour is not directly observable, Lipsey used the level of unemployment as a proxy or surrogate measure for excess demand in the labour market. He postulated that a negative (non-linear) relationship exists between excess demand and unemployment, as shown in Figure 10.2. Reference to Figure 10.2 reveals that when the demand for and supply of labour are equal (that is, excess demand is zero) there will still be, as discussed in Chapter 9, some positive amount of unemployment. As excess demand for labour increases, unemployment will fall (for example as vacancies increase and jobs become easier to find) but by increasingly smaller amounts. Unemployment will never actually fall to zero because of various factors such as those individuals who change their jobs and who will be unemployed while they are searching for new employment.

A combination of two hypotheses, namely that:

- the rate of increase in money wages depends positively on excess demand for labour
- excess demand for labour and unemployment are negatively related provided the economic rationale for the Phillips curve shown in Figure 10.1.

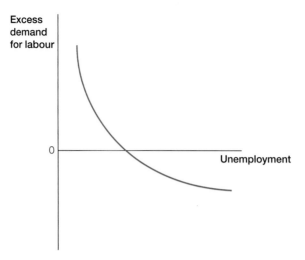

Figure 10.2 The relationship between excess demand for labour and unemployment

The Phillips curve can also be described by the equation:

$$\dot{W} = f(U) \tag{10.4}$$

where $\dot{W}$ = rate of change of money wages

U = unemployment (a proxy measure for excess demand for labour)

The original Phillips curve as a menu for policy choice

During the 1960s the Phillips curve was quickly adopted as part of the then-prevailing Keynesian economic orthodoxy, not least because it provided the authorities with a menu of possible inflation–unemployment combinations for policy choice. Given the apparent *stable trade-off* between inflation and unemployment policymakers were faced with a clear-cut choice. If they decided to run the economy at a lower level of unemployment they would have to accept a cost in terms of a higher rate of inflation. Alternatively, reducing the rate of inflation would involve a cost in terms of higher unemployment. Although some Keynesians argued that inflation was caused by rising costs (a cost-push theory), most Keynesians adhered to a theory of **demand-pull inflation**. In this view, inflation was caused by an excess demand for goods and services when the economy was at, or above, full employment.

Demand-pull inflation: inflation caused by an excess demand for goods and services when the economy is at, or above, full employment.

The breakdown of the original Phillips curve

By the late 1960s the original Phillips curve had broken down and in the early 1970s Western economies experienced a simultaneous increase in both the rate of inflation and unemployment (so-called stagflation). Broadly speaking, economists reacted to the breakdown of the original Phillips curve in one of two main ways. Some Keynesian economists abandoned the demand-pull theory of inflation and turned to a theory of **cost-push inflation** (see below). Other

Cost-push inflation: inflation caused by cost increases even though there are no shortages of goods and services and the economy is below full employment.

economists sought to modify the demand-pull theory by arguing that inflation is caused by excess demand *and* expectations of future rates of inflation. We first turn to discuss the expectations-augmented Phillips curve and how this fits into the monetarist view of inflation.

The expectations-augmented Phillips curve

In Chapter 7 we discussed how within orthodox microeconomic analysis of the labour market the demand for and supply of labour are specified in real, not money, terms. In other words, although money wages are set in wage negotiations, what really matters to both firms as employers and workers as employees is the **real wage** that is negotiated. In addition, given that wage bargains are struck for an advance period (for example lasting for one year), the rate of inflation expected throughout the period of the contract has a crucial bearing on the real wage negotiated. In the light of these considerations, Friedman augmented the original Phillips curve with the expected rate of inflation as an additional variable determining the rate of change of money wages.

Real wage: the money wage divided (or deflated) by the price index; the amount of goods and services that a money wage can buy.

REFLECTING ON ECONOMICS

Milton Friedman's and Edmund Phelps's pioneering insights into the trade-off between inflation and unemployment

The expectations-augmented Phillips curve derives from the pioneering work undertaken by two Nobel Laureates: Milton Friedman (1912–2006), a prominent monetarist, and Edmund Phelps, a leading new Keynesian, who won the Nobel Prize in Economics in 1976 and 2006 respectively. In the late 1960s both economists independently challenged the then-conventional wisdom of there being a stable, negatively sloped long-run Phillips curve relationship between inflation and unemployment. The main differences between Friedman's and Phelps's analyses is that Phelps

Courtesy of Edmund Phelps

Edmund Phelps

offered a theory of the natural rate of unemployment that was based on *microeconomic* foundations, and which revolved around quit rates specified as a decreasing function of a firm's relative wage. While most economists today accept that there is no trade-off between inflation and unemployment in the long run there are some notable exceptions. For example, George Akerlof, the 2001 Nobel Laureate – who you will recall from our discussion in Chapter 2 is famous for his analysis of asymmetric information, especially regarding poor-quality cars (so-called lemons), in the used-car market – has suggested that when inflation is low it may not be 'salient' and that, in consequence, inflationary expectations have a negligible role in wage bargaining. According to Akerlof, the result is that there is a permanent trade-off between inflation and unemployment in the presence of low inflation.

Deriving a whole family of short-run Phillips curves and a vertical long-run Phillips curve

The introduction of the expected rate of inflation as an additional variable that determines the rate of change of money wages modifies the original Phillips curve. As we will now discuss, the expectations-augmented Phillips curve implies that there is no longer a single unique Phillips curve; rather there exist a whole family of **short-run Phillips curves**. Each short-run Phillips curve is associated with a different expected rate of inflation. As the expected rate of inflation increases, the short-run Phillips curve will shift upwards. In other words, each level of unemployment corresponds to a unique rate of change of real wages.

Short-run Phillips curve: depicts the relationship between inflation and unemployment that exists for a given expected rate of inflation.

This analysis is illustrated in Figure 10.3 where both to simplify the analysis and for ease of diagrammatic presentation two assumptions are made, namely that:

- productivity growth remains constant at zero with the result that firms will pass on any wage increases in the form of price increases, in order to maintain their profit margins
- the short-run Phillips curves are linear.

Figure 10.3 maintains the same axes as the original Phillips curve of Figure 10.1 and shows three short-run Phillips curves, each associated with a different expected rate of inflation, and a *vertical long-run Phillips curve* (LRPC) at the natural rate of unemployment (U_N).

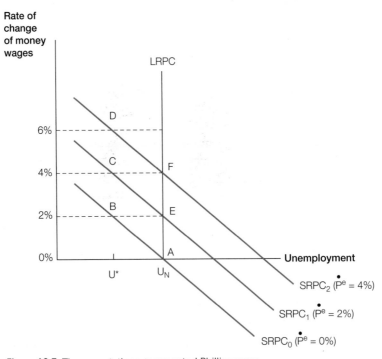

Figure 10.3 The expectations-augmented Phillips curve

Suppose the labour market is initially in equilibrium (that is, there is zero excess demand) at the natural rate of unemployment (see Chapter 9, Section 9.4) with a zero rate of increase in money wages. Assuming productivity growth is zero, a zero rate of increase in money wages ($\dot{W}$) will be matched by a zero rate of increase in prices ($\dot{P}$) and the expected rate of increase in prices ($\dot{P}^e$) will also be zero. In this situation the real wage is constant, as the rate of increase in money wages is exactly equal to the rate of increase in prices. Furthermore, inflation is perfectly anticipated with the actual and expected rates of inflation equal at zero. In Figure 10.3 this initial situation is indicated by the short-run Phillips curve $SRPC_0$ which cuts the horizontal axis at point A, at the natural rate of unemployment.

Now suppose that the government decided to increase aggregate demand in the economy by embarking on a policy of monetary expansion in an attempt to *maintain* unemployment below U_N at U^*. As firms increased their production to meet the increase in aggregate demand for goods, the demand for labour would increase and money wages would start to rise at a rate of 2 per cent. Given recent experience of zero actual and expected inflation rates, workers would interpret the 2 per cent increase in their money wages as a 2 per cent increase in their real wages and respond by increasing the supply of labour. As the demand for and supply of labour increased, unemployment would fall from U_N to U^*, a movement along the short-run Phillips curve ($SRPC_0$) from point A to point B.

Assuming productivity growth is zero, a 2 per cent rate of increase in money wages would lead to a 2 per cent rate of increase in prices. Sooner or later workers would start to adapt their expectations of future inflation in the light of such changed circumstances and take their revised expectations into consideration when negotiating money wage increases. As individuals fully revised their expectations of inflation upwards from zero to 2 per cent, the short-run Phillips curve would shift upwards from $SRPC_0$ to $SRPC_1$. In other words, once the 2 per cent rate of actual inflation is fully anticipated ($\dot{P} = \dot{P}^e = 2$ per cent) money wages would have to increase at a rate of 4 per cent, in order to achieve the 2 per cent increase in real wages necessary to maintain unemployment at U^*; that is, point C on $SRPC_1$. In this situation the authorities would have to increase further the rate of monetary expansion in order to finance the 4 per cent rate of wage and price inflation.

As individuals revised upwards their expectations of inflation, the short-run Phillips curve would again shift upwards, this time from $SRPC_1$ to $SRPC_2$. At an expected inflation of 4 per cent, money wages would have to increase at a rate of 6 per cent, in order to achieve the 2 per cent rise in real wages required by the continued existence of excess demand in the labour market at U^*; that is, point D on $SRPC_2$. In this situation the authorities would have to increase the rate of monetary expansion still further in order to finance the 6 per cent rate of wage and prices inflation, and so on.

As such, the expectations-augmented Phillips curve can be described by the equation:

$$\dot{W} = f(U) + \dot{P}^e \qquad (10.5)$$

where $\dot{W}$ = rate of change of money wages
U = unemployment
$\dot{P}^e$ = the expected rate of inflation

When the economy is in equilibrium at the natural rate of unemployment and there is no excess demand for labour, the rate of increase in money wages ($\dot{W}$) will equal the rate of increase in prices ($\dot{P}$) and the expected rate of increase in prices ($\dot{P}^e$). In this situation the real wage will be constant. The vertical long-run Phillips curve traces a locus of possible points where inflation is perfectly anticipated (that is, $\dot{W} = \dot{P} = \dot{P}^e$) at the natural rate of unemployment. The intersection of the short-run Phillips curve ($SRPC_0$) with the vertical long-run Phillips curve at point A represents our initial starting point where the rate of wage and price inflation, and the expected rate of inflation are all equal to zero. Points E and F represent other potential long-run equilibrium situations.

Summing up

In the monetarist view, inflation is *initiated* by excessive monetary expansion, which leads to excess demand in the labour market. This causes a rise in money wages, which firms then pass on to consumers in the form of higher prices. Expectations of further price increases lead to increased wage claims, resulting in an inflationary 'wage–price' spiral. For monetarists, the chain of causation runs from changes in the money supply (and its rate of expansion) to changes in prices (and their rate of increase, namely inflation). As we will shortly come to discuss, in the non-monetarist view this chain of causation is reversed. Before discussing the non-monetarist view we need to consider the policy implications of the expectations-augmented Phillips curve.

Policy implications of the expectations-augmented Phillips curve

The danger of triggering accelerating inflation

One of the main policy implications of this analysis is that, as illustrated in Figure 10.3, any attempt to *maintain* unemployment below the natural rate will result in an accelerating rate of inflation, which can only be financed by accelerating monetary growth. If, however, the authorities refused to increase continuously the rate of monetary expansion, unemployment would return to U_N and in line with the quantity theory of money, in equilibrium in the long run, the rate of monetary expansion would equal the rate of inflation ($\dot{P} = \dot{M}$). At U_N the real wage will be restored to its original level and there will be no disturbance in the labour market. As discussed above, when joining together all such points of equilibrium (that is, points A, E, F and so on) a vertical long-run Phillips curve (LRPC) is obtained at the natural rate of unemployment.

In summary, monetarists argue that while an inflation–unemployment trade-off exists in the short run along a given short-run Phillips curve, once economic agents have fully adjusted their inflationary expectations the trade-off disappears, resulting in a vertical long-run Phillips curve at the natural rate of unemployment. The natural or equilibrium level of unemployment is associated with a stable (or non-accelerating) rate of inflation which is itself determined by the rate of monetary expansion. You should also recall from what we discussed in Chapter 9, Section 9.4 that, in the monetarist view, if the authorities want to reduce the natural rate of unemployment they need to pursue supply-management policies – designed to improve the structure and functioning of the labour market – rather than aggregate demand-management policies.

The output–employment costs of reducing inflation

As we have seen, in the monetarist view, inflation is essentially a monetary phenomenon propagated by excessive monetary growth. It follows from this analysis that inflation can only be reduced by slowing down the rate of monetary expansion. Reducing the rate of growth of the money supply will, in the short run, result in an increase in the level of unemployment above the natural rate. The extent and duration of the rise in unemployment depends on two main factors, namely:

• whether the authorities pursue a policy of rapid or gradual monetary contraction
• the speed at which economic agents revise their expectations of inflation downwards in the light of changed circumstances.

We can illustrate why this is the case using Figure 10.4. Assume that the economy is initially operating at point A, with a 6 per cent (stable) rate of wage and price inflation (determined by a 6 per cent rate of monetary expansion) and unemployment is at its natural level (U_N). At point A, which is both a short-run and a long-run equilibrium position, inflation is perfectly anticipated with the actual and expected rates of inflation equal at 6 per cent. Now suppose the authorities decide that they want to reduce the rate of wage and price inflation to 2 per cent and move to point B on the long-run Phillips curve (LRPC). One option open to the authorities would be to rapidly reduce the rate of monetary expansion from 6 per cent to 2 per cent in order to attain their new inflation target of 2 per cent. Such a policy stance would initially result in a relatively large increase in unemployment from U_N to U_1; that is, an initial movement along the short-run Phillips curve associated with an expected rate of inflation of 6 per cent, from point A to point C. As the rate of wage and price inflation fell, individuals would revise downwards their expectations of inflation and the short-run Phillips curve would shift downwards. Eventually unemployment

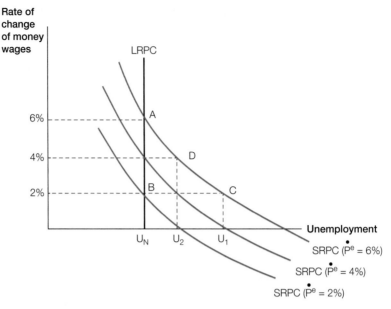

Figure 10.4 The unemployment costs of reducing inflation

would return to U_N and a new short-run and long-run equilibrium would be established at point B.

Alternatively, the authorities might choose to gradually reduce the rate of monetary expansion from 6 per cent to 4 per cent and thereafter from 4 per cent to 2 per cent. Such a policy stance would involve a smaller initial increase in unemployment above the natural rate from U_N to U_2; that is, an initial movement along the short-run Phillips curve, associated with an expected rate of inflation of 6 per cent, from point A to point D. The short-run Phillips curve would, as before, shift downwards as individuals revised downwards their expectations of inflation in line with the fall in the actual rate of wage and price inflation. As the authorities gradually reduced the rate of monetary expansion further from 4 per cent to 2 per cent, they would reduce inflation to their target of 2 per cent, and eventually unemployment would return to U_N. In contrast to the policy option of rapid **disinflation**, sometimes referred to as **cold turkey**, reducing inflation by **gradual** monetary contraction would take longer. Recognition of this has led some economists to advocate the use of supplementary policy measures, such as **prices and incomes policy** (see Section 10.3), to accompany gradual monetary contraction. Such supplementary policy measures would speed the adjustment process to a lower rate of inflation *if* they succeeded in reducing individuals' expectations of inflation. The faster individuals revise their expectations of inflation downwards, the shorter the period of time unemployment will remain above the natural rate following a decrease in the rate of monetary

Disinflation: a decrease in the rate of inflation.

Cold turkey: a rapid and permanent reduction in the rate of monetary growth aimed at reducing the rate of inflation.

Gradualism: an approach to disinflation that involves a slow and gradual reduction in the rate of monetary growth.

Prices and incomes policy: measures that establish guidelines or controls for wage and/or price increases.

Credibility: the degree to which people believe the authorities' announcements about future policy.

expansion. Of particular importance in this context is the **credibility** of any anti-inflation strategy pursued by the authorities.

In the chapter's final 'Reflecting on Economics' feature we outline the form that anti-inflation policy took in the early 1980s in the United Kingdom and shed some light on the output–employment costs of reducing inflation. Students whose studies are pitched at a higher level – for example those on MBA programmes – can find a discussion of the main differences between Keynesians, monetarists and new classicists with respect to the expectations-augmented Phillips curve and the policy implications that derive from it in the appendix to this chapter.

REFLECTING ON ECONOMICS

Polices adopted in the United Kingdom to reduce inflation in the early 1980s

The monetarist view that inflation can only be reduced by slowing down the rate of monetary expansion had an important bearing on the course of anti-inflation policy pursued in many countries during the 1980s. For example, in the UK the Conservative government elected into office in 1979 sought to reduce progressively the rate of monetary growth in order to achieve its overriding economic policy objective of reducing the rate of inflation. As part of its medium-term financial strategy, first introduced in the March 1980 budget, the Thatcher government announced declining targets for monetary growth. Such targets reflected an *explicit* acceptance of the monetarist view that a reduction in monetary growth is both necessary and sufficient to reduce the rate of inflation. At the same, time the pre-announcement of declining monetary growth targets reflected an *implicit* acceptance of the view that economic agents form their expectations of inflation rationally and would quickly revise their inflationary expectations downwards, thereby

minimizing the unemployment costs associated with monetary disinflation.

The Thatcher government achieved some measure of success in reducing inflation in the UK in the early 1980s. Between 1979 and 1983 inflation fell from 13.4 per cent to 4.6 per cent and most economists agree that the domestic monetary (and fiscal) policies pursued contributed substantially to reducing the rate of inflation in the UK. However, most economists also agree that the restrictive domestic policies pursued made a significant contribution to the rise in unemployment experienced in the early 1980s. Between 1979 and 1983 unemployment rose from 4.7 per cent to 11.1 per cent. *Prima facie* evidence from other economies also suggests that the unemployment costs of reducing inflation are not insignificant. For example, the pursuit of restrictive monetary policy in the US economy in the early 1980s was also associated with deep recession. While inflation fell from 11.3 per cent to 3.2 per cent in the US economy between 1979 and 1983, over the same period unemployment rose from 5.8 per cent to 9.6 per cent. Most economists agree that the restrictive domestic policies pursued significantly contributed to the rise in US unemployment, along with other contributory factors including the second oil price shock.

Inflation as an international monetary phenomenon

So far we have discussed the monetarist view of inflation implicitly in the context of a closed economy in which no international trade takes place. In a closed economy (or an open economy operating under flexible exchange rates – see Chapter 14), the domestic rate of inflation is held to be determined by the domestic rate of monetary expansion relative to the rate of growth of

Fixed exchange rate: an exchange rate that is fixed at a predetermined level by intervention by the country's central bank in the foreign exchange market.

Bretton Woods system: a fixed exchange rate system established at the end of the Second World War. The system broke down in the early 1970s.

domestic real output. However, in a regime of **fixed exchange rates**, such as the **Bretton Woods system** (see Chapter 14), which operated from the mid-1940s until the early 1970s, inflation is viewed as an international monetary phenomenon.

Under a regime of fixed exchange rates, monetarists argue that nations are linked together in a world economy in which the aggregate world money supply (and its rate of change) determines world prices (and their rates of change). Domestic monetary expansion will influence the domestic rate of inflation only to the extent that it influences the rate of growth of the world money supply and in consequence the rate of growth of world prices. An increase in the world rate of monetary expansion (due to the rapid monetary expansion by either a large country relative to the rest of the world, or a number of small countries simultaneously) would create excess demand and result in inflationary pressure throughout the world economy. On the basis of this analysis, monetarists have argued that the acceleration of inflation that occurred in Western economies in the late 1960s was primarily the consequence of an increase in the rate of monetary expansion in the US to finance increased expenditure on the Vietnam War. As such, inflationary pressure initiated in the US was then transmitted to other Western economies via the US balance of payments deficit.

Flexible exchange rate: an exchange rate that is determined in the foreign exchange market by the forces of demand and supply; also known as a floating exchange rate.

For an economy operating under a regime of **flexible exchange rates**, monetarists argue that a country's domestic rate of inflation will be determined, as in the case of a closed economy, by its domestic rate of monetary expansion (relative to the rate of growth of domestic real output). If the domestic rate of monetary expansion in an economy is greater than that in the rest of the world, then it will experience a faster domestic rate of inflation compared to that prevailing in other countries and its currency will depreciate.

Having discussed in some detail the monetarist view of inflation we now turn to discuss the second main conflicting explanation of inflation, the non-monetarist view.

10.3 The non-monetarist view

Wage increases as the initiating force of inflation

In contrast to the monetarist view, in the non-monetarist view (also sometimes referred to as the cost-push or sociological explanation of inflation) wage increases are regarded as the initiating force of inflation. Furthermore such wage increases can occur *independently* of the state of demand and supply conditions in the labour market. Adherents to this view argue that there exist various social pressures that lead to largely *exogenous* wage increases. Given these social pressures, the common theme in the non-monetarist approach is that, because wages are such an important component of firms' costs of production, if money wages continually rise at a faster rate than the growth of productivity, then an inflationary wage–price spiral will result in a similar manner to that analysed in the monetarist view. In the absence of monetary expansion, unemployment will increase as inflation reduces the real value of the money supply. Proponents of the non-monetarist view argue that, in the past, governments have increased the money supply in order to prevent unemployment from rising. This response by the government explains, in this view, the strong correlation between changes in the money supply and changes in prices. In contrast to the monetarist view, in the non-monetarist view causation runs from changes in prices to changes in the money supply, rather than the other way round.

In what follows we outline some of the social pressures that, it is alleged, lead to wage increases and initiate the inflationary process. Two examples will suffice.

- Some writers argue that class conflict is inevitable in a capitalist society and that inflation results from the struggle between workers and capitalists as each group strives to achieve a bigger share of national income for themselves. If workers succeed in securing wage increases above productivity growth, capitalists' profit margins will be reduced. In order to maintain the share of profits in national income, capitalists will react by increasing their prices. Workers then react by pressing for wage increases, resulting in the familiar inflationary wage–price spiral. The more workers' aspirations for real income growth exceed productivity growth, the faster will be the ensuing inflation.
- Other writers suggest that inflation results from the attempts of unions to improve or maintain their members' position in the league table of wages. If one union succeeds in improving its *relative* wage position, other unions seeking to restore or improve on the previous order of wage differentials will react by pushing for wage increases. Such a process will lead to leapfrogging as each union tries to improve its relative wage position, resulting in an inflationary wage–price spiral.

In the two examples of the non-monetarist view cited above, the common theme is that trade unions continually push for increases in money wages above the growth of productivity. Such wage increases feed into price increases, which in turn leads to further wage increases and so on. If this is the case then it is important to ask why firms are willing to accede to such inflationary wage claims. The usual answer given to this question by adherents of the non-monetarist view is that the balance of power in negotiating wage increases has tended to move away from firms in favour of unions. Among the reasons put forward to explain this is that increased welfare benefits have enabled workers to resort to longer periods of strike action if their wage claims are not met. Furthermore, given the changing nature of the production process, firms are more willing to accede to claims for wage increases rather than resist and face 'costly' strike action. As production has become more capital-intensive in many industries, firms have become more vulnerable to their whole production process being disrupted by

© iStockphoto/Tacojim

Non-monetarists think trade unions may contribute to inflation

a small number of workers threatening strike action. In addition, greater foreign competition has meant that in the event of strike action output may be lost as customers turn to foreign markets. In these circumstances it is argued that it is less costly for firms to give in to wage claims than to face the severe costs that result from strike action that disrupts the production process.

The non-monetarist view of inflation outlined above emphasizes rising wage costs as the initiating force of the inflationary process. Before considering the policy implications of this view, mention should also be made of the role of increases in other production costs in triggering higher prices. Some writers have drawn attention to rising costs of imported raw materials and fuels, which firms pass on to consumers in the form of higher prices. As domestic prices rise, unions demand money wage increases in order to maintain their members' real wages. As a result an inflationary wage–price spiral develops which is then accommodated by monetary expansion in order to prevent a rise in unemployment. In particular the two oil price hikes that occurred in 1973–74 and 1979 are highlighted as triggering the high rates of inflation experienced in many Western economies in the mid-1970s and early 1980s. Furthermore, the widening gap between the production and consumption of oil in the mid-2000s resulted in a third significant rise in the price of oil, which impacted firms' production costs. Oil prices, however, fell sharply from their record high levels following the 2008–9 recession before recovering again. More recently they have plummeted and at the time of writing (early 2015) had fallen more than half from their mid-2014 level.

Policy implications of the non-monetarist view

Let us now turn to examine the policy implications of this non-monetarist view of inflation. Given the belief that money wage increases, or other increased costs of production, initiate inflation, the introduction of a *permanent* prices and incomes policy is seen as the best way to control the inflationary spiral. Such a policy involves implementing a series of *direct controls* or rules that govern the extent to which wages and prices can increase. For example, for wage increases not to be inflationary, money wage increases need to be controlled to ensure that they do not exceed the average increase in productivity. Of note is that past policy has traditionally focused on *wage control*, rather than income control, in part because other forms of income, such as dividends and interest, are much more difficult to influence.

Despite the simple logic behind the introduction of prices and incomes policy, such a policy involves a number of potentially important problems and is not without its critics. In what follows we outline four main difficulties associated with prices and incomes policy:

- There are a number of problems involved with the implementation of both a wages and a prices policy. For example, both workers and firms may find ways of evading wage and price controls respectively.
- A wages policy operates *outside* the market mechanism and in consequence may result in a misallocation of resources. For example, firms in growth industries may find it difficult to expand production if they are not allowed to offer wage increases that are necessary to attract additional workers required.
- If a prices and incomes policy is accompanied by excessive monetary expansion, the policy will ultimately be doomed to failure. Unless the extreme view is taken that excess demand never affects wages and prices, excessive monetary expansion must result in inflationary pressures, which will inevitably lead to the breakdown of a policy seeking to control wage and price increases.
- While a prices and incomes policy may succeed in moderating the rate of wage and price increase during the period in which it is operated, once the policy is relaxed, or breaks down, wages and prices may subsequently 'catch up' by increasing at a faster pace.

10.4 A case study: maintaining price stability in the euro area

The European Central Bank

Within the euro area, the responsibility for achieving price stability – which since 2003 has been defined as maintaining inflation rates below, but close to, 2 per cent over the medium term – lies with the European Central Bank (ECB). With respect to this objective four observations are worthy of note.

© European Central Bank/ Claudio Hils

- First, although the ECB has a mandate to support policies that contribute to other macro objectives – such as high employment and sustained growth – it does not have *direct* responsibility for achieving any objective other than price stability. In line with the expectations-augmented Phillips curve analysis, this reflects the widely held view that while monetary policy can influence output and employment in the short run, it cannot exert any lasting influence on real variables.

- Second, underlying the primacy given to the objective of price stability is the now widely accepted view that price stability is a *necessary precondition* for sustainable growth of output and employment.

Deflation: a sustained fall in the general price level.

- Third, reference to inflation rates *below,* but close to, 2 per cent in the *medium term* reflects a consensus view that it is also important to avoid **deflation** (a situation where the general price level falls over time) and that monetary policy cannot completely eliminate (some inevitable) short-term variation in inflation.
- Fourth, as is evident from Figure 10.5, from 2000 until the deflationary impact of the 2008–9 recession and its aftermath, inflation in the euro area more often than not *exceeded* 2 per cent. This has led some commentators to suggest that *in practice* the ECB has been prepared to operate as if 2 per cent was the midpoint of a symmetrical inflation range.

In pursuing its inflation objective, the ECB adopts a 'two-pillar' approach to the risks to price stability by undertaking both:

- an **economic analysis** focusing on real economic activity and financial conditions in the euro area. The economic analysis involves reviewing a wide range of economic data from different sources including movements in output, demand conditions, conditions in the labour market, various price and cost indicators and the balance of payments. It also contains projections of key macroeconomic variables. As such, the economic analysis focuses its attention on factors that can affect inflation in the short-to-medium term; and

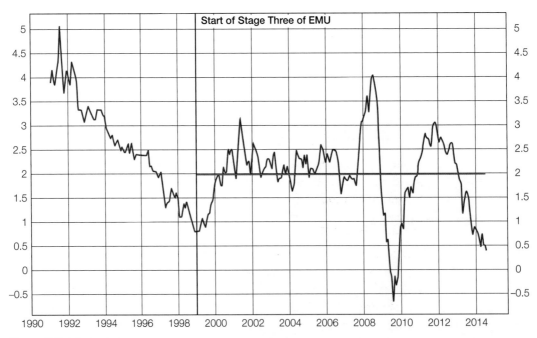

Figure 10.5 Inflation in the euro area

Source: Courtesy of the ECB. Data is available free of charge via the ECB's home page © European Central Bank, Frankfurt am Main, Germany

- a **monetary analysis** monitoring a set of key indicators, with prominence given to monetary aggregates. In the latter case this involves analysing the rate of growth of a broad monetary aggregate (M3) deemed to be compatible with price stability over the medium-to-long term. The money growth pillar reflects the consensus view that inflation is a monetary phenomenon, and that over the *long run* the rate of growth of the money supply and inflation are closely related. Indeed a substantial body of evidence exists which suggests that periods of high and prolonged inflation tend to be associated with high and sustained monetary growth. As such, a significant and sustained rise in the rate of monetary growth would signal a medium to long-term risk to price stability. It is important to note, however, that the growth of M3 is generally considered to be a poor indicator of short- to medium-term inflationary pressure within the euro area.

This two-pillar approach provides a crosscheck of the risks to price stability from the *shorter-term* economic analysis and the *longer-term* monetary analysis, and is used to inform monetary policy decisions that allow the ECB to set interest rates with the primary objective of maintaining price stability in the euro area.

Finally it is interesting to note that inflation in the euro area has declined steadily since 2012 and at the end of 2014 actually became negative. This situation has triggered a lively debate over whether the decision taken by the ECB in January 2015 to launch quantitative easing in the euro area will succeed in successfully combating deflation and enable the ECB to fulfil its price stability mandate. For up-to-date examples of policy discussion – including that relating to quantitative easing in the euro area – the reader should access www.voxeu.org. This site – established 'to promote the dissemination of research-based policy analysis and commentary by leading economists' – provides a rich source of reading material.

10.5 Concluding remarks

In this chapter we have considered two competing explanations of the cause of, and cure for, inflation. In the monetarist view the cause of inflation is excessive monetary expansion – a case of 'too much money chasing too few goods'. Since governments cause inflation they also have it within their power to reduce inflation through monetary contraction. In contrast, in the non-monetarist view, inflation is caused primarily by largely exogenous wage increases, which arise from various social pressures. In this view the best way to control inflation is through the introduction of prices and incomes policy. While our presentation has highlighted the difference between these two competing explanations, it is important to note that some economists take an eclectic or compromise stance, suggesting that inflation can be caused by both excessive monetary expansion and various cost-push pressures. Indeed, the consensus view is that while *sustained* inflation is not possible without excessive monetary expansion, *temporary* bouts of inflation can be attributed to non-monetary causes arising from the supply side of the economy.

SUMMARY

- The debate over the causes of, and cures for, inflation can be divided between two main competing explanations involving monetarist and non-monetarist views.
- In the monetarist view the rate of inflation, in the long run, is determined by the rate of monetary expansion relative to the rate of growth of real output. While an inflation–unemployment trade-off exists in the short run, in the long run the Phillips curve is vertical at the natural rate of unemployment. The natural rate of unemployment is associated with a stable rate of inflation which is itself determined by the rate of monetary expansion.
- In the short run, monetary disinflation results in an increase in the level of unemployment above the natural rate. How much unemployment increases depends on whether the authorities pursue a policy of rapid or gradual monetary contraction and how quickly inflation expectations are revised downwards. Prima facie evidence from the UK and US economies in the early 1980s suggests that the unemployment costs of monetary disinflation are significant.
- Under a regime of fixed exchange rates, inflation can be regarded as an international monetary phenomenon.
- In the non-monetarist view of inflation wages increases, which can occur independently of labour market conditions, are seen as the initiating force of an inflationary wage–price spiral. As the balance of power in negotiating wage increases has changed in favour of trade unions, firms have become more willing to accede to claims for wage increases. Prices and incomes policy is seen as the best way to control the inflationary spiral according to proponents of the non-monetarist view.
- Some economists take an eclectic stance between the monetarist and non-monetarist views, and argue that inflation can be caused by both excessive monetary expansion and various cost-push pressures.

KEY TERMS

- Quantity theory of money
- Phillips curve
- Inflation–unemployment trade-off
- Expectations-augmented Phillips curve
- Monetary disinflation
- Gradualism versus cold turkey
- Credibility
- Cost-push inflation
- Prices and incomes policy
- Eclecticism

QUESTIONS FOR DISCUSSION

1. What are the main differences between the monetarist and non-monetarist views of inflation?
2. Do governments or trade unions cause inflation?
3. Is there a permanent trade-off between inflation and unemployment?
4. What factors determine the unemployment costs of reducing inflation?
5. Before the onset of the 2008–9 recession the Bank of England's Monetary Policy Committee had, on a number of occasions, increased interest rates in order to dampen inflationary pressures in the UK economy. How might higher interest rates adversely affect firms?
6. What initiates inflation in the non-monetarist view? What are the main problems that may arise in implementing prices and incomes policy?

ONE THING YOU SHOULD READ

At www.econlib.org/library/Columns/y2006/ Friedmantranscript.html you can access the transcript of an interview undertaken by Russell Roberts, the Features Editor of EconTalk – part of the Library of Economics and Liberty – with Milton Friedman in 2006, the year he died. Alternatively, you can listen to the podcast conversation on EconTalk. Of particular interest is the first part of the interview – this focuses on Friedman's views on the role of money which can be found in his seminal 1963 book, co-authored with Anna Schwartz, *A Monetary History of the United States, 1867–1960*. Having read or listened to part 1 (Milton Friedman on Money) of the interview consider the following questions:

1. What happened to the quantity of money in the US during the Great Depression? What lessons were learned from this episode, which resulted in governments around the world supporting banks following the financial crisis and associated 2008–9 recession?
2. Why did Friedman advocate that the authorities should pursue a monetary growth rule in order to maintain price stability?
3. In practice, how does the Federal Reserve Board control the money supply in the US?
4. What happened in the early-to-mid 1970s which helped to change people's views on the trade-off between inflation and unemployment?
5. Which country first adopted inflation targeting?

Appendix

Keynesians, monetarists and new classicists and the expectations-augmented Phillips curve

In section 10.2 we discussed how augmenting the original Phillips curve with the expected rate of inflation results in a whole family of short-run Phillips curves and a vertical long-run Phillips curve. In this appendix we consider *four important differences* between Keynesians, monetarists and new classicists with respect to the expectations-augmented Phillips curve and the policy implications that derive from it.

- *Nowadays* while most Keynesian economists accept that the long-run Phillips curve is vertical, some Keynesians believe that there is a long-run trade-off between inflation and unemployment, although one that is less favourable (steeper) than that predicted by the short-run Phillips curve. As such they argue that the long-run (non-vertical) Phillips curve still offers the authorities a menu of possible inflation–unemployment combinations for policy choice.
- In contrast to monetarists and new classicists, Keynesian economists tend to be more favourably disposed towards the use of prices and incomes policy as an anti-inflationary weapon. Some Keynesians advocate the *temporary* use of prices and incomes policy as a supplementary policy measure to accompany gradual monetary contraction. Other Keynesians, who assign a role to wage increases made independently of the state of excess demand, advocate the *permanent* use of prices and incomes policy as an anti-inflationary weapon. In the latter case, if the long-run (non-vertical) Phillips curve could be shifted downwards by the adoption of a prices and incomes policy, the trade-off between inflation and unemployment could be improved, allowing the authorities to achieve a lower rate of inflation at any given target level of unemployment.
- In marked contrast to monetarists and new classicists, new Keynesians argue that the natural rate of unemployment (or, as discussed in Chapter 9, what they would prefer to refer to as NAIRU) is affected by the path taken by the actual rate of unemployment. In other words new Keynesians argue that the natural rate (NAIRU) is affected by the level of aggregate demand. If,

following monetary disinflation, the economy experiences a prolonged recession, the natural rate or NAIRU will tend to increase as hysteresis effects pull the long-run Phillips curve to the right.

- In contrast to the views held by most Keynesians and monetarists, new classicists do not see the need to follow a policy of gradual monetary contraction in order to reduce inflation. According to the new classical view, the unemployment costs associated with monetary disinflation will be non-existent or negligible provided policy is credible. If the authorities announce a reduction in the rate of monetary growth and the policy announcement is believed to be credible, rational economic agents would immediately revise downwards their expectations of inflation in line with the anticipated effects of monetary contraction on the rate of inflation. In terms of Figure 10.4, inflation would be reduced from 6 per cent to 2 per cent without any increase in unemployment. As such, the short-run Phillips curve associated with a 6 per cent expected inflation would immediately shift downwards to that associated with a 2 per cent expected inflation; that is, the economy would immediately adjust from point A to point B on the long-run Phillips curve. In such circumstances, the authorities might just as well announce a rapid reduction in the rate of growth of the money supply in order to reduce inflation to their new target rate. If, however, there is widespread scepticism that the authorities are not fully committed to disinflation through monetary contraction, individuals will not adjust their inflation expectations downwards. In such a situation, the unemployment costs involved with the adjustment process will be more severe than the case where the authorities have no such credibility problem.

11

economic growth and business cycles

KEY ISSUES

What factors determine economic growth over time?

What role can the government play in promoting growth?

What are business cycles?

What are the main theories that economists have put forward to explain business cycles?

Can the authorities control business cycles?

CONTENTS

11.1	Introduction	**342**
11.2	Economic growth: an overview	**342**
11.3	The Solow growth model	**346**
11.4	The new endogenous growth models	**348**
11.5	Wider influences on economic growth	**349**
11.6	Main features of business cycles	**351**
11.7	The debate over the cause and control of business cycles	**352**
11.8	Concluding remarks	**363**
Appendix	The Solow growth model	**366**

11.1 Introduction

In Chapter 8 we discussed the nature and measurement of economic growth. You will recall that economic growth, the source of *sustained* increases in material living standards over time, refers to an increase in real GDP. Not only is economic growth important for raising living standards but so too is the rate of growth actually achieved in an economy. Even small differences in growth rates can have a tremendous impact on the growth of living standards and the level of potential output over the course of a few decades. As a rough rule of thumb, the number of years it takes for an economy to double its productive capacity can be found by dividing 72 by its rate of growth. For example, an economy will take approximately 36 years to double its output of goods and services if its growth rate is 2 per cent, but only 18 years if its growth rate is 4 per cent. Quite remarkably, between 1992 and 2009 China achieved an average growth rate of more than 10 per cent per annum. As a result China's output approximately doubled every 7 years over this period.

> **Potential output:** the maximum output that can be produced in an economy, given its factor endowments, without generating inflation; also known as full employment output.

Periods of sustained economic growth provide a stable economic environment in which firms can plan, grow and develop. In such circumstances firms are more likely to invest in new plant and machinery given their expectations of rising demand and increased future sales. Now clearly there are close links between economic growth, employment and unemployment. When an economy grows consistently close to its potential output level, its resources – including labour – are near to being fully utilized; there is, in other words, near-full employment. Conversely, in periods of slow growth or outright recession resources are under-utilized and unemployment emerges as a policy problem which impacts upon the profitability of firms.

In Chapter 8 we discussed how an economy will experience short-term fluctuations in output (real GDP) around its secular or long-term trend path, a phenomenon referred to as the business cycle. During an upturn in economic activity output increases, unemployment falls, and the potential for firms to raise their profits increases, and vice versa. Because, over long periods of time, short-term fluctuations in output are dominated by the growth of potential output as the productive capacity of the economy increases, we begin this chapter with a discussion of those factors that determine an economy's rate of economic growth over time. In the second half of the chapter we consider the main theories put forward by economists to explain periodic fluctuations in economic activity and the question of whether or not the authorities can control business cycles.

> **Aggregate production function:** a functional relationship between the quantity of aggregate output produced and the quantities of inputs used in production.

11.2 Economic growth: an overview

Our starting point in discussing the causes of economic growth is consideration of the aggregate production function. The aggregate production function is a function that relates the quantity of aggregate output that can be produced to a *given* quantity of factor inputs. This relationship can be written as:

$$Y = A(t)\, F(K, N) \tag{11.1}$$

Where Y is real output; A (t) represents technological know-how at time t; and F is a function that relates real output to K, the quantity of capital inputs and N, the quantity of labour inputs. Real output will increase over time if there is an increase in the quantity of factor inputs (capital and/or labour) and/or if there is an increase in the *productivity* of capital and labour inputs (that is, an increase in output per unit of factor input) due to an increase in technological know-how.

This analysis can be illustrated graphically using either the short-run aggregate production function (Figure 11.1) or the production possibility frontier (Figure 11.2). The short-run aggregate production function depicted in Figure 11.1 relates real output (Y) to the quantity of labour inputs (N) for *given* technological know-how (A) and quantity of capital inputs (K). The

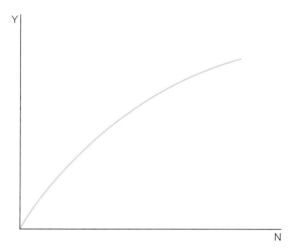

Figure 11.1 The short-run aggregate production function

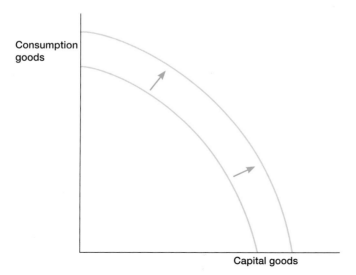

Figure 11.2 The production possibility frontier

decreasing slope of the aggregate production function reflects diminishing returns to the factor input, N. Over time as economic growth occurs, the function will shift upwards following an increase in the quantity of capital inputs and/or an increase in the productivity of factor inputs K and N due to an increase in the value of A, for example following an improvement in the state of technology.

Economic growth, which involves an increase in real output over time, can also be conceptualized using the production possibility frontier shown in Figure 11.2. This figure illustrates two production possibility frontiers, namely before and after economic growth has taken place. Each frontier shows production possibilities involving various combinations of consumption and capital goods when an economy's resources are efficiently employed. Economic growth involves an outward movement of the production possibility frontier, thereby increasing the economy's capacity to produce goods. Such a movement in the frontier results from an increase in the quantity of factor inputs available and/or an improvement in the quality of those factor inputs.

What the above analysis illustrates is that economic growth depends on increases in the quantity *and* quality of both capital and labour inputs. 'Reflecting on Economics', below, summarizes the results of a study by Edward Denison of *Trends in American Economic Growth* over the period 1929 to 1982 and gives some indication of the relative importance of various sources of economic growth.

REFLECTING ON ECONOMICS

Sources of US economic growth 1929–82 (per cent)

Annual growth rate of output	2.9
Percentage of growth due to	
Growth in labour input	32
Growth in labour productivity	
Education per worker	14
Capital	19
Technological change	28
Economies of scale	9
Other factors	–2

Source: Denison, E.F. (1985) *Trends in American Economic Growth,* Washington, DC: The Brookings Institution.

Some indication of the relative importance of various sources of economic growth is contained in Edward Denison's study of *Trends in American Economic Growth* over the period 1929 to 1982. Denison's findings concerning the sources of US economic growth over this period are summarized above. Between 1929 and 1982 real output grew at an annual rate of 2.9 per cent. Denison estimated that 32 per cent of US economic growth over this period was due to growth in the quantity of labour input, while 68 per cent came from growth in labour productivity, itself due to four main factors. According to Denison's estimates, 28 per cent of US economic growth was due to technological change (the most important influence on labour productivity), 19 per cent resulted from capital formation, 14 per cent was due to increased education per worker and 9 per cent resulted from economies of scale.

We now turn to consider what role the government can play in promoting increases in the quantity and quality of K (capital input) and N (labour input). At the outset it is important to stress that this issue is the subject of considerable controversy and economists disagree over what role the government can play in promoting economic growth.

Let us consider the quantity of capital inputs. The physical stock of capital in the form of plant, machinery and infrastructure can only be increased by investment. One option open to the government is to stimulate private-sector investment by increasing the rate of return on, or reducing the cost of, capital by changing company taxation. For example, the cost of capital can be reduced by changing investment and depreciation allowances. However, whether or not tax changes would succeed in stimulating private-sector investment depends in part upon a detailed knowledge of a country's tax system in order to establish how different firms would be affected. Within the system of corporate taxation of any economy there are a variety of investment and depreciation allowances and this means that the cost of capital can vary from one company to another.

Supply-side policies: policies directed towards increasing aggregate supply by altering the response of firms and individuals to changing conditions.

Discussion of such supply-side policy measures are the subject matter of more advanced specialized courses which are beyond the scope of this text. Another option open to the government is to increase public-sector investment by infrastructure provision such as road and rail networks. While noting this option, it is important to remember that economists differ in their views over the degree that the private and public sectors should be involved in the provision of infrastructure.

In addition to increasing the quantity of capital, investment in research and development is required in order to increase the *quality* of capital by discovering, developing and diffusing new technical knowledge. As noted earlier, improvements in technological know-how increase the productivity of both capital and labour, generating an increase in output per unit of factor input. The government can seek to influence the supply of technology either *directly* by, for example, financing research and development itself, or *indirectly* by, for example, encouraging the private sector to engage in research and development through such initiatives as research grants, tax incentives and patent rights. In the latter case patent rights allow monopoly profits to accrue to their inventors and thereby provide an incentive for individuals and firms to engage in research and development.

Human capital: the knowledge and skills of workers in an economy.

So far we have outlined the importance of physical capital to the growth process. Some theories of economic growth have stressed the accumulation of human capital – the knowledge and skills of a country's workers – as the key to achieving economic growth. As human capital is acquired through education, training and experience, one option open to the government is to encourage investment in human capital by, for example, the provision of subsidized university education. Investment in human capital may also have wider social benefits by generating 'ideas' for the development of new goods. Such

Human capital: a key determinant of economic growth

theories, in part, help explain the lack of convergence of per capita income levels and growth rates between poor nations and industrial nations. Poor nations with little human capital cannot hope to catch up industrial nations simply by accumulating physical capital. These theories also point to another reason why poor nations may fail to catch up industrial nations, namely because of 'idea gaps'.

● **Think Point**

Theory suggests that economic growth is boosted by improvements in human capital. What implications does this have for the highly charged debates in many economies over immigration?

11.3   The Solow growth model

The best analytical framework to start studying economic growth is provided by a model developed in the 1950s and 1960s by Robert Solow, who is Emeritus Professor of Economics at Massachusetts Institute of Technology. For his important and influential work on the theory of economic growth, Solow was awarded the Nobel Prize in Economics in 1987.

Robert Solow

The Solow growth model identifies which factors determine growth in output over time and also sheds light on some of the reasons why standards of living (real GDP per person) vary so widely between countries. As knowledge of the model is beyond the scope required for first-year students, in this section we will merely outline the main predictions of the model. Other student readers, for example those on MBA programmes whose studies are pitched at a higher level, can find a more detailed discussion of the model in the Appendix to this chapter.

The bedrock of the Solow growth model is provided by the aggregate production function, which we considered in the previous section. Among the key assumptions made about the properties of the aggregate production function are that:

● Factor inputs experience diminishing returns. For example, while an increase in the quantity of capital inputs with a fixed labour force will result in an increase in real output, output will increase at an ever-declining rate. In consequence, increasing growth rates cannot result from increased capital accumulation due to diminishing returns.

- When factor inputs increase in some proportion, real output will increase in the same proportion. For example, if both the quantity of labour and capital input were doubled, the amount of real output would also be doubled. In other words, the aggregate production function exhibits constant returns to scale.

You will recall from equation (11.1) that growth in output over time depends on both the rate of technological change and the rate at which factor inputs (the labour force and the capital stock) grow over time. One of the most important implications of Solow's model is that the economy will approach a long-run equilibrium or steady-state growth rate, where output, labour input and capital input all grow at the same rate. When the economy reaches a steady state in the long run, output per worker and capital input per worker are constant or unchanging over time. For example, if the labour force grows at 5 per cent then capital will also have to grow at 5 per cent to keep capital input per worker constant. In the steady state, the growth rate depends on the rate of growth of the labour force and the rate of technological progress.

Steady state: a situation in which output per worker and capital input per worker are constant or unchanging over time.

Some of the most important predictions of the model (which are discussed more fully in the Appendix to this chapter) are:

- Countries with higher saving rates will have higher steady-state levels of capital input per worker and therefore higher levels of output per worker, giving a higher standard of living.
- Countries with higher rates of growth in their labour force will have lower steady-state levels of capital input per worker and therefore lower levels of output per worker.
- Sustained growth of output per worker requires, and can only be explained by, technological progress since without it growth of output per worker will eventually cease due to the impact of diminishing returns to capital accumulation.

During the 1970s, economists' interest in the theory of long-run economic growth waned, in large part due to a number of problems with the Solow growth model. Here we highlight two such problems. The first is that, as noted above, technological change is exogenous. Given that the Solow growth model does not explain or consider the determinants of technological change, it provides no insight into how government policy could raise the long-run equilibrium growth rate of output. Furthermore although government policies can influence the saving rate (for example via tax incentives), the model predicts that a (policy-induced) increase in the saving rate will only lead to a *temporary* period of faster growth as the new steady state is approached but it will not affect the

Exogenous variable: a variable that is not explained within a particular model; its value is taken as given.

long-run sustainable or equilibrium growth rate. The long-run equilibrium growth rate depends on the rate of growth of the labour force and technological change, both of which are exogenous.

The second problem with the Solow growth model concerns the *non-convergence* of levels of per capita income of advanced industrial nations and poor nations *over time*. If technological change is freely available, poor nations should be able to close the gap in living standards between themselves and industrial nations by using the technology developed in industrial nations. Moreover, poor nations have less capital input per worker and in consequence their marginal product of capital is higher than in advanced industrial nations. Higher returns to capital in poor nations should attract foreign investment and cause their capital stock to grow more quickly than in industrial nations. As a result, output per worker in industrial and poor nations should converge over time. However, rather than converging, the difference in living standards between advanced industrial nations and the poorest nations has widened.

Convergence: the tendency for output per worker in different countries to converge over time.

Technology spurs growth: Japanese Maglev trains (running on magnets) have reached speeds of more than 370 mph. What will this kind of innovation do for the Japanese economy and Japanese industry?

Endogenous variable: a variable that is explained within a particular model.

11.4 The new endogenous growth models

The late 1980s witnessed a resurgence of interest by economists in the theory of long-run economic growth, which was marked by the development of three new approaches to modelling growth. While the so-called endogenous growth models are highly technical and are beyond the scope of this text, it is useful to briefly outline some of the main ideas involved.

One approach – largely associated with the work of Paul Romer of Stanford University – has abandoned the assumption of diminishing returns to capital accumulation by introducing positive externalities from capital accumulation. Investment in capital by an individual firm – which includes investment in knowledge (research and development) as well as the accumulation of physical capital goods – increases the production potential of other firms by enhancing the economy-wide stock of knowledge. In consequence, diminishing returns to capital accumulation may not apply in the aggregate. In this approach technological progress occurs as an unintended by-product of capital accumulation by individual firms and economies will experience different growth rates depending on the creation of productivity-enhancing positive externalities.

A second approach – also associated with the work of Paul Romer – in line with the Solow growth model has technological change as the driving force

Courtesy of Paul Romer

Paul Romer

behind economic growth. However, unlike the Solow model, technological change is endogenously determined by the activities of self-interested economic agents acting largely in response to financial incentives. In this approach improvements in technology (new ideas) must generate benefits to individuals that are at least 'partially excludable' – for example by the application of patent rights and copyrights – so that agents can earn a reward for their new ideas. In short the approach stresses endogenous innovation in which the development of 'ideas' for new goods is seen as the key to achieving economic growth. As such, poor nations may fail to catch up industrial nations because of 'idea gaps'.

The third new approach to modelling growth has entailed broadening the concept of capital to include human capital. This approach stresses the accumulation of human capital – the knowledge and skills of a nation's workers – as a key to achieving economic growth. In these models the level of output per worker depends on *both* the amount of physical capital input per worker *and* human capital input per worker. Poor nations with little human capital cannot hope to catch up industrial nations simply by accumulating physical capital. As such, different levels of investment in human capital – through training and education – help explain the lack of convergence of per capita income levels and growth rates over time.

In summary, the new endogenous growth models have gone beyond the basic Solow growth model by making the rate of technological change endogenous. Growth is driven by broad capital accumulation (both physical and human capital) together with the creation of new knowledge through research and development. In addition the new models have abandoned the assumption that all nations have the same access to technological opportunities. In doing so the new endogenous growth literature has helped explain differences in living standards among nations and given insights into how government policy can influence long-term growth rates by, for example, encouraging education, training, capital formation and research and development.

11.5 Wider influences on economic growth

So far we have focused our discussion on the aggregate production function in order to highlight the *proximate* sources of economic growth, namely the accumulation of factor inputs (capital and labour) and variables that influence their productivity, such as technological change. In recent years economists have turned their attention to considering the *fundamental* sources of economic growth that influence a country's ability and capacity to accumulate factor inputs and produce new knowledge. These wider influences on growth include the impact of:

- institutions
- international economic integration
- geography

Institutions

Among the factors highlighted are property rights, contract enforcement, the legal system, corruption, the regulatory framework and the quality of governance. Individually and collectively these factors have a marked bearing on the ability and willingness of people to save and invest productively, and the incentive to innovate and participate in entrepreneurial activity. In short there is widespread acceptance that good institutions, and incentive structures, are an important *precondition* for successful growth and development.

International economic integration

Some economists argue that 'globalization' (see Chapter 15) has a positive influence on economic growth. One example frequently cited is the outstanding growth performance of the East Asian 'tiger' economies, which is positively linked to their open trading regimes. Prima facie evidence such as this cannot be explained solely by export-led growth. Other economists argue that, in line with the endogenous growth literature, which emphasizes the importance of new ideas in stimulating technological change, countries that have greater exposure to the rest of the world are more likely to benefit from and absorb new ideas emanating from the research and development activities of other countries.

Paul Krugman

Courtesy of Princeton University, Office of Communications [Brian Wilson]

Geography

Not only may geography have a direct impact on growth through climate, natural resources and topography, in addition some economists – including the 2008 Nobel Laureate Paul Krugman – have stressed the importance of trade patterns and location of economic activity in what has been called a 'new economic geography'. Among the factors highlighted in the literature on the new economic geography is the impact of cumulative effects whereby success breeds success.

Having discussed the factors that determine economic growth over time, we now turn to consider the business cycle. Before considering the main approaches to the cause and control of business cycles we first describe the main features of business cycles.

11.6 Main features of business cycles

Business cycle:
fluctuations in
aggregate economic
activity; in particular
movements in output
around its trend.

The business cycle (or trade cycle as it is sometimes called) can be defined as periodic fluctuations in the pattern of economic activity. While recurrent cycles in a number of aggregate economic series such as employment, consumption and investment can be observed, the business cycle is usually defined as deviations of output (real GDP) from its secular or long-term trend path. Figure 11.3, which depicts a stylized business cycle employing this definition, can be used to describe the main features of business cycles.

The *period* of the cycle, or length of time it takes to complete a full cycle, can be measured by the time gap between any two points at the same stage of the cycle. Reference to Figure 11.3 reveals that it may be measured by the time between successive:

- troughs, for example A and E
- peaks, for example C and G
- up-crosses (of the trend), for example B and F
- down-crosses (of the trend), for example D and H

Only in the hypothetical case of a *perfectly* regular cycle depicted in Figure 11.3 will these alternative measures of the period of the cycle coincide. The *amplitude* of the cycle, which gives an indication of the severity of the cycle, may be

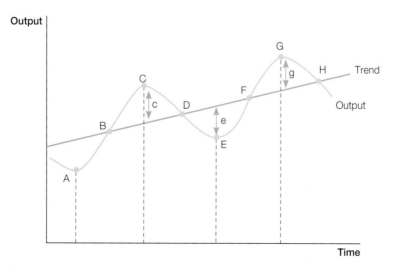

Figure 11.3 A stylized business cycle

measured by the total difference of successive peaks and troughs from the trend path of output, for example c + e or e + g and so on. It should be noted that the amplitude of the cycle will only remain constant where the deviations of output above and below the trend are perfectly regular from one time period to the next, as depicted in Figure 11.3. In practice, cycles will vary both in their timing and amplitude.

Figure 11.3 can also be used to distinguish between the different phases of the cycle. The *expansionary phase* refers to the movement from a trough or lower turning point (for example point A) to a successive peak or upper turning point (for example point C) in the cycle; while the *contractionary phase* refers to the movement from a peak (for example point C) to a successive trough (for example point E). The terms 'boom' and 'slump' are also often used in connection with the business cycle. These terms refer to the periods of rapid expansion (boom) and contraction (slump) before the movement of output from the trend begins to flatten out near the top and bottom of the cycle respectively. In addition, it should be noted that with respect to the contractionary phase of the cycle, the term recession is generally used to describe a slowdown in the growth rate of output below the trend growth rate, while the term depression is usually reserved for the most severe recessions.

Having described the main features of business cycles, we are now in a position to consider alternative explanations of the cause of the cycle. Before considering five main approaches to the cause and control of cycles it is important to stress that, unlike the stylized cycle depicted in Figure 11.3, in practice business cycles are characterized by recurrent fluctuations in output/real GDP from its trend of varying length and amplitude. Furthermore, this pattern of behaviour is also observed in a number of other aggregate economic series. While controversy exists over the duration of cycles, economists usually have in mind short cycles of approximately 3–10 years in length when they refer to the business cycle.

11.7   The debate over the cause and control of business cycles

At the centre of the debate over the cause and control of business cycles lie a number of fundamental questions, most notably:

- Is the economy inherently stable?
- What is the main source of shocks that affect the economy?
- How long does it take for the economy to self-equilibrate once subjected to a shock?
- Can the authorities intervene to reduce fluctuations in economic activity?

In attempting to answer these questions it is possible to identify the development of *five* main approaches within mainstream economics, namely the:

- Keynesian approach
- monetarist approach
- new classical approach
- real business cycle approach
- political business cycle approach

The Keynesian approach

Keynesians believe that the economy is *inherently unstable* and is subject to erratic shocks that cause it to fluctuate between periods of rapid expansion and contraction. The erratic shocks that cause these fluctuations in economic activity are attributed primarily to a change in autonomous expenditures. Furthermore, Keynesians contend that, after being subjected to some disturbance, the economy can take a long time to return to the neighbourhood of full employment/potential output.

In the Keynesian approach the expansionary and contractionary phases of the business cycle are explained by the interaction of the multiplier process and the accelerator. Let us now examine why periods of economic expansion and contraction, once begun, tend to develop their own momentum. Starting from a position of less than full employment, suppose there is an increase in the amount of autonomous investment expenditure undertaken in the economy. An increase in investment expenditure will result in an increase in employment in firms that produce capital goods. Newly employed workers in capital-goods industries will spend some of their income on consumption goods. The rise in demand for consumer goods will lead to increased employment in consumer-goods industries and result in further rounds of expenditure. In consequence, an initial rise in autonomous investment produces a *more than* proportionate rise in income, a process known as the multiplier (see the following 'Reflecting on Economics' feature). The rise in income will *induce* a further increase in investment as new capital equipment is needed to meet the increased demand for output. Since the cost of capital equipment is usually greater than the value of its annual output, new investment will be *greater than* the increase in output that brought it about. This latter phenomenon is referred to as the accelerator (see the chapter's final 'Reflecting on Economics' feature). The *interaction* of the multiplier process and the accelerator explains why periods of economic expansion or contraction will tend to develop their own momentum. Following an initial increase in autonomous investment, the rise in income due to the multiplier process will be reinforced by an increase in new investment, via the accelerator, which will in turn have a further multiplier effect on income and so on.

Multiplier: the ratio of the change in income to a change in autonomous expenditure.

Accelerator principle: the theory that the level of net investment depends on the change in output.

The multiplier: an algebraic derivation and numerical example

Consider first a hypothetical economy in which there is no government sector or international trade undertaken. The output (Y) of such an economy would be split between the production of consumption (C) and investment (I) goods:

$$Y = C + I \qquad (11.1B)$$

Let us further assume that investment expenditure is autonomously determined, while consumer expenditure depends positively upon income. As discussed in Chapter 9, Section 9.3, the form of the consumption function can be represented by a simple linear equation:

$$C = \alpha + \beta Y \qquad (11.2B)$$

If we substitute equation (11.2B) into equation (11.1B) we obtain:

$$Y = \alpha + \beta Y + I \qquad (11.3B)$$

Rearranging equation (11.3B) and factorizing we obtain:

$$Y(1 - \beta) = \alpha + I \qquad (11.4B)$$

Finally, dividing both sides of equation (11.4B) by $(1 - \beta)$ we obtain:

$$Y = \frac{1}{1 - \beta}[\alpha + I] \qquad (11.5B)$$

Equation (11.5B) determines the equilibrium level of income. The multiplier is given by:

$$\frac{1}{1 - \beta}$$

and is equal to the reciprocal of 1 minus the marginal propensity to consume (β). Alternatively in this hypothetical economy, with no government or foreign trade, the multiplier is equal to the reciprocal of the marginal propensity to save. For example, with a marginal propensity to consume of 0.8 (and by definition a marginal propensity to save of 0.2), the multiplier would be equal to 5. Following a change in investment, income will change (ΔY) by some multiple of the original change in investment expenditure (ΔI). For example, if investment expenditure increased by £2 million, income would increase by £10 million; that is, $\Delta Y = \Delta I \times 5$.

The above analysis needs to be modified if we consider an economy with a government sector that engages in international trade. While an initial increase in investment spending will lead in exactly the same way to successive rounds of increased expenditure, some part of the *extra* income will be withdrawn, not only in the form of savings (marginal propensity to save), but also on import spending (marginal propensity to import) and taxes paid to the government (marginal tax rate). The multiplier will, in consequence, depend on the fraction of income withdrawn from the circular flow (see Chapter 8) via savings, imports and taxes, and can be generalized as:

$$\frac{1}{w}$$

For example, if the fraction of income withdrawn (w) from the circular flow is 0.5, then the multiplier will be equal to 2. Finally, it is interesting to note that the same multiplier process will apply following a change in exports or government expenditure.

Although the interaction of the multiplier process and the accelerator can explain both the expansionary and contractionary phases of the cycle, the Keynesian approach requires the addition of *ceilings* and *floors* to account for turning points in the cycle. Periods of rapid expansion cannot continue indefinitely. As the economy approaches its full employment or potential output 'ceiling', the rate at which income/output increases will slow down due to resource constraints. As the rate of increase in income slows down this leads to a reduction in new investment, through the operation of the accelerator (see 'Reflecting on Economics' below), which in turn leads to a fall in income, through the multiplier process and so on. The cycle now passes into its contractionary phase as it moves from an upper turning point to a lower turning point.

Stabilization policy:
policy aimed at
stabilizing output
and employment
at, or near, their
full employment
or natural levels by
influencing the level
of aggregate demand.

Discretionary policy:
a situation in which
the authorities are
free to vary the
strength of fiscal and/
or monetary policy, in
any way they see fit, in
order to achieve their
desired objectives.

The movement of output from trend will eventually flatten out near the bottom of the cycle. The contractionary phase of the cycle will be reversed when the economy hits a 'floor'. Sooner or later, as the existing capital equipment wears out, it will fall to a level where it needs replacing in order to produce the current sales/production of annual output. New investment for replacement orders will, through the interaction of the multiplier and accelerator, start the expansionary phase of the cycle again, and so on.

What are the implications of the Keynesian approach for stabilization policy and the control of business cycles? Given the belief that the economy is inherently unstable and is not rapidly self-equilibrating, Keynesians stress the *need* to stabilize the economy. Furthermore, in their view, governments *can* and therefore *should* use discretionary aggregate demand (especially fiscal) **policies** to offset fluctuations in autonomous expenditures (such as private-sector investment) and stabilize the economy (see Chapters 9 and 12).

REFLECTING ON ECONOMICS

The simple accelerator theory of investment: a numerical example

The relationship between output (Y) and the amount of capital (K) required to produce it can be described by the equation:

$$K = \alpha Y$$

The capital–output ratio (α) is also referred to as the accelerator coefficient. New investment (I) will be required to increase the capital stock (ΔK), to meet an increase in output/sales (ΔY).

$$I = \Delta K = \alpha \Delta Y$$

The following numerical example illustrates the 'simple' accelerator theory of investment.

Columns (2) and (3) show that the value of capital equipment is three times the value of annual output produced and sold. The capital–output ratio is fixed at 3:1. An increase in the production and sales of annual output requires new investment to increase the required capital stock. Columns (4) and (5) show

that new investment is proportional to the *change* in output sales. For example, as sales of annual output increase by £5 from year 4 to 5, new investment of £15 is required. Reference to columns (4) and (5) also reveals that as the increase in sales of annual output slows down in years 6 and 7, new investment falls.

(1) Year	(2) Output (Y)	(3) Required capital stock (K)	(4) Change in output (ΔY)	(5) Change in required capital stock (ΔK)
1	£50	£150	£0	£0
2	£51	£153	£1	£3
3	£53	£159	£2	£6
4	£56	£168	£3	£9
5	£61	£183	£5	£15
6	£63	£189	£2	£6
7	£64	£192	£1	£3
8	£64	£192	£0	£0

**Capital–output
ratio:** the ratio of the
amount of capital to
the amount of output
produced by it.

The monetarist approach

In contrast to Keynesians, monetarists believe that the economy is *inherently stable*, unless disturbed by erratic monetary growth. Most of the actually observed instability is attributed to fluctuations in the money supply induced by the authorities. Furthermore, monetarists contend that, when subjected to some disturbance, the economy will return fairly rapidly to the neighbourhood of the natural level of output and employment. The dominant position assigned to monetary shocks in determining the course of economic activity is embodied in the quantity theory approach to macroeconomic analysis. In Chapter 10 we discussed how the effects of a change in the rate of monetary expansion are divided between real and nominal variables in the monetarist view. You will recall that this involves a distinction between short-run and long-run effects. While an inflation–unemployment trade-off exists in the short run, in the long run the trade-off disappears. In the monetarist view, changes in the rate of monetary growth result in short-run fluctuations in output and employment around their natural levels. However, in the long run, the trend rate of monetary growth only influences movements in the price level and other nominal variables.

The monetarist view that monetary shocks are the dominant cause of business cycles is based on two kinds of empirical evidence. The first kind of evidence is the empirically observed tendency for monetary changes to *precede* changes in economic activity. One of the earliest studies concerning the timing of monetary changes was undertaken by Milton Friedman in the late 1950s. In his study, Friedman compared rates of monetary growth with turning points in the level of economic activity. On the average of 18 non-war cycles in the US since 1870, he found that:

- peaks in the rate of change of the money supply had preceded peaks in the level of economic activity by an average of 16 months
- troughs in the rate of change of the money supply had preceded troughs in the level of economic activity by an average of 12 months.

While accepting that timing evidence, such as this, is by no means decisive, monetarists argue that it is *suggestive* of an influence running from monetary changes to changes in economic activity.

The second kind of evidence to support the monetarist belief that monetary shocks are the dominant cause of business cycles was presented by Milton Friedman and Anna Schwartz in their influential study of the *Monetary History of the United States, 1867–1960*, published in 1963. In this work they found that the *rate of growth* of the money supply had been slower during cyclical contractions than during cyclical expansions in the level of economic activity. Indeed, the only times when there was an appreciable *absolute* fall in the money stock coincided with the six *major* US recessions identified over the period examined. Examining the specific historical circumstances surrounding events, Friedman and Schwartz concluded that the factors producing the absolute fall in the money supply during these major recessions were mainly independent of contemporary or prior changes in nominal income and prices. In other words, monetary changes were the *cause*, rather than the consequence, of all major American recessions. For example, Friedman and Schwartz argue that the severity of the Great Depression, 1929–33, was due to a dramatic decline in the money stock. Between October 1929 and June 1933 the money stock in the US fell by about a third. An initial mild decline in the money stock from 1929 to 1930, was, they argue, converted into a sharp decline by a wave of bank failures beginning late in 1930. Those bank failures produced a loss of faith on the part of both the public, in the banks' ability to redeem their deposits, and the banks, in the public's willingness to maintain their deposits with them. In Friedman and Schwartz's interpretation of events, the Federal Reserve System could, by adopting alternative policies, have prevented the banking collapse and the dramatic fall in the money stock which coincided with the period of severe economic contraction.

Given the belief that the main cause of economic fluctuations is policy-induced changes in the rate of monetary growth, monetarists advocate that the authorities should pursue a monetary **rule**, rather than attempt to use monetary policy in a discretionary manner. Several rules have been suggested, the best known of which is Friedman's rule that the authorities should pursue a *fixed* rate of monetary growth in line with the long-run growth potential of the economy. It should be noted that a monetary growth rule is not submitted as a panacea to fluctuations in the level of economic activity. While instability may arise from sources other than the mismanagement of the money supply, monetarists believe that by avoiding sharp swings in monetary policy the authorities can remove the main source of economic disturbances.

Rules: pre-specified guidelines that determine the conduct of policy.

The monetarist way to run the economy

Even when the economy is subjected to shocks that can be identified as arising from other sources, monetarists argue against the use of discretionary monetary policy to stabilize the economy. Their fear that discretionary monetary policy could turn out to be destabilizing is based on a number of arguments including the length and variability of time lags associated with monetary policy, and the inflationary consequences of maintaining unemployment below the natural rate, a problem compounded by uncertainty over what precise value to attribute to the natural rate (see Chapter 10). In the former case, monetarists argue that stabilization policy could in reality make economic fluctuations more severe because, by the time monetary policy changes affect economic activity, the underlying state of the economy may have changed making the measures adopted inappropriate (see Chapter 12).

In summary, given their belief that the economy is inherently stable and is rapidly self-equilibrating, monetarists question the need to stabilize the economy

Are economies inherently stable, or not?

Getty Images/iStockphoto/Thinkstock/TooTH_PIK

via discretionary aggregate demand policies. Furthermore, even if there were a need they tend to argue that discretionary aggregate demand policies cannot, and therefore should not, be used to stabilize the economy.

The new classical approach

During the 1970s a new classical approach to explaining business cycles was developed. This approach derives largely from the influential work of Robert Lucas, Jr of the University of Chicago who was awarded the Nobel Prize in Economics in 1995. The theory developed by Lucas and other leading new classical economists is similar to the monetarist explanation in that business cycles are viewed as being primarily caused by monetary shocks. However, in the new classical approach it is *unanticipated monetary shocks* that are the dominant cause of business cycles. As we will now discuss, in the new classical *equilibrium theory*, economic agents respond optimally to the prices they perceive and markets continuously clear.

Consider an economy that is initially in a position where output and employment are at their natural levels. Suppose the authorities announce that they intend to increase the money supply. According to the new classical approach, rational economic agents would take this information into account in forming their expectations and fully anticipate the effects of the announced increase in the money supply on the general price level. In this situation, output and employment would remain unchanged at their natural levels. Now suppose that the authorities *surprise* economic agents by increasing the money supply without announcing their intentions. In this situation, firms and workers with *incomplete information* would *misperceive* the resultant increase in the general price level as an increase in relative prices and respond by increasing the supply of output and labour respectively. A central element of this approach is the structure of information available to economic agents. To illustrate the role that incomplete information plays in the new classical approach, we focus on the supply decisions of firms.

A firm's production plans are made on the basis of information on the price of its output. When a firm experiences a rise in the current market-clearing price of its output it must decide how to react to the rise. Where the price rise reflects a *real* increase in demand for its product, the firm should respond to the increase in the current price of its output *relative* to the price of other goods, by increasing production. In contrast, where the change in price merely reflects a *nominal* increase in demand across all markets, producing a *general* increase in prices, no supply response is required. In other words, a firm is faced by what is referred to as a *signal extraction problem* in which its supply response depends on its distinguishing between relative as opposed to absolute price changes. In the new classical approach it is assumed that a firm has information both on the current price of its own goods and on prices in the limited number of markets in which it trades. However, information on the general price level for other markets only becomes known after a time lag. Suppose an unanticipated monetary shock occurs that leads to an increase in the general price level and therefore prices in all markets throughout the economy. In this situation, individual firms with incomplete information will, it is argued, misperceive the increase in the current price of their goods as an increase in the relative price of their output and respond by increasing their output.

Why will output and employment remain above (or below) their natural levels for a succession of time periods? The fact that output and employment levels in any one time period are correlated with their preceding values can be explained by the inclusion of an accelerator mechanism into the analysis. As before, consider an economy that is initially in a position where output and employment are at their natural levels. Following an unanticipated monetary shock, which causes an unexpected rise in prices, firms will respond by increasing output. In a situation where no spare capacity exists, new investment will be required to increase the capital stock in order to produce extra output following the perceived real increase in demand for firms' output. Given the durability of capital goods, errors made in one time period will, in consequence, continue to affect output in subsequent time periods.

What are the implications of the new classical approach for stabilization policy and the control of business cycles? The new classical approach suggests that changes in monetary or fiscal policy can only affect output and employment if they are unanticipated. For example, suppose the money supply is determined by the authorities according to some rule, and the public *know* the rule and base their behaviour and decision-making on the anticipated growth of the money supply. In this situation the authorities will be unable to influence output and employment even in the short run by pursuing a systematic monetary policy. Only departures from a known monetary rule, resulting from policy errors made by the monetary authorities or unforeseen changes in policy, will have real effects because they are unanticipated. Any attempt to influence output and employment by random or non-systematic aggregate demand policies would, it is argued, only increase the variation of output and employment around their natural levels and increase uncertainty in the economy. Stabilization policy would only be beneficial in two situations. First, if the authorities had superior information, compared to the private sector, then they could exploit this information to influence the economy. Second, if the authorities were able to react to shocks more quickly than the private sector, there would be scope for discretionary intervention to stabilize the economy. Nevertheless, having noted these two possible situations, it is the case that the new classical approach, in line with the monetarist approach, maintains a non-intervention position with respect to macroeconomic policy.

The early 1980s witnessed the demise of the 'monetary surprise' version of the new classical approach to business cycles. A number of criticisms were raised against the new classical approach, involving both theoretical and empirical failings. In the former case, for example, critics of the approach drew attention to the fact that both aggregate price level and money supply data are published within a short time lag and are readily available to economic agents. Given the availability of such data, they questioned how business cycles could be caused by supposed information gaps. In the latter case, the results of a number of empirical tests suggested that both unanticipated *and* anticipated money supply shocks have real output and employment effects. The depth of the recessions in both the US and the UK in the early 1980s (see Chapter 10), following announced monetary disinflation policies, provided further ammunition to the critics that systematic monetary policy has real effects. Criticisms of the monetary surprise version of the new classical approach led a number of economists who were sympathetic to the 'equilibrium' approach to develop a new version in which business cycles are predominantly caused by persistent *real* (supply-side) shocks, rather than unanticipated monetary (demand-side) shocks, to the economy. This approach – which is largely associated with the work of American economists, most notably Finn Kydland of the University of California, Santa Barbara and Edward Prescott of Arizona State University, the 2004 Nobel Laureates – is commonly referred to as the real business cycle approach.

The real business cycle approach

According to proponents of the real business cycle approach, business cycles are driven by persistent *supply-side shocks* to the economy. These *random* supply-side shocks can originate from such sources as changes in raw material or energy prices, natural disasters, the development of new products and the introduction of new techniques of production. Despite the wide variety of potential supply-side shocks, most real business cycle models are based on the premise that these shocks mainly result from *large* random fluctuations in the rate of technological progress. In the real business cycle approach, observed fluctuations in output and employment are *equilibrium* phenomena and are the outcome of rational economic agents responding *optimally* to unavoidable changes in the economic environment. Furthermore, observed fluctuations in output are viewed as fluctuations in potential output, not as deviations of actual output from the trend. In the real business cycle approach, the distinction between actual and potential output is abandoned. Given the belief that the economy is subjected to large random fluctuations in the rate of technological progress, the fluctuating path of output over time follows a so-called random walk and is nothing more than a continuously fluctuating, full employment/potential output equilibrium. As such, the approach integrates business cycle theory with the theory of economic growth.

What are the implications of the real business cycle approach for stabilizing economic fluctuations? As fluctuations in output and employment are held to reflect the Pareto efficient responses to a succession of supply-side shocks hitting the economy, the approach provides no role for monetary and

Random walk: the path of a variable whose changes over time are unpredictable.

Pareto efficiency: a situation in which it is impossible to make someone better off without making someone else worse off; also known as Pareto optimality.

fiscal policies for stabilization purposes. On the one hand, monetary factors are regarded as being irrelevant in explaining such fluctuations, with monetary policy having no influence on real variables. On the other hand, attempts to stabilize fluctuations in output and employment through fiscal policy would, it is claimed, reduce welfare because government taxation and spending policies would distort output and employment from the optimal amounts chosen by firms and workers.

The real business cycle approach to business cycles and the implication that stabilization policy has no role to play is *highly* controversial and has been subjected to a number of criticisms. Two examples will suffice. First, most economists question whether supply shocks are large enough or frequent enough to explain observed aggregate fluctuations in output and employment. With the exception of the two OPEC oil price shocks that occurred in 1973–4 and 1979, it is difficult to identify adverse supply shocks that are powerful enough to explain major recessions, especially episodes such as the Great Depression in the 1930s. The idea that major recessions are caused by technological *regress* strikes many critics as being particularly implausible. Second, real business cycle models assume wage and price flexibility so that markets continuously clear and equilibrium always prevails. Critics of the new classical approach have put forward a variety of reasons to explain wage and price stickiness that prevents continuous market clearing. For example, as discussed in Chapter 9, new Keynesians have put forward various explanations of real wage rigidity in the labour market that can account for the existence of involuntary unemployment as an equilibrium phenomenon. Indeed, most economists believe that demand shocks, arising from changes in monetary policy, can have significant real effects in the short run, because of the nominal price and wage rigidities which characterize actual economies.

The political business cycle approach

Political business cycle: fluctuations in the level of output and employment caused by the manipulation of the economy for electoral gains or due to partisan differences.

In the political business cycle approach, business cycles are policy-induced and reflect the objectives of politicians either in terms of getting re-elected or in terms of partisan differences.

Consider first the possibility of a political business cycle resulting from a government manipulating the state of the economy just before an election, in order to improve its chances of being re-elected. This particular approach, which is associated with the work of William Nordhaus in the mid-1970s, is based on the beliefs that: (a) the main goal of political parties is winning the next election and (b) the state of the economy has a strong influence on voters. As an election approaches, the government pursues expansionary policies (for example increasing its expenditure and/or reducing taxes) in order to reduce unemployment and gain votes. Once re-elected, contractionary policies will be required to dampen down inflationary pressures that arise as output rises above its full employment/potential level. As inflation subsides and unemployment increases, the stage is set once again for the government to engineer expansionary policies to reduce unemployment and gain popularity before the next election. Changes in macroeconomic policy produce a political business cycle.

Although this approach is intuitively appealing, it suffers from a number of weaknesses. Three examples will suffice. First, the approach would seem to be more appropriate for countries with fixed election dates, such as the US, rather than countries where election dates are variable, such as the UK. Second, the approach implies that in a two-party system, political parties will offer similar policies to attract voters at the centre of the political spectrum (so-called median voters) and ignores the fact that political parties are likely to have ideological or partisan aims in addition to that of obtaining power. Third, the approach implies that voters are myopic or short-sighted and do not learn from past experience that politicians generate a pre-election boom, followed by a post-election slump.

Since the mid-1980s, interest in the political business cycle approach has been rekindled, most notably by the work of Alberto Alesina of Harvard University. Alesina has put forward a partisan model in which political parties do not pursue a simple vote-maximizing strategy and differ in their priorities and preferences. In particular, right-wing parties are assumed to attach more importance to keeping inflation in check than left-wing parties, who care more about unemployment. Voters know that given such priorities parties will pursue different polices when they are in office. In this model, what drives the cycle is the fact that election results are unknown before they occur. Wage contracts set before an election will be determined by the rate of inflation expected after the election. The expected rate of inflation will depend on which party is expected to form the next government. For example, if wage negotiators expect that a left-wing government currently in office will be re-elected, they will form contracts that have a high expected rate of inflation built into them. If a right-wing party then gains office, it will tighten monetary policy in order to reduce inflation. In a situation where contracts cannot be instantly renegotiated unemployment will rise. The opposite sequence of events would follow if a right-wing government in office was replaced by a left-wing party. In this case, after the election a left-wing government would expand the economy and reduce unemployment. In both cases, once inflation expectations had adjusted to the new situation, at a later stage in the government's term of office, output and employment would return to their natural levels (see the discussion of the expectations-augmented Phillips curve in Chapter 10). Unlike Nordhaus's political business cycle model, which predicts a pre-election boom and a post-election slump, Alesina's partisan model predicts a slump after a change in policy regime to a right-wing government and a boom after a change of regime to a left-wing government.

The political business cycle approach provides another reason for those economists who favour giving central banks greater independence, enabling monetary policy to be conducted free from consideration of electoral gain and partisan influences (see Reflecting on Economics: central bank independence and inflation performance in Chapter 12).

11.8 Concluding remarks

In this chapter we have considered the factors that determine economic growth over time and the debate over the cause and control of business cycles. Clearly, economic growth is the result of extremely complex processes involving economic, political and institutional considerations. As a starting point only, in Section 11.3 we outlined a model that identifies *some* of the main determinants of economic growth over time. Like all economic models, the Solow growth model simplifies reality and omits many important considerations. Nevertheless, as we have seen, the model sheds light on some of the reasons why standards of living vary so widely between countries. The resurgence of interest in the theory of long-run growth has produced more sophisticated models in which the rate of technological change is endogenous. These models provide a rationale for governments to adopt policies that encourage education, training, capital formation and research and development in order to increase the economy's productive capacity. Despite these further insights, exactly what role the government can and should play in encouraging growth remains the subject of intense controversy.

Education helps fuel growth

As to the main theories of business cycles, four theories suggest that cycles are primarily caused by demand shocks. In the Keynesian approach, the main cause of cycles is changes in autonomous expenditures. Monetarists emphasize changes in the rate of monetary growth as the main source of cycles, while the new classical approach highlights unanticipated monetary shocks as the dominant cause of cycles. The political business cycle approach ascribes the existence of cycles to government macroeconomic policy. In contrast to these approaches, proponents of the real business cycle approach suggest that business cycles are primarily caused by supply shocks. While our presentation has highlighted the differences between these competing explanations, it is important to remember that many economists take an eclectic stance, recognizing that no one key causal factor can account for all business cycles. Some cycles will be triggered by demand shocks, others by supply shocks. On some occasions demand and supply shocks will *both* be important. Whether governments cause cycles and what policies they should pursue to reduce fluctuations in economic activity remain highly controversial issues. In the next chapter we turn to consider the issue of stabilizing the economy more fully.

SUMMARY

- Economic growth can be defined as an increase in real GDP. The annual percentage increase in real GDP represents the rate of economic growth.

- Real output will increase over time if there is an increase in the quantity of factor inputs and/or in the productivity of inputs.

- In the Solow growth model, a long-run equilibrium or steady-state growth rate occurs where output, capital input and labour input all grow at the same rate. The model allows us to examine the relationship between a nation's output per worker and its saving rate, labour force growth and rate of technological progress. *Ceteris paribus*, an increase in the saving rate, a decrease in the rate of growth of the labour force or an improvement in technology increases the level of capital input and output per worker. The long-run equilibrium growth rate depends on the rate of growth of the labour force and technological change and is not affected by a change in the saving rate. As both the rate of growth of the labour force and technological change are exogenous, the Solow model provides no insight into how government policy could raise the long-run equilibrium growth rate of output.

- In the new endogenous growth models, the rate of technological change is endogenous and growth is driven by broad capital accumulation together with the creation of new knowledge through research and development. The models help explain the lack of convergence of per capita income levels and growth rates over time and provide a number of insights into how government policy can influence the long-run growth rate.

- Recent literature on the fundamental sources of economic growth has highlighted a number of wider influences including the impact of institutions, economic integration and geography.

- The business cycle can be defined as deviations in output from trend. Cycles that vary both in their timing and amplitude involve expansionary and contractionary phases, and upper and lower turning points.

- In the Keynesian approach, the main cause of business cycles is fluctuations in autonomous expenditures.

Expansionary and contractionary phases are explained through the interaction of the multiplier process and the accelerator, while ceilings and floors account for turning points in the cycle. Keynesians believe that governments need to, can and therefore should stabilize the economy.

- In the monetarist approach, the main cause of business cycles is held to be monetary actions that result in changes in the rate of growth of the money supply. By pursuing a monetary growth rate rule, monetarists argue that the authorities can remove the major source of economic disturbances.

- In the new classical approach, unanticipated monetary shocks are the dominant cause of business cycles. Surprised by such shocks, economic agents, with incomplete information, mistake general price changes for relative price changes and react by changing the supply of output and labour. Governments can only influence output and employment by pursuing random or non-systematic monetary policy. New classicists claim that such policy will, however, only increase the variation of output and employment around their natural levels, and increase uncertainty in the economy. In line with the monetarist approach, the new classical approach maintains a non-interventionist position with respect to macroeconomic policy.

- In the real business cycle approach, business cycles are primarily caused by persistent real supply shocks to the economy, mainly large random fluctuations in the rate of technological progress. Fluctuations in output and employment are held to reflect the optimal response of economic agents to such shocks. Because cycles are due to a succession of supply shocks hitting the economy, there is no role for the government to stabilize fluctuations in output and employment through aggregate demand policies.

- The political business cycle approach suggests that cycles are policy-induced and reflect the objectives of politicians either in terms of getting re-elected or in terms of partisan differences.

- No one key factor can account for all business cycles. On some occasions demand and supply shocks will both be important.

KEY TERMS

- Aggregate production function
- Production possibility frontier
- Quantity and quality of factor inputs
- Solow growth model
- Steady-state growth
- Convergence
- Endogenous growth models
- Human capital
- Fundamental sources of economic growth
- The period of the cycle
- The amplitude of the cycle
- Expansionary and contractionary phases
- Multiplier process
- Accelerator
- Multiplier–accelerator interaction
- Ceilings and floors
- Monetary shocks
- Monetary rule
- Unanticipated monetary shocks
- Signal extraction problem
- Real shocks
- Politically induced cycles
- Partisan priorities and preferences

QUESTIONS FOR DISCUSSION

1. What factors determine economic growth over time?
2. What role can the government play in promoting growth?
3. According to the Solow model, what effect will each of the following have on the level of output per worker:

   i.   an increase in the saving rate
   ii. an increase in labour force growth
   iii. a technological improvement?
4. Explain why the saving rate does not affect the steady-state growth rate in the Solow model.
5. What determines the long-run equilibrium growth rate in the Solow model?
6. Explain why according to the Solow model *sustained* growth of output per worker depends on technological progress.
7. What are the main problems with the Solow growth model?
8. What drives growth in the new endogenous growth models?
9. What is the main cause of business cycles in the Keynesian approach? How are the expansionary and contractionary phases of the business cycle explained in the Keynesian approach?
10. What is the main cause of business cycles in the monetarist approach?
11. Compare and contrast the main policy implications of the Keynesian and monetarist approaches for the control of business cycles.
12. What is the main cause of business cycles in the new classical and real business cycle approaches?
13. What role is there for stabilization policy in the new classical and real business cycle approaches?
14. What is the main cause of business cycles in the political business cycle approach?

ONE THING YOU SHOULD READ

At http://www.econlib.org/library/Enc/EconomicGrowth.html you can access a non-technical overview of economic growth written by Paul Romer – one of the leading architects of the new endogenous growth theory – as an entry for *The Concise Encyclopedia of Economics*, a volume edited by David R. Henderson and first published by Liberty Fund in 2007. Having read the entry you should consider the following questions.

1. What does Romer argue is the driving force behind economic growth: objects or ideas?
2. What factors does he identify as being particularly important in the acquisition and adoption of ideas by poor countries from the rest of the world?
3. What role do incentives play in the discovery of new ideas?
4. Why does Romer support subsidies for education to increase the supply of scientists and engineers?
5. What fundamental challenge does Romer suggest now faces all industrialized countries?

Appendix

The Solow growth model

In this appendix we consider the Solow growth model in more detail. Our starting point is consideration of the aggregate production function, which forms the bedrock of the model.

The aggregate production function

The aggregate production function is a function that relates the quantity of aggregate output that can be produced to a *given* quantity of factor inputs. This relationship can be written as:

$$Y = A(t) F(K, N) \tag{11.1}$$

Where Y is real output; A (t) represents technological know-how at time t; and F is a function that relates real output to K, the quantity of capital inputs and N, the quantity of labour inputs. Real output will increase over time if there is an increase in the quantity of factor inputs (capital and/or labour) and/or there is an increase in the productivity of capital and labour inputs (that is, an increase in output per unit of factor input) due to an increase in technological know-how.

At the outset it is important to highlight three key properties exhibited by the neoclassical production function used by Solow in his analysis.

- First, factor inputs of labour and capital can be smoothly *substituted* for each other in the production process. In other words, firms can use more capital inputs and fewer labour inputs, or vice versa, to produce the same quantity of output.
- Second, factor inputs experience diminishing returns. For example, while an increase in the quantity of labour inputs with the quantity of capital inputs held constant will result in an increase in real output, output will increase at an ever-declining rate. Similarly, diminishing returns will result from increase in the capital stock to a fixed labour force.
- Third, it is assumed that the aggregate production function exhibits constant returns to scale. Constant returns to scale mean that when all factor inputs increase in some proportion, real output will increase in that same proportion.

Diminishing returns: occur when successive increases in the use of a factor input, holding other factor inputs constant, eventually result in a fall in the additional output derived from a unit increase in that factor input.

Constant returns to scale: occur where a given percentage increase in all factor inputs results in the same percentage increase in output.

For example, if both the quantity of labour and capital inputs were doubled, the amount of real output produced would also be doubled.

Given the assumption of constant returns to scale, then for a given technology we can express the aggregate production function in per capita terms. As such output per worker (Y/N) will depend on the amount of capital input per worker (K/N) or what is sometimes referred to as the capital–labour ratio. This relationship is depicted in Figure 11.4 and can be written as:

Capital–labour ratio: the amount of capital per worker; the ratio of the quantity of capital inputs to the number of workers.

$$Y/N = A (t) f (K/N) \qquad (11.2)$$

The astute reader will have noticed that in order to highlight that the aggregate production function is expressed in terms of output and capital input *per worker* we use a small letter f in equation (11.2) rather than a capital letter F used in equation (11.1).

The aggregate production function depicted in Figure 11.4 relates output per worker (Y/N) to the amount of capital input per worker (K/N) for a given technology at a point in time t. For example, with a given technology at time t_0, y_0 output per worker $(Y/N = y)$ can be produced with k_0 capital input per worker $(K/N = k)$. The decreasing slope of the aggregate production function reflects diminishing returns to increases in the amount of capital input per worker. In other words, increases in capital input per worker result in increases in output per worker, but at an ever-declining rate. Finally, it is important to note that technological change over time (for example from t_0 to t_1) would shift the aggregate production function upwards, increasing output per worker for a *given* amount of capital input per worker. For example, as illustrated in

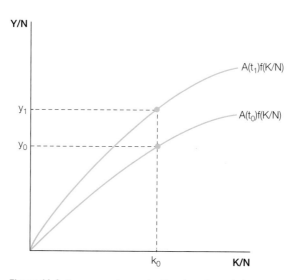

Figure 11.4 An aggregate production function relating output per worker to capital input per worker

Figure 11.4, technological change would allow a higher level of output per worker (y_1) to be produced with k_0 capital input per worker.

The steady state

We now turn to consider the long-run *equilibrium* or steady-state growth rate within the neoclassical model developed by Solow. From equation (11.1), it can be seen that growth in output over time depends on both the rate of technological change and the rate at which factor inputs (the capital stock and the labour force) grow over time. One of the most important implications of the Solow growth model is that the economy reaches a steady state in the long run. A long-run equilibrium or steady state occurs when output per worker and capital input per worker are constant or unchanging over time. In the simplest case, when there is no change in the state of technology, output (Y), capital input (K) and labour input (N) all grow at the same rate.

In Figure 11.5 a steady state in the long run is achieved at point X with a constant level of output per worker (y_0) and a constant amount of capital input per worker (k_0). Steady state is achieved at the intersection of the steady-state investment line (I) and the saving curve (S). Each point along the steady-state investment line indicates how much investment per worker is *required* to keep the amount of capital input per worker *constant* after taking account of labour force growth and the need to replace the fraction of the capital stock that wears out each year due to depreciation. The line slopes upwards because the faster is labour force growth (and depreciation), the more investment per worker is needed to equip new workers with the current level of capital input per worker and replace depreciating capital. The saving curve (S), which represents saving per worker, has the same shape as the per worker production function

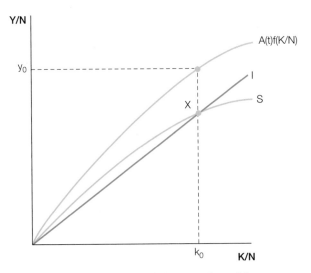

Figure 11.5 Steady state in the Solow growth model

because saving is assumed to be proportional to income in the Solow model. As capital input per worker increases so too does output per worker, resulting in an increase in saving per worker. All saving is assumed to be channelled into investment so that saving and actual investment are equal at all times, maintaining good market equilibrium.

In Figure 11.5 the steady-state level of capital input per worker (k_0) is achieved at point X, the intersection of the steady-state investment line (I) and the saving curve (S). Reference to Figure 11.5 reveals that if capital input per worker is below k_0, saving per worker is greater than investment per worker necessary to maintain capital input per worker constant. As the extra savings are invested and converted into capital, capital input per worker will rise towards k_0. Conversely, if capital input per worker is above k_0, then saving per worker is less than the amount of investment per worker required to maintain capital input per worker constant and capital input per worker will fall towards k_0. In the steady state the positive effect of investment (determined by saving) on the amount of capital input per worker balances the negative effects of labour force growth and depreciation. When capital input per worker is constant at k_0, output per worker is also constant at y_0 over time. In this simple case, output (Y), capital input (K) and labour input (N) all grow at the same rate and all ratios are constant; that is, the steady state.

The model we have outlined allows us to examine the relationship between a nation's output per worker and factors such as its saving rate, labour force growth and rate of technological progress. We first consider what the Solow growth model predicts will happen following an increase in the nation's saving rate. Suppose the economy is initially in steady state with capital and labour inputs growing at the same rate with a steady-state capital input per worker established where the steady-state investment line (I) and saving curve (S_0) intersect. In Figure 11.6 this initial situation is achieved at point X with k_0 capital input per worker and y_0 output per worker. Assuming that saving is channelled into actual investment, an increase in the saving rate will *initially* increase the rate of capital formation. In the absence of any change in the rate of growth of the labour force or in technological progress, an increase in the rate of capital formation will result in an increase in the amount of capital input per worker. In terms of Figure 11.6, an increase in the saving rate will raise the saving curve from S_0 to S_1 and capital input per worker will rise from k_0 to k_1 until the economy reaches a new steady state at point Y. Once the economy has made the adjustment from point X to point Y, there will be no further increases in either capital input per worker or output per worker. In the new steady state both capital input per worker and output per worker will be stable. The Solow model predicts that countries with higher saving rates will have higher steady-state levels of capital input per worker and therefore higher levels of output per worker, giving a higher standard of living. However, the model predicts that, while an increase in the saving rate will lead to a *temporary* period

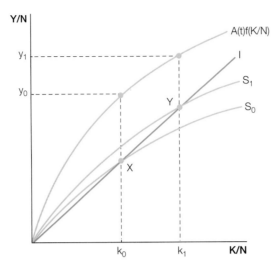

Figure 11.6 The effects of an increase in the saving rate on capital input per worker and output per worker

of faster growth (when output per worker is increasing from y_0 to y_1), it will not affect the long-run equilibrium or steady-state growth rate. Once the new equilibrium has been reached the rate of capital formation and growth rate in output will have returned to their initial levels equal to the rate of growth of the labour force.

We finally turn to briefly consider the effects of a change in the rate of growth of the labour force (Figure 11.7) and technological change (Figure 11.8) in the Solow growth model. In Figure 11.7 the economy is initially in steady state at point X with a steady-state capital input per worker k_0 established where the

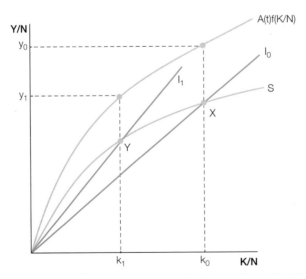

Figure 11.7 The effects of an increase in the rate of growth of the labour force on capital input per worker and output per worker

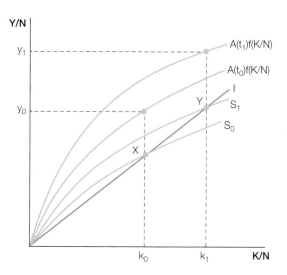

Figure 11.8 The effects of an improvement in technology on capital input per worker and output per worker

saving curve (S) and steady-state investment line (I_0) intersect. If the rate of growth of the labour force increases, the amount of investment per current member of the labour force will have to rise to maintain a given capital input per worker. In other words, an increase in the labour force growth rate will cause the steady-state investment line to pivot up to the left from I_0 to I_1. In the new steady state, point Y, the level of capital input per worker is lower (k_1), generating a lower level of output per worker (y_1). The Solow model consequently predicts that countries with higher rates of growth in their labour force will have lower steady-state levels of capital input per worker and therefore lower levels of output per worker.

Figure 11.8 illustrates the effects of an improvement in technology on capital input per worker and output per worker. In Figure 11.8 the economy is initially in steady state at point X with a steady-state capital input per worker k_0 established where the saving curve (S_0) and steady-state investment line (I) intersect. As discussed, an improvement in technology shifts the aggregate production function upwards from $A(t_0)$ f (K/N) to A (t_1) f (K/N) increasing output per worker for any given amount of capital input per worker. Since saving per worker is assumed to be proportional to output per worker, the saving curve also shifts upwards from S_0 to S_1 at any given amount of capital input per worker. A new steady state will eventually be reached at point Y where the new saving curve (S_1) intersects the steady-state investment line (I) with a higher level of capital input per worker (k_1) and output per worker (y_1). In the Solow model, *sustained* growth of output per worker can only be explained by technological progress. The model predicts that in the steady state both capital input per worker and output per worker grow at the rate of technological progress.

12

stabilizing the economy

KEY ISSUES

Why do economists disagree over the issue of whether the authorities need to, can and should stabilize the economy?

Should macroeconomic policy be operated at the discretion of the authorities or on the basis of rules?

What are the main problems encountered by policymakers in implementing stabilization policy?

CONTENTS

12.1 Introduction **374**

12.2 Discretionary policy and policy rules **374**

12.3 The rules versus discretion debate: problems of stabilization policy **375**

12.4 Changing views on stabilizing the economy **386**

12.5 Concluding remarks **389**

12.1 Introduction

In the preceding three chapters we examined the debate over the causes of and appropriate policy responses to unemployment, inflation, economic growth and the business cycle. Given the nature of our discussion, it should be evident that there is much controversy among macroeconomists over these important issues, all of which impact upon the business environment and – as we highlighted in the introductions to the three preceding chapters – have a substantial effect on the success and profitability of firms. The purpose of this chapter is to draw together a number of themes addressed in Chapters 9 and 11, and consider the continuing debate over **stabilization policy**. The authorities use stabilization policy to try to keep output and employment at, or near, their full employment or natural levels by influencing the level of aggregate demand. Our particular focus is on the controversy over whether, in their conduct of macroeconomic policy, the authorities should be given *discretion* to change the strength of fiscal and monetary policy in the light of particular economic circumstances, or whether monetary and fiscal policy should be conducted by *rules*.

> **Stabilization policy:** policy aimed at stabilizing output and employment at or near their full employment or natural levels by influencing the level of aggregate demand.

12.2 Discretionary policy and policy rules

Before proceeding to discuss alternative views on stabilization policy we need first to highlight the difference between discretionary policy and policy rules.

Discretionary policy

Discretionary policy takes place when the authorities are given the *freedom* to vary the strength of fiscal and/or monetary policy in any way they see fit in order to achieve their desired objectives. In monitoring the course of the economy, policy may be changed either:

- frequently, in an attempt to maintain output and employment at, or near, their full employment or natural levels, so-called *fine tuning*; or
- occasionally, in response to a large divergence in output and employment from their full employment or natural levels, so-called *rough tuning*.

Policy rules

In contrast, where policy is conducted by rules, the authorities are *committed* to follow a *pre-specified* rule that determines the conduct of fiscal and/or monetary policy. Rules themselves may, or may not, be linked to changes in economic conditions. With a **passive policy rule** the pre-specified rule for the policy instrument is not linked to prevailing economic circumstances. An example of a passive monetary policy rule is where the authorities are committed to pursuing a *constant* rate of monetary growth. Whatever the state of the economy, the authorities would pursue a given fixed rate of monetary growth of, say, 3 per cent per annum.

> **Passive policy rule:** a pre-specified rule for the conduct of policy not linked to prevailing economic circumstances.

Activist policy rule: a pre-specified rule for the conduct of policy that is linked to the state of the economy; also known as a **feedback rule**.

An **activist policy rule**, however, involves **feedback** from the state of the economy to the policy instrument. An example of an activist monetary policy rule would be where the money supply is targeted to grow at a rate of, say, 3 per cent per annum if unemployment is 6 per cent, but monetary growth is automatically increased (decreased) by 1 per cent per annum for every 1 per cent unemployment rises above (falls below) 6 per cent. If unemployment rose to 8 per cent, monetary growth would be increased to 5 per cent. Conversely, if unemployment fell to 4 per cent, monetary growth would be reduced to 1 per cent. Both active and passive policy rules tie the hands of the authorities to pursue pre-specified rules without leaving them any discretion to change the strength of fiscal and/or monetary policy.

As we shall now discuss, the debate over stabilization policy critically depends on whether one views the economy as inherently unstable, subject to frequent shocks that lead to inefficient fluctuations in output and employment; or whether one views the economy as naturally stable. Broadly speaking, those economists (namely Keynesians) who subscribe to the former view emphasize the need for stabilization policy and argue that the authorities should be given discretion to use fiscal and monetary policy to offset shocks and keep output and employment close to their full employment or natural levels. Other economists (monetarists and new classicists), who subscribe to the latter view, tend to question the need for stabilization policy and favour rules over discretion, blaming ill-conceived policies for inefficient departures of output and employment from their natural levels experienced from time to time.

12.3 The rules versus discretion debate: problems of stabilization policy

The Keynesian view

In the *orthodox* Keynesian view, the economy is *inherently unstable*, experiencing frequent shocks that lead to inefficient fluctuations in output and employment. The main sources of instability that cause these fluctuations in economic activity are *aggregate demand* shocks. Furthermore, orthodox Keynesians contend that, after being subjected to such disturbances, the economy will not rapidly self-equilibrate and will take a long time to return to the neighbourhood of full employment output. Given these beliefs, orthodox Keynesians stress the *need* for stabilization policy and argue that the authorities *can* and therefore *should* use discretionary fiscal and monetary policies to stabilize the economy.

Using the Keynesian model first introduced in Chapter 9, we can illustrate how the authorities would, via discretionary policy activism, seek to stimulate the economy after it had been subjected to some contractionary aggregate demand shock and deflate the economy when it was overheating. In Figure 12.1 we assume that the economy is initially operating at its full employment level of output (Y_F). Following some contractionary aggregate demand shock, which

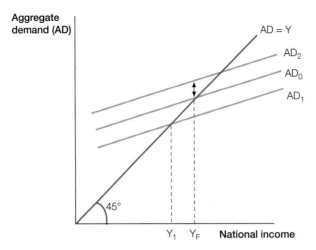

Figure 12.1 Stabilization policy in the orthodox Keynesian model

shifts the aggregate demand curve from AD_0 to AD_1, the economy could, if left to its own devices, come to rest below full employment at Y_1 for a prolonged period of time. By taking appropriate corrective action (that is, expansionary fiscal and/or monetary policy), which offsets the contractionary shock and shifts the aggregate demand curve back from AD_1 to AD_0, orthodox Keynesians argue that the authorities can stabilize the economy at, or close to, its full employment level. Alternatively, the economy might be subjected to an expansionary aggregate demand shock, which shifts the aggregate demand curve from AD_0 to AD_2, causing the economy to overheat as aggregate demand exceeds national income at the full employment level of output. The resulting *inflationary gap*, indicated by the arrows in Figure 12.1, would require deflationary fiscal and/or monetary policy to close the gap and offset the expansionary shock, shifting the aggregate demand curve back from AD_2 to AD_0.

In both situations analysed above, it is clearly important that the authorities exert the *correct dosage* of stimulus or restraint. Consider, for example, the former case of the economy experiencing a contractionary aggregate demand shock. If the authorities fail to stimulate aggregate demand sufficiently, the economy will come to rest below its full employment equilibrium. In contrast, if the authorities overstimulate aggregate demand beyond that required to establish full employment, an inflationary gap will ensue. While acknowledging this potential problem, orthodox Keynesians believe that the authorities can and therefore should use discretionary fiscal and monetary policies to stabilize the economy at, or close to, its full employment level. Indeed, in the 1950s and 1960s, when Keynesian economics was the conventional wisdom, many Western governments attempted to *fine tune* their economies using discretionary aggregate demand policies. However, by the late 1960s/early 1970s, many Western governments began to experience a steady rise in unemployment and inflation, leading some economists to question the ability of conventional Keynesian economics to deal with the problem of so-called stagflation.

Before discussing subsequent developments associated with monetarist and new classical views, which provide a critique of discretionary policy activism involving fine tuning, we need to mention the views of *new* Keynesians. New Keynesians accept that the economy is not as unstable as once believed. Nevertheless, they argue that the economy does experience shocks, from both the demand side *and* the supply side, which cause undesirable and inefficient economic fluctuations. As such, in line with orthodox Keynesians, they recognize the need for stabilization policy and believe that the authorities can and therefore should use discretionary aggregate demand policies to stabilize the economy. However, unlike orthodox Keynesians, new Keynesians do not support what they regard as overambitious attempts to fine tune the macroeconomy and have instead championed the case for rough tuning. In particular, as discussed in Chapter 9, hysteresis effects provide new Keynesians with a strong case that the authorities should stimulate aggregate demand during a prolonged recession.

Even new Keynesians agree it's not advisable to try to fine tune the economy

The manner in which governments responded to the 2008–9 recession is clearly in line with the Keynesian view (see, for example, 'Applying Economics to Business' box in Chapter 9).

The monetarist view

During the late 1960s and early 1970s, a monetarist counter-revolution took place (most notably in the US), which fed into what has become a continuing debate over stabilization policy. As outlined in Chapter 11, monetarists, in stark contrast to Keynesians, believe that the economy is *inherently stable*, unless disturbed by erratic monetary growth. Furthermore, they contend that, when subjected to some disturbance, the economy is rapidly self-equilibrating and will return fairly quickly to the neighbourhood of the natural level of output and employment. Given these beliefs, monetarists question the need for stabilization policy involving the management of aggregate demand. Even if there were a need, they argue that discretionary fiscal and monetary policies cannot, and therefore should not, be used to stabilize the economy. We now consider more fully the monetarist case against discretionary policy activism.

Crowding out

While monetarists accept that fiscal policy can be used to influence the level of output and employment in the short run, they argue that in the long run fiscal expansion (for example an increase in government expenditure) will replace or crowd out components of private-sector expenditure so that real income remains unchanged at its natural level. **Crowding out** will be complete where private-sector expenditure is reduced by the same amount that government expenditure is increased, so that the long-run government expenditure multiplier is zero. The monetarist view contrasts with the Keynesian view in which an increase in government expenditure will, through the multiplier process, lead to an increase in income by some multiple of the original change in government expenditure (for an example of the multiplier, see box 'Reflecting on Economics: the multiplier' in Chapter 11).

A number of reasons have been put forward to explain why crowding out may occur. Two examples will suffice. First, crowding out may arise as a direct result of the way in which an increase in government expenditure is financed, a so-called financing effect. Consider the case where an increase in government expenditure is financed by increased sales of government bonds. In order to induce the public to buy more government bonds, the rate of interest on new bond issues will have to increase. When the cost of borrowing funds rises, the level of private-sector investment will be reduced as firms cancel investment projects they had planned to finance by borrowing before interest rates increased. Second, crowding out may occur in an open economy operating under a regime of **fixed exchange rates** (see Chapter 14) due to a price level effect. If the domestic price level increases following an increase in government expenditure and the exchange rate is fixed, exports will become less competitive with foreign-produced goods, while imports will become more competitive with domestically produced goods (again, see Chapter 14). In other words, an increase in government expenditure will result in a fall in exports and an increase in imports.

Tax changes

In discussing fiscal policy we have so far considered only why monetarists typically argue that an increase in government expenditure will, in the long run, replace or crowd out some components of private-sector expenditure. We next need to consider why monetarists question the likely impact of tax changes as a stabilization instrument. In contrast to the Keynesian view, in which consumption expenditure depends on current income, Milton Friedman argued that consumption spending depends on **permanent** (long-run average) **income** that people expect to receive. Tax changes that people believe will be in effect for only a year or two will have only a negligible effect on permanent income. In consequence, temporary tax changes will have only a small effect on consumption and are useless for stabilization purposes.

Finally, turning to monetary policy, as discussed in Chapter 10, monetarists argue that discretionary monetary policy can also influence output and employment, but again only in the short run. In the long run, monetary policy can determine only nominal variables and their rates of change.

Crowding out: the reduction in private-sector expenditure that results following an increase in government expenditure.

Fixed exchange rate: an exchange rate that is fixed at a predetermined level by intervention by the country's central bank in the foreign exchange market.

Permanent income: the average income that people expect to receive over a period of years in the future; also known as normal income and average expected income.

Problems associated with stabilization policy

If both fiscal and monetary policy can influence output and employment in the short run, why are monetarists against discretionary policy activism? In summary, monetarists argue that, due to numerous problems associated with stabilization policy (including time lags, forecasting errors and uncertainty), the authorities should refrain from attempting to stabilize the economy in the short run, by discretionary aggregate demand management policies, for fear they do more harm than good. We first examine how, given the existence of time lags, it is possible for discretionary policy activism to be destabilizing. In discussing time lags in the conduct of stabilization policy, it is customary to divide the lags into an inside lag and an outside lag.

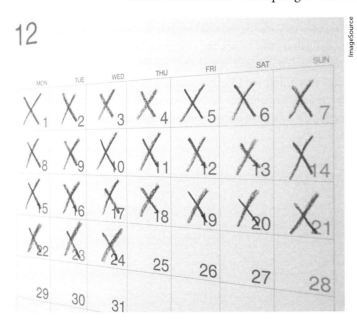

Monetarists argue that time lags make stabilization policy dangerous

The *inside lag* is the period of time it takes to initiate a policy change, such as a tax cut or an increase in the money supply. The inside lag can be divided into two components: a recognition lag, and an administrative lag. The *recognition lag* is the time lag between when a disturbance or shock affects the economy and when the authorities recognize that some kind of corrective action is needed. This lag will be the same for both fiscal and monetary policy. The *administrative lag* is the time lag between recognizing that action is required and actually planning, and implementing, the corrective policies. Unlike the recognition lag, the administrative lag will not be the same for fiscal and monetary policy. In the US, the administrative lag associated with fiscal policy is longer than that for monetary policy. While monetary policy actions can be implemented fairly swiftly by the Federal Reserve System, most fiscal policy changes require the approval of both Houses of Congress and the legislative process involved can sometimes be painfully slow. In contrast, in the UK, the legislative process required to implement fiscal policy changes is much quicker as long as the government in office can command a parliamentary majority.

Once a policy change has been implemented, we move on to the outside lag. The *outside lag* is the time between an initiated policy change and its influence on the economy. Unlike the inside lag, the outside lag is a *distributed* lag in that the effects of a policy change on the economy will be spread out over time. A policy change, such as a tax cut or a change in the money supply, will not lead to an immediate increase in spending and employment in the economy and its effects are likely to continue over several periods. The length of the outside lag will vary depending on a number of factors including the state of the economy at the time when the policy change is implemented, the way the private sector responds to the policy change and whether fiscal or monetary policy changes are implemented. In the latter case, for example, it is generally accepted that monetary policy has a relatively long outside lag. Monetary policy works through interest rate changes, which in turn influence investment spending in the economy. Given that many firms will plan new investment far in advance, their response to interest rate changes is likely to be slow and may take many months. Due to the length of the inside lag associated with fiscal policy (especially in the US) and the length and variability of the outside lag associated with monetary policy (see Chapter 11), monetarists argue that any attempt to use discretionary fiscal and/or monetary policy to stabilize the economy could do more harm than good. This possibility is illustrated in Figure 12.2.

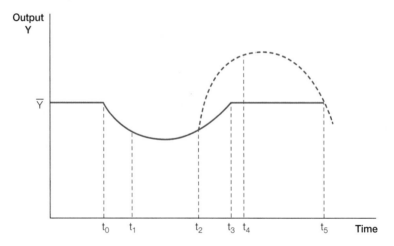

Figure 12.2 Time lags and stabilization policy

Figure 12.2 depicts a situation where output is initially at its full employment or natural level ($\overline{Y}$). At time t_0, a disturbance affects the economy, which reduces output below $\overline{Y}$. However, given the inside lag, it is not until time t_1 that the authorities actually implement an expansionary policy. There then follows a further outside time lag before the initiated policy change starts to affect the economy at time t_2 and thereafter. Without discretionary stabilization policy, output would return to $\overline{Y}$ by time t_3. With discretionary stabilization policy, output rises above its full employment/natural level. At time t_4, the authorities initiate contractionary policy, which again only begins to affect the economy after a further period of time has elapsed. With stabilization policy, output now falls below its full employment/natural level at time t_5 and thereafter. It can be seen that, in this example, due to time lags stabilization policy has actually destabilized the economy, resulting in more severe fluctuations in output than would otherwise have occurred if the authorities had not engaged in activist discretionary policy intervention.

In addition to the problems raised by time lags, uncertainty over both the size of policy multipliers associated with fiscal and monetary policy in the short run and what precise value to attribute to the natural rate of unemployment make it possible for discretionary policy activism to be destabilizing. In the latter case, given the belief that the long-run Phillips curve is vertical, any attempt to *maintain* unemployment below the natural rate by discretionary aggregate demand policies will result in accelerating inflation (see Chapter 10). In consequence, monetarists advocate that discretionary aggregate demand policies should be replaced by some form of monetary rule. Finally, it is interesting to note that, in addition, some monetarists justify their position that policy is best conducted by rules rather than discretion by explaining that opportunistic politicians cannot be trusted not to use activist discretionary policy to manipulate the economy for political gain.

ImageSource

Rational agents make the best use of all the information available to them

The new classical view

The 1970s witnessed the development of the new classical approach to macroeconomics, an approach that cast further doubt on whether traditional Keynesian aggregate demand policies can be used to improve overall economic performance and stabilize the economy. Underlying the new classical model of the macroeconomy is the joint acceptance of three main tenets:

- rational expectations
- the assumption that all markets in the economy continuously clear
- the Lucas surprise supply function

Rational expectations: an approach that assumes people make the best use of all available information to forecast the future.

Rational expectations assume that agents make the best use of all available information – including information on current and prospective policies – to form their forecasts or expectations of the future value of a variable. For example, if economic agents believe that the rate of inflation is determined by the rate of monetary expansion then they will make the best use of all publicly available information on rates of monetary expansion in forming their expectations of future rates of inflation. The Lucas surprise supply function states that output only deviates from its natural level in response to deviations of the actual price level from its expected value. As discussed in Chapter 11, in the absence of price surprises, which arise from incomplete information, output will remain at its natural level. The combination of the rational expectations hypothesis, the assumption of continuous market clearing and the Lucas surprise function produces a number of important implications for macroeconomic policy. In what follows we outline three insights associated with the new classical approach that are relevant to the debate over stabilization policy, namely the:

- policy ineffectiveness proposition
- time inconsistency of discretionary policy
- Lucas critique of traditional methods of policy evaluation

Policy ineffectiveness proposition

Policy ineffectiveness proposition: the proposition that anticipated changes in monetary policy have no effect on output and employment.

In line with monetarists, new classicists believe that the economy is inherently stable and that when subjected to some disturbance will quickly return to its natural level of output and employment. While the main source of disturbances is attributed to monetary shocks in both approaches, according to the new classical view, only *unanticipated* monetary shocks affect output and employment and then only in the short run (see Chapter 11). Furthermore, rational economic agents will react *very* quickly to aggregate demand shocks, returning the economy to its long-run equilibrium in a very short period of time. Not only is stabilization policy totally unnecessary but the authorities will also be unable to influence output and employment, even in the short run, by pursuing systematic aggregate demand policies. According to the so-called policy ineffectiveness proposition, which was first put forward in the mid-1970s by Thomas Sargent and Neil Wallace, anticipated monetary policy will be completely ineffective. The proposition implies that only random or arbitrary policy actions undertaken by the authorities have real effects, because they cannot be anticipated by rational economic agents. However, given that such actions would only increase the variation of output and employment around their natural levels and increase uncertainty in the economy, the policy ineffectiveness proposition provides new classicists with a strong argument against discretionary policy activism and in favour of rules.

Time inconsistency

Time inconsistency: the temptation of policymakers to deviate from a previously announced policy once private decision-makers have adjusted their behaviour to the announced policy.

In the mid-1970s, the influential work of Finn Kydland and Edward Prescott (the joint recipients of the 2004 Nobel Prize in Economics) on the problem of time inconsistency of policy provided another argument in the case for fixed rules over discretion. In some situations, in order to influence the expectations of private decision-makers, the authorities may announce that they intend to pursue a particular policy or course of action. However, once private decision-makers have reacted to the announced policy, the authorities may then be tempted to renege on their previous announcement. Time inconsistency describes a situation where an announced policy that is optimal today may not remain optimal in subsequent periods once private decision-makers have adjusted their behaviour accordingly. The problem of time inconsistency can be illustrated with a simple example. To encourage students to work hard, a lecturer announces that his course will end with a hard exam. After students have responded by studying hard and learning the course material, the lecturer may then be tempted to cancel the exam in order to avoid having to spend time marking the exam scripts.

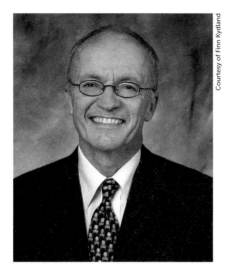

Finn Kydland   Edward Prescott

In macroeconomics one of the best examples of the problem of time inconsistency concerns the Phillips curve trade-off between inflation and unemployment. In Chapter 10 we discussed how the expectations-augmented Phillips curve implies that while the long-run Phillips curve is vertical at the natural rate of unemployment, there exists a whole family of short-run Phillips curves, each associated with a different expected rate of inflation. For example, as the expected rate of inflation decreases, the short-run Phillips curve will shift downwards so that, for any given rate of unemployment, inflation will be lower the lower are expectations of inflation.

In Figure 12.3 we assume that the economy is initially operating at point A with a 4 per cent rate of inflation and unemployment at its natural rate (U_N). Now suppose that the authorities want to reduce inflation to 0 per cent and move to point B on the long-run Phillips curve (LRPC). The authorities announce a policy of monetary contraction in order to reduce expectations of inflation held by workers and firms. However, once workers and firms have reduced their inflation expectations, shifting the short-run Phillips curve downwards from $SRPC_0$ to $SPRC_1$, the authorities will have an incentive to renege or cheat on their previously announced policy and implement expansionary monetary policy in order to reduce unemployment. By exercising their discretionary powers and engaging in monetary stimulus, the authorities can create an 'inflation surprise' and move to point C on $SRPC_1$. Point C is, however, unsustainable since unemployment (U^*) is below its natural rate (U_N) and the actual rate of inflation is greater than expected. As rational economic agents revise their inflation expectations upwards, shifting the short-run Phillips curve back from $SRPC_1$ to $SRPC_0$, the economy will return to point A on the LRPC with an *inflationary bias*. In situations where the authorities

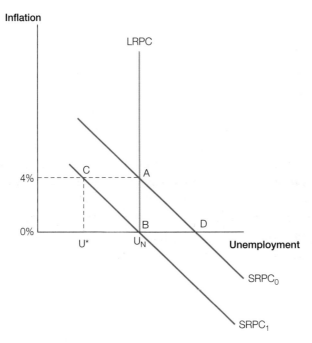

Figure 12.3 The problem of time inconsistency

have such discretionary powers and have in consequence an incentive to cheat, the credibility of announced policies will be significantly weakened. Aware that the authorities may be inconsistent over time, workers and firms are likely to distrust policy announcements. In circumstances where the announced policy of monetary contraction lacks credibility, agents will not revise their inflation expectations downwards. If the authorities actually carry out their announced policy, unemployment will rise above the natural rate; that is, a movement along $SRPC_0$ from point A to D.

The implication of the analysis we have discussed is that economic performance may be improved if discretionary powers are taken away from the authorities and the authorities make a commitment to pursue a fixed monetary growth rate rule. In this case, policy will be seen to be credible and agents will reduce their inflation expectations downwards, making possible a policy of lower inflation without higher unemployment. The inflationary bias present when the authorities are given discretion in the way they conduct monetary policy has led some economists to advocate giving the responsibility for anti-inflation policy to a central bank that is *independent* from the government. In 'Reflecting on Economics', below, we discuss the relationship between central bank independence and inflation performance.

The Lucas critique

In 1976, the leading new classical economist Robert Lucas, Jr (the 1995 Nobel Laureate) put forward a further criticism of traditional policy evaluation,

Lucas critique:
the argument that traditional policy evaluation may be misleading as it fails to take into account that people may change their expectations and behaviour when policy changes.

popularly known as the **Lucas critique.** In order to understand the significance of this critique we must first explain briefly the role of a macroeconometric model in providing forecasts and simulations of the effects of policy changes. A macroeconometric model consists of a set of equations that describe the behaviour of the economy as a whole. The estimated numerical values for the parameters of the model, such as the marginal propensity to consume, are themselves based on past behaviour. Once constructed, macroeconometric models can be used not only to provide forecasts of the future course of key macroeconomic variables, such as output, unemployment and inflation, but also to study the effects of various policy changes on these variables. Lucas, however, argues that traditional macroeconometric models should not be used to predict the consequences of alternative policy changes, since the parameters of such models may change as economic agents adjust their expectations and behaviour in response to the policy change.

REFLECTING ON ECONOMICS

Central bank independence and inflation performance

A number of economists have undertaken research that has examined the relationship between central bank independence and macroeconomic performance in advanced industrial countries for the period from the 1950s to the late 1980s. These studies have uncovered two main results.

- First, there appears to be no relationship between central bank independence and real macroeconomic performance, such as average unemployment and real output growth.
- Second, there is a striking *inverse* relationship between central bank independence and inflation performance. More central bank independence is strongly associated with lower, and more stable,

inflation. Countries with more independent central banks – such as the US, Switzerland and Germany – have experienced the lowest average inflation. In contrast, countries with less central bank independence – such as Spain and Italy – have experienced higher average inflation.

No doubt with these findings in mind, and also to help establish the *credibility* of monetary policy, a number of countries over more recent years have given a higher degree of independence to their central banks. For example, in the early 1990s the central bank of New Zealand was given greater independence *and* accountability for its actions. In the latter case, if the head of the central bank of New Zealand fails to fulfil pre-agreed low inflation targets, he/she is fired. Interestingly, since being given greater central bank independence (and accountability) New Zealand has achieved lower inflation performance.

One example of the Lucas critique concerns the role of rational expectations in determining the output/employment costs of reducing inflation. According to the new classical view, the output/employment costs of monetary disinflation will be non-existent or negligible provided a policy change is credible. If the authorities announce a reduction in the rate of monetary expansion and the policy announcement is believed to be credible, rational economic agents will immediately revise their expectations of inflation downwards, in line with the anticipated effects of monetary contraction on the rate of inflation (see Chapter 10). New classicists claim that traditional estimates of the output/employment costs of reducing inflation are unreliable because they do not take into account how agents adjust their expectations and behaviour to a policy change. The traditional approach incorporates **adaptive expectations**, where economic agents form their expectations of the future value of a variable solely on the basis of recent past values of the variable. For example, agents' expectations of inflation will depend solely on past inflation and will not alter following a policy change. In consequence, new classicists argue that traditional policy evaluation overestimates the output/employment costs of reducing inflation because it is subject to the Lucas critique. In summary, the Lucas critique has cast doubt on the reliability of traditional estimates of the impact of various policy changes on key macroeconomic variables.

The real business cycle view

While both monetarists and new classicists question not only the need for stabilization policy but also whether the authorities can stabilize output and employment by discretionary policy intervention, a much more radical view emerged in the 1980s associated with the real business cycle approach to economic fluctuations. As discussed in Chapter 11, according to this approach economic fluctuations are the optimal response of the economy to supply-side shocks. In the real business cycle view, monetary factors are irrelevant in explaining fluctuations in output and employment, and monetary policy cannot influence real variables in either the short or the long run. Turning to fiscal policy, adherents of the approach contend that governments should not attempt to reduce economic fluctuations through stabilization policy as they could do a great deal of harm if their taxation and spending distorted output and employment from the optimal amounts chosen by firms and workers. In short, in the real business cycle view there is no role for the authorities to stabilize fluctuations in output and employment through conventional aggregate demand policies.

12.4 Changing views on stabilizing the economy

From what we have discussed in both this chapter and Chapters 8–11, it should be apparent that policymakers' views on stabilizing the economy changed in the period after the Second World War as a result of changing macroeconomic problems and perspectives on the macroeconomy. In the 1950s and 1960s Western governments sought to manage aggregate demand – through frequent changes in the stance of fiscal policy and, to a lesser extent, monetary policy – in order to stabilize output and employment at, or near, their full employment levels. This policy response was informed by the then-dominant Keynesian view of the macroeconomy and the belief that policymakers could successfully fine tune their economies.

In the 1970s when the problem of rising inflation and unemployment (stagflation) emerged, policymakers were forced to turn their attention to curbing inflation. As a result of the arguments put forward by monetarists, most notably

Milton Friedman (the 1976 Nobel Laureate), and developments in macroeconomics associated with economists belonging to the new classical school, policymakers began to switch the *main focus* of macroeconomic policy away from aggregate demand management towards aggregate supply management to help achieve their growth and employment objectives, and they highlighted the role of monetary policy to achieve low and stable inflation. At the same time much greater attention was paid to the question of whether the authorities should be given discretion or follow rules in the way they conduct fiscal and monetary policy.

In the UK, for example, from 1997 – when a 'New Labour' government, under PM Tony Blair, was elected to office – until the onset of the 2008–9 financial crisis and associated recession, the government's macroeconomic framework could be described as one involving 'constrained discretion'.

Post-1997 the conduct of fiscal policy in the UK was conditioned by the adoption of two rules:

- the *golden rule*, where over the economic cycle the government was committed to borrow only to invest and not to fund current expenditure
- the *sustainable investment rule*, where public-sector debt was to be maintained at a 'prudent' level below 40 per cent of GDP over the economic cycle.

Blair's government also introduced a new monetary policy framework in the UK that gave greater independence to the Bank of England. The key features of this framework include:

- An inflation target – currently 2 per cent – set by the government. The inflation target is symmetric, meaning that deviations above or below target are deemed equally unacceptable.

The Bank of England: independent interest rate setting since 1997

- Operational independence for the Bank of England. This allows the Monetary Policy Committee (MPC) to set the level of interest rates it deems necessary to meet the government's inflation target.
- An open letter system. If inflation deviates 1 per cent either above or below the 2 per cent target the governor of the Bank of England, on behalf of the MPC, must write an open letter to the Chancellor of the Exchequer explaining why the target has not been met and what actions the MPC intends to take to bring inflation back on target.

The monetary policy framework is based on the view that:

- Price stability is an essential *precondition* to achieve high and stable levels of growth and employment.
- In the *long run* there is no trade-off between inflation and unemployment.

In response to the 2008–9 recession, both fiscal rules were put on hold. As discussed in Chapters 8 and 9, the then-Labour government, under PM Gordon Brown, sought to mitigate the depth of the recession by pursuing both expansionary fiscal and monetary policy – a policy response that has been described by many commentators as a rebirth of Keynesian economics. On the fiscal side, for example, extra government spending was financed by unprecedented levels of government borrowing.

In 2010, the newly formed coalition government between the Conservatives and Liberal Democrats, with David Cameron as PM, created the Office for Budget Responsibility (OBR) with the aim of providing 'independent' and 'authoritative analysis' of the UK's public finances. The four main responsibilities of the OBR are to:

- produce (twice a year) five-year forecasts for the economy and public finances. The forecasts incorporate the impact of any tax and spending measures announced by the Chancellor of the Exchequer in his Budget and Autumn statements
- use its forecasts on public finances to assess the extent to which the Government's performance is likely to meet its fiscal targets
- scrutinize and challenge the Treasury's costing of tax and welfare spending measures
- assess the long-term sustainability of the public finances

At the time of writing (early 2015) it is clear that the deficit reduction plan announced after the 2010 general election (which included substantial reductions in public sector spending) will not be achieved over the original time span envisaged. It remains to be seen whether the present up-turn in economic activity in the UK economy translates into a sustained and robust recovery. Finally it is interesting to note that the political consensus in favour of austerity by governments in office in many economies, including the UK, in order to balance the books is not universally accepted among politicians and economists. Firstly, even among those who accept that government budgets deficits need to be reduced there is a wide range of opinion regarding the speed at which public spending cuts should be implemented. Secondly, if growth in the euro area remains weak and deflation persists there are likely to be increasingly vociferous calls for more expansionary (Keynesian) macroeconomic policy, rather than austerity.

12.5 Concluding remarks

In this chapter we have outlined various views concerning the debate over stabilization policy. Two main views can be identified. One view, held by orthodox Keynesians and new Keynesians, is that the authorities need to, can and therefore should stabilize the economy using aggregate demand policies. Even though nowadays most Keynesian economists accept that the long-run Phillips curve is vertical, they justify discretionary policy intervention to stabilize the economy on the following grounds: (a) the period of time required for the economy to return to the natural rate of unemployment having been subjected to some shock or disturbance; and (b) the potential to identify and respond to major shocks which periodically hit the economy.

The other main view, held by monetarists and new classicists, is that there is no need for stabilization policy involving the management of aggregate demand and that, in any case, discretionary fiscal and monetary policies cannot and therefore should not be used to stabilize the economy. Given the divide between these two broad groupings of economists, the debate over stabilization policy is likely to continue and remain a controversial area in macroeconomics.

SUMMARY

- One of the key questions that divide macroeconomists is whether the authorities need to, can and therefore should stabilize the economy at, or near, the full employment or natural level of output by influencing the level of aggregate demand.
- Discretionary policy takes place in circumstances where the authorities are free to vary the strength of fiscal and/or monetary policy in any way they see fit at the time. In contrast, the authorities may be committed to follow a pre-specified rule that determines the conduct of fiscal and/or monetary policy. Rules may or may not be linked to prevailing economic circumstances.
- The debate over stabilization policy critically depends on whether one views the economy as being inherently unstable or naturally stable. While both orthodox Keynesians and new Keynesians subscribe to the former view, arguing that there is a need for stabilization policy, new Keynesians regard attempts to fine tune the macroeconomy as being overambitious and instead advocate rough tuning.
- Both monetarists and new classicists, believing the economy to be inherently stable, question the need for stabilization policy involving the management of aggregate demand. Highlighting a number of problems associated with stabilization policy, most notably those associated with time lags, monetarists argue that discretionary policy activism may make matters worse and advocate that discretionary aggregate demand policies should be replaced by some form of monetary rule. New classicists' support for rules over discretion is based on the insights provided by policy ineffectiveness, the problem of time inconsistency and the Lucas critique.
- In the real business cycle approach there is no role for stabilization policy.

KEY TERMS

- Discretionary policy
- Fine tuning and rough tuning
- Policy rule: active and passive
- Inflationary gap
- Crowding out
- Inside and outside lags
- Rational expectations
- Policy ineffectiveness
- Time inconsistency
- Macroeconometric model
- Lucas critique

QUESTIONS FOR DISCUSSION

1. What is the difference between 'fine tuning' and 'rough tuning'? Which is the more realistic option?
2. Why do economists disagree over the issue of whether the authorities need to, can and should stabilize the economy?
3. What are the main problems encountered by policymakers in implementing stabilization policy?
4. What are the main time lags associated with fiscal and monetary policy? Why does the existence of these lags make it possible for policy intervention to have a destabilizing effect on the level of economic activity?
5. Why do monetarists question the use of changes in government expenditure and taxes as instruments to influence the level of economic activity in the long run?
6. In what ways will a change in interest rates affect firms?
7. What is meant by the term 'time inconsistency'? Why does time inconsistency imply that economic performance may be improved if discretionary powers are taken away from the authorities?
8. Should macroeconomic policy be operated at the discretion of the authorities or on the basis of rules?

ONE THING YOU SHOULD READ

Paul Krugman, who is currently Professor of Economics and International Affairs at Princeton University in the US, won the Nobel Prize in Economics in 2008 'for his analysis of trade patterns and location of economic activity'. Aside from his academic career and influential contributions to the development of economics, Krugman has, over the years, sought to communicate his views on a wide range of issues to non-economists. Since 1999 he has been an Op-Ed columnist for the *New York Times*, which has allowed him to present his views on current economic issues, in an accessible and lively manner, to a broad public audience. His thought-provoking and often controversial columns have won him both many admirers and critics. His blog, with its American orientation, can be accessed at http://krugman.blogs.nytimes.com

One blog entry you should read is, 'How Did Economists Get It So Wrong?' published in the *New York Times* in September 2009. In the article – which can be accessed at: http://www.nytimes.com/2009/09/06/magazine/06Economic-t.html – he considers the state of macroeconomics, criticizing the building blocks of new classical economics while making a passionate plea for a return to the insights of Keynesian economics in combating recessions and depressions. Having read the article you should consider the following questions.

1. Why are economists in the US sometimes referred to as belonging to 'saltwater' and 'freshwater' camps?
2. Which leading freshwater economists – referred to both in this chapter and in the article – won the Nobel Prize in Economics in 1995 and 2004 respectively?
3. What views – in particular regarding the way markets work and the behaviour of agents within markets – characterize freshwater economists?
4. How and why did President Obama seek to counter the effects of the financial crisis?
5. As a direct consequence of the 2008–9 recession, which view of the macroeconomy has seen a resurgence?

For an alternative opinion to Krugman the reader should access John Cochrane's article, 'How did Paul Krugman get it so Wrong?' at http: faculty.chicagobooth.edu/john.cochrane/research/Papers/krugman_response.htm

iStockphoto.com/John Steele

13

international trade

KEY ISSUES

Why do countries trade with one another?

Can *all* countries gain from trade?

How have patterns of trade changed since 1945?

How has trade policy unfolded since 1945?

CONTENTS

13.1 Introduction   **394**

13.2 The theory of
     comparative advantage   **396**

13.3 Reflecting on
     comparative advantage:
     further developments in
     trade theory   **401**

13.4 Patterns of trade since
     1945   **408**

13.5 International trade policy   **413**

13.1 Introduction

International trade is simply the extension of the market process across international boundaries: the buying and selling of goods and services in foreign markets rather than in the domestic economy. To begin our discussion of international trade it is useful to consider the following three basic questions:

- What advantages does trade offer over and above the confinement of economic activity to the domestic market alone?
- What is the economic basis for trade?
- Is trade always a mutually advantageous process or are some economic agents potentially disadvantaged by it?

The advantages of trade

The most obvious advantage of international trade is that it provides access to a range of goods and services that might otherwise be denied to domestic populations. The residents of Germany, for example, cannot easily produce and consume tropical fruits or lie on a tropical beach on holiday except through trade: the German economy and German factors of production are not suited to the production of either of these things, so demand for them must be met from abroad. More significantly, countries often have few means of meeting certain basic material needs out of domestic resources. For example, many economies are importers of basic foodstuffs such as wheat. This, the *consumption* motive for trade, is however not restricted solely to items that are beyond the powers of the domestic economy to adequately produce. A growing number of countries have industries that sell their outputs into each other's markets. For example, French cars are sold in Britain and British-made cars are bought in France. Some British residents clearly prefer French cars to those produced at home and vice versa. Such preferences for foreign goods over their home-produced counterparts may simply reflect differences in taste but can also be based on price or quality factors. Whatever the motivation, trade makes much wider consumption choices possible in comparison to those available under *autarky* (which means self-sufficiency).

If trade opens up new opportunities for consumption, what of its effects upon *production*? It should be clear that goods and services sold abroad provide incomes and employment for those who produce them. As we will see, the relatively rapid rates of economic growth enjoyed by the advanced industrial

Trade: here come the goods

Getty Images/iStockphoto/EvrenKalinbacak

countries in the two decades after the Second World War, together with the more exceptional growth performances of the industrializing countries of the Pacific Rim, such as South Korea and more recently China, have their basis, at least in part, in international trade. There is a close affinity between success in foreign markets and domestic economic progress that is perhaps best expressed by the phrase 'export-led growth'. Of course, trade also gives access to the global range of raw materials and technologies upon which production rests. As few countries, if any, are completely self-sufficient in raw materials or technology, trade provides a vital conduit through which the earth's resources and the ingenuity and capacities of its inhabitants can be put to productive use.

The economic basis for trade

Having briefly reviewed the advantages of international trade, we now introduce the economic principles upon which it rests. We begin with the notion of *specialization and exchange* associated with the work of the British classical economists Adam Smith (1723–90) and David Ricardo (1772–1823).

In his book, *An Inquiry into the Nature and Causes of the Wealth of Nations*, published in 1776, Smith argued that labour can be made more productive by allocating it *specialist* tasks. He famously used the example of pin making to demonstrate that a group of workers, each with a particular and complementary skill in which they are well versed, will collectively be much more productive than they would be if each alone tried to master the full repertoire of pin-making skills. In other words, it is better to be adept at a small number of tasks than to undertake many with questionable competence. As for individuals, Smith declared, so for nations. It is appropriate for countries to limit the range of economic activities to those to which they are *best* suited and to engage in international trade to obtain those goods and services that they desire but cannot or choose not to produce.

■ **Concept:** **Free trade** implies an absence of government regulation in international markets for goods and services.

Smith also provided a rationale for **free trade**, unregulated and unchecked by government interference. His argument was that individuals freely enter into transactions which benefit them; hence, the greater the number of transactions, the greater the benefit. At the international level the same reasoning applies: the greater the volume of trade, the greater the benefit derived by those engaging in it. Thus trade should be allowed to flourish unconstrained. Note the mutually supportive link here between the notion of an **international division of labour** (nations specializing in what they are best at) and the argument for free trade. In a free and open international economy, countries will be motivated to push their productive specialisms as far as they are able, utilizing the factors of production in the most appropriate ways.

■ **Concept:** The **international division of labour** describes patterns of specialization in the production of goods and services between nations.

Ricardo's contribution to this analysis, published in 1817 in his book *On The Principles of Political Economy and Taxation*, was to demonstrate that *all* countries can gain from specialization and exchange and not just those that have reached a certain level of economic development. In such circumstances there

Comparative advantage: the ability of a country to produce a commodity at a lower opportunity cost, in terms of other commodities forgone, than another country.

are no sustainable arguments to confound the general case for free trade. We review the Ricardian notion of **comparative advantage**, which is at the heart of this thinking, in Section 13.2 below.

Some negative consequences of trade

The free trade arguments advanced by Smith and Ricardo have become a cornerstone of modern economic orthodoxy but this is not to say that international trade is not without its problems or that the case for *managed* trade can find no advocates. Later in this chapter we will provide some examples of instances in which the international division of labour has shifted over time between nations. When this happens countries with long-standing specialisms in the production of particular goods can find themselves 'outcompeted' in those specialisms by emergent rivals.

■ **Concept: Protectionism** occurs where the principle of free trade is compromised. Usually, protectionist policies are implemented by governments concerned to promote domestic industries over their foreign rivals.

This situation requires the newly uncompetitive nations to shift factors of production out of their threatened specialisms and reallocate them to uses in which they retain or can develop a competitive edge. However, while in theory the reallocation of resources can proceed in a smooth and timely manner, the reality is usually rather different and may involve bankruptcies and unemployment in industries with deteriorating competitiveness. This is because opportunities for the reinvestment of capital and re-employment of labour in new sectors usually emerge slowly and not at a pace sufficient to offset the original industrial decline. This kind of adjustment problem may give rise to calls for domestic industries to be **protected** by governments from the full force of international competition that completely free trade would unleash. We examine the contemporary validity of this position in Section 13.5 of this chapter.

13.2 The theory of comparative advantage

■ **Concept: Mercantilism** is an economic philosophy advanced by merchants and politicians prior to the rise of industrial capitalism. Mercantilism emphasized the importance of accumulating bullion from balance of trade surpluses and advocated tariffs and other protectionist measures to achieve that end.

Ricardo's theory of comparative advantage suggests that all countries will have some particular efficiency in the production of a good or service *relative to another country*. This means that every country can gain from specialization and trade. It does not matter if a given national economy is economically advanced or backward in comparison to its neighbours: it can still find an appropriate avenue of production upon which to concentrate.

At the time of its publication Ricardo's work, together with that of Smith, constituted a radical attack on the then-prevailing philosophy of international trade – **mercantilism**. Mercantilists thought that the key to national prosperity was the accumulation of gold and silver bullion. Bullion was, of itself, manifest wealth but it could also be used to finance wars with other foreign powers. The key to the accumulation of bullion was strong export performance – in order to maximize the inflow of gold and silver arising from payments for goods sold abroad – together with import restraint to minimize bullion outflow. The mercantilists argued that the state had a duty to implement policies to promote exports and protect domestic industry from import penetration; both were a means of furthering national prosperity. This establishes mercantilism as a profoundly interventionist philosophy. Finally, in the mercantilist view, international trade could only ever be attractive to one group of nations: those consistent net exporters who followed an aggressive trade policy, accumulated bullion and were prosperous. In contrast, nations less successful in the drive for exports tended to lose bullion and were economically enfeebled.

Ricardo thought that this idea of strong nations carving out overseas markets at the expense of the weak was wholly mistaken. Indeed, he argued that there were no economically strong or weak nations in the mercantilist sense: all were possessed of a comparative advantage in the production of some good or service. The truly striking element in his approach, compared with what had gone before, was its demonstration that international trade could no longer be considered to be a 'zero sum game' in which the strong nations elbowed aside the weak. Instead, trade was a 'positive sum' process that actually raised the production and consumption possibilities of participant nations, leaving them *all* better off.

The theory of comparative advantage is best explained with the help of a simple example. We begin by identifying two countries: Germany and Ukraine, each of which, fully using the resources available to it, can produce some combination of two goods: cameras and beer. Let us assume that the *production possibilities* in Table 13.1 apply: Germany, in other words, can produce either 20 million cameras or 20 million units of beer (in a given time period) if all its resources are allocated to either camera or beer production respectively, or some combination of both products in between these two values. Similarly, Ukraine can produce either 5 million cameras or 15 million units of beer or some combination in between. Figure 13.1 graphs the possible production combinations for both countries, assuming, to keep things simple, constant returns to scale.

Table 13.1 Hypothetical production possibilities

		Cameras		Beer
Germany:	⟶	20 million units	*or*	20 million units
Ukraine:	⟶	5 million units	*or*	15 million units

For each country we can now express the opportunity cost of one good in terms of the other. Recall that opportunity cost refers to the amount of one good that must be given up in order to obtain a given increase in the output of the other good. In the case of Germany it can be seen, for example, that the opportunity cost of producing 1 camera is 1 unit of beer (20 million cameras would 'cost' 20 million units of beer; 20m ÷ 20m = 1). Therefore, to produce *one* million more cameras (for example from 10m to 11m cameras), *one* million units of beer must be sacrificed (that is, from 10m to 9m units). In Ukraine, however, the opportunity cost of the amount of beer that must be forgone to produce one more camera is higher. Here, the maximum of 5 million cameras that can be

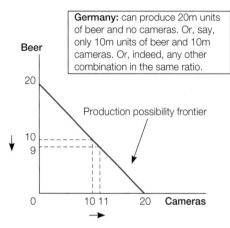

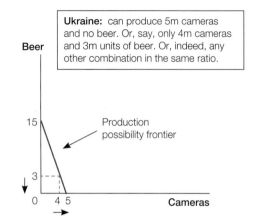

Figure 13.1 Production possibility frontiers

produced would cost the forgone production of 15 million units of beer. Thus, the opportunity cost of a camera in Ukraine is 3 units of beer (15m ÷ 5m = 3). To produce *one* million more cameras (for example from 4m to 5m cameras), *three* million units of beer must be sacrificed (that is, from 3m units to zero).

This means that Germany can produce cameras at a lower opportunity cost in terms of beer production that must be forgone than Ukraine. Germany, in other words, has a *comparative advantage in camera production* over Ukraine. On the other hand, it is apparent that Ukraine has a comparative advantage in beer production over Germany. In Germany, each extra unit of beer produced involves the loss of 1 camera; but in Ukraine it is possible to produce 3 extra units of beer for the loss of a camera (that is, the opportunity cost of producing one unit of beer is the loss of a third of a camera). *In opportunity cost terms, Ukraine can produce beer at a lower opportunity cost compared to Germany*; in other words, it has a comparative advantage in beer production over Germany.

The different opportunity costs suggest that there is scope for specialization in the two countries. Germany could produce only cameras, at which it appears adept, and no beer, while Ukraine could do the reverse. Each country would be producing the commodity in which it has a comparative advantage (that is, producing at the lowest opportunity cost) in comparison to

How many cameras to produce; how many to export?

© iStockphoto/ellobo1

the other country. We now need to demonstrate that, in this situation, there is scope for trade between Germany and Ukraine that is mutually advantageous.

Consider Germany first. Suppose the German economy produced *only* cameras: 20 million of them, some of which it wished to exchange for beer from Ukraine. The crucial issue is the exchange ratio that needs to be agreed. We know that to obtain 1 unit of beer in Germany there is a 'price' to be paid of 1 camera. If Germany could persuade Ukraine to let it have, say, 2 units of beer per camera, then this would represent a huge improvement on what was available domestically. The obvious question now concerns the receptiveness of Ukraine to this offer.

In Ukraine, the opportunity cost of producing a camera is 3 units of beer. If Germany offers to exchange its cameras for only 2 units of beer this is a very acceptable arrangement for Ukraine. It would be advantageous for Ukraine to produce only beer (that is, 15 million units) and to exchange some of its beer production for German cameras. The important point to notice is that there is a different international exchange ratio (or price) for cameras and beer compared to that prevailing in the two domestic economies.

Table 13.2 summarizes the position of both countries in autarky with an arbitrary division of production between the two goods. Note the *total* output levels for cameras and beer in this situation, namely 19 million cameras and 8 million units of beer.

Table 13.2 Germany and Ukraine in autarky

	Production and Consumption	
	Cameras (millions)	Beer (millions of units)
Germany	15	5
Ukraine	4	3
'World' output in autarky	19	8

We will now consider complete specialization in both countries, where some of the output of each is traded at an exchange ratio of 2 units of beer per camera. Again, the volumes traded are selected arbitrarily simply for illustrative purposes. The results are summarized in Table 13.3. Here it can be seen that both countries have gained from the process. In Germany, camera consumption has remained at the same level as in autarky but the consumption of beer has doubled from 5 to 10 million units. In Ukraine, camera consumption has increased by 1 million units and beer consumption by 2 million units. World production and consumption has increased by 1 and 7 million units of cameras and beer respectively.

It is evident then that specialization and exchange has indeed improved the consumption positions of both countries and Ricardo's critique of the

Table 13.3 Specialization and trade

	Produces	Exports		Imports	Consumes
Germany	20m cameras	5m cameras	←——→	10m beers	15m cameras; 10m beers
Ukraine	15m beers	10m beers	←——→	5m cameras	5m cameras; 5m beers
'World' output and consumption after trade ————→					20m cameras; 15m beers

Absolute advantage: the ability of a country to produce more of a particular commodity than another country, using an equal quantity of factor inputs.

mercantilist view – that countries can gain through trade only at the expense of their rivals – appears vindicated. Similarly, the Ricardian case for free trade is equally well founded. Note also that in our example Germany is capable of producing more of *both* commodities than is Ukraine. It is said to possess an **absolute advantage** in the production of both. Adam Smith had originally supposed that trade could only take place between countries that each had an absolute advantage in the production of particular goods. Ricardo's great contribution was to show that the important criterion was the existence of comparative, not absolute, advantage. Now, because all countries have a comparative advantage in something, all may gain from the trade process. This means that free trade looks to be in the interest of *all* countries and that, as a corollary, its inverse – the kind of protectionism recommended by the mercantilists – may be inimical to the general economic good.

● **Think Point**

Reflect on these two scenarios. What does the theory of comparative advantage suggest about each?

- Imagine yourself in 20 years. You're a highly qualified and experienced business consultant. You hire yourself out by the hour at a very lucrative rate. You're also quite creative and adept at DIY. This raises a question: should you do your own decorating and house maintenance or pay someone to do it for you?
- You're managing a large company that makes and sells kitchenware. You have a large complement of sales and marketing people who do a lot of travelling. The industry standard is that all such employees are provided with company cars. Is it better for your company to buy and maintain a fleet of cars or lease them?

The comparative advantage rationale in both cases would be to concentrate on the core activity. As a business consultant you're a very high earner. The opportunity cost of maintaining your property yourself is very high in the sense that you have to give up lucrative working hours to do it. So it is better to work more and pay someone to do your DIY. Similarly, your kitchenware company is adept at making and selling kitchenware. This is a market that you know intimately. The purchase and maintenance of a fleet of cars would be manageable but it might also be a diversion for you and some of your colleagues from your core business. So better to stick to what you know you do best.

To test your understanding of the sources of comparative advantage have a look at Everyday Economics 13.1. Can you identify the nature of comparative advantage illustrated in these photos?

EVERYDAY ECONOMICS 13.1

Each of the images below illustrates a type of comparative advantage. Can you work out what these are?

Answers are at the end of the chapter.

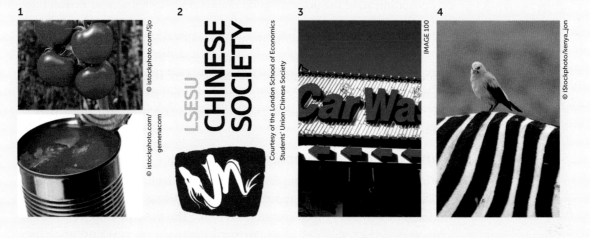

13.3 Reflecting on comparative advantage: further developments in trade theory

The basic message that emerges from the theory of comparative advantage is very clear: the best way to organize the international economy is to allow specialization and trade to flourish. Yet there are still some questions that our description of the principle so far has left unanswered:

- Are there really *no* problems whatsoever with the process of free trade in the Ricardian view?
- What factors determine a country's comparative advantage?
- How are we to reconcile Ricardo's expectation of specialization with the fact that, as noted, many countries produce the *same* goods (the car was the example used earlier) and sell them in each other's markets?

Problems with the free trade process?

To begin with the first of these questions, it is the Ricardian case that for each country *as a whole* trade offers no threats, only opportunities. However, Ricardo himself acknowledged that, for some groups inside the national economy, problems could arise as a result of free trade. His specific reference was to the losses free trade might visit upon British landowners at the end of the Napoleonic wars in 1815 (recall that Ricardo's book was published in 1817). War had raised British food prices to the benefit of the landowners on whose property the food was produced. Because free trade threatened to open the British market to imports of cheaper foreign food, landowners were in favour of the protection, by government, of the domestic food market. However, a second British interest group – the newly emerging manufacturing class – wanted a liberal trading environment that would allow them to profit from open overseas markets. Ricardo's suggested compromise was that the free-trade enriched manufacturers should compensate the disadvantaged landowners. In this way, internal objections to the effects of trade could be overcome and its larger benefits secured. We consider further potential problems associated with free trade later in the chapter.

What determines comparative advantage?

What of the source of comparative advantage? In his original formulation, Ricardo highlighted the importance of *labour productivity* as the key determinant of a country's specialization decision. The more productive its labour becomes in the fashioning of one particular commodity as against an alternative, the lower the opportunity cost of the commodity. Returning to our earlier example (summarized in Table 13.1 and Figure 13.1), consider the impact of a fivefold increase in productivity in the German camera industry. Instead of 20 million cameras in a given time period, it is now able to produce 100 million cameras. We assume conditions in the German beer industry are unchanged. Formerly, the opportunity cost of a camera was one unit of beer. Now, given the improvement in camera industry productivity, one camera costs only a fifth of a unit of beer (20m ÷ 100m = 1/5). If Ukraine is still happy to trade at the existing international ratio of 1 camera for 2 units of beer, then the leap in German camera productivity provides the basis for an even better deal for the Germans. Domestically, they can now get only 1/5 of a unit of beer for every camera they sacrifice (instead of one unit as previously) but internationally they can still obtain 2 beers per camera, and they're producing many more cameras.

Although the concept of comparative advantage still survives as the underlying essence of modern international trade theory, Ricardo's emphasis on labour productivity as its (sole) source has fared less well. In particular, given the existence of several factors of production, it seems reasonable to question the validity of elevating only *one* factor as a means of explaining patterns of trade. This concern eventually prompted a further important step in the development of trade theory with the emergence, in the 1920s, of the **Heckscher–Ohlin** model of international trade, named after its Swedish originators, Eli Heckscher (1879–1952) and Bertil Ohlin (1899–1979), the 1977 Nobel Laureate.

■ **Concept:** The **Heckscher–Ohlin** approach to international trade holds that a country's production and trade specialisms will reflect its particular factor endowments.

The Heckscher–Ohlin model supposes that a country's comparative advantage will reflect its particular *endowments* of factors of production. Because, globally, factors are not evenly spread the basis for specialization and exchange is established. For example, those countries that are richly endowed with fertile land will find it beneficial to devote resources to the production of agricultural output. For countries with a relative abundance of labour, specialization in the production of labour-intensive goods and services will be preferable.

The advantage of this kind of approach is that it has expectations that appear to conform to some very obvious real-world general trading patterns. 'Land-rich' countries such as New Zealand and Brazil do tend to specialize in outputs that exploit their natural resource endowments, while a country like Japan, which has fewer natural resources but a relative abundance of capital (in the shape of technologically advanced factories and machines), specializes in manufactured goods. Unfortunately, despite the stamp of realism which the Heckscher–Ohlin model appears to possess, its formal construction required that only *two* factors of production could be considered, rather than the four that microeconomic theory identifies. The preferred two factors were labour and capital. Despite such simplification, the model was still regarded as an advance upon the foundations provided by Ricardo.

In 1947 the central hypothesis of the Heckscher–Ohlin model was famously subjected to an empirical test by the economist Wassily Leontief (1906–99), the 1973 Nobel Laureate. Using a model of the American economy, Leontief expected to be able to demonstrate specialization by the US in capital-intensive goods and, therefore, that US exports were similarly capital intensive. Given that the US was by far the most technologically advanced nation in the world at that time, this was a reasonable hypothesis. However, Leontief's results were the reverse of those anticipated. His work suggested that the US was an exporter

Heckscher–Ohlin in action: the world's major coffee producers depicted by their ranking. To produce coffee you need lots of land at suitable altitudes and the right climate

of labour-intensive goods and an importer of capital-intensive goods; in other words, the US was *not* specializing in the production of goods that required the use of its most abundant factor. Because the Heckscher–Ohlin model was supported by an apparent wealth of casual empirical evidence, concerning the kind of international division of labour noted above, economists, including Leontief himself, were reluctant to dismiss it and his findings subsequently became known as the **Leontief paradox**.

This impasse between an intuitively defensible model and apparently contradictory empirical evidence subsequently resulted in a number of analyses that attempted to reconcile the two. The most widely accepted of these have usually involved some acknowledgement that comparative advantage must have its roots in something a little more complex than two simple categories of labour and capital. For example, Leontief thought that his results might be explained by the higher quality of labour in the US. This subsequently became known as the *human capital* argument and rests upon the proposition that the relatively heavy investment in education and training that takes place in the advanced economies makes labour there much more productive than elsewhere. The specialization of the US in labour-intensive industries, as discovered by Leontief, can therefore be explained by the abundance of high-quality labour in the US. In this sense, there is no paradox: it is just that the basis of comparative advantage is indeed more complex than the formalities of the Heckscher–Ohlin model can allow. The model itself, with due deference to its Ricardian foundations, remains a central element of orthodox trade theory in modern economics.

Why don't countries specialize to the extent that comparative advantage predicts?

In our third question reflecting upon comparative advantage, we raised a further facet of real-world trade complexity. In his original formulation, Ricardo argued that countries specialize in *particular* goods, which they then trade for *different* goods the domestic economy either cannot or chooses not to produce. This is known as **inter-industry trade**. The Heckscher–Ohlin model was a slightly more sophisticated endorsement of this same view. But, of course, the world is not that simple. A large proportion of trade takes place between countries that make the same products. As noted, the car industry is an obvious case in point. There is little sign of specialization and exchange of the kind Ricardo expected here: an increasing number of countries make cars and sell them to each other. Trade between nations in the same goods is known as **intra-industry trade** and the rapid increase in this kind of activity in the postwar period has prompted new developments in trade theory.

Although it might at first appear that the growth of intra-industry trade serves to undermine the traditional Ricardian approach, with its emphasis on the development of patterns of specialization, this is not the case. Some contemporary contributions to trade theory recognize that Ricardo's rather rigid

■ **Concept:** The **Leontief paradox** refers to the finding by the economist Leontief that, for the US, the predictions of the Heckscher–Ohlin model did not appear empirically verifiable.

■ **Concept: Inter-industry trade** refers to the tendency for countries to produce and trade different kinds of goods and services.

■ **Concept: Intra-industry trade** refers to the tendency for countries to produce and trade the same kinds of goods and services.

demarcation between 'country A producing good X and country B producing good Y, with trade between them' is increasingly outdated, but they continue to respect the essence of comparative advantage: *that different forms of production will be more efficiently conducted in different places.* Because everywhere is not the same in terms of economic attributes, it makes sense to use some places for one (suitable) form of production and other places for other (suitable) forms.

Product life-cycle theory

This kind of thinking has provided the basis for a number of advances in international trade theory. One of these, **product life-cycle theory**, describes the relationship between, on the one hand, the initial launch of a new good and its subsequent path to the status of a mature and recognized product, and on the other, its evolving *geography* of production. Let us take the car as an example of the application of this theory. When the car was first invented, the location of its production was constrained by a number of factors. First, as a new and expensive good, its market was initially small, and prospective customers needed to be affluent. Second, its technical complexity demanded a skilled labour force. Finally, new carmakers may have gained from close proximity to one another: perhaps from sharing information or resources, or simply by 'keeping an eye on the competition'. Taken together, these factors tended to mean that car production was restricted to certain economically advanced locations.

Eventually, the car became a mature commodity. Its form was no longer experimental and changing but established and stable. The way in which it was produced changed too. Skilled labour was no longer pre-eminent as the introduction of the assembly line allowed cars to be produced in vast numbers by semi-skilled or even unskilled labour. Such efficient production – taking advantage of scale economies – lowered the price of cars to within reach of the pockets of the people who made them. Finally, in a large and established market, car manufacturers began to compete much more heavily on price than they had done in the earliest stages of production. These new circumstances meant that the location of production became much more flexible. The old imperatives restricting it to economically advanced locations disappeared and, indeed, there were positive benefits to be reaped from seeking out places where costs could be minimized.

The stylized analysis above permits us to grasp the notion of a **shifting comparative advantage**, which favours different locations as a product moves from a stage of innovation to one of maturity. At first, because certain factors – such as skilled labour inputs – are crucial, production must be retained in the innovating areas; for carmaking, these are the advanced industrial nations. Later, when other factors become more important upon the maturing of the product, a wider distribution of production is favoured and may encompass, for example, less developed country locations. More generally, this analysis enables us to understand some of the reasons for the growth of intra-industry trade. If

■ **Concept: Product life-cycle theory** understands patterns of international trade by referencing the development of commodities over time. As they move from a stage of innovation through to maturity, products have different international geographies of production and, therefore, varying trade patterns.

■ **Concept: Shifting comparative advantage** implies that patterns of comparative advantage are not stable over time. Countries may lose and gain comparative advantage in different products.

product life-cycle theory is applicable to many consumer goods then it is possible to conceive of a highly complex patterning of trade (such as actually exists in the real world) that reflects the processes of innovation and maturation of many different products as their production migrates to, and they are exported from, newly appropriate locations. Again, however, we should be aware that the essence of 'locational appropriateness' is captured in Ricardian comparative advantage.

The new theory of international trade

The most recent innovation in understanding international trade has been provided in Nobel Prize–winning work by Paul Krugman.[1] This, the so-called new theory of international trade, is based on the interaction between two readily observable features of real economies: that bigger firms can produce at a lower cost as a result of economies of scale; and that consumers have a wide variety of tastes and preferences. The principal feature of the new trade theory is that it predicts intra-industry trade rather than the patterns of national specialization anticipated in the Ricardian model.

Krugman's approach centres on the framework of monopolistic or imperfect competition introduced in Chapter 5. To recap, a major feature of imperfectly competitive markets is the presence of firms producing goods that are *differentiated*: for example, beer is not just beer, it's Heineken, Carlsberg, Budweiser or Guinness. Because goods are to some extent unique, firms have a degree of market power – that is, they can set their own prices, rather than simply accept a uniform market price. This is possible because of the other noted characteristic of real economies – differences in consumer tastes. You might prefer Heineken but I like Guinness. The producers of these beers can therefore charge differently for them knowing that brand loyalties won't – up to a point – be compromised.

What happens when monopolistically competitive firms in different economies are exposed to the possibilities of international trade? One of the attractions of Krugman's model is that the answer is the same regardless of the characteristics of these economies. They may have different factor endowments, as in the Heckscher–Ohlin refinement of the Ricardian approach, or they may be identical in resources and technological sophistication. In either eventuality, as trade develops all firms enjoy potential access to a larger but more competitive international market where they may or may not be successful. Those firms that thrive in this environment will grow bigger and therefore enjoy scale economies that allow them to lower prices. Consumers in the now internationally articulated market gain both from lower prices *and* more choice. Are there any losers? Yes, firms that are forced to cede ground in the more intensely competitive market and go out of business – the usual penalty for failure under capitalism.

---

1 Krugman, P. (1979) 'Increasing Returns, Monopolistic Competition and International Trade', *Journal of International Economics*, 9: 469–79.

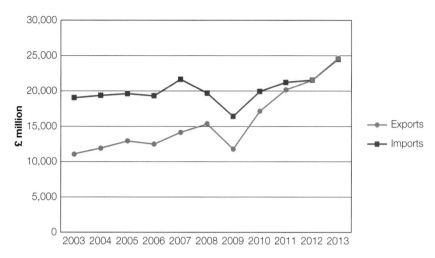

Figure 13.2 UK trade in cars, 2003–13

Source: Data from ONS: The Pink Book, 2014

New international trade theory provides very plausible explanations for developments in intra-industry trade in many markets. Think again about the car market. In the UK some decades ago there were several major British-*owned* car producers: Austin, Morris, Hillman, Humber, Jaguar. Now there are none. All these firms to a greater or lesser extent found it very difficult to compete in an increasingly open European car market with intense competition from German, French, Italian, Swedish, American and Japanese carmakers. So British-owned car manufacturing became a casualty of intra-industry trade. Of course, there are still a number of major foreign-owned car producers in the UK: Honda, Nissan, Ford, Vauxhall and Indian-owned Jaguar, for example. Their exports to Europe and elsewhere contribute to the credit side of the UK's intra-industry trade in cars. And this trade is significant. Figure 13.2 depicts UK car trade since 2003. Two things stand out. First, the sheer extent of intra-industry trade; for example, in 2013 the UK exported just under £25bn worth of cars while simultaneously importing cars also worth just under £25bn. Second, for most of the period as a whole the UK experienced a deficit in car trade. We explore trade deficit issues in Chapter 14.

Cars ready for export

13.4 Patterns of trade since 1945

We referred earlier to the rapid growth in international trade that has occurred since the end of the Second World War. In this section we will briefly describe the scale of this process and demonstrate its economic importance. We will also describe the striking changes in the patterns of trade that have emerged over the period.

It is generally agreed that there is a positive relationship between trade and economic growth: the more rapid the annual rate at which trade expands, the faster the growth in world output. There is in fact a *causal* link between these two variables: it is the opening up of new and bigger international markets for goods and services which motivates firms to increase output levels.

In Chapter 8 we described the years 1945–70 as the *postwar boom*: a period during which most of the advanced economies experienced unprecedented rates of economic growth, together with full employment and low inflation. Growth in world trade made a central contribution to this 'golden era'. Between 1950 and 1973 trade grew at an annual average rate of 8.6 per cent: more than double that in any previous period; while output expanded at 4.9 per cent, again about twice the best previous rate. However, a more modest expansion of trade since the beginning of the 1970s has, not unexpectedly, been associated with slower growth in world output. This was most acutely evident during the 2008–9 recession. In 2009 world trade fell by more than 10 per cent, while world output was virtually flat.

If world trade has generally expanded at a rapid if uneven rate over the postwar period, which countries have been the biggest participants in this process? Table 13.4 summarizes the shares of *world merchandise exports* since 1948. A country's export performance is the ultimate indicator of its competitive strength in international markets. From the two bottom rows of the table we can see, first, that the overall export share of the developed economies was reasonably stable between 1948 and 1993 within a range of 66.4 per cent to 76.3 per cent but declined to a low of 48 per cent in 2013. However, that a relatively few advanced nations in Europe and North America still account for a clear majority of world merchandise exports suggests that, despite the purported success of many less developed countries in the trade process, the international economy remains the preserve of established interests. The developing economies' share of world exports reached a nadir of 20.2 per cent in 1973 but then increased to a high of 52 per cent in 2013.

The main body of Table 13.4 describes the export performance of different regional groups in the international economy. Here some of the patterns described above are broadly replicated. North America and Western Europe (consisting only of developed economies) saw their export shares decline slightly over the last decade or so. However, there are some striking differences in long-term export performance between the remaining regional groups.

Table 13.4 World merchandise exports by region and selected economy, 1948–2013 (%)

	1948	1953	1963	1973	1983	1993	2003	2007	2013
World	100.0	100.0	100.0	100.0	100.0	100.0	100.0	100.0	100.0
North America	28.1	24.8	19.9	17.3	16.8	18.0	15.8	13.6	13.2
United States	21.7	18.8	14.9	12.3	11.2	12.6	9.8	8.5	8.6
Canada	5.5	5.2	4.3	4.6	4.2	4.0	3.7	3.1	2.5
Mexico	0.9	0.7	0.6	0.4	1.4	1.4	2.2	2.0	2.1
South and Central America	11.3	9.7	6.4	4.3	4.4	3.0	3.0	3.7	4.0
Europe	35.1	39.4	47.8	50.9	43.5	45.4	46.0	42.4	36.3
Germany	1.4	5.3	9.3	11.7	9.2	10.3	10.2	9.7	7.9
France	3.4	4.8	5.2	6.3	5.2	6.0	5.3	4.1	3.2
United Kingdom	11.3	9.0	7.8	5.1	5.0	4.9	4.1	3.3	3.0
USSR/CIS (from 1993)	2.2	3.5	4.6	3.7	5.0	1.5	2.6	3.7	4.3
Africa	7.3	6.5	5.7	4.8	4.5	2.5	2.4	3.1	3.3
Middle East	2.0	2.7	3.2	4.1	6.8	3.5	4.1	5.6	7.4
Asia	14.0	13.4	12.6	15.2	19.1	26.1	26.1	27.9	34.4
China	0.9	1.2	1.3	1.0	1.2	2.5	5.9	8.9	12.1
Japan	0.4	1.5	3.5	6.4	8.0	9.9	6.4	5.2	3.9
Six East Asian traders[a]	3.4	3.0	2.4	3.4	5.8	9.7	9.6	9.3	9.6
Developing countries	*31.4*	*28.3*	*22.6*	*20.2*	*26.8*	*25.2*	*30.3*	*34.7*	*52.0*
Developed countries	*66.4*	*68.2*	*72.9*	*76.3*	*68.2*	*73.3*	*67.1*	*61.6*	*48.0*

[a]Hong Kong China, Malaysia, Republic of Korea, Singapore, Chinese Taipei, Thailand

Source: Adapted from WTO World Trade Reports, 2007 and 2014

Consider first the more successful participants in the trade process. Taken together, the Asian nations, for example, managed to increase their collective share of world exports from 15.2 per cent in 1973 to 34.4 per cent by 2013. Given that the relative slowdown in the growth of trade overall during the last three decades (compared to the postwar boom) has meant that overseas markets have become much more keenly contested, this is a remarkable achievement.

Of the Asian group of economies, Japan consistently accounted for the largest export share between 1963 and 1993. In 1993 this was just under 10 per cent of the world total, making it then the world's third largest exporter behind the US and Germany. Japan's status as the leading Asian exporter has been since challenged, initially by the so-called Six East Asian traders – Hong Kong, Malaysia, South Korea, Singapore, Taiwan and Thailand – and more recently and most spectacularly by China.

Since 1973, the collective share of world exports of the six East Asian traders has increased almost threefold, and the achievements of these economies in opening up foreign markets have resulted in rates of economic growth consistently above those of any of the established advanced industrial nations.

China's explosion onto world markets has been even more dramatic. In 1983 its share in world merchandise exports was about a *tenth* of that of the US. Since then its share has increased more than tenfold, allowing it to overtake the US in the mid-2000s and Germany in 2009 to become the world's largest goods exporter.

How can the unparalleled modern expansion in export trade shares enjoyed by the Asian economies be explained? The answer lies in the Ricardian notion of *shifting* comparative advantage. Several of these nations managed to cast off long-established patterns of specialization in favour of others that have allowed them to enter new and growing world markets. In particular, economies like the Republic of (South) Korea reallocated resources away from the production of primary commodities (foodstuffs and raw materials) initially towards the production of basic manufactured goods. This was possible because these *newly industrializing countries* (NICs) were able to fashion certain kinds of manufactured items more efficiently than the advanced countries. By taking advantage of lower labour costs, for example, the NICs began to produce a range of labour-intensive manufactures, which they were able to price extremely competitively in world markets. More controversially, the NICs also tended to protect their new industries from foreign competition. We will say more about this shortly. Later, South Korea and others developed capacities in more advanced forms of production and produced more sophisticated outputs, to the extent that they are now classed as simply industrial – rather than newly industrializing – economies. Indeed, in 2013 South Korea was ranked 7th in the table of the world's leading exporters of merchandise goods – one place above the UK in 8th position. China has since followed much the same general path but, given the size of its economy (the world's second largest, with a fifth of the global population), it has done so faster and with a giant's momentum.

Of the other regions in the main body of Table 13.4, the story until recently was mostly one of declining export shares. To some extent this has been recently reversed by dramatic increases in commodity prices. We reviewed the extent

Relatively low labour costs and shifting comparative advantage: a garment factory in South East Asia

of the third oil shock in Chapter 2, but rocketing oil prices were accompanied in the mid-to-late 2000s by sharp increases in the prices of raw materials such as copper and tin and in the prices of foodstuffs such as wheat and rice. These developments – which are at least in part demand driven (and the Chinese economy itself makes a telling contribution here as a commodities buyer) – have in turn pushed up the values of exports from commodity-dependent regions such as Africa, South and Central America, and the CIS (Commonwealth of Independent States). Finally, the recurrent ebbs and flows evident in the export shares of the Middle East are simply a reflection of the medium-term path of the price of oil.

We have spent some time considering merchandise export performance as trade in goods accounts for around 75 per cent of total international trade; trade in services accounts for the remaining 25 per cent. Table 13.5 ranks the world's leading exporters in commercial services. Notice from the table that the UK comes in second; much higher than its 8th place in the merchandise export rankings. This primarily reflects the long-standing prowess of the City of London as a purveyor of financial services in international markets.

Table 13.5 Leading exporters in world trade in commercial services 2013 ($billion and %)

Rank	Country	Value ($bn)	Share (%)
1	United States	662	14.3
2	United Kingdom	293	6.3
3	Germany	286	6.2
4	France	236	5.1
5	China	205	4.4
6	India	151	3.2
7	Netherlands	147	3.2
8	Japan	145	3.1
9	Spain	145	3.1
10	Hong Kong China	133	2.9
11	Ireland	125	2.7
12	Singapore	122	2.6
13	Korea, Republic of	112	2.4
14	Italy	110	2.4
15	Belgium	106	2.3
16	Switzerland	93	2.0
17	Canada	78	1.7
18	Luxembourg	77	1.7
19	Sweden	75	1.6
20	Denmark	70	1.5

Source: WTO World Trade Report 2014

Simply, the UK has an established comparative advantage in financial services. Note that China is ranked 5th; in 1997 it was in 16th place. India, to take another rapidly developing economy, was outside the top 20 in 1997; in 2013 it was 6th. These examples suggest that the competitive edge long enjoyed by the old industrial nations is as much under challenge in services as it is in merchandise trade.

We are now aware of the distribution of international trade: we know something about which countries and regions enjoy most of it and which are enjoying the fastest growth in trade shares. But what of the *pattern* of trade: who trades mostly with whom? Some answers to this question can be found in Figure 13.3. The evidence here is that the world economy is characterized by heavy *intra*-regional trade processes. In 2012 internal trade in North America, Europe and Asia accounted for about half of global trade; while trade between these regions accounted for only about 20 per cent. Internal trade in Central and South America, the CIS, Africa and the Middle East is much more modest in scale, accounting in each case for a very small percentage of total world trade. For these regions trade relations with markets in North America, Europe and Asia are more important than markets in neighbouring countries. This is especially so in the case of Africa. Intra-regional African trade in 2012 was of the order of $81bn but African trade with Europe was almost six times as large at $451bn.

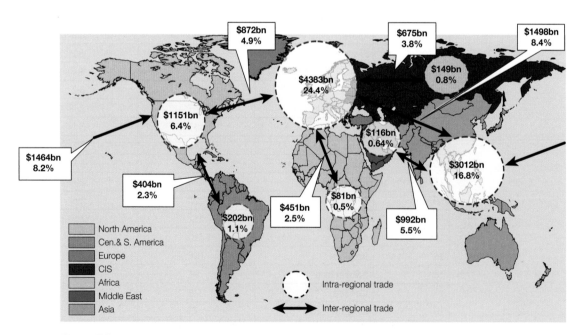

Figure 13.3 Selected intra and inter-regional merchandise trade flows, 2012

Source: Authors' calculations based on data from WTO International Trade Statistics, 2012

13.5 International trade policy

On the basis of the theory and evidence offered so far in this chapter, the issue of trade policy should, for all nations, be a relatively uncontentious one. Because it permits the deployment of resources in their most productive uses, together with the mutually advantageous exchange of the resulting maximized output and wider consumer choice, free and unrestricted trade should generally be the preferred option. This is one of the cast iron certainties of orthodox economics. Yet *all* nations *do* engage in many forms of protectionism. Indeed, in the post-1970 period protectionism has become more widespread than at any time since the interwar years. The obvious question arises: if free trade is so mutually advantageous, why protect?

Understanding protectionism

One of the most instructive ways to think about the development of trade policy involves use of the framework provided by *Institutionalist Economics*. The work of this school was first introduced in Chapter 5 in the context of a discussion of the theory of the firm. In Chapter 5, we described the institutionalist emphasis – exemplified in the writings of J.K. Galbraith (1908–2006) – on the evolutionary development of capitalist economies. Very simply, this approach suggests that because the world's economies are not all at the same stage of development they require different kinds of policy to help them flourish. In terms of trade policy, this means that for some nations, at particular stages, elements of protectionism are indeed appropriate.

In advancing this view Galbraith draws on the work of an early institutionalist and critic of Smith and Ricardo: the German economist Friedrich List (1789–1846). List was an advocate of German protectionism in the first half of the nineteenth century. His concern, reflecting the idea of different stages of national economic development, was that the strong industrial base of the then more advanced British economy would suppress the growth of new German industries. The development of the German economy as a whole would therefore be constrained unless its industries could be insulated from their superior British competitors. Such insulation was available through the imposition of **tariff**-based protection, which would raise the prices of imports from Britain. However, once German industrialization had attained a level of maturity that would permit it to compete on a more equal basis with Britain, then a liberal German trading regime would be appropriate. The important point here is that the form of trade policy an economy adopts must be in keeping with its particular stage of development; as the economy matures so the choice of trade policy will change. This conclusion is clearly at odds with the free trade recommendations of Smith and Ricardo. List memorably indicted free trade, from the perspective of the German economy, as a 'British racket'.

Tariff: a tax on traded goods. When levied on imports, the assumption is that importers will pass the tax on in the form of higher prices to domestic customers, thus reducing the quantity of imports demanded.

■ **Concept:** The **infant-industry argument** suggests that nascent domestic industries may need to be protected from mature foreign competitors until such time as they have acquired the necessary scale or expertise to compete openly with them.

As Galbraith notes, such views made List an early advocate of the **infant-industry argument** for protection. This supposes that protection is legitimate in cases where industrial development in an economy might be denied because of the presence of superior foreign competition. In these circumstances, protection offers a respite to infant domestic industries until they achieve a degree of maturity and self-sufficiency that allows them to survive and grow independently. Recall our recent reference to protection by East Asian NICs (such as South Korea) of their emerging industries a few decades ago. The 'Applying Economics to Business' box below contains a more recent example of trade policy in China, which is based on the infant-industry argument.

APPLYING ECONOMICS TO BUSINESS
China's exports of rare earths and infant-industry protection

China now produces 95 per cent of the world's rare earth elements. There are 17 of these, including neodymium, promethium, europium, terbium and dysprosium. Chances are, like us, you've never heard of them but they're an essential component of many of the hi-tech products we use every day such as mobile devices, fluorescent lighting and televisions.

Other countries, notably the US, have in the past been major producers of rare earths but comparative advantage has passed to China because it employs cheaper production techniques than are feasible elsewhere.

That's the recent history of specialization and trade in rare earths.

But there have recently been interesting developments in Chinese rare earths trade policy.

China has been accused by the US and others of limiting its exports of rare earths. Such a policy could cause difficulties for non-Chinese manufacturers who find it hard to get the supplies they need.

The US claims that China:

- imposes tariffs on rare earth exports;
- imposes quotas on the quantity of rare earths that can be exported in a given period;
- limits export permissions to certain kinds of firm.

Why might China do these things? One answer centres on the protection of infant industries in China. The Chinese economy is growing rapidly but a lot of economic activity has been in the form of low-cost low-tech production.

Like everyone else, China has aspirations to continue to develop more sophisticated forms of production too. Retaining rare earths might be a way to help bring this about.

We'll return to this story later in the chapter when we discuss the activities of the World Trade Organization (WTO), the body that oversees and tries to liberalize international trade.

Although the infant-industry argument gained wide currency in the nineteenth century when many economies were industrializing in the wake of the British lead, it is by no means absent from contemporary economic debate. Indeed, it is a curious irony that it is now interest groups in the *advanced nations* that have adopted the idea that temporary protection for acutely threatened domestic industries is a sensible form of trade policy. The notion of shifting comparative advantage is again relevant here.

Earlier we noted that the basis of the economic success of the newly industrializing countries (NICs) has been the development of new manufacturing industries that are able to compete in world markets against the formerly dominant industries of the advanced nations. The concern in the advanced countries is the loss of jobs, incomes and profits that this more intense competitive environment brings. As an illustration we briefly consider the imposition of tariffs by the European Union on shoe imports from China and Vietnam. Recall that a tariff is a tax on traded goods. In imposing tariffs of 16.5 per cent on China and 10 per cent on Vietnam respectively the EU expected the prices of imported footwear from these countries to rise as importers passed on the costs of the tariffs to European consumers. The EU's argument was that both countries had been **dumping** shoes at artificially low prices on its markets and thus competing unfairly with EU shoe producers.

Dumping: the export of goods to foreign markets with prices set below those normally charged in the home market.

But there is also a second issue here. This concerns the weakness of the EU's shoe industry against which comparative advantage has shifted. The problem lies in the nature of shoe making and where it is most efficiently conducted. Shoemaking is a labour-intensive process – it requires some materials and equipment certainly, but mostly it needs people with cutting and stitching skills; skills that while not particularly demanding to learn are hard to mechanize. This means that the cost of labour is a crucial consideration and, given that people are generally less costly to employ in China and Vietnam than they are in the EU, shoe production is more efficiently done in the former countries rather than the latter.

A telling illustration of the changing economics of footwear production is provided by the recent history of the UK shoemaker Clarks. This firm once produced shoes in 15 plants across the UK; now it sources much of what it sells in its UK shops from the Far East with operations in, as you might have guessed, China and Vietnam. An irony here then is that EU shoe tariffs may have raised the business costs of a UK firm. This, of course, was not the EU's intention; rather its purpose was to try to protect the last outposts of EU-based shoe production and employment in countries such as Portugal and Italy from what it saw as unfair competition.

One final explanation of protectionism concerns the relative influence and power of different interest groups in an economy. Protectionism protects whom? The answer is particular interest groups that lobby government to implement policies that will help *them*. Google image the phrase 'French farmers protest'. If you do you'll see a series of photos of tractors blocking roads, of milk and manure being dumped or even sprayed in public places and so on. We met the policy that French and other European farmers are worried they're about to lose when we discussed agricultural protection in Chapter 2. It's the EU's common agricultural policy (CAP). This subsidizes agriculture across the EU and so protects farmers' incomes.

We can make two useful points here about the CAP that follow from the work of Anne Krueger. First, the very fact that the policy exists may galvanize an interest group that gains from it. So creating the policy may be a lot easier than unwinding it. Second, the benefits of the CAP are focused on EU farmers but the costs of the policy are widely dispersed across the whole EU population.

This means that political lobbying in favour of the CAP is likely to be vociferous (manure in the road) and without any great countervailing pressure. Without the CAP the average citizen of Finland or Austria might get cheaper sugar (because it is cheaper on world markets than in the protected EU market) and pay a fraction less in taxes (their share of the cost of the CAP) but these are probably not things they are going to take to the streets about. So the narrow interests of the protectionist lobby tend to win out.

We now have a nuanced understanding of protection:

- It appears defensible in cases where new infant industries require less than full exposure to open competition for a period in order that they might mature.
- It may be demanded by firms when they are threatened by unfair forms of competition such as dumping.
- It also arises from political lobbying where the benefits of protection are concentrated but the costs diffuse.

We should also note that protection has in the past provided the springboard for the development of some of the most ardent of the modern free-trade promoting economies such as the United States and the UK (for more on this see Ha-Joon Chang's *Bad Samaritans*, our one thing you should read at the end of this chapter).

Where does all this leave the 'cast iron' case for free trade? We can further explore this question by reflecting upon the history of the main vehicle for the development of world trade policy over the postwar period: the General Agreement on Tariffs and Trade (GATT) (1947–1994), and its successor body, the World Trade Organization (WTO) (1995–).

The institutions of international trade policy: from GATT to the WTO

The GATT originated in the early postwar years as a means of securing tariff reductions and preventing new tariffs emerging among its original 23 signatory countries. The interwar period witnessed a huge escalation in retaliatory tariff protection involving many nations, causing a *two-thirds* fall in the value of world trade in the early 1930s. As international markets were closed off and world demand fell, producers cut back on the output of goods they could no longer sell and unemployment rose everywhere: the world economy entered its deepest ever *slump*. It was the connection between the slump and high tariffs that provided the motivation for the creation of the GATT so soon after the end of the Second World War: nations were determined that they would not repeat the protectionist mistakes of the 1930s.

Initially, the GATT was intended solely as an interim measure that would begin the process of cutting the vast array of tariffs accumulated in the 1930s; it was soon to have been superseded by the creation of a new international trade body. In the event, plans for this organization collapsed and instead the GATT matured from a mere treaty into an organization in its own right. In 1995 the GATT's permanent secretariat in Geneva and its membership, which now embraces 160 countries or so-called 'contracting parties', were inherited by its successor body: the World Trade Organization.

The GATT had three main objectives. These were to:

- Prevent an immediate postwar resumption of the kind of protectionism that had done so much damage in the 1930s.
- Dismantle the tariff structures built up during this period.
- Provide rules and protocols that would ensure that international trade relations were conducted on an *open* and *multilateral* basis.

In the 1930s too many nations had begun to act unilaterally and bilaterally: segmenting and preserving 'their' markets for themselves and their preferred partners. It was thought that the promotion of a multilateral environment was the natural way to prevent the same thing happening again. The work of the GATT over the postwar period as a whole was largely conducted in a series of negotiating 'rounds', each of which has attempted to address an agenda of tariff reduction. The rounds also provided a forum for the refinement of rules, which the GATT nations agreed would govern trading relations between them. We do not need to go into the detail here of each of the *eight* rounds that took place during the life of the GATT but it is useful to give a brief overview of the general course of their development.

The first half of the life of the GATT coincided with the postwar boom. As noted, during this period growth rates for the advanced nations were at an historic high and full employment ambitions were consistently fulfilled. These conditions provided a fertile background for the GATT rounds – six in all – which took place before 1970. Countries are more likely to lower trade barriers and expose domestic industries to international competition if the level of economic activity is generally high. In such circumstances, factors of production released from declining industries will be more quickly absorbed by new and expanding ones.

The longest and most notable of the pre-1970 rounds was the 1964–7 *Kennedy Round*. Although earlier meetings had succeeded in implementing significant tariff reductions, the Kennedy Round is credited with finally dismantling the tariff structures erected during the 1930s. This was clearly an important milestone in the development of the GATT as it meant that two out of three of its objectives had been achieved: there had been no resumption of the kind of protectionism that typified trade policy in the 1930s and the barriers to multilateral trade which had emerged during that decade had now gone.

Unfortunately, the Kennedy Round also marked the high water mark of GATT's achievements. After 1970, new problems of protectionism emerged onto the world stage. We emphasize the word 'new' here to distinguish post-1970 protectionism from the 'old' tariff structures of the 1930s. But where did the **new protectionism** come from? Part of the answer lies in the ending of the postwar boom. The benign economic climate associated with strong growth and full employment was replaced after 1970 by a much more sombre one conditioned, in the advanced nations in particular, by much slower growth rates and rising unemployment. Now, whereas the boom period made tariff concessions easier to justify, the new recession-seeded era made nations much more reluctant to expose their economies to more intense international competition when lower levels of economic activity meant that alternative sources of employment would be harder to find for factors released from uncompetitive industries.

The end of the boom was not the only issue affecting trade policy from the early 1970s; important shifts in comparative advantage were also evident at this time. In particular, the noted tendency of *industrialization* among formerly 'less developed' nations was decisively underway. We described earlier how the NICs were able to start competing with the advanced nations in certain labour-intensive branches of manufacturing – textiles, clothing, footwear and sports goods are among the most typical examples – by using the relatively low-paid labour available to them. This process posed clear difficulties for the equivalent industries in the advanced nations and at a time when the advanced economies as a whole were experiencing an economic slowdown.

How then did threatened interests in the advanced nations react? The simple answer is that they lobbied governments for protection from the NICs but because of the presence and authority of GATT this had to be implemented in a *non-tariff* form. Recall again the difference between the old and the new protectionism. The old protectionism of the 1930s was tariff based; the new protectionism post-1970 is not. In fact the new protectionism assumes a variety of guises. Its purpose is to enhance the competitive position of domestic industry vis-à-vis its rivals. This means that protection can include measures such as:

- state subsidy (which reduces the costs of production to industry and allows it to lower prices)
- preferential state procurement (where governments make their purchases from *domestic* industry alone)
- discriminatory administrative action (where imports are discouraged by the imposition of arduous bureaucratic procedures)
- quota restrictions on imports
- and, finally, 'persuading' exporters to voluntarily limit their exports.

The latter form of new protection – the so-called *voluntary export restraint* (VER) – was particularly insidious. The GATT trade rules explicitly committed member nations to a multilateral philosophy. This made it very difficult for individual nations to be selected as *particular* targets of protection. For example, the EU could only legally place tariffs on footwear imports from China and Vietnam if these countries are demonstrably guilty of competitive practices – such as dumping – that GATT recognized as unfair. The EU could not simply discriminate against footwear from China and Vietnam because the EU's own firms were unable to compete with their Far Eastern rivals on price or quality. If it had wanted to protect its domestic market from competition it could have legally imposed non-discriminatory tariffs on footwear imports as a whole. But this might have provoked other countries to take entirely legal retaliatory measures against the EU.

However, if the EU had been able to persuade China and Vietnam to *voluntarily* limit their exports then this potential problem would have been solved. A bilateral agreement on the *export* side would have allowed the EU to discriminate against Far Eastern imports alone without formally breaking GATT principles. China and Vietnam might have been amenable to this course of action because it would have presented them with a securely open export market (albeit a smaller one) and for fear of more draconian EU protection should this option fail.

The discriminatory potential of the VER made it an increasingly popular measure with the advanced nations in the context of shifting comparative advantage. Because they were selectively threatened by particular NICs in particular industries, they required the kind of finely tuned protection the VER offers. Moreover, the VER increasingly became a tool for the management of trade between the *advanced* nations. For example, Japanese car exports to the EU and the US were periodically limited by VER agreements. Recognizing the threat to openness in international markets posed by VERs, the *Uruguay GATT Round* (1986–94) agreed that they should be phased out over a 10-year period: VERs became illegal in 2004.

That many countries resorted to the use of VERs did not mean that discriminatory action in trade policy was forbidden under the GATT institutional framework. It was possible for contracting parties to protect their markets in the face of illegal or destabilizing competition from particular countries. This means that, *in certain circumstances*, if (say) Canada thought that electrical goods imported from France were edging out its own electrical goods firms in the Canadian market, it could take action against France. There were three main grounds for such discriminatory retaliation. These were to:

- Combat dumping, as in the case of our example of EU tariffs on shoes from China and Vietnam.
- Offset subsidies by foreign governments in support of their industries. Here countervailing duties could be levied on goods from offending countries.
- Facilitate *temporary* protection from a surge in imports that may have seriously injured domestic industries.

What was *not* permitted, though, was discriminatory tariff protection by Canada against France or any other economy because some Canadian firms were outcompeted by their rivals. A loss of competitiveness in the Ricardian sense is not a bad thing and should not be resisted. It merely denotes that a country needs to reallocate its resources away from areas where it is less efficient and towards those areas in which it has or may develop a comparative advantage.

● Think Point

Given the Ricardian insistence that shifting comparative advantage be embraced rather than resisted why do you think that so many countries around the world still resort to protectionism when their domestic industries are threatened?

The main problem here is the *speed* at which comparative advantage may shift and the relatively slow and painful process of resource reallocation. As countries like China, Vietnam, India and others continue to develop they are going to get better at producing lots of goods and services. When this process happens demand will switch rapidly in their favour leaving the former producers of these things in other countries unemployed. This *is* an opportunity for resource reallocation but such a process hardly ever occurs without a protracted and painful period of adjustment. This is the hard truth that protectionism often seeks to delay.

The Uruguay Round (1986–94): extending trade liberalization and dealing with the new protectionism

The Uruguay Round was the final GATT programme of trade liberalization. It was notable for three features:

- The World Trade Organization replaced the GATT
- The EU and US/Cairns Group dispute
- Creation of the dispute settlement process

World Trade Organization replaces the GATT

The Uruguay Round provided for the replacement of the GATT with the World Trade Organization (WTO). Essentially, the WTO now presides over a *framework of agreements* for the continuing liberalization of the international trading environment. Figure 13.4 sketches out this framework. Note that the GATT itself continues as an *agreement* alongside the newer parts of the liberalization agenda such as the *General Agreement on Trade in Services* (GATS). The emergence of GATS reflects the increasing importance of service trade in the world economy. This now accounts for about one quarter of total trade. The agreement on *Trade Related Aspects of Intellectual Property Rights* (TRIPS) is intended to provide international safeguards for copyrights, patents and trademarks.

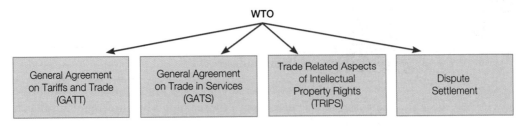

Figure 13.4 The World Trade Organization's agreements

The EU and US/Cairns Group dispute

For all the popular adulation given to its successful completion the Uruguay Round very nearly ended in crisis and collapse. The uncertainty was the result of a long-running dispute between, on the one hand, the European Union and, on the other, the United States and a disparate group of food-producing countries known as the **Cairns Group**. The EU, which heavily subsidizes agricultural production, was reluctant to concede the principle of completely free trade in agriculture that the US/Cairns Group preferred. Ultimately, a compromise position acceptable to both sides did emerge but not before the Uruguay Round had been brought to the brink of disaster.

The significance of this dispute lies less in its own seismic proportions, though these were considerable, than in its general form. Both the EU and the US/Cairns Group are collective representations of very powerful trading interests of which there are an increasing number in the international economy. The previously mentioned North American Free Trade Agreement (NAFTA), for example, which came into force in 1994, binds together the markets of the US, Canada and Mexico; while the Asia-Pacific Economic Co-operation (APEC) forum plans a similar arrangement for an even larger number of countries, including the US and Japan at some time in the future. Now although such groupings are organized on the basis of *internal* free trade, they offer no similar external commitments and there is a natural concern, reflecting the experiences of the Uruguay Round, that the segmentation of the international economy into *trading blocs* of this type might provide an environment in which large-scale (inter-bloc) protectionism becomes a distinct possibility. The last time the world economy witnessed equivalent segmentation was in the 1930s when rampant protectionism severely threatened the integrity of the world economy.

Cairns group: comprises Argentina, Australia, Brazil, Canada, Chile, Columbia, Fiji, Hungary, Indonesia, Malaysia, Philippines, New Zealand, Thailand and Uruguay.

The dispute settlement process

Dispute settlement: the jewel in the WTO's crown

Finally, the Uruguay Round created what the WTO considers to be the jewel in its crown: a legal process for the settlement of trade disputes between members. The ambition here is to try to help countries resolve differences in trade matters without the need for protectionism, and, crucially, to time-limit protectionism when it arises.

The dispute settlement process had by the end of 2014 dealt with almost 500 individual cases. Of these about 200 were in process while around a further 200 had been resolved by WTO-facilitated negotiation between the countries concerned or by the implementation of a dispute settlement ruling. Only in five cases had

© Chris Mulhearn

there been a failure on the part of a member country to fully comply with a WTO ruling.

The WTO's dispute settlement process is potentially a powerful tool for dealing with protectionism. All WTO members now have an avenue that can be quickly used to test the legality of any form of trade restriction that they feel is unfair and breaks the principle of a free and open trading environment. But note that the spirit of the process is not to judge and punish errant countries but to try to help them cooperatively resolve issues. The first stage in the dispute settlement process involves the complainant and respondent countries in consultations that can last up to 60 days, during which they may attempt to settle their differences without resorting to legal formalities. More than 150 cases so far dealt with by the WTO have been resolved by this kind of interaction. The 'Applying Economics to Business' box below considers a case where the dispute settlement process ruling was reached and accepted by the interested parties. This updates our earlier discussion of China's trade restrictions on rare earth elements.

APPLYING ECONOMICS TO BUSINESS

WTO dispute settlement in the case of China's rare earths trade policy

You will recall our earlier 'Applying economics to business' box and its discussion of China's possible infant-industry-inspired protection of its hi-tech industries. This may be done by restricting exports of rare earth elements. China controls 95 per cent of the world market in rare earths.

In 2012 the US initiated consultations with China under the terms of the WTO's dispute settlement process. Subsequently a WTO dispute settlement panel found that China's duties and quotas on exports of rare earths and its limits on the rights of firms to trade in these commodities were all inconsistent with China's WTO obligations.

China did not contest the findings but did seek some clarifications on the rights of WTO members to take steps to protect and conserve their exhaustible natural resources.

In 2014 China agreed to implement the dispute settlement recommendations and ruling, but stated that it would take some time to do so.

If countries cannot be reconciled, cases like the one above are usually speedily decided on their behalf by the WTO and the crucial point is that, *whatever the outcome*, trade restrictions should be lifted. In tandem with the wider WTO rules that prohibit forms of new protection, such as the voluntary export restraint, dispute settlement offers the promise of a significant leap forward in the quest for a more open trade relations between WTO members.

The WTO's first test: the Doha Round crisis

But whether or not the WTO will live up to these expectations is for the moment an open question. A new *Millennium Round* of trade negotiations was to have been launched in Seattle in December 1999. However, the WTO's Seattle conference was the focus of vociferous and disruptive lobbying by direct action groups. Even more significantly, stark differences between the developed and less developed countries over the nature and purpose of the Millennium Round meant that little progress was made.

The developing countries harboured understandable resentments that the Uruguay Round mostly addressed the concerns of the rich nations and paid little attention to their interests. For example, the agreements on trade in services (GATS) and intellectual property rights (TRIPS) principally benefit the developed countries. It is they who have the sophisticated economic infrastructures capable of producing service exports, and they who most require their considerable investments in intellectual property to be defended. Countries in the poorest parts of the world have more modest trade aspirations.

For example, the developing countries might have been more impressed by the Uruguay Round had it promoted greater liberalization of *agricultural trade*. It is through agricultural exports that many poor countries pay their way in the international economy. Such exports are, for many, the principal source of the foreign currencies necessary to buy vital foreign goods. Unfortunately, as noted, agricultural issues appeared to be shakily resolved in the Uruguay Round by an agreement primarily between the EU and the US; the less developed country agenda was sidelined. That the developed countries failed to realize a much more liberal trading environment in agriculture is hardly surprising. The EU, to take one example, spent almost €40bn on agricultural and related subsidies in 2012. Such subsidies help to keep the produce of farmers from the developing countries out of the developed world's markets (see Chapter 2 for details of the EU's common agricultural policy).

However, agriculture was revisited in the *Doha Round* (the revised name for the Millennium Round), which was designed to promote both global trade and express an explicit *development agenda* – one intended to reflect the trade concerns and aspirations of the world's poorer countries. Unfortunately, as in the case of the Uruguay Round, progress has been neither timely nor smooth. The Doha Round was supposed to have concluded by 1 January 2005 but it staggered on past that date and actually collapsed in 2008, with the divisive issue of agricultural protection once again proving one of several stumbling blocks. At the time of writing there are renewed attempts to revive the Round but whether or not these will be successful is unclear.

The difficulty the WTO now faces hinges on the tension between what it appears to have achieved in creating a mechanism for tackling specific trade disputes between its members, and the grander conceptualization of an international trade environment that is more open and that fairly respects the particular interests and concerns of developing and developed country groups. Dispute settlement may be the jewel in the WTO's crown but that won't count for very much if the crown itself begins to look tarnished and rusted. Because agreement about fair answers to the big questions in international trade, such as agricultural protection, cannot for the moment be reached – and the collapse of the Doha Round is clear evidence that they can't – the WTO's legitimacy may increasingly become an issue.

SUMMARY

- International trade permits economies to push the boundaries of specialization and exchange beyond the confines of their own borders. The Ricardian theory of comparative advantage suggests that all participant economies can gain from trade. This conventional wisdom contrasts strongly with older mercantilist notions that trade is a zero sum game.
- The policy implication of comparative advantage is that free trade offers benefits to all trading economies. However, where comparative advantage is shifting, there may be claims for protection arising from threatened interests in particular countries or regions.
- Since 1945, international trade policy has been possessed of a broad liberalizing ethos under the auspices of the GATT and latterly the WTO. However, the ending of the postwar boom and shifting comparative advantage between the developed and less developed countries led to the re-emergence of protectionism in a new, non-tariff, form.
- The WTO's dispute settlement process appears to be a promising mechanism for the resolution of particular trade disputes.
- The collapse of the Doha Development Round poses a serious threat to the legitimacy of the WTO.

KEY TERMS

- International trade
- Specialization and exchange
- Protection
- Mercantilism
- Comparative advantage
- Shifting comparative advantage

- Trade policy
- The General Agreement on Tariffs and Trade
- Uruguay Round
- The World Trade Organization
- Dispute settlement
- Doha Round

QUESTIONS FOR DISCUSSION

1. What are the advantages of trade?
2. Explain the arguments underlying the theory of comparative advantage.
3. What were the later developments in trade theory that built upon Ricardian notions of comparative advantage?
4. Describe the major patterns of world trade that have evolved since 1945 and explain the notion of shifting comparative advantage.
5. Why does protectionism arise and what are its main forms?
6. What are the main issues confronting the WTO?

EVERYDAY ECONOMICS 13.1 ANSWERS

1. **Tinned tomatoes** Italy exports around 75 per cent of the world supply of tinned tomatoes. The basis of comparative advantage here is a Mediterranean climate particularly suited to tomato cultivation.

2. **The London School of Economics Students' Union Chinese Society** Universities in the UK and US attract large numbers of students from all over the world. Both are countries with long experience and heavy investment in higher education. They also teach in English, the world's most popular second language. These factors suggest that the UK

and the US have a comparative advantage in higher education.

3. **A car wash** Do you or your family own a car? Do you wash it yourself? The proliferation of car washes in many economies suggests that a lot of car owners feel they do not have a comparative advantage in the struggle to keep their cars clean. They would rather spend a relatively small sum of money to have someone else do it quickly for them rather than spend a longer time with effort doing it themselves.

4. **An oxpecker sitting on a zebra** Oxpeckers are birds that feed on

the parasites infesting animals such as zebra and oxen. They provide an example of comparative advantage in nature. Zebra and oxen might relieve the itch of parasites by rubbing themselves against a tree or the ground. But it's more convenient to allow oxpeckers to do the job instead. Oxpeckers also warn their hosts of the approach of predators. The oxpeckers' reward for these services is food.

This is an example of what in natural history is called a mutually advantageous symbiotic relationship. In economic terms it's simply comparative advantage.

ONE THING YOU SHOULD READ

'My Six-Year-Old Son Should Get a Job' (Chapter 3 of *Bad Samaritans* by Ha-Joon Chang)

Ha-Joon Chang's book is about economic development – how the world's rich countries managed to grow in the way that they did and how the world's poor economies are mostly prevented from doing the same. The book's title – *Bad Samaritans* – is the name Chang gives to the rich countries and the major international economic policy institutions such as the WTO. His argument is that these countries – such as Britain and the US – owe their own development to protectionist trade policy and other forms of state intervention in the economy as practised in the nineteenth century and earlier. But now that they're rich and powerful this is conveniently forgotten as the rich countries seek to impose free trade as the sole route to development on everyone else. Chang thinks that free trade won't work for the poorer nations. Instead they should protect their infant industries until they are strong enough to compete with the rich and powerful.

Chapter 3 of the book gives a good summary of this argument.

After reading the chapter, answer the following questions.

1. Why is the suggestion that Ha-Joon Chang's six-year-old son should get a job a good critique of the case for universal free trade?
2. Even if liberalized trade brings some benefits to poorer countries, why might they be worse off in overall terms? (Hint: this has to do with the adequacy of compensation mechanisms in poorer countries.)
3. Ha-Joon Chang is South Korean. What does he have to say about the trade policies that enabled the stunning development of his own economy?
4. Why is the North Korean experience an illustration that isolationism is not good for economic development?
5. Is Ha-Joon Chang anti-trade?

14

the balance of payments and exchange rates

KEY ISSUES

What is the balance of payments?

Why does balance of payments imbalance matter and what are its implications for business?

What are exchange rates?

How are exchange rates determined?

What are the main forms of exchange rate policy?

Why do exchange rates and exchange rate policy matter for business?

CONTENTS

14.1 Introduction — **428**

14.2 The balance of payments accounts — **428**

14.3 The balance of payments and business — **440**

14.4 Exchange rates and exchange rate determination — **442**

14.5 Exchange rate systems — **449**

14.6 Exchange rate systems in practice — **457**

14.7 The euro — **465**

14.8 The balance of payments, exchange rates and business — **472**

14.1   Introduction

Having discussed a number of general issues of international trade, we now turn to consider the trading relationships of individual economies. The balance of payments provides both a way of thinking about how a country connects to the wider global environment and a means of measuring that connection. In what follows we first discuss the nature of the balance of payments accounts and notions of balance of payments equilibria and disequilibria, before offering a brief overview of the recent balance of payments performances of some selected economies. Because international markets, like all others, are coordinated by price signals it is also necessary to develop an understanding of the role played in the international economy by the different currencies in which prices are quoted. Accordingly, this chapter offers some discussion of exchange rates and different exchange rate systems.

Both the balance of payments and exchange rates are important for business. The condition of an economy's balance of payments may give rise to different forms of government policy that have significant implications for domestic firms inside the economy and for foreign ones outside it. Exchange rates have a strong bearing on firms' capacities to sell goods and services in both domestic and foreign markets.

14.2   The balance of payments accounts

Balance of payments: a record of the transactions that take place between the residents of one country and the rest of the world over a given time period (usually one year).

The balance of payments accounts record the transactions that occur between the residents of one country and the rest of the world over a given period, usually one year. Such transactions take the form of trade in *goods* and *services*, *capital movements*, and *financial flows*. These three forms of transaction give rise to a compartmentalization of the balance of payments accounts. Trade in goods and services is recorded in the *current account,* capital movements are recorded in the *capital account,* and financial flows are recorded in the *financial account.* Table 14.1 summarizes the main components of the UK balance of payments accounts; we briefly review each below.

Current account

As is evident from Table 14.1, the current account has two main components: visible trade in goods and invisible trade in services. Because they are associated with monetary *inflows*, exports of goods produced in the UK are recorded as *positive* visible trade entries. Imports of goods on the other hand, because they give rise to monetary *outflows*, are recorded as *negative* entries. Thus, if visible trade is in overall surplus (value of exports > value of imports) its value will be positive, reflecting a net monetary inflow from trade in goods. If the situation is reversed then the resultant deficit (a net monetary outflow) on visibles will have a negative sign.

Table 14.1 Structure of the UK balance of payments

Current Account
Visible trade
• Exports of goods [*monetary inflow*]
• Imports of goods [*monetary outflow*]
Invisible trade
• Services (financial; transport and travel; military) [*inflow and outflow*]
• Investment income (interest, profits and dividends) [*inflow and outflow*]
• Transfers (non-pecuniary and EU contributions) [*inflow and outflow*]
Capital Account
Transfers (migrants' transfers, EU regional fund etc.)
Financial Account
Foreign Direct Investment (FDI) [*inflow and outflow*] ⎫
Portfolio investment [*inflow and outflow*] ⎬ Usually considered long-term flows
Financial Derivatives [*inflow and outflow*] ⎭
Other investment [*inflow and outflow*]
Use of Reserves of Foreign Currency [*inflow and outflow*]
Net errors and omissions

Invisible trade includes trade in services, income arising from investments, and transfers. Similar positive and negative entry conventions apply here. The cost of a holiday taken in the UK by a resident from another country is an exported UK service and, because it is associated with a monetary *inflow*, is recorded as a *positive* invisible trade entry; while the transport costs of shipping using a foreign carrier is an imported service (a monetary outflow) and is recorded as a *negative* service trade entry. Again, if the value of service exports exceeds the value of service imports, then the resultant invisibles surplus has a positive sign, reflecting a net monetary inflow. If the situation is reversed then the resultant deficit on invisibles (a net monetary outflow) will have a negative sign.

Capital account

The capital account contains a number of relatively less significant capital flows associated with, for example, EU regional fund transfers, transfers by UK migrants back to the UK, and transfers by foreign migrants living in the UK to their home economies.

Financial account

The financial account contains five broad kinds of transaction:

- *Foreign direct investment:* Foreign direct investment (FDI) is investment capital provided to a firm from a source in another country where the investor has a direct influence on the business activities of the recipient firm. FDI transactions include those in real assets such as factories, machinery and equipment, retail infrastructure and so on.

● *Portfolio investment:* Portfolio investment is the buying or selling of British and foreign share capital. In contrast to foreign direct investors, portfolio investors have no entitlement to make executive decisions about the activities of firms in which they have an interest.

● *Transactions in financial derivatives:* Financial derivatives are instruments that may be used for risk management purposes. For example, for a fee, a firm may buy an *option* to purchase a given amount of a particular currency at a particular exchange rate at some specified time in the future, thus insuring itself against the possibility of excessive exchange rate movements.

● *'Other' investment* – mostly borrowing and lending: The other investment category mainly covers borrowing and lending by the banking and non-banking private sector. Because it is associated with a monetary inflow, borrowing is usually recorded as a positive item, while lending outflows are usually recorded as negative items. However, very occasionally, the repayment of liabilities can result in these signs being reversed.

● *The use of reserve assets:* The final form of transaction recorded in the financial account mainly concerns changes in the foreign exchange reserves of the Bank of England. For reasons that we will explain shortly, an increase in reserves is recorded as a negative item and a decrease in reserves as a positive one.

Foreign exchange reserves: stocks of foreign currencies held by central banks.

How the balance of payments works

There is another way to interpret the structure of the balance of payments. This entails the identification of two broad elements that we can distinguish by reference to their principal purpose in the balance of payments accounts. These are autonomous and accommodating transactions.

Autonomous transaction: one undertaken for its own sake.

Autonomous transactions are transactions undertaken spontaneously for their own sake. All transactions on the current account are autonomous in nature; a UK resident, for example, buys an imported good because he or she finds some personal benefit in doing so. Similarly, capital account transactions such as migrants' transfers can be considered to be autonomous. On the financial account, both FDI and portfolio investment are autonomous because they originate in the profit- and dividend-related ambitions of those who make them. Now, the remaining items in the financial account – mostly other investment, which is borrowing and lending – are accommodating transactions. These are undertaken mainly in order to make international trade possible and, therefore, to help the balance of payments to actually balance. Table 14.2 illustrates how they work.

Accommodating transaction: one undertaken for balance of payments purposes.

In Table 14.2 we show a hypothetical deficit of –£1bn for each of the current account and the long-term investment element of the financial account. For ease of analysis we assume the capital account to be in balance (that is, it sums to zero). Overall then, autonomous transactions are in deficit to the tune

Table 14.2 How the balance of payments works

Current balance		Because autonomous transactions are in a combined deficit of −£2bn, accommodating transactions must be made to cover the deficit. Here the suggestion is that the UK must borrow to cover the amount it owes to foreign residents. However, the deficit could be alternatively accommodated using currency reserves.
all are *autonomous* transactions	net deficit of −£1bn [*outflow*]	
Capital balance		
autonomous transactions	zero	
Financial balance of which:		
autonomous transactions (FDI & portfolio investment)	net deficit of −£1bn [*outflow*]	
accommodating transactions	borrowing of +£2bn [*inflow*]	
Net errors and omissions	zero	

of −£2bn. This means that economic agents in the UK have sold goods, services, firms, shares and so on abroad worth £2bn *less* than foreign agents have managed to sell in the UK over the period in question. The −£2bn is in effect a collective debt owed by the UK to the rest of the world: a *net monetary claim* on UK residents. How is this debt settled, bearing in mind that foreign residents will want to be paid in their own currencies rather than British pounds sterling? The answer is that payment is facilitated by (positive) accommodating transactions of £2bn. The UK must either borrow the £2bn equivalent of foreign currency that it requires, draw on the reserves of foreign currency that it already holds, or undertake some combination of both. This action leaves the balance of payments accounts as a whole in *balance* (that is, neither in surplus or deficit).

What happens if the situation is reversed and the UK runs a surplus on its autonomous transactions? Here, UK residents have a *net monetary claim* on the rest of the world: foreign residents owe a debt that must be settled in pounds sterling. In this case the UK can conduct (negative) accommodating transactions that involve lending the necessary sterling abroad. In addition or alternatively, the Bank of England may supply sterling abroad in exchange for foreign currencies, thus increasing its reserves of foreign currency (but note that, as suggested, the increase must be by convention represented by a negative sign).

Regardless of the precise course of action taken, it should be clear that, once again, net autonomous transactions are counterbalanced by equivalent net accommodating transactions. In the situation (and its inverse) depicted in Table 14.2, *net errors and omissions* must be zero. Net errors and omissions indicate any measurement discrepancies between autonomous and accommodating transactions. In our example there are none, but this is seldom the case in reality. Thus, the net errors and omissions entry permits the balance of payments to balance in an 'accounting' sense.

Surplus and deficit on the balance of payments

Table 14.3 describes the actual UK balance of payments position for 2012. To understand the table, note that panel (a) sums all autonomous transactions; that is, current balance + capital balance + net FDI + net portfolio investment + net financial derivatives. This gives a figure of –£248,777m, meaning that, in 2012, the UK had a net monetary liability with the rest of the world of this amount. To meet this liability the UK undertook accommodating transactions as described in panel (b). Here, the accommodating transactions total is found by summing net other investment + reserve assets, giving a figure of £241,586m. In the absence of any errors and omissions, the autonomous total (–£248,777m) and the accommodating total £241,586m would balance out at zero. Clearly

Table 14.3 UK balance of payments 2012 (£m)[1]

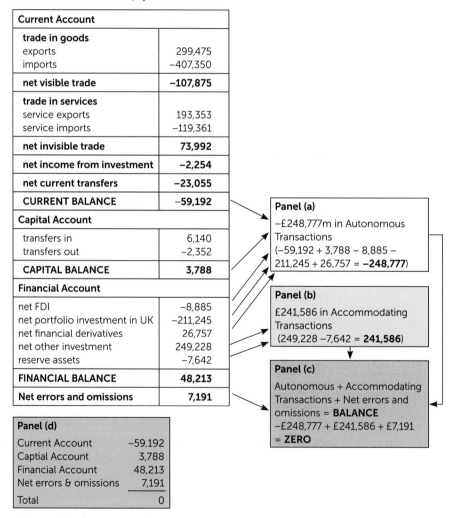

Current Account	
trade in goods	
exports	299,475
imports	−407,350
net visible trade	**−107,875**
trade in services	
service exports	193,353
service imports	−119,361
net invisible trade	**73,992**
net income from investment	**−2,254**
net current transfers	**−23,055**
CURRENT BALANCE	**−59,192**
Capital Account	
transfers in	6,140
transfers out	−2,352
CAPITAL BALANCE	**3,788**
Financial Account	
net FDI	−8,885
net portfolio investment in UK	−211,245
net financial derivatives	26,757
net other investment	249,228
reserve assets	−7,642
FINANCIAL BALANCE	**48,213**
Net errors and omissions	**7,191**

Panel (a)
−£248,777m in Autonomous Transactions
(−59,192 + 3,788 − 8,885 − 211,245 + 26,757 = **−248,777**)

Panel (b)
£241,586 in Accommodating Transactions
(249,228 −7,642 = **241,586**)

Panel (c)
Autonomous + Accommodating Transactions + Net errors and omissions = **BALANCE**
−£248,777 + £241,586 + £7,191 = **ZERO**

Panel (d)	
Current Account	−59,192
Captial Account	3,788
Financial Account	48,213
Net errors & omissions	7,191
Total	0

[1]Some minor accounts have been subsumed into major ones for ease of presentation

Source: ONS: The Pink Book, 2013

they don't and the difference between them is accounted for by net errors and omissions of £7,191. Panel (c) shows that when net errors and omissions are taken into account the balance of payments does indeed sum to zero. Panel (d) simply sums each of the three balance of payments accounts together with net errors and omissions; the total is again zero.

Table 14.3 also allows us to comment on an element of apparent ambiguity in the balance of payments. It is true that, in any given period, the balance of payments must balance as overseas debts or credits are settled, but how does this square with the notions of balance of payments surplus and deficit introduced in Chapter 8? How can the balance of payments always balance and simultaneously be in surplus or deficit? A balance of payments surplus or deficit in fact refers only to autonomous transactions and then, as Table 14.1 indicates, because FDI and portfolio investment flows tend to be long term and thus may be more stable, to autonomous transactions on the current account. Capital account transactions are typically small in relative terms (see Table 14.3). Thus balance of payments surplus or deficit often focuses on the current account only.

Finally, we should note that the notions of balance of payments surplus and deficit introduced here rest on the assumption of a prevailing fixed exchange rate system or an environment in which exchange rates are managed by the authorities rather then left to market forces. In Section 14.5 we demonstrate that a market-determined flexible exchange rate system has the effect, in theory, of automatically eliminating balance of payments disequilibria.

Fixed exchange rate: one that is fixed at a predetermined level by intervention by the country's central bank in the foreign exchange market.

Influences upon the current and financial accounts

What are the main determinants of *autonomous* current and financial account transactions as depicted in Table 14.1? What factors influence imports, exports and longer-term investment flows?

To take the current account first, the demand for imports and exports may be analysed in exactly the same way as the demand for any good or service. In Chapter 2 we demonstrated that a picture of demand – quite literally a picture in the shape of a demand curve – is built up using *price* as a starting point. Other factors, such as *income* and *tastes*, are then admitted for consideration.

The demand for imports

Following the same process, we can say that the demand for imports will be determined, in part, by their prices relative to the prices of home-produced alternatives that can act as import substitutes. The obvious complication here is that the relative price of imports is influenced by:

- the price-setting behaviour of domestic and foreign producers
- changes in the *exchange rate*.

In the former case, if the price of imports is increasing at a slower rate than that for home-produced alternatives (that is, the rate of inflation in the rest of the world is below that in the home economy) then imports will become more competitive.

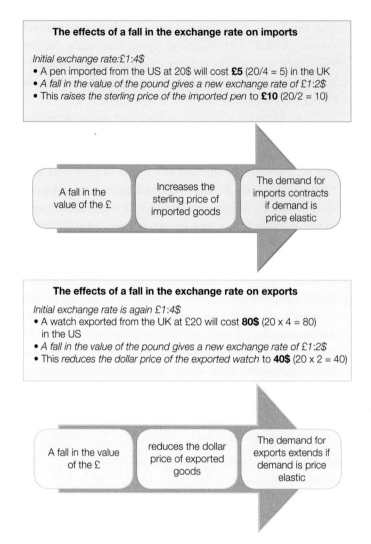

The effects of a fall in the exchange rate on imports

Initial exchange rate:£1:4$
- A pen imported from the US at 20$ will cost **£5** (20/4 = 5) in the UK
- *A fall in the value of the pound gives a new exchange rate of £1:2$*
- This *raises the sterling price of the imported pen* to **£10** (20/2 = 10)

| A fall in the value of the £ | Increases the sterling price of imported goods | The demand for imports contracts if demand is price elastic |

The effects of a fall in the exchange rate on exports

Initial exchange rate is again £1:4$
- A watch exported from the UK at £20 will cost **80$** (20 x 4 = 80) in the US
- *A fall in the value of the pound gives a new exchange rate of £1:2$*
- This *reduces the dollar price of the exported watch* to **40$** (20 x 2 = 40)

| A fall in the value of the £ | reduces the dollar price of exported goods | The demand for exports extends if demand is price elastic |

Figure 14.1 The effects of a fall in the exchange rate

In considering the influence of the exchange rate on import demand, it will be sufficient to proceed by means of a simple example. Figure 14.1 demonstrates the effect of a fall in the sterling exchange rate upon the price, expressed in pounds, of an import from the US.

Because the fall in the pound's value means that *more* pounds are required to obtain a given amount of dollars, the price of an import from the US must *increase*. Assuming that demand is price elastic (that is, greater than 1), it follows *ceteris paribus* that a fall in the sterling exchange rate will precipitate a contraction in the demand for imports. Conversely, on the same assumptions, an increase in the sterling exchange rate will be associated with an extension in the demand for imports, as their domestic price falls.

The level of demand for imports is also affected by changes in domestic incomes. Higher domestic incomes facilitate additional expenditure on goods and services

© Royalty-Free/Corbis

Britain has a taste for tea so a lot of it is imported

generally, some of which will be on imports. As will be recalled from Chapter 9, this involves the concept of the marginal propensity to import, which generally implies that the demand for imports varies positively with domestic incomes. Finally, the tastes and preferences of domestic consumers will clearly influence the demand for imports. For example, British residents drink more tea than residents of other European countries. The demand for imports will also be affected by other non-price factors such as their quality, design, degree of innovation and delivery time. Take the really big global brands: Apple, Samsung, BMW, Microsoft and so on. How did they acquire such elevated status? By getting their economics right in the world markets in which they compete and answering correctly (think back to Chapter 1) the three basic economic questions: what should we produce, how and for whom?

The demand for exports

Export demand is similarly governed by the price of exports relative to the prices of goods produced by competitors abroad, and by income and tastes. To begin with relative prices, we may say that if inflation in the home economy is greater than that prevailing in the rest of the world, then export demand will contract due to declining international price competitiveness. On the other hand, lower domestic inflation will be associated with improving international price competitiveness and an extension in export demand.

The exchange rate also remains an important influence but in the case of export demand it works in the opposite direction to that described earlier. From Figure 14.1, it can be seen that a fall in the exchange rate, because it reduces the number of dollars that have to be exchanged to obtain a given number of pounds, has the effect of *lowering* the price of UK exports to the US. Assuming that demand is price elastic, it follows *ceteris paribus* that a fall in the sterling exchange rate will precipitate an extension in the demand for UK exports. Conversely, on the same assumptions, an increase in the sterling exchange rate will be associated with a contraction in the demand for exports, as their price (in foreign markets) rises. Export demand is also a function of *foreign* incomes, tastes and other non-price factors. If incomes overseas are rising or foreign consumer preferences favour exports, then clearly demand will increase and vice versa.

Factors affecting investment flows

Turning to the financial account, it is possible to identify three main influences upon autonomous investment flows: expectations of exchange rate changes, nominal interest rate differentials between countries and differences in the perceived profitability of investments overseas.

- First, where exchange rate changes can be anticipated, it is possible for adroit investors to sell a currency about to fall in value or to buy one about to increase in value. In both cases it is possible to reap capital gains. For example, holders of sterling in the run up to the European exchange rate mechanism crisis in the autumn of 1992 (which forced down the value of the pound) would have been able to realize a sterling profit had they bought German marks before the crisis and then sold them afterwards when marks quickly became worth more in sterling terms. This means that expectations of a fall in the value of a currency will lead to a capital outflow, while expectations of an increase in the value of a currency will be likely to prompt a capital inflow.

- Second, because *ceteris paribus* higher domestic nominal interest rates improve the returns on financial assets, it follows that they will be associated with capital inflows. Lower nominal interest rates, presaging poorer returns, will result in capital outflows.

- Finally, a perceived improvement in the profitability of new overseas investments relative to the anticipated returns on new foreign investments in the domestic economy will be associated with a net capital outflow and vice versa.

Disequilibria in the balance of payments

We know that there are two ways that the balance of payments can be out of balance: the current account can be either in surplus or deficit. Neither eventuality is actually a policy problem unless it becomes *persistent*. If a deficit in one year is counterbalanced by a surplus in the next, then, over the medium term the balance of payments will remain broadly in balance and this, as suggested earlier, is the object of policy (see Chapter 8).

What is the difficulty posed by a persistent deficit? In such a situation we know that the deficit economy – say the UK – will be piling up net monetary liabilities with the rest of the world for each year the deficit persists. The UK is consistently importing a greater value of imports of goods and services than it is managing to export. In each year, these liabilities are settled (that is, accommodated) by some combination of borrowing from abroad and drawing upon the UK's reserves of foreign currency. *The crucial point is that neither of these avenues of debt settlement can be kept open indefinitely.*

A country that tries to run a persistent balance of payments deficit is, in effect, asking the rest of the world to continually lend it more money, or it is hoping that its foreign currency reserves will never reach the point of exhaustion. In the end, of course, lenders will lose patience and reserves must dwindle away (besides borrowing, the only way to replenish reserves, as we will see, is by running a surplus). A persistent balance of payments deficit is, therefore, a policy problem because it cannot be sustained and it may precipitate a crisis of international confidence in the deficit nation. Figure 14.2 shows that the same kind of persistent deficit problem can apply to individuals as well as countries.

● **Think Point**

What happens to the balance of payments on current account when an economy experiences rapid economic growth?

The current account is likely to worsen as higher incomes in the economy boost demand, including the demand for imported goods. This is especially the case if growth in competitor economies is sluggish, weakening demand including the demand for imports.

A persistent surplus appears at first sight to be much less of a problem and, indeed, this is usually considered to be the case, not least by some creditor nations themselves as they enjoy the fruits of export-led growth. However, a

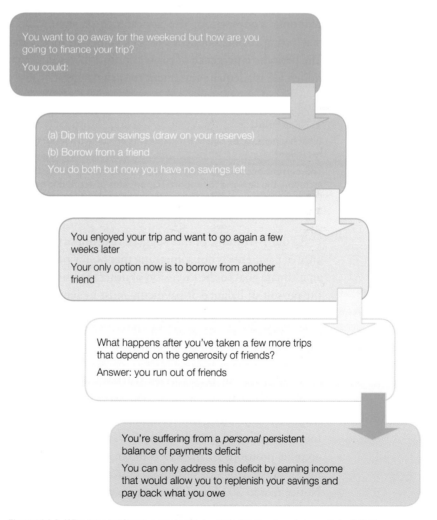

Figure 14.2 Why you can't run a personal persistent balance-of-payments deficit

policy response to persistent surplus may still be required for two reasons. First, balance of payments surplus is associated with the steady accumulation of net monetary claims on the rest of the world. For the surplus country, this can involve the acquisition of more and more foreign currency reserves as its credits are settled. Alternatively, it may continually make accommodating loans abroad to indebted nations. The point here is that both forms of balance of payments accommodation mean that opportunities for *current consumption* are being sacrificed. The accumulating reserves and the foreign loans could be converted into spending on imports: consumption would be higher at home and balance of payments deficits in other countries would be reduced or eliminated entirely.

The second reason that balance of payments surplus may require a policy response arises from the fact that, in balance of payments terms, the world economy is a 'zero sum game': one nation's surplus necessitates equivalent deficits elsewhere. Now, given that the growth of the world economy since 1945 has been based on openness in trading relationships and general international economic cooperation, the appearance of significant surpluses and deficits may prompt some countries to seek refuge in highly damaging introspection. The periodic emergence of protectionist lobbies in the current account deficit-ridden US is adequate testament to such dangers.

● **Think Point**

What happens to the balance of payments on current account when an economy experiences recession?

The current account is likely to improve as falling domestic incomes constrain demand, including the demand for imports. Good rates of economic growth in competitor economies will mean an even greater improvement as demand in these economies increases, including the demand for imports.

As our two think points suggest, it is important to emphasize that the balance of payments is not something that policymakers can elevate to the status of an ultimate goal to the exclusion of other macroeconomic considerations. Thus, the pursuit of balance of payments must be tempered by the competing claims of full employment, price stability and a satisfactory rate of growth. To grow only slowly, for example, burdened by high unemployment in order to maintain a given balance of payments position is really no achievement at all.

The balance of payments performance of selected economies

As means of elaborating upon some of the themes introduced above, it will be helpful, in concluding this section, to briefly review the balance of payments performances of some actual economies. Figures 14.3 and 14.4 describe the current account positions of the G5 economies plus China, 1990–2014. Figure 14.3 measures the deficit or surplus on current account in each case in absolute terms. Notice that in 2014 the US current account deficit of $431bn dwarfed the relatively modest UK deficit of about $122bn. But absolute data may not provide the most appropriate interpretation of the deficit positions of these economies.

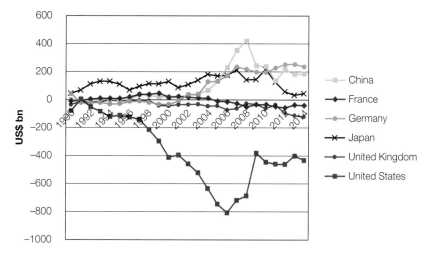

Figure 14.3 Current account balances 1990–2014

Source: Data from IMF's World Economic Outlook Database
Note: Data for China from 1998; estimates for 2014

Figure 14.4 measures the current account positions of the economies as a percentage of GDP. This approach may be preferred because it scales each deficit or surplus in terms of the size of the economy that must accommodate it. Now the US deficit does not look quite so much out of line. Because the American economy is itself much bigger than the British economy, the *relative* significance of the US deficit was actually smaller than in the British case. In 2014 the US deficit was 2.5 per cent of GDP; the figure for the UK was 4.2 per cent.

Figure 14.4 shows the major and consistent current account debtors among the G5 to be the US and the UK. For the period as a whole, the US deficit averaged just less than 3 per cent of GDP per annum, while for the UK the equivalent figure was just under 2 per cent. France experienced some combination of deficit

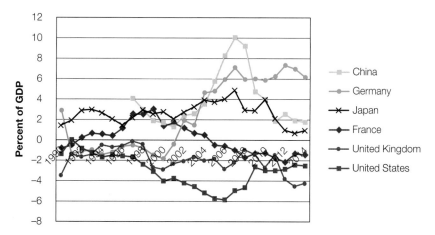

Figure 14.4 Current account as percentage of GDP 1990–2014

Source: Data from IMF's World Economic Outlook Database
Note: Data for China from 1998; estimates for 2014

and surplus: its overall average at 0.1 per cent is the closest of all the countries to medium-term balance (that is, zero). Germany also combined deficit and surplus positions over the period as a whole though it has been in strong surplus for more than a decade now. China's and Japan's performances are of consistently strong surplus, with average annual surpluses of 3.9 and 2.6 per cent of GDP respectively.

Figures 14.3 and 14.4 starkly demonstrate the symmetry between the current account performances of the US and the UK on the one hand and China, Germany and Japan on the other. Because these are some of the world's largest economies (accounting together for approximately 54 per cent of world GDP in 2014) it is highly improbable that a large absolute current account deficit in one would not be reflected in the counterweight of large surpluses in the others. For example, from 2002–6, when the US deficit deteriorates sharply, increasing surpluses were recorded in Japan, Germany and China.

We can now relate these real-world balance of payments performances back to our earlier theoretical discussions. There we argued that a persistent balance of payments deficit poses an adjustment problem for deficit nations. This is certainly the case for the US, which has in fact been in current account deficit since 1982. Indeed, we might reasonably wonder at the ability of the US to run a deficit for so long; how has this been possible? Part of the answer lies in the noted size and importance of the US economy. While lesser nations might find their accommodating credit lines running dry in the presence of a persistent balance of payments deficit sooner rather than later, because the US is responsible for about a fifth of world GDP, it is deemed to be more credit-worthy than most. But this is not to imply that the US deficit is unproblematic. Balance of payments adjustment will be required eventually and, as we will see later, this can have painful economic consequences for the adjusting economy.

Finally, although there is an evident symmetry between the surpluses of countries like China and Germany and the deficits of the US and UK we should emphasize that there is no simple cause and effect here. While it is true that the emergence of China and others has intensified competition in the global economy the struggles of the UK economy in particular indicate that there are deep and long-standing challenges to British industry to effectively allocate the scarce resources at its command: to produce goods and services that the rest of the world wants to buy at a price it is prepared to pay.

14.3   The balance of payments and business

Why does the balance of payments matter to business? For the moment we can only partly answer this question. Later, we will see that government balance of payments policy can have serious consequences for firms of all kinds, regardless of whether or not they are directly involved in international trade. However, on the basis of what we have learned so far we can say that balance of payments issues may have a negative effect upon business if payments *imbalances* in the world economy become large or sustained enough to raise the possibility of protectionism. This has become a potential issue given tensions in the trade relations between the US and China.

The US complains that part of the reason for its huge trade deficit with China is the unfair manipulation of the yuan (the Chinese currency) by the Chinese authorities. As Figure 14.5 illustrates China has for some time pegged its currency to the US dollar at what the US argues is a series of artificially low rates, making China's goods relatively cheap in American markets, and making American goods expensive in Chinese markets. China's argument is that its monetary policy objective 'is to maintain the stability of the value of the currency and thereby promote economic growth'.

Until 2005 the target rate was 8.26 yuan per dollar but between 2005 and 2008, partly in response to pressures from the US and other economies, the Chinese authorities allowed the currency to *appreciate* to a target rate of around 6.83 yuan per dollar (since Figure 14.5 expresses the exchange rate as the quantity of yuan a dollar will buy, the appreciation is depicted as a declining curve). However, this did not satisfy the Americans. In testimony to the US Senate Finance Committee in June 2010, Timothy Geithner, the Secretary of the Treasury, argued that 'Reform of China's exchange rate is critically important to the United States and to the global economy. And it is in China's own interest to allow the exchange rate to reflect market forces.' Mr Geithner clearly wanted an abandonment of China's fixed exchange rate policy and a further appreciation of the yuan. In the end he got the second but not the first. In 2014 China announced a further appreciation of the target rate for the yuan to 6.1521 yuan per US dollar.

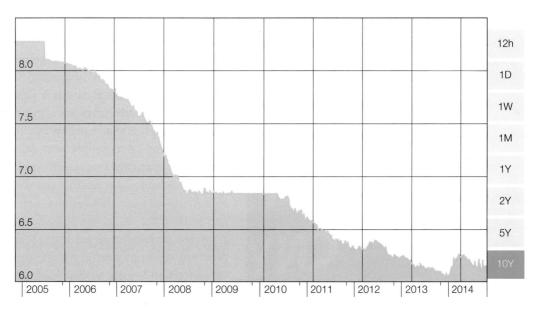

Figure 14.5 Chinese yuan per US dollar, 2005–2014

Source: XE.com

We do not intend to adjudicate in this continuing dispute here but its consequences are potentially profound, particularly in the context of the failure of the WTO's Doha Round trade talks discussed in Chapter 13. A world economy seriously out of trade balance and at a trade policy impasse may be one edging towards more generalized protectionism. We also know from Chapter 13 that protectionism is a threat to output and incomes in the world economy. More trade means more growth and higher incomes; constraints on trade limit output and income growth. This suggests that payments imbalances, even if they are initially between other apparently remote economies, can still impact upon *your* economy and *your* business.

14.4   Exchange rates and exchange rate determination

Exchange rate: the price of one currency expressed in terms of another.

An **exchange rate** is simply a *price*: the price of one currency expressed in terms of another. For instance, on 4 January 2011 one pound sterling was valued at 1.16 euros and 1.55 US dollars. These are two of the wide range of current prices at which sterling is bought and sold. In all likelihood, on the following day different prices prevailed. In the remainder of this chapter we will explain how exchange rates are determined and why they vary over time. We will also describe the fundamentals of different exchange rate systems and their implications for the balance of payments. For a long time, two basic forms of exchange rate system have operated:

An exchange rate is the price of one currency in terms of another

© iStockphoto.com/narviikk

- fixed regimes, which have limited the tendency of exchange rates to change;
- flexible regimes, which have been much more tolerant of exchange rate variation.

We will examine the relative arguments for these different kinds of arrangement.

Because an exchange rate is a price, it is determined, like any other price, by the interaction of supply and demand. What, then, are the influences upon supply and demand in the foreign exchange market? To explain this simply in what follows we limit our discussion to current account transactions. Let us take the Swiss franc as an example. Why would a foreign demand arise for francs? The simplest answer is, of course, that non-residents of Switzerland wish to purchase goods or services from Swiss residents. Because Swiss residents require payment in francs, foreign buyers must obtain (demand) francs in exchange for their own currencies. On the other hand, the supply of francs arises from the purchases of foreign goods and services made by Swiss residents. As foreign suppliers similarly require payment in their own currencies, Swiss residents must obtain these in exchange for (a supply of) francs. In this way, the foreign exchange market can be understood as a mechanism that facilitates the trade process: it allows economic agents resident in different countries holding different currencies to buy and sell goods and services to each other.

A diagrammatic representation of the demand and supply sides of the foreign exchange market for francs is given in Figure 14.6. Here panel (a) demonstrates the negative relationship between the demand for francs and the value of the franc expressed in terms of other currencies (that is, the franc exchange rate). As the value of the franc falls (from 0a to 0c), so do the prices of Swiss goods in foreign markets. Assuming that the foreign price elasticity of demand for Swiss goods is greater than 1, this leads *ceteris paribus* to an increase in the foreign demand for Swiss goods and an *extension* in the quantity of francs demanded (from 0b to 0d). Alternatively, if the franc's value increases, the prices of Swiss goods in foreign markets rise leading *ceteris paribus* to a fall in the demand for these goods and a *contraction* in the quantity of francs demanded.

In Figure 14.6 panel (b), the supply curve for francs is derived in a similar manner. A fall in the value of the franc (again from 0a to 0c) causes the price of foreign goods and services in Swiss markets to rise and, therefore, the demand for them to fall. Assuming that the Swiss price elasticity of demand for foreign goods is greater than 1, this prompts a *contraction* in the quantity of francs supplied on the foreign exchanges (from 0b to 0d) as Swiss residents require less foreign currency for imports. On the other hand, a rise in the franc's value makes foreign goods in Switzerland cheaper, causing an increase in the demand for them and an *extension* in the quantity of francs supplied.

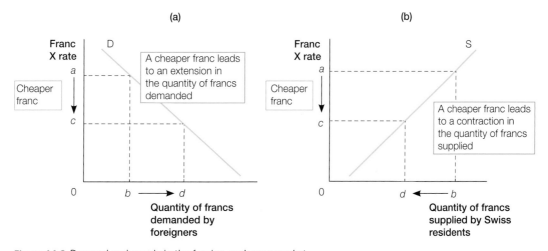

Figure 14.6 Demand and supply in the foreign exchange market

We can now put the two sides of the foreign exchange market together to see how it works. This is done in Figure 14.7. The general principles of operation here are identical to those of any normal market. A market-clearing equilibrium is defined by the intersection of the demand and supply curves. At this point, the exchange rate 0*b* gives rise to a quantity of francs demanded 0*d* and an identical quantity supplied, also 0*d*. Because the exchange rate produces an exact fusion of interest between the two sides of the market – no demand is unmet and no supply is ignored – there are no pressures for it to change: hence the equilibrium.

At *all* other possible exchange rates there can be no such stability. Above the market-clearing equilibrium exchange rate 0*b*, a stronger franc gives rise to an extension in the quantity supplied as domestic residents increase their demand for cheaper foreign imports. At the same time, however, the quantity of francs demanded contracts as its higher value makes Swiss exports more expensive in foreign markets. Thus, at the exchange rate 0*a*, for example, there is an *excess supply* of francs of the order marked in the diagram. The elimination of excess supply conditions will require a weakening of the franc. As the franc falls in value from 0*a*, the quantities demanded and supplied come closer together but they will not be finally harmonized until the market-clearing equilibrium exchange rate 0*b* has been reached. It should be clear that exchange rates below 0*b*, such as 0*c*, will stimulate conditions of *excess demand*. A cheap franc makes Swiss goods more desirable in foreign markets and therefore foreign residents demand more francs. But it also reduces the Swiss interest in imports and thus causes a contraction in the quantity of francs supplied. The unsatisfied demand for francs that now prevails in the market allows the exchange rate to rise. Again, this pressure is fully relieved only when the equilibrium rate 0*b* is attained.

In Figure 14.7 the demand and supply curves for foreign exchange were derived by reference to the usual market relationships between prices and quantities, with other influences held constant. For the sake of completeness, we should note here that the *positions* of the curves themselves depend on a range

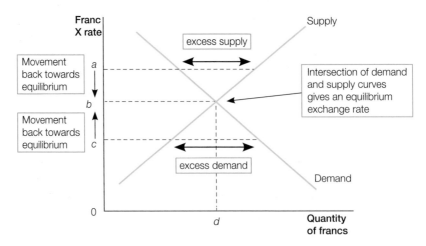

Figure 14.7 Equilibrium in the foreign exchange market

of other relevant factors. Some of these were discussed in our introduction to market dynamics in Chapter 2 and include, for example, income and tastes. A fall in incomes in the rest of the world would cause the demand curve for the franc to shift to the left as world demand for all imports falls; whereas a more favourable disposition towards Swiss goods on the part of foreign consumers would shift the franc demand curve to the right as more Swiss goods are sold on world markets.

We can also use this framework to illustrate the effects of changes that impact on the financial account. For example, changes in the domestic interest rate also greatly influence the demand for francs, especially over the shorter run. Because it makes interest-bearing assets denominated in francs more attractive (as returns on them become higher), an increase in the Swiss interest rate, compared to that prevailing in the rest of the world, would be associated with a rightward shift in the demand curve for francs. On the other hand, a reduction in the Swiss interest rate, because it lowers the attractiveness of franc-denominated interest-bearing assets, would cause the demand curve for francs to shift to the left.

Having explained the process of exchange rate determination and the notion of equilibrium, we also need to understand why exchange rates *vary*. The underlying connection between trade and the demand and supply of foreign currencies is significant here. If there were no trade, there would be no demand for specifically *foreign* currency; all material needs and desires could be financed using domestic currency. But there *is* trade. The rest of the world does have a taste, for example, for Swiss watches and this must involve a foreign demand for francs. Now, which of all the world's currencies would we expect to be in the greatest demand? The obvious answer is the currency of the nation that produces the greatest value of exports. Conversely, there would be less demand for the currencies of nations that exported relatively fewer goods and services.

We are now in a position to begin to understand *secular* (slow but persistent) movements in exchange rates. These are partly conditioned by the long-term trade performances of nations. Countries that gradually lose shares in world export markets will *ceteris paribus* see demand for their currencies fall. If, at the same time, these countries maintain healthy appetites for imports, thereby underwriting a consistent supply of their currencies onto the foreign exchanges, then the inevitable outcome will be *excess* currency supply and currency depreciation over the long term. Graphically, this would involve something approximating a steady leftward shift of the demand curve for a typical currency, consistently dragging down the market-clearing equilibrium exchange rate (see Figure 14.8(a)). For nations that are able to improve their shares in world export markets, the associated strong currency demand would most likely be associated with long-term currency appreciation. Graphically, this would involve a steady rightward shift of the demand curve for the typical currency, consistently pulling up the market-clearing equilibrium exchange rate (see Figure 14.8(b)).

Recall that we have confined our analysis here to the current account only. Clearly, currency supply and demand will also be conditioned by transactions

Depreciation: the depreciation of a currency involves a decrease in its value in terms of other currencies. The term depreciation is used when the currency is *not* part of some formal fixed exchange rate system. When a currency decreases in value as a result of government policy inside a fixed system, the term *devaluation* is used.

Appreciation: the appreciation of a currency involves an increase in its value in terms of other currencies. The term appreciation is used when the currency is *not* part of some formal fixed exchange rate system. When a currency increases in value as a result of government policy inside a fixed system, the term *revaluation* is used.

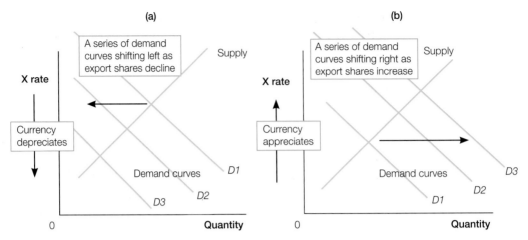

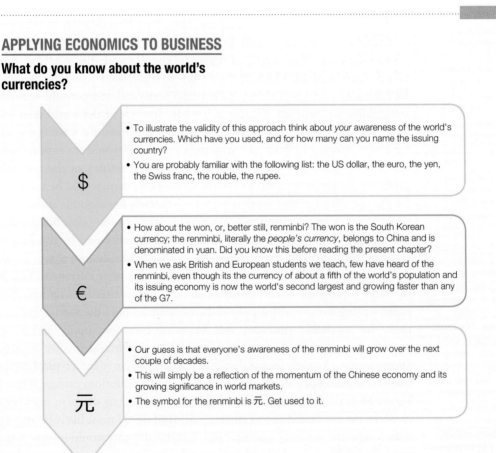

Figure 14.8 Long-term change in the foreign exchange market

APPLYING ECONOMICS TO BUSINESS

What do you know about the world's currencies?

$
- To illustrate the validity of this approach think about *your* awareness of the world's currencies. Which have you used, and for how many can you name the issuing country?
- You are probably familiar with the following list: the US dollar, the euro, the yen, the Swiss franc, the rouble, the rupee.

€
- How about the won, or, better still, renminbi? The won is the South Korean currency; the renminbi, literally the *people's currency*, belongs to China and is denominated in yuan. Did you know this before reading the present chapter?
- When we ask British and European students we teach, few have heard of the renminbi, even though its the currency of about a fifth of the world's population and its issuing economy is now the world's second largest and growing faster than any of the G7.

元
- Our guess is that everyone's awareness of the renminbi will grow over the next couple of decades.
- This will simply be a reflection of the momentum of the Chinese economy and its growing significance in world markets.
- The symbol for the renminbi is 元. Get used to it.

that appear elsewhere in the balance of payments accounts. In particular, FDI and portfolio investment transactions on the financial account will also influence long-term currency movements for an economy. Have a look at 'Applying Economics to Business', below, for a prediction about a currency of growing importance in the world economy.

Nominal and real exchange rates

So far we have focused on the nominal exchange rate – the rate at which different currencies can be traded. We demonstrated in Figure 14.1 that changes in nominal exchange rates affect the price competitiveness of traded goods. A fall in the value of the pound, for example, makes UK exports cheaper in foreign markets and imported goods more expensive in the UK. But there is another factor that may affect the price competitiveness of UK goods: the rate of UK inflation compared to inflation rates in rival economies. In Chapter 8 we suggested that one of the problems typically associated with inflation was its potential to erode international price competitiveness. This means that price competitiveness is affected by changes in nominal exchange rates *and* relative inflation rates.

Figure 14.9 depicts the nominal exchange rate for sterling versus the US dollar and the euro between 2007 and 2014. Also shown is the effective exchange rate index for sterling (ERI). The ERI is the nominal exchange rate for sterling against a basket of currencies weighted to reflect the importance of their issuing economies in trade in goods and services with the UK. The striking feature of Figure 14.9 is the sharp depreciation of sterling against the euro and the ERI after the middle of 2007, and against the dollar in the last quarter of 2008. Overall, the depreciation is of the order of about 20 per cent. One positive

Figure 14.9 Sterling exchange rates

Source: Bank of England Inflation Report, November 2014

implication of sterling's fall was the potential boost it gave to UK exporters and UK firms competing with foreign firms in UK markets.

However, this is not the end of the story. To better understand what happened to UK price competitiveness over this period we also need to reflect on relative inflation rates. These are depicted in Figure 14.10. Notice here that while inflation in the UK and the euro area fell sharply in 2008–9, in the UK there was a much more modest reduction. UK inflation remained above inflation in the euro area for the remainder of the period and above US inflation until 2014. Overall then, improved UK competitiveness arising from a significant depreciation of the nominal exchange rate was marginally offset by slightly higher UK inflation.

Taking into account both the nominal exchange rate and the prices of goods in different economies produces a variable known as the real exchange rate. The real exchange rate measures the real purchasing power of a currency. In our example the real exchange rate for UK goods and services was falling because of the nominal depreciation of sterling but it did not fall as far as the nominal rate because UK inflation was mostly a little higher than in the US and the euro area.

Euro area: comprises the 19 economies that have replaced their national currencies with the euro.

Real exchange rate: measures the real purchasing power of a currency.

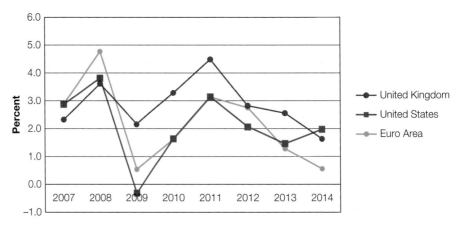

Figure 14.10 UK, US and euro area inflation, 2007–14

Source: Data from IMF's World Economic Outlook Database

Purchasing power parity

The relations between nominal exchange rates and relative inflation rates that we've just discussed bring us onto a well-known basic model of exchange rate determination: the theory of purchasing power parity (PPP). PPP is often thought to provide a means of explaining the path of nominal exchange rates in the long run.

PPP holds that the nominal exchange rate adjusts to offset differences in inflation rates between economies in the long run. Thus over several years an inflation-prone economy should see its nominal exchange rate depreciate against the currency of a low-inflation economy. The theory is based on the argument that differences in the price of goods in different economies create

Purchasing power parity: predicts that the nominal exchange rate will adjust to offset differences in inflation rates between economies in the long run.

opportunities for *arbitrage*; that is, buying goods cheaply in one economy and selling them on at a profit in another.

To take an example, in the 1970s and 1980s Britain's was typically an inflation-prone economy in comparison to the US and (West) Germany. It was possible for entrepreneurs to buy goods relatively cheaply in the US and Germany and ship them to the UK at a profit. But this opportunity would itself be undermined by its effects on the nominal sterling exchange rate. As UK residents bought more American and German goods to sell cheaply at home they would necessarily push up the demand for the dollar and the deutschmark and simultaneously increase the supply of pounds on the foreign exchanges. Arbitrage in goods prompted by inflation differentials therefore provokes countervailing nominal currency adjustments. Assuming inflation in the UK did not *continuously* soar away from US and German inflation, the falling pound would eliminate the arbitrage opportunity, meaning that there is no difference between what a given amount of sterling will buy at home or abroad. This is why the theory is called purchasing power parity. It predicts that a given amount of any currency will buy the same quantity of goods across different economies.

Exchange rates are multiply determined

If longer-term currency movements can be attributed to trade performances and differences in countries' inflation rates, what of very short-term movements? The value of currencies changes on a daily and even minute-by-minute basis. On occasion, short-term movements can be abrupt; how are these to be explained? Short-term currency movements often reflect market reactions to a wide variety of economic and even political factors. For example, the euro's sharp fall in the spring of 2010 reflected concerns about the condition of the Greek government's finances. The weakness of sterling in 2008 can be explained by a combination of steep interest rate cuts by the Bank of England – which reduced the demand for sterling – and worries about the particular exposure of the UK economy's relatively large financial sector to the world financial crisis. Overall then we must conclude that exchange rates are *multiply* determined by a wide range of long- *and* short-term factors. In most circumstances this makes them hard to model or predict with any degree of confidence, which in turn raises the question of how they should be treated in policy terms. Whether governments should try to control exchange rates, leave them to the markets, or try something in between is a subject to which we now turn.

14.5   Exchange rate systems

Flexible exchange rates

At the beginning of Section 14.4 we characterized two general forms of exchange rate system: those that embraced exchange rate flexibility and those that imposed some degree of restriction on exchange rate movements. A flexible system is one that follows free market principles. Exchange rate determination is left entirely to the processes of currency supply and demand described earlier, and governments do not attempt to manipulate the market in order to achieve particular exchange rate outcomes.

A flexible exchange rate system confers a number of advantages upon economies that adopt it. The first and most important of these relates to the balance of payments. We know that one of the central objectives of macroeconomic policy is the achievement of balance of payments balance over the medium term. A flexible exchange rate system *automatically* provides for this objective without the need for any action whatsoever by policymakers. How?

Consider the implications for the foreign exchange market of a balance of payments deficit in, say, the UK. Assuming, for the moment, that all foreign exchange transactions are trade-related, the deficit will necessarily be associated with conditions of *excess supply* of sterling. This is because UK residents will be supplying more sterling to the foreign exchange market than there is demand for. Remember that, here, sterling demand is conditioned by the rest of the world's demand for UK exports. Because the value of imports is greater than the value of exports, there must be a greater volume of sterling supplied than demanded: hence, excess supply. By the familiar market processes identified in Figure 14.7, a currency in excess supply will depreciate in value.

Now, the sterling depreciation has important implications for the relative price competitiveness of exports and imports. *Ceteris paribus*, exports become cheaper in foreign markets and, because import prices rise, import substitutes become more attractive to domestic consumers (see Figure 14.1 for an example of this process at work). Assuming that the price elasticity of demand for exports *plus* imports is greater than 1 (that is, demand is sufficiently price elastic), there will be an improvement in the UK's trade balance. This is known as the Marshall–Lerner condition. We must also presume that there are spare resources so that export industries and import-substituting industries are able to respond to the extra domestic demand stimulus that results from the depreciation.

Marshall–Lerner condition: states that a currency depreciation or devaluation will improve the current account of the balance of payments so long as the sum of the price elasticities of the demand for imports and exports is greater than 1.

If depreciation facilitated by a flexible exchange rate system impacts upon a deficit in the way described, at what point does the process end? Given that depreciation itself is prompted by, in our example, an excess supply of sterling on the foreign exchanges, it should be clear that this condition will persist so long as the deficit itself is present. This means that the deficit will continue to exert downward pressure on sterling until balance of payments balance is achieved.

A flexible exchange rate also provides an automatic panacea for balance of payments surplus. An excess of UK exports over UK imports in value terms gives rise to an *excess demand* for sterling and an *appreciation* of the sterling exchange rate. This adversely affects the price competitiveness of UK exports and import substitutes and, on the Marshall–Lerner assumption, worsens the trade balance and erodes the surplus. Again, the process continues until balance of payments balance has been achieved and equilibrium in the market for sterling prevents further appreciation of the currency.

The late Milton Friedman was the most famous advocate of the case for flexible exchange rates. He held that flexible rates offer nations the opportunity to enjoy *consistent* balance of payments balance. Friedman argued that any early or 'incipient' (the word he used) deficit or surplus that might arise will be swiftly dissipated by appropriate corrective exchange rate movements. Flexible rates also offer two other advantages. First, they allow nations to pursue their own *independent* economic goals in respect of the other objectives of macro policy. As we will see, membership of a *fixed* exchange rate system restricts the ability of participant countries to conduct macroeconomic policy autonomously. Second, flexible rates, because they reflect the free interplay of market forces, offer the most appropriate framework for the international allocation of resources through the trade process. The alternative – rates manipulated by governments – Friedman considered to be inimical to the very desirable objective of free trade.

Fixed exchange rates

There are three sets of issues to be explored in respect of fixed exchange rate systems:

- How can rates be fixed in the first place?
- How can a persistent balance of payments deficit be corrected under a regime of fixed exchange rates?
- If exchange rates can be fixed and if balance of payments deficits can be corrected with fixed rates, what are the *additional* merits of fixed systems that might make them preferable to a flexible system?

On the first of these questions, it is important to realize that fixity cannot be achieved by simple government decree. As we have seen, there are powerful economic forces at work in the foreign exchange markets; restricting the movement of currencies requires equally decisive countervailing action by the authorities. This can take two broad forms: direct intervention in the foreign exchange markets to alter supply and demand conditions, or the less direct option of interest rate manipulation.

The fixing of an exchange rate rarely involves the establishment of a single point away from which a currency is not permitted to move. The usual approach is to define a *target zone* for the currency. The authorities then respond with appropriate measures when market forces threaten to move the currency above or below the zone. For example, the Danish central bank maintains its currency in a zone around a declared central rate with the euro. The Danish krone is maintained inside a 2.25 per cent zone.

Figure 14.11 depicts a hypothetical case in which, for the sake of illustration, a target zone has been defined above the market equilibrium. The boundaries of the zone are points *a* and *c* on the vertical axis, while point *b* marks its midpoint and is the *central parity* of the currency. The market-clearing equilibrium here is given by point *d*. Under free market conditions, should an exchange rate emerge somewhere in the target zone, say because of a sudden surge in import demand in the domestic economy (which, remember, would lead to an excess supply of the currency), market forces would tend to drive the rate back down towards the equilibrium at *d*.

To prevent this happening and retain an exchange rate above *d*, the authorities themselves could buy the excess currency supply that is the driving force of the depreciation process. If, for example, the authorities wished to hold the exchange rate at *b*, they would need to buy the excess supply of currency *xy*, which arises at this rate. The purchase would, of course, have to be made using reserves of foreign currency. On the other hand, should market conditions change such that there are *excess demand* pressures that threaten an appreciation of the currency *above* the upper limit of the target zone at *a*, then the authorities might undertake open market operations to *sell* domestic currency in exchange for additional reserves. Theoretically then, it is possible to hold a currency at any given rate, so long as the associated excess demand or supply of the currency at that rate can be met.

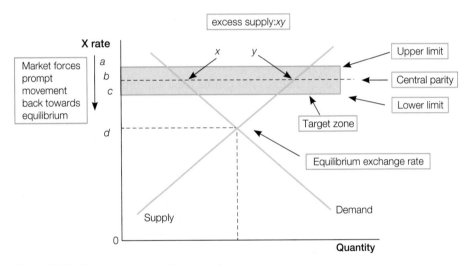

Figure 14.11 A target zone in the foreign exchange market

The second policy measure that can be used as an alternative or supplement to direct market intervention involves the use of interest rates. If the European Central Bank (ECB), for example, raises interest rates, investments denominated in euros become more attractive to overseas investors. This means that they are more likely to demand euros for investment purposes. The stronger demand for euros leads to a rise in its value against other currencies. In terms of Figure 14.11, this would involve a shift in the demand curve to the right, such that the demand for euros is higher at every exchange rate and a higher-rate equilibrium is established. Conversely, if the ECB elected to reduce interest rates, the lower associated demand for euros would shift the demand curve to the left and force down the exchange rate. The interest rate is therefore a potentially powerful weapon that the authorities can use to try to maintain a currency, for a time, at a selected level in defiance of the will of the market.

Correcting balance of payments disequilibria under fixed exchange rates

It might well be possible to periodically stabilize exchange rates but how are balance of payments disequilibria to be corrected under more rigid frameworks of this kind? In answering this question, we concentrate upon the most pressing problem of balance of payments current account deficit. There are two possible courses of action open to any deficit economy:

- *Expenditure reduction policy*, or
- *Expenditure switching policy* (or some combination of both).

Expenditure reduction policy: involves reducing the level of aggregate demand in the domestic economy in order to improve the balance of payments position on the current account.

The aim of expenditure reduction policy is to dampen the level of aggregate demand in the domestic economy so that the demand for imported goods and services is reduced. Because the level of exports is unrelated to domestic demand – export demand depends on such factors as foreign incomes, the prices of exports relative to the prices of rival goods produced by competitors abroad, foreign tastes and so on – it follows that the balance of payments position should improve. Moreover, as lower domestic demand may ease domestic inflationary pressures, the international competitiveness of home-produced goods and services should rise, thereby further improving the current account. Domestic demand may be reduced by contractionary monetary or fiscal policy or some combination of both. Unfortunately, dealing with a balance of payments deficit in this way may have harmful consequences for some of the other major macroeconomic objectives. Thus, a lower level of demand is likely to constrain output and effect an increase in unemployment. Recall our caution that balance of payments equilibrium should not be relentlessly pursued at the expense of other goals or objectives.

Expenditure switching policy: policy that is intended to switch domestic and foreign demand away from foreign goods and towards home-produced goods.

Devaluation: the devaluation of a currency involves the lowering of its value in terms of other currencies when the currency in question is part of some formal fixed exchange rate system.

Turning to expenditure switching policy, the objective here is to encourage overseas residents to buy more exports and to induce domestic residents to purchase home-produced goods and services instead of imports. How are such modifications in consumption behaviour to be achieved? The most obvious method is to *devalue* the domestic currency. (To recap, devaluation involves lowering the price of a currency inside a fixed exchange rate system; as such, it is necessarily an action of the monetary authorities. Depreciation, on the other hand, is the word used to describe the lowering of the price of a currency inside a flexible exchange rate regime. This can be either wholly market driven or can be managed by the authorities. The antonyms of devaluation and depreciation are revaluation and appreciation.)

Devaluation requires the monetary authorities to revise downwards the declared central parity for the currency inside the relevant fixed exchange rate system. This has the effect of reducing the price of exports in foreign markets, as overseas buyers have to part with fewer units of their own currency to obtain a given amount of the devalued currency. The domestic price of imports is simultaneously increased, as home consumers must part with more of their currency to obtain a given amount of foreign currency (see Figure 14.1 for an illustration). In this way currency devaluation induces relative price changes that favour the products of the devaluing economy.

For the devaluation to work – for it to improve the trade balance – two additional conditions must be observed. These were introduced earlier in our discussion of balance of payments adjustment under flexible exchange rates. They are: first, that there must be sufficient spare capacity in domestic industries to enable them to respond to greater demand pressures both at home and abroad. Second, the relative price changes themselves must stimulate appropriate behaviour among consumers; in other words, there must be a reasonable degree of price elasticity of demand for exports and imports. For a current account deficit to ease following a devaluation, it is generally recognized that the price elasticity of demand for exports plus the price elasticity of demand for imports must be greater than 1 (the noted Marshall–Lerner condition).

It should be clear that the devaluation will also have a positive influence on the levels of output and employment in the domestic economy in that demand has been raised. However, there may be a potentially adverse effect on inflation. Rising import prices, particularly for strategically important commodities such as oil, may introduce cost-push pressures into domestic industry. Finally, we should be aware that there are several additional measures available to governments each of which also have expenditure-switching properties. These include import controls, export promotion and the promotion of domestic industry by fiscal or other means.

The advantages of fixed exchange rates

Our analysis so far in this section suggests that exchange rates can be fixed and that balance of payments deficits can be corrected inside fixed rate regimes. Yet, in themselves, these findings hardly amount to a recommendation of exchange rate fixity; a market-based system also provides for deficit correction. Why then might fixed regimes be actively preferred by policymakers? There are two arguments for exchange rate fixity: the *integration argument* and the *anchor argument*.

The integration argument

The integration argument proceeds by analogy. An economy is thought to gain certain advantages from its ability to issue a single currency that is uniformly acceptable throughout its territory. In the US, for example, the dollar serves equally well in transactions in every state. This means that (say) a New Jersey food-processing firm can pay for Californian oranges in dollars and that a resident of Texas can buy a coffee machine manufactured in Pennsylvania and

Getty

Californian oranges are priced in dollars in every US state, helping the US market cohere; in the European market, where the euro, the pound, the zloty, the forint, etc., circulate there is less clarity and coherence

also pay in dollars. In this way, the dollar provides *monetary coherence* throughout the US: all transactions are patently transparent.

However, if the four US states just mentioned issued their own *individual* currencies then a degree of coherence would immediately be lost. The New Jersey orange buyer would need to obtain the Californian currency, while the Texan would require Pennsylvanian currency to pay for the coffee machine. The inconvenience, uncertainty and risk associated with this more complex situation would clearly be much worse were these separate currencies free to fluctuate in value against each other. In fact, the more complex the monetary arrangement becomes, the greater the potential *fragmentation* of the economy. The danger is that producers and consumers may begin to retreat and confine their activities to their own 'monetary region', thus segmenting and impoverishing the competitive process itself. Consumers may not choose to buy what offers them the best value simply because it comes from another region and the associated transaction might be inconvenient, or the price might be unclear or suddenly prohibitive because of currency fluctuations. Economic fragmentation of this sort reduces the exposure of less efficient producers to the full rigours of the competitive process. If greater competition is a desirable objective – and we presume that it is – then the benefit to the US economy of the highest possible degree of monetary coherence is clear.

Let us retain the essence of this conclusion and move back to the international level. Different national economies usually have different currencies, which means, in terms of our US example, that there is a choice to be made over the degree of *incoherence* the prevailing international monetary system should have. On the one hand, fixed exchange rates do not offer the same level of simplicity and transparency that a single currency does; but on the other hand it can be argued that they certainly appear preferable to the more opaque and uncertain environment often associated with flexible rates.

The anchor argument

The second argument for fixed exchange rates – the anchor argument – is based on the proposition that membership of a fixed regime restricts the freedom policymakers have to pursue expansionary monetary and fiscal policy. This means that participant economies become *anchored* to a policy of monetary discipline. Consider the implications of a decision by one member of a fixed system to adopt a relatively loose fiscal and monetary stance compared to those of its partners. Such a shift in policy might be motivated by the need to engineer faster growth and lower unemployment. A looser monetary stance would normally involve a reduction in interest rates. However, as we have already seen, lower interest rates may well induce a fall in the international demand for an economy's financial assets (because their returns are falling), and therefore in the demand for its currency. This in turn would be likely to result in currency depreciation. In other circumstances depreciation might not matter but it certainly does for an economy that has agreed to fix its currency against the currencies of a group of partners. So fixed systems are intolerant of any kind of deviant monetary policy, meaning that a pay-off of membership is a good monetary policy – in fact one that is anchored to the best in the system – delivering low and stable inflation.

Managed rates

Although we have so far framed exchange rate policy in terms of a rather stark choice between market determination and absolute fixity imposed by government, there are a several qualifications that must be made here. In the first place, there is the third option of the managed exchange rate, sometimes referred to as a 'dirty' float. It is unlikely that the authorities in any country could remain completely indifferent to the behaviour of the exchange rate and yet this is what the advocates of completely flexible rates recommend. The continuous depreciation of the currency of a deficit nation, for example, would clearly raise concerns over *how* far it could tolerably sink. Notwithstanding the fact that the strength of a currency is sometimes popularly interpreted as a measure of national economic vitality, a pronounced depreciation would, for example, have extremely serious *inflationary* consequences for the domestic economy as the prices of imports with typically low price elasticities of demand (such as oil) were forced up. Dangers of this kind mean that managed or dirty floating is the more usual alternative to participation in a fixed exchange rate system. In practice, a managed float permits the authorities to intervene in the foreign exchange markets, using direct intervention, interest rates, or some combination of both, when market imperatives threaten particularly unwelcome currency movements; in all other circumstances the market is the preferred mechanism of control.

If absolute flexibility is not usually a practical option, what of exchange rate fixity: can this tend towards the absolute? We have already noted the possible use of intervention zones around a central exchange rate parity, such as that depicted in Figure 14.11. This means that *some* movement of rates is tolerated but what of the parities themselves, are they immutably fixed? In terms of the history of actual exchange rate systems, the simple answer here is that, in cases where parities have been *fixed but adjustable*, the systems themselves appear more robust than the alternative hard *fixed and not adjustable* parity systems. In order to illustrate this point we now turn to consider some important examples of actual exchange rate systems.

Managed exchange rate: one that is influenced by the country's central bank intervening in the foreign exchange market.

14.6 Exchange rate systems in practice

In this section we review the nature and performance of two major *fixed* exchange rate systems:

- the Bretton Woods system (1945–71)
- the European exchange rate mechanism (1979–99)

We also examine a flexible exchange rate regime:

- the 'non-system' (1973 to date)

The Bretton Woods system

In Chapter 13 we explained how the GATT multilateral trade framework emerged as a response to the chaotic protectionism of the 1930s. Although in trade policy terms the protectionism was tariff-based, it also had an exchange rate dimension. This took the form of a series of *competitive* devaluations in which individual countries lowered the values of their currencies in an attempt to encourage domestic economic recovery. However, as with the tariff, devaluation at this time tended to spawn retaliation and monetary chaos rather than recovery and, as more and more countries took part, none was left in a better general economic position than when it started. This kind of disorder greatly influenced the architects of the postwar international monetary system when they met at Bretton Woods, an imposing country hotel in the US state of New Hampshire, in July 1944.

The Bretton Woods Hotel in New Hampshire

The Bretton Woods conference gave rise to an agreement that the postwar world economy would be best served by the adoption of a framework of fixed exchange rates. This, it was believed, would both obviate the dangers of a new round of competitive devaluations and – on the assumption that trade is enhanced by exchange rate stability – stimulate a general environment in which export-led growth could flourish. The new system was to be based on the US dollar, which was fixed in value by the US authorities against gold (at $35 per ounce). All other currencies in the system could then be tied to the dollar – and each other – at fixed values. The British pound, for example, had an initial central parity with the dollar of $4.03.

The US dollar was accorded such a pivotal role because of the enormous economic advantage that the US enjoyed over the rest of the world at the end of the war: at this time fully half of the world's output was produced in America and the US Federal Reserve held two thirds of the world's gold stock. The purpose of fixing the value of the dollar to gold was to limit the ability of the US authorities to indulge in unwarranted monetary expansion. Because the American commitment to gold meant that all other participants in the system could exchange dollar holdings for gold with the Federal Reserve at $35 per ounce, the US authorities could only issue (print) dollars commensurate with their ability to redeem them from other central banks using gold. The general intention here was to ensure inflation control via sober American monetary policy.

The target zone for the Bretton Woods system was set at 1 per cent, which meant that currencies could fluctuate against each other up to a 1 per cent margin above or below the declared parity (see Figure 14.11 for a reminder of what a target zone looks like). To keep currencies inside their target zones it was recognized that active management of the foreign exchange markets was required. Accordingly, the Bretton Woods agreement established the *International Monetary Fund* (IMF) which would lend participant nations intervention currencies in order that they might fulfil their obligations regarding the stability of their own currencies. The IMF was itself resourced by subscriptions from system members.

Finally, and most importantly, it was recognized that currencies would need to be *realigned* from time to time, as, for example, new trading patterns and relationships evolved. Accordingly, the rules of the system permitted devaluations by countries in balance of payments deficit of up to 10 per cent of the value of a currency but larger movements required IMF approval. Note that a clamour for the right to *revalue* was not anticipated. As we have seen, the pressures upon deficit nations are generally more intense than on those in surplus; moreover, surplus nations are often understandably reluctant to allow revaluation to undermine export-led growth.

In summary then, the Bretton Woods system was envisaged as one that would provide a framework of stable exchange rates conducive to trade development. Participant nations, with the help of the IMF, would manage their currencies in this spirit but periodic realignments were anticipated so that changes in real economic circumstances – especially the emergence of persistent balance of payments deficits – could be addressed.

As we shall see, the actual development of the Bretton Woods system during the 1950s and 1960s differed from this agreed blueprint in some important ways but the most fundamental element – exchange rate stability – remained in place and was associated with the most sustained and trade-based economic boom in human history.

Given this kind of achievement, why did the system not last? One answer is that it became an *overly* fixed exchange rate system – something its founders had been concerned to avoid. In part, this reflected a view that emerged from the IMF that, especially for the most important currencies, *any* movement beyond the agreed target zones was undesirable. More generally, it also became apparent that declared parities were widely interpreted as tokens of economic vitality, to the extent that devaluation came to be associated with national weakness and incompetence on the part of policymakers in the countries experiencing persistent deficits. This had the effect of forestalling currency realignments that were necessary to the healthy functioning of the system: deficit countries that needed to devalue were reluctant to do so for fear of the consequences of appearing weak, and surplus countries would not revalue because they had no wish to imperil their growth prospects. In this way, the Bretton Woods system ossified, unable to make the periodic currency adjustments that would allow the whole currency grid to retain its integrity. Ultimately, something was bound to snap, as indeed the US dollar did in 1971.

This brings us to the second and ultimately fatal weakness of the system: the so-called dollar dilemma. We know that the US dollar was selected as the system's pivotal currency at the Bretton Woods conference because of the great strength of the American economy at the time. The overwhelming scale of American production also made the dollar the world's most heavily demanded currency: dollars were necessary to finance the rest of the world's imports of American and other countries' goods. The imperatives of postwar reconstruction served only to accentuate this situation. In 1948, to begin to meet the huge demand for dollars, the US initiated the *Marshall Plan*, a programme of dollar grants to European countries. However, despite this action, what became known as the period of the *dollar shortage* persisted until the end of the 1950s. Thereafter, the gap between the supply of and demand for dollars began to be closed by other changes in the US economy itself. There was, for example, a significant increase in American foreign direct investment. This raised the flow of dollars abroad as US firms opened foreign production facilities. But herein lay the essence of the problem for the Bretton Woods system. What if the outflow of dollars from the US became so large that it swamped the American capacity – to which it was committed – to continue to redeem dollars using its gold stock? In such a situation the system would fail because the entire exchange rate framework proceeded from the established gold valuation of the dollar. On the other hand, the greater availability of dollars was important as it provided the extra volume of *the* key currency necessary to finance the continued unprecedented growth in world trade. *In effect this meant that the world economy was balanced on the knife-edge between a dollar shortage and a dollar glut, and a policy to address one risked advancing the other.* The problem became known as the *Triffin Dilemma*, after the economist Robert Triffin who (presciently) identified it in 1960.

Unfortunately, from the mid-1960s there was a burgeoning dollar

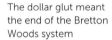

■ Concept: The dollar dilemma referred to the contradictory needs inside the Bretton Woods system for, on the one hand, a sufficient supply of dollars to finance the growth in world trade and, on the other, some constraints on the supply of dollars in order to maintain market confidence in the dollar.

The dollar glut meant the end of the Bretton Woods system

© iStockphoto.com/Jezperklauzen

glut. The most notable cause was the domestic economic expansion associated with both the escalation of the Vietnam War and President Johnson's 1964 announcement of the 'Great Society' programme (which involved, inter alia, increases in government spending on education and housing, and measures to tackle poverty). This caused a serious deterioration in the US balance of payments on current account resulting in significant increases in dollar holdings by foreign central banks. While confidence in the gold basis of the dollar held, the central banks were happy to accumulate dollar assets. In fact, because they could not obtain sufficient gold for reserve use purposes (as the world supply of gold was growing too slowly) they greatly needed this alternative prime reserve asset. But the threat of a dollar crisis loomed ever larger as these holdings increased. At the beginning of the 1970s, a further and even more severe deterioration in the US balance of payments appeared to convince the foreign exchange markets that the dollar would have to be devalued: consequently the dollar was sold heavily in favour of more robust currencies such as the deutschmark and the yen. This meant that the German and Japanese central banks had to buy dollars using their own currencies in order to prevent them from rising in value (in other words they had to meet higher demand with an equivalent increase in supply). This very quickly became an impossible task.

The tide of speculation against the dollar continued unabated until 15 August 1971 when President Nixon effectively dissolved the Bretton Woods system by announcing that the US would no longer honour the agreement to exchange dollars for gold. As the fixed gold value of the dollar was at the very heart of the framework of interconnected currency rates, the entire structure simply melted away, ultimately to be replaced by the present non-system of flexible exchange rates.

Non-system: refers to the broad system of flexible exchange rates prevailing in the world economy since 1973.

The non-system

Although it had been operating informally for some time, the non-system was officially endorsed by the IMF at a meeting in Jamaica in January 1976. That the IMF survived the demise of the system it was designed to oversee is, together with the spirit of international economic cooperation this institution embodies, one of the lasting legacies of Bretton Woods. The Jamaica meeting gave permission for the former Bretton Woods participants to assume any exchange rate policy they found appropriate, subject to the exhortation that they should not seek to manipulate exchange rates for unilateral competitive gain: a clear reference to the regrettable currency dispositions of the 1930s. In fact, as we saw in Chapter 8, the major macroeconomic policy preoccupation of this period was not exchange rates and the balance of payments but *inflation*. Indeed, it is worth pausing for a moment here to explain how the resurgence in worldwide inflation actually *necessitated* a return to a more flexible exchange rate environment.

Figure 14.12 illustrates the high and *uneven* incidence of inflation among the advanced nations in the 1970s and the first half of the 1980s. Compare, for example, the British and German experiences. The average inflation rate in Britain from 1973–79 was 14.8 per cent; in Germany over the same period the inflation rate averaged 5.0 per cent. As we have seen, differing inflation rates have important effects upon the relative international price competitiveness of nations. The high inflation rate in Britain meant *lost* price competitiveness vis-à-vis Germany and other economies with a similar capacity for greater price stability. In a fixed exchange rate system, Britain could only have regained international price competitiveness by imposing relatively severe expenditure reduction policies. Domestically, this makes the option of expenditure switching much more attractive. The main form of expenditure switching policy is currency devaluation or depreciation. Now, under fixed exchange rate conditions, it is simply not possible to engineer the *series* of devaluations required to confront the lost international price competitiveness implications of an inflationary environment. To do so would clearly undermine any pretence of exchange rate stability. This means that a period of high and unevenly experienced inflation will tend to lever countries away from an adherence to exchange rate fixity so that they can use currency depreciation both to protect their international price competitiveness and to stave off the need for severe expenditure-reducing policies.

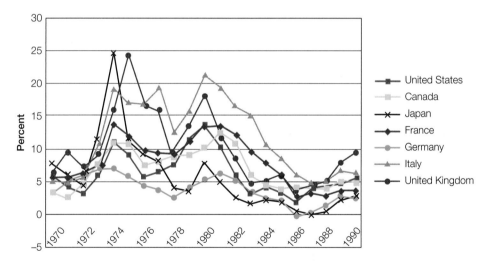

Figure 14.12 Inflation for the G7 1970–90

Source: Data from IMF's World Economic Outlook Database

Although the non-system provides for exchange rate flexibility, this is generally recognized to be a *managed* flexibility. We argued earlier that no country can afford to be entirely indifferent to the behaviour of its exchange rate. Pronounced depreciation can, for example, have severe inflationary consequences for the domestic economy as import prices are forced up, while pronounced appreciation will clearly impinge upon the prospects for exports and growth. It has been a feature of the non-system that exchange rates have, at times, moved to positions that appear to be at variance with conditions prevailing in, and the longer-term interests of, domestic economies.

For example, in 1980–81, the sterling exchange rate climbed rapidly to $2.45 on the back of high domestic interest rates and because North Sea oil caused the markets to take a more favourable view of the currency. This can partly help to explain the abrupt contraction in British manufacturing output of some 20 per cent as firms found themselves less able to compete on price in foreign markets and as the relative price of manufactured imports fell. The recessionary impact on the economy as a whole was of an order not seen since the 1930s. Yet just a few years later in the sterling crisis of 1984–85, the value of the pound plummeted to $1.04 at its lowest point as speculative sentiment turned sour. The central point here is that there was nothing in the 'real' economy that could justify such wild oscillations in the value of the pound over a relatively short period and the damage they caused. It was this kind of experience which helped to prompt the evolution of forms of collective management of the non-system.

While the tribulations of sterling might be a serious problem for the British economy, they have limited impact upon the fortunes of the rest of the world. However, this is not true of the US dollar, which, reflecting the absolute size of the American economy, remains the world's most important currency. In the mid-1980s the dollar was generally recognized to be *overvalued*, given the presence of a large US current account deficit, but, contrary to the expectations of theory, there was little sign of the necessary and corrective dollar depreciation. This meant, of course, that in the absence of US expenditure reduction policy, the deficit would in all likelihood become even larger. It is at this point that the issue becomes a more generalized one. The intractability of the deficit gave rise to increasingly strident calls for *protection* from American industrial and labour lobbies and the major economies recognized that the possibility of a retaliatory trade war existed unless some ameliorative action could be taken.

Accordingly, the G5 group of nations, in the 1985 *Plaza Agreement*, declared their collective intention to orchestrate an appropriate managed depreciation of the dollar. This amounted to a general recognition that the non-system could not be coordinated on the basis of market sentiment alone. In 1987, the G5 plus Canada moved a stage further by recognizing – in the *Louvre Accord* – that a greater degree of stability among the world's major currencies would bolster the prospects for trade growth and, therefore, for general economic expansion. The Accord established undisclosed target zones for the currencies of its signatories. The zones themselves were informed by an awareness of the basic economic circumstances of each economy such that currency levels would be both stable and appropriate.

The European exchange rate mechanism (ERM)

It would seem from the experiences of Bretton Woods and the non-system that both overly fixed and highly flexible exchange rate regimes have limitations.

One of the critical failings of the Bretton Woods system was the absence of any formal mechanism of currency adjustment. It had been envisaged that devaluations would periodically occur in order to dissipate evident balance of payments imbalances, but this simply did not happen on a sufficient scale. Similarly, theoretical predictions that the non-system would be typified by smooth, orderly and appropriate currency movements have not been realized and substantial intervention has occurred as a result. In practice, what might be required is some kind of compromise between near-absolute fixity and limitless flexibility. The ERM, at least for part of its life, can be seen to have been the institutional embodiment of such a compromise. Although it was eclipsed by the creation of the euro in 1999, a review of the ERM is still instructive for the wider lessons it carries for exchange rate management.

The ERM was launched in 1979 as a 'zone of monetary stability in Europe'. It was conceived as a fixed but *adjustable* exchange rate system which would do two things.

- First, it would provide the exchange rate stability conducive to trade growth in an integrating EU (see Chapter 2).
- Second, by binding their monetary policies to the highly successful policy operated by the German Bundesbank, it would provide a means of inflation control for participant nations.

Recall the anchor argument for fixed exchange rates. This suggests that members of a fixed system cannot use monetary policy independently of their partner economies. To do so would threaten the stability of agreed currency parities as, for example, lower interest rates prompt a fall in the demand for the currency of a deviant member.

The parity grid of the ERM was based on a specially created hybrid currency – the European currency unit (ECU). The ECU was a weighted average of the currencies of all member states. Inside the ERM, each central bank declared a parity with the ECU and through it with all other participant currencies. In this way a parity grid for the entire ERM was formed. The target zone for most currencies was initially set as a ±2.25 per cent band around the central parity. In the event of a pair of currencies threatening to move too far apart, *both* central banks were required to intervene in the foreign exchange markets to re-establish the integrity of the target zone. This approach established a degree of *symmetry* in the ERM that had been lacking in Bretton Woods; there, the responsibility for currency defence had fallen primarily upon countries with weaker currencies.

Our main interest here is in the evolution of the ERM. Between 1979 and 1987, the system functioned, as intended, in a fixed but adjustable manner. In other words, the dominant concern was for currency stability within the prescribed limits but appropriate currency realignments were made from time to time. This meant that the kinds of tensions associated with overdue adjustment, which had typified the Bretton Woods system, did not have the chance to build up. However, from 1987, following the advent of the *Basle Nyborg Agreement*, the ERM ossified to produce sets of parities which were in effect *non-adjustable*. This meant that the system had no way to relieve tensions created by exchange rates that became misaligned: they had simply to be defended using the familiar tools of currency management.

Ironically, the Basle Nyborg Agreement was actually an attempt to strengthen the integrity of the ERM by more forcefully equipping its members to with-stand speculative attacks upon their currencies. It established a new protocol of parity defence – facilitating, for example, the coordinated use of interest rate changes – and enhanced the pooled resources available for intervention in the foreign exchange markets. However, the agreement also relegated the option of currency realignment to the status of 'last resort'. Now, insofar as the last resort of realignment fused into a policy of *no* realignment, the ERM became possessed of a fundamental shortcoming as divergent economic performances among member states raised inevitable and increasingly stark questions as to the sustainability of established parities.

The integrity of the post-Basle Nyborg 'unadjustable' parity grid eventually foundered upon problems associated with the reunification of Germany in 1989. Reunification sparked a huge reconstruction programme in the old East Germany, which was funded by an expansionary fiscal policy in Germany as a whole. Fears that this policy might have inflationary consequences prompted the Bundesbank to operate a tighter – that is, higher interest rate – monetary policy. In turn, higher interest rates had the effect of putting upward pressure on the deutschmark and downward pressure on other major European currencies such as sterling and the French franc. Eventually, the markets seized first upon

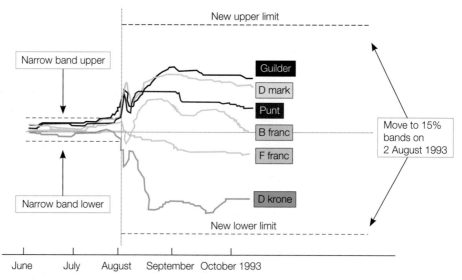

Figure 14.13 The widening of the ERM band in 1993

Source: Adapted from Bank of England *Quarterly Bulletin*, November 1993

sterling and, despite heavy intervention by the Bank of England in its favour and the raising of UK interest rates to emergency levels, speculators forced the pound out of the ERM in October 1992, two years after it had belatedly joined. The Italian lira and the Spanish peseta were floated at the same time. The following summer, renewed tensions in the ERM, which again favoured the deutschmark, were only dissipated by a widening of the margins of fluctuation inside the parity grid from ± 2.25 to ±15 per cent. Figure 14.13 illustrates the movement from the narrow target zone to the (very much) wider band.

14.7 The euro

We conclude this chapter with a brief overview of the issue of European monetary integration. What kind of context does the preceding discussion provide for the notion of the single currency in Europe? Given the advent of the euro in 1999, there can be *no* exchange rate fluctuations inside the euro area and, moreover, the balance of payments relationships that formerly existed between these countries now appear in a wholly different form. Why are such developments thought desirable, and what are the possible costs of the euro to its member countries?

The first thing to say is that we have been part way down this road before. In 1970, the *Werner Plan* anticipated that monetary union for the six original members of the European Economic Community (EEC) would be completed by 1980. However, the resurgence of worldwide inflation over the course of the 1970s prompted differing policy responses among the Six and this prevented the kind of monetary policy convergence and gradual tightening of exchange rates that was to presage full monetary union.

19 European economies have now abandoned their own currencies in favour of the euro

© iStockphoto.com/MARIA TOUTOUDAKI

Ambitions for monetary union were revived in the EU's Single European Act (SEA) in 1986. As discussed in Chapter 2, this was the legislation that provided for the European single market. Recognizing that a *fully* integrated market requires as high a degree of monetary coherence as possible, the SEA committed member states to the principle of a single currency. Recall the *integration argument* for fixed exchange rates discussed in Section 14.5. This states that a market will operate most efficiently and competitively when it is served by one currency. In Section 14.5, we used the hypothetical example of the US to show that the presence of different regional currencies inside the American economy would be likely to prompt the fragmentation of markets, reducing efficiency and competition to levels below those prevailing when the single national currency – the dollar – is employed. The SEA simply applied the same principle to Europe as a whole: that the evolution of a *single market* in Europe should be mirrored by the emergence of a *single currency* in Europe.

The path to the single currency was laid down by the *Delors Report* (1989) and the *Maastricht Treaty* (1991). The Delors Report set the tone for the general form and evolution of monetary union, while the Maastricht Treaty formally endorsed Delors in its key respects and established the timetable and criteria for the introduction of the single currency. The Delors Report outlined three important and interconnected principles:

- The first concerned the nature of the new European Central Bank (ECB), which would oversee EU monetary policy upon the advent of the single currency. This institution would replace the national central banks, which had hitherto been responsible for the conduct of policy in each euro area country. Thus, it would set the *one* euro area interest rate and manage the exchange rate of the new single currency against others outside the euro area. What we might term the 'general disposition' of the ECB would therefore be of crucial importance. The Delors Report left no room for doubt as to what this should be. The ECB would be modelled on the German Bundesbank; it would, in other words, be committed to *price stability* and would operate *independently*, free of political control as exercised by either national governments or EU authorities.
- Because the ambition was for the single currency to exhibit a tendency towards low inflation, rectitude in monetary policy (on the part of the ECB) would have to be matched by similar parsimony in the conduct of fiscal policy, which is to remain in the hands of national governments. The second principle of the Delors Report was, therefore, that national budget deficits in the EU should be limited and that national fiscal policies should be set on a path of convergence.
- Finally, the Report recognized that setting an austere tone for the conduct of macroeconomic policy at the European level could have negative implications for employment prospects, particularly in the less economically advanced regions of the EU, such as parts of Portugal, Greece, southern Italy and some northern areas of the British Isles. The third and final principle of Delors was, therefore, that EU *structural intervention funds* be doubled in size. The purpose of these funds is to assist the economic development of EU regions in chronic decline. However, the structural funds remained extremely modest in absolute terms; this was inevitable given that the EU spends only about 1 per cent of European GDP – it is not a wealthy institution.

Building upon the Delors Report, the Maastricht Treaty agreed that monetary union would begin on 1 January 1999 for those EU nations able to meet a series of economic *convergence criteria*. The convergence criteria were necessary to ensure that member economies were able to live with the single monetary policy that would be set for the euro area as a whole as soon as the new currency and its institutions were created. Monetary union was to initially involve the irrevocable fixing of national exchange rates with a view to their physical replacement by the single currency – the euro – by 2002. The convergence criteria established at Maastricht were that:

- The inflation rate in each national economy should not exceed that of the average of the best three EU national performances by more than 1.5 per cent.
- Long-term interest rates in each national economy should not exceed the average of the lowest three rates in the EU by more than 2 per cent.
- The indebtedness of national governments should be limited: expressed as a 3 per cent ceiling on annual budget deficits, and a ceiling on accumulated debt equivalent to 60 per cent of GDP.
- National currencies must be maintained in the *narrow* (that is, 2.25 per cent) band of the ERM for two years, without undue tensions arising.

The position established at Maastricht was that, for a country to be entitled to participate in monetary union, all four criteria would have to be met. However, developments after 1991, not least the successive crises of the ERM, prompted the emergence of more flexible interpretations. Thus, the exchange rate criterion was ultimately based on the post-1993 version of the ERM, with its much wider margins of fluctuation, and there was tacit acceptance of 'creative accounting' on the part of some governments in order to allow them to clear the indebtedness hurdles. It is not unreasonable to conclude, on the basis of these manoeuvres, that the wider *political* will favouring monetary union in Europe came to override what were perceived as narrower technical objections to this process. It is also worth pointing out that the convergence criteria have a macroeconomic orientation. We will say more in a moment about whether macro criteria are an appropriate way to assess whether a country is ready for euro area membership.

On 1 May 1998, of those countries deemed to have met the Maastricht criteria, 11 elected to adopt the euro. These were Austria, Belgium, Finland, France, Germany, Ireland, Italy, Luxembourg, Netherlands, Portugal and Spain. Of the remaining four EU member states at the time, the UK and Denmark had negotiated opt-outs that freed them of the obligation to join, while Sweden and Greece did not meet all the Maastricht criteria. Sweden *chose* not to meet the ERM criterion and a subsequent Swedish referendum on euro membership produced a decisive 'no' vote. Greece, on the other hand, initially *failed* a number of the criteria but was deemed to have met them all soon afterwards and joined the euro area in 2001. Following the expansion of the EU in 2004, Cyprus, Malta, Slovenia, Slovakia, Estonia, Latvia and Lithuania also subsequently met the Maastricht criteria and joined, bringing the present membership of the euro area to 19 economies. All non-euro area members of the EU (except Denmark and the UK) are obliged to take steps to join in a timely fashion.

What, then, are the great advantages of a single currency in Europe: the bigger prize which allowed some of the 'technicalities' of Maastricht to be swept aside? We saw in Chapter 2 how the European single market was conceived as the EU's response to the fragmentation of the customs union created by the 1957 Treaty of Rome. Recall that the poorer collective performance of the EU economy, relative to the US and Japan in particular, had prompted concerns in the EU that it had lost something of its competitive edge. This was to be restored by raising the level of economic *integration* in the EU: substituting the customs union for a single market. The addition of the single currency entails even *deeper* integration and, its proponents claim, will confer specific benefits on Europe as a whole.

The benefits of the euro

The positive claims of the euro assume both microeconomic and macroeconomic forms. There are three main *micro* benefits:

- The elimination of the *transaction costs* associated with currency exchange. No one travelling from the Netherlands to Germany ever again has to incur the cost associated with changing money – the same currency circulates in both countries, indeed in all 19 member countries. This benefit is generally recognized to be relatively modest.
- The elimination of *exchange rate risk* inside the euro area. Because all 19 economies use the same currency, the exchange rate in one will never again move against the currency of any fellow member. So, for example, firms in Finland can plan medium-term investments without any risk that adverse currency movements will suddenly push up the cost of components or raw materials sourced in the euro area, or the price of their exports to other euro area economies.

Price transparency: arises in an international context when countries use the same currencies or, to a lesser extent, when exchange rates are fixed.

- Finally, the euro brings perfect price transparency. Because the transactions that UK consumers and firms undertake in other countries involve prices and contracts denominated in foreign currencies they are less clear than transactions in the UK conducted in pounds. To some extent this may make UK residents less willing to do business abroad because it's a little harder. This is the UK's loss if such opacity prevents it from undertaking the *best* set of transactions that it could. Because of the euro this no longer applies for countries like Ireland. Irish consumers and firms no longer have to convert German marks, French or Belgian francs, Italian lire and so on into punts to see if they're being quoted a competitive price; they know instantly because they use and think in the same currency. Figure 14.14 indicates why price transparency and reduced exchange rate risk are so highly prized for the euro area economies – simply because they trade so heavily with one another. Thus, Austria, to take the first entry in the figure, has 67 per cent of its exports bought by fellow EU members, most of whom are already in the euro area with most of the rest obliged to join. Austria's next biggest market, the United States, takes just 5.4 per cent of its exports.

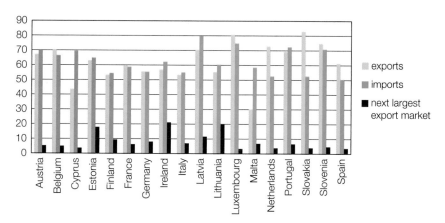

Figure 14.14 Euro area members' share of trade with EU 28, 2013 (%)

Source: Data from WTO

At the *macro* level the euro offers two main benefits:

- The design of the ECB means that the euro area should be a low inflation economy. This is certainly a potential boon to those countries that struggled with inflation in the past (Figure 14.12 suggests that Italy and France might be in this group).
- The euro may provide for a stronger presence in the global monetary system than was achieved by many national EU currencies and countries. Should it begin to eclipse the dollar as the world's key currency, the financial markets may accept lower interest rate premiums as the price of holding the euro; this may mean a lower euro zone interest rate than would otherwise prevail and consequent stimuli to investment and consumption in Europe.

The costs of the euro

The single currency has two main types of cost associated with it:

- First, there are the obvious costs of *redenomination*. The financial and wider economic systems of each euro area country were tailored to national currencies. The introduction of the euro required the recalibration of all these systems. Redenomination costs are generally thought to be modest; and they are one-off costs but the benefits of the euro go on forever.
- The second cost is potentially much more serious. This is *the loss of macroeconomic policy independence*. Inside the euro area, interest rates are set by the ECB in the light of prevailing economic conditions in the area as a whole. What happens if (say) euro area interest rates appear too low given circumstances in one particular country? Arguably, this was the case in Ireland when the euro was introduced. Irish interest rates fell from 6 to 3 per cent *overnight* when the Irish central bank's monetary writ passed to the ECB. In the ECB's view, sluggish economic conditions in the euro area in 1999 demanded the lower rate but the Irish authorities thought that the fast-growing Irish

economy needed the higher rate in order to keep inflationary pressures in check. Because the ECB sets euro area interest rates, Ireland had an interest rate imposed upon it that its policymakers clearly perceived as inappropriate.[1]

This example illustrates what is sometimes referred to as the 'one size fits all' problem of euro area interest rates, and indeed of macro policy more generally. The euro seems to require that ECB decisions should suit all euro participants. However, that this may not always happen – as our Irish example illustrates – is not necessarily a fundamental weakness of the euro. This is because the long-term success of the currency is dependent upon the real integration of the euro area nations. They need over time to behave much more like *one* economy; if they do, a unified macro policy framework will actually be appropriate in that one size will fit all because that size – the prevailing interest rate level – will be the right one.

This issue is neatly summed up by the question of whether or not the euro area can become an optimum currency area. This concept originated in the Nobel Prize–winning work of Robert Mundell. Briefly, an optimum currency area is a grouping of economies or regions within which goods, capital and labour markets are sufficiently integrated and flexible to allow the effective operation of a single currency and unified macro-policy framework across them. We return to our example of the Irish economy to illustrate the significance of this concept. Already fast, Irish economic growth was further stimulated by the lowering of interest rates from 6 to 3 per cent when Ireland joined the euro area at its inception. On the face of it this appears to be a regrettable and possibly disastrous development. However, what if the euro area labour market was flexible to the extent that unemployed people from, say, a hypothetically depressed Spain began to migrate to Ireland attracted by relatively high wages – the product of full employment – and greater job opportunities?

Moreover, what if at the same time, encouraged by EU regional policy, firms began to seek out locations in Spain in which to invest because slower growth there had lowered investment costs and because, unlike perhaps in Ireland, there were no labour shortages? In these circumstances, the differences in economic growth between Ireland and Spain would not be a major issue because labour and capital market flexibility would tend to reduce them. Labour would gravitate to Ireland thus 'cooling' its economy; new investment would tend to focus on low-cost Spain, driving up its economic prospects. This also means that Ireland and any other euro area economy or region can 'live' with whatever ECB macroeconomic policy framework is set.

Here is where the Maastricht criteria in a sense 'got it wrong'. Recall that these are macro in orientation. They ask questions about inflation, interest rates and exchange rates. They don't ask about the level of flexibility of the labour and capital markets of euro area candidates – the things that matter if the euro area is to become an optimum currency area. The difficulties of the Greek, Irish and

Concept: An optimum currency area is a grouping of economies within which markets are sufficiently integrated and flexible to make the use of one currency more desirable than separate national currencies.

---

1 Interest rate movements in the advanced economies are usually of the order of a fraction of 1 per cent. A cut from 6 to 3 per cent is almost unprecedented outside emergency conditions in recent times.

Spanish economies highlight the extent of the problem. In Spain, for example, unemployment is presently 24 per cent – a stunning figure and a stunning waste of that country's most important resource: its people. How can Spain recover? Because it is in the euro area we know what Spain *can't* do:

- It cannot cut interest rates (they're the domain of the ECB).
- It cannot devalue its currency against the currencies of its main trading partners (they use the same one).
- It cannot, like the British government, engage in quantitative easing – this again is the prerogative of the ECB.
- It cannot increase government spending (it hasn't the money but even if it was in a better fiscal position the euro rules limit what it can do with fiscal policy).

In fact the only thing it *can* do is hope that its labour markets become flexible enough to make its goods and services competitive in the European market where it sells more than 60 per cent of its exports (see Figure 14.14). It almost certainly needs to implement unpopular microeconomic polices to help raise labour market competitiveness. Crudely, this means Spanish people working harder, longer and more cheaply than they do now, and for a number of years. The euro makes austerity Spain's way forward. It also demonstrates what happens to balance of payments problems inside a monetary union: they are transformed into regional problems. In this case the problem region is the whole Spanish economy.

The problems of Greece, Ireland and Spain raise another question about the euro's design. We noted that the Delors Report urged that more resources be put into the EU's regional policy framework. Though this was done, the sums involved were very small because the EU is a meagrely funded institution. The overwhelming majority of state spending in Europe is undertaken by national governments. This means that when euro area economies get into Greek-style difficulties they are in a double bind: they have no meaningful macro tools available to them, nor is there any supra-national authority at hand to help. There is a contrast here with the US, where troubled states – similarly lacking in macro powers – can be given resources by the Federal government.

In response to this design deficiency, in 2010 the EU established a European Financial Stability Facility (EFSF), which provides a €750bn fund on which euro members can draw should their fiscal positions become threatened. Greece, Ireland and Portugal were all forced to accept EU assistance as their governments ran out of cash. This kind of federal apparatus through which pooled resources can be used to aid members as they move down the slow road of adjustment-by-austerity are a belated recognition of some fundamental flaws in the euro's architecture.

Estonia joined the euro area on 1 January 2011 but not all Estonians were happy about it

14.8   The balance of payments, exchange rates and business

We conclude this chapter with a discussion of the relevance of the balance of payments and exchange rates to business. In Section 14.3 we saw how balance of payments problems in the world economy, if they foment a rise in protectionist sentiment, have the potential to adversely impact upon other economies, many of which may not be themselves involved in the initial payments problems. Here we consider the more localized problem of the policy reaction to payments imbalance by the authorities in an individual economy. What implications does such balance of payments policy have for business?

An initial issue here is the nature of the exchange rate regime under which the economy is operating. Consider first balance of payments imbalance under fixed exchange rates.

Fixed exchange rates

Under fixed exchange rates we know that persistent balance of payments imbalance will eventually need to be tackled by some combination of expenditure reduction policy and expenditure switching policy. In the case of a deficit, this involves slowing down the rate of growth in order to reduce the demand for imports, and currency devaluation to both lower the price of exports in foreign markets and increase the price of imports in the domestic market. Assuming the Marshall–Lerner condition holds and domestic industry has sufficient capacity to respond to the demand stimulus resulting from the devaluation, the deficit should be eroded.

For some domestic firms, the implications of this policy response will be positive. Those that sell in foreign markets may find their position improved as the devaluation makes their products cheaper in comparison to goods and services sold by foreign competitors. For firms active in the domestic market, outcomes are more ambiguous. On the one hand, they may find their price competitiveness improves as the devaluation raises the price of imported goods, but on the other, the domestic market as a whole will come under pressure as economic growth slows and demand slackens. For domestic firms that use imported commodities in their own production processes and sell into the domestic market, matters are even more serious. The devaluation raises the price of imports, putting upward pressure on their own final prices, and they find the size of their market shrinking.

Flexible exchange rates

Under flexible exchange rates remember that all the strain of balance of payments imbalance is borne by the exchange rate. For example, should a deficit begin to emerge, excess supply of the domestic currency on the foreign exchanges will tend to promote a depreciation of the currency in question. In turn, this alters export and import prices in a manner that favours firms in the country with the depreciating currency. The main difference between balance of payments deficit correction under fixed and floating exchange rates is thus the absence of any need for expenditure reduction under floating rates. For domestic firms this has the obvious advantage that there will be no depression of demand in the domestic market.

Fixed versus flexible exchange rates in a business context

Our discussion would seem to suggest that, from a business perspective, flexible rates might be the preferred option. However, there is one additional issue that complicates matters. It is a commonplace that many firms prefer stable economic conditions to less stable ones. Business planning – decisions about how much to produce, how much to invest, which markets to target, and so on – is clearly best conducted in an environment of certainty. Now, given that a major source of instability and uncertainty for business has its roots in currency fluctuations, it may be that business interests are best served by the active management of exchange rates. In other words, fixed exchange rates may be preferred by firms because they help foster more stable conditions for business. Yet it is also the case that firms can protect themselves from the vagaries of currency movements by using forward markets for currencies.

Consider the following example. If a German manufacturer of printing machinery contracts to export a machine, priced in euros, to a British printing firm in six months' time, the British firm knows the price it will have to pay in sterling today. However, the British firm cannot know what the euro/pound exchange rate will be in six months' time. Perhaps the euro will weaken against sterling, making the sterling price of the machine lower when it is actually delivered. Alternatively, sterling could weaken, making the sterling price faced by the firm on delivery higher. This kind of uncertainty can be eliminated if the British firm agrees a forward exchange rate with its bank for sterling against the euro at the same time as the contract for the machine itself is signed (there will, of course, be a charge for this service by the bank). So, when the machine arrives, so too do the euros required to pay for it at an exchange rate the printing firm has agreed to in advance. It seems then that firms can insulate themselves from some of the uncertainty associated with exchange rate variability under a flexible exchange rate regime. However, this option is not costless and forward markets usually range only up to 180 days into the future; certainly beyond a year or two they are much more expensive to participate in. This means that, for example, it is difficult to insure that an income stream earned in a foreign economy will not be vulnerable to depreciation in the long term against the domestic currency.

What are we to make of this process of argument and counter argument? Are fixed or flexible rates better from a business perspective? Possibly the best conclusion is to accept that these are open questions. Currently, the world economy is *generally* organized along flexible lines but many countries choose to manage their currencies sometimes unilaterally – like China – and sometimes in partnership with other countries. We might characterize this environment as one in which many countries find some advantage in a degree of currency management.

Check your understanding of some of the issues around currencies by answering the questions posed in Everyday Economics 14.1.

EVERYDAY ECONOMICS 14.1

Exchange rate regimes, policy options and business planning

What might each of these images suggest about the following:

- Policymakers' options over currency devaluation or depreciation?
- The ability of firms in international markets to make effective business plans?

Answers are at the end of the chapter.

SUMMARY

- An economy's balance of payments and its exchange rate are inextricably linked. In theory, a floating exchange rate will automatically produce balance of payments balance; policy may then be concentrated on other objectives free of any concern for the external account. However, where exchange rates are fixed or managed, the emergence of balance of payments disequilibria requires active forms of policy correction. Expenditure reduction involves internal deflation and invokes movement out of deficit by virtue of lower domestic aggregate demand and a reduced demand for imports. In the face of a deficit, the second form of policy – expenditure switching, usually involves currency devaluation or depreciation, which improves the price competitiveness of exports and import substitutes.
- Since 1945 the world economy has relied upon both fixed exchange rates (under the Bretton Woods system) and flexible rates (under the 'non-system'). The non-system has, however, not been characterized by freely floating exchange rates. Indeed, at times during the 1980s, exchange rates were collectively managed by the major industrialized nations. Moreover, inside the non-system, regional fixed exchange rate regimes, such as the ERM, have been developed. The ERM was succeeded in 1999 by the euro.
- From a business perspective there is no definitive answer to the question of whether fixed or flexible exchange rate regimes are preferable.

KEY TERMS

- Current account
- Capital account
- Financial account
- Autonomous transactions
- Accommodating transactions
- Appreciation/ revaluation
- Flexible exchange rates
- Fixed exchange rates
- Expenditure reduction policy
- Balance of payments disequilibria
- Exchange rate
- Depreciation/ devaluation
- Expenditure switching policy
- Currency speculation
- European monetary union
- Optimum currency area

QUESTIONS FOR DISCUSSION

1. Outline the structure of the balance of payments accounts.
2. Explain the significance of autonomous and accommodating transactions in the balance of payments.
3. What is meant by balance of payments surplus and deficit and which general forms of policy are appropriate to each?
4. How are exchange rates determined?
5. Explain the differences between fixed and flexible exchange rate systems and the advantages and disadvantages of each.
6. What is the economic case for the euro?

EVERYDAY ECONOMICS 14.1 ANSWERS

1 and 2. The exchange rate regime for each country is what counts. France and Germany use the same currency, the euro. There is no difference between a euro circulating in Paris and a euro in Berlin. This means that the French authorities cannot devalue their currency against the German currency to try to make French goods more competitive against German goods. On the other hand, French businesses may find the certainty over the value of their currency in their major export market immensely helpful. They know that in the 18 other euro countries the prices they charge will be extremely transparent and that there can be no tricky exchange rate risks lurking around the corner.

3. Things in Denmark are a little different. Denmark is in the EU's single market but it has retained its currency, the krone. This means that in principle it is possible for the Danish authorities to alter the value of their currency against Denmark's competitors. However, Denmark has chosen to fix the krone against the euro, which indicates that the authorities have no wish to engage in currency manipulation inside the single market. Danish businesses can plan securely on this basis. Note, however, that although they don't have to worry about exchange rate risk against the euro there is less price transparency for Danish businesses. Foreign customers still have to work out Danish prices in unfamiliar krone.

4. Finally, in the UK the authorities are free to try to condition the value of the pound on the foreign exchange markets should they choose to do so. During the aftermath of the global financial crisis the UK benefited from a substantial depreciation of sterling against other major currencies (see Figure 14.9). For UK businesses a floating currency is perhaps a mixed blessing. It can certainly help to keep UK goods price competitive in difficult times but it makes business planning more challenging. There is always the risk that careful plans can be wrecked by unanticipated adverse currency swings. The UK's ability to present transparent prices to the rest of the world may also be undermined.

ONE THING YOU SHOULD READ

John Cassidy, 'Why chaos in the currency markets might be good news', *The New Yorker*, January 16, 2015 (newyorker.com)

This short article was prompted by the abandonment by the authorities in Switzerland of the peg of the Swiss franc to the euro. The value of the Swiss franc had been fixed against the euro for three years. The principal reason for the peg was to stop the Swiss franc appreciating sharply against the euro and the peg was maintained by low Swiss interest rates and direct intervention in the foreign exchange market by the Swiss central bank. As soon as the peg was abandoned the Swiss franc appreciated against the euro, initially by about 40 per cent. The euro also slumped against other currencies such as the US dollar. John Cassidy reflects on the implications of these developments for the euro area, the US and Switzerland. After reading the article answer the following questions.

1. Why does the euro area desperately need a fall in the value of its currency?
2. At the time he wrote this article Cassidy reports that the market expected the ECB to begin quantitative easing (QE). Find out if this happened. What are the likely effects of QE on the euro area's exchange rate and its inflation rate? Why are these effects desirable?
3. Why might the US not be too concerned about the dollar's appreciation against the euro?
4. Cassidy expresses some sympathy towards the Swiss authorities. Why in his view were they within their rights to abandon their currency peg to the euro? What are the dangers to Switzerland of abandoning the peg?

PhotoDisc/Getty Images

15

globalization

KEY ISSUES

What is meant by globalization?

How far has globalization progressed?

What are the attractions of globalization?

What threats might globalization pose?

Has globalization always been with us?

CONTENTS

15.1 Introduction **478**

15.2 What is globalization? **478**

15.3 How far has globalization progressed? **481**

15.4 What are the attractions of globalization? **490**

15.5 What threats might globalization pose? **492**

15.6 On reflection, how new is globalization anyway? **498**

15.1   Introduction

In Chapters 13 and 14 we introduced the 'open economy' concepts of the balance of payments and exchange rates. Our discussion in part concentrated on the problems and issues such concepts posed for *national* economies. We saw that because a country cannot ignore a persistent balance of payments imbalance it may choose to confront potential balance of payments problems by, for example, allowing its currency's exchange rate to float freely against other currencies.

In this final chapter we move beyond national economic concerns of this nature to further explore one of the key international economic issues of our time: *globalization* and the supposed emergence of a new 'global' economy. This concept is often invoked, but what exactly does it mean and what is its basis in reality?

15.2   What is globalization?

Aspects of globalization

The world has become a very different place over the past 30 or so years. Many of the borders, boundaries and differences that segmented and gave shape to our economies and societies have become porous or melted away entirely. Here's one example. When the authors of this book were students, travel to places such as Russia, China or even Poland was not easy. A large chunk of the world was riven between the capitalist West and the communist East and the mutual suspicion and hostility between these two groupings left relations between them – economic, political, cultural, technological – somewhere between difficult and non-existent. And even if we had been able to gain permission to visit Moscow or Beijing, the expense would have been exorbitant. No cheap flights then, or Internet to sort out visas and arrange accommodation.

Borders are in many ways less forbidding than in the twentieth century

Now we live in a world that is much more accessible and where space and time seem to have been compressed. From the PC on which this chapter is being written we can quickly and easily book a flight to virtually anywhere, arrange visas and reserve a hotel room, all for a sum of money that is nowhere near as prohibitive as it once was – the planet seems to be a *smaller* place. It is also more uniform. What have become global brands saturate near and very distant localities: McDonald's in Manchester and Moscow, Tesco in Birmingham and Beijing, and Starbucks in Hull and Hiroshima.

While globalization might be welcomed by many as it spreads markets and economic opportunities to new places, it is also resisted by others. And, confusingly, globalization might often be simultaneously welcomed *and* resisted by some groups or institutions. Think back to Chapter 13 and our example of the tariffs that the EU placed on shoe imports from China and Vietnam. European residents wanted to buy these cheap and fashionable shoes but because their arrival in the market threatened the few remaining European shoe producers the authorities tried to make things difficult for China and Vietnam. Another example? French farmers have been fined and even imprisoned for ransacking the site of a planned McDonald's restaurant in France. Many French citizens like McDonald's – its business continues to grow in France – but some see it as a threat to the distinctiveness of French culture and way of life. Globalization also poses a threat where it facilitates the rapid transmission of wider economic problems. The 2008–9 recession was a global event that involved the spread of the fall-out from the collapse of a real estate bubble in the United States to the rest of the world. Had the world's financial system been less interdependent or better regulated, this catastrophe might have been contained.

Conceptualizing globalization from a business perspective

So globalization embraces a range of economic, political, cultural and technological processes that appear to make the world a more compact and integrated place. But in this book we're interested in economics for business and it will be helpful to express our interpretation of globalization more concisely.

Globalization: the spread of international trade and foreign direct investment to new parts of the world.

From a business perspective, **globalization** refers to the spread of international trade and foreign direct investment to new parts of the world, though, as above, much of this has been facilitated by the rapid growth of financial markets, unprecedented changes in the world's political landscape and seismic shifts in technology.

As an example of the contemporary importance of financial markets in particular consider their scale in relation to national economies. Figure 15.1 depicts the daily turnover of the global foreign exchange market and the weekly global turnover in company shares set against GDP data for four selected economies. At $5.3tn a single day's foreign exchange trading is at least twice the yearly output of each of the UK, Brazil and Australia and it takes this market only four days to exceed annual US GDP. The value of the weekly turnover in the global share market is smaller – at about $1tn – but it exceeds the annual GDP of each of the UK, Brazil and Australia in just three weeks and US annual output in a little over four months.

Not surprisingly a corollary of the globalization process is sometimes thought to be a weakening of the sovereignty of nation states. As markets and firms continue to grow and migrate across international borders, the power of the authorities to condition the development of their own economies is eroded; and this may be true for even the traditionally large and powerful states. For

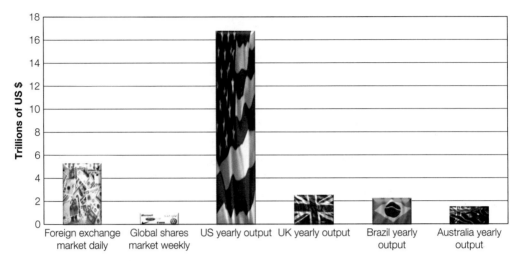

Figure 15.1 Estimated size of the daily turnover of the global foreign exchange market, weekly turnover of global share market vs GDP of selected economies, 2013, $tn

example, although the UK is still a major car-manufacturing economy, there are no longer any major UK-owned car companies. This means that the British economy's future in carmaking is entirely dependent on decisions taken in boardrooms in places such as the US, Japan, Germany and India, and the British government has little option but to make life as comfortable as it can for the foreign car firms upon which so much investment and jobs in Britain depend. For 'comfortable life' read low taxes and forms of state support such as the car scrappage scheme introduced to boost the industry in the aftermath of the 2008–9 financial crisis.

ECONOMICS AT WORK

Jaime Marshall, Palgrave (Macmillan Education), www.palgrave.com

Jaime is the Managing Director of Palgrave, a Macmillan Education business. Palgrave develops books and learning resources, in both print and digital formats, for university-level students in the humanities, social sciences and engineering. Jaime has worked extensively in sales, marketing and editorial.

Visit **www.palgrave.com/companion/mulhearn3** to watch Jaime talking about the challenges and opportunities faced by operating globally, and how a basic knowledge of economics is useful in day-to-day working life.

15.3   How far has globalization progressed?

The world economy has dramatically changed in many ways but has it really globalized? This is an empirical question – we have to go and look. If it were evident that most parts of the globe had been recently and decisively embraced by the twin processes of trade and investment then the case for the advent of a global economy would be strong. However, although *some* of the world's formerly peripheral regions have become heavily integrated with the incumbent developed economies, other regions, containing many economies and large populations, have yet to gain an extensive share in either trade or investment. What is the evidence for this claim?

Recent patterns in world trade

The ability of a country to successfully export some of the goods and services it produces is important for a number of reasons. For example, a country's exports generate an inflow of foreign currencies that condition its capacity to import. Without foreign currencies countries cannot buy food, machinery, technology, medicines or anything else from abroad. Exports and the demand they generate for a nation may also be an important source of economic growth and job generation. Figure 15.2 describes the shares in exports of the world's major regions in 1983 and 2013. One aspect of the two pie charts is their depiction of a striking degree of *continuity* in the pattern of world exports. In 1983 Europe and North America respectively generated 43.5 and 16.8 per cent of all exports. Just over 30 years later, during the period in which the world has supposedly globalized, these shares stood at 36.6 and 13.0 per cent respectively – a loss in each case but still leaving these regions in first and third place in the shares in the export pie.

Asia has seen a simply stunning growth in export share – from 19.1 per cent in 1983 to 32.9 per cent by 2013. There are a number of forces at work here but mostly this change can be explained by the extraordinary improvement in the export performances of the six East Asian Tiger economies (Hong Kong, Malaysia, South Korea, Singapore, Taiwan and Thailand), and above all by China, which saw its share of world exports grow from about 1 per cent in 1983 to 12.6 per cent in 2013. China is now the world's single largest export-ing nation.

Turning to South and Central America, the CIS (Confederation of Independent States), Africa and the Middle East, it is evident that all but one of these regions has *lost* some export share. In a globalizing world the reverse might be expected to happen, with trade activity spreading to regions that had in the past been relatively excluded from it.

So where does this leave an assessment of the extent of progress towards globalized trade? What we seem to have found is dramatic change in *one* of the world's regions, and especially in its most populous country (China has about

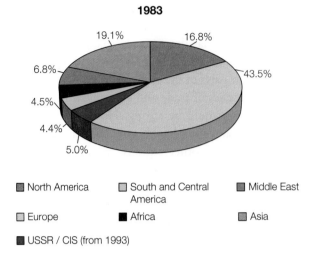

1983

- ■ North America
- ☐ South and Central America
- ■ Middle East
- ☐ Europe
- ■ Africa
- ☐ Asia
- ■ USSR / CIS (from 1993)

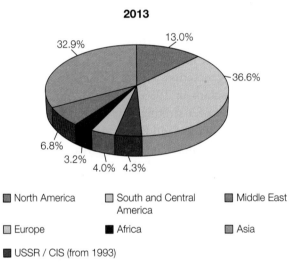

2013

- ■ North America
- ☐ South and Central America
- ■ Middle East
- ☐ Europe
- ■ Africa
- ☐ Asia
- ■ USSR / CIS (from 1993)

Figure 15.2 Regional shares in world merchandise exports 1983 and 2013 (%)

Source: Data from World Trade Organization, www.wto.org

a fifth of the world's people) but limited evidence of much progress elsewhere. The rich countries in Europe and North America have lost some share in world exports but so too have the poorest regions with, for example, Africa's export share falling from 4.5 per cent in 1983 to 3.2 per cent in 2013.

Recent patterns in world investment

If trade patterns offer limited evidence of a globalizing world what about investment patterns? As noted in Chapter 14, foreign direct investment (FDI) is investment capital provided to a firm from a source in another country where the investor has a direct influence on the business activities of the recipient firm. FDI transactions include those in real assets such as factories, machinery and equipment, retail infrastructure and so on. Inward streams of FDI can be important as they may be associated with the transfer of new technologies and production know-how to recipient economies, particularly if these are less developed. Investment also lays the basis for wider economic growth and job generation.

Figures 15.3 and 15.4 provide some evidence on the distribution of FDI inflows since 1990. Thinking again about globalization, what patterns might we expect to see here? One popular view is that multinational firms have both helped to shape and taken advantage of a more open global environment in moving production to new parts of the world and away from the long-established industrial centres in Europe and North America. In doing so they look to profit by the productivity advantages associated with, for example, low labour cost locations. Why pay a relatively high minimum wage in Western Europe when workers can be hired for a lot less in North Africa or the Indian sub-continent?

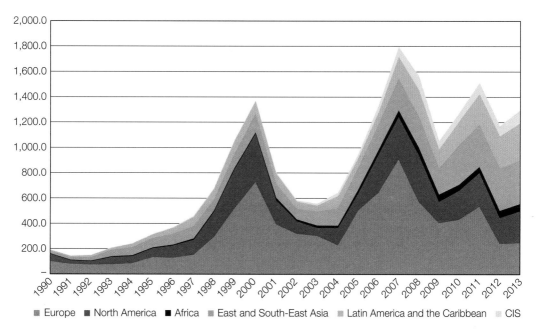

Figure 15.3 FDI inflows by region 1990–2013, US$bn

Source: Data from UNCTAD, http://unctad.org

So how far has this process gone? Figure 15.3 describes FDI inflows by region. One thing that seems to be apparent from the figure is the *continuing* attraction of Europe and North America as places where foreign firms want to open production and distribution facilities. Between 1990 and 2013 Europe took somewhere between 17 and 50 per cent of global FDI, while the North American share fluctuated between 10 and 28 per cent. However, complementing to some extent our evidence in Figure 15.2, South, East and South-East Asia and Latin America and the Caribbean are now major recipients of FDI

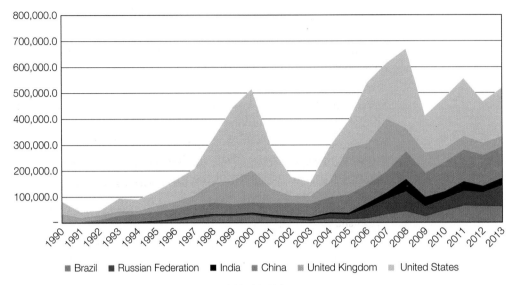

Figure 15.4 FDI inflows by selected countries 1990–2013, $m

Source: Data from UNCTAD, http://unctad.org

with average respective shares since 2009 of 22 and 16 per cent. Finally, notice the relatively small shares of Africa and the CIS. Although these have been generally rising since 2000 they cannot yet be said to be part of any great global shift in the patterns of multinational investment.

Figure 15.4 shows FDI inflows for selected countries and more specifically for two major types of country: on the one hand, two representatives of the industrial nations – the US and the UK – and, on the other, the large and rapidly developing **BRIC economies** (BRIC is an acronym for **B**razil, **R**ussia, **I**ndia and **C**hina). The US is the world's major recipient of FDI. The UK also enjoys a historically healthy share of investment inflows (which are comparable to flows to France and Germany – other large economies of a similar size but which we have not shown to prevent a cluttering of the figure). More recently, however, the UK's share of FDI has fallen. In 2013 it was 2.6 per cent. Among the BRIC economies, China has been the focus of increasingly strong investment inflows since 1990 but the shares of Brazil and the Russian Federation have also grown. These data provide some evidence for the decisive spread of the tentacles of capitalist development to new economies.

BRIC economies: Brazil, Russia, India and China.

São Paulo in Brazil, one of the BRICs

PhotoDisc/ Getty Images

● **Think Point**

The ride-hire firm Uber was only founded in 2009 but has spread rapidly to more than 200 locations in over 50 countries. Its app connects people with smartphones who want a ride with drivers. A price for a journey is quoted, accepted and paid for via the app. It's a revolutionary business model for the global taxi industry. In which regions of the world do you think Uber has made most ground and why? What does your answer say about globalization?

Of Uber's 200 locations so far only three are in Africa – in Lagos, Cape Town and Johannesburg. This may in part be a reflection of the differences in infrastructure available between the highly developed and less-developed parts of the world. Uber's needs include:

- the recruitment of sufficient numbers of drivers with their own vehicles;
- reliable network coverage;
- an adequate base of potential customers with smartphones and the capacity for electronic payment.

It will certainly find these more easily in some places which suggests that, for this new form of economic activity, global reach may eventually happen but it will take time.

Some reflections on the distribution of world GDP

Figure 15.5 shows the shares of G5 and BRIC economies in world GDP in 1992, 2000, 2009 and 2013. The continued dominance of the US economy is particularly striking; the US still produces more than 20 per cent of the world's output. This makes it a particular magnet for investment as it is clearly the world's biggest national market and the home of many large firms that may be the targets of merger or acquisition of non-US corporations (as well as home-based ones). Figure 15.5 is also notable for the unfolding story it tells about the BRIC economies. In 1992 each of the BRIC economies was less than half the size of the UK, then the smallest member of the G5. By 2009 China's

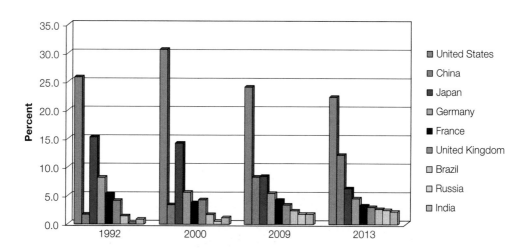

Figure 15.5 Shares in world GDP: G5 and BRIC economies

Source: Data from IMF's World Economic Outlook Database

spectacular growth saw it challenging Japan for second place behind the US, while the gaps between Germany, France and the UK on the one hand and Brazil, Russia and India on the other had narrowed considerably. Just five years later in 2013 China had eclipsed Japan and the gap between it and the US was narrowing fast, as were the gaps between the major European economies and the BRICs. What will Figure 15.5 look like with observations added for 2025 and 2050? An intriguing and, for the G5, probably a worrying question.

However, before we get too carried away with what may happen, consider Figure 15.6, which depicts gross national income per capita for the G5 and BRICs in 2013. Although the BRICs, and China in particular, are gathering economic momentum, the size of the populations of these countries for the moment continues to limit their relative affluence and therefore their attractiveness as markets in which to invest. Although China is the world's second largest economy, the income that it generates has to be spread around a vast population of 1.3 billion (compared, for example, to the UK's 61 million). This contextualizes the progress that China and the other BRIC economies have made: a very positive start but some way yet to go.

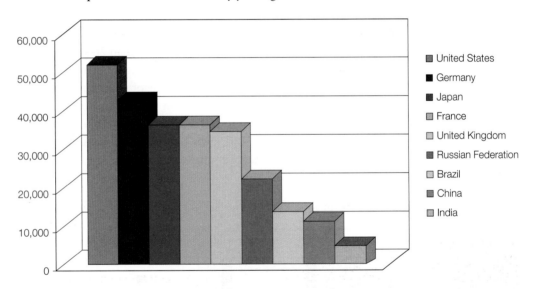

Figure 15.6 Gross national income per capita 2013 (PPP 2011 US$)

Source: Data from UN Human Development Report 2013, hdr.undp.org

This point is further exemplified by the data in Table 15.1 which has been extracted from the United Nations 2013 Human Development Index (HDI). The HDI offers a ranking of the world's nations based on a combination of three measures of human development: life expectancy, education and income. These measures reflect, respectively, the extent to which people are able to live long lives, their capacities for self-improvement; and their material living standards. Not surprisingly the G5 enjoy relatively high HDI

Table 15.1 United Nations Human Development Index 2013, top 10 and selected economies

		Life expectancy at birth (years) 2013	Mean years of schooling (years) 2012	Gross national income (GNI) per capita (2011 PPP $) 2013
1	Norway	81.5	12.6	63,909
2	Australia	82.5	12.8	41,524
3	Switzerland	82.6	12.2	53,762
4	Netherlands	81.0	11.9	42,397
5	United States	78.9	12.9	52,308
6	Germany	80.7	12.9	43,049
7	New Zealand	81.1	12.5	32,569
8	Canada	81.5	12.3	41,887
9	Singapore	82.3	10.2	72,371
10	Denmark	79.4	12.1	42,880
14	United Kingdom	80.5	12.3	35,002
17	Japan	83.6	11.5	36,747
20	France	81.8	11.1	36,629
57	Russian Federation	68.0	11.7	22,617
79	Brazil	73.9	7.2	14,275
91	China	75.3	7.5	11,477
135	India	66.4	4.4	5,150

Source: UN Human Development Report 2014, hdr.undp.org

rankings. Although the United States leads the group in 5th place, each G5 member has long life expectancy, mean years of schooling above 11 or 12 years and, as per Figure 15.6, high income levels. For the BRIC economies, although life expectancy in Russia is lower than in Brazil, its greater investment in schooling and higher per capita income give it a slightly higher ranking: 57th compared to Brazil's 79th. India is the lowest-ranked of the BRIC economies, given its combination of lower life expectancy, relatively meagre schooling and lower per capita income. The human development gap between the G5 and the BRICs is mostly a reflection of the more sustained growth of the industrial economies over past generations. Should the economic momentum of the BRICs be sustained over future generations the gap will narrow.

Children in rural India: what's their share of the global cake?

© iStockphoto.com/Vikram Raghuvanshi Photography

If the BRIC economies can aspire to move up the HDI rankings in the coming decades, it is often harder to say the same for economies with low-to-medium human development such as those in Table 15.2. In some of these countries life expectancy fails to reach 60 or even 50 years. Think of the ages of some of your older relatives in the context of those figures. Sierra Leone and Niger have minimal schooling, and income per capita is less than $3 a day in Niger. How does the concept of globalization fit with the broad experiences of many people in these economies? Perhaps it doesn't.

Table 15.2 United Nations Human Development Index 2013, selected economies with medium and low human development

HDI rank		Life expectancy at birth (years) 2013	Mean years of schooling (years) 2012	Gross national income (GNI) per capita (2011 PPP $) 2013
136	Cambodia	71.9	5.8	2,805
141	Zambia	58.1	6.5	2,898
183	Sierra Leone	45.6	2.9	1,815
187	Niger	58.4	1.4	873

Source: UN Human Development Report 2014, hdr.undp.org

Recent patterns in human migration

While globalization is primarily associated with shifts in international trade and investment, the movement of people might also be a consideration. If trade and investment patterns have changed in relatively limited ways perhaps human migration might add to the global fluidity of resource allocation. For example, as FDI flows from developed countries to Africa are relatively weak, can African residents move instead to developed countries to take advantage of greater economic opportunities there?

The evidence suggests that while human migration has increased over the past 20 years it has not done so in any grand globalizing sense. As of 1990, 155 million people had left their home country to live abroad for at least a year; by 2013 the estimated figure was 232 million. Figure 15.7 illustrates the pattern of migrant flows by destination from 1990 to 2013. The world's three major migrant destinations are Northern America, Europe and Asia. Between 1990 and 2013 each of these regions increased its migrant stock; Asia by 20 million, Europe by 23 million and Northern America by 26 million. Table 15.3 places these numbers into context showing international migrants as a percentage of regional population. In Europe, for example, the proportion of migrants in the population was 6.8 per cent in 1990, rising to an estimated 9.8 per cent in 2013. For Northern America, the equivalent figures were 9.8 per cent rising to 14.9 per cent. It appears that the world centres of economic activity in Europe

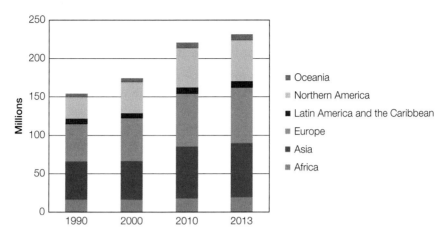

Figure 15.7 Estimated international migrants at mid-year by destination

Source: Data from United Nations, Department of Economic and Social Affairs (2013)

Table 15.3 International migrants as a percentage of the population

	1990	2000	2010	2013
Africa	2.5	1.9	1.7	1.7
Asia	1.6	1.4	1.6	1.6
Europe	6.8	7.7	9.3	9.8
Latin America and the Caribbean	1.6	1.2	1.4	1.4
Northern America	9.8	12.8	14.8	14.9
Oceania	17.3	17.3	20.0	20.7

Source: United Nations, Department of Economic and Social Affairs (2013)

and North America are as attractive to human migrants as they are to mobile capital, the only difference being that, especially after the 2008–9 recession, governments in these places may be less receptive towards migrants than they are to inward investment.

Globalization – has it happened?

So has the world economy globalized? Possibly this remains an open question given some of the continuities we have seen in the patterns of world trade and investment and the discontinuities we continue to see in income and human development. Certainly, there have been some notable achievements by a handful of Asian Tiger economies and China. But elsewhere changes have been relatively modest. Brazil, Russia and India enjoy growing shares of world GDP but, given the apparent lack of momentum in, for example, Africa and much of South and Central America, it may still be premature to refer to a globalized world economy.

15.4   What are the attractions of globalization?

Free and open trade is beneficial to all

Globalization, in the view of its proponents, has the potential to spread economic opportunity to parts of the world that have hitherto been denied it; opportunity for entire economies, particular communities, and individual women and men. In part, this goes back to the work of David Ricardo we discussed in Chapter 13. Ricardo was a supporter of free trade. Ricardo's lasting contribution to the canon of economic theory – comparative advantage – demonstrates that all nations can gain from participation in a free and open world economy. In such an environment resources will be efficiently allocated by markets that are articulated at a global level. Should globalization make international trade a more inclusive process, the big gainers will be the world's poorer economies which will find new markets for the goods and services they produce; and they will be incentivized to produce more efficiently. Just as important, there will be no losers.

To take one example, think of the resources that the European Union presently uses in subsidizing inefficient agricultural production. We discussed why the EU does this in Chapter 2: it's mostly to protect the jobs and incomes of European farmers. Without subsidies fewer of them would be in business and European countries would have to import more food from other parts of the world. And this would be a good thing in the view of the proponents of globalization because food production is more efficiently conducted elsewhere and without government subsidy. In a globalized world, Europeans would benefit from cheaper imported food. But wouldn't European farmers lose out? In the short term yes, even Ricardo recognized this. But were the EU not paying farmers to stay on the land it might use some of the resources released from defunct subsidies to encourage them to redeploy into other forms of economic activity where Europe retains a comparative advantage. In time *everyone* wins.

Trade and investment are complements in a globalized world

Where economic activity is borderless, investment too can flow to places of greater opportunity. Foreign direct investment brings a range of advantages to host countries that serve to underpin their longer-term economic prospects. New production facilities, technology, know-how and jobs may all be associated with FDI inflows.

Globalization may also positively fuse the processes of trade and investment. A good example is the recent relationship between China and Zambia. We've already said a bit about China in this chapter but little so far about Zambia beyond noting, in Table 15.2, its relatively limited levels of human development. Zambia is one of the world's major producers of copper but, more importantly from its own perspective, Zambia is heavily dependent on copper exports. These generate about 70 per cent of its overall export revenues. So to

An open-pit copper mine in Zambia. Copper is Zambia's main export

pay for its imports of cars, trucks, medicines, computers, mobile phones and everything else it doesn't produce, Zambia principally sells copper to the rest of the world.

Such dependence on a single export leaves Zambia highly vulnerable to swings in the international price of copper of which there have been a few in recent years. As Figure 15.8 illustrates, from 2000 until 2003 the copper price was flat, hovering between $1500 and $2000 per tonne, but thereafter it climbed steadily to $5000, and then sharply to $8000 per tonne in 2006.

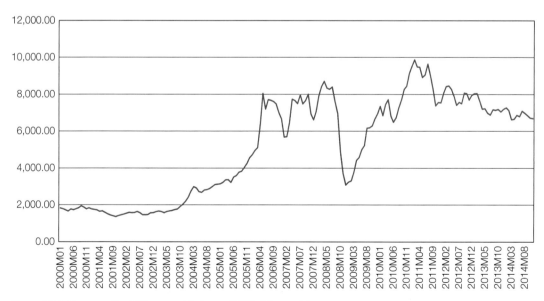

Figure 15.8 Copper price US$ per metric tonne 2000–14, monthly

Source: Data from IMF's World Economic Outlook Database

After peaking again in 2008 at close to $9000, the price collapsed during the world recession to around $3000. Since then it has recovered and at the time of writing stands at around $7000. The 2008 copper price collapse was potentially very dangerous for Zambia as some Western foreign investors in its mining industry took fright and left the country entirely. Several copper mines were closed as a result.

However, some might argue that this is actually a success story for globalization in general and Zambia in particular because of what happened next. One of Zambia's most important export markets is China, which has a strong demand for copper, given its surging industrialization. Western disinvestment in Zambian copper was the signal for Chinese investors to move in. China is now Zambia's biggest source of FDI and its copper industry is once again thriving as the world economy and the copper price recover. Had it not been for the growing Chinese presence in the world economy Zambia's economic outlook might have appeared bleaker. As it is Zambia has moved sharply up the United Nations HDI rank from 150th to 141st. The UN presently classifies Zambia as a country with medium rather than low human development.

And there's a footnote that might be added here by those who assert that the world has indeed become global. Why might China's demand for copper affect a Yorkshireman's ability to switch on a light? No, it's not a joke. The soaring demand-driven world price of copper is thought to be behind an increase in thefts of the metal from electricity power stations in Yorkshire and power cuts have happened there as a result.

15.5 What threats might globalization pose?

An unbalanced and less stable world economy?

Major changes in the world economy, whether these amount to globalization or not (or not yet), raise serious questions for national economies, wider regions, and the businesses and people in them. This is because change implies shifts in the patterns of resource allocation. Some countries or regions may be threatened by these shifts because they find themselves, at least for a time, allocated relatively fewer resources than before. On the other hand, some countries and regions will find themselves better off. One vital consideration, then, becomes how the losers and winners react to their new or emerging positions.

We can highlight the importance of this issue in the unfolding relationship between China and the West, especially the United States. China's growth has implications for the US, some of which it finds unpalatable. For example, we noted in Chapter 14 the US government's concern over what it sees as China's unwelcome manipulation of its exchange rate. Keeping the renminbi fixed at a cheap rate against the US dollar is good for China – it makes Chinese exports extremely price competitive in American markets. But the US is unhappy about the large trade deficit it currently bears (look back at Figure 14.3) and it partly blames this on China's exchange rate policy. We can make two observations about this simmering dispute.

- The US reaction to its difficulties may have regrettable implications for everyone. The former director-general of the World Trade Organization, Pascal Lamy, expressed concern that tensions over key international currencies could spill over into the kind of trade-protectionist wars associated with the Great Depression of the 1930s, where countries erected tariff barriers and competed in driving down the values of their currencies. He said: 'What should be avoided is a domino effect, where you get a beggar-my-neighbour, or tit-for-tat, chain and it sours and sours.'[1]

- If the first point is about what could happen, the second is much more about what has *already* happened. The huge trade surpluses of China and other economies such as Japan and Germany generate incomes that have to be spent or used somehow. One possibility is to lend them to other economies. The question then becomes who in the world economy most needs to borrow; and the unfortunate answer is the US and others (such as the UK) with large trade deficits that require financing. Of course, it might be better if China revalued the renminbi and the US also took appropriate expenditure switching and expenditure reducing measures to address its deficit, but as the economist Benjamin Cohen memorably observed, loans to large debtor nations by their creditors are an easy way out; *bribes may be preferred to genuine adjustment.*

And it gets worse. We've touched on the financial crisis several times in this book. One undeniable issue here is that before the crisis Western financial institutions, particularly but not exclusively those in the US and the UK, were awash with cash which they invested in increasingly exotic and risky ways. But why were credit conditions so easy in the run-up to the financial crisis? One answer is that the unbalanced world economy allowed creditor nations such as China to push mountains of money into the debtor nations such as the US. None of this excuses bankers' stupidity or regulators' credulity but it does hint at a context for the financial crisis and subsequent world recession: it was facilitated by a world economy which was and continues to be seriously out of balance.

Figures 15.9 and 15.10 offer some evidence on the extent of this imbalance. Figure 15.9 shows the deficit and surplus current account positions of the world's economies. The notable deficit nations, importing goods and services in net terms from other countries are, especially, the US and some countries in Europe such as the UK and Spain. The net surplus exporters include China, Germany and Japan as well as other Asian economies and some oil-producing nations. Note that the extent of imbalance is greatest around the time of the global financial crisis.

---

[1] *Guardian* interview, 14 October 2010

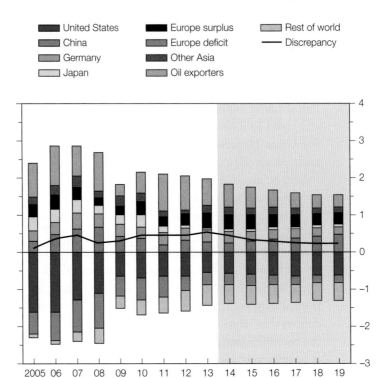

Figure 15.9 Global current account imbalances

Source: IMF World Economic Outlook, Legacies, Clouds, Uncertainties (October 2014)

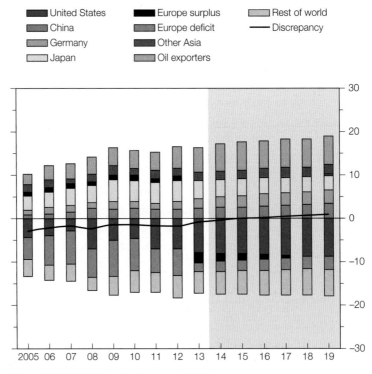

Figure 15.10 Global net foreign asset imbalances

Source: IMF World Economic Outlook, Legacies, Clouds, Uncertainties (October 2014)

Figure 15.10 depicts imbalances in the *stock* of foreign assets held by different countries. These are accumulations of assets and liabilities that result from current account performance. A similar ordering of deficit and surplus economies is evident here with, for example, the UK and some of Europe in deficit and China, Germany and Japan in surplus. Note that whereas current account flow imbalances (Figure 15.9) have narrowed since the global financial crisis and are expected to continue to do so, the stock of asset imbalances has widened and is expected to widen further. Following the argument of the IMF (the source for both figures), this is because the continued current account surplus of (say) Germany, even though it may fall, will continue to add to the stock of German foreign assets so long as it is positive. For the stock imbalances to begin to reverse the likes of the US and UK would need to run current account surpluses, something the UK has not done for more than 30 years! Insofar as globalization facilitates such imbalances it continues to generate conditions that have the potential to make the world a much less stable place.

Issues of exclusion and exploitation

We have already seen evidence that some economies and regions have not participated or gained much in the momentous changes that have happened in the world economy in recent decades. For example, Africa's share of world trade has actually fallen (see Figure 15.2), its share in foreign direct investment inflows has risen but only modestly (see Figure 15.3), and human development in some African countries remains very low (see Table 15.2). We know some of the reasons why this has happened. Many Western markets continue to be protected, making it harder for developing economies to export the goods they produce. FDI inflows to poorer economies may be limited by the priorities investors attach to access to major markets, or their need to recruit a skilled or highly educated workforce. Both of these criteria are easily satisfied in Europe or North America but not in Africa or parts of South America.

If *not* being part of a changing world economy is a problem for some of the world's poorer economies, becoming integrated with it may also be something of a mixed blessing. The need to be efficient, to drive down production costs, can lead to externalities that, in reality, amount to forms of exploitation. Recall from Chapter 6 that an externality is a cost or benefit arising from economic activity that impacts upon a third party. A negative general externality that may be stimulated by the spread of production to developing countries is that associated with child labour.

Child labour is not new – it happened in nineteenth-century Britain as anyone who has read *Oliver Twist* will know. Nor is it uniquely linked to today's more open world markets. Child labour often simply happens where needs, whether from poverty, family breakdown or parental death, are intense and opportunities for work in the home, on the street or in a factory arise. UNICEF (the United Nations International Children's Emergency Fund) has estimated that more than 170 million children under the age of 15 are employed in the 'worst forms' of unhealthy or dangerous work.

Why is child labour a negative externality? Because, unlike adults, children are not free to make an informed choice about their decision to participate in the labour market (and the decision may often be made for them). Consequently, the third party in this case is the child. There have been several instances of Western firms breaking contracts with their suppliers in less developed economies where it has become evident that suppliers have employed child labour. For example, Primark has dismissed suppliers in India for subcontracting embroidery to children working at home.

Information economics, counteracting institutions and globalization

Would you buy a good or service if you knew that the producer was not receiving a fair price for his or her work? Possibly not, but most of the time we don't know how, by whom, and for what reward the things we eat, drink, wear and use are produced. In this sense we're participating in markets with asymmetric information. We pay £2.50 for a latte and don't think about how this is divided between the coffee farmer, distributor or retailer. In Chapter 2 we saw how problems associated with asymmetric information may be ameliorated by the presence of counteracting institutions such as product guarantees that reassure us about the quality of goods, or educational qualifications that reassure employers about the quality of job applicants.

In an era when global considerations have come to the fore it is interesting to see examples of counteracting institutions that help us to make consumption choices that may redress some of the iniquities global markets throw up. One of these that you may be familiar with is *Fairtrade*. Fairtrade is a system that guarantees producers in developing economies a minimum price for their output. For example, if you choose to buy Fairtrade coffee you can be sure that an agreed level of revenue gets back to the farmers who grew the beans in the first place.

One of the problems with coffee production is that the price of coffee is variable – reflecting shifting conditions in world demand and supply. Typical price-taking coffee farmers can do

Ever thought about who gains from buying Fairtrade coffee?

© istockphoto/RyanJLane

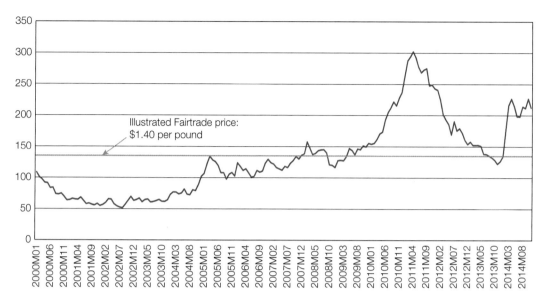

Figure 15.11 Coffee price (arabica) US cents per pound 2000–14, monthly and illustrated Fairtrade price

Source: Data from IMF's World Economic Outlook Database

little about this. So when coffee prices fall they suffer. The Fairtrade principle is an attempt to address the problem. Figure 15.11 illustrates fluctuations in the price of coffee between 2000 and 2014. Coffee farmers would clearly have struggled in the early 2000s when coffee prices more than halved from their 2000 level.

However, producers of Fairtrade coffee are guaranteed a minimum price – presently $1.40 per pound – as exemplified in Figure 15.11, so any fall in world coffee prices below this level does not affect them. Should the market price rise above the Fairtrade price, as has happened since 2007 in Figure 15.11, then the Fairtrade price matches it. In addition coffee farmers are paid a Fairtrade premium: an extra amount of money to invest in their businesses and communities.

Has Fairtrade encouraged UK consumers to make more ethical purchases and fewer purely market-driven ones; does it impact upon the lives of developing

● **Think Point**

Though it impresses and influences the shopping behaviour of the authors of this book, Fairtrade is not without its critics. Their argument centres on the concept of monopoly. Can you suggest what it might be?

Recall from Chapter 5 that the basis of monopoly lies in market exclusion: when a firm is able to keep rivals out it generates a degree of market power not available to competitive firms. The Fairtrade brand bestows some elements of market exclusion: other goods are not Fairtrade (are they then by implication unfair trade?). This raises a question about the effects of Fairtrade on non-Fairtrade producers in poor countries. Are they left behind and worse off because of the creation of this brand?

country producers? In 1998 Fairtrade reported that it made sales worth an estimated £16.7m in tea, coffee and cocoa. By 2012 *annual* sales had increased to about £1.57bn across an extended range of products including honey, wine, bananas and cotton, though to put this in perspective modal *weekly* retail sales in the UK were around £7bn.

15.6 On reflection, how new is globalization anyway?

We'll begin to conclude this chapter with a short quotation. We've omitted the place mentioned in the first line and the device in the second line. Read the quotation and add your preferences in the square brackets as you go along.

> *The inhabitant of* [insert place – city or country] *could order by* [insert device – iPhone, iPad or laptop], *sipping his morning tea in bed, the various products of the whole earth, in such quantity as he might see fit, and reasonably expect their early delivery upon his doorstep; he could at the same moment and by the same means adventure his wealth in the natural resources and new enterprises of any quarter of the world, and share, without exertion or even trouble, in their prospective fruits and advantages …*

The language might sound a little strange but the actions described are familiar. You're in bed with a cup of tea and you'd like to order a book from France, a scarf from Italy or reserve a hotel room in Sydney. Or you'd like to invest in an American software company, or even a Zambian copper mine. These things are all possible, even commonplace in the world we've come to think of as shiny, new, wired and *globalized*. So when was this written? In 2011 or 2005? No, in 1920, by Keynes in *The Economic Consequences of the Peace*. And he was writing about the period just before the outbreak of the First World War in 1914! The missing words are London and telephone.

The point of this little example is to suggest that global economic relationships such as they are may not be all that new. Modern global trade and investment began in the nineteenth century supported by global institutions such as the Gold Standard – a fixed exchange rate system that preceded the euro by more than 125 years. The Great Depression of the 1930s, introduced in Chapter 1, was a global phenomenon and a global catastrophe that produced new global institutions of economic management and regulation such as the GATT and the Bretton Woods system, which we discussed in Chapters 13 and 14. Arguably, the recent global financial crisis and world recession were arrested short of calamity because of the policy lessons of the 1920s and 1930s: we did not have a new global depression in 2008–9 because we'd had one 80 years before and learned from it.

The world economy now *is* very different from the recent past in many ways; but in some key respects it really hasn't changed much at all.

SUMMARY

- While there is some evidence of change in the international economy, the case for 'globalization' may be overstated. Globalization implies the widest possible articulation of market forces and this hasn't yet happened.
- There appears to be some degree of continuity in the international patterns of trade and foreign direct investment.
- Globalization is attractive in that it has the potential to spread markets, investment and economic activity to new parts of the world.
- If global processes leave the world economy unbalanced, nations may make short-sighted policy decisions that could leave us all worse off.
- More open international markets may increase the likelihood of exploitative externalities such as child labour.
- Counteracting institutions may help consumers make more ethical choices in the global marketplace.
- Globalization may have actually begun in the nineteenth century.

KEY TERMS

- Globalization
- Global economy
- International trade
- Foreign direct investment
- BRIC economies
- Human development
- Human Development Index
- Protectionism
- Exploitation
- Counteracting institutions

QUESTIONS FOR DISCUSSION

1. What would be the main characteristics of a 'global' economy?
2. What evidence is there against the existence of a global economy?
3. What are the advantages of globalization for developing economies?
4. What threats and opportunities might globalization pose for you personally?

ONE THING YOU SHOULD READ

Joseph Stiglitz, *Making Globalization Work*, Chapter 2: 'The promise of development'

Stiglitz won the Nobel Prize for work on asymmetric information problems in markets. He has also been chief economist at the World Bank. *Making Globalization Work* draws on both these foundations. In Chapter 2, Stiglitz reflects on the kinds of economic policy that will in his view help poor countries develop in the shifting sands of today's global economic environment where markets are clearly not perfect and where some regions — such as Africa — continue to flounder despite the attentions of agencies like the World Bank and the International Monetary Fund.

After reading the chapter answer the following questions.

1. Stiglitz singles out economic policies adopted by countries in East Asia for particular praise. How and why are these policies different to what has been done elsewhere?
2. What does Stiglitz mean by a 'comprehensive' approach to development?
3. Stiglitz criticizes Thomas Friedman's notion of a 'flat' world. What does this term mean? Do you think Stiglitz or Friedman is nearer the truth? What is the evidence for your conclusion?

glossary

A

Absolute advantage: the ability of a country to produce more of a particular commodity than another country, using an equal quantity of factor inputs.

Accelerator principle: the theory that the level of net investment depends on the change in output.

Accommodating transaction: one undertaken for balance of payments purposes.

Activist policy rule: a pre-specified rule for the conduct of policy which is linked to the state of the economy; also known as a feedback rule.

Adaptive expectations: an approach which assumes that people's expectations of the future value of a variable are based solely on recently observed values of that variable.

Adverse selection: arises in a market when asymmetric information problems drive out higher-quality goods or services.

Aggregate demand (AD): the total planned expenditures of all buyers of final goods and services; made up of consumer expenditure, investment expenditure, government expenditure and net exports.

Aggregate demand management: the use of fiscal and monetary policies to influence the level of aggregate demand.

Aggregate production function: a functional relationship between the quantity of aggregate output produced and the quantities of inputs used in production.

Aggregate supply (AS): the total planned output in the economy.

Appreciation: the appreciation of a currency involves an increase in its value in terms of other currencies when the currency in question is not part of a formal exchange rate system.

APR: annual percentage rate of interest.

Asymmetric information: arises when one party to a transaction has more information about a product than his or her counterpart.

Austerity: a programme of public expenditure reduction.

Autonomous expenditure: expenditure that does not depend on the level of national income.

Autonomous transaction: one undertaken for its own sake.

Average cost: the total cost of producing any given output divided by the number of units produced; average cost can be divided into average fixed costs and average variable costs.

Average product of labour: the average quantity of output produced by each worker employed.

Average revenue: the total revenue divided by the number of units sold; also equals price.

B

Balance of payments: a record of a country's international transactions.

Barriers to entry: barriers or restrictions that prevent the entry of new firms into an industry.

Base rate: the interest rate on loans the Bank of England makes to the banking sector.

Behavioural economics: a branch of economics that studies sub-rational human decision-making.

Bretton Woods system: a fixed exchange rate system established at the end of the Second World War. The system broke down in the early 1970s.

BRIC economies: Brazil, Russia, India and China.

Broad money: notes and coins plus a range of deposits held by individuals, firms and other organizations in banks and similar financial institutions.

Business cycle: fluctuations in aggregate economic activity; in particular movements in output around its trend.

C

Cairns Group: comprises Argentina, Australia, Brazil, Canada, Chile, Columbia, Fiji, Hungary, Indonesia, Malaysia, Philippines, New Zealand, Thailand and Uruguay.

Capital-labour ratio: the amount of capital per worker; the ratio of the quantity of capital inputs to the number of workers.

Capital-output ratio: the ratio of the amount of capital to the amount of output produced by it.

Cartel: a group of firms or producers that agree to act as if they were a single firm or producer, for example with regard to pricing or output decisions.

Centrally planned economy: one in which resource allocation is predominantly organized by the state.

Ceteris paribus: all other things being equal or remaining constant.

Classical economics: a pre-Keynesian approach based on the assumption that wages and prices adjust to clear markets and that monetary policy does not influence real variables, such as output and employment.

Coase theorem: states that where private parties can bargain in the absence of transaction costs, externality issues may be resolved without the need for government intervention.

Cold turkey: a rapid and permanent reduction in the rate of monetary growth aimed at reducing the rate of inflation.

Collective bargaining: involves negotiations between a trade union and one or more employers over pay or workplace conditions.

Collective provision: the provision of goods and services by the state.

Comparative advantage: the ability of a country to produce a commodity at a lower opportunity cost, in terms of other commodities forgone, than another country.

Competition policy: policy aimed at promoting competitive practices between firms in markets.

Complement: a good which complements another good.

Constant returns to scale: occur where a given percentage increase in all factor inputs results in the same percentage increase in output.

Consumers' expenditure: the aggregate purchases of goods and services by households for their own use.

Consumer sovereignty: implies that the consumption choices of individuals collectively determine production patterns.

Consumer surplus: the amount consumers would be willing to pay for a good or service above the price they actually pay.

Consumption function: the relationship between aggregate consumer expenditure and aggregate income.

Contractions in the quantity demanded: movements along a demand curve that reduce the quantity demanded.

Contractions in the quantity supplied: movements along a supply curve that reduce the quantity supplied.

Convergence: the tendency for output per worker in different countries to converge over time.

Cost-push inflation: inflation caused by cost increases even though there are no shortages of goods and services and the economy is below full employment.

CPI: Consumer Price Index.

Credit crunch: the seizure in the world's financial system in 2008–9 when financial institutions greatly reduced their lending to one another and to their customers.

Credibility: the degree to which people believe the authorities' announcements about future policy.

Crowding out: the reduction in private sector expenditure that results following an increase in government expenditure.

Cyclical unemployment: *see* demand-deficient unemployment.

D

Deadweight loss: arises in the case of monopoly when society is denied output it would prefer to see produced and consumed.

Decrease in demand: a decrease in the quantity demanded at all possible prices resulting from an inward shift of the demand curve.

Decrease in supply: a decrease in the quantity supplied at all possible prices resulting from an inward shift of the supply curve.

Decreasing returns to scale: occur where a given percentage increase in all factor inputs results in a smaller percentage increase in output.

Deflation: a sustained fall in the general price level.

Demand: the quantity of a good or service that consumers wish to purchase at each conceivable price, other things being equal.

Demand-deficient unemployment: unemployment that results because aggregate demand is insufficient to provide employment for everyone who wants to work at the prevailing real wage; also known as cyclical unemployment.

Demand-pull inflation: inflation caused by an excess demand for goods and services when the economy is at, or above, full employment.

Depreciation: the depreciation of a currency involves the lowering of its value in terms of other currencies when the currency in question is not part of some formal exchange rate system.

Depression: a very severe and prolonged recession.

Derived demand: arises for factor of production because of the demand for the output the factor helps to produce; the factor in itself does not generate demand.

Devaluation: the devaluation of a currency involves the lowering of its value in terms of other currencies when the currency in question is part of some formal exchange rate system.

Diminishing marginal returns: occur when the extra output produced from employing additional units of a variable factor alongside the fixed factors of production diminishes.

Diminishing marginal utility: the decline in marginal utility that occurs as more and more of a good or service is consumed.

Diminishing returns: a situation where successive increases in the use of a factor input, holding other factor inputs constant, eventually results in a fall in the additional output derived from a unit increase in that factor input.

Dirty flexible/floating exchange rate: *see* managed exchange rate.

Discretionary policy: a situation in which the authorities are free to vary the strength of fiscal and/or monetary policy, in any way they see fit, in order to achieve their desired objectives.

Diseconomies of scale: occur where the average cost per unit of output increases as the scale of production increases.

Disinflation: a decrease in the rate of inflation.

Disposable income: income that households have at their disposal after the payment of tax.

Diversified or conglomerate growth: occurs when a firm engages in activity in another market or industry in which it has no prior interest.

Dividends: sums of money paid by a firm to shareholders; each shareholder receives a dividend for each share held.

Division of labour: the separation of economic activity into different but complementary tasks.

Dollar dilemma: referred to the contradictory needs inside the Bretton Woods system from the US to rein in and continue the flow of dollars to the rest of the world.

Dominant strategy: a course of action that a player in a game follows regardless of the decisions of other players.

Dumping: exporting goods to foreign markets with prices set below those normally charged in the home market.

E

Eclectic approach: one which combines themes and policies from different schools of thought.

Economic growth: an increase in real GDP over time.

Economic rent: payment to a factor of production above that necessary to retain it in its present use.

Economically active: economically active individuals are those people of working age who are either in work or actively seeking it.

Economies of scale: occur where the average cost per unit of output falls as the scale of production increases.

Economies of scope: arise when firms are able to provide goods and services *collectively* at a lower cost than would be possible were they to provide them discretely.

Efficiency wage: a real wage paid by firms, above the market-clearing real wage rate, because it is both profitable and rational for them to do so.

Elasticity of labour supply: measures the responsiveness of the quantity of labour supplied to changes in the wage rate.

Endogenous variable: a variable that is explained within a particular model.

Entrepreneur: the risk-taking individual producer who perceives a demand in the market and organizes resources to meet that demand in the anticipation of profit.

Equilibrium price: the price at which the quantity demanded equals the quantity supplied.

Equilibrium quantity: the amount of a good that is bought and sold at the equilibrium price.

Euro area: comprises the 19 economies which have replaced their national currencies with the euro.

European Central Bank (ECB): the monetary authority for the euro area.

European Free Trade Association (EFTA): a free trade area which was formed under British leadership to rival the EEC; created in 1960, it has more recently been absorbed by the EU single market.

European Union: a political and economic union between 28 European countries.

Eurosclerosis: a term used to describe the belief that Europe suffers from excessive labour market rigidities.

Excess demand: occurs when the quantity demanded exceeds the quantity supplied at some given price.

Excess supply: occurs when the quantity supplied exceeds the quantity demanded at some given price.

Exchange rate: the price of one currency expressed in terms of another.

Exchange rate mechanism (ERM): the fixed but adjustable exchange rate element of the European Monetary System (EMS).

Exogenous variable: a variable that is not explained within a particular model; its value is taken as given.

Expenditure reduction policy: involves a reduction in the level of aggregate demand in the domestic economy in order to improve the balance of payments position on the current account.

Expenditure switching policy: switches domestic and foreign demand away from foreign goods and towards home-produced goods.

Extensions in the quantity demanded: movements along a demand curve that increase the quantity demanded.

Extensions in the quantity supplied: movements along a supply curve that increase the quantity supplied.

Externalities: the costs incurred by, or benefits received by, other members of society not taken into account by consumers or producers. Externalities are also known as third-party effects.

F

Factor inputs: any goods and services used in the process of production.

Factor intensity: the emphasis in production towards the use of one particular factor of production above others.

Factor markets: markets in which factors of production – in land, labour and capital – are bought and sold.

Feedback rule: *see* activist policy rule.

Final output: goods and services which are sold to their ultimate users.

Fiscal policy: measures which alter the level and composition of government expenditure and taxation.

Fixed costs: costs which do not change with the quantity of output produced; also referred to as overhead costs or unavoidable costs.

Fixed exchange rate: an exchange rate which is fixed at a predetermined level by intervention by the country's central bank in the foreign exchange market.

Flexible exchange rate: an exchange rate which is determined in the foreign exchange market by the forces of demand and supply; also known as a floating exchange rate.

Floating exchange rate: *see* flexible exchange rate.

Foreign direct investment (FDI): investment capital provided to a firm from a source in another country where the investor has a direct influence on the business activities of the recipient firm.

Foreign exchange reserves: stocks of foreign currencies held by central banks.

Free market economy: one in which resource allocation is predominantly market based.

Free rider problem: refers to the possibility that public goods will be underprovided by the market because individuals rely on others to pay for them.

Free trade: implies an absence of government regulation in international markets for goods and services.

Frictional unemployment: unemployment that results because it takes time for workers to search for suitable jobs; also known as search unemployment.

Full employment: a situation in which all unemployment is frictional and structural, and cannot be reduced by increasing aggregate demand.

Full employment output: *see* potential output.

G

G5: the world's five leading industrial nations: the United States, Japan, Germany, France and the United Kingdom.

G7: the seven main industrial economies in the world: the United States, Japan, Germany, France, Italy, the United Kingdom and Canada.

GDP in current prices: *see* nominal GDP.

GDP in real prices: *see* real GDP.

Globalization: the spread of international trade and foreign direct investment to new parts of the world.

Goods: tangible products.

Goods markets: markets in which goods and services are bought and sold.

Gradualism: an approach to disinflation that involves a slow and gradual reduction in the rate of monetary growth.

Gross domestic product (GDP): the total value of goods and services produced in a country by the factors of production located in that country regardless of who owns them.

Gross national product (GNP): the value of final goods and services produced by domestically owned factors of production; GDP plus net property income from abroad.

H

Heckscher–Ohlin approach: holds that a country's production and trade specialisms will reflect its particular factor endowments.

Horizontal growth: occurs when a firm expands its existing form of activity.

Horizontal merger: arises when two firms in the same industry and stage in the production process merge together.

Human capital: the knowledge and skills of workers in an economy.

Hyperinflation: a situation in which the rate of inflation is extremely high.

Hysteresis: the proposition that the equilibrium value of a variable depends on the history of that variable; if the actual rate of unemployment remains above the natural rate for a prolonged period the natural rate will tend to increase, and vice versa.

I

Information economics: is concerned with issues that arise in economic decision-making which are affected by access to information.

Imperfect competition: a market structure in which there are a large number of firms selling similar but differentiated products; also known as monopolistic competition.

Imperfectly anticipated inflation: a situation in which the actual rate of inflation differs from the anticipated or expected rate of inflation.

Income elasticity of demand: the proportionate change in the quantity of a good demanded divided by the proportionate change in consumers' incomes.

Increase in demand: an increase in the quantity demanded at all possible prices resulting from an outward shift of the demand curve.

Increase in supply: an increase in the quantity supplied at all possible prices resulting from an outward shift of the supply curve.

Increasing returns to scale: occur where a given percentage increase in all factor inputs results in a larger percentage increase in output.

Industrial policy: policy aimed at enhancing the performance of firms in markets.

Infant-industry argument: suggests that nascent domestic industries may need temporary protection from foreign competition until they mature.

Inferior good: one for which demand decreases when income increases.

Inflation: a situation in which the overall or general level of prices rises over time.

Inflation rate: the rate at which the general level of prices increases; expressed as a percentage on an annual basis.

Inter-industry trade: refers to the tendency for countries to produce and trade different kinds of goods and services.

International division of labour: describes patterns of specialization in the production of goods and services between nations.

International Monetary Fund (IMF): an international agency, located in Washington, which promotes stability of member countries' exchange rates and assists them in correcting balance of payments disequilibria.

Intra-industry trade: arises when countries trade the same kinds of goods and services.

Investment expenditure: purchases of capital goods, such as plant, machinery and buildings.

K

Keynesian economics: an approach based on the belief that capitalist economies are inherently unstable and can come to rest at less than full employment for prolonged periods; Keynesian economists favour the use of discretionary aggregate demand policies to stabilize the economy at, or near, full employment.

L

Labour market segmentation: arises when labour faces barriers to entry to a particular labour market.

Laissez-faire: a situation in which there is little or no state interference in the market economy.

Law of diminishing returns: states that if more of a variable input is employed, holding the quantity of other inputs constant, the marginal product of the variable input will eventually decrease.

Legal monopoly: as defined in the UK, a legal monopoly arises where a firm enjoys a market share of 25 per cent or more.

Leontief paradox: refers to the finding that for the United States the predictions of the Heckscher–Ohlin model did not appear empirically verifiable.

Limited liability: a situation where in the event of losses incurred by a firm the personal wealth of its owners is not at risk; liability is limited to the value of the firm.

Long run: a period of time in which all inputs may be varied.

Loss aversion: suggests that people become more attached to an item or asset once they own it and value it more highly as a consequence.

Lucas critique: the argument that traditional policy evaluation may be misleading as it fails to take into account that people may change their expectations and behaviour when policy changes.

M

Macroeconomics: the study of the economy as a whole.

Macroeconomic policy: policies governments use to try to influence overall economic performance.

Managed exchange rate: an exchange rate which is influenced by intervention of the country's central bank in the foreign exchange market; also known as a dirty flexible, or dirty floating, exchange rate.

Marginal cost: the change in total cost resulting from increasing production by one unit.

Marginal physical product: the change in total output resulting from a unit change in the variable factor.

Marginal product of labour: the change in total output produced as a result of employing one more worker.

Marginal propensity to consume: the change in consumption expenditure resulting from an additional unit of income.

Marginal propensity to import: the change in import expenditure resulting from an additional unit of income.

Marginal propensity to withdraw: the fraction of an additional unit of income which is withdrawn from the circular flow of income.

Marginal revenue: the amount of money that a firm receives from the sale of one more unit of its output.

Marginal revenue product: the change in a firm's total revenue resulting from the sale of output produced by one more unit of the variable factor.

Marginal social benefit: the money value of the benefit from one additional unit of consumption.

Marginal social cost: the cost of producing one additional unit of output. It includes both the marginal cost incurred by the producer and any marginal costs incurred by other members of society in the form of externalities.

Marginal utility: the change in total satisfaction resulting from a one-unit change in the consumption of a good or service.

Market: a framework which brings buyers and sellers together.

Market clearing: occurs when all goods or services supplied in a market are sold.

Market concentration: the extent to which a market is dominated by a small number of firms.

Market failure: arises where the market fails either to provide certain goods, or fails to provide them at their optimal or most desirable level.

Market power: the capacity of a firm to influence the market price of a good or service.

Market segmentation: the division of a market by the producer into a number of discrete parts between which consumers cannot easily move.

Market structure: a market structure characterizes a market according to the degree of competition in it.

Marshall–Lerner condition: states that a currency depreciation or devaluation will improve the current account of the balance of payments if the sum of the price elasticities of the demand for imports and exports is greater than 1.

Medium of exchange: an instrument that is accepted in exchange for goods and services.

Mercantilism: a policy of state-protected trade.

Merger and acquisition: the process in which one firm combines with or takes over another.

Microeconomics: the study of the behaviour of individual households and firms, and the determination of the relative prices of particular goods and services.

Minimum wage: a legally binding obligation on employers to pay at least a given hourly rate.

Mismatch unemployment: *see* structural unemployment.

Mixed economy: one which combines market and state forms of resource allocation.

Monetarism: an approach based on the belief that capitalist economies are inherently stable, unless distributed by erratic monetary growth and will return fairly rapidly to the neighbourhood of the natural level of output and employment when subjected to some disturbance.

Monetary policy: measures which alter the money supply and/or interest rates.

Money: anything which is generally accepted in exchange for goods and services and in the settlement of debt.

Monopolistic competition: *see* imperfect competition.

Monopoly: a market structure in which there is a sole supplier of a good or service that has no close substitutes and for which there are barriers to entry into the industry.

Monopoly power: monopoly power arises where potential competitors can be excluded from a market.

Monopsony: arises where there is a dominant buyer in a market.

Moral hazard: undesirable or reckless behaviour in an economic context where there are no incentives to avoid such behaviour.

Multinational: a firm which owns and controls assets in more than one country.

Multiplier: the ratio of the change in income to a change in autonomous expenditure.

N

NAIRU: *see* non-accelerating inflation rate of unemployment

Narrow money: notes and coins in circulation plus reserve balances held by banks at the central bank.

Nash equilibrium: a situation where economic agents optimize their actions given the choices made by other parties.

National income: the income that originates in the production of goods and services supplied by residents of a nation.

Natural monopoly: arises where a single firm is the most efficient structure for the production of a particular good or service.

Natural rate of unemployment: the rate of unemployment that exists when the labour market is in equilibrium; composed of frictional and structural unemployment.

Net exports: exports minus imports.

New classical economics: an approach based on the three assumptions of continuous market clearing, incomplete information and rational expectations.

New Keynesian economics: an approach which explores a variety of reasons for wage and price stickiness that prevents market clearing.

New protectionism: the non-tariff-based protection that emerged after the end of the postwar boom at the beginning of the 1970s.

Nominal GDP: the value of gross domestic product measured in terms of the prices prevailing at the time; also known as GDP in current prices.

Non-accelerating inflation rate of unemployment (NAIRU): the rate of unemployment at which inflation is stable.

Non-system: the broad system of flexible exchange rates prevailing in the world economy since 1973.

Normal good: one for which demand increases when income increases.

Normal profit: the minimum amount of profit a firm must earn to induce it to remain in the industry.

Normative issues: those which are a matter of opinion.

North American Free Trade Agreement (NAFTA): a free trade area that covers the US, Canadian and Mexican economies.

O

Oligopoly: a market structure in which there are a small number of firms.

Open market operations: the purchase and sale of government bonds by the central bank.

Opportunity cost: the cost of an action measured in terms of the best forgone alternative action.

Optimum currency area: a grouping of economies within which markets are sufficiently integrated and flexible to make the use of one currency more desirable than separate national currencies.

Organic growth: the growth of a firm from its own resources.

Organization for Economic Co-operation and Development (OECD): an intergovernmental organization, based in Paris, which provides a policy forum for the major industrialized countries for the promotion of economic growth, expansion of multilateral trade and provision of foreign aid to developing countries.

Overhead costs: *see* fixed costs.

P

Pareto efficiency: a situation in which it is impossible to make someone better off without making someone else worse off; also known as Pareto optimality.

Participation rate: the proportion of economically active workers in a particular group of the population.

Passive policy rule: a pre-specified rule for the conduct of policy not linked to prevailing economic circumstances.

Pay differentials: exist where there are wage rate premiums attached to particular kinds of work.

Perfect competition: a market structure characterized most notably by a situation in which all firms in the industry are price-takers and there is freedom of entry into and exit from the industry.

Perfectly anticipated inflation: a situation in which the actual rate of inflation is equal to the anticipated or expected rate of inflation.

Perfectly elastic demand: arises where the response of quantity demanded to a price change is infinitely large; price elasticity of demand is ∞ (infinity).

Perfectly inelastic demand: arises where the quantity demanded does not respond to a change in price; price elasticity of demand is 0.

Permanent income: the average income that people expect to receive over a period of years in the future; also known as normal income and average expected income.

Phillips curve: the relationship between the inflation rate and the unemployment rate.

Policy ineffectiveness proposition: the proposition that anticipated changes in monetary policy will have no effect on output and employment.

Political business cycle: fluctuations in the level of output and employment caused by the manipulation of the economy for electoral gains or due to partisan differences.

Positive issues: those which are factually based.

Potential output: the maximum output that can be produced in an economy, given its factor endowments, without generating accelerating inflation; also known as full employment output.

Price discrimination: charging customers different prices for the same product

Price elastic: a situation where the proportionate change in quantity demanded is greater than the proportionate change in price; elasticity is greater than one.

Price elasticity of demand: the proportionate change in the quantity demanded of a good divided by the proportionate change in its price which brought it about.

Price elasticity of supply: the proportionate change in quantity supplied of a good divided by the proportionate change in its price that brought it about.

Price inelastic: a situation where the proportionate change in quantity demanded is less than the proportionate change in price; elasticity is less than one.

Price index: a measure of the average level of prices of a set of goods and services relative to the prices of the same goods and services in a particular base year.

Price maker: a firm that can determine the price it charges for its goods.

Price taker: a firm that has to take the market price of its product as given.

Price transparency: arises in an international context when countries use the same currencies or, to a lesser extent, when exchange rates are fixed.

Prices and incomes policy: measures that establish guidelines or controls for wage and/or price increases.

Private good: one that is wholly consumed by an individual.

Producer surplus: the total amount suppliers in a market receive above that necessary to induce them to supply the goods in question.

Product life-cycle theory: understands the changing patterns of international trade by referencing the development of commodities and their production locations over time.

Production function: a functional relationship between the output of goods or services produced and the quantity of inputs used in the production process.

Profit: the difference between total revenue and total cost.

Protectionism: occurs where the principle of free trade is compromised.

Public good: one that once produced can be consumed by everyone.

Public sector borrowing requirement (PSBR): the amount by which the expenditure of the public sector exceeds its revenue.

Purchasing power parity: predicts that the nominal exchange rate will adjust to offset differences in inflation rates between economies in the long run.

Pure monopoly: a pure monopoly is a market structure in which there is a sole supplier of a good or service which has no close substitutes and for which there are barriers to entry into the industry.

Q

Quantitative easing: a policy that injects money directly into the economy in order to boost spending and prevent inflation falling below target.

Quantity demanded: the amount of a good or service that consumers wish to purchase at a particular price, other things being equal.

Quantity supplied: the amount that producers wish to sell at a particular price, other things being equal.

Quota: a quantitative limit on goods.

R

Random walk: the path of a variable whose changes over time are unpredictable.

Rational expectations: an approach which assumes that people make the best use of all available information to forecast the future.

Real business cycle approach: an approach in which fluctuations in aggregate output and employment are driven by persistent supply-side shocks to the economy, most notably random fluctuations in the rate of technological progress.

Real exchange rate: measures the real purchasing power of a currency.

Real GDP: the value of gross domestic product measured in terms of the prices that prevailed in some particular base year; also known as GDP in constant prices.

Real wage: the money wage divided (or deflated) by a price index; the amount of goods and services a money wage can buy.

Recession: a decline in real GDP that lasts for at least two consecutive quarters of a year.

Relative price: the ratio of the price of one good to the price of another good; expressed as the number of units of one good that one unit of another good will buy.

Reserve requirements: the minimum amount of reserves banks must hold against deposits.

Reservation wage: the minimum rate required to induce an individual to accept a job.

Resource allocation: the commitment of a society's productive endowments, such as labour and machinery, to particular uses or patterns of use.

Resource scarcity: implies that *all* resources are scarce in relation to the limitless wants present in every society.

Revaluation: the revaluation of a currency involves an increase in its value in terms of other currencies when the currency in question is part of some formal exchange rate system.

Rules: pre-specified guidelines that determine the conduct of policy.

S

Say's Law: states that supply creates its own demand.

Search unemployment: *see* frictional unemployment.

Services: intangible products.

Shifting comparative advantage: implies that patterns of comparative advantage are not stable over time.

Short run: a period of time in which some inputs like capital are fixed, while others like labour may be varied.

Short-run Phillips curve: the relationship between inflation and unemployment that exists for a given expected rate of inflation.

Signalling: measures taken by economic agents to indicate their value to third parties; for example, educational qualifications signal the potential productivity of workers.

Social provision: *see* collective provision.

Specialization: a focus on one form of activity by an economic agent.

Stabilization policy: policies aimed at stabilizing output and employment at, or near, their full employment or natural levels by influencing the level of aggregate demand.

Stagflation: a situation in which high unemployment and high inflation occur simultaneously; a combination of stagnation and inflation.

Steady state: a situation in which output per worker and capital input per worker are no longer changing.

Structural unemployment: unemployment that results from a mismatch between the skills or location of existing job vacancies and the present skills or location of the unemployed; also known as mismatch unemployment.

Substitute: a good which can be substituted in place of another good.

Supernormal profits: profits which exceed the minimum amount a firm must earn to induce it to remain in the industry.

Supply: the quantity of a good or service producers wish to sell at each conceivable price, other things being equal.

Supply-side policies: policies directed towards increasing aggregate supply by altering the response of firms and individuals to changing conditions.

T

Tariff: a tax on traded goods.

Third-party effects: *see* externalities.

Tiger economies: Hong Kong, Malaysia, South Korea, Singapore, Taiwan and Thailand.

Time inconsistency: the temptation of policymakers to deviate from a previously announced policy once private decision-makers have adjusted their behaviour to the announced policy.

Total cost: the sum of the costs of all inputs used in producing a firm's output; can be divided into total fixed and total variable costs.

Total product of labour: the total output produced by a given number of workers.

Total revenue: the amount of money a firm receives from the sale of its output; it equals the price of output multiplied by the number of units sold.

Trade union density: the percentage of employees in an economy that are members of a trade union.

Transaction costs: costs associated with undertaking business activities or other forms of economic exchange.

Transfer earnings: payments to a factor necessary to retain it in its present use.

Transition economy: an economy in the process of changing from central planning to capitalism.

U

Unemployed: people who are available for work and are actively seeking jobs but cannot find them.

Unemployment rate: the percentage of the labour force unemployed.

Unit of account: an instrument that allows us to measure the values of different goods and services.

Unit elasticity: where the proportionate change in quantity demanded is equal to the proportionate change in price; unit elasticity is 1.

Unlimited liability: places the entire personal wealth of the owner of a firm at risk in respect of losses that the firm may incur.

Utility: the satisfaction that a consumer receives from the consumption of a good or service.

V

Variable costs: costs which vary with the quantity of output produced; also referred to as direct costs and avoidable costs.

Vertical growth: occurs when a firm engages in activity in another part of the production process or market in which it has an interest.

Vertical merger: when two firms in the same industry but at different stages in the production process merge.

index

A

absolute advantage   400
accelerator principle   353–5, 359
accepted sequence   184
accommodating transaction   430–2
activist policy rule   375
adaptive expectations   386
adverse selection   78–9
advertising   51, 77, 104, 150, 175, 183, 196, 213, 306
aggregate demand (AD)   270, 282, 284, 288–90, 293, 296–9, 302, 304, 307–8, 311, 325, 338, 355, 358–9, 374–7, 381–2, 386, 389, 453
aggregate demand management   298, 327, 379, 387
aggregate production function   296, 342–4, 346–7, 349, 366–7, 371
Akerlof, George   78–9, 110–11, 243, 323
Alesina, Alberto   362
allocation of resources *see* resource allocation
Amazon   44, 93, 103, 147, 171–2
anchor argument   454–5, 463
Apple   6, 48, 93, 103, 148, 166–7, 173, 180–1, 435
appreciation   44, 445, 450, 452–3, 461
APR   78–9
asymmetric information   66, 77–81, 83, 108, 110–12, 114–17, 243, 305, 323, 496
austerity   280, 285, 388–9, 471
Austrian economics   7, 117–19
autonomous expenditure   294, 353, 355, 363
autonomous transaction   430–3
average cost   129, 131–5, 153–7, 163, 173
average product of labour   126

average revenue   136, 148, 153, 155–7, 163, 172

B

BA   105–6, 148, 180
balance of payments   27, 255, 263–4, 276, 278–80, 282–3, 330, 334, 428–33, 438–42, 460, 478
   accounts   428–36
   adjustment   440, 450–1, 453–4
   business and   472–3
   disequilibria in   436–40, 458, 460, 463, 471
   and fixed exchange rates   453–4
   and flexible exchange rates   450–1
barriers to entry   159–60, 164, 173, 224, 226
Basle Nyborg Agreement   464
Baumol, William,   102
behavioural economics   81–3, 112
Berman, Marshall,   9–10
Blinder, Alan   242
Branson, Sir Richard   106
Breaking Bad,   5
Bretton Woods system   330, 457–60, 462–3, 498
BRIC economies   72, 484–8
business
   importance of economics for   6–10
   macroeconomic context of   27–31, 254
   public goods, externalities and   204–6
business cycles   78, 342
   Keynesian approach to   353–5
   main features of   351–2
   monetarist approach to   355–8
   new classical approach to   358–60

political business cycle approach to   361–3
   real business cycle approach to   360–1

C

Cairns Group   420–1
cap-and-trade approach   199–200
capital account   428–33
capital-labour ratio   355
capital-output ratio   314
car industry   18–19, 118–19, 278, 311, 404
   assembly line and   92, 360
   European   407
   innovation in   6, 38, 181–2
   labour relations in   109–10
cartel   169, 179–80
central bank independence and inflation performance   385
centrally planned economy   16, 278
ceteris paribus   40–1
circular flow of income   257–61, 354
classical economics   282, 289–90, 299–300, 317–18, 395
Coase, Ronald   91, 202–4
cold turkey   328
collective bargaining   224
collective provision   208
Common Agricultural Policy (CAP)   58–60, 415–16
comparative advantage   396–406, 410, 412, 414–15, 118–20
competition
   imperfect   146, 151–2, 172–3, 177, 181–2, 406
   examples of limits to   11–13, 103–5, 118, 149–51
   perfect   117, 131–8
competition policy   189–90, 214–15
complement   44

constant returns to scale   133–4, 347, 366–7, 397
consumers' expenditure   298
consumer sovereignty   15, 17, 19–20, 24, 38–9, 88, 93, 118, 169, 182–4, 188, 214
consumer surplus   113–14, 167–8
consumption function   293–4, 354
contractions in the quantity demanded   41–2, 45, 61, 176, 227, 434–5, 443–4
contractions in the quantity supplied 46–8
convergence   346, 348–9
convergence criteria for euro area membership   466–7
Cooper, Olly   61
cost-push inflation   322, 330, 335, 454
costs
    fixed   125, 129
    marginal   129–32, 134, 140–1, 153–8, 163–5, 172, 177, 226
    menu   273
    total   101, 124, 129–31, 154–6, 164, 172
    variable   128–9, 131, 144
Consumer Prices Index (CPI)   270–2
copyrights   160, 162, 170, 201, 349, 420
credibility   329, 339, 384–5
credit crunch   30, 114–16, 216, 311
crowding out   208, 377–8
currency depreciation   29, 445, 447–8, 450, 452–3, 456, 461–2, 472–3, 474, 476
currency speculation   460
current account of the balance of payments   428–30, 432–3, 436–40, 442, 445, 450, 453–4, 460, 462, 493–5
cyclical unemployment see demand-deficient unemployment
Cyert, Richard   101

D
deadweight loss   166
decrease in demand   42–3, 47
decrease in supply   47
decreasing returns to scale   133–4
Delors Report   466, 471
demand
    aggregate (AD)   270, 282, 284, 288–90, 293, 296–9, 302, 304, 307–8, 311, 325, 327, 338, 355, 358–9, 374–7, 379, 381–2, 386–7, 389, 453

    derived   226, 236, 248
    excess   49–50, 222, 224, 226, 321–3, 325–6, 330, 333, 338, 444, 450, 452
    income elasticity of   72–4
    perfectly elastic   65–6, 75–6, 137, 153, 235, 249
    perfectly inelastic   64–5, 75–6
demand curve
    derivation of   40–2
    kinked   176–7
    movements along   41, 45
    shifts in   42–5
demand-deficient unemployment 288, 293–300
demand-pull inflation   322–3
Denison, Edward   344
depression   282, 311, 352, 498
derived demand see demand, derived
design rights   162, 170
devaluation   445, 450, 453–4, 457–8, 461, 463, 472, 474
differentiated product   150–1, 184, 229
diminishing marginal returns   125–9, 132
diminishing returns, law of   154, 227
dirty flexible/floating exchange rate see managed exchange rate
discretionary policy   282, 355, 357–9, 374–84, 386–7, 389
diseconomies of scale   134
disinflation   328
disposable income   298
diversified or conglomerate growth 106
dividends   95–6, 101–2, 206, 332, 429
division of labour   36, 38, 74, 91–2, 133, 211, 395–6, 404
dollar dilemma   459
dominant strategy   178–81
dumping   415–16, 419
Dyson, James,   174, 201

E
easyJet   57, 106
eclectic approach   310, 335, 363
economic growth   341–9
    definition of   261, 342
    endogenous growth models 348–50
    in G5 economies   264–5, 485–6
    overview of   342–6
    real GDP, living standards and welfare   255, 262–4, 266

Solow growth model   346–9, 363, 366–71
economic rent   248–52
economically active individuals   231–2
economics
    Austrian   7, 117–19
    classical   282, 288–90, 293, 299, 317–18, 395
    institutionalist   181–4, 413
    Keynesian   7, 9, 282–5, 289–300, 302, 322, 338, 353–5, 363, 375–8, 381, 386, 388–9, 498
    new classical   289, 301–3, 339, 353, 358–61, 363, 377, 381–7
    new Keynesian   289, 303–11, 323
economies of scale   57–8, 104, 117, 133–4, 212, 344, 406
economies of scope   104
economy
    centrally planned   16, 210, 278
    free market   15–18, 54, 58–60, 158, 189–90, 206, 208, 211, 449, 451
    mixed   16–18, 20, 24
    transition   9, 16, 247
efficiency wage model   304–6
elasticity of labour supply   234
elasticity, unit   64–5, 76
endogenous variable   348
entrepreneurship   88–9, 215–16, 220
    Austrian view of   117–19
equilibrium see market equilibrium
euro   9, 29, 54, 56–7, 446–7, 451, 455, 463, 465–71, 473, 476, 498
euro area   272, 278, 308, 319, 333–5, 389, 448
European Central Bank (ECB)   333–5, 452, 466, 469–71
European Union (EU)
    Delors Report   466, 471
    European single market   54–8, 104, 134, 224, 277–8, 468, 476
    Maastricht Treaty   231, 466–8, 470
    Single European Act (SEA)   465–6
    Treaty of Rome   56, 468
eurosclerosis   309
excess demand   49–50, 222, 224, 226, 321–3, 325–6, 330, 333, 338, 444, 450, 452
excess supply   49–50, 59, 68, 222, 224, 244, 289–90, 299–300, 304, 306, 444, 450, 452, 472
exchange rate
    determination of   442–7, 448–9

fixed   330, 378, 433, 451, 472–4,
    476
    flexible   330, 449–51, 472–4
    managed   433, 453, 456, 461–2
    systems   428, 442, 449–65
exchange rate mechanism (ERM)
    462–5, 467
exogenous variable   347
expectations
    adaptive   386
    rational   339, 358, 360, 381–3, 385
expenditure
    autonomous   294, 298, 353, 355,
    363
    consumers'   298
expenditure reduction policy   453,
    461–2, 472
expenditure switching policy   453–4,
    461, 472, 493
exports   8, 29, 57–8, 60, 74, 256,
    258–9, 275–7, 279–80, 282–3,
    293, 295–6, 354, 378, 397,
    400, 403, 407–11, 414, 418–19,
    422–4, 428–9, 432–5, 444–5,
    447, 450, 453–4, 461, 468–9,
    471–2, 481–2, 490, 492
extensions in the quantity demanded
    41–2, 45, 61
extensions in the quantity supplied
    46–8, 61
externalities   194–206, 209, 495–6
    negative   194–9, 203, 217, 496
    positive   194, 199–202, 217

F
Facebook   3, 97–100, 103, 152, 291
factor inputs   46, 75–7, 133, 342–4,
    346–7, 349–50, 366, 368, 400
factor intensity   89
factor markets   220–51, 258
feedback rule see activist policy rule
final output   256
fine tuning   374, 377
firms
    competition between   11, 38,
    117–19, 151–2
    different kinds of   93–100
    growth strategies of   105–8
    objectives of   5, 10, 100–2
    role in markets   10, 15, 17, 45–8,
    88, 91–4
fiscal policy   298, 355, 359, 361,
    374–81, 386–9, 453, 455, 464,
    466, 471
fixed costs   129

Ford, Henry   92, 133, 182
Ford Motors   19, 93, 150, 183, 256,
    292, 407
Fordism   92, 182
foreign direct investment (FDI)   8–9,
    429–33, 447, 482–4, 488, 490,
    492, 495
foreign exchange reserves   279–80,
    429–31, 436–8, 452
free market economy see economy
free rider problem   190–1, 201
free trade   58, 277–8, 395–6, 400–2,
    413, 416, 421, 451, 490
frictional unemployment   270, 288,
    290–1, 298–301
Friedman, Milton   32, 209, 218, 274,
    283–4, 300, 307, 317, 320, 323,
    337, 356–7, 378, 387, 451
full employment   270, 282–3,
    289–90, 293, 296–9, 304, 318,
    322, 342, 353–5, 360–1, 374–6,
    380, 386, 408, 417–18, 438, 470
full employment output see potential
    output

G
G5   225, 264–5, 268–9, 275–7,
    438–9, 462, 485–7
Galbraith, J.K.   182–4, 186, 413–14
game theory   177–81
General Agreement on Tariffs and
    Trade (GATT)   416–20, 457, 498
globalization
    benefits of   350, 485–7, 490–2,
    498
    defined   478–80
    development of   9–11, 481–5, 489
    threats posed by   492–6
goods
    inferior   73
    normal   42–3, 73
    private   190–2
    public   190–2
goods markets   10, 36–50, 228, 290
Google   3, 93, 103–5, 119, 148
Gorst, Geoff   95
gradualism   328
Great Depression   9, 28, 32, 34, 89,
    264, 282, 303, 357, 361, 493, 498
gross domestic product (GDP)   28,
    255–8, 260–1, 264–6, 479,
    485–6
    nominal   261, 277
    real   261–2, 269, 342, 346
gross national product (GNP)   257

growth, economic   13, 27, 53–4, 74,
    107, 255, 261–5, 280, 282–3,
    342–51, 366–71, 437–8
Gunawardene, Nileeka   6

H
Heckman, James   33
Heckscher-Ohlin approach   402–4,
    406
Hoover   25–6, 174
horizontal growth   105–6
horizontal merger   105–6
human capital   216, 240–2, 247, 307,
    345–6, 349, 404
hyperinflation   273–4, 286
hysteresis   306–8, 310, 339, 377

I
information economics   77–81, 83,
    85, 110–12, 114–17, 242–3, 305,
    323, 496–8
imperfect competition   146, 151–2,
    172–3, 175, 177, 181–2, 184,
    406
imperfectly anticipated inflation   273,
    275
income
    circular flow of   257–61, 354
    disposable   298
    national   30, 98, 183, 293–7, 331,
    376, 486–8
    permanent see permanent
    income
income effect   233–4
income elasticity of demand see
    demand, income elasticity of
increasing returns to scale   133
individualism   190
industrial policy   189, 215–16
infant-industry argument   414, 416,
    422, 425
inferior good   73
inflation
    and central bank independence
    362–3, 384–5, 387–8
    cost-push   322, 330, 335, 454
    costs of   272–5
    definition of   270
    demand-pull   322–3
    in G5 economies   275–6
    imperfectly anticipated   273
    as an international monetary
    phenomenon   329–30
    measurement of   270–1
    monetarist approach to   272–3

inflation (*Continued*)
  non-monetarist approach to
    330–3
  perfectly anticipated   272–3
inflation rate   270–2
innovation   4, 6, 38, 93, 105, 119, 160–1,
    170, 271, 348–9, 405–6, 435
inside lag   379–80
insider-outsider model   304, 306,
    308, 310
institutional economics   181–4, 413–14
integration argument   454–5
inter-industry trade   404
international division of labour   74,
    395–6, 404
International Monetary Fund (IMF)
    458, 460, 495
international trade
  economic basis for   23, 74, 258,
    274, 276–7, 395–6, 490
  patterns of trade since 1945   9,
    58, 408–12, 479, 481–2
  problems associated with   396,
    401–2, 492–6
  and theory of comparative
    advantage   396–407, 424
international trade policy   20, 56–60,
    278, 413–23, 425, 441–2
intra-industry trade   404–6
investment expenditure   259, 282,
    293–9, 353–4

J
Jobs, Steve,   180

K
Kahneman, Daniel   81
Keynesian economics   7–9, 282–6,
    290–300, 322, 338–9, 353–5,
    363, 375–7, 386–9, 391
Keynesian model   290–300
kinked demand curve   176–7
Krueger, Anne   415–16
Krugman, Paul   286, 350, 391, 406
Kydland, Finn   360, 382–3

L
labour
  average product of   126
  demand for   222, 224, 226–9,
    236–7, 245, 289, 298, 300–1,
    304, 321–2, 325–6
  division of   36, 38, 91–2, 133, 211
  international division of   74,
    395–6, 404

marginal product of   126–7,
    130–1, 134
  supply of   222, 230–5, 244, 247,
    252, 261, 289–90, 298–302,
    304, 306, 321, 323, 325
labour market segmentation   224, 234
labour supply, elasticity of   234
laissez-faire   55, 57, 188, 209
law of diminishing returns   134, 154, 227
legal monopoly   160
Lehman Brothers   114–17
Leontief paradox   404
limited liability   94–6
living standards   21, 255, 262–4, 266,
    342, 348–9, 486
long run   125
long-run costs   133–5, 144
long-run Phillips curve   323–4, 326–7,
    338–9, 381, 383, 389
loss aversion   112
Louvre Accord   462
Lucas critique   382, 384–6
Lucas, Robert   302–3, 358, 381–2

M
Maastricht Treaty   231, 466–8, 470
MacKinnon, Ben   140
macroeconometric model   385
macroeconomic policy   28, 254, 255,
    263–4, 280, 288, 359, 362–3,
    374, 381, 387, 389, 450–1, 460,
    466, 469–70
  since 1945   282–5
macroeconomics   27–8, 254–5, 261,
    282, 316, 389
managed exchange rate *see* exchange
    rate, managed
manufacturing industry   74, 108–9,
    225, 241, 407, 414, 418, 462, 480
March, James   101
marginal cost   129, 131–2, 140–1,
    153–8, 163–5, 172
marginal physical product   227, 229
marginal product of labour   126–7,
    130–1, 134
marginal propensity to consume   294,
    354, 385
marginal propensity to import   295,
    354, 435
marginal propensity to withdraw   354
marginal revenue   136–41, 153–7, 163,
    172, 177
marginal revenue product   227–8,
    236, 238, 241, 244–5, 248–9
market   10–21, 27, 36–40

market clearing   50, 119, 137, 156, 226,
    289–90, 299, 300, 302–6, 358,
    361, 381, 444–5, 451
market concentration   150
market equilibrium   48–50, 117, 119,
    300, 369, 451
market failure and government
    failure   170, 188–211, 216
market integration   54–60, 277–8,
    468
market power   13, 136, 138, 146–51,
    158–61, 166, 171, 182–4, 186,
    226, 406, 497
market segmentation   166–7, 224,
    234, 421
market structure   88, 136, 138, 142, 146,
    149–52, 157–8, 160, 163, 165,
    172–3, 175, 177, 181–4
Marris, Robin,   102
Marshall, Jaime   480
Marshall-Lerner condition   450, 454,
    472
Marshall Plan   459
Marx, Karl   7, 9–10, 25, 252, 291
menu costs *see* costs
mercantilism   396–7
merger and acquisition   105–8
Merton, Robert   33
microeconomics   27–8, 261
Millennium Round   422–3
minimum wage   27, 209, 243–6, 252,
    305, 309, 483
Mirrlees, James   32
mismatch unemployment *see*
    structural unemployment
mixed economy *see* economy
monetarism   283, 300–2, 317–29,
    338–9, 377–81
monetary policy   282, 298, 311,
    329, 333–5, 355, 357, 359–62,
    374–6, 378–88, 441, 456, 458,
    463–7
money
  creating   319
  functions of   316–17
monopolistic competition *see*
    imperfect competition
monopoly   20, 39, 88, 138, 146–8,
    152, 158–60, 162–4, 169–70,
  and allocative efficiency   164–6
  regulation of   170–2
  sources of   160–2
monopsony   171–2
moral hazard   31, 85, 305
multinational firms   92, 483–4

multiplier   298, 353–5, 378
Mundell, Robert   470
Murdoch, Rupert   186

N
NAIRU *see* non-accelerating inflation
    rate of unemployment
Nash equilibrium   176
national income   30, 98, 293–7, 331,
    376, 486–8
natural monopoly   160, 165–6
natural rate of unemployment   288,
    300–2, 307–8, 310–11, 323–8,
    338–9, 357, 381, 383–4, 389
net exports   280, 282, 293
new classical economics   289, 302–3,
    339, 358–61, 363, 381–7
new Keynesian economics   289,
    303–8, 323
new protectionism   418, 420
nominal GDP   261, 277
non-accelerating inflation rate of
    unemployment (NAIRU)   288,
    307–8, 310–11, 338–9
non-system   457, 460–3
Nordhaus, William   361–2
normal good   42–3, 73
normal profit *see* profit
normative issues   32, 194, 210, 243
North American Free Trade Agreement
    (NAFTA)   277–8, 421
Norway   183, 195, 198

O
Obama, Barack   5, 313, 391
Ohlin, Bertil   402–4, 406
oligopoly   146, 151–2, 172–82, 184,
    188, 213
opportunity cost   21–5, 34, 89, 91,
    195, 197, 232–3, 396–400, 402
optimum currency area   470
organic growth   100, 105–6, 173
Organization of Petroleum Exporting
    Countries (OPEC)   66, 69–72,
    90, 148, 169–70, 179, 262, 310,
    361
Ostrom, Elinor   203–4
output, final *see* final output
outside lag   379–80
overhead costs *see* fixed costs

P
Pareto efficiency   360
participation rate   231
passive policy rule   374–5

patents   160–1, 170, 180–1, 201, 420
pay differentials   244
perfect competition   136–8, 146,
    151–8, 163–6, 172, 175, 177, 181,
    220–1
perfectly anticipated inflation   272–3,
    325–7
perfectly elastic demand   65–6,
    137, 153
perfectly elastic supply   75–6, 235, 249
perfectly inelastic demand   64–5
perfectly inelastic supply   75–6
permanent income   378
PEST   13, 103
Pfizer   93, 161, 201
Phelps, Edmund   323
Phillips curve
    expectations-augmented   316,
        323–9, 338–9, 362, 383
    long-run   323–4, 326–7, 338–9,
        381, 383, 389
    original   320–4, 338
planning system   183–4
Plaza Agreement   462
policy ineffectiveness proposition   382
political business cycle   353, 361–3
Porter's five forces model   103–5
portfolio investment   429–33, 447
positive issues   32, 244
postwar boom   283–4, 408–9, 417–18
potential output   342, 353–4, 360
Prescott, Edward   360, 382–3
price
    equilibrium   48–53, 59, 119, 153,
        156, 167, 198, 217
    relative   274, 295, 358–9, 433,
        435, 450, 454, 462
price competition   149–52, 174, 210
price elasticity
    of demand   62–9, 139–40, 167,
        176, 210, 434–5, 443, 450,
        454, 456
    of supply   74–6, 235
price index   270, 289, 323
price maker   136–42, 146, 163, 166,
    172, 175, 184
price taker   136–8, 140–2, 146, 152–3,
    156, 163, 175
price transparency   56, 468, 476
prices and incomes policy   328,
    332–3, 335, 338
principal-agent problem   108–10, 114,
    116, 121
principle of net advantages   223, 249
private good *see* goods

privatization   4, 160, 188–90, 203–6,
    210–13, 301
producer sovereignty   184
product life-cycle theory   405–6
production function   125–8, 296,
    342–4, 346–7, 349, 366–71
production possibility frontier   343–4,
    398
profit
    normal   156, 158, 172
    supernormal   155–6, 163–4, 172
profit-maximizing output   140–2,
    153–7, 162–4, 177, 226
protectionism   13–14, 396, 400,
    413–18, 420–2, 441–2, 457
public good   188, 190–4, 204–6,
    208–9, 215
purchasing power parity   448–9
pure monopoly   152, 160, 163, 170, 184

Q
quantitative easing   30, 311, 335, 471,
    476
quantity demanded   40–2, 45, 48–50,
    52–3, 58–9, 61–6, 68, 73, 113,
    139, 156, 167, 176, 221
quantity supplied   45–50, 61, 74–6,
    234–5, 244, 444
quantity theory of money   316–20,
    326, 356
quota   194, 203, 414, 418, 422

R
random walk   360
rational expectations   381, 385
ratios
    capital-labour   367
    capital-output   355
real business cycle approach   353,
    360–1, 363, 386
real wage   246–7, 288–90, 293,
    299–306, 309, 323–6, 332, 361
recession   6–7, 282, 298, 307–8, 311,
    329, 339, 342, 352, 356, 360–1,
    418, 462
    definition of   262
    effect on the balance of payments
        263–4, 280, 438
    2008–09 financial crisis and
        12–13, 19, 25, 28–31, 53, 72,
        108, 114, 231, 257, 264–5, 269,
        284–6, 311, 332, 334, 337, 377,
        387–8, 408, 479, 489, 492–3,
        498
relative price *see* price

reservation wage   232
resource allocation
    collective   4–5, 15–21, 23–4,
        190–4, 260–1
    individualist   10–15, 36–8,
        118–19, 206–10
    market versus the state   38–9,
        194–204, 206–13
resource scarcity   21–4
returns to scale   133–4, 347, 366–7
revaluation   445, 453, 458
revised sequence   184
Ricardo, David   395–7, 399–404,
    413, 490
road pricing   193–4
Romer, Paul   348–9, 365
rough tuning   374, 377
Rowling, J.K.   162, 201
rules   357, 374–7, 381–2, 387–8
    activist   375, 380–1
    passive   374–5
Ryanair   106

S
Samsung   173, 180, 435
Sargent, Thomas   382
Say's law   290, 299
scarcity *see* resource scarcity
Schelling, Thomas   82–3, 178, 180–1
Schumpeter, Joseph   7, 9, 25, 170
Schwartz, Anna   337, 356–7
search unemployment *see* frictional
    unemployment
Sen, Amartya   32
services   2–3
shifting comparative advantage   405,
    420
shoe leather costs   273
short run   125
short-run costs   128–32
short-run Phillips curve   323–8,
    338–9, 383
single market programme   54–8, 104,
    134, 224, 277–8, 465–6, 468,
    476
signalling   243, 305
Simon, Herbert   101, 121
Smith, Adam   37, 189, 213, 395, 400
Singapore   8, 74, 193–4, 196
social provision *see* collective
    provision

Solow growth model   346–9, 363,
    366–71
Solow, Robert   346
Sopranos, The   79
Spence, Michael   243
stabilization policy
    defined   374
    Keynesian view   375–7
    monetarist view   377–81
    new classical view   381–6
    real business cycle view   386
stagflation   283, 322, 377, 386
state failure   188, 206–10
steady state   347, 368–71
Stiglitz, Joseph   111, 499
structural unemployment   270, 286,
    291–2, 298–301, 307
substitute   43, 103, 105, 169, 198
supernormal profit *see* profit
supply
    excess   49–50, 59, 68, 222, 224,
        244, 252, 289–90, 299–300,
        304, 306, 444, 450, 452, 472
supply curve
    derivation of   45–7
    movements along   46, 48
    shifts in   46–8
supply-side policies   345

T
target zone   451–2, 458, 462–5
tariff   56, 59, 278, 396, 413–20, 457,
    479, 493
Tesco   6, 10–14, 25, 171, 221
Tesla   6, 181
Thatcher government   329
third-part effects *see* externalities
tiger economies   350, 481, 489
time inconsistency   382–4
total cost   101, 124, 129–31
total product of labour   126–7
total revenue   101, 124, 136–40
trademarks   7, 161–2, 170, 174, 420
trade union density   225, 310
transactions
    accommodating   430–2
    autonomous   430–3
transaction costs   91–2, 202–4, 468
transfer earnings   249–50, 252
transition economy   16, 247
Tversky, Amos   81

U
unemployment
    classical approach to   289–90
    costs of   269–70
    defined   265
    demand-deficient   290, 293,
        298–99, 301, 313
    in Europe   308–11
    frictional   270, 290–1, 299
    in G5 economies   268–9
    Keynesian approach to   290–300
    measurement of   267
    monetarist approach to   300–2
    natural rate of   288, 300–2,
        307–8, 310, 323, 324–7, 338,
        381, 383, 389
    new classical approach to   302–3
    new Keynesian approach to   303–8
    non-accelerating inflation rate of
        (NAIRU)   288, 307–8, 310–11,
        338–9
    structural   270, 286, 291–2,
        298–301, 307
unemployment rate   231, 254, 267–9,
    308, 320
unit elasticity   64–5, 76
unlimited liability   94
Uruguay Round   419–21, 423
utility   83, 102, 112
    marginal   40–1

V
variable costs   128–31
variables
    endogenous   348
    exogenous   347
vertical growth   106
Virgin group   106,   180
voluntary export restraint
    (VER)   418–19

W
wage determination   237–40
Wallace, Neil   382
Werner Plan   465
Willamson, Oliver   102
World Trade Organization (WTO)   414,
    416–23, 425

Z
Zuckerberg, Mark   98–100